Palgrave Studies in Global Higher Education

Series Editors
Roger King
School of Management
University of Bath
Bath, UK

Jenny Lee
Centre for the Study of Higher Education
University of Arizona
Tuscon, Arizona, USA

Simon Marginson
Institute of Education
University College London
London, UK

Rajani Naidoo
School of Management
University of Bath
Bath, UK

This series aims to explore the globalization of higher education and the impact this has had on education systems around the world including East Asia, Africa, the Middle East, Europe and the US. Analyzing HE systems and policy this series will provide a comprehensive overview of how HE within different nations and/or regions is responding to the new age of universal mass higher education.

More information about this series at
http://www.palgrave.com/gp/series/14624

Jeroen Huisman • Anna Smolentseva
Isak Froumin
Editors

25 Years of Transformations of Higher Education Systems in Post-Soviet Countries

Reform and Continuity

Editors
Jeroen Huisman
University of Ghent
Ghent, Belgium

Anna Smolentseva
National Research University
Higher School of Economics
Moscow, Russia

Isak Froumin
National Research University
Higher School of Economics
Moscow, Russia

Palgrave Studies in Global Higher Education
ISBN 978-3-030-09604-5   ISBN 978-3-319-52980-6   (eBook)
https://doi.org/10.1007/978-3-319-52980-6

© The Editor(s) (if applicable) and The Author(s) 2018 This book is an open access publication
Softcover re-print of the Hardcover 1st edition 2018
Open Access This book is licensed under the terms of the Creative Commons Attribution 4.0 International License (http://creativecommons.org/licenses/by/4.0/), which permits use, sharing, adaptation, distribution and reproduction in any medium or format, as long as you give appropriate credit to the original author(s) and the source, provide a link to the Creative Commons license and indicate if changes were made.
The images or other third party material in this book are included in the book's Creative Commons license, unless indicated otherwise in a credit line to the material. If material is not included in the book's Creative Commons license and your intended use is not permitted by statutory regulation or exceeds the permitted use, you will need to obtain permission directly from the copyright holder.
The use of general descriptive names, registered names, trademarks, service marks, etc. in this publication does not imply, even in the absence of a specific statement, that such names are exempt from the relevant protective laws and regulations and therefore free for general use. The publisher, the authors, and the editors are safe to assume that the advice and information in this book are believed to be true and accurate at the date of publication. Neither the publisher nor the authors or the editors give a warranty, express or implied, with respect to the material contained herein or for any errors or omissions that may have been made. The publisher remains neutral with regard to jurisdictional claims in published maps and institutional affiliations.

Cover credit: Utamaru Kido / Getty Stock Images

Printed on acid-free paper

This Palgrave Macmillan imprint is published by the registered company Springer International Publishing AG part of Springer Nature.
The registered company address is: Gewerbestrasse 11, 6330 Cham, Switzerland

This volume is dedicated to the memory of our colleagues, Dmitry Semyonov, Evgeny Kniazev and Natalya Drantusova, in recognition of their original contribution to the study of post-Soviet higher education and its institutional landscape.

Preface: Challenges and Advantages of Exploring Post-Soviet Higher Education

The Soviet Union fell apart a quarter of a century ago. Fifteen newly born countries started their independent development in 1991 and a formerly unified higher education system was divided up. The basic commonality of Soviet design at the beginning of the independent era and the dramatic transformations of the post-Soviet period serve as the point of departure for this study.

Post-Soviet countries have different histories, and their socialist past is not the only thing that builds their identities. Yet, it would be incorrect to deny the significance of such a long and intense period in their national histories. This experience is still on the table. Politicians, experts and academics still often discuss the present while referring to the past. However, such references are not enough to grasp the effect of the Soviet past on modern states and bring insights to understand the further development of these societies. Both academic and pragmatic discourse lack a wide systemic picture.

The studies of post-socialist countries are especially crucial as they debunk the myths. Soviet society was not monolithic. Norms and practices changed over time and varied among communities. Identification of the real differences and similarities beyond the proclaimed statements is important and requires a generous amount of ambitious studies. Nevertheless, even very general assumptions about the Soviet past can result in great contributions to the discussion, especially if the research is comparative. Juxtaposition can reveal the core rationales for changes and the foundations of the current state of affairs. The simultaneous start of countries' own trajectories makes the observed period the field of 'natural experiment' which should be described.

In studies of post-Soviet higher education, researchers usually focus on particular issues. Academic discourse consists of a number papers that investigate several topics of higher education development (e.g. outcomes of reforms, internationalization, academic profession); they often consider several countries of the post-Soviet space. Yet, we rarely see articles which elaborate on higher education systemic development in its entirety. In order to investigate a given problem, researchers naturally have to limit the comprehensiveness of view. We therefore saw a niche for a book that would contribute to building the background for further studies.

Context matters. That is why the design of this book reflects the diversity of national pathways in higher education. At the start, we were faced with several alternatives to proceed with the book composition. On the one hand, the narrative could have flowed around particular aggregated categories, with the chapters covering as many countries as possible. The topics could have been major sets of reforms, fluctuations in basic system indicators, or problems to be resolved in the context of higher education development. However, after several discussions, we selected a more demanding approach which, on the bright side, promised a deep and profound contribution. This book is a collection of country cases, each of them shaped in accordance with a common framework, yet each country chapter provides a comprehensive view. The introduction chapter aims to reveal a cumulative understanding of the object of study and the topic of the higher education landscape in general.

Writing in this manner demanded extensive expertise from the contributors as well as their being personally embedded in the contexts. The search for authors was a tricky task. The complicated process of finding academically relevant people required enlisting the efforts of several layers in our professional networks. Fortunately, the idea behind the study and the ambition to cover the whole set of post-Soviet countries appealed to a number of people around the globe, to whom we are thankful for their help.

The states examined have gone through hard times. We did not purposefully pick the moment for the start of the project, but by chance the two years of the study turned out to be an extraordinary period for this part of the world. Under these conditions, the outstanding academic integrity and ethics of the authors and editors became a real asset for the project.

The second major challenge in the fulfilment of this task was obviously the lack of data. First of all, due to a number of reasons, data is not likely to be available for the countries studied. Our retrospective view intended to involve some dynamic pictures. We faced difficulties in collecting and comparing even aggregate numbers. At the beginning we were lacking such common characteristics as number of higher education institutions and student body in private sector, funding and research performance in higher education, and so on.

Moreover, investigation of the institutional landscape requires a capability to differentiate the types of HEIs and their roles in the system. The wide variations between countries, especially in the size of their higher education systems, make it impossible to rely on a universalistic approach to data collection and analysis. Such an approach might have weakened the results. Due to these reasons a mixed approach was selected. The authors used both qualitative and quantitative methods. Analyses were based on a number of expert interviews, fragments of data and literature reviews. In every case, the choice of relevant techniques and methodology resulted from numerous discussions between the respective authors, editors and the coordination team.

We hope that this study will make one more step in the gradual movement towards opening up opportunities for research on the post-Soviet space built on transparent data and keen academic interest. Based on results of the project, we created a web timeline of higher education key policy events in all post-Soviet countries. We expect that the scope of this tool will expand, and it will aggregate more useful information for further work.

The demand for a thorough grasp of post-Soviet higher education transformations in each former Soviet Republic seemed natural at the start. Basically, we assumed that national higher education systems reflect changes in societies and the economic and political environment. The institutional landscape of higher education, the structure of the system and the set of 'rules of the game' can tell us a great deal about the society in which they are rooted.

Moscow, Russia   Dmitry Semyonov
                                             Daria Platonova

Acknowledgements

This book is a result of the international research project 'Higher Education Dynamics and Institutional Diversity in Post-Soviet Countries'. The idea of a study covering the national higher education systems of the entirety of the former USSR emerged at the National Research University Higher School of Economics (HSE) in 2012–2013.

This project continued two previous HSE studies. In 2012, Evgeny Knyazev and Natalya Drantusova reopened the discussion about the institutional landscape in Russian higher education. They started to develop a project framework to explore higher education institution types and their transformations and released several papers on the issue. Regretfully, in November 2013, a sudden tragedy in the sky terminated their lives. We dedicate this book to the memory of our colleagues.

In 2013, Isak Froumin, Yaroslav Kouzminov and Dmitry Semyonov attracted attention to the issue of the evolution of higher education institutions in Russia. In their paper they conceptualized the idea of studying institutional diversity as a result of transformations in the broader environment and higher education policy in particular. Obviously, the Soviet legacy became a natural object to address, as well as the post-dissolution period. This retrospective approach became the core for the post-Soviet research.

Hence, in 2014, thanks to the inspiration and tremendous support of the Institute of Education (HSE), we took the opportunity to launch research on higher education development in all 15 countries. From the very beginning, we received full endorsement and strong support for the study from Yaroslav Kouzminov, rector of the HSE, who shared his expertise and participated in discussions.

Such a voluminous and complex study would not be meaningful without discussions with our colleagues around the world. Martin Carnoy (Stanford University) took a significant part in shaping the idea.

With such a scale and diversity of cases, it is hard to overestimate the heroic work of the editors: Anna Smolentseva, Jeroen Huisman, Isak Froumin. After several rounds of discussions with them, the research became focused on the two key issues—higher education policy changes and institutional diversity in all post-Soviet countries.

Jeroen Huisman came up with a framework which laid out the ground for all the authors. The straightforward and consistent design of the comparative research vitalized the whole idea. Thanks to his efforts, the case studies remained focused on the most important issues. His accurate and careful attention to each chapter has ensured that this book complies with modern academic standards.

The enormous efforts of Anna Smolentseva, both in content development and communication with the authors, made this book come to life. Her ability to assemble the whole picture gave the common output its consistency. The extensive expertise and enthusiasm of Isak Froumin widened the book's ambition and outlook. His passionate approach pushed the matter through even the most problematic situations.

We would like to thank the World Bank Moscow Office for its organizational support. Our personal thanks are extended to Denis Nikolaev and Kirill Vasiliev for their help in the recruitment of the research teams, as well as for fruitful discussions and participation in the project workshops. Support from the Basic Research Programme of the National Research University Higher School of Economics is also gratefully acknowledged.

We would also like to thank Amanda Schimunek for her high-quality language editing and Natalia Rosyaikina for the administrative support.

The team of the Laboratory for University Development (Institute of Education, HSE) backed us throughout. Their engagement imparted a lot of confidence and provided the solid base for thoughts and coordination.

The spin-off of the study, the web timeline of higher education changes, was developed by Lukas Bischof as a leader, Zumrad Kataeva and Daria Platonova.

In 2016 the summary articles on the country cases of the prospective book were published in the newsletter *Higher Education in Russia and Beyond* (HERB), #2(8)-2016.[1] The issue *Higher Education Landscape in Post-Soviet Countries: 25 Years of Changes* gained a lot of interest from the readers around the globe, which reassured our belief in the relevance of the book to the academic demand. The credit for this goes to the HERB editorial team and coordinators, who came up with an idea and got the issue perfectly fulfilled.

Our greatest acknowledgement is reserved for the 31 researchers for the country case studies, who committed themselves to this project for two years, who were so involved in discussions, who hunted down the precious data and who so patiently worked through the several versions. Thanks to their energies, the project was enriched by the several workshops and panels around the world. During the Conference of the Russian Association of Higher Education Researchers (RAHER) in 2014 and in 2015, we held project workshops in Moscow (Russia), where all the research teams presented the results. We would like to thank Mark Johnson for his great contribution to the discussion and fruitful comments.

With active participation of the research teams, we had project panels and roundtables at the CIES Annual Conference in Washington D.C. (USA) in 2015, where Stephen Heyneman (Vanderbilt University) provided very helpful feedback to the idea and preliminary findings. Also, some reflections had been presented at the session at the European Conference on Educational Research (ECER) in 2015 in Budapest (Hungary).

This book could only have happened thanks to the efforts of this large and diverse team of ambitious researchers.

Postscript

When this book was ready for print we received tragic news. Dmitry Semyonov, director of our research project, died in a car crash at the age of 31. During his short life he created the strong academic unit at the Institute of Education – Laboratory for Universities Development focused on higher education studies. He was a very creative leader who proposed exciting new topics for study. His studies and publications informed Russian higher education policies.

He was a real leader of our project. He managed to mobilize 15 research teams and the editors. He raised funds, organized seminars and workshops, was involved in data collection and initiated substantive discussions. We will always remember the joy of working with him.

Note

1. https://herb.hse.ru/en/2016--2(8).html

Contents

1 Transformation of Higher Education Institutional
   Landscape in Post-Soviet Countries: From Soviet Model
   to Where? 1
   Anna Smolentseva, Jeroen Huisman, and Isak Froumin

2 Common Legacy: Evolution of the Institutional
   Landscape of Soviet Higher Education 45
   Isak Froumin and Yaroslav Kouzminov

3 Armenia: Transformational Peculiarities of the Soviet
   and Post-Soviet Higher Education System 73
   Susanna Karakhanyan

4 Higher Education Transformation, Institutional Diversity
   and Typology of Higher Education Institutions
   in Azerbaijan 97
   Hamlet Isakhanli and Aytaj Pashayeva

5 Belarus: Higher Education Dynamics and Institutional
   Landscape 123
   Olga Gille-Belova and Larissa Titarenko

6 Inverted U-shape of Estonian Higher Education: Post-Socialist Liberalism and Postpostsocialist Consolidation   149
Ellu Saar and Triin Roosalu

7 Georgia: Higher Education System Dynamics and Institutional Diversity   175
Lela Chakhaia and Tamar Bregvadze

8 Looking at Kazakhstan's Higher Education Landscape: From Transition to Transformation Between 1920 and 2015   199
Elise S. Ahn, John Dixon, and Larissa Chekmareva

9 Institutional Strategies of Higher Education Reform in Post-Soviet Kyrgyzstan: Differentiating to Survive Between State and Market   229
Jarkyn Shadymanova and Sarah Amsler

10 Latvia: A Historical Analysis of Transformation and Diversification of the Higher Education System   259
Ali Ait Si Mhamed, Zane Vārpiņa, Indra Dedze, and Rita Kaša

11 Lithuanian Higher Education: Between Path Dependence and Change   285
Liudvika Leišytė, Anna-Lena Rose, and Elena Schimmelpfennig

12 Moldova: Institutions Under Stress—The Past, the Present and the Future of Moldova's Higher Education System   311
Lukas Bischof and Alina Tofan

13	Russia: The Institutional Landscape of Russian Higher Education Daria Platonova and Dmitry Semyonov	337
14	Higher Education in Tajikistan: Institutional Landscape and Key Policy Developments Alan J. DeYoung, Zumrad Kataeva, and Dilrabo Jonbekova	363
15	The Transformation of Higher Education in Turkmenistan: Continuity and Change Victoria Clement and Zumrad Kataeva	387
16	Ukraine: Higher Education Reforms and Dynamics of the Institutional Landscape Nataliya L. Rumyantseva and Olena I. Logvynenko	407
17	Uzbekistan: Higher Education Reforms and the Changing Landscape Since Independence Kobil Ruziev and Umar Burkhanov	435
Appendix		461

LIST OF FIGURES

Fig. 2.1	Governance of Soviet higher education and research in the 1980s (Source: Zinov'ev and Filippov 1983)	54
Fig. 2.2	Number of HEIs in the USSR (Source: Authors using data from Narodnoye obrazovaniye i kultura v USSR: Statisticheskiy ezhegodnik [Education and Culture in the USSR: Statistic Yearbook] (1989). Moscow: Finansy i statistika)	61
Fig. 2.3	Graduates by form of education (Source: Authors using data from Narodnoye obrazovaniye i kultura v USSR: Statisticheskiy ezhegodnik [Education and Culture in the USSR: Statistic Yearbook] (1989). Moscow: Finansy i statistika)	65
Fig. 3.1	Number of HEIs with total enrolment figures (in thousands) at the start of selected academic years (Data collected from different sources: UNESCO, HE in the USSR, Monographs on HE edited by L. C. Barrows; Khudaverdyan, K. S, 1960)	75
Fig. 3.2	Enrolment in tertiary education institutions in Armenia (*Statistical Yearbook of Armenia*: http://www.armstat.am/en/?nid=45&year=2014)	80
Fig. 3.3	Student enrolment per major (BA level) (*Statistical Yearbook of Armenia*): http://www.armstat.am/en/?nid=45&year=2014)	80
Fig. 3.4	Official labour force demand submitted by employers (*Statistical Yearbook of Armenia*: http://www.armstat.am/en/?nid=45&year=2014)	81
Fig. 3.5	Distribution of HEIs and number of students (*Statistical Yearbook of Armenia*: http://www.armstat.am/en/?nid=45&year=2014)	89

Fig. 4.1	Student enrolment in higher education (1960–2014) (Source: SSC 2014)	104
Fig. 4.2	Number of private and public HEIs in Azerbaijan, 1960–2014 (Source: State Statistical Committee 2014)	105
Fig. 4.3	International students based on home country (2013–2014) and Dynamics in International Student Participation since 2000 (Source: SSC (2014), *Commonwealth of Independent States)	109
Fig. 4.4	Student body characteristics for 2014/2015 (Source: State Statistical Committee 2014)	112
Fig. 5.1	Change in the number of HEI students in Belarus (thousands), 1940–2015 (Source: MORB 2001, 2013b; NSCRB 2013, 2014, 2015)	130
Fig. 5.2	Change in the number of HEIs in Belarus, 1940–2015 (Source: MORB 2001, 2013a; NSCRB 2013, 2014, 2015)	130
Fig. 5.3	Change in the number of students by study profile between 1990–1991 and 2012–2013 (Source: MORB 2001, 2013a)	134
Fig. 6.1	Number of HEIs in Estonia 1990–2015 (Source: Statistics Estonia; Estonian ministry of education)	156
Fig. 6.2	Number of students in Estonian HEIs, 1980–2015 (Source: Statistics Estonia)	158
Fig. 6.3	Number of state-financed and fee-paying students in Estonian HEIs, 1993–2015 (Source: Ministry of education and research)	159
Fig. 7.1	Number of HEIs and enrolments in Soviet Georgia (Source: Savelyev et al. 1990)	176
Fig. 7.2	Number of HEIs	182
Fig. 7.3	Absolute student enrolments	183
Fig. 7.4	Classification of Georgian HEIs in the 1990s by prestige and rank	187
Fig. 7.5	Number of admitted students in HEIs	191
Fig. 8.1	Demographic trends (1985–2012) (Source: Adopted from the Agency of Statistics of the Republic of Kazakhstan (2013))	204
Fig. 8.2	Education reform timeline (1991–2020) (Source: Adopted from OECD (2007, 112))	205
Fig. 8.3	HEI trends over time by institutions 1940–2014 (Sources: Adopted from Brunner and Tillett (n.d.); MoES (2014, 2015); Ministry of Economics (2015); Moskva-Finansy i Statistika [Moscow Finance and Statistics] (1989, 202); OECD (2007, 40); Zhakenov (n.d.))	207
Fig. 8.4	Distribution of universities in Kazakhstan in AY2014–15 (Source: MoES (2015))	208

Fig. 9.1	Number of HEIs in the Kirgiz Soviet Socialist Republic, 1932–1991 (Source: Authors using data from Orusbaeva 1982 and NSC 2008)	232
Fig. 9.2	The HEI landscape in Kyrgyzstan (Source: Authors using data from Orusbaeva 1982)	234
Fig. 9.3	Number of HE students in the Kirgiz Soviet Socialist Republic, 1932–1991 (Source: Authors using data from Orusbaeva 1982 and NSC 2008)	235
Fig. 9.4	Secondary school graduates and student enrollment in vocational and higher education institutions, 1991–2013 (Source: Authors using data NSC 2014c)	239
Fig. 9.5	Part-time and full-time, day, and evening-class students (Source: Authors using data from NSC 2014a)	244
Fig. 9.6	Dynamics of higher education enrollment by fields of study, 2000–2014 (Source: Source: Authors using data from NSC 2008, 2015)	245
Fig. 9.7	The HEI landscape in Kyrgyzstan, 2015 (Source: Authors using data from NSC 2008, 2015)	246
Fig. 10.1	Milestones in the development of the higher education system in Latvia, 1990–2014 (Source: Authors)	264
Fig. 10.2	The dynamics of HEIs in Latvia, 1990–2014 (Source: Authors based on data from MoES, 1991 to 2014)	265
Fig. 10.3	The dynamics of HE student enrolment in Latvia, 1990–2014 (Source: Authors based on data from MoES, 1991 to 2014)	266
Fig. 10.4	Proportion of the number of students in different fields of study (Source: Authors based on data from MoES 1998 to 2014)	271
Fig. 10.5	Proportion of students by age group (Source: Authors based on data from MoES 1998 to 2014)	272
Fig. 11.1	Number of schools of higher education and number of students in Lithuanian SSR (1970–1990) (Source: Statistics Lithuania: Official Statistics Portal)	288
Fig. 12.1	Timeline of important developments in higher education policy in the Republic of Moldova	316
Fig. 12.2	Number of public and private HEIs in the Republic of Moldova	320
Fig. 12.3	Development of the total number of students enrolled on a budget and tuition-fee basis (in both private and public HEIs)	321
Fig. 12.4	Government expenditure on education 2000/2005–2013	327

Fig. 12.5	Admission numbers by type of prior schooling (2000/2005–2013)	328
Fig. 13.1	Timeline of key higher education reforms in Russia, 1991–2015 (Source: Developed by the authors)	342
Fig. 13.2	Number of graduates by study field (Source: Aggregative groups calculated by authors based on data from the Federal State Statistics Service (2015))	343
Fig. 13.3	Number of students in HEIs and age cohort participation (17–25), 1991–2014, Russia (Source: Calculated by the authors. Data from Federal State Statistics Service (2015))	344
Fig. 13.4	Enrolment by source of financing and type of HEIs, 1995–2013, Russia (Source: Calculated by authors. Data from: before 2000, Education in the Russian Federation (2006); for 2000–2010, Education in the Russian Federation (2012); after 2010, Federal State Statistics Service (2015))	346
Fig. 13.5	Public spending on higher education as a share of total public expenditure on education and public spending on education as a share of total public expenditure (*per cent*) (Source: Calculated by authors. Data for expenditure from: before 2003, Education in the Russian Federation (2006); after 2003, Roskozna (2015) and FSSS (2015)) Note: Due to the reform of the financial system in 2003, the data before and after 2003 cannot be directly compared.	347
Fig. 13.6	Russian HEIs by nominal types, 1998–2012 (Source: Education in the Russian Federation 2006; Federal State Statistics Service, 2015)	352
Fig. 14.1	HEIs in Tajikistan, 1991–2013	369
Fig. 14.2	Student enrolments in Tajikistan (in thousands): 1991–2013	369
Fig. 14.3	Number of enrolled students by specialization, 1991 and 2010 (Source: The Ministry of Education and Science)	374
Fig. 14.4	Higher education institutions by presidential quota, 2014/2015	375
Fig. 15.1	Higher education participation rate 1991–2011, in % (age cohort 20–24) (Sources: http://www.cisstat.com)	395
Fig. 16.1	Numbers of HEIs by levels of accreditation, 1990–2015 (The data for 2014–2015 and 2015–2016 are not fully comparable to data from previous years as they do not take into account institutions that remained in the occupied territories and the zone of military conflict in Donetsk, Lugansk and Crimea. Source: State Office of Statistics of Ukraine (2016))	415

Fig. 16.2	Numbers of students in HEIs by levels of accreditation, 1990–2015 (The data for 2014–2015 and 2015–2016 are not fully comparable to data from previous years as they do not take into account institutions that remained in the occupied territories and the zone of military conflict in Donetsk, Lugansk and Crimea. Source: State Office of Statistics of Ukraine (2016))	415
Fig. 17.1	Share of GDP by industrial origin in Uzbekistan, 1993–2012 (Source: ADB (2015))	439
Fig. 17.2	Employment by economic sector in Uzbekistan, 1991–2012 (Source: ADB (2015))	440
Fig. 17.3	Timeline of key changes in HE since independence	443
Fig. 17.4	Hierarchical structure of the higher education system in Uzbekistan	450
Fig. 17.5	Geographic distribution of HEIs and student population in 2012–13 (Source: MHSSE (2013))	453
Fig. 17.6	Demand for and supply of higher education places, 1996–2014 (Source: MHSSE (2015))	454

List of Tables

Table 1.1	The key reforms in higher education in post-Soviet countries	21
Table 2.1	State HEIs in Russia in 1913	48
Table 2.2	Number of HEIs in the USSR by the specialization of the institution	59
Table 3.1	Higher education landscape in Armenia in 1991	76
Table 3.2	Armenian HEIs by legal status: regulatory landscape	91
Table 3.3	Higher education landscape in Armenia in 2015	92
Table 4.1	Main credentials awarded during the Soviet period	99
Table 4.2	Types of HEIs that emerged between 1919 and 1990 with student numbers for 2013–2014	100
Table 4.3	State defined characteristics of HEIs	107
Table 4.4	State defined typology of HEIs	113
Table 4.5	Classification of HEIs in Azerbaijan	115
Table 5.1	Main types of HEIs in the Byelorussian Republic, 1990/1991 academic year	127
Table 5.2	Typology of Belarusian HEIs at the beginning of the 2010s	136
Table 5.3	Characteristics of various HEI types (based on data for 2012–2013)	138
Table 6.1	Main types of HEIs in Estonia in 1990/1991 and 1993/1994 academic year	153
Table 6.2	Number and share of students in Estonian HEIs by study field	161
Table 6.3	Main types of HEIs in Estonia in the 2013/2014 academic year	162
Table 7.1	Classification of Georgian HEIs by the end of the 1980s	178
Table 7.2	Performances of private HEIs	187
Table 7.3	Current typology of Georgian HEIs	190

Table 8.1	Kazakhstani HEIs (AY1988–89)	202
Table 8.2	Types of Kazakhstani HEIs in AY1990–91	203
Table 8.3	HEIs by type based on the law "On Education" (2007)	210
Table 8.4	The Kazakhstani HE landscape between 1993 and 2010	217
Table 8.5	Characteristics of HEIs	218
Table 9.1	Higher education institutions in the Kirgiz Soviet Socialist Republic, 1980	233
Table 9.2	Dynamics of institutional growth in Kyrgyz higher education, 1991–2016	237
Table 9.3	Dynamics of student population, public and private HEIs, 1991–2013	238
Table 9.4	Classification of higher education institutions in Kyrgyzstan, 2015	247
Table 10.1	Types of HEIs in Latvia by 1989 characteristics	262
Table 10.2	Types of HEI in Latvia by 2015 characteristics and ministerial affiliation	274
Table 11.1	Typology of higher education institutions in Lithuania in 1990	291
Table 11.2	Typology of higher education institutions in Lithuania in 2016	301
Table 12.1	HEIs in Moldova during the Soviet period	314
Table 12.2	Types of HEIs in 2015	324
Table 13.1	Expenditure on education (total and higher education) in the USSR and Russian SFSR in 1981 and 1987 (in billion rubles and %)	338
Table 13.2	Number of HEIs by type, number of students by form of learning and their shares, 1990	340
Table 13.3	Types of HEIs in Soviet Russia	341
Table 13.4	Structural transformations of the Russian economy 1991–2014	343
Table 13.5	Distribution of HEIs by ministry and other agencies, Russia, 2014	349
Table 13.6	Indicators and measurement	355
Table 13.7	Classification of HEIs in Russia, 2015	356
Table 14.1	Classification of HEIs as of 1989/1990	367
Table 14.2	Typology of higher education institutions as of 2014/2015	370
Table. 15.1	Number of higher education institutions in Turkmenistan during 1940–1990	390
Table 15.2	Distribution of higher education institutions by sector (1988)	391
Table 15.3	Classification of Soviet HEIs (1988)	392

Table 15.4	Number of higher education institutions and number of students from 2000 to 2011	395
Table 15.5	Current classification of higher education institutions (2016)	400
Table 16.1	Typology of HEIs by specialisation in 1941	410
Table 16.2	Typology of HEIs by type of specialisation in 1988	411
Table 16.3	Typology of higher education institutions in Ukraine in 2016	418
Table 17.1	Horizontal diversity by HEI type in 1988–89	442
Table 17.2	Horizontal diversity by HEI type in 2015	448
Table 17.3	HE quality diversity based on demand, selectivity and public perception	452
Table 17.4	Academic qualification of full-time HEI staff in 2013	456
Table A.1	State HEIs in Russia in 1913	462
Table A.2	Non-governmental HEIs in 1913	462
Table A.3	State and non-state HEIs, number of students and share of women by types of HEIs in the Russian Empire in 1914/15	463
Table A.4	Number of HEIs and students by types of HEIs in the USSR in 1922 and 1925	464
Table A.5	Number of HEIs in the USSR in 1940–1988	465
Table A.6	Share of enrolment by the types of HEIs, %	465
Table A.7	Engineers in the USSR, thousand students	466
Table A.8	Graduates by the forms of education, thousand students	466
Table A.9	Number of HEIs in the Soviet Republics	466
Table A.10	Number of HEIs in 1988	467
Table A.11	Number of universities and university students in 1988	468
Table A.12	Number of students in 1988	469
Table A.13	Number of students and share of full-time students in 1990	470
Table A.14	Dynamics of student number in the Soviet Republics, thousand	470
Table A.15	Dynamics of student number per 10,000 population in the Soviet Republics	471
Table A.16	Age cohort participation in higher education (20–24 age cohort) in Soviet Republics	471
Table A.17	Competition at entrance exams per 100 places in 1988	472
Table A.18	Share of women in student body in the Soviet Republics in 1988	472
Table A.19	Number of higher education institutions	473
Table A.20	Number and share of non-state HEIs	474
Table A.21	Number and share of enrolment in non-state HEIs	475
Table A.22	Share of students paying tuition fees	476

Table A.23	Number of students in 1991–2013	477
Table A.24	Share of full-time students, %	478
Table A.25	Age cohort participation in higher education (17–25 age cohort) in 1991–2013	478
Table A.26	Gross enrolment ratio, tertiary, %	479

CHAPTER 1

Transformation of Higher Education Institutional Landscape in Post-Soviet Countries: From Soviet Model to Where?

Anna Smolentseva, Jeroen Huisman, and Isak Froumin

INTRODUCTION

In 1991, the Soviet model of higher education in 15 republics of the USSR, with its 5.1 million students and 946 higher education institutions, started 15 independent journeys. All post-Soviet systems shared the legacies of the single Soviet approach to higher education provision: a centrally planned organization and financing, subordination to multiple sectoral ministries, a national curriculum, a vocational orientation based on the combination of strong basic education and narrow specialized job-related training, a nomenclature of types of higher education institutions, tuition-free study places and guaranteed employment upon graduation combined with mandatory job placement. Despite these commonalities, the sociocultural and economic disparities across the republics were

---

A. Smolentseva (✉) • I. Froumin
National Research University Higher School of Economics, Moscow, Russia

J. Huisman
University of Ghent, Ghent, Belgium

© The Author(s) 2018
J. Huisman et al. (eds.), *25 Years of Transformations of Higher Education Systems in Post-Soviet Countries*, Palgrave Studies in Global Higher Education, https://doi.org/10.1007/978-3-319-52980-6_1

remarkable: for example, in the structure of the economy, the level of urbanization, the cultural and ethnic diversity and demographic trends, as well as the number of higher education institutions, the number of students and higher education participation rates.

After gaining their independence, all new countries faced similar challenges. First of all, there were the challenges of the consolidation of the new nation and the introduction of a market economy. Second, the collapse of the centrally planned economy was associated with economic decline, political instability, a drastic drop in public funding and brain drain from higher education and research institutions to other sectors of the economy or overseas. Many post-Soviet countries—Armenia, Azerbaijan, Georgia, Kyrgyz Republic, Moldova, Russia, Tajikistan and recently Ukraine—experienced armed conflicts, which deeply affected their societies and economies. The similarities and differences between the national contexts, together with the challenges of the independence period, created a unique constellation of political, economic, sociocultural and demographic conditions in each country.

In higher education, almost all the new nations adopted a similar package of reforms, many of these neo-liberal in nature (Silova and Steiner-Khamsi 2008; Smolentseva 2012) that aimed to "normalize" their higher education systems. This would be achieved through the establishment of a non-state sector, the introduction of tuition fees in the public sector, national standardized tests for admission exams to higher education, decentralization of the governance and—although not in all countries—loans for students and performance-based funding. The argument in favour of this particular set of reforms was socially constructed (Fourcade-Gourinchas and Babb 2002), in terms of the perceived need to follow a certain ideal type. Reform was presented as following the ideal type of the single model of excellence in higher education (Heyneman 2010), or catching up, not lagging behind other countries (Silova and Steiner-Khamsi 2008) in the context of an increasing interest in and greater opportunities to attend higher education. The main features of the ideal type of higher education were taken from the Western world. The implementation of the reforms varied in speed and timing across countries. Some countries were not so much affected in the early years of independence (in particular, Turkmenistan), but in recent years that country too has become more responsive to international policy trends.

Other important reforms across the region included efforts to overcome Soviet ideological legacies and align higher education systems with the goals of new nation building. Thus, Soviet ideological courses were excluded from curricula. Along with the change of the official language in all countries, titular nation language became predominant in higher education instruction, and the higher education programmes were supplemented by courses on national history and culture.

All of these transformations have dramatically affected individuals, social groups and institutions of post-Soviet societies, including higher education. All have had to adapt to their rapidly changing environments. That has eventually resulted in a range of changes in the structure of national higher education systems and in—what we term—their institutional landscapes, the overall institutional composition of the higher education system.

Despite the scale and importance of the changes that have taken place, there are only few comparative studies of post-Soviet higher education transformation. In many countries, the weakness of the social sciences due to a lack of research funding, together with the long-standing isolation from international research communities, partly explains that absence. Interestingly, comparative research with a focus on secondary education in post-Soviet systems seems more prolific than research on higher education (e.g. Phillips and Kaser 1992; Silova 2010a). There are publications which aim to analyse several countries of the region and/or the nature of post-Soviet transformations (see Heyneman 2010; Johnson 2008; Silova 2009, 2010a; Silova and Steiner-Khamsi 2008). There appear to be no comparative higher education studies on the region based on primary data collection and analysis, as distinct from studies consisting of reviews of literature and policy documents (but see Silova 2010b; Slantcheva and Levy 2007).

This book is the outcome of the first ever study of the transformations of the higher education institutional landscape in 15 former USSR countries following the disintegration of the Soviet Union (1991). It explores how the single Soviet model that developed across the vast and diverse territory of the Soviet Union over several decades changed into

15 unique national systems, systems that have responded to national and global developments while still bearing significant traces of the past. This study is distinctive in that (a) it presents a comprehensive analysis of the higher education reforms and transformations in the region in the last 25 years; (b) it focuses on institutional landscape through the evolution of the institutional types established and developed in pre-Soviet, Soviet and post-Soviet times; (c) it embraces all 15 countries of the former USSR; and (d) it provides a comparative analysis of the drivers of transformations of institutional landscape across post-Soviet systems.

The institutional landscape of higher education is one of the key characteristics of higher education systems. Approaching higher education transformations through the lens of changes in the institutional landscape enables several goals to be achieved. First, it makes it possible to incorporate the dynamic dimension, to trace the processes of change. Second, it includes an analysis of the drivers of change, which opens up the opportunity for systematic analysis of higher education system transformations and the factors behind them, including governmental policies, institutional behaviour, demographic change, global forces and others. Third, it allows the researcher to look at system level while keeping in mind the diversity of the institutions.

Despite an increasing interest in studying institutional landscapes and institutional diversity in higher education around the world (Huisman 1998; Huisman et al. 2007; van Vught 2009), very little research has been focused on the institutional landscape in post-Soviet systems, despite the major transformations in those landscapes (for Russia, see Knyazev and Drantusova 2014; Froumin et al. 2014).

In the remainder of this chapter we present a conceptual framework which guided the project. Following a short introduction to the Soviet model and an overview of the reforms that took place across the 15 systems, the chapter focuses on the project findings—the changes in the institutional landscape, its drivers and a brief reflection on what the future may bring. This chapter also introduces all country cases included in the study and highlights their main points, after which it concludes with our final reflections on the changes in higher education institutional landscapes in 15 post-Soviet countries.

The Conceptual Approach and Research Design

The concept of the institutional landscape covers two aspects. First, it denotes the idea of institutional (or organizational) diversity. Higher education systems consist of a variety of institutions. These institutions may differ in various respects. Birnbaum (1983) distinguished various dimensions of diversity, and many of these will also figure in our description and analysis of the post-Soviet systems. Particularly, three dimensions are key to our project: systemic diversity, differences in size, type and control within a higher education system; structural diversity, differences in historical and legal foundations; and programme diversity, differences in degree level, area, mission and emphasis of programmes within the institutions.

The second aspect of the landscape signifies how the different dimensions of diversity play out in a particular system. That is, various stakeholders classify higher education institutions on the basis of the various diversity dimensions. Governments are key players by, for example, labelling certain higher education institutions as polytechnics or universities of applied sciences or—as we will see in the subsequent chapters—as academies, institutes and (research) universities. Whereas governments are key, there are other actors that may figure, for instance, representatives of certain types of institutions (e.g. the Russell Group in the UK, the Group of Eight in Australia).

Two concepts are helpful to make more sense of this second aspect: *vertical* and *horizontal* differentiation (Teichler 1988). Horizontal differentiation refers to making distinctions between types of higher education institutions on the basis of their function within the broader fabric. Such differentiation likely reflects the needs and demands of different groups in society, including the government (see also Taylor et al. 2008). As such, the landscape or configuration could be seen as a reflection of a social pact (Gornitzka 2007). Following this logic, it makes sense to distinguish, for example, *hogescholen* from universities in the Netherlands, because they fulfil different roles, professional education versus academic education, and applied research versus basic research, respectively. That such distinctions are not watertight (as the demise of the binary systems in, e.g. the UK and Australia shows) is beyond the point: there is (or has been) a functional reason to label higher education institutions differently.

Vertical differentiation refers to differences in status and prestige, with further connotations like "elite" and "high quality". Such differences are less tangible and likely more dynamic than horizontal differences. This is because status and prestige are in the eye of the beholder and therefore malleable. Across the globe, the globally oriented comprehensive research university (sometimes called the world-class university) is quite often seen as the type of institution at the top of the status hierarchy. The underlying dynamics are quite different from horizontal differentiation and sometimes at odds. Through processes of academic drift those institutions lower in the pecking order may emulate higher-status institutions and this could undermine the functional differentiation. Obviously, academic drift is not the sole driver of changes in the landscape. On the basis of our understanding of the literature (e.g. Teichler 1988; Huisman 1998), there are various factors that would affect the institutional configuration: the government's steering approach, the level of marketization, demographic developments, internationalization and so on.

With these conceptual tools in mind, we asked our country authors to reflect on the following questions: How did the landscape look like at the moment of (or just before) independence? Which developments took place in the system since independence and which drivers can be discerned that impacted the landscape? And, finally, how do the new landscapes look like (and are they much different from those in place around 1990)? We asked authors to rely on available classifications and statistics to arrive at landscape descriptions that would do justice to the state of the art in their systems.

Assuming distinctive features of each national context, the project benefits from the unique institutional classifications developed for each chapter by their authors. The institutional types and classifications established in the late Soviet time serve as a starting point for the analysis of the transformations of the independence period. The post-Soviet classifications embracing state of art of each national system enable to catch the nature of the current institutional landscape and to trace the transformations of the institutional landscape since gaining the independence.

The institutional classifications are developed using a wide range of national- and institutional-level data: affiliation, number of HEIs/students within types, distribution over the country, size, age of the institutions, disciplinary composition, student body characteristics, faculty characteristics, research activity (grants, R&D revenues, publication activity), international activity (international students, faculty, programmes), interrelations with business/production (funding, grants, agreements) and interrelations with other HEIs (net of branches, agreements, mergers).

In their overall analysis, most authors relied on analyses of policy developments in higher education and hence made significant use of policy papers and existing secondary literature. Some authors supplemented these methods with interviews. Some authors analysed higher education landscape using institutional-level data.

THE POINT OF DEPARTURE: SOVIET HIGHER EDUCATION SYSTEM

The USSR was a unique combination of peoples and cultures stretching from the Eastern Europe to the Siberian Far East, from Northern Russia to the Caucasus and Central Asia. Over 70 years (for the Baltic republics and Moldova which became a part of the USSR later it was about 50 years) the Soviet system evolved according to common principles that aimed at the building of a new political, socioeconomic and cultural system, that of communism. The sociocultural project of the USSR—the construction of the new Soviet man—became interwoven with the pragmatic purpose of accelerated economic development, in order to overcome the devastating consequences of the two world wars and outpace the capitalist countries in military excellence. The Soviet higher education system was an important player in both of these arenas: as an instrument of the formation of a new type of man and as an instrument of economic progress (Smolentseva 2016).

The Soviet system of higher education had a number of distinctive characteristics. First of all, as is well known, it was characterized as mainly state-centred, with central planning and a top-down command method of administration (Froumin et al. 2014; Kuraev 2016). The higher education system was built into a larger economic planning system and had to respond to orders from higher authorities. Higher education institutions were required to train a specified number of people in certain fields, while the larger economic planning system was responsible for graduates' job assignments. The control and supervision of higher education institutions were distributed among a large number of sectoral ministries that were responsible for administering specific industries. This structure was created in the Stalin era. From 1929 to 1930 onwards, most higher education institutions were transferred from the ministry of education (*Narkompros*) to various sectoral ministries and state departments (David-Fox 2012; Ryzhkovskiy 2012). That type of organization was considered to be a more effective way of linking the training of higher educated cadre with the needs of industrialization and military mobilization.

Second, as higher education was a system of training professional, "highly qualified" cadre for the national economy (Kuraev 2015; Smolentseva 2016), it was in many ways predominantly vocational. The need to bring higher education and research closer to "life" and the requirements of the national economy was much discussed during the Soviet years. This affected organization and curricula in higher education. The turn towards a technical and vocational orientation started in the early Soviet period (David-Fox 2012; Ryzhkovskiy 2012) and was maintained over the succeeding decades.

Third, uniformity, the application of the same principles and requirements to all institutions and individuals, was another key feature of the Soviet system (Ovsyannikov and Iudin 1990; Kuraev 2015). This approach contributed to the consolidation of the diverse country in social and cultural terms, including the creation of a "common educational space" via the introduction of the Russian as a common language and the use of standard curricula and textbooks.

The Soviet programme of continuous expansion of the educational system across all republics had results. Each Soviet republic had at least one comprehensive university and a number of specialized higher education institutions. The number of students increased from 811 thousand in 1940 to 5.2 million in 1991. Trends in the number of institutions are less straightforward, due to the ongoing process of opening up, closing down, merging and disintegrating particular higher learning establishments. There were 817 HEIs in 1940, 739 in 1960, 805 in 1970 and 883 in 1980 (see Table A.5 in Appendix). Even in the last decade of the USSR the government kept establishing new HEIs.

Despite the application of similar principles to organization and administration, uneven socioeconomic conditions of the republics were a historical legacy which the Soviet government had to grapple with from its beginning, but did not overcome. There was a special effort to build higher education institutions outside the European part of the country where they were mostly concentrated (Matthews 1982; Ovsyannikov and Iudin 1990). However, one official Soviet indicator, competition for HE admissions per 100 places, suggests that in many republics the interest of the population in higher education was much higher than the system could meet (Table A.16 in Appendix). Higher education systems in the Baltic republics experienced the least pressure, with 154–164 applications per

100 vacancies in 1988. The competition in Central Asia was on average much fiercer, with 291–328 applications per 100 vacancies (but 226 in Kazakhstan). In Georgia the indicator was even higher at 394.

Free higher education (except in the period 1940–1956) and the continuing expansion of higher education were important achievements of the USSR. Many of the barriers to higher education were removed. Social groups previously underrepresented in higher education received increasing opportunities: workers, peasants, women and members of various nationalities. Women comprised 52 per cent of students by the end of the Soviet era, with the lowest gender ratios in Azerbaijan (33 per cent) and Turkmenistan (36 per cent).

The participation rate in higher education, calculated as a gross enrolment ratio (the number of students as compared to the number of people in the 20–24 age cohort), was relatively high in the USSR in general at about a quarter of the age group, but again, it varied significantly across the Republics (Table A.15 in Appendix). The European part of the country had the higher participation with the Central Asian republics and Azerbaijan demonstrating relatively modest indicators (12 per cent for Turkmenistan, 15 per cent for Tajikistan, 16 per cent Kirgizia (Kyrgyz Republic), 15 per cent for Azerbaijan). Using Trow's division of three stages of massification process (Trow 1973), some Republics had reached the mass stage (15–50 per cent), while in others participation in higher education was still in the elite stage of development (less than 15 per cent).

Another prominent characteristic of the Soviet system was the institutional separation of higher education from research (Johnson 2008; Froumin et al. 2014). From the early Soviet period onwards this structural division played an important role in weakening the Soviet higher education sector. Most research was conducted in sectoral institutes that were directly linked to particular industries and subordinated to the corresponding ministries, as were most of the higher education institutions. The need to connect higher education and research, basic and applied, was constantly discussed in Soviet policy documents (Smolentseva 2016), but the dominant role of higher education remained the same, that of teaching highly qualified manpower (Kuraev 2015). The higher education sector's share of research was small. For example, in Russia in 1990 it comprised just 6 per cent of all research, while the great bulk of which took place in academies, sectoral institutes and industries (Nauka Rossii v tsifrakh 1994, 41[1]).

The Soviet higher education landscape consisted of universities (comprehensive HEIs) and specialized institutions—institutes, academies, factory-HEIs (*zavod-VTUZ*) and others. The comprehensive universities comprised a small minority of HEIs (8 per cent) and enrolled 12 per cent of all students by the end of the Soviet era (see Appendix). These universities had two tasks: the reproduction of research and teaching staff in certain fields "humanities, natural sciences, psychology and political economy" (Yagodin 1990) and training for "practical work in national economy, schools and technic, cultural institutions, government departments and corporate bodies (such as trade unions, the Party, etc.)" (Severtsev 1976). The comprehensive universities were supposed to play an important role in research, and their graduates were expected to make use of their research-oriented education in their professional activities.

However, this group of universities was not homogenous. A small number of them had their origins in the imperial period, while the majority was established in the Soviet period, with some of them being upgraded from pedagogical institutes (and keeping the characteristics of those institutes, according to Ovsyannikov and Iudin 1990). In the case of Russia, the biggest higher education system among Soviet republics, including 69 universities in 1988, only 17 out of 37 universities subject to statistical analysis were regarded as well positioned as universities, characterized by well-qualified academic staff, a traditional profile of university fields or a strong research orientation (Ovsyannikov and Iudin 1988). Indeed, despite the official approach of uniformity, a vertically differentiated system of higher education was evident in the USSR.

As noted, the majority of higher learning was organized in specialized institutions for particular jobs: engineers of various kinds, doctors, teachers, economists, lawyers and so on. Engineering students enrolled in HEIs servicing industry, construction, transportation and communication comprised 43 per cent of the total student population (see Table A.6 in Appendix). That group of HEIs comprised almost one third of all HE establishments in the country. Another big group, also about one third of HEIs, were the pedagogical institutions, with 19 per cent of total number of students. The engineering and technical fields dominated in the official list of specialties: 243 out of 381 (64 %) in the ministry list as of 1975 (Ministry of Higher and Secondary Vocational Education 1975) and 177 out 289 (61 %) in 1987 (Ministry of Higher and Secondary Vocational Education 1987). Admissions in philosophy were available in 13 HEIs, in psychology in 12 HEIs and in sociology in only 11 institutions (Ovsyannikov and Iudin 1990).

In the Soviet period, the pre-Soviet orientation towards engineering and technical fields was continued and deepened. "Industrialization" was evident in many universities (Ovsyannikov and Iudin 1988). In this work we set aside the larger question of the nature of the Soviet university, whose characteristics were very different from the traditional notion of the European university (for this topic see Kuraev 2015). Nevertheless, as early as in the Soviet period it was noted that the two distinct higher education sectors, universities and specialized institutes, were developing in converging ways: university education was moving towards more specialized instruction with the inclusion of applied sciences, while specialized educational institutions tend to embrace more academic research in their foundations, becoming more like universities, and paid more attention to research. The "modern technical university" was an example of such converging trends (e.g. the Moscow Institute of Physics and Technology, Moscow Institute of Electronic Engineering, Moscow and Kharkov Institutes of Radio Engineering, Electronics and Automatics and others (Severtsev 1976)). The drift to greater vocationalism within the university sector was fairly common (see Ovsyannikov and Iudin 1988, 1990), but the intensification of research activities within the specialized sector mostly developed within a small group of elite engineering institutions.

By the time of *perestroika* in the mid-1980s, many issues in the Soviet system of higher education had become evident and were explicitly discussed (Ovsyannikov and Iudin 1990; Smolentseva 2016), and the first movements towards changing the educational system had started. The legalization of cooperatives (1988) as a Soviet form of entrepreneurship opened an opportunity to create alternative educational provision. For example, in Estonia by 1989 two non-state higher education institutions were already established (see the chapter on Estonia in this volume). That period also introduced the term "customer" into the public policy domain (Smolentseva 2016), where the production sector served in this role, being called upon to evaluate the quality of training of specialists. The differentiation of the large higher education system was already noted. It was acknowledged that there were genuine education and research centres but also many without quality in either theoretical or practical training.

The 25 Years of Changes: Higher Education Reforms and Contexts

After the disintegration of the USSR, the new independent nations were looking for quick solutions to stabilize and develop their economies. Some declared themselves as "normal" Western market-based democracies;

some adhered to more conservative and isolationistic approaches. In all countries, the economic collapse, transformational recessions, the breakdown of economic ties with the other former republics in what was a large federal network and political changes had dramatic effects on the economy and living standards. Measures that introduced market mechanisms into the ruined centrally planned economies were supposed to revive the economic development.

In his comparative analysis of the transitional economies of Central and Eastern Europe, the Baltics, and 12 CIS countries, Izyumov (2010) finds that in all CIS countries the reforms were implemented by inconsistent shock therapy, ineffective privatization and highly inflationary monetary policies. Public participation in the reform agenda was narrow, which prevented those countries from developing policies that would reduce the negative effects of reform for the population. The transition to a market economy had a high human cost, especially in the countries of the former USSR. Despite the different political regimes that emerged within the former USSR, ranging from more democratic to autocratic, the drastic decline in the standards of living was evident in all countries. In the first 5–10 years of reforms, GDP and GDP per capita dropped dramatically, while the Gini coefficient increased (again, with some variations: e.g. for poor countries like Uzbekistan that change in indicators was not significant). In the absence of supportive governmental policies, private initiatives to cope with transformation often took destructive forms, boosting the informal economy, corruption, crime and drugs use (Izyumov 2010). Neo-liberal ideology, which asserted a limited role of the state and individuals' responsibility for their own well-being, was timely in the countries trying to overcome the legacies of the overwhelming state/central control.

Against this dramatic backdrop, liberalization also took place in higher education. The opening up of the educational system, like the entire society, had started in the *perestroika* period. At the beginning of the period of independence, it was expected that private property, market mechanisms and the absence of state and party control would help to overcome the problems of socialist education (in some countries, including corruption at admissions—see chapter on Azerbaijan, for instance). It was hoped that a change from total state control to autonomy, from uniformity to diversity, from the engineering and vocational bias towards greater humanitarization and personal development would have a crucial impact on the political, economic, social and cultural progress of the society. Education was seen as a key to the new society, and eliminating the state monopoly in education was often seen as an instrument of the expected positive development.

Marketization

Accordingly, the earliest reforms in most of the countries of the region were the introduction of a **non-state/private sector in higher education and tuition fees** in the public sector for both full-time and part-time programmes. The latter was not something that all transitional countries of Central and Eastern Europe did. They either kept their higher education public (e.g. Slovak Republic) or charged fees only for part-time programmes (e.g. in Poland). In all post-Soviet countries, including the Baltics and except for Turkmenistan which only introduced fees recently in a few higher education institutions (HEIs), the impoverishment of the public sector economy inevitably led HEIs to seek for funding elsewhere. Taking tuition fees from the population was essential to the survival of higher education. Tuition fees not only directly brought money into the public HEIs, they also supported largely the same faculty from public HEIs when they took supplemental teaching jobs at non-state HEIs.

As the comparative data show (see Table A.19 in Appendix), in the first ten years after independence, the non-state institutions in many countries of the region have grown very fast, and in five countries (Armenia, Georgia, Kazakhstan, Latvia, Moldova) exceeded the number of public institutions. Two countries (Turkmenistan, Uzbekistan) do not have non-state providers of higher education. Tajikistan closed down most non-state providers, except for one.

However, as case studies in this book will also show, the non-state sector in an absolute majority of the countries was unable to gain the same level of prestige and demand for attendance as the traditional public sector. In the absolute majority of countries, the enrolments continued to be concentrated in the public institutions (Table A.20 in Appendix).

Perhaps the only deviation from this trend is visible in Kazakhstan, where the course of neo-liberal reforms was more explicit than in other countries of the region. In 2015, 52 per cent of students in Kazakhstan enrolled in non-state institutions (Table A.20 in Appendix). Kazakhstan went further in privatization by not only shifting the costs of higher education to the families of students enrolled but also by changing the legal status of several Soviet institutions of higher education into joint stock companies (see the chapter on Kazakhstan).

Therefore, the more striking change took probably not place through the creation of non-state/private sectors but through the transformation of public sectors, which largely changed their economic basis to private funding. In public HEIs in most of the countries, except for Estonia and Turkmenistan, more than half of all students pay fees. Fee payers comprise up to 85 per cent in the Kyrgyz Republic. The share of student population of the region that pays fees to either state or non-state providers further illustrates this point, demonstrating the big change from the full public provision to the privatization of costs of higher education in the region.

Marketization of higher education had another important implication for most of the higher education systems of the region: students and their families became an important source of revenues, and higher education became more consumer-oriented. It led to a rapid expansion of enrolments in the fields of business studies, economics, foreign language studies and law. The public sector immediately started to offer degrees in those fields (either with or without tuition fees). The non-state/private sector was also mostly built around these fields, as these types of programmes were cheaper to provide and had a high demand. As our case studies show, the change from predominantly engineering education to the domination of "soft" fields had significantly changed the higher education landscape. A "consumerist turn" (Naidoo et al. 2011) has taken place in this part of the world too.

Following Kwiek, who reflects on the particular path of marketization in Poland (2008, 2011), we argue that in the case of post-Soviet states, marketization of higher education was dual: both internal to the public sector (through tuition fees) and external (through the emergence of non-state providers). We also argue that unlike in Poland, where internal privatization was limited to the part-time programme domain, "creeping marketization" in the post-Soviet states was much more severe, as the level of penetration of quasi-market forces through user fees was implemented at a larger scale. Public higher education institutions could "sell" the most prestigious "commodity": a full-time degree in highly desirable fields stamped by established HEI "brands", hardly limited by governmental regulations, especially in the first years of independence.

The privatization of costs opened the way to a remarkable expansion in higher education. In most countries, higher education enrolments at least doubled by the mid-late 2000s: in Belarus, Estonia, Kazakhstan, Kyrgyz Republic, Latvia, Lithuania, Moldova, Russia, Tajikistan and Ukraine. Significant growth also took place in Armenia, Azerbaijan and Georgia. In just two countries, Turkmenistan and Uzbekistan, enrolment numbers declined. In Turkmenistan, the absolute enrolment decreased twice at the beginning of the reforms and is still far behind the situation in the Soviet period (currently about 20,000 students compared to 40,000 in the Soviet period). In Uzbekistan, the enrolment also decreased sharply at first and the system has yet to achieve the Soviet level of student numbers (about 260,000 now versus over 300,000 in the Soviet era) (see Tables A.22 and A.24 in Appendix; for massification, see, e.g. Smolentseva 2012; Platonova 2016).

In this way countries that already achieved Trow's mass stage of higher education by the end of the Soviet era moved towards and beyond Trow's threshold of 50 per cent for 'universal' higher education. As such, attending higher education more or less became the social norm, especially in the countries of the European part of the region—the three Baltics states, Belarus, Russia and Ukraine. However, by the mid-late 2000s those systems faced the demographic decline due to the low birth rates of the turbulent 1990s. This resulted in decreasing enrolments in non-state and public sectors. Overall, the demographic change has led to system contraction: in Belarus, the Baltics, Russia and Ukraine (also Moldova, but by participation rate this country is in another group). De-privatization (an increasing role of public funding in contrast to the previous trend to privatization) has become a new trend in the region (Kwiek 2014), which dramatically affects all dimensions of national landscapes of higher education (see respective country chapters).

The two Central Asian countries, Uzbekistan and Turkmenistan, have demonstrated quite the opposite case. They have seen a unique process of de-massification, accompanied by tight government control over higher education and a pattern of demographic growth. The access bottleneck created in the Soviet time (e.g. see the above indicators on competition per 100 places and the chapter on Uzbekistan) has built up more pressure in the independence period, and that contradiction has not yet been resolved.

The other countries—Armenia, Azerbaijan, Georgia, Moldova, Kazakhstan, Kyrgyz Republic and Tajikistan—have experienced various fluctuations over the independence period, but all of them have tended to remain in the mass phase of the massification process. In most of them there has been a recent decline in participation because of governmental policy, including quality assurance mechanisms (including programme and institutional accreditation), in combination with demographic trends. In this group of countries, except for European Moldova, the demographics are rising. This creates additional pressure on the educational system.

Admissions Reform: Introduction of National Standardized Tests

One of the key transformations of higher education systems in the region was the reform of admission system. In the Soviet period, each HEI held written and oral examination in subjects corresponding to the field of study. Examinations took place in person, at the same time in all HEIs, with a couple of exceptions. For instance, Moscow State University conducted admissions earlier than the majority of the other institutions. An applicant could take exams only at one institution at a time. Failing the exams meant one had to wait for another year to try again. The Soviet admission system was widely criticized as restricting equity (talented students could not travel to other cities to take exams) and enabling corruption (lacking transparency).

Standardized tests have been introduced in all post-Soviet countries, except for Turkmenistan. Even in Uzbekistan the national test was introduced quite early—in 1994, unlike, for example, Russia, where it became a prevailing form of admissions only in mid-late 2000s or Tajikistan (in 2014). The subject tests enable candidates to apply to a higher education programme and—if scores would be sufficiently high—to be eligible for a tuition-free place (in some countries, it is called "grants"). The test was considered as an instrument to overcome shortages in the Soviet system and ensure quality and transparency of admissions, decrease corruption and enhance educational equity. It was a significant change of the traditional system and its introduction was accompanied with lots of discussions and tensions. Assessments of the outcomes of these reforms were ambiguous. In some countries the new test system addressed the corruption issue (see chapter on Georgia) or failed to ensure transparency (see chapter on Uzbekistan). In some countries it probably increased social mobility somewhat, but also fostered inequities by advantaging those from better-off families (see chapters on Georgia, Kyrgyz Republic). In addition, the new admission system has become a market mechanism introducing competition among HEIs for "better prepared" students, and thus more public funding, as in most countries academic merit is linked to governmental support. That indeed has led to an increasing vertical institutional differentiation within higher education systems. In many countries the average score of the national university entrance test became one of the key indicators of the prestige and status of a university (see chapters on Azerbaijan, Belarus, Georgia, Russia).

Bologna Reforms

Most of the countries of the region joined the Bologna process, starting with the three Baltic states (1999), Russia (2003), then Armenia, Azerbaijan, Georgia, Moldova, Ukraine (2005), Kazakhstan (2010) and Belarus (2015). Kyrgyz Republic applied, but was turned down. Only four countries, all in Central Asia (Kyrgyz Republic, Tajikistan, Turkmenistan, Uzbekistan), are outside of the Bologna group.

Along Bologna lines, all 15 countries, including those outside the European Higher Education Area, have adopted a two-cycle degree system and introduced bachelor and master degree programmes (3–4 plus 1–2 years). In some countries this system still co-exists, at least in some fields, with the traditional Soviet 5-year degree for specialists (e.g. in Russia and Turkmenistan). In terms of advanced qualifications, several countries, including Estonia, Latvia, Lithuania, Georgia and Kazakhstan, have abolished the second Soviet doctorate, so that their third cycle now only consists of one doctoral degree (PhD).

EHEA member states formally comply with the agreement requirements and have introduced quality assurance bodies for programme and/or institutional accreditation and established a system of credits (ECTS), all measures to support increasing mobility within the EHEA. This is a large-scale transformation for national higher education systems. Adoption of the new policies has created many tensions and uncertainties for higher education and employers' communities, as the value and status of the degrees, especially at bachelor level, have been unclear. In many cases, traditional 5-year curricula were simply shortened in order to meet the new length of studies requirements, which generated a lot of discussion about "incomplete higher education" in the first cycle. In case of countries with binary systems, like Lithuania, the transition to the new system created challenges for colleges awarding professional degrees, especially in regard to internal quality assurance and the disjunction between professional bachelor degree and opportunities of further learning at master's level (Leisyte et al. 2014).

Bologna transformation of the higher education systems for the post-Soviet states meant another wave of adoption of foreign/Western model of higher education with, for many, unclear purposes and advantages.

Internationalization

The USSR became a pioneer of a particular form of internationalization of higher education early in the twentieth century (Kuraev 2014). "Academic internationalization was continually a mission of the national government, reflecting general political strategy of the Soviet state", and aimed at the "global promotion of the Soviet order" (p. 251). In preparation for the world revolution after the advent of global capitalism (imperialism), the Soviet government created a substantial programme of international education. This included full government support for international students to study in the USSR and very limited and highly controlled exchange programmes. Imposing the Soviet model of higher education on the other countries of the socialist bloc was also a part of Soviet international strategy. In the last years of the Soviet period it was already understood that the national economy was unable to continue to bear the costs of large-scale internationalization. But by the time of *perestroika*, the deteriorating Soviet system had opened up opportunities for genuine internationalization. The idea of joining global academia as an equal partner became appealing for Soviet academics. After decades of disseminating the Soviet model worldwide, as Kuraev points out, the new Soviet government suggested to study Western values and to adopt Western principles of academic freedom, institutional autonomy and self-governance. The "Open doors" policy resulted in international agreements and exchanges.

However, those policies had little financial support from the collapsing economy. Internationalization has increasingly become a tool of commercialization, offering a way to supplement institutional budgets with tuition fees from international students. In that respect, Russia was in a "privileged" position, as it inherited the international ties from the Soviet times and had HEIs in major cities where international students traditionally studied. However, also in other countries of the region internationalization has become an important aspect of the transformation of higher education.

Drawing on three case studies of internationalization in post-socialist countries, including former Soviet Georgia and Kazakhstan, Orosz and Perna (2016) found that internationalization has become an important dimension in these countries, especially in government rhetoric, but it lacks consistency and clarity in definitions. In both Georgia and Kazakhstan internationalization indicators became a part of accreditation procedures and the promotion of student mobility.

It can be argued that one of the key questions about internationalization in post-Soviet countries is what are its purposes, and to what extent are they related to the genuine improvement of higher education system by learning from other cultures? How is it interpreted by governments and academic communities of the region? To what extent does internationalization go beyond a single focus on commercialization or degree recognition? We argue that in many cases the role of internationalization is largely seen as a way to secure financial revenues for the sector, but also as an instrument of the further state control, linking internationalization with accreditation procedures and accountability.

International Assistance

An important role in post-Soviet transformations was played by international assistance. This included numerous Western government agencies, multilateral institutions (such as World Bank, OECD, Council of Europe), private non-profit foundations and exchange organizations (Open Society/Soros Institute, Ford Foundation, etc.) and also individual universities, consortia and professional associations (Johnson 1996). In the case of the international financial organizations international aid came as part of the package associated with conditional loans to the governments. Mostly the aid was focused on secondary school reform, but some was targeted towards higher education. International assistance contributed not only to the internationalization of higher education by supporting direct academic exchanges, the publication of international textbooks and literature and training programmes, but also helped to support infrastructure development and academic staff. In Central Asia these international agencies largely supported structural reforms, such as establishing national test systems (see chapter on Tajikistan). However, as Johnson (1996) notes for the case of Russia—and the point is applicable to other countries of the region—often both the reformers and the providers of international aid (including World Bank) were guided by idealized Western practices, rather than local needs and realities. International assistance agents underestimated the power of traditional institutional structures and inherited professional practices from the Soviet system, and the need to work with them, instead of trying to "develop" the systems as they did in educational programmes in other regions.

Summary of Reforms

Table 1.1 summarizes key reforms in higher education, which have been implemented in the post-Soviet period. It shows both commonalities and differences across countries. Even countries close to each other historically and culturally demonstrate different combinations of the reforms (e.g. the countries of Central Asia).

It is important to note that this comparative table does not include the research dimension of higher education systems. It mostly focuses on the teaching function. Although research has been a concern for many governments and international aid providers, it has not become a focus of reform in most of the countries. As the case studies in this book show, none of the systems were able to build a strong system of research universities. This is not only because of the chronic underfunding of research over the last 25 years but also because of the structural legacies inherited from the Soviet system, particularly its separation of teaching and research. Nevertheless, research funding has become an instrument of the state (see chapters on Lithuania, Russia), and this has contributed to the vertical differentiation of higher education systems.

LANDSCAPE CHANGES

The changes in the landscape that took place from the 1990s on—note that some of the changes overlap—are as follows.

First, **many new higher education institutions emerged**, particularly the growth of non-state/private higher education was impressive (but note our earlier comment that the "privatization" of public higher education should not be overlooked). Obviously, under the communist regime, higher education provision was public and planned and regulated by the state. In the post-Soviet period, from the mid-1990s on, in many higher education systems, private initiatives loomed largely. In some countries, the number of institutions doubled between 1990 and now, in others growth was steeper, amounting to sixfold the number of institutions in 2015 compared to the beginning of the 1990s (see Table 1.1). Growth has been even more impressive if the dynamics between 1990 and 2015 are taken into account. Many more non-state higher education institutions emerged in that period, but governmental regulations—licensing and accreditation—led to the closing down of many private initiatives. The current private higher education institutions are generally smaller,

Table 1.1 The key reforms in higher education in post-Soviet countries

	Non-state sector	Fees in public sector; full- and part-time	Standardized test (admissions) reform)	Privatization of public HEIs and new legal forms	Bologna signatory	2-tier degree system (bachelor-master)	Soviet 5-year specialist degree	Replacement of the Soviet two doctorates by single doctorate (PhD)	Stage of massification in Soviet time and now (mass, elite, universal)
Armenia	+	+	2005[a]	+[b]	2005	+	+	–	M –> M
Azerbaijan	+	+	1992/2004	–	2005	+	+[c]	–	M –> M
Belarus	+	+	2004	–	2015	+/–[d]	+	–	M –> U
Georgia	+	+	2005	+[e]	2005	+	–	+	M –> M
Estonia	+	+[f]	1997	–	1999	+	–	+	M –> U
Kazakhstan	+	+	2004	+	2010	+	–	+	M –> M
Kyrgyz Republic	+	+	2002/2012	–	–	+	+	–[g]	M –> M
Latvia	+	+	+	–	1999	+	–	+	M –> U
Lithuania	+	+	2004	–	1999	+	–	+	M –> U
Moldova	+	+	2006/2011[h]	–	2005	+	+[i]	–	M –> M
Russia	+	+	2005–2009	–	2003	+	+	–	M –> U
Tajikistan	+	+	2014	–	–	+	+	–[j]	M –> M
Turkmenistan	–[k]	+	–	–	–	+	+	–	E –> E
Ukraine	+	+	2006	–	2005	+	+[c]	–	M –> U
Uzbekistan	–	+	1994	–	–	+	–	–[l]	E –> E

Source: L. Bischof, Z. Kataeva, D. Platonova, A. Smolentseva using this project's data and analysis.

[a]Since 2012 it is also used for non-state admissions
[b]For example, a new legal form of a foundation

(continued)

Table 1.1 (continued)

cSpecialist degree is being phased out
dNo bachelor degree so far
eIn Georgia, in 2011, the Georgian Agrarian University in Tbilisi was privatized to billionaire Kakha Bendukidze in return to a guarantee of significant investment into the university
fFrom 2013, Estonia cancelled fees for Estonian-language public HE
gA couple of HEIs have PhD programmes
hThe central baccalaureate exam mandatory for lyceum students. Until 2011 a diploma of general secondary education also served as higher education entry qualification
iSpecialist degree kept only for pharmacy and medicine
jIn 2016/2017 academic year, several HEIs have started admissions to PhD programmes
kFees only at one HEI
lReplacement by Doctor of Science—According to the President's Resolution of July 24, 2012, the two-stage postgraduate education (two scientific degrees "Fanlar Nomzodi" and "Fanlar Doktori") replaced by a single level of Doctor of Sciences that is active starting from January 1, 2013

focusing on economics, business studies and foreign language studies. They are often deemed of a lower reputation, although there are important exceptions found in some of the countries and it must also be acknowledged that the popularity of private higher education in many states was due to a lack of trust in public institutions and due to public institutions being reluctant or relatively slow to adjust to the new expectations.

Second, the growth of number of institutions is not only due to the emergence of non-state providers. Also, in all countries, the **number of public institutions grew**, although at a steadier pace than the number of privates. This was partly a spontaneous process with grass-root changes taking place (see also e.g. Tomusk 2004), including existing universities that set up branches elsewhere in the country (e.g. in Tajikistan, Russia, Armenia, Turkmenistan and Uzbekistan). Sometimes governments played a determining role in setting up new higher education institutions in regions that until then did not have universities or other higher education institutions. The governments of the new countries also established new universities to serve the needs of the states in such areas as security, public administration and international relationships.

A third change has been the **upgrading of Soviet specialized institutes into universities**: comprehensive or specialized (technical, medical, agricultural, pedagogical), in both cases with a greater number of fields of study (for specialized universities, going beyond their formal specialization). This resonates with an almost universal trend of "non-university" institutions trying to achieve university status noted in the literature by academic drift (e.g. Neave 1979; Birnbaum 1983). In post-Soviet countries, with the introduction of market-led or market-driven economies, many higher education institutions broadened their portfolio, particularly by adding "popular" disciplines and fields, like economics and business studies. In most higher education systems, there was a significant shift from enrolments in sciences and engineering towards economics, management and social sciences. As a consequence, many single-discipline institutions evolved into multidisciplinary institutions, even though many institutions kept their original names (or just changed from "institute" to "university") and corporate identities. Although we do not have the exact data to support this point empirically, a corollary is that the differences between the higher education institutions—in terms of programme provision—became smaller over time. The Russian and Lithuanian cases particularly refer to the process of upgrading of some of the institutes and academies to universities. It should be noted however that this dynamic played out differently in the cases in this book: for example, the Azerbaijan case reports the blurring of boundaries between the three types, whereas other cases seem to suggest that the distinctions, even though they may be largely symbolic, remained (Tajikistan, Latvia).

A fourth change relates to **vertical differentiation**. Despite the norms and values of equity of the Soviet system, undeniably there were status differences between the institutions. Several chapters allude to the term "flagship" university, signalling there were particular institutions in their systems that were distinctive, for instance because they were educating the next generation of elites (see the chapter on Lithuania). Also some chapters argued that some disciplines had a higher status than others, giving subsequent prestige and status to the institution that specialized in those disciplines. In the period after independence, these status differences continued to exist and were even more profound. In some countries this is partly due to the attempts to (re)integrate research into the universities (in Soviet times carried out at the Academies of Sciences and sectoral institutes), with the level of research activities being used as a sign of excellence and reputation (in the case of Russia, there was an explicit excellence initiative). As noted, funding regimes and the introduction of national entrance exams have also affected the emergence of stronger vertical differences between HEIs in the region. In addition, some countries have employed various procedures to divide HEIs into different tiers by the level of awarded degrees: only first degree (bachelor) awarding institutions, bachelor and master institutions and three cycle HEIs (see chapters on Azerbaijan, Georgia, Kyrgyz Republic, Latvia, Lithuania, Tajikistan, Ukraine). That inevitably contributed to the formal vertical differentiation in the sector.

Some other changes may have been less omnipresent and smaller in terms of impact, but nevertheless worth mentioning. In some countries, governments explicitly aimed at creating a **binary structure** (Lithuania and Estonia). It is interesting to see that such a policy solution was only visible in a minority of systems, whereas this solution was implemented quite often in European countries. Western European countries may have been in a different stage of development and more keen to "offload" universities and establish "cheaper" alternative pathways in higher education (see, e.g. Taylor et al. 2008), but also some Central and Eastern European countries adopted binary systems after independence (see Dobbins 2011).

Another small difference relates to the emergence of **transnational or international providers** (particularly in Armenia and Kyrgyzstan).

Despite the small size of the segment of these new institutions, they occupy high prestige positions in the landscape. In many ways, the establishment of international providers reflects the geopolitical situation and contest within each country. For example in Belarus, there are no international providers, except for two Russian branches, while in Central Asia and Caucuses countries, the international HEIs come from not only Russia and the USA but also Turkey and other neighbouring countries.

In some countries, the Soviet structure has been changed through **mergers**. In Russia, for example, performance indicators have led the government to propose mergers and in Armenia there are recent plans for mergers. In Lithuania, mergers have been planned, but they have been largely unsuccessful. Some mergers have also been found in cases of Georgia, Estonia and Kazakhstan.

In the project it was not always possible to get data on the size of the institutions; however, the findings suggest that it was one of the ways in which the institutional landscape changed. For instance, in Russia system expansion has happened mostly due to the increase of the number of institutions, while in Belarus, the expansion has resulted in an increase of the size of institutions, rather than their number (Platonova 2016).

A final smaller difference is that in some countries existing educational providers, not yet belonging to the higher education fabric, were **included into** the higher education sector, for example, **vocational schools** in Ukraine. Alongside the latter change, we note a blurring of the distinctions between two parts of the tertiary sector: higher education and vocational colleges. The students' pathways between these two levels became less restrictive.

Interestingly such an important feature of the institutional landscape as the separation of **research** and higher education (which manifested in the almost non-existence of research universities) was not changed significantly. Only few countries (e.g. Russia or Kazakhstan) made deliberate attempts to transform existing universities according to the model of the global research university (Mohrman et al. 2008) or establish new research universities.

This brings us to a final comment on the changes, already stressed in previous paragraphs, but important to stress again. Not all changes took place in all countries at the same level and, neither at the same time. There were remarkable differences between the countries, for instance with respect to the occurrence of mergers (to some extent reported in Azerbaijan and Russia), the phenomenon of international branch campuses (primarily in Armenia and Kyrgyzstan) and the emergence of private providers (not in Turkmenistan and Uzbekistan). It is also noteworthy to share that in some countries the distinctions between private and public providers were not as sharp as they appear to be. In all countries the public universities appeared on the market competing with private universities for fee-paying students. In Kazakhstan, public universities were allowed to change their status into joint-stock companies, and in other countries, private higher education institutions were restricted in their operations by national regulations.

The Drivers of the Landscape Changes

As suggested earlier, it is not easy to distinguish drivers of landscape changes from contextual conditions, neither is it easy to disentangle major and minor drivers, but it is safe to argue that the foremost important driver has been the **change from a planned economy towards societies in which market forces were incorporated**. The overall response to the new economic setting was twofold. First, a new balance was sought between demand and supply. The Soviet mechanism of regulating demand and supply through advanced planning of numbers of seats in about 300 specializations and mandatory job placing was abandoned. Many narrow specializations were merged into broader areas. There was an increasing interest among students in disciplines and fields that were not offered in big numbers during Soviet times. This led to the transformation of many formerly highly specialized institutes and academies into multi-profile universities. The higher education institutions undertook action to broaden their supply, and governments contemplated whether new institutions needed to be set up to cater for the rising demand. And, importantly, the new economic context allowed for entrepreneurship in higher education, which led, on the one hand, to opening fee-paying places in public institutions and, on the other hand, to the emergence of many new (non-state/private) providers. Whereas the case studies may not have been fully clear on how initiatives for private higher education emerged, it appears that the ideas were developed mainly by those already working in public higher education institutions or by the former government or party servants seeking for status and income (e.g. see chapter on Belarus).

A second driver relates to **international influences**. Under this broad driver, several elements can be distinguished. International and supra-national agencies became involved in domestic policies. The case studies report the activities of the World Bank, the Asian Development Bank, the

International Monetary Fund and the European Union's Structural Funds. Powerful international NGOs like the "Open Society Institute" and Aga Khan Foundation also played a role in shaping national higher education systems. The international support came with strings attached in the form of certain conditions. These institutions, on the one hand, promoted neo-liberal ideas in financing higher education and in higher education governance. On the other hand, they promoted greater equality and access in higher education (e.g. through national university entrance exams). These policies usually did not have direct elements of the institutional landscape changes in the system except the support for private providers. They however had overall strong influence on the landscape through supporting policies that encourage competition and entrepreneurial behaviour of the universities.

Second, bilateral international relations and partnerships also played the role of driver of the changes in the institutional landscape. Branches of international universities or "national- international" universities like Russian-Armenian or British-Kazakh were established with the support of the respective governments, NGOs or business companies. These universities played an important role of setting new examples and models for "old" universities.

Third, the Bologna process figured to a large extent as an element of supranational influence. Most of the signatories have adjusted their higher education system by implementing a three-cycle degree structure, implementing a quality assurance system in line with the expectations formulated in the European Standards and Guidelines, and implementing diploma supplements and qualification frameworks. In addition, it seems reasonable to assume that the quality assurance and accreditation developments (partly under the influence of the Bologna Process) have paved the way for regulations to deal with minimum standards for higher education provision.

Demographic changes have been the fourth driver in the case studies, although it is difficult to pinpoint how exactly they impacted the changes. During the early years after independence, demographic factors in some countries contributed to the growth of unmet demand. That is, in that period a new balance was sought for—by governments, students and higher education institutions—between needs and supply. In some countries this dynamic was later dampened by decreasing birth rates and decreasing numbers of secondary school-leavers. These demographic changes interacted with governmental policies (particularly accreditation).

That is, higher education institutions started to struggle to survive, partly due to stringent accreditation requirements and demand dropping because of a smaller pool of potential students.

The Role of Governments

One might expect that there should or could have been a significant role of the governments in shaping the higher education landscapes. Indeed the governments lead the development of the legislation that made possible the implementation of the reforms discussed above. One could agree with Carnoy et al. (2013) that the governments in most post-Soviet countries (except more authoritarian) were driven by global and national legitimacy agendas. It drove them to borrow some policies, to open access to higher education.

However, most case studies report that there was limited action from the government directly aimed at changes in the landscape. There is no country of the former Soviet Union that came with its own master plan to restructure the higher education system, to create a new differentiation of higher education institutions. Furthermore, many of the policies that were implemented were more reactive than deliberately proactive.

However, the governments of independent states did consider higher education to be an important tool of building new states. They established new (often specialized) universities to meet new human resources needs. Almost all states established their own military, police and public administration academies and higher education institutions to train cadres for diplomatic fields. Some governments established high prestige and quality higher education institutions in economics and finance. The governments also closed or transformed Soviet institutions that were useless for the independent countries like the Communist party schools and technical institutes that served the Union as a whole.

The need to strengthen the new national (ethnic) identity of young countries required language and culture policies in higher education. In 14 countries, the Russian language (that used to be the dominant language of instruction in higher education) was gradually replaced by local languages. It affected the vertical differentiation of universities. It also led in some cases to the establishment of new universities specialized in national culture and language. During the last years some countries added a new dimension into the vertical differentiation by establishing new or converting old institutions into world-class universities. Another set of the reforms enabled the transformation of existing universities into "niche" universities and establishment of the branches of universities. It contributed to both vertical and horizontal differentiation. The governments also supported the growth of new forms of delivery of education through part-time and distance programmes. It led to emergence of special type of institutions where these forms would be prevalent. The university branches in many countries radically changed the institutional landscape and opened a new level of the territorial accessibility in HE.

The governments also devised new legislation that defined new types of universities. They introduced national exams. Also, accreditation and licensing rules impacted the landscape to some extent. But overall—especially in the early years of independence—much change in the institutional landscape was due to grass-root innovations and entrepreneurship outside the government. Some cases explicitly point at a lack of capacity at the governmental level to develop strategies and policies for higher education in the new economic setting (e.g. Georgia and Armenia).

Interestingly the post-Soviet countries, unlike China, failed to concentrate the overwhelming majority of HEIs under the education ministry. The fact that higher education was steered not only by education ministers but that also ministers of health, defence, agriculture and so on were involved may have limited the scope for coherent governmental action as well.

Probably not a key reason, but it must be mentioned that some universities got their own specific acts and regulations, which may have further hampered the power of the governments or ministries.

In addition, it must be stressed that the economic crises in many countries may have led the governments to focus on more pressing issues than the shape, structure and size of their higher education systems. On the other hand, some countries had relatively stable economies built around the oil and gas industry. In some countries, the lack of attention to higher education was obviously also due to political constraints mentioned earlier. The second type of constraints relates to the political climate as such. Many case studies report on the ongoing practices of corruption and fraud in public administration (e.g. Georgia, Kyrgyzstan, Kazakhstan and Uzbekistan) and obviously we cannot close our eyes to the democratic deficits in many of the countries. Transparency International reports annually on the corruption perceptions in countries across the globe, and it is important to note that only the Baltic states and Georgia are in the upper half and 11 countries appear in the bottom half of the ranking of 168 countries (2015). Also the Democracy Index (composed by the Economist Intelligence Unit) reports major deficits in the level of democracy in the former Soviet states, with seven of these being qualified as "authoritarian". Undoubtedly, these features of the political climate affect the way policies are developed and implemented.

Structure of the Book

The discussion of the transformation of the institutional landscape in the region begins with an analysis of the institutional landscape in the USSR. Isak Froumin and Yaroslav Kouzminov note that by the revolution of 1917 the institutional landscape in imperial Russia has already been diverse. In the 1920s–1930s, Soviet economy took on the form of a megacorporation aiming at industrialization and military power building, where higher education had a role of manpower training, among others. Specialization of its parts and their vertical, rather than horizontal, integration (between higher education and research, among various fields and disciplines) have become key features of that system. The authors argue that the system has remained almost unchanged since the 1930s until the 1980s.

Further the book presents the discussion of the institutional landscape transformation in 15 countries in alphabetical order. Each of the chapters provides an historical evolution of the national higher education systems since their beginning, showing continuities and discontinuities in their development. The chapters also try to place higher education developments in the larger societal context of major social transformations.

In the chapter on Armenia, Susanna Karakhanyan finds that the higher education landscape has become more diverse. It includes not only public and private institutions, but also intergovernmental and transnational institutions. An unusual development in the country is related to the introduction of a new legal form of public HEIs, in the form of foundations, which enjoy more financial freedoms. Transition to a market economy, resurrection of national identity and internationalization agenda developed by government are listed as most important factors behind the HE landscape changes. The recent decline in the number of HEIs (mostly, private) was a result of governmental initiatives to increase educational quality by strengthening accreditation and licensing (since 2008) as well as the extension of the national test to admissions in private sector (since 2012).

In Azerbaijan, as Hamlet Isakhanli and Aytaj Pashayeva note, an expanded HE system has also transformed into a more diverse system, which includes 5 public and 11 private comprehensive universities as well as a number of specialized HEIs. The institutional landscape has been also affected by governmental policies leading to increased vertical differentiation, including the early introduction of a distinction between different levels of HEIs (those awarding only bachelor degrees and those allowed to confer also master- and doctoral-level degrees) and by the use of institutional rankings based on admission test results.

Olga Gille-Belova and Larissa Titarenko argue in their chapter that the Belarusian higher education system expanded horizontally and changed vertically due to governmental policy and various rankings. The transformations at the inter-organizational level were also a result of a change in governmental policy rationales—from the logic of complementarity in the Soviet time to the logic of competition for students and resources. However, the government did not have the ambition to build a brand new higher education model. Rather it tried to adapt an existing Soviet model to the new political, economic, social and international reality.

In Georgia, as Lela Chakhaia and Tamar Bregvadze state, the higher education transformations can be divided into two periods: a chaotic development until 2004, associated with the expansion of both the public and especially the private sectors, followed by more strict governmental regulation aimed at achieving transparency and efficiency. However, the institutional landscape has become more diverse than in the Soviet time. Vertical differentiation has been strengthened by using national tests directly linked to the amount of governmental funding received.

In the chapter on Estonia, Triin Roosalu and Ellu Saar identify four periods in higher education development: from chaotic liberalization until 1993, to expansion and regulation in the next five years, then the Bologna reforms, and the more recent efficiency and excellence agenda. The transition from a demand-driven to supply-driven approach has been primarily determined by demographic decline. The authors argue that early post-Soviet years had more impact on the current state of higher education than did the entire socialist period. The current institutional landscape resembles the one of 1993. We might have to replace the concept of 'post-socialism' with the 'post-post-socialism concept'.

In the case of Kazakhstan, Elise S. Ahn, John Dixon and Larissa Chekmareva find that despite different and in some ways comparatively radical reforms in higher education, which affected all dimensions of higher education—there were departures from the Soviet institutional types and the Soviet degree system; and there were changes in relation to educational funding, the privatization of public institutions, admission reforms, Bologna reforms, excellence programme and others—the administrative, teaching and learning legacies of the Soviet time continue to be prominent, and the government retains the full power to implement changes.

Jarkyn Shadymanova and Sarah Amsler argue that in the Kyrgyz Republic rapid system expansion did not result in an immediate diversification of institutional forms. Many Soviet institutions have kept their positions. Soviet and Bologna degree structures co-exist. However, diversification is taking place in many dimensions—public/private, central/regional, international/regional, horizontal/vertical and others. The authors find that diversification has become a strategy for survival of HEIs, where the best position is defined by historically accumulated prestige and association with governmental or international power.

In the case of Latvia, as Ali Ait Si Mhamed, Indra Dedze, Rita Kasa and Zane Cunska maintain, the expansion and diversification of the higher education system was driven largely by liberalization of the sector, and increased demand for higher education, as well as Latvia's EU accession agenda. The factors differentiating the system vary from public/private, capital/regional, university/non-university sector to the language of instruction (English). The comparative autonomy of Latvian HEIs also contributes to the unique higher education pattern of the country.

Lithuanian higher education system has transformed from an elite system with one flagship university to a mass system that includes both university and non-university sectors, as Liudvika Leisyte, Anna-Lena Rose and Elena Schimmelpfennig argue. It experienced three periods of change: a period of regained autonomy and sporadic expansion; then further expansion, especially in the college sector, and changes related to the EU accession; and most recently, a period of increasing autonomy, competition and internationalization under conditions of demographic decline. During the post-Soviet period horizontal differentiation has been continuous, while vertical differentiation has strengthened, due to the introduction of a binary system, a private sector and competitive research funding. The role of the state, as authors point out, has shifted from a "sovereign state" to a "corporate state". There is a somewhat high degree of HE organizational autonomy.

Alina Tofan and Lukas Bischof find that in the case of Moldova the pattern of higher education development can be described as ongoing consolidation. The first period of reform witnessed the disappearance of governance structures and led to the rapid expansion of HE system, which often under-delivered on quality. Since the demographic decline in 2005 and after, the government's new admission rules and quality assurance initiatives resulted in a decrease in enrolments and in the number of private HEIs.

Russian higher education system sporadically expanded during the first period of independence, as Daria Platonova and Dmitry Semyonov demonstrate. However, from the 2000s onward, the government introduced a number of reforms which have contributed to a mostly vertical differentiation of the system. These include admission reform, new degree structures and new kinds of university status (the federal university and the national research university). Most recently, governmental policies were aimed at the "optimization" of the system by closing down and merging HEIs. Employing statistical analysis the authors interrogate various types of HEIs, showing that there are gaps between formal status and the actual institutional activity.

In Tajikistan, the first years of independence saw a dramatic civil war, as Alan J. DeYoung, Zumrad Kataeva and Dilrabo Jonbekova note. That delayed the process of enrolment growth until the 2000s. Before that the number of HEIs had begun to increase. The doubling of student numbers and the tripling of the numbers of HEIs constituted significant expansion of the system. The system has also diversified. Yet it still carries the Soviet structures and frameworks.

Victoria Clement and Zumrad Kataeva analyse two periods of reform in Turkmenistan. The key goal of the new state was consolidation of the nation. Under the new state ideology, this resulted in a shortening of educational programmes (in higher education, from 5 to 2 years) and discontinuing part-time education. Enrolments dramatically decreased, being already among the lowest for Soviet republics. They still have not returned to the Soviet level. However, the state has been building a new system of HEIs. The total number of HEIs has increased. Since 2007, the country has begun to restore some of the previous developments and has started to embrace certain international policy agendas, including diversification of the institutional landscape.

In Ukraine, the key drivers of the transformations were fascination with developments in the neighbouring EU and the need to overcome or incorporate Soviet legacies, as Nataliya Rumyantseva and Olena L. Logvynenko suggest. The authors argue that reform was guided by three rationales: nation and state building, comparison and critique, and catch-up Europeanization. The chaotic expansion of the early independence period has led to a more diversified higher education system, mostly due to the growing role of private and municipal institutions. Later the state regained its crucial position in shaping higher education sector, which is now being challenged by the increasing role of the academic staff, students and employers.

The case of Uzbekistan presented by Kobil Ruziev and Umar Bukhanov is another interesting example of the central role played by the state in post-Soviet higher education development. They also argue that the transformations in Uzbekistan were driven by the demands of the market economy and the requirements of building and strengthening state HEIs to support the process of transition. Despite the increase in the number of HEIs, enrolments have not increased. There has been a continued bottleneck at the entrance to the HE system. The authors note that the governmental top-down approach has failed to improve higher education sector.

The book concludes with an Appendix prepared by Daria Platonova. It presents relevant statistical data for all countries for each of the pre-Soviet, Soviet and post-Soviet periods collected by the author from various national and international sources.

Conclusions

This project has contributed significantly to our understanding of landscape change and system dynamics in post-Soviet higher education systems. There are no previous studies that analysed all post-Soviet higher education systems from a comparative perspective, based on a framework guiding all case study work. Nevertheless, the project has not answered all of its own questions fully and it has posed new and additional questions that deserve the attention of higher education scholars.

First, it turned out to be difficult to find reliable data in many of the countries in the project, which limited us to some extent in gaining insight into developments in the systems. It was particularly challenging to find robust longitudinal data on the characteristics of higher education institutions. These data form the backbone for classifications of higher education institutions and are crucial to detect patterns of convergence or divergence in higher education (see e.g. Huisman et al. 2015). Although we were very pleased to see the chapter authors arrived at solid classifications, future efforts should be made to gather reliable organization-level data to allow for in-depth insight in system dynamics over time.

Second, we think there is scope for addressing questions of agency in-depth. Many of the developments in our 15 higher education institutions are adequately described, but at the same time it has not always been clear which agent(s) has or have been involved in the various stages of the system developments and the various policy stages. For example, the case studies do reveal that new laws were developed and that quality assurance procedures were implemented. From a policy process perspective, it would be very interesting to understand in much more detail which stakeholders were involved in the different stages of the policy process. Have new (framework) laws largely been developed at the responsible ministries, or have various stakeholders—ranging from representatives from the higher education institutions to external advisers—been involved? Have policy ideas been discussed in broader contexts? Were policies instigated because of concerns stemming from powerful societal groups and institutions? Again, our study has revealed the main patterns, but deeper insight into policy actors and processes could lead to additional insights in policy dynamics (see e.g. De Boer et al. 2016).

Our overall reflection on the landscape changes, and the drivers and contextual factors that have led to the changes, suggests that landscape developments in the post-Soviet states can be divided into two larger periods, at least in most of the countries.

The first period of independence in many countries was characterized by chaotic or sporadic liberalization and expansion. At that time the changes were largely organic, driven by external factors: demand from students for places and demand from the labour market for graduates, and also many bottom-up processes within the states such as the role of private or academic entrepreneurs in the existing higher education institutions. The roles of the respective governments were relatively limited and embodied by general framework laws and accreditation regulations that were used to enable some institutional autonomy and the introduction of market mechanisms, particularly in the form of fee-charging in the public HEIs, and private providers. No longer-term visions of the shape and structure of the higher education systems were evident, apart from the transition to the bachelor-master degree system, and the introduction of a national standardized admission test. This first period was essentially an outcome of general liberalization after the breakdown of the Soviet sociopolitical, economic and cultural system. The new post-Soviet ideology largely followed a global neo-liberal agenda, which implied a diminished role of the state. This lack of political determination (Tomusk 1998; Kwiek 2008) or "policy of non-policy" (Kwiek 2008) in regard to higher education, as in Poland, but unlike many other Central and Eastern European countries, was a principal contributor to internal and external privatization. Partly, also, the policy of non-policy was an outcome of the economic and political turbulence of the time. Higher education was not a priority of government; and governmental resources were very scarce. The government was unable to support many other policies that post-Soviet countries needed: higher education was not the only area in which necessary state action was weak or absent. Thus, the 'solution' was to loosen governmental control and give institutions freedom that would enable them to survive by raising their own money. That window of opportunities in many countries was used by the administration of HEIs to consolidate their control over the institutions, and their vanishing budgets. It might have contributed to the subsequent growth of informal economy in the higher education sector. Hence, marketization "worked" both for the state and HEIs at that time. But perhaps, not for higher education as one of the key social institutions of society.

The second period emerged in the mid-2000s or later. In many countries the approach to higher education steering changed to greater governmental intervention or supervision. The needs of the much larger systems in many countries, including the problem of quality, became impossible to ignore. In addition, many governments joined the worldwide trend towards new public management. The policy goals could be described as efficiency, excellence, better matching higher education with the labour market and international visibility. In most countries, new accreditation and accountability procedures resulted in a declining number of HEIs and students. National and international rankings, and competitive funding models, where applied, contributed to increased vertical differentiation. The introduction of the national test, along with marketization in some countries, led to increased educational inequalities.

International academic discussion about the role of markets in higher education has been prolific in recent decades (see, e.g. Marginson 1997; Olssen and Peters 2005; Klees 2008; Marginson 2013). This literature suggests there is a mismatch between the idea or goal of rule of the market and the nature of higher education. However, nothing of that critical literature has been taken on board by post-Soviet government reformers. Despite the prevailing neo-liberal ideology in the region, alternative views were available even at the beginning of the reforms. A group of experts, consisting mostly of leading social science professors, prepared a report to the Russian government. This was not published in Russia until 18 years later (Castells et al. 2010). That report warned the reformers about overestimating the role of the market and neglecting the role of the state. But countries tend to borrow policies that best fit their own immediate domestic policy agendas (Steiner-Khamsi 2014).

At present in all the countries the role of government remains crucial for the development of higher education sector. In that respect, Soviet legacies have continuities. Only in a few countries, such as Lithuania, have other actors—academic staff, rectors' unions—held some power over the direction of the changes to higher education. This suggests that the role of government should be an important theme for further research on higher education in the region. So far it has not received sufficient scholarly attention in the literature internationally (Carnoy et al. 2013).

The consumerization of higher education in post-Soviet countries also makes a case of further re-considering the link between higher education and employment, as suggested by human capital theory. Enrolments in soft fields have grown without regard for labour market needs, pointing to the non-vocational, socialization-related and credential-creating roles of higher education.

Comparative studies in education and higher education often address the question of convergence or divergence of systems, within larger regions or at the global scale (Dobbins and Knill 2009). Differentiated outcomes can be partly explained by the critical role of local institutional conditions in determining the way in which neo-liberal transformations were carried out (Fourcade-Gourinchas and Babb 2002). Our study, like many other studies, suggests that there are trends towards both convergence and divergence. The role of the diverse national contexts, which can be traced back to pre-Soviet times, has been continuously profound.

However, the question of whether the systems have moved or are moving to a common model or not is not that important. More important is what is happening to each country. The current state of higher education in the countries of the region can only be understood in historical perspective. Their transformations have historical roots. Over the first decades of the reforms the countries of the region were called "transitional". The implication was that they were transiting from totalitarianism and the planned economy to democracy and the market. Nowadays, looking back at the variety of trajectories of these countries, we can see that the goal of democracy was certainly not achieved in the majority of them, and their economic regime can hardly be compared to, for example, Western European or even the Eastern European economies. So are they still transitional, and if so, where are they in transition to? Do they still use ideal Western types as models of reform? If so, where would such models lead them?

In some ways, the countries of the region are still looking at Western models, considered as leaders in higher education in terms of such models (e.g. with reference to often misleading university rankings), but exactly what they are now, where they are going and why is a question for further research into their societies, economies, political systems and cultures. In turn this research would throw a clearer light on the changes so far in higher education and the likely trajectory of higher education in each country in the future.

Acknowledgements The authors express their gratitude to Dmitry Semyonov and Daria Platonova for their continuous work on this project from the very beginning: formulation of the project goals, contributions to the project design, communication with all teams and ongoing organizational and administrative support. Without their genuine commitment and excellent contribution, the project would not exist and could not have succeeded.

The authors are also most grateful to Daria Platonova for her tremendous help with the data collection for all post-Soviet countries using various national and CIS statistical resources. The tables putting together all relevant statistics are presented in the Appendix.

The authors would like to thank all the teams and all the colleagues from many countries whose brilliant work made the project possible. We do appreciate their time and energy throughout many phases of the project and multiple revisions over the last two years. We finally thank Amanda Shimunek for proofreading most of the chapters. Obviously any remaining mistakes in the chapters are ours.

Note

1. The same indicator for the USSR was not available in the official statistical books, even those on R&D.

REFERENCES

de Boer, H., J. File, J. Huisman, M. Seeber, M. Vukasovic, and D.F. Westerheijden, eds. 2016. *Policy Analysis of Structural Reforms in Higher Education: Processes and Outcomes*. Basingstoke: Palgrave.

Carnoy, M., P. Loyalka, M. Dobryakova, R. Dossani, I. Froumin, K. Kuhns, J. Tilak, and R. Wang. 2013. *University Expansion in a Changing Global Economy Triumph of the BRICs?* Stanford, CA: Stanford University Press.

Castells, M., F. Cardoso, M. Carnoy, S. Cohen, and A. Touraine. 2010. "Report to the Russian Government of the International Advisory Group on the Social and Political Problems of Economic Reform and Structural Transition in Russia", as of 1992. *Mir Rossii* 19 (2): 3–18. (In Russian).

David-Fox, M. 2012. Nastuplenie na universitety i dinamika stalinskogo velikogo pereloma (1928–1932) [The Assault on the Universities and the Dynamics of Stalin's 'Great Break', 1928–1932]. *Raspisanie peremen: ocherki istorii obrazovatel'noi i nauchnoi politiki v Rossiiskoi imperii i SSSR (konets 1880–1930e gody) [Timetable of the Changes: Essays on the History of Educational and Research Policy in Russian Empire and the USSR: Late 1880s–1930s]*, 523–563. Moscow: Novoe literaturnoe obozrenie.

Dobbins, M. 2011. *Higher Education Policies in Central and Eastern Europe. Convergence Towards a Common Model?* Basingstoke: Palgrave Macmillan.

Dobbins, M., and C. Knill. 2009. Higher Education Policies in Central and Eastern Europe: Convergence Toward a Common Model? *Governance: An International Journal of Policy, Administration, and Institutions* 22 (3): 397–430.

Fourcade-Gourinchas, M., and S. Babb. 2002. The Rebirth of the Liberal Creed: Paths to Neoliberalism in Four Countries. *American Journal of Sociology* 108 (3): 533–579.

Froumin, I., Y. Kouzminov, and D. Semyonov. 2014. Institutional Diversity in Russian Higher Education: Revolutions and Evolution. *European Journal of Higher Education*. doi:10.1080/21568235.2014.916532.

Heyneman, S. 2010. A Comment on the Changes in Higher Education in the Former Soviet Union. *European Education* 42 (1): 76–87.

Huisman, J. 1998. Differentiation and Diversity in Higher Education Systems. In *Higher Education: Handbook of Theory and Research*, ed. J.C. Smart, vol. 13, 75–100. Edison: Agathon Press.

Huisman, J., V.L. Meek, and F. Wood. 2007. Institutional Diversity in Higher Education: A Cross-National and Longitudinal Analysis. *Higher Education Quarterly* 61 (7): 563–577.

Huisman, J., B. Lepori, M. Seeber, N. Frølich, and L. Scordato. 2015. Measuring Institutional Diversity Across Higher Education Systems. *Research Evaluation* 24 (4): 369–379.

Izyumov, A. 2010. Human Costs of Post-communist Transition: Public Policies and Private Response. *Review of Social Economy* 68 (1): 93–125.

Johnson, M. 1996. Western Models and Russian Realities in Postcommunist Education. *Tertium Comparationis: Journal für Internationale Bildungsforschung* 2 (2): 119–132.

Johnson, M.S. 2008. Historical Legacies of Soviet Higher Education and the Transformation of Higher Education Systems in Post-Soviet Russia and Eurasia. *The Worldwide Transformation of Higher Education. International Perspectives on Education and Society* 9: 159–176.

Klees, S.J. 2008. A Quarter Century of Neoliberal Thinking in Education: Misleading Analyses and Failed Policies. *Globalisation, Societies and Education* 6 (4): 311–348. doi:10.1080/14767720802506672.

Knyazev, E., and N. Drantusova. 2014. "Evropeiskoe izmerenie i institutsional'naya differentsiatsia v rossiiskom vysshem obrazovanii" [European Dimension and Institutional Differentiation in Russian Higher Education]. *Voprosy obrazovania [Educational Studies]* 2: 109–131.

Kuraev, A. 2014. *Internationalization of Higher Education in Russia: Collapse or Perpetuation of the Soviet System? A Historical and Conceptual Study*. PhD dissertation, Boston College, Newton, MA.

Kwiek, M. 2008. Accessibility and Equity, Market Forces and Entrepreneurship: Developments in Higher Education in Central and Eastern Europe. *Higher Education Management and Policy* 20 (1): 89–110.

———. 2011. Creeping Marketization: Where Polish Public and Private Higher Education Sectors Meet. In *Higher Education and the Market*, ed. R. Brown, 135–145. New York/London: Routledge.

———. 2014. Structural Changes in the Polish Higher Education System (1990–2010): A Synthetic View. *European Journal of Higher Education* 3: 266–280.

Leisyte, L., R. Zelvys, and L. Zenkiene. 2014. Re-contextualization of the Bologna Process in Lithuania. *European Journal of Higher Education*. doi:10.1080/21 568235.2014.951669.

Marginson, S. 1997. *Markets in Education*. Sydney: Allen and Unwin.

———. 2013. The Impossibility of Capitalist Markets in Higher Education. *Journal of Education Policy* 28 (3): 353–370.

Matthews, M. 1982. *Education in the Soviet Union: Policies and Institutions since Stalin*. London/New York: Routledge.

Mohrman, K., W. Ma, and D. Baker. 2008. The Research University in Transition: The Emerging Global Model. *Higher Education Policy* 21: 5–27.

Naidoo, R., A. Shankar, and V. Ekant. 2011. The Consumerist Turn in Higher Education: Policy Aspirations and Outcomes. *Journal of Marketing Management* 27 (11/12): 1142–1162.

Nauka Rossii v tsifrakh: statisticheskii sbornik 1994 [Research in Russia: statistical yearbook 1994]. 1995. Moscow: TsISN.

Ministry of Higher and Secondary Vocational Education of the USSR. 1975. Ob utverzhdenii perechnya deistvuyuschi special'nostei i specializatsii vysshikh uchebnykh zavedenii SSSR. [On approval of the list of current specialties and specialisations at HEIs of the USSR]. Order #831. Moscow.

Ministry of Higher and Secondary Vocational Education of the USSR. 1987. Ob utverzhdenii perechnya special'nostei vuzov SSSR. [On approval of the list of current specialties at HEIs of the USSR]. Order #790. Moscow.

Olssen, M., and M.A. Peters. 2005. Neoliberalism, Higher Education and the Knowledge Economy: From the Free Market to Knowledge Capitalism. *Journal of Education Policy* 20 (3): 313–345.

Orosz, K., and L. Perna. 2016. Higher Education Internationalization in the Context of Ongoing Economic-Political Transitions: Insights from Former Soviet and Eastern Bloc Nations. *Hungarian Educational Research Journal* 6 (1): 3–20.

Ovsyannikov, A.A., and A.A. Iudin. 1988. *Universitety Rossii: problemy i spetsifika [Universities in Russia: Issues and Special Features]*. Analytical Report. Moscow: Goskomitet SSSR po narodnomu obrazovaniyu/Golovnoi sovet po programme "Obschestvennoe mnenie".

———. 1990. *Ukrupnennyi structurnyi analiz vuzovskikh tsentrov SSSR [Aggregative Structural Analysis of Higher Education Centers in the USSR]*. Analytical report. Gorkiy: Goskomitet SSSR po narodnomu obrazovaniyu/ Golovnoi sovet po programme "Obschestvennoe mnenie"/Gorkiy State University.

Phillips, D., and M. Kaser. 1992. *Education and Economic Change in Eastern Europe and the Former Soviet Union*. Oxfordshire: Triangle Books.

Platonova, D. 2016. *The Expansion and Transformation of Higher Education: A Comparative Analysis of Post-Soviet Countries*. Master's thesis, National Research University Higher School of Economics, Moscow.

Ryzhkovskiy, V.V. 2012. Genealogia "spetsa": vysshaya spetsial'naya shkola I technicheskaya nauka v usloviyakh sotsial'noi mobilizatsii [Genealogy of the "Spets": Higher Vocational School and Technical Science under Social Mobilization]. *Raspisanie peremen: ocherki istorii obrazovatel'noi i nauchnoi politiki v Rossiiskoi imperii i SSSR (konets 1880–1930e gody) [Timetable of the Changes: Essays on the History of Educational and Research Policy in Russian Empire and the USSR: Late 1880s–1930s]*, 682–774. Moscow: Novoe literaturnoe obozrenie.

Severtsev, V. 1976. *Case Study of the Development of Higher Education in the USSR*. Paris: UNESCO. ED/76/WS/1.

Silova, I. 2009. Varieties of Educational Transformation: The Post-Socialist States of Central/Southeastern Europe and the Former Soviet Union. In *International Handbook of Comparative Education*, ed. R. Cowen and A. Kazamias, 295–320. Dordrecht: Springer.

———., ed. 2010a. *Post-Socialism Is Not Dead: (Re)Reading the Global in Comparative Education, International Perspectives on Education and Society.* Vol. 14. Bingley: Emerald Group Publishing.

———. 2010b. Rediscovering Post-Socialism in Comparative Education. In *Post-Socialism Is Not Dead: (Re)Reading the Global in Comparative Education, International Perspectives on Education and Society*, ed. I. Silova, vol. 14, 1–24. Bingley: Emerald Group Publishing.

Silova, I., and G. Steiner-Khamsi. 2008. Unwrapping the Post-Socialist Reform Package. In *How NGOs React: Globalization and Education Reform in the Caucasus, Central Asia and Mongolia*, ed. I. Silova and G. Steiner-Khamsi. Bloomfield: Kumarian Press.

Slantcheva, S., and D. Levy. 2007. *Private Higher Education in Post-communist Europe. In Search of Legitimacy.* Basingstoke: Palgrave Macmillan.

Smolentseva, A. 2012. Access to Higher Education in the Post-Soviet States: Between Soviet Legacy and Global Challenges. Salzburg Global Seminar, Session 495, Optimizing talent: Closing educational and social mobility gaps worldwide. October 2–7, 2012. http://www.salzburgglobal.org/fileadmin/user_upload/Documents/2010-2019/2012/495/Session_Document_AccesstoHigherEducation_495.pdf

———. 2016. Transformations in the Knowledge Transmission Mission of Russian Universities: Social vs Economic Instrumentalism. In *Re-becoming Universities? Critical Comparative Reflections on Higher Education Institutions in Networked Knowledge Societies*, ed. D.M. Hoffman and J. Välimaa, 169–200. Dordrecht: Springer.

Steiner-Khamsi, G. 2014. Cross-National Policy Borrowing: Understanding Reception and Translation. *Asia Pacific Journal of Education* 34 (2): 153–167. doi:10.1080/02188791.2013.875649.

Teichler, U. 1988. *Changing Patterns of the Higher Education System.* London: Jessica Kingsley.

Trow, M. 1973. *Problems in the Transition from Elite to Mass Higher Education.* Berkeley: Carnegie Commission on Higher Education.

van Vught, F., ed. 2009. *Mapping the Higher Education Landscape: Towards a European Classification of Higher Education.* Dordrecht: Springer.

Yagodin, A., ed. 1990. *Higher Education in the USSR*, Monographs on Higher Education Series. Bucharest: UNESCO CEPES.

Anna Smolentseva is a Senior Research Fellow at the Institute of Education at National Research University Higher School of Economics, Moscow, Russia. She is a sociologist focusing on the changing role of higher education in societies, issues of globalization, educational inequality, the academic profession and transformations in post-socialist higher education systems. A. Smolentseva received a

PhD in sociology from Moscow State University and has been a US National Academy of Education/Spencer postdoctoral fellow, recipient of a Fulbright New Century Scholar grant, visiting scholar at the CSHPE at the University of Michigan, Ann Arbor, and a Salzburg Global Seminar faculty. She is an author of about 50 publications in Russian and English.

Jeroen Huisman is a Professor of Higher Education, Ghent University, Belgium. His work focuses on policy, governance and organizational change. He worked in the Netherlands (1991–2005) and the UK (2005–2013) and is currently directing a research centre on higher education at Ghent University. He is editor of *Higher Education Policy* (Palgrave), co-editor of the *Theory and Method in Higher Education Research* series (with Malcolm Tight, for Emerald) and co-editor of the *SRHE Higher Education* book series (with Jenni Case, for Routledge). He is member of various editorial boards of higher education journals.

Isak Froumin is an Academic Supervisor of the Institute of Education at National Research University Higher School of Economics, Moscow. Prof. Froumin was leading the World Bank education programme in Russia from 1999 to 2011, including the projects in Kazakhstan, Kyrgyzstan, Afghanistan, Nepal, Turkmenistan and India. In 2011 he was co-chair of the education part of the "Russia Strategy 2020" expert group. Since 2012 he is an advisor to the Minister of Education and Science of Russia Federation and the member of the Russian delegation at OECD Education Policy Committee. Prof. Froumin is the author of more than 250 publications including articles and books in Russian and English.

Open Access This chapter is distributed under the terms of the Creative Commons Attribution 4.0 International License (http://creativecommons.org/licenses/by/4.0/), which permits use, duplication, adaptation, distribution and reproduction in any medium or format, as long as you give appropriate credit to the original author(s) and the source, provide a link to the Creative Commons license and indicate if changes were made.

The images or other third party material in this chapter are included in the chapter's Creative Commons license, unless indicated otherwise in a credit line to the material. If material is not included in the chapter's Creative Commons license and your intended use is not permitted by statutory regulation or exceeds the permitted use, you will need to obtain permission directly from the copyright holder.

CHAPTER 2

Common Legacy: Evolution of the Institutional Landscape of Soviet Higher Education

Isak Froumin and Yaroslav Kouzminov

The objective of this chapter is to present the common legacy basis for the chapters devoted to specific post-Soviet countries.

"Classical" Western literature on Soviet higher education paid little attention to the institutional landscape and its evolution. It focused mainly on ideological training, limited autonomy and narrow specialization. Recent advances in higher education studies call us to re-examine the Soviet experience from the angle of institutional differentiation. We shall explore the following questions: How was the structure of the Soviet higher education system designed and how did it evolve? What were the drivers of horizontal and vertical differentiation within the system? How did this structure manifest itself in different Soviet republics?

I. Froumin (✉) • Y. Kouzminov
National Research University Higher School of Economics, Moscow, Russia

The literature on the issue of institutional diversity (e.g., Huisman 1995; Reichert 2009) suggests that the process of differentiation (both vertical and horizontal) accelerates with the massification of higher education. The Soviet experience shows that this is not a universal rule. We argue that the Soviet authorities used differentiation as a powerful tool of the state to build a socialist higher education system almost from scratch.

This was one of the first attempts in history to materialize the utopian socialist ideal of a "correct" system that operates not by the influence of individual and institutional choices but as a machine—through clear and universal rules and prescriptions.

Clark called this "the purest case of the triumph of the state over oligarchical and market interaction" (Clark 1983, 142). In our view, this is a simplification. The key feature of the Soviet system was not just state control over the higher education system. It was rather the fact that the state combined the functions of manpower producer and principal employer that defined the system. This is the case, for instance, in corporate systems of staff training. One might therefore call such a system "quasi-corporate" higher education.

This was an element in a grand social engineering project—a master plan[1] for a system where higher education institutions (HEIs) were specialized parts of a state-controlled machine for manpower production, for the production of a "new man" and for reshaping the social and ethnic structure of the country. We use the metaphor of a machine not simply because higher education was constructed by social engineers. For us, this metaphor stresses the integrity of the system, reflecting Lenin's notion of a socialist economy as a rationally organized "single common factory" (Lenin 1967, 101) as well as Stalin's conception of Soviet society as a "socially unified camp…using education as a weapon" (cited by Kuraev 2016, 8). The carefully forged links between this machine and other parts of the "factory" or "camp" allow us to call this system "quasi-corporate", with reference to modern corporate universities. We agree with the researchers who stress the deep difference between the classical Western idea of a university and the Soviet university model (Kuraev 2016). Our analysis confirms that it was the main organizational principles of Soviet universities that defined this difference. At the same time, we consider that not only limited academic autonomy but also the inclusion of higher education institutions into the planning and distribution of manpower was the key organizational principle defining both the nature of academic work and the institutional landscape.

Some parts of the manpower production machine were broken in 1991, leaving the rest to spontaneously adapt to the new conditions and challenges. The individual compositions of different types of universities and their connections with the external environment that had existed in the various republics of the Soviet Union determined the path dependence of post-Soviet development of higher education in 15 countries.

This chapter starts with a discussion on the different attempts to find the right design for the higher education system. It describes the emerging variety of the types of the institutions and their externally managed relationship with the environment. We then discuss how the rigid structure of the higher education system in the country as a whole evolved over time. Finally, we present the structural features of higher education on the level of the constituent Soviet republics.

STARTING POINT: THE HIGHER EDUCATION LANDSCAPE BEFORE THE REVOLUTION

The Soviet Union was created in 1922 as a federation of four founding republics. By the end of the 1930s it had almost come to occupy the same borders as the old Russian Empire. This enables us to look at the state of higher education in 1916 in the Russian Empire as a starting point for the future transformations. The table below provides some information about the higher education institutional landscape before the socialist revolution.

From Table 2.1 (see also the data on pre-Soviet higher education in Tables A1–3 in the Appendix), we see that the traditional "comprehensive" universities represented only half of the total higher education scene. Half of all students attended a variety of professional HEIs.

Four structural features are particularly important in the context of further discussion.

First of all, the initial initiative to establish higher education institutions came from the Emperor. These institutions invited the first professors from abroad. The autonomy of these universities was very limited (Andreev 2014). Secondly, the Russian authorities considered the universities as an important instrument for holding Imperial Russia together. This is why they had a kind of master plan and founded universities in a number of provincial

Table 2.1 State HEIs in Russia in 1913

Types of HEIs	Number of HEIs	Number of students
Comprehensive universities	10	35,695
Law	4	1036
Oriental studies	3	270
Health care (medical)	2	2592
Teachers' colleges (pedagogical)	4	894
Military and naval	8	894
Theological	6	1185
Engineering	15	23,329
Agriculture	6	3307
Veterinary	4	1729
Art	1	260
Total	63	71,379

Source: Russia 1913 year (1995)

cities, including those in "ethnic" territories. The first universities were opened in Ukraine and Tatarstan in the early nineteenth century. Two universities were re-established in the Baltics (Andreev 2014). However, modern higher education did not appear in Central Asia, the Caucasus or Belarus until the first post-revolutionary years.

Thirdly, the monopoly of imperial universities ended in the second half of the nineteenth century as other ministries began the establishment of more specialized higher education institutions, for example, the Mining Institute, Institute of Technology, Agriculture Academy and so on (Saprykin 2012). The establishment of these institutions manifested the government's attention to the needs of the new industrial economy. Fourthly, at the end of the nineteenth century, non-governmental organizations also joined the state in higher education provision for groups that had previously been declined access. Women and representatives of the lower social classes received the opportunity to study in the non-governmental non-profit sector (Kassow 1989).

Thus, by 1917, Russia had developed a higher education system which included a number of features of the French and German universities (Avrus 2001). The Empire had quite a diverse system of higher education institution. From 1859 to 1914, the number of higher education students grew from 8,750 to 127,000, seeing the number of students per 10,000 population increase from 1.4 to 7.6 (Kassow 1989).

The Russian universities (including the specialized establishments) became strong centres of research. These universities trained several future Nobel Prize laureates and famous inventors, and helped Russia to become one of the strongest producers of new knowledge.

In Search of a Perfect Design: From "Utopia" to Real Socialism—1917–1928

The first anthem of the young Soviet state was "The International", with its famous line "We will destroy all the world of violence/ Completely, and then/ We will build the new world./ – He who was nothing will become everything". This reflected the intentions of the Soviet leaders to demolish all capitalist institutions and to implement the idealistic ideas of Marx and his predecessors (the utopian socialists) in the real world. Two obvious questions emerged after the Revolution with regard to higher education: what should an ideal higher education system be like, and what should be done with the "old" universities?

The first question was particularly difficult. Orthodox Marxism and the utopian socialists had not said much about higher education in particular. They had focused on mass (school) education. Their ideas reflected the general values of the Enlightenment and aimed for the wide dissemination of knowledge (Vasilkova 1989). The Russian Marxists had not devoted much thought to the specific form of higher education that would serve the new "state of workers and peasants" either. Three distinctive answers to the first question appeared after the Revolution (McClelland 1971). All these solutions had in common the idea that "education cannot help but be connected with politics" (Lenin 1957, 354) and that education should be linked with the real world. They also agreed that the "proletarianization" of the universities was an important goal (Safronov 2013, 55). However, the proposed institutional (organizational) forms for these three versions were quite different.

The strongest (initially) group suggested that higher education should be part of the general system of proletarian cultural dissemination. One of their intellectual leaders, Alexander Bogdanov, insisted that the Revolution should bring the proletariat broad possibilities to master knowledge to the highest level. His ideas about higher education reflected the European ideal of universalist education opened up for underprivileged groups. After the 1917 Revolution, he promoted and established the so-called Workers'

University—a system of programmes "built on cooperation between the teachers and students and leading proletariat, aiming towards mastering the highest achievements of science" (Bogdanov 1911). The supporters of this idea also promoted local higher education initiatives to establish "Proletariat Universities" in various cities, including several without any tradition of higher education (David-Fox 1997). They insisted on open admission to HEIs and a broad curriculum. As a result of this policy the number of HEIs had reached 278 by 1921—a threefold increase from 1914 (McClelland 1971). This group of new universities did not last long. The Communist Party leadership did not support grassroots movements. They also saw little value in the unregulated dissemination of broad knowledge for the "building of socialist society". They started to close these universities or transform them into other types of institution. The students and professors of the Workers' Universities protested as they thought that such universities should exist as "laboratories of new forms". Their voices were not heard (Lapina 2011).

The second approach was based on Lenin's idea of the party as the vanguard of the working class: "If one wants the working class to understand its interests and its situation, to control the political process, there is an immediate need for a leading group of this class, to be achieved by all means" (Lenin 1967, vol. 24, 37). The new Soviet leadership regarded a special type of higher education to be the main instrument in the training of new leaders, of a new Soviet elite. The first "communist university named after Sverdlov" was established in 1919 on the basis of several small higher schools for party leaders. The experience of this university was considered positively. The 10th Party Congress of 1921 directed the establishment of a wide network of Soviet-Communist higher schools in each region (including communist universities in the big cities) (Ivantsov 2011). This was a prototype for the Soviet system of higher education—a centrally controlled (by the Central Committee of the Communist Party) hierarchical system of organizations of several types with a standardized curriculum and rules for each type. Admission to these schools was restricted to those who had obtained a recommendation from the local party committee. The mechanism of mandatory job placement was also piloted within this system of training. The system had its intellectual centres: the Institute of Marx and Engels Studies and the Institute of the Red Professoriate (est. 1921). These institutions provided quality control and trained professors for the party higher education system (Leonova 1972). "The rise of this party system bifurcated higher learning, in policy as in perception, as the Party created Bolshevik equivalents of academies, research institutes, universities, middle schools, and so on. It was party schools – more Marxist, more communist, and more proletarian than the old institutions" (David-Fox 1997, 3).

It is important to stress that one special type of these higher education institutions was developed to serve the "ethnic" regions—to train local political leaders. Two communist universities for active workers from foreign communist parties in the East and the West were also established in Moscow in 1921. After the establishment of the Soviet Union, the system was expanded to all Soviet republics. There were 45 communist universities in the Soviet Union by 1931.

Similar in structure and even larger in scale, a network of higher education institutions also emerged in the military sector. The old military colleges and academies were closed. The first Soviet military academy was established as early as 1918. In a couple of years the system of higher education under the Ministry of Defence included not only Artillery or Naval Academies but also Military-Medical and Military-Political Academies. Taking into account the place of the military in the Soviet system, it is not surprising that by 1980 there were 164 military higher education institutions in the USSR (Feskov et al. 2013). This constituted a significant sector of higher education—about 15 % of the whole system.

The third approach to the development of a new higher education system was similar to the second but had a very different objective. The leaders of the young Soviet state admitted that they needed trained specialists for the state-owned economy. The main principle of the higher education policy of the early 1920s was "the rigorous subordination of all other possible functions of education to the economic function. Gone was the effort by Narkompros to stimulate the general development of the individual and to achieve a psychological transformation of the masses. Greatly minimized was the attempt to achieve significant social change by means of a drastic increase in educational opportunities for working-class youth" (McClelland 1971, 828). This idea was in full correspondence with the dominant ideology of the planned economy and social engineering (Avrus 2001). The idea behind this new approach was clearly presented by the first minister of education: "We will not consider the desire, or the declaration, 'I want to be a builder, and you are making me into a chemist'; we will say, 'Here it is necessary to do what the Red Army does; it sends to specialized work those whom it deems necessary to send, and not according to individual desire' (Lunacharskiy 1958, 135). The military analogy reflected the built-in enforcement mechanisms within the higher education system, including the recruitment of students and their job placement. Interestingly, this vocation orientation somewhat contradicted the Marxist view that narrow specialization has a dehumanizing impact and reflects the capitalist division of labour. This led the theorists of Russian education to the idea of polytechnic education, which implies the combination of a variety of practical skills and the theoretical basis for them (Fitzpatrick 1979). This could be called vocational orientation, but we would prefer to call it specialized practical orientation.

The implementation of this approach made the issue concerning the use of the universities inherited from the pre-revolutionary period even more pressing. The discussion in the party leadership ended in a practical solution—to use the existing network of HEIs as the basis for a future industry-oriented system while keeping rigid political control over them. This decision, supported by Lenin, strongly influenced the institutional landscape of the future higher education system. Instead of building the whole system from scratch as a "greenfield project", the Soviet government decided to start the system with the socialist transformation of the existing universities. This determined the path dependence within the system and gave additional prestige to (and influenced vertical differentiation in) the "old imperial" institutions.

Soviet higher education also performed an important function of creating the Soviet intelligentsia and bureaucracy—"whole-hearted" supporters of socialism that had to occupy leadership positions in the economic and social sectors. Lenin believed that a good education is a prerequisite for leadership (Fitzpatrick 1979). This function was expanded from the party higher education institutions to the higher education systems as a whole. It determined a number of unique features of the Soviet system, with its mandatory (for all students) ideologically designed courses on Marxism and Communist Party history, massive affirmative action mechanisms, including remedial courses for children from working-class families to prepare them for university. Such orientation "also provided a significant source of compensatory legitimacy among a large and influential segment of the Soviet population" (Johnson 2008, 163). At the same time, this function did little to influence the institutional landscape.

The idea of manpower production as the dominant function of higher education institutions directed Soviet policy makers in their search for an optimal organizational model in higher education. The Ministry of Education (the 'People's Commissariat of Enlightenment', rather) fought with the Supreme Economic Council for control over higher education institutions. To make a long story short, one could say that these discussions almost ended with the beginning of the implementation of the first five-year plan in 1928.

Since then, the Soviet economy took on the form of a mega-corporation focusing on industrialization and military power building, which acted according to detailed and long-term planning, including manpower planning. The main parts of the Soviet higher education model were by this point in place.

The key role of the state in the economic sphere has been associated with planning production output, something which also applied to the higher education sector: the quantity of students and programmes for each institution was planned in accordance with the anticipated needs of different industries. In other words, the development of higher education was subordinated to the manpower needs of the economy. The most important link between the universities and industry that ensured higher education's function as a producer of manpower was mandatory job placement for graduates, as regulated by planning the staffing needs through a list of specialties. Graduates who did not want to work at their assigned jobs could face criminal charges.

A fundamental feature of this quasi-corporate system was the specialization of its parts. This refers to the strict separation of elements, and their vertical rather than horizontal integration. The separation of research and educational activities reflected this principle (Graham 1967, vii; Clark 1983, 98–99). Industrial research institutes, defence laboratories, the Academy of Sciences, universities and subject-oriented educational institutions made up the research and education landscape. This peculiarity did not allow universities to link research and education in a consistent manner (Johnson 2008, 160). At the same time, the separation secured the directed and vivid development of science in the interests of national defence and the economy of the USSR.

Another type of separation was based on differences between fields and disciplines. Almost every sectoral ministry in the Soviet Union and its republics had its own specialized HEIs. These specializations reflected the extensive list of narrowly defined occupations within different sectors of the Soviet economy. Industrial universities (university factories) were an important element of the Soviet system (Ushakov and Shuruev 1980), training students not just for a specific role in industry but also for a specific role at a specific factory. Along with strong coordination between higher education and the industrial agenda, this led to parallelism, an inefficient use of financial and human resources and often insurmountable barriers to movement within the system (Johnson 2008, 163). By 1990, 896 Soviet universities fell under the jurisdiction of one of over 70 agencies and organizations (Avis 1990, 6).

The complex structure of the Soviet higher education system is presented in Fig. 2.1.

Obviously such a complex "machine" could work only in a very rigid management model. Institutional autonomy was unnecessary in this "perfect" mechanism. The first Soviet university charter was exemplary "in its complete denial of autonomy, and in its subordination of university administration to the central governmental apparatus" (McClelland 1971, 828).

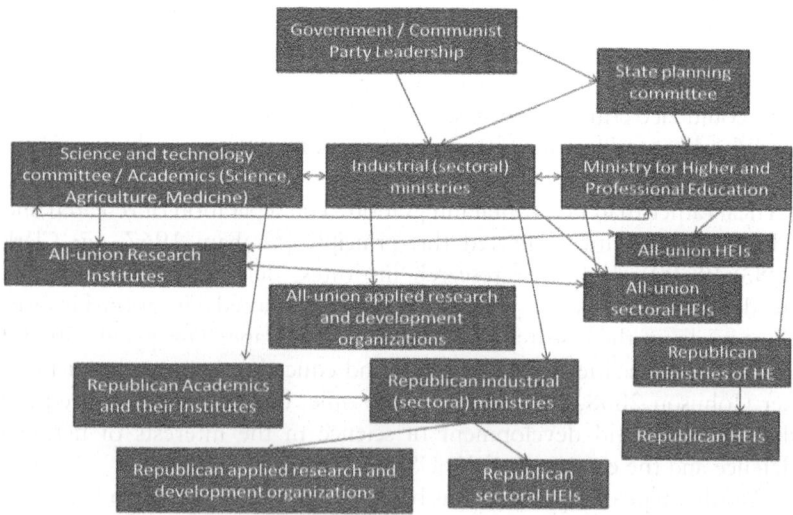

Fig. 2.1 Governance of Soviet higher education and research in the 1980s (Source: Zinov'ev and Filippov 1983)

Tuning the Machine 1928–1940

The time between the start of the five-year plan and 1940 was a period of further enhancement of the organizational structures and mechanisms described above. The Soviet leadership considered higher education to be an important instrument for accelerating economic and social development. It was looking for the best governance and organization mechanisms not just in education but in the economy as a whole. Below, we discuss the various different directions to the further development of the quasi-corporate organization of higher education.

The main efforts of the higher education designers were focused on strengthening the linkages between higher education and industry. In April 1931, Stalin made a strong statement at the plenum of the Central Committee of the Communist Party: "Soviet industry needs Engineers, who are not only strong theoretically but strong in practical experience and in their link with production" (cited by Fitzpatrick 1979, 123).

The desire to build even closer links between higher education and industry led to the invention of a new type of higher education institution, the *zavod-VTUZ* ("factory university") . The essential features of this type are organizational integration of the higher education institution into a particular enterprise and inclusion of the practical work of students at this enterprise into the mandatory curriculum. In the late 1920s, a Central Committee resolution raised the status of in-factory training, allowing enterprises to adopt the title of *zavod-VTUZ* and to award degrees and diplomas. "For the radical communist theorists who wished to see a merging of education and production, the recognition of the *zavod-VTUZ* was a milestone on the road to socialism" (Fitzpatrick 1979, 201). This radical model did not receive wide dissemination (there were only eight such institutions by 1989) (Lyusev 2009). However, it influenced the whole system by stressing the role of practical experience in higher education. The VTUZ issue was not simply a question of institutional control, but was associated with a dispute on the kind of engineers that ought to be trained. The Narkompros[2] and engineering professors were in favour of the "broad" engineer according to the German model, which meant in effect that they were for the type of training currently offered in the engineering schools. The Vesenkha[3] took the position that industry needed only a small number of "broad" engineers for planning and senior supervisory positions. The majority of engineers should be trained on the "narrow" profile to be "specialists in a definite concrete and limited branch of industry" (Fitzpatrick 1979, 125).

As a result, a rigid and rich system of practical work as part of the mandatory curriculum was developed and introduced. Enterprises were obliged to take students and supervise them. The placement of students for this practical work in many cases became part of the overall planning process. These *links between the HEIs and enterprises became an important part of the higher education landscape.*

The idea of the *zavod-VTUZ* also influenced the opening of new narrowly specialized HEIs near the centres of corresponding industries. The Institute of the Linen Industry was established in the small town of Kostroma in 1932 by the Ministry of Light Industry and the Institute of Fruit and Vegetable Production in the town of Michurinsk in 1931.

For the autumn admissions of 1931, higher education institutions were instructed to enrol workers into *evening and correspondence courses* rather than as full-time day students (Fitzpatrick 1979). This marked an important step in enriching the institutional landscape by opening evening and correspondence courses at HEIs, and by establishing separate "correspondence universities". By 1940, 18 such HEIs and correspondence courses in 383 HEIs were operating in the Soviet Union (Bim-Bad 2002). The links between industry and this form of education were ensured by the requirement that these programmes could enrol only those students working in a particular sector and that workers could only attend the programmes that trained for their sector of work.

The main changes in the institutional landscape in this period were primarily caused by experimentation in the establishment of specialized institutes and their separation from large multidisciplinary universities. This phenomenon was accompanied by these institutes being transferred to the jurisdiction of sectoral ministries. The implementation of this new educational policy, suggesting a large-scale reorganization and redesigning of curricula, led to an even more sophisticated and complex system that included a large number of relatively small and highly specialized institutions. Two new words captured the essence of the changes: *otraslirovaniye*, that is, the distribution of HEIs among sectoral ministries, and *vtuzirovaniye*, that is, the widespread dissemination of operating forms and methods of factory-specific higher technical schools (Andreev et al. 2012, 544). The restructuring was remarkable because of the way in which fundamental and applied disciplines were continuously and consciously detached from universities.

The examples are very clear. In 1930, the Moscow Mining Academy was divided into six specialized HEIs: geology, mining, oil, non-ferrous metals, steel and peat. Three faculties of Moscow's famous Bauman Higher School of Technology became separate institutes: aviation, energy and construction engineering. The Moscow Institute of Zootechnics was divided into even more specialized institutes: of horse breeding, meat cattle, sheep and goats, veterinary science and the breeding of animals for fur (Froumin et al. 2013). In some cases, "higher education engineers" from the government would not just divide existing universities into separate HEIs but put together parts from different institutions to create something new—the Moscow Institute of Bread Baking was formed on the basis of one faculty of the Bauman Higher School of Technology and one from the Moscow Chemical Technology Institute.

This process in the beginning of the 1930s gave rise to a burst in the number of new HEIs. While there had been 152 HEIs in the 1929/30 academic year, there were 579 of them in 1930/1931 and 701 in the 1931/1932 academic year (Chanbarisov 1988, 193–194). New universities were opened in the capitals of almost all Soviet republics between 1931 and 1934 (ibid).

The 17th Congress of the Communist Party in 1934 (known as the Congress of the Winners) summed up the results of the implementation of the first five-year plan and approved the second five-year plan. The Congress approved 14 main sets of measures to accelerate the social and economic development of the country. "Manpower training" was one of these key sets of measures linked with future economic victories. It gave a further impetus for the improvement of the higher education machine and its links with the external environment.

As research and development were moved from the universities, inconsistencies and intra-system contentions grew. In order to mitigate the risks, the authorities built special mechanisms to involve university staff in contractual research for state enterprises, and to involve specialists from the research institutes in part-time teaching at universities. Enterprises had to allocate some part of their funds to support contractual research and development at HEIs.

The authorities understood the risks of stagnation and deterioration of education quality in the absence of competition between universities and graduates. Therefore, the government created the so-called socialist competition between the universities and between similar faculties in different universities (Korotenko 2009; Kurasov 2015). It also created incentives for the best students to enrol at the best respective institutions. Few leading HEIs had special right to run the admission exams one month earlier than all others.

This mechanical but orderly system, which satisfied the needs for staffing specialized research and development in the planned economy, was mainly formed in the late 1930s. The All-Union Congress of Higher Education Staff concluded in 1938 that "the goal of the reorganization of the network of the higher education institutions in the country has been completed. The new institutional landscape finally corresponds with the needs of the socialist state" (Bolshevik 1938, 3). This Congress specifically stressed that 3 HEIs be established in Kyrgyzstan, 14 in Kazakhstan, 16 in Georgia and 26 in Uzbekistan. The Soviet economic development plan became the only real driving force to transform the system. The universities did not provide feedback for this plan. They did not have any room for initiative in either their own development or the development of the economy and society.

As a result of this reorganization, three main types of HEIs then emerged (Froumin et al. 2014):

HEIs established on the territorial production principle. The essence of these institutions was the staffing needs of specific sectors at the regional level. Specialized universities, such as teacher training, medical institutes, polytechnics and so on, were established in each region or group of regions to correspond to their economic and social needs.

Some HEIs and groups of HEIs were subordinated to specialized ministries, for example, agricultural universities reported to the Ministry of Agriculture of the USSR. We call this type of institution *regional infrastructural HEIs*, as the primary function of this group was to staff relatively homogeneous economic sectors in the regions. These institutions were focused on local labour markets. Each specialized group of such universities included a few "leaders", which were specialized infrastructural universities in the regional capital cities. These universities enjoyed additional benefits, such as methodological leadership and staff support from other institutions in the same field, such as the Moscow Medical Institute.

Specialized industrial HEIs focused on staffing a specific sector of industry on the national level. This group of institutions included specialized universities affiliated with the Soviet industrial clusters (e.g., transport engineering universities or aviation universities in the regions) and technical HEIs affiliated with particular factories or enterprises. This group also included designated leaders who performed the role of methodological centres for other institutions in the same field.

Classical (comprehensive) universities that trained staff for other HEIs (especially in the basic sciences), staff for research institutes and personnel for local managerial elites (in economics, journalism, history and law).

Some universities were associated with mixed rather than pure types (probably as a result of specific historical circumstances). At the same time, if we try to relate each HEI to one particular type, the following picture emerges: the system comprised 6 % universities, 17 % specialized institutions of macro-regional significance and 77 % regional infrastructural HEIs in the end of 1980th.

Table 2.2 shows the formal classification of HEIs according to their field of specialization.

The specialization of HEIs reflected in this table was an important element of their horizontal differentiation. The prevalence of the specialized HEIs was an important feature of the Soviet system. A large share of the engineering training was also a peculiar characteristic aimed at rapid industrialization—almost 30 % of students in 1940 have been enrolled in engineering-related programs (see Tables A.6 and A.7 in Appendix).

Another important factor for the horizontal differentiation was the proportion of full-time, part-time (evening) and correspondence higher education programmes. Almost 4 % of the students were enrolled in evening programmes and almost 20 % in programmes delivered by correspondence in 1940 (see Table A.8 in Appendix). Moreover, there were some

Table 2.2 Number of HEIs in the USSR by the specialization of the institution

	1940/41
Total	817
Industry and construction	136
Transportation and communications	28
Agriculture	91
Economics and law	47
Healthcare, physical culture and sport	78
Education (including universities)	407
Art and cinema	30

Source: Narodnoye obrazovaniye i kultura v USSR: Statisticheskiy ezhegodnik [Education and Culture in the USSR: Statistic Yearbook] (1989). Moscow: Finansy i statistika

HEIs that had only evening and correspondence programmes (at least six HEIs in 1940).

This structure mainly reflects a very rich horizontal differentiation. It would be wrong to say that the *vertical differentiation* simply put comprehensive universities on the top of the hierarchy. The vertical differentiation had a number of dimensions.

The most obvious was that of administrative vertical differentiation. Part of the higher education institutions were subordinated to the All-Union Ministry of Higher Education or sectoral all-union ministries. The status (and often the funding) of these institutions was higher than under the republics' ministries. In various periods there were about 25–35 HEIs under the All-Union Ministry of Higher Education (Zinov'ev and Filippov 1983). Specialized HEIs were distributed between All-union and republican sectoral ministries. Their superiority was supported by special functions related to other universities. Usually these "central" universities performed quality assurance for similar universities; they provided in-service training and concentrated doctoral programmes not just for their own graduates but for those who had completed a "specialist" programme[4] at another university. Graduates of these programmes were often sent back to their "alma maters" to become professors. This system was well structured: second-tier HEIs had quotas for sending their future professors for doctoral training.

Another dimension of the vertical differentiation was based on *prestige*. One could say that there were two prestige hierarchies: the all-union and the republic level. At the Union level, some universities were famous for training political or professional elites. They had particular support from the state. Some of these even scheduled their entrance exams earlier than those of other universities, to allow those who failed the chance to go to less prestigious places. At the republic level the comprehensive universities in the republican capital cities were usually more prestigious than other HEIs. It was very rare that less popular universities challenged the status quo. Such initiatives would not be supported.

Finally, we have to note another important feature of the Soviet higher education landscape—*territorial (geographical) distribution*. This aspect of the network's structure was influenced by two ideas: access and proximity to the production site. Broad access had been one of the major ideas of the Soviet master plan from its very beginnings. It was implemented through the "norms" of deploying regional infrastructural HEIs in almost all regions of the country. As one US geographer noted, "The distribution of Soviet higher educational institutions conforms generally to the distribution of population... Large ethnic areas have universities, as do all large cities of Russia. ASSRs usually have universities, while autonomous oblasts have pedagogical institutes and autonomous okrugs have no higher educational institutions at all" (Andrews 1978, 456).

Many cities of sufficient population had their own teacher-training institutions. Some smaller cities that emerged around one big enterprise had branches or evening course sites affiliated to the specialized HEIs based in the big cities. The town of Novomoskovsk, for instance, built around a huge chemical plant, had a branch of the Moscow Chemical-Technical Institute; and the town of Stary Oskol, built around a metallurgical plant, had a branch of the Moscow Institute of Steel and Alloys. Some researchers counted the number of such branches at 300–400 by the end of the 1970s (Andrews 1978).

This structure and differentiation remained almost unchanged until the late 1980s. The number of HEIs in the USSR grew from 817 in 1940 to only 898 in 1989 (Statisticheskiy sbornik 1989) (Fig. 2.2).

Since 1940 the higher education machine was running in the USSR within a "single common factory" on the basis of stable and clear rules and mechanisms.

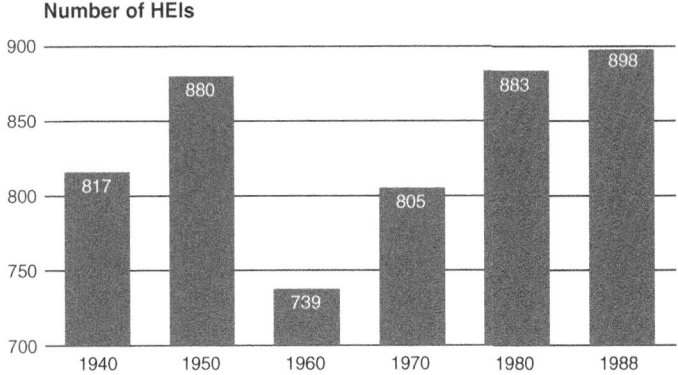

Fig. 2.2 Number of HEIs in the USSR (Source: Authors using data from Narodnoye obrazovaniye i kultura v USSR: Statisticheskiy ezhegodnik [Education and Culture in the USSR: Statistic Yearbook] (1989). Moscow: Finansy i statistika)

From Development to Stagnation 1940–1991

After 1940 there were no major innovations in institutional differentiation or in the instruments linking higher education with the external environment. At the same, there were several drivers for change.

Political changes included a degree of democratization and internationalization after Stalin's death in 1953—the "thaw period". This created at least some opportunities for initiative and for bringing in international students. Some universities gained special departments for foreign students (helping them to raise their informal prestige and status and contributing to vertical differentiation). A special HEI for foreign students—the Peoples' Friendship University—was established in 1960.

Technological challenges associated with military competition with NATO called for the development of new fields of training. The period 1945–1980 saw the appearance not just of new departments within the established universities but also new HEIs specializing in these fields such as the Moscow Institute of Physics and Engineering aimed at supporting the Soviet nuclear research and industry.

The separation of research and higher education was a permanent issue for the Soviet higher education policy. The authorities insisted on the specialization of different organizations and on constructing formalized links between them. Researchers argued for more organic connection that could be achieved within the model of the research university. In 1938 the newspaper of the Central Committee of the Communist Party published an open letter of a group of leading scientists suggesting the establishing of the Higher Institute of the Technology to train engineers-researchers because existing HEIs train only those who can use existing technologies. They suggested that this Institute should employ only research-active professors and should give them all conditions for the research (Pravda 1938, #334). This letter did not have a big impact. However, the idea survived—in 1946 leading Russian physicist P. Kapitsa (Nobel Prize laureate) wrote to Stalin suggesting to establish the Moscow Institute of Physics and Technology that should train future engineers-researchers on the basis of the leading research institutes. He convinced Stalin with the arguments that only such training could assure the Soviet competitiveness in space and military industry. This institute was established in 1951 (it existed as a school at Moscow State University since 1946). However, it remained a rare example. Later Novosibirsk University was established with a special relationship with the Academy of Science. The closeness between these

HEIs and the Academy manifested in a simple fact—the majority of their professors were adjuncts belonging to the Academy. This model brought into question the separation that was embedded into the system.

In the late 1950s, the Soviet leadership became unhappy with the poor links between HEIs and the economy. They saw the problem as lying in weak planning and weak enforcement of administrative requirements. They "also seemed dissatisfied with an involuntary and seemingly often ineffective system for the "distribution" of graduates to job placements after their university training" (Johnson 2008, 164)

Two new laws were adopted to improve the links between higher education and "real life", providing a regulatory framework for increased practical training in industry and agriculture, and to expand the network of *zavod-VTUZ* (Yelyutin 1980). Two provisions were specifically made in these laws to change the institutional landscape.

The first law suggested "making better order in the network of HEIs, aiming at the increase of the number of HEIs in the territories of rapid industrial growth, moving HEIs closer to production facilities, and the merger of HEIs working for the same sector" (USSR Law – 24.12.1958). This decision was not fully implemented, but a number of highly specialized HEIs were established in the regions of the Soviet Union. The idea of specialization as a solution to the inefficiency of the quasi-corporate system became even stronger than it had been in the 1920s. The implementation of this law led to changes in the distribution of HEIs in the country. Despite weak opposition from the professors, the Moscow Institute of Non-Ferrous Metals was moved to Siberia, and the Moscow Peat Institute was moved to one of the regions of Central Russia—closer to the industry concerned.

Western researchers positively noted the ability of the Soviet state to restructure the system: "Another undeniable dimension of the distinctive strengths of the Soviet system of higher education and research was the powerful (if often ponderous) bureaucracy that could "force" educational resources and professional talent "out and down," out into the rural regions and nationality areas (Rosen 1963, 9).

The second provision could be considered as contradicting the first. It called for further development of universities in Russia to increase the supply of specialists in the basic sciences and to increase the role of universities in research. It also stated the necessity of "strengthening the network of universities in Russian Federation, especially in the eastern part of the country" (USSR Law—16.04.1959). In making this decision, the authorities recognized the weaknesses of the "machine"—the problems that emerged from the separation between research and higher education. They also noted that the closed sub-systems of highly specialized higher education institutions prevented the building of links between technological development and the advancement of the basic sciences. These sub-systems did not feel the importance of linkages with comprehensive universities, so the government interfered once again to correct the imperfections in the machine's operation. As a result of this policy, the number of HEIs in the country grew by 12 % from 1966 to 1975 and the number of comprehensive universities by 50 % (from 42 to 63) (Zykin 1992).

Opening new universities in the eastern part of Russia also demonstrated that the authorities regarded the establishment of higher education institutions as an important step in territorial development. The needs of regional development became a stronger driver for changes in the distribution of HEIs in the country. As a result of this policy, the total number of students in HEIs in the eastern part of the USSR grew almost twofold (Zykin 1992). Table A.5 in Appendix reflects the outcomes of the discussions and attempts to align the structure of the system constituted from highly specialized parts to the needs of the economy.

One could observe quite dramatic increase (almost 50 %) of the number of universities specialized in the "real economy" from 1940 to 1988. At the same time the number of teacher-training institutions declined at the same rate. Also the share of enrolment in industrial HEIs increased from 17 % in 1940 to around 38 % during 1960–1988 (Table A.6 in Appendix).

The growing number of students in evening and correspondence programmes (Fig. 2.3 and Table A.8 in Appendix) also contributed to the changes in the landscape (both in the horizontal and the vertical dimension). Eighteen "correspondence HEIs" and eight "evening HEIs" operated as separate institutions in 1963 (Kairov and Petrov 1964).

These changes in the institutional landscape stimulated a new round in the discussion about the governance of the system. "The administration of Soviet higher education has inevitably exacerbated inefficiency and inertia. 896 HIEs come under the jurisdiction of over 70 different ministries and organisations – a clear recipe for duplication and increased specialization of courses, sectional resistance to broader national goals and wasted resources, not to mention horrendous bureaucracy. Nor have branch ministries and economic managers generally been very eager to supply funds and equipment to the HEIs which provide them with a free supply of highly qualified workers. In particular, support for research in HEIs has

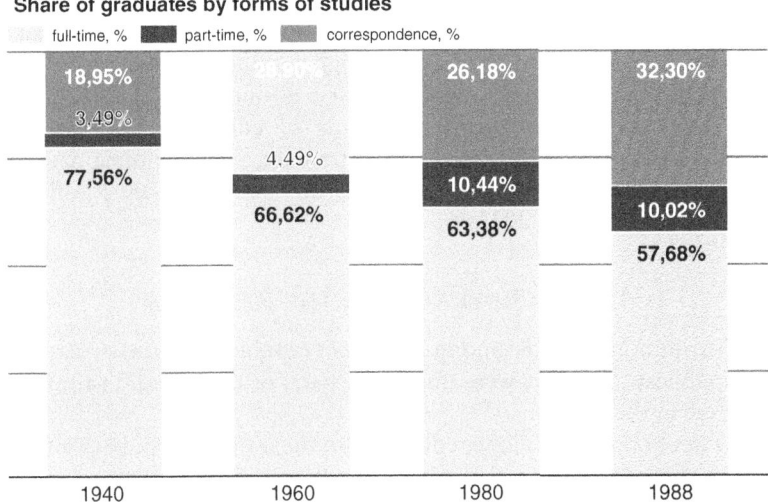

Fig. 2.3 Graduates by form of education (Source: Authors using data from Narodnoye obrazovaniye i kultura v USSR: Statisticheskiy ezhegodnik [Education and Culture in the USSR: Statistic Yearbook] (1989). Moscow: Finansy i statistika)

been weak" (Avis 1990, 6). The Ministry of Higher and Secondary Professional Education was not happy with the way the sectoral ministries ran "their" universities. The minister recognized that there was a contradiction between two trends: "the trend to concentrate the HEIs under the all-union and republican ministries of higher education…and the trend to govern higher education through individual sectors of national economy" (Yelyutin 1980, 46). He called for a compromise which would include a clear distribution of the responsibilities between the Ministry of Higher Education and the sectoral ministries. The machine had become too complex to function.

The compromise included stronger attention to "academic quality in the 1970s and 1980s, as the Soviet regime attempted to strengthen the role of regional universities and engaged in fitful attempts to combine research and education in new ways, for example by fostering cooperation between Academy of Sciences research institutes and universities. The nearly 900 exceedingly narrow specializations of the Stalinist era were narrowed to 300, and the policy emphasis was shifted to training 'specialists of a broad profile'" (Matthews 1982, 43).

These discussions in the Soviet leadership confirm the attention paid to institutional differentiation. As M. Johnson noted, "Thus, while rigid and dogmatic in many ways, the Soviet higher education system at least attempted to sustain and, in its later years, to improve "systemic coherence," between the various components of education and research; between higher education, professional training, and economic development; and between the union republics and various other constituent parts of the U.S.S.R." (2015, 6)

HIGHER EDUCATION IN THE REPUBLICS

The distribution of HEIs among the Soviet republics and the structure of the republican networks were important parts of the overall institutional landscape in the Union.

The development of higher education in the different republics gives us an idea of what the main elements of the Soviet higher education master plan were. The republican systems of higher education performed four major functions: economic development, ethnic cultural development, Russification and equalization of access.

Firstly, the Soviet leadership aimed at creating in each Republic a *higher education system sufficient for the functioning of the main existing sectors of economy,* including the social sector. This meant that each republic was to have a "normal" set of infrastructural HEIs. If the republic had a specific industry central to its economy, specialized HEIs were established to serve this industry. Ivano-Frankovsk in Ukraine had an Institute of Oil and Gas, Andizhan in Uzbekistan had an Institute of Cotton Culture, and Sukhumi in Georgia had an Institute of Subtropical Economy (Andrews 1978).

Another important aim was *to support the development of the ethnic culture* central for each particular republic. This meant the establishment of musical conservatories and institutes for ethnic cultural studies in almost every republic. It also led to the use of the local language as a language of instruction in higher education. In the 1920s and 1930s, there were even special institutions with the local language of instruction. Thus, in 1931, about half of the instruction at Ukrainian HEIs took place in Ukrainian (Martin 2001, 109). Even some branches of all-union HEIs started to use Ukrainian as a language of instruction. However, this trend was not supported politically—the Soviet leadership found that Russification was an important prerequisite for industrialization and closed or transformed these universities, leaving local language instruction mostly for the "culture-specific" departments.

As a result, the higher education systems in the republics also became an *instrument for Russification* and for maintaining the Union. This function was supported not just by teaching in Russian but by keeping major Russian higher education institutions as mentor institutions for similar HEIs in the republics.

The fourth objective was *equalizing access* to higher education between the republics. All republics had lagged behind Russia in the development of higher education in the early Soviet years. The Soviet leadership made large-scale efforts to develop higher education systems outside of Russia, to equalize the access to higher education in all parts of the Union.

Table A.14 in Appendix presents the changes in size of higher education systems within the Soviet republics counted in absolute numbers of students from 1940 to 1990. The Soviet higher education system expanded by more than six times, going from 811,700 students in 1940 to 5,161,600 students in 1990. In such republics as the Kazakh, Moldavian and Tajik SSRs, the rate of expansion in terms of absolute student numbers was higher than 2000 %. The lowest growth was in the Georgian (265 %), Ukrainian (348 %) and the Latvian SSRs (364 %) (Platonova forthcoming).

Up until 1970, the participation rate (measured as the number of students per population in the age cohort 20–24) grew dramatically in all republics. Nine republics (the Uzbek, Georgian, Azerbaijani, Lithuanian, Moldavian, Kyrgyz, Tajik, Armenian and Turkmen SSRs) gained the highest rates by the 1970s, and six other republics (The Russian SFSR, Ukrainian, Belorussian, Kazakh, Latvian and Estonian SSRs)—by the 1990s (see Table A.15 in Appendix) (Platonova forthcoming).

Table A.15 in the Appendix shows that success in equalizing access depended significantly on the share of rural population. This was more obvious in the capitals of the republics, where the number of students per 10,000 population ranged (in 1970) from 78 in Dushanbe and 81 in Ashkabad to 100 in Tashkent and Alma-Ata (with the exception of Tbilisi (177) and those capitals with a large number of HEIs subordinated to All-Union Ministries (as in Moscow or Kiev (146)) (Andrews 1978).

One could ask why such big differences in access existed for such a long time. Or, moreover, why they continued to grow over the years despite all efforts? First of all, the republics experienced different demographic trends. All republics with declining enrolment had to accommodate quickly growing young populations. Secondly, the development of higher education in the Eastern parts of Russia was the priority in the 1970s and 1980s.

Despite these differences in scale, the analysis confirms that the structure of the higher education network in each republic (including horizontal and vertical differentiation, as well as the links with the external environment) reflected in large degree the principles of the construction of the higher education system in the Union as a whole.

Conclusions

The evolution of the higher education landscape in the Soviet Union reflects the attempts to implement the utopian ideal of a rational social order. The Soviet higher education master plan was part of an ambitious social engineering project. As M. Johnson noted, "many of those systemic "strengths" were logical and functional only within the highly centralized and bureaucratized system of Soviet state socialism and the planned economy" (Johnson 2008, 165). This alignment between higher education and the economy worked relatively well within large-scale mobilization projects. However, the system suffered from bureaucratic automatism where "little or no allowance was made for professional initiative or institutional adaptability in the provision of higher education" (Johnson 2008, 165)

This quasi-corporate system could perform only in a specific enabling environment. The collapse of the USSR and the shocking marketization of higher education changed this environment, and quasi-corporatism had no chance of survival.

Acknowledgements We are grateful to D. Semyonov, co-author of the idea of "quasi-corporate" higher education system, and to K. Romanenko and D. Platonova for the help with the data obtaining and processing.

Notes

1. The editors of this books discussed if the use of the expression "master plan" is appropriate to describe the Soviet experience because there are big differences between the Californian master plan and that of the Soviet approach. However, the authors of the chapter use this expression because the Soviet authorities had quite clear rules of the rationing of higher education and included the plans of the development of the higher education institutions in the implementation of the 5-year plans of economic development in USSR. In a sense they had a few higher education master plans within these larger economic planning processes.
2. Ministry of Education.
3. Supreme Economic Council.
4. Equivalent to a master's degree.

References

Andreev, A. 2014. *Rossiyskie universitety XVIII–pervoy poloviny XIX veka v kontekste universitetskoy istorii Evropy.* [*Russian Universities XVIII–1st half XIX century in the context of the European University History*]. Litres.

Andrews, A. 1978. Spatial Patterns of Higher Education in the Soviet Union. *Soviet Geography* 19 (7): 443–457.

Avis, G. 1990. The Soviet Higher Education Reform: Proposals and Reactions. *Comparative Education* 26 (1): 5–12.

Avrus, A. 2001. *Istoriya rossiyskikh universitetov.* [*History of Russian Universities*]. Moscow: Moskovskiy obshchestvenny nauchny fond.

Bim-Bad, B.M. 2002. *Pedagogical Encyclopedic Dictionary*, 528. Moscow: Great Encyclopedia of Russia.

Bogdanov, A.A. 1911. *Kul'turnye zadachi nashego vremeni.* [*Cultural Challenge of Our Time*]. Moscow: Izd. S. Dorovaovskogo i A. Charushnikova.

"Bol'shevik" magazine, TsK VKP(b), №10–11. 1938.

Chanbarisov, Sh.Kh. 1988. *Formirovanie sovetskoy universitetskoy sistemy.* [*Establishing of Soviet Higher Education System*]. Moscow: Vysshaya shkola.

Clark, B.R. 1983. Governing the Higher Education System. In *The Structure and Governance of Higher Education*, 31–37. Guildford: Society for Research into Higher Education.

Feskov V.I., V.I. Golikov., K.A. Kalashnikov., and S.A. Slugin. 2013. *Vooruzhennye Sily SSSR posle Vtoroy Mirovoy voyny: ot Krasnoy armii k Sovetskoy.* [*USSR Military Forces: from Red to Soviet Army*]. Tomsk: Izdatelstvo NTL.

Fitzpatrick, S. 1979. Stalin and the Making of a New Elite, 1928–1939. *Slavic Review* 38 (3): 377–402.

Froumin, I., Kouzminov, Y., and D. Semyonov. 2014. Institutional Diversity in Russian Higher Education: Revolutions and Evolution. *European Journal of Higher Education* 4 (3): 209–234.

Frumin, I.D., I. Kuz'minov, Y., and D.S. Semenov. 2013. Nezavershennyy perekhod: ot gosplana — k master-planu. ["Unfinished Transition: From Gosplan to Masterplan"]. *Otechestvennye zapiski* 4: 55.

Graham, P.A. 1967. *Progressive Education.* New York: Teachers College Press, Columbia University.

Huisman, J. 1995. *Differentiation, Diversity and Dependency in Higher Education: A Theoretical and Empirical Analysis.* Utrecht: Uitgeverij Lemma BV.

Ivantsov, I.G. 2011. Sistema partiynogo obrazovaniya v SSSR v 1930-e gody (na primere Severnogo Kavkaza). ["System of Communist Education in the USSR in 1930s (on the Example of the North Caucasus)"] *Vestnik Adygeyskogo gosudarstvennogo universiteta: Regionovedenie: filosofiya, istoriya, sotsiologiya, yurispudentsiya, politologiya, kul'turologiya* 1 (4): 99-105.

Johnson, M.S. 2008. Historical Legacies of Soviet Higher Education and the Transformation of Higher Education Systems in Post-Soviet Russia and Eurasia. *The Worldwide Transformation of Higher Education* 9: 159–176.

Kairov, A.I., and F.N. Petrov. 1964. *Pedagogicheskaya entsiklopediya. [Pedagogical Encyclopedia]*. Vol. 1. Moscow: Sovetskaya Entsiklopediya.

Kassow, S.D. 1989. *Students, Professors, and the State in Tsarist Russia*. Vol. 5. Berkeley: University of California Press.

Korotenko, N.M. 2009. Organizaciya socialsticheskikh zmagan' v universititetakh USRR-URSR v period 1933–1941 ["Organization of socialist competition at universities in Ukrainian Soviet Republic in 1933–1941"]. *Visnik* 5: 114–119.

Kuraev, A. 2016. Soviet Higher Education: An Alternative Construct to the Western University Paradigm. *Higher Education* 71 (2): 181–193.

Kurasov, S.A. 2015. Socialisticheskoe sorevnovanie kak sposob organizacii povsednevnoy zhizni sovetskikh vuzov [Socialist Competition as an Instrument of the Organization of Everyday Life of the Soviet HEIs]. *Istoricheskie, filosofskie, politicheskie i yuridicheskie nauki* 3 (3): 96–100.

Lapina, I.A. 2011. Proletkul't i proekt «sotsializatsii nauki». [Proletkult and a Project on «Socialization of Science»]. *Obshchestvo. Sreda. Razvitie (Terra Humana)* 2: 43-47

Lenin V.I. 1957. *Lenin o narodnom obrazovanii: stat'i i rechi. [Lenin About National Education: Articles and Speech]*. Moskva: APN RSFSR

———. 1967. Gosudarstvo i revolyutsiya. ["State and Revolution"]. In *Polnoe sobranie sochineniy* by Lenin V. I., T. 24. Moskva: Izd-vo politicheskoy literatury.

Leonova, L.S. 1972. *Iz istorii podgotovki partiynykh kadrov v sovetsko-partiynykh shkolakh i kommunisticheskikh universitetakh (1921–1925 gg.). [From the History of Communist Staff Training in the Soviet Party Schools and Communist Universities]*. Moskva: Izd-vo MGU Moskva

Lunacharskiy, A.V. 1958. *O narodnom obrazovanii. Stat'i i rechi za period 1917–1929 gg. [About a National Education. Articles and speech for the period 1917–1929 yy]*. Moskva, Izd–vo Akad. ped. nauk RSFSR.

Lyusev, V.N. 2009. Zavod-vuz kak forma integratsii vysshego tekhnicheskogo obrazovaniya i proizvodstva. ["Factory-HEI as a form of Integration of Engineering Education and Industry"]. *Pedagogicheskoe obrazovanie i nauka* 10: 70–75.

Martin, T.D. 2001. *The Affirmative Action Empire: Nations and Nationalism in the Soviet Union, 1923–1939*. Ithaca/London: Cornell University Press.

Matthews, M. 1982. *Education in the Soviet Union Policies and Institutions Since Stalin*. Vol. 9. London: Routledge.

Mcclelland, J.C. 1971. Bolshevik Approaches to Higher Education, 1917–1921. *Slavic Review* 30 (4): 818–831.

Platonova, D. Forthcoming. Expansion and Transformations of Higher Education: Case of Post-Soviet Countries [Rasshirenie dostupa i transformatsiya sistem vysshego obrazovaniya: keys postsovetskikh stran]. *Voprosy obrazovaniya.*
"Pravda" newspaper, TsK and MK VKP(b), №334 (7569). 04.12.1938.
Reichert, S. 2009. *Institutional Diversity in European Higher Education.* Brussels: EUA.
Rosen, S.M. 1963. *Higher Education in the USSR: Curriculums, Schools, and Statistics.* Washington, DC: U.S. Department of Health, Education, and Welfare, Office of Education.
Russia 1913 Year. (1995). *Statistical and Document Handbook [Rossiya 1913 god Statistiko-dokumental'nyy spravochnik].* Russian Academy of Science Institute of Russian History [Rossiyskaya Akademiya Nauk Institut Rossiyskoy istorii]. Saint-Petersburg.
Safronov, P.A. 2013. Posle demodernizatsii. ["After De-Modernization"]. *Otechestvennye zapiski* 4: 22–30.
Saprykin, D.L. 2012. Istoriya inzhenernogo obrazovaniya v Rossii, Evrope i SShA: razvitie institutov i kolichestvennye otsenki. ["History of Engineering Education in Russia, Europe and the United States: Development of the Institutes and Quantitative Assessment"]. *Voprosy istorii estestvoznaniya i tekhniki* 4: 51–90.
Statisticheskiy sbornik Narodnoe obrazovanie i kul'tura v SSSR. 1989. [Statistical Collection "National Education and Culture in the USSR"]. Moskva, "Finansy i statistika".
Ushakov, G.I., and A.S. Shuruev. 1980. *Planirovanie i finansirovanie podgotovki spetsialistov. [Planning and Funding of Specialist Training].* Moscow: Ekonomika.
Vasilkova, Y.V. 1989. *Sotsialisty-utopisty ob obrazovanii i vospitanii. [Utopian Socialists about Education]* Pedagogika.
Yelyutin, V.P. 1980. *Higher School in Developed Socialist Society [Vysshaya shkola obschestva razvitogo sotsializma].* Moscow: Vysshaya shkola.
Zakon RSFSR ot 16.04.1959 *Ob ukreplenii svyazi shkoly s zhiznyu i o dal'neyshem razvitii sistemy narodnogo obrazovaniya v RSFSR.* [RSFSR Law 16.04.1959 on Strengthening the Connection Between the School and the Life and on Further Development of the Public Education System in the RSFSR].
Zakon SSSR ot 24.12.1958 *Ob ukreplenii svyazi shkoly s zhizn'yu i o dal'neyshem razvitii sistemy narodnogo obrazovaniya v SSSR.* [USSR Law 24.12.1958 on Strengthening the Connection Between the School and the Life and on Further Development of the Public Education System in the USSR].
Zinov'ev, A.L., and P.I. Filippov. 1983. *Vvedenie v spetsial'nost' radioinzhenera. [Introduction to the Profession of Radio Engineer].* Moskva: Izdatel'stvo «Vysshaya shkola».
Zykin, V.A. 1992. *Razvitie universitetskogo obrazovaniya v Sibiri i na Dalnem Vostoke (1966–1975 gg.). [University Education Development in Siberia and Far East (1966–1975)].* Moscow.

Isak Froumin is Academic Supervisor of the Institute of Education at National Research University, Higher School of Economics, Moscow. Prof. Froumin was leading the World Bank education programme in Russia from 1999 to 2011, including the projects in Kazakhstan, Kyrgyzstan, Afghanistan, Nepal, Turkmenistan and India. In 2011 he was co-chair of the education part of the "Russia Strategy 2020" expert group. Since 2012 he is an advisor to the Minister of Education and Science of Russia Federation and the member of the Russian delegation at OECD Education Policy Committee. Prof. Froumin is the author of more than 250 publications including articles and books in Russian and English.

Yaroslav Kouzminov is Rector of the National Research University, Higher School of Economics (HSE), Moscow, Russia. He is a Professor, Head of the Department of Institutional Economics and Academic Supervisor of the HSE Center for Institutional Studies. Dr Kuzminov is the author of more than 50 academic works published in Russia and abroad and a co-author of over 10 monographs and textbooks on institutional economics, economics of education and institutional reforms. He is the Editor-in-Chief of the journal *Voprosy Obrazovania* (Educational Studies) and member of the editorial boards of the *HSE Economic Journal* and *Mir Rossii* (Universe of Russia).

Open Access This chapter is distributed under the terms of the Creative Commons Attribution 4.0 International License (http://creativecommons.org/licenses/by/4.0/), which permits use, duplication, adaptation, distribution and reproduction in any medium or format, as long as you give appropriate credit to the original author(s) and the source, provide a link to the Creative Commons license and indicate if changes were made.

The images or other third party material in this chapter are included in the chapter's Creative Commons license, unless indicated otherwise in a credit line to the material. If material is not included in the chapter's Creative Commons license and your intended use is not permitted by statutory regulation or exceeds the permitted use, you will need to obtain permission directly from the copyright holder.

CHAPTER 3

Armenia: Transformational Peculiarities of the Soviet and Post-Soviet Higher Education System

Susanna Karakhanyan

INTRODUCTION

Schools of higher learning were initiated in Armenia as early as the ninth century and one of the first schools was Tatev Academy. From the thirteenth through the fifteenth century, the fame of some schools spread beyond the borders of the country. This included the University of Gladzor, which celebrated its 700th anniversary in 1980 under the aegis of UNESCO (2000). Historically, schools of higher learning were located in churches. Strict management rules were applied as early as the thirteenth century to ensure adequate qualifications for teachers and admission of the best students. In medieval Armenia, schools of higher learning had already begun conferring the scientific degrees of "Archimandrite" and "Rabbi" upon successful completion of oral and written examinations, and thesis defence (ibid).

Armenian schools of higher learning saw a major expansion between the eighteenth and nineteenth century to various worldwide locations

S. Karakhanyan (✉)
ANQA Accreditation Commission, Yerevan, Armenia

© The Author(s) 2018
J. Huisman et al. (eds.), *25 Years of Transformations of Higher Education Systems in Post-Soviet Countries*, Palgrave Studies in Global Higher Education, https://doi.org/10.1007/978-3-319-52980-6_3

such as Venice (Mkhitarian College), India (Calcutta College), Moscow (Lazarian Seminary), Tiflis (Nersisian School), Echmiadzin (Gevorkian Seminary), Madras and Rostov (ibid).

In 1920, schools were separated from the church and the whole system of education became state-owned. As elsewhere in the Soviet republics, primary, secondary and tertiary education was free, and tertiary education was elite in both social and intellectual dimensions. Considering that education has always been a central value of Armenian culture, the country enjoyed a 100 % literacy rate as early as 1960 (Suny 1996, 36).

With the fall of the Soviet Union (SU) in 1991 and the sudden cessation of Soviet standards and rules, the first years of Armenia's independence were marked by a vacuum in education and culture. The abrupt absence of a dominating power created social and political confusion, thus filling the vacuum with the standards of a new and more powerful country (Terzian 2010) mainly influenced by educational policies from Anglophone and Anglo-centric systems. In the early 1990s, Armenia made substantial changes to a centralised and regimented system that evolved with advantages and disadvantages.

The aim of this chapter is to explore the HE landscape in Armenia before and after the fall of the Soviet regime and the respective transformations reflected by social needs, economic demands and political goals. In particular, we will look at the Soviet model of institutional diversity in Armenia, followed by the main drivers of transformation after the fall of the Soviet regime and the factors that stimulated or impeded institutional differentiation (van Vught 2007). The chapter will culminate in a presentation of the current institutional landscape and the contextual factors affecting it.

THE SOVIET MODEL OF INSTITUTIONAL DIVERSITY IN ARMENIA

Armenia became part of the SU in December 1923. Consequently, at the start of the twentieth century, the whole concept and ideology of education radically changed to become permeated with one idea: the collective self, which became more important than the individual self (Sarafian 1930). By becoming part of the SU, the higher education (HE) system in Armenia witnessed a cessation of the ecclesiastical era and the beginning of horizontal differentiation with the emergence of professionally oriented schools, new professionally oriented institutes, universities and art schools to serve societal needs (Sarafian 1930). The only university from the Soviet era in Armenia, the National University of Armenia, was renamed Yerevan State University (YSU) in 1922. It was founded in 1919 by Ministerial decree and was established based on a rich history of higher learning preserved by the church; it "renewed the ancient traditions of Armenian scholarship in language and history that during 600 years of foreign occupation had flourished only among the diaspora abroad" (NAS 2004, 11).

From the 1920s to the fall of the Soviet regime, the system evolved in line with Communist Party (CP) directives, socialist and communist ideology and the demands of the *industrialisation* agenda. Higher education institutions (HEIs) in that period were purely public and free of charge. As early as at the beginning of the 1920s in tandem with the Cultural Revolution reforms that swept the USSR, technical and agricultural schools as well as workers' universities gradually evolved into new professionally oriented institutes (e.g. in 1922 Armenian State Pedagogic Institute and in 1933 Yerevan Polytechnic Institute).

In 1930, in accordance with the government and on the basis of YSU faculties, independent professionally oriented institutes were established. Among these were the State Medical Institute, the Armenian Construction Institute, and the Yerevan Agriculture Institute. In the 1970s, a major boom in HE enrolment was recorded (Fig. 3.1). This could be partly explained by industrialisation policy requiring more educated employees and partly by the full transition from seven-year education to ten-year secondary education as well as massive provision for compulsory secondary education (with consideration of vocational education) for all citizens (Chabe 1971).

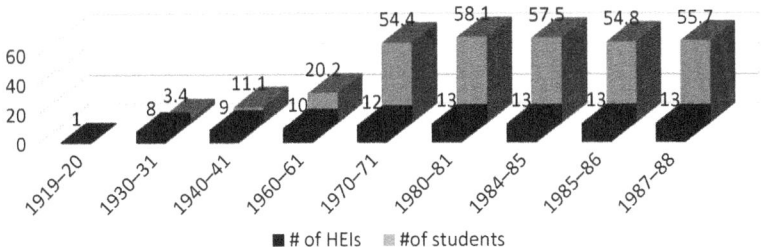

Fig. 3.1 Number of HEIs with total enrolment figures (in thousands) at the start of selected academic years (Data collected from different sources: UNESCO, HE in the USSR, Monographs on HE edited by L. C. Barrows; Khudaverdyan, K. S, 1960)

Based on a strictly centralised model, the HE system was uniform. In 1988 just before the fall of the Soviet regime, there were 13 HEIs in Soviet Armenia, of which only YSU was qualified as a full university. The others were 11 professionally oriented institutes and 1 conservatorium. The schools of higher learning had a combined student body of 55,700 specialising in 103 professions leading to a 5-year diploma specialist qualification (Table 3.1).

During the Soviet regime, Armenia had one of the highest percentages of HE attendees per capita in comparison to other USSR republics, and science was a particularly popular field of study (NAS 2004). One major development during Soviet times that drastically affected HEI research capacity was the removal of research from HEIs. It was placed under the Armenian Branch of the Academy of Sciences of the USSR in 1935. As a result of this separation, the boundaries between professional and research HEIs gradually blurred, as the only distinction between the HEIs was whether they comprehensively covered a variety of study fields or only one

Table 3.1 Higher education landscape in Armenia in 1991

Type of HEIs	Number of HEIs	Specific example	Description
Full university	1	Yerevan State University	Higher, postgraduate and supplementary education in *a wide variety of* natural and sociological fields, science, technology and culture, as well as providing opportunities for scientific research and studies
Professionally oriented institute	11	Yerevan Polytechnic Institute	HEI conducting specialised and postgraduate academic programmes and applied research in a number of field-related scientific, economic and cultural branches
Conservatorium	1	Yerevan Komitas State Conservatorium	HEI preparing specialists in the field of music, providing qualifications, development and postgraduate academic programmes

single field. Although the separation strictly served the Soviet agenda of supporting military-industrial complexes, it also resulted in the establishment of a rich tradition in research activities, particularly in physics, and ensured strong government support to promote education in science and engineering in Armenia. The Academy of Sciences became a centre of science and technology research providing support services to the entire SU (NAS 2004). Just before the fall of the regime, there were about 36 research institutions within and outside the Academy. In 1940, 11 of the 36 belonged to the Armenian Branch of the Academy of Sciences of the USSR and directly reported to either federal agencies in Moscow or to local Armenian ministries (Khudaverdyan 1960) (NAS 2004).

All the HEIs were under the auspices of the Ministry of Education and Science (MoES), with respective line ministries for the Medical Institute and the Agriculture Institute. They were state funded and followed the model of curriculum and teaching methods imposed from Moscow. The HE system was unitary with no differentiation between professional and academic programmes/qualifications and a strong bias towards the provision of practical knowledge directly linked with industry (Sarafian 1930).

Further, HE system uniformity was spelled out in a centralised and unified approach to HEI governance, since the only directives eligible for implementation came from a higher level, the Central CP in Moscow, and were imposed on HEIs without any right to deviate. In fact, the CP considered education too important to delegate to education professionals, and it was thus the political leaders who designed education policies and steered the respective developments (Chabe 1971). One of the negative impacts of such a centralised approach was a decrease in system capacity to develop and innovate. The isolated system gradually turned the HE leaders in Armenia and other Soviet republics into mere implementers with no opportunities to reflect on the imperatives coming from Moscow or question approaches related to content and methodology.

Although paralysed in the sphere of social sciences, the technical and natural sciences proliferated in Armenia. Just before the fall of the SU, Armenia enjoyed a strong body of professionals advancing research in the fields of hydro-energy, nuclear energy, radio-electronics, machinery production, precise machine-making, laser technology, biochemistry, microbiology, and light and heavy textile industry. The number of persons per 10,000 enrolled in Armenian HE was 161, compared to the overall average of 177 for the USSR (UNESCO 1990). From every thousand employed people, 192 and 222 had a higher and secondary professional education, respectively (UNESCO 2000).

Post-Soviet Transformations

After the dissolution of the SU, Armenia faced challenges related to resurrection of its identity and recovery of its economic, cultural and educational values. The country was in major need of transformation at different levels to ensure its survival and later competitiveness at the international level. The economic crisis and political tensions were priority issues to be dealt with, as they were caused by the radical change in the political system.

Firstly, the country experienced a drastic earthquake in 1988 followed by political tension with neighbouring Azerbaijan over a historically Armenian territory, Mountainous Karabagh. This geared the major investments of the Armenian government from development towards a vision of preserving the national identity and resurrecting rich historical and cultural legacy. Two major trends related to political tension evolved, which eventually had a major impact on the socio-economic development of the country. One was an inflow of refugees from Azerbaijan, and the other was the "brain drain" of Armenian human capacity to countries offering more opportunities for growth. According to CARIM, major social changes resulted from hosting refugees from Azerbaijan and other Soviet republics; there were over 420,000 between 1988 and 1991, with 360,000 from Azerbaijan alone (UNHCR 2004; CARIM 2013). The trend is still persistent with a refugee inflow from Syria. Further, a major outflow of both citizens and refugees has been registered. The 2004 *UNHCR Statistical Yearbook* estimates the number of outflowing people from Armenia to developed countries to be above 13,000. According to the State Migration Authority data as of 2013, about 42,800 people left the country in 2012 without returning. Thus, the two trends have contributed immensely to the existing lag in economic development and consequently reflected in government investment into HE.

While popular during Soviet times, Armenian industry has now declined and the country has experienced a major blow to the economy. Caused by political tension, war and blockades, most industries were closed, which led to rising unemployment and economic paralysis. In addition to economic, political and social issues, the system had to deal with the legacy of several decades of a communist regime that was deeply rooted in all aspects of life and therefore the culture, beliefs and values of Armenia (Kozma and Polonyi 2004) (Zelvys 2004). Formed throughout the 70 years of the Soviet regime, exceptionally peculiar culture and values made the transformations to the market economy and democracy complicated, leading to distortions in many cases. These factors included Soviet trust vs. Western responsibility, nihilism and negotiation vs. competition, humanity vs. professionalism, truth vs. rules, faith vs. stimulus, "universalism" vs. individualism, spirituality vs. interests and charity vs. justice (Khrushcheva and Benvenuti 2002).

In the 2000s, Armenia demonstrated steady economic growth until the global crisis hit the economy. According to the *Index of Economic Freedom 2009*, Armenia was ranked the 39th most economically free nation in the world, and as of 2012 it had made a full transfer to the market economy (MoES 2014). In 2009, the real GDP rate declined by 14.1 %, followed by a slow recovery, registering a GDP growth of 2.2 % in 2010 and 4.7 % in 2011.

So, what were the changes in the HE arena based on these trends? In tandem with the changes in the political system, changes took place in HE. After the fall of the communist regime, the liberalisation of the country and a move towards a market-driven economy was the apparent trend. The first step was related to the resurrection of the Armenian identity and was registered with curricula emphasising Armenian language, history and culture. The Armenian language became the dominant language of instruction followed by English, although Russian was still widely taught as a foreign language. Because of the political tension, few and fragmented changes were possible in HE in the early 1990s.

As seen from the figure below, the enrolment of students in the HE sector remained unchanged up to 1999. Starting with the 1999–2000 academic year, a move from "elite" HE to mass education became apparent. This trend was also conditioned by the appearance of private sector providers enforced by the Law on Education adopted in 1999. The same cannot be said about vocational education providers (so-called technicums or professional colleges/*uchilishe*). This sector has remained relatively constant since Soviet times (Fig. 3.2).

Massification of HE is explained by several factors: the demand for a more qualified workforce in the market, the growing prestige of HE enrolment over Vocational Education and Training (VET) and the country's strategic priority of establishing a knowledge economy.

As can be seen from Fig. 3.3, among the most preferred programmes offered by HEIs predominance is in humanities, education and pedagogy, economics and management, the agro/food sphere, public health and culture and arts. To a lesser extent, programmes in physical-mathematical and natural sciences are also registered as preferred. There has been a steady

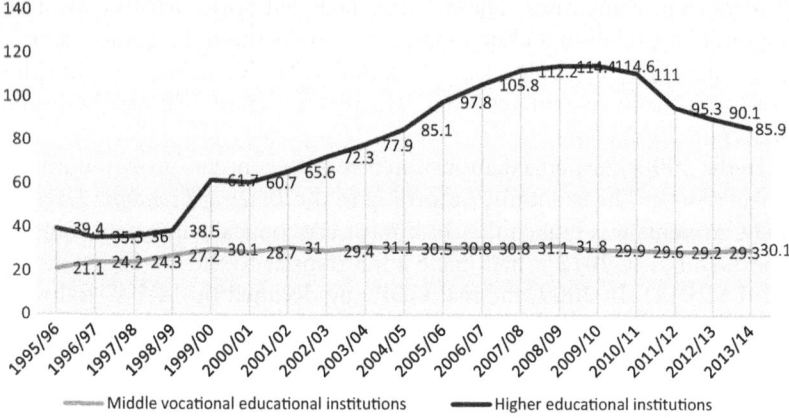

Fig. 3.2 Enrolment in tertiary education institutions in Armenia (*Statistical Yearbook of Armenia*: http://www.armstat.am/en/?nid=45&year=2014)

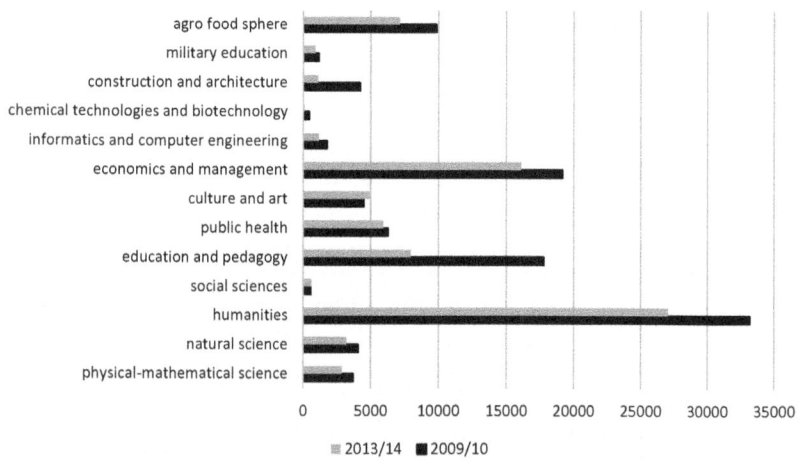

Fig. 3.3 Student enrolment per major (BA level) *(Statistical Yearbook of Armenia)*: http://www.armstat.am/en/?nid=45&year=2014)

rise in information technologies throughout the last 6 years, which is a good sign of demand on the HE system by the labour market.

One of the consequences of the granted freedom in HE provisions is the overabundance of professionals in management and economics, law, humanities and some spheres of engineering. This adds to unemployment to a major extent, taking it from 3.8 % in 2008 to 18.7 % in 2009 and beyond (NSSRA 2014).

According to the *Statistical Yearbook of Armenia* (2014), only 62.8 % of HE graduates were actually employed in 2013.

Further in terms of employment, the official demand from the labour force (for wage earners) as submitted by employers is steadily growing, while there are fewer and fewer applicants per vacant position. A high degree of unemployment is apparent and it has marred the economy of the country for two major reasons. Firstly, HEIs have continued offering traditional study programmes based on the academic standards stipulated by the government without harmonising the offered qualifications with market needs. Secondly, the market itself was and still is in the process of formation with high reliance on the personal capacities of the workforce to manage environmental and organisational changes, rather than on the education and qualifications received (Fig. 3.4).

The period after 1998 can be characterised as a recovery period for the country in all the dimensions: economic, political and cultural. One sign was a steady increase in public spending on education until the late 2000s when the next economic crisis hit in 2009. The education sector suffered with a drastic cut of about 15 % from the original budget with no indication of recovery (WB 2013). Overall, according to the *WB Public Expenditure Review* (WB 2011), public funding for tertiary education was well below the regional average of 1.3 % and the OECD average of 2.0 %, taking it down to 0.3 % of GDP and 10–12 % of total education spending,

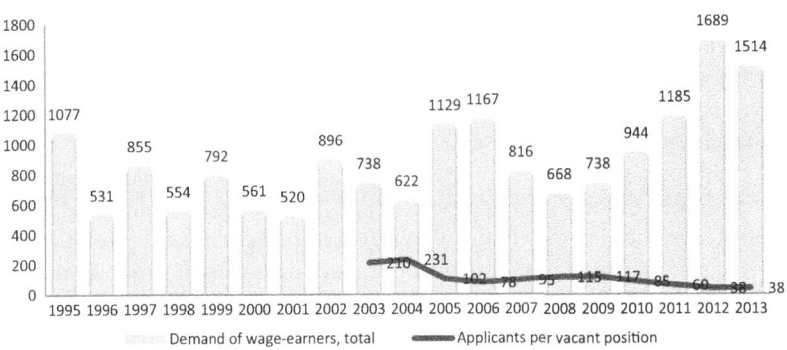

Fig. 3.4 Official labour force demand submitted by employers (*Statistical Yearbook of Armenia*: http://www.armstat.am/en/?nid=45&year=2014)

respectively. Public funding for research and development (R&D) is as low as 0.2 % of GDP and the priority allocation is for the NAS, which doubly limits HEI research capacity. The 2010–2013 state budget allocated for education and science underwent a steady decline, taking the share for education and science to 2.4 % of GDP in 2013.

Considering that state allocation amounts to 23 % of the public HEI budget on average, HEIs generally cover capital expenditures and salaries from tuition fees. The budget of private HEIs is primarily based on tuition fees and amounts to 94–100 %. According to the WB Report 2013, the tuition level in Armenia is considered relatively high if measured against the GDP and compared with lower-middle income countries on the OECD list. It is calculated at 7–37 % of GDP per capita PPP, whereas the maximum is 14 % of GDP per capita PPP in the USA (OECD, Education at a Glance, 2012). Despite the steady increase in HEI gross enrolment from 19.6 % in 2001 to 28.6 % in 2008, which compares well with the countries at a similar economic level in the ECA region (WB report 2013), equity of access is still a challenge.

HE Landscape in Armenia: Current State of Affairs

The reform of Armenian HE was initiated bottom-up in the early 1990s by leading scholars and top management at some leading universities. The first steps taken through pilot projects were the introduction of a two-tier degree structure, changes to curricula, and student assessment systems. In some cases, the changes were supported by international projects such as Tempus, Open Society Institute Assistance Foundation Armenia, the World Bank and the United States Departments of State and Education. However, ambiguity with regard to what should be done in what sequence, as well as how and why, resulted from a lack of clear vision for educational reforms (Zelvys 2004) and insufficient administrative capacity for change management, coupled with a lack of MoES guidance. In fact, the trend was predominant reliance on international consultants instead of building the capacities of local change owners. This, according to Fullan and Scott (2009), may have made things worse instead of better as the use of external consultants was not cost-effective and has caused overreliance on external support at the expense of developing inner capacity (Karakhanyan et al. 2011).

Further, the newly introduced approaches raised the issue of legitimacy; this was caused by lack of inquiry into the context in which the diffused policy was planted (Karakhanyan et al. 2011). One example is the revision of the approach to governance, which authorises public HEIs to be governed by a Governing Board (GB) with equal representation by stakeholders, state employees, renowned individuals, faculty members and students. While democratic in nature, an absent preparatory phase enabling the meaningful participation of such key stakeholders combined with negligence of contextualisation later resulted in decision-making manipulation.

Another trend was the unprecedented decline in the status and prestige of scholars and researchers conditioned by decades of low payment, overload, insufficient and inadequate resources for teaching and research, and demoralising management. The once highly prestigious profession lost its attraction among youth, which resulted in an aging faculty and therefore non-relevant methods and content delivery. One of the consequences of this trend is a tendency for highly qualified staff to leave academia for more lucrative positions so that vacancies are filled by less qualified individuals.

Bologna Reforms

In the 2000s, geared towards the establishment of an independent country and a democratic society, the Armenian government began to reconsider the whole architecture of the HE system. In 2003, the MoES developed the Strategy of HE Reforms, which led Armenia to join the Bologna Process in 2005. The MoES took the initiatives at the major policy making level, while giving HEIs some autonomy to make institutional and programme level changes. In May 2005 (Bergen Communiqué), the *Development Strategy of Education for 2008–2015* was adopted and put into practice. The document was revised and reinforced through adoption of the *Law on the Republic of Armenia Education Development Strategy* on June 23, 2011. The main objectives were reflected in the *State Program for Education Development 2011–2015*, which sets key objectives and strategic directions for HE revolving around widening access to HE, a national qualifications framework, enhancement of quality assurance, revising funding mechanisms, recognition and comparability of degrees, student mobility, strengthening the ties between HE and the labour market and ensuring effective governance and financial management of HEIs.

Drawing on the *Strategy*, the shift to a two-tier degree system (MoES decree, 2004) has been completed and almost 100 % of students below the doctoral level are enrolled in two-cycle programmes. All HEIs issue Diploma Supplements and implement the European Credit Transfer and Accumulation System (ECTS) as of 2008, although with some difficulties. However, the move towards a two-tier degree has proved to have insufficient legitimacy for many professional sectors across the system (e.g. medicine) and required a necessary revision in 2015–2016 to align with market needs.

A new actor in the HE sector appeared as a direct result of joining the Bologna Declaration. A buffer body, the National Center for Professional Education Quality Assurance (ANQA), was established in 2008 as a new governmental tool to hold all HEIs accountable for their operations and outcomes. ANQA policies and procedures are aligned with the *European Standards for Quality Assurance in the European HE Area* (ESGs) of the European Network of Quality Assurance (ENQA) as well as the *Guidelines of Good Practices* (GGP) of the International Network for Quality Assurance Agencies in HE (INQAAHE). At HEI level, with major support from ANQA, internal quality assurance systems have been put in place and HEIs have completed the first round of institutional self-assessments. This is a move towards programme level self-assessment.

In 2011, the Armenian government adopted the National Education Qualifications Framework of the Republic of Armenia (ANQF) consisting of eight levels, and the responsibilities for the operation and maintenance of the ANQF are within the jurisdiction of the MoES. Currently, the ANQF is under revision based on the first round of its implementation and pilot evaluation.

Armenia is pursuing a strong internationalisation policy. Currently, it is a member of the United Nations, the Commonwealth of Independent States, the Council of Europe and more than 40 other international organisations including OSCE, the World Bank, the International Monetary Fund, WTO, WHO and UNESCO, to name but a few. Supported by international missions, the leading HEIs are geared towards internationalisation and have been revamping their approaches to governance, administration and overall programme delivery. Internationalisation is pursued through development and integration of such dimensions as:

- Integration of an international dimension into the teaching, learning and research functions of universities by developing and implementing respective policies and procedures
- Identification and development of new skills, attitudes and knowledge in students, faculty and staff to promote internationalisation

- Promoting scholar and student exchange and technical cooperation of HEIs
- Development of ethos and culture that values and supports intercultural and international perspectives, initiatives and their quality assurance

Among the current priorities on the government agenda is the refinement of the ANQF to move to the next step of self-certification, its full implementation and respective recognition internationally. Also included are a move from academic standards to a learning outcome approach to programme development and delivery as well as a revision of funding mechanisms.

Legal and Regulatory Developments

At the legal framework level, Armenian HE is regulated by the *Law on Education* adopted in 1999 and the *Law on Higher and Postgraduate Professional Education* adopted in 2004. The two documents clearly state the vision of HE, which is aimed at international recognition, competitiveness and full integration into the European Higher Education Area (EHEA). As for regulations related to the research dimension, a new *Law on the National Academy of Sciences* was adopted in 2011 to ensure an autonomous legal status for the NAS. This sort of division actually created a gulf between HE and research and thus deprives HEIs of the opportunity to strengthen research functions.

The Law on Education (1999) and the Law on HE (2004) define the overall governance framework for HE in detail, but with ambiguity in favour of government control (WB 2013). However, due to their status, some HEIs are also regulated by the *Law on State Non-Commercial Organizations* and the *Law on State Governing Institutions* (SGIs), both adopted in 2001. The latter was not specifically developed for HEIs and does not take into account governance, autonomy and academic freedom guaranteed in education laws, thus contributing even more controversy. Given the current legal framework, the governance model can be defined as semi-autonomous (WB 2013).

Recently, a new trend of transitioning to foundation status has been observed. A foundation is a not-for-profit independent legal entity that enjoys the following privileges (Hasan 2007):

(i) It is an independent legal entity.
(ii) It has a mission (or charter or mandate) to serve defined public (or national and societal) interests in HE and research.
(iii) As a not-for-profit public interest legal entity, it has favourable tax treatment on its incomes, assets and trading activities undertaken in pursuit of its foundation goals.
(iv) It has the autonomy to raise funds and manage its assets in pursuit of the foundation goals, for which it receives favourable tax treatment (2007, p.7).

Throughout the last couple of years, six state HEIs have changed their legal status to foundation, each by individual MoES decree. Thus, public HEIs in Armenia are now legally differentiated between State Non-Commercial Organizations (SNCOs) and foundations.

The same cannot be said for private and intergovernmental HEIs, since they are less restricted in their operations. Private HEIs, depending on their status, are regulated by the Law on Education, the Law on HE, the Law on Enterprises and Entrepreneurial Activity, the Law on Foundations, the Law on LLCs, the Law on Cooperatives and/or the Law on Joint Stock Company (JSCs). Intergovernmental HEIs are regulated by the Law on Education, the Law on HE and the respective legal frameworks of their counterparts in home or host countries. Table 3.2 summarises the types of Armenian HEIs by legal status as of 2015.

Funding

Diversification also affected the funding of HEIs. Public HEIs, which were previously run 100 % on the state budget, now have legal authorisation to charge tuition fees. This has been the case since 1999. By the late 2000s, the average proportion of HEI budget share coming from the government was only 20 %, with the rest coming predominantly from student fees. Paradoxically, "public" HEIs in Armenia actually receive very little state contribution (WB 2013). New funding mechanisms include competitive innovation funds with a target to promote HEI competitiveness. Funding mechanisms are currently under revision with a diversification goal in mind.

New Admissions Policy

The next major change was the revision of admissions policy, which moved from exams given by individual HEIs to a Centralised Admission Exam (CAE), which is both a school final and a university entrance examination. From 2005 to 2012, only state HEIs utilised a centralised admission exam process, which is organised and administered by the MoES's State Admission Commission (SAC). In the academic year 2012–2013, private HEIs were also subject to CAE for the first time, which was a major blow to the private sector threatening a total closure of some institutions. Exceptions apply to some public HEIs that still reserved the right to conduct subject specific exams as supplementary to the CAE.

Admissions to foreign-affiliated institutions are governed by individual HEIs, although these schools may choose to use state exam scores in their admission decisions.

With the introduction of unified exams, the landscape has transformed significantly due to intensified competition among HEIs for students. As a result, weaker public and most private HEIs are now forced to revise their approaches. The choice is whether or not to merge or revise their missions and concentrate mostly on life-long learning or further education courses to become more competitive in the market.

Classification and Ranking of HEIs

With regard to the vertical stratification of HEIs, under the Soviet approach distinctions in quality were reflected in the privileged status of a university vs. an institute. Recently, the MoES has come up with new mechanisms to classify HEIs:

- Ranking Web of Universities, which provides rankings per country as well[1]
- National classification of HEIs and ranking of programmes, based on a pilot project conducted by the MoES to classify and then rank HEI programmes within each classification.

The same trend could be observed implicitly, through the reputational stratification of HEIs broadly discussed at the society level. Such a stratification mainly places public and intergovernmental HEIs on top as the most prestigious HEIs. Recently, to move forward on the international visibility agenda, highly prestigious universities have been invited to establish branch campuses in Armenia as exemplified by the MoES's invitation of Moscow State University. Despite a history of about 25 years, private HEIs have not been able to live up to the standards expected by society. The main indicator for the public at large is the quality of teaching staff, availability of resources and, most importantly, national and international recognition of awarded degrees.

Vertical stratification could also be described as promoted by national accreditation, which serves as an accountability tool for the government and a tool for financial allocation. According to the ANQA revised procedures (2015), regardless of HEI legal status, those that fail to obtain accreditation will be deprived of state funds and will have limits set on tuition fees to be charged. This will become effective as of 2018. Thus, the new stratification tool has the potential to substantially change the HE landscape.

Organisational Interrelationships

Last but not least, an aspect of diversity worth elaborating on is organisational interrelationships. Although not very significant in the context of the developing Armenian system, these alliances create synergies in teaching and learning, research and community outreach activities. Interrelationships in the context of Armenia are promoted in the following ways:

- Static—empowered by buffer bodies or international organisations;
- Dynamic—natural evolutions based on the needs of the HE system and society at large.

With regard to the static, in its quest to develop a quality culture, ANQA tirelessly invests in the capacity building of different stakeholders. Capacity building events and peer reviews organised by ANQA actually create a collaborative culture and establish a firm platform for a quality education dialogue.

SCS,[2] through its grants, promotes research projects that bring together faculty members from different HEIs and, in some cases, industries. The same applies to international projects like Tempus, Erasmus+ and Twinning, which actually bring together HEIs to collectively pursue project objectives. As a natural evolution to this process, for example, the International Association of Educationalists (IntAE) has been established to bring together professionals from Armenia, Georgia and Europe.

The dynamic form of interrelationships revolves around the establishment of industry-university collaborative partnerships, merging HEIs and partnership agreements. A prominent example of an industry-university collaborative partnership is Synopsis, which is the Silicon to Software™ partner for innovative companies developing electronic products and software applications. Additionally, it offers courses in microelectronics at the bachelor and master levels and the degree is awarded with its collaborative partners which include such IT leaders as YSU, SEUA, and RAU (Slavonic). Most graduates of this partnership are then hired by Synopsis itself.

A recent trend of merging HEIs is gradually becoming apparent. Currently, this form of interrelationship has been registered only in the private sector with some HEIs merging to serve the same purposes. However, at the government level there are also plans to merge public HEIs to achieve economies of scale.

Classification of HEIs 2014–2015

The HE system in the 1990s was characterised by only 1 full university, 11 professionally oriented institutes and 1 conservatorium. The new *Law on Education* adopted in 1999, however, allowed for a diversity of HE providers to enter the market. Thus, as seen from Fig. 3.5, from 1999 to

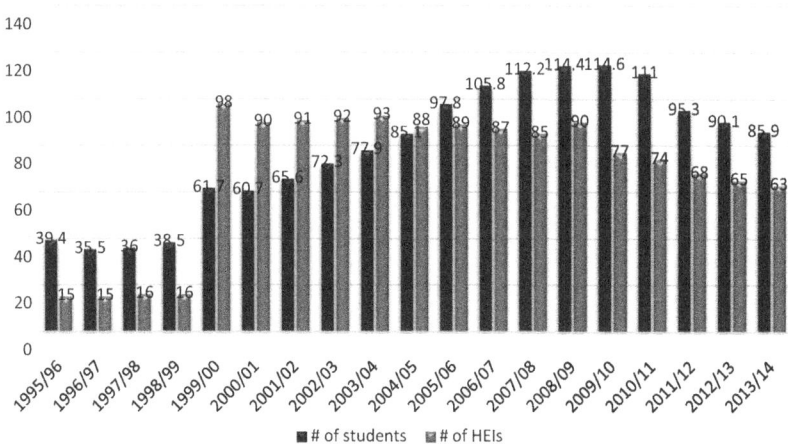

Fig. 3.5 Distribution of HEIs and number of students (*Statistical Yearbook of Armenia*: http://www.armstat.am/en/?nid=45&year=2014)

2008 a new type of HEI mushroomed. The initiators were mainly private entrepreneurs (e.g. Armenian diaspora to the USA, leading professionals in different fields like law and economics) and former leaders of public HEIs. Table 3.2 illustrates the diversity of HE providers as of 2015.

However, having set no boundaries on private initiatives, the system found itself with an abundance of private providers with quality levels that are still largely questioned. Starting in 2008 with persistent MoES efforts, the number of private HEIs was reduced from 98 in 1999 to 63 in 2013 and 57 in 2015. The decline in the number of private HEIs was due to (1) toughening licensure criteria; (2) university mergers, which were applied in very few cases; and (3) imposing state unified entrance exams on private HEIs. The steady decline in enrolments is mainly explained by the decline in birth rates throughout the 1990s and beginning of the 2000s.

Currently, the HE system in Armenia consists of public, private, intergovernmental and transnational HEIs. At the national level, the executive authority to elaborate and implement government policies is the MoES, which tends to its mandate in cooperation with regional and municipal authorities. State HEIs operate under the responsibility of several ministries but most of them are under the supervision of the MoES. In total there are 26 state HEIs, of which 16 with 14 branches are under MoES jurisdiction; 4 HEIs were founded by intergovernmental agreements and partly funded by the MoES; 2 HEIs are under the Ministry of Defence, and one HEI is under each of the following ministries/bodies: Police, Ministry of Emergency Situations and Mother See of Holy Etchimiadzin.[3] Of all the public HEIs, YSU has a special distinction as the only Armenian HEI with its own separate provision in the Law on Higher and Professional Education and a separate mention in the national budget (Table 3.3).

As demonstrated above, driven by the vision of internationalisation and the demands of the market economy, the HE landscape is gradually becoming diverse with three full universities qualified as comprehensive as well as specialised universities, institutes, academies, a conservatorium and research institutes to meet a diversity of needs.

Private HEIs are out of the scope of MoES jurisdiction to a considerable extent; however, the government imposes accountability mechanisms. Intergovernmental institutions are universities established on the basis of agreement between two countries, for example, the American University of Armenia, the Russian-Slavonic University of Armenia and the French University of Armenia. The trend of promoting transnational providers is escalating with the introduction of academic programmes within the

Table 3.2 Armenian HEIs by legal status: regulatory landscape

Types	State			Private		
	Public	Intergovernmental		Local		Foreign
	SNCOs	Foundation	Intergovernmental	Interstate foundations	For-profit foundations	Not-for-profit foundations	branches of foreign universities/transnational providers
No. of HEIs	14	6	2	2	31	2	9
Major governing laws	Law on SNCOs, Law on Education, Law on HE	Law on Foundations, Law on Education, Law on HE	Law on Foundations and Agreement between two countries, Law on Education, Law on HE	Law on Foundations, Civil Code, Law on Education, Law on HE	Law on LLCs; Law on Coops, Law on JSCs, Law on Education, Law on HE	Law on Foundations, Law on Education, Law on HE	Law on registering of Legal Entities and Records on Separate Units of Legal Entities, respective counterpart institutions and Law on Private Enterprises, Law on Education, Law on HE

Source: WB Report 2013, modified by author in 2015

Table 3.3 Higher education landscape in Armenia in 2015

Full university	Specialised university	Institute	Academy	Conservatorium	Research institute
Offer higher, postgraduate and supplementary education in a wide variety of branches of natural and sociological fields, science, technology and culture, as well as providing opportunities for scientific research and studies	Offering specialised and postgraduate academic programmes and scientific research in a number of field-related scientific, economic and cultural branches	Offering professional/applied programmes and conducting field-specific research	Offer applied programmes in specific fields (arts, police), leading to bachelor, master and candidate of Science qualifications, as well as conduct research in the field	Offers programmes in the field of music, leading to bachelor, master and candidate of Science qualifications	Offer master degrees and above all conduct scientific research

PUB[a]	PRV	IG	TN	PUB	PRV	IG	TN	PUB	PRV	IG	TN	PUB	PRV	IG	TN	PUB	PRV	IG	TN	Public (within NASRA)	Public (outside NASRA)
1	0	1	1	10	24	2	8	3	6	0	0	4	3	1	0	1	0	0	0	34	1
Total 3				Total 44				Total 9				Total 8				Total 1				Total 35	

66 HEIs + 35 RIs

[a]PUB Public, PRV Private, IG Intergovernmental, TN Transnational

framework of existing HEIs (e.g. the Armenian University of Economics is hosting a programme from the United Kingdom). This also involves Armenia hosting worldwide leading university branches (e.g. Moscow State Lomonosov University), thereby bringing in a more diverse range of HEI providers.

All the HEIs are degree-awarding entities. All the private HEIs accredited by the MoES starting from 1999 under the old accreditation policy issue state-standard diplomas, which qualifies the graduates as the same level as those from public HEIs. However, the trust in degrees awarded by private HEIs is much lower in the labour market and society at large.

Conclusions

For the last century and a half, HE in Armenia has been driven by ideological and political factors and undergone major transformations resulting in system differentiation at horizontal and to some extent vertical level.

The first major transformation was compelled by the change to a Soviet and socialist ideology and industrialisation agenda when joining the USSR in 1923. Driven by the imperatives of the Soviet regime, there was a radical cessation of the ecclesiastic nature leading to the establishment of professionally oriented HEIs outside the church to meet the demands of society. As shown in Table 3.1, this resulted in the emergence of a full university as well as professionally oriented institutes and a conservatorium. The system was predominantly characterised by uniformity and was centrally planned and controlled by the government, with no opportunity for any other types of HE providers (e.g. private).

With the collapse of the Soviet system, HE in Armenia has undergone a major transformation at the horizontal level. The institutional landscape has expanded, not only in numbers but also in types, to include such HEIs as academies, professionally oriented universities, educational centres (foundations) and research institutes within National Academy of Sciences of the Republic of Armenia (NASRA); this is very different to the landscape in 1991 (Table 3.1 vs. 3.2). Further, the system evolved to host HEIs with diversity in terms of legal status: public, intergovernmental, transnational and private, which could further be differentiated between for-profit and not-for-profit providers. The contextual factors affecting the alteration of the institutional landscape are mainly related to the move to a market economy, national identity resurrection and the internationalisation agenda promoted by the government.

To achieve international visibility and respond to the changing trends in HE, the transformations entailed the encouragement of private, intergovernmental and transnational providers. On the other hand, concerned with the rapidly increasing number of private providers with questionable quality, the government took steps to regulate the market newcomers by introducing accountability tools, for example by setting strict regulations and licensing and accreditation policies. This has led to the closure or merger of private and poorly performing public providers. Another example is the extension of centralised admission policy to private providers, which eventually compelled the latter to reorient their missions. Thus, the stimulators for horizontal differentiation could be summed up as driven by market demands for modernisation of qualifications and massification of HE as well as the government agenda for accountability, funding, internationalisation and recognition of qualifications.

Vertical differentiation is increasingly becoming a major concern for the government, HEIs and stakeholders. HEIs are becoming part of international and national rankings and classifications to enable measurement of achievements and comparative analysis of those achievements throughout time and across systems. Among the steps leading to vertical differentiation is the government attempt to invite highly ranked HEIs to establish branch campuses in Armenia (e.g. Moscow State University).

In sum, the transformations in the Armenian HE system have come in the form of differentiation at diverse levels. Considering that the drivers behind this differentiation are predominantly market requirements and political strategies at the government level leading to international visibility, the HE system is predominantly governed by a balance of national and global forces leading to convergence. Although it is still premature to speak about the level of convergence in actual implementation practices, HEIs in Armenia are becoming more convergent with those at the European level through such major tools as the NQF and its alignment with EQF, the independent quality assurance and accountability system, operationalisation of the credit transfer and accumulation system and a move towards two-tier education (bachelor and master).

Notes

1. http://www.webometrics.info/en/europe/armenia
2. State Committee of Science, established within the MoES in 2008 with a mandate to improve the science sector in Armenia. The body mainly promotes research by offering grants.
3. http://studyinarmenia.org/hea

References

CARIM. 2013. *Refugees, Displaced Persons and Asylum Seekers in Armenia.* RSCAS, CARIM East Project, European University Institute, Florence, Italy.

Chabe, A.M. 1971. Soviet Educational Policies: Their Development, Administration and Content. *Association for Supervision and Curriculum Development, 525–531 in August, 2015.* www.ascd.org/ASCD/pdf/journals/ed_lead/el_197102_chabe.pdf

Hasan, A. 2007. *Independent Legal Status and Universities as Foundations.* Paris: UNESCO, International Institute for Educational Planning.

Karakhanyan, S., K. van Veen, and T. Bergen. 2011. Higher Education Policy Transfer and Diffusion: The Case of Armenia. *Higher Education Policy* 24: 53–83.

Khrushcheva, N., and A. Benvenuti. 2002. *Lessons of Transition: The Cultural Contradictions and the Future of Russian Liberalization.* New York: World Policy Institute.

Khudaverdyan, K.S. 1960. Cultural Changes in the Soviet Armenia During Prewar Five-Year-Time-Spans. *Izvestiya Academii Nauk Armyanskoi SSR* 3–17.

Kozma, T., and T. Polonyi. 2004. Understanding Education in European-East Frames of Interpretation and Comparison. *International Journal of Education Development* 24 (5): 467–477.

MoES. 2014. *Education for All 2015 National Review Report: Armenia.* Paris: UNESCO.

NAS. 2004. *Science and Technology in Armenia: Toward a Knowledge-Based Economy.* Washington, DC: National Academy of Sciences, The National Academies Press.

NSSRA. 2014. National Statistical Services of the Republic of Armenia. *Yearbooks,* March 2015. http://www.armstat.am/en/?nid=45&year=2014

Sarafian, K. 1930. *History of Education in Armenia.* California: La Verne Leader.

Suny, R. 1996. *Armenia, Azerbaijan, and Georgia: Country Studies.* Dane Publishing, Washington D. C.

Terzian, M.S. 2010. *Curriculum Reform in Post-Soviet Armenia: Balancing Local and Global Contexts in Armenian Secondary Schools.* Dissertations/107, Loyola University Chicago.

UNESCO. 1990. *Higher Education in the USSR.* Bucharest: CEPES.

———. 2000. *The EFA 2000 Assessment: Country report, Armenia.* Paris.

UNHCR. 2004. *UNHCR Statistical Yearbook.* UNHCR Refugee Agency, Geneva, Switzerland.

van Vught, F. 2007. *Diversity and Differentiation in Higher Education Systems.* CHET Anniversary Conference, Cape Town.

WB. 2011. *Public Expenditure Review.* Washington, DC: World Bank.

———. 2013. *Addressing Governance at the Center of Higher Education Reforms in Armenia*. Washington, DC: World Bank.

Zelvys, R. 2004. Development of Education Policy in Lithuania During the Years of Transformations. *International Journal of Educational Development* 24 (5): 559–571.

Susanna Karakhanyan is one of the founders of the National Center for Professional Education Quality Assurance in Armenia (ANQA) as well as the first President and current member of the (ANQA) Accreditation Commission. She is the current President of the International Network for Quality Assurance Agencies in Higher Education (INQAAHE). Dr. Karakhanyan holds an M.S.Ed. in Educational Administration from the University of Pennsylvania, USA, and Ph.D. in Social Sciences from the Radboud University Nijmegen, the Netherlands. Her research interests evolve around higher education policy development, diffusion and transfer, HE governance, administration and management in general and its quality assurance, in particular.

Open Access This chapter is distributed under the terms of the Creative Commons Attribution 4.0 International License (http://creativecommons.org/licenses/by/4.0/), which permits use, duplication, adaptation, distribution and reproduction in any medium or format, as long as you give appropriate credit to the original author(s) and the source, provide a link to the Creative Commons license and indicate if changes were made.

The images or other third party material in this chapter are included in the chapter's Creative Commons license, unless indicated otherwise in a credit line to the material. If material is not included in the chapter's Creative Commons license and your intended use is not permitted by statutory regulation or exceeds the permitted use, you will need to obtain permission directly from the copyright holder.

CHAPTER 4

Higher Education Transformation, Institutional Diversity and Typology of Higher Education Institutions in Azerbaijan

Hamlet Isakhanli and Aytaj Pashayeva

INTRODUCTION

Azerbaijan is a transcontinental country located at the crossroads of Eastern Europe and Western Asia, and bound by the Caspian Sea to the east. The country borders Iran and Turkey to the south, Russia to the north, Georgia to the northwest and Armenia to the west. It is the largest country in the South Caucasus region with a majority Muslim and Turkic population speaking the Azerbaijani (Azeri) language. In 2014, the population of the nation was equal to 9.5 million with more than half living in urban areas (53%). Azerbaijanis constitute the majority of the nation (91.6%), while Lezgins (2%), Armenians[1] (2%), Talysh (1.3%) and Russians (1.3%) make up the biggest minority groups. There has been

H. Isakhanli
Khazar University, Baku, Azerbaijan

A. Pashayeva (✉)
Institute of Education of the Republic of Azerbaijan, Baku, Azerbaijan

moderate population growth due to a sharp reduction in the birth rate since the beginning of the 1990s. However, it is a young country with around 28% of the population aged 19–24.

The development of the Azerbaijani education system mirrors the country's historical transformations. The country first announced its independence in 1918 with the establishment of the Azerbaijan Democratic Republic (ADR). The first university in the country, Baku State University, was founded by the ADR in 1919. The new democratic republic was established by the Azerbaijani elite, who were educated in Europe and understood the necessity of building a national higher education system. The short life of the ADR did not allow the founders to expand the university and establish a full-blown higher education system; however, the first university in the country continued to function after the fall of the ADR. It was later enlarged during the Soviet period and became the major research and higher education institute in Azerbaijan (Isakhanli 2014).

Soviet forces ended the democratic republic in 1920 and established the Azerbaijan Soviet Socialist Republic (SSR). From then on, low literacy levels and minimal participation by women in social and economic life were major development issues in the country (Avakov and Atakishiev 1984). The primary goal for educational development was to increase literacy levels by providing free schooling for all. Teacher 'technicums'[2] began providing teacher training and the school system expanded throughout the country. This reform increased literacy levels up to 90% during the first two decades of the Soviet period (1920–1940).

Alongside general educational development, the higher education system began to form as well. Industrialisation and economic development were the leading forces impacting higher education development in the Azerbaijan SSR. The emergence of new industries and branches in the 1920s and 1930s necessitated the establishment of new educational programmes and institutions. Higher education had to adapt to the national economy and industrialisation. This was the main reason for the establishment of specialised higher education institutions (HEIs), such as the Petroleum Institute, the Agrarian Institute and the Azerbaijan Polytechnic Institute. The Azerbaijan State University[3] and the Azerbaijan Petroleum Institute[4] were the main research-oriented institutions in the country during the Soviet period. Industrialisation and labour market demands also shaped modes of higher education provision, which are still practiced today: evening and part-time (correspondence) classes were introduced during this time. Azerbaijan higher education planning was identical to many other countries within the Union of Soviet Socialist Republics (USSR) and stemmed from the idea of the planned economy.

Depending on the length of studies and prior educational experiences, four types of degrees were awarded during the Soviet period (Table 4.1). Post-secondary institutions provided vocational training, which led to the junior specialist diploma. Higher education institutions (HEIs) granted graduates the specialist diploma. Research degrees were awarded by the Academy of Science, which included *Kandidat Nauk* and *Doktor Nauk*.

A major expansion in the number of HEIs during the Soviet period took place between 1970 and 1980; while in 1970 there were 80,000 students studying 138 specialisations at 13 HEIs, in 1980 the number increased to 107,000 students specialising in 158 areas at 17 HEIs (Mehdizade 1980; Salakov 1990). The system included one university, two institutes of art, the Baku Higher Party School (see Table 4.2) as well as institutes of engineering, agriculture, medical studies, physical education and economics. This was explained by the development of the economy and an increased population with a growing need for specialists with high-level qualifications. In 1990, just before the collapse of the Soviet Union, there were 17 HEIs providing education to 105,000 students in Azerbaijan. Between 1990 and 2014, the number of students increased to 150,000 while the number of HEIs expanded to 53.

Table 4.1 Main credentials awarded during the Soviet period

Degree and diploma	Type of institution	Admission requirement	Length
Diploma of Junior Specialist	Post-secondary, non-university institutions (*Ucilishe, Technicums*)	Completion of basic secondary education	2–4 years
Diploma of Specialist	University, Academy Institute, Polytechnic	Completion of secondary education	4 years (technology and economics) 5 years (all disciplines) 6 years (medicine)
Kandidat Nauk	Academy of Science	Diploma of Specialist	3 years
Doktor Nauk (Doctor of Science)	Academy of Science	*Kandidat Nauk*	5–15 years

Source: World Education News & Reviews (2015)

Table 4.2 Types of HEIs that emerged between 1919 and 1990 with student numbers for 2013–2014

Type/focus of training	Year	Name	Loc.	Student
Republic's leading university/ training of academic and research staff for other HEIs as well as chief public sector employees	1919	Azerbaijan State University	Baku	16,566
Specialised HEIs/training specialists in specific area of industry (engineering, agriculture, technology, etc.) or sector of economy (medical studies, teaching, art, etc.)	1920	Petroleum Institute	Baku	7,357
	1921	Baku Musical Academy	Baku	270
	1923	Theatrical Institute	Baku	2,120
	1929	Agrarian Institute	Ganja	5,040
	1929	State Pedagogical Institute	Baku	8,941
	1930	Medical Institute	Baku	6,725
	1930	Institute of Sport and Physical Ed.	Baku	3,721
	1930	Trade-Cooperative Institute	Baku	18,000
	1936	Painting Institute	Baku	854
	1950	Polytechnic Institute	Baku	8,589
	1972	Pedagogical Institute of Foreign Languages	Baku	5,501
	1972	Nakhchivan State Pedagogical Institute	Nakhchivan	5,403
	1973	Khankendi Pedagogical Institute	Khankendi	n.a
	1975	Construction Institute	Baku	5,576
	1980	Technological Institute	Ganja	2,244
Specialised/ideological, political	1939	Baku Higher Party School	Baku	n.a

Source: State Statistical Committee (2014), Mehdizade (1980), Salakov (1990)

Although the first university in Azerbaijan was established before the country was integrated into the Soviet Union, the higher education system developed and expanded during the Soviet period as shaped by economic planning, the emerging needs of industry and the ideological priorities of the system. Higher education continued changing and developing during the independence years as driven by various social, economic and political as well as international factors.

Higher Education Since Independence

With independence in 1991, Azerbaijan continued to maintain its well-developed educational system, with high levels of literacy as a legacy of the Soviet period. As soon as independence was obtained, the country repudiated the traditions of the Soviet past and started building policies for immediate changes to adapt to the new economic and political structure. This was accompanied by market privatisation and liberalisation. Yet economic decline and resource scarcity in all areas of social development, especially education, prevented the full implementation of reforms and adversely affected all levels of schooling. Moreover, educational institutions were often reluctant to embrace changes and maintained Soviet traditions of management, administration and teaching.

The country experienced a sharp economic decline between 1991 and 1994 that resulted in the loss of about 60% of its pre-independence gross domestic product (GDP) (World Bank 1997). Failures in the implementation of reform policies and the economic turmoil in this period (1991–1994) are related to the war in Karabakh (1988–1994) and the political instability in the country (Allahveranov and Huseynov 2013). Armed conflict with Armenia over Nagorno Karabakh escalated in the early 1990s, resulting in the occupation of about 20% of Azerbaijani territory; this issue remains unresolved. As a result of the war, Azerbaijan received about 1 million refugees from the occupied territory, which made up 11% of the total population. It was the largest Internally Displaced Persons (IDP) burden in the world at that time (UNECE 2010). Currently, Nagorno Karabakh is internationally recognised as Azerbaijani territory; however, the country is not in control of the disputed area. Therefore, this chapter does not include any information on HEIs in the occupied territory.

After agreeing to a ceasefire with Armenia in 1994, Azerbaijan started along a new development path. It signed oil and gas exploration contracts with foreign companies in 1995 that led to an extraordinary amount of international investment flowing into the sector. As a resource-rich country, the oil and gas sector comprises a major part of the economy. The share of the oil sector in the state budget has reached 78% and accounts for 65% of GDP, with oil and gas products making up more than 92% of exports (Bayramov et al. 2014).

Despite the growth of the economy, educational funding did not keep pace with the overall economic improvements: the percentage of GDP allocated to education was 2.5% in 2013 with just 0.2% apportioned to higher education and science. This lack of resources led to lower quality at all levels of education. Corruption practices at universities that had roots in the later years of the Soviet period became more common during the early years of independence. Bribery was often practiced in student admission to universities and in obtaining diplomas. Hence, newly emerging private universities became alternatives for corrupt state institutions. Limited funds also urged universities to start charging student fees and establishing new educational programmes.

The participation of international organisations in the field of education was another factor impacting the development of the education sector, specifically higher education. Since the early 1990s, organisations such as the World Bank, the European Union, UNICEF, the Soros Foundation, IREX and the Eurasia Foundation have contributed to the development of the education sector through activities like direct grants and credits, technical assistance in launching programmes and sponsoring Azerbaijani students abroad.

These changes were also supported by legislation. The three-cycle degree system, permission to establish private universities, the right to own property and permission to set tuition fees were introduced in the Education Law. This was the first national legislative provision on education, which was adopted in October 1992. The Law reflected the first post-communist government plans regarding the modernisation and updating of the education system to meet international standards. It spelled out the educational structure, the main concepts of higher education and the unification of science and education within higher education institutions. Most importantly, it legalised revenue diversification for universities.

The Law also made a clear division between Bachelor and Master degrees and classified institutions based on the degrees they offered. HEIs are typified as one-tier institutions if they provide Bachelor degrees only (institutes, conservatories and higher colleges). Two-tier universities are those offering Master and Doctoral studies in addition to Bachelor degrees. For instance, Baku State University (BSU) is an example of a two-tier HEI providing higher education in all three levels, while Mingechevir Polytechnic provided Bachelor degrees only. In line with the Law, both private and public universities were exempted from taxation and were independent in student recruitment and granting degrees. The Law did not include major changes to Doctoral studies, leaving the post-graduate landscape rather intact.

The establishment of new public universities was carried out by merging and separating existing higher education institutions as well as non-university institutions, colleges[5] and 'technicums' in early 2000. For instance, 11 teacher technicums in the different regions of Azerbaijan were upgraded to higher education institutions as branches of the Azerbaijan Teachers Institute. The National Conservatory was established on the foundations of the Baku Musical Academy. Two colleges of art and music were integrated into the Conservatory and the Painting Academy, respectively.

The increase in the number of HEIs was also related to the expansion of private and cross-border universities: more than 100 private post-secondary (vocational colleges) and higher education institutions were established during the first 5 years of independence. The key factor driving the expansion was increasing societal interest in privatisation and private enterprise. Corruption issues and low educational quality in public HEIs also contributed to the appeal of private institutions. Rather than launching studies with uncertain costs due to bribery in a public university, parents and students started viewing private universities as a better alternative (Catterall and McGhee 1996). Growing demand for graduates with English language skills trained in important fields such as business, management and administration combined with the failure of public universities to meet this demand due to outdated institutional traditions and low marketplace agility created fertile conditions for private universities. Another factor impacting increased interest in higher education stemmed from the degraded quality of vocational education and its decreased value in the country. Within 15 years after independence (1990–2005), the Gross Enrolment Ratio (GER) in vocational education fell from 38.9% to 14.2% (Azerbaijan Economists' Union and UNICEF 2008).

The increase in the number of HEIs and interest in higher education was not followed by rapid and prominent growth in student enrolment (Fig. 4.1). On the contrary, the GER declined in the first years after independence and reached 1980s levels again, but not until 1998.

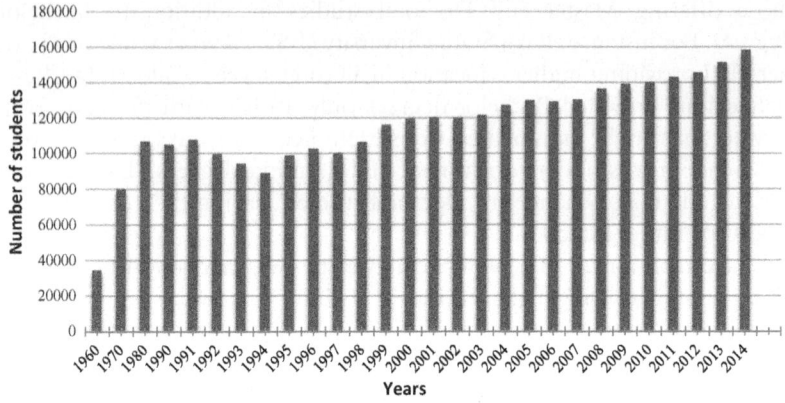

Fig. 4.1 Student enrolment in higher education (1960–2014) (Source: SSC 2014)

The decrease in enrolment was primarily due to the introduction of tuition fees and a new admissions system, which replaced Soviet institutional admission with standardised testing throughout the country. Families could afford neither tuition fees nor tutoring costs for admission exams (Silova and Kazimzade 2006).

In addition to educational legislation, changes in student admission procedures also marked a major turning point in higher education development. Accelerated corruption levels as a consequence of the general crisis in the country was the main driving force for altering student recruitment. To fight corruption, Azerbaijan was the first former Soviet Union country to introduce standardised testing in university admission processes in 1992 (Drummond and Gabrscek 2012). The State Commission for Student Admission (SSAC) was established as the major administrative body for these tests. SSAC operates independently from the Ministry of Education (MoE) and reports directly to the President. Currently, SSAC administers school graduation exams, organises Bachelor and Master admission exams for both private and public HEIs, and implements student placement at HEIs.

The mushrooming of private institutions also ceased with the introduction of new quality assurance mechanisms. In 1995, only 10 out of 100 newly established private institutions acquired formal legal status after being evaluated by a Ministry of Education expert commission and obtaining permission from the Cabinet of Ministers (Catterall and McGhee 1996).

It was not only the decline in HEI numbers but also limited resources, centralised admission processes and educational quality that resulted in low participation rates in tertiary education (Aliyev 2011). In 2014, the GER for tertiary education was 23%.

Hence, higher education development in the first 10 years after Azerbaijani independence was associated with increased institutional diversity and differentiation. Loose regulations regarding the establishment of private institutions, increased demand for higher education and interest in private enterprise led to higher education attracting more students. Although the number of HEIs in the country skyrocketed initially with more than 100 new university and non-university institutions entering the market, differentiation in the Azerbaijani higher education system has been relatively slow since 2000.

In the early 2000s, the number of private HEIs dropped from 18 to 15 as some were closed down (Fig. 4.2). The number of public HEIs, however, increased from 29 to 37 due to newly established universities and academies with diverse study areas, such as the Azerbaijan Diplomatic Academy and the Baku Higher Oil School. Stagnation in the number of private universities since the 2000s can be explained by increased requirements for establishing HEIs and social favouritism for public institutions

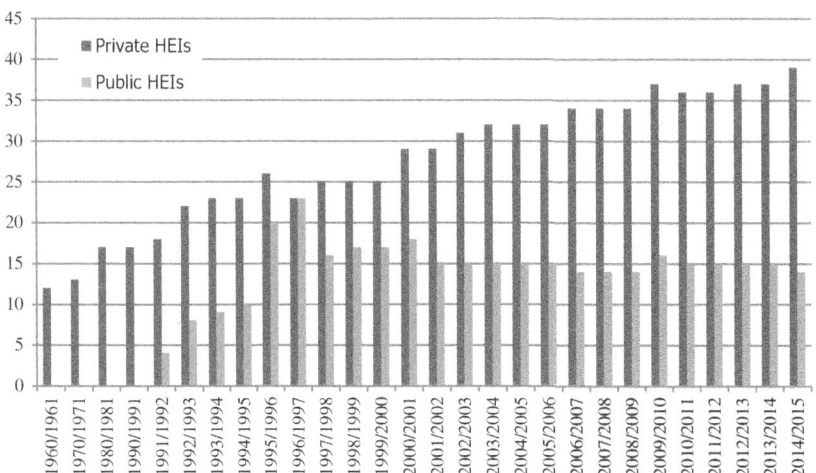

Fig. 4.2 Number of private and public HEIs in Azerbaijan, 1960–2014 (Source: State Statistical Committee 2014)

as stable establishments stemming from mistrust in short-lived private ones, as well as ministry and state demands. While public institutions grew in number and profile, many HEI branches dropped off. Four branches of the Azerbaijan Institute of Teachers were closed due to alleged corrupt practices in 2014–15.

Harmonising the higher education system with the Bologna Process requirements and the need for more clarity in HEI management necessitated updates in legislation. The Second Education Law was adopted in 2009 after 15 years of discussion. The transition period was accompanied by political turmoil and the adoption of the new Law was delayed until the late 2000s, when the country started benefiting from the oil boom and developing fast.

The Second Law established a new system for Doctoral education, culminating in either a Doctor of Philosophy (PhD) or Doctor of Science, the latter being an amalgam of Soviet and Western Doctoral degrees. As the leading educational document, the Law also aimed to clarify education structure and the educational system. It determines the characteristics of HEIs (Table 4.3) that divides HEIs into universities, academies and institutes based on their research and teaching focus. In the document, universities represent multi-profile institutions and, in addition to teaching, function as research institutes. Academies included primarily specialised HEIs with a narrow focus of study like military schools, the Academy of Painting and the Azerbaijan Diplomatic Academy. Institutes encompassed specialised institutions that provided professional training. However, the title of "institute" is slowly being phased out in the current Azerbaijani higher education system. By Presidential decree, "institute" is being replaced with "university" in HEI titles. The only HEI still carrying the "institute" title is the Nakhchivan Institute of Teachers.

It is also worth mentioning that the distinction between universities and academies is vague in reality. In September 2015, the Azerbaijan State Oil Academy was renamed the Azerbaijan State University of Oil and Industry with no major structural or institutional changes. University representatives explained the inclusion of the word "industry" in the title by pointing out that the HEI's focus is not limited to the oil sector, but this does not explain why the institution was upgraded from an academy to a university. Again by Presidential Decree in December 2014, the Azerbaijan Tourism Institute was renamed the Azerbaijan University of Management and Tourism. Similarly, in July 2015, Mingechevir State University was established on the foundations of the former Mingechevir Polytechnic

Table 4.3 State defined characteristics of HEIs

Education/teaching and learning	Research
Student body (bachelor, master, and doctoral degree students studying part time and full time) Teaching staff (tenure and adjunct professors) Country ranking Average SSAC scores Choice of high scorers Presidential scholarship winners Eight group programmes and required scores Top ten programmes	Total budget for research and science funding Number of articles published in local scientific journals Number of articles published in international peer reviewed journals Number of patents and patent applications Number of international research science projects partnered/joined Number of national and regional science projects partnered/joined Number of professors who are members of ANAS, PhD/ DSc programme offering universities Number of research institutes under the HEI
Financing	**Internationalisation**
Universities with rights to independent funding allocation Sources of income other than from tuition and state funding Income from research activities Income from tuition	Number of international students (bachelor, master and doctoral degree Number of international students sponsored by the HEI Number of exchange programmes administered by the HEI Number of professor exchange programmes Number of international programmes Number of international exchange projects, number of contracts with foreign universities, institutions, organisations, etc., number of international faculty

Source: Education Law (2009)

Institute. The purpose of this was to provide one comprehensive state university in each big city in the country. The latest upgrade was the inclusion of the Azerbaijan Institute of Teachers under the Azerbaijan Pedagogical University. This was to optimise the number of HEIs in the country and increase the efficiency of their governance.

Admission plays an important role in shaping HEI diversification and the higher education market in Azerbaijan. Although universities set their admission cut-off scores, the bar fluctuates based on general student test performance. Student placement is carried out based on an HEI admission plan designed by the MoE and confirmed by the Cabinet of Ministers. HEI ranking is a new phenomenon for the higher education system in Azerbaijan, and the ranking system was established in 2013 to increase competition among HEIs. The ranking is issued by SSAC based on applicant HEI preferences and the average admission score of enrolling students. Recently, the MoE commissioned a study that yielded another country ranking of HEIs with the purpose of creating more competition in the higher education market. The study not only produced a country ranking of HEIs, but also proved a positive relation between ranking and student choice (Ahmadov 2014). For instance, Khazar University and Qafqaz University are private HEIs often chosen by high scoring students (on the admission test), despite requiring a lower passing score than public HEIs. Hence, the admission process is the major driver of vertical diversity in the system.

EUROPEANISATION AND INTERNATIONALISATION OF HIGHER EDUCATION

Not only socioeconomic and political changes within the country but also global trends have affected the system in Azerbaijan. From the initial reforms and decrees, Azerbaijan clearly aimed to transform Soviet education by establishing and following Western educational values and modes to discard the remnants and values of socialist education. Other higher education systems and institutions were observed for insight and good examples, and were used as a basis for benchmarking. Moreover, educational policies in the country were closely associated with foreign policy. Azerbaijan joined the Council of Europe in 2001 and has been a part of the European Neighbourhood Policy since 2004. Accession to the Bologna Process in 2005 took higher education on a more defined development path. Many important reforms following the accession were directed towards harmonising the higher education system with European standards.

Joining the Bologna Process also increased student mobility in higher education and positively affected internationalisation by opening opportunities for participation in various exchange programmes, expanding university partnerships and transferring credits to other universities. Currently, Azerbaijani universities participate in European Union educational programmes such as Trans-European Mobility Programme for University Studies (TEMPUS) and Erasmus+.

Increased political relations with neighbouring countries after independence brought about increased student mobility within the region and contributed to the movement of students among the former Soviet republics. After independence, relations with neighbours such as Iran became stronger and closer than in Soviet times. Most international students in Azerbaijan currently come from Turkey (57%) and Iran (13%). There are also many students from the former Soviet Union (12%), mostly from Turkmenistan and Kazakhstan as well as neighbouring Georgia (Fig. 4.3).

Universities are free to attract and recruit international students. In 2013, there were more than 3,971 international students studying in Azerbaijan, which comprised 2.6% of the total student body. Although some universities provide international programmes in English, the state mandates the provision of core courses in the Azerbaijani language. Therefore, in case they do not master Azerbaijani or Russian, international students are expected to take a preparatory Azerbaijani language course for one or two semesters. The majority of international students in Azerbaijan opt for studies in fields such as medicine, economics, humanitarian and technical studies.

In line with inbound student mobility, the number of Azerbaijani students studying abroad grew as well. Shortly after joining the Bologna Process, an order to launch a scholarship programme for Azerbaijani citizens to study abroad (between 2007 and 2015) was signed by the President in 2006. Programmes of study are defined and listed by the MoE based on assumed labour market need. Most of these students study in the fields of medicine, economics and technology and the most attractive destinations for studying abroad are the United Kingdom, Turkey and Germany. In 2015, a total of 3,558 students received the state scholarship to study in 32 countries at 379 universities.

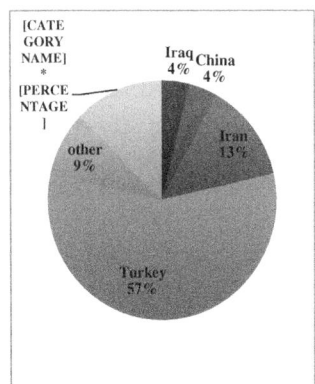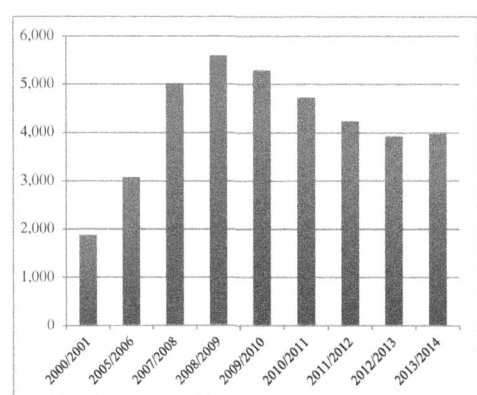

Fig. 4.3 International students based on home country (2013–2014) and Dynamics in International Student Participation since 2000 (Source: SSC (2014), *Commonwealth of Independent States)

Governance of Higher Education: Role of the State

According to the Education Law of the Republic of Azerbaijan (2009), the major goal of higher education is to provide education that integrates the demands of society and the labour market to develop highly specialised experts, researchers and academic staff for the country. The governance of higher education remains quite centralised, with all policies and reforms decided and very often imposed by the Cabinet of Ministers and the MoE. The MoE is the central executive body governing the education system. It participates in the development and implementation of state policy for education.

There are six universities that have obtained autonomy from the state. Such HEIs acquire funding directly from the Ministry of Finances and are not steered by any other governmental institution. Universities with this level of autonomy are allowed to define the contents of education, set their own admission plan in all three degree levels and independently award scientific degrees and scientific titles. Ten HEIs are under the auspices of other ministries, state companies and other affiliated institutions. For instance, the Azerbaijan Medical University is under the Ministry of Healthcare, while the State Academy of Sports and the University of Management and Tourism are under the Ministry of Youth and Sports.

Curricula, teaching methodologies and course priorities in higher education are defined at the national level and built around state-level higher education standards. All HEIs including public, private and international institutions as well as autonomous universities are obliged to follow these standards. State standards also outline the different higher education degree levels, higher education management, HEI infrastructure, quality standards for education providers and measurement tools for student competences as well as educational programmes.

The state budget is the basis for public HEIs, while private HEIs heavily depend on tuition fees. Such institutions also obtain resources from trustees, partnerships with industry, bank loans and various local and international grants. Both public and private HEIs are free to define their tuition fees. The fee amount is usually based on the reputation of the HEI and its place on the ranking list. Starting in 2010, the state uses a funding model based on the number of students admitted and defines the amount per student, varying by field of study within a range of 1500–1800 AZN[6]; there is an exception for medical students (2500 AZN). In 2013, the state started paying public HEIs for students who scored sufficient points to make them eligible for free state university seats, but chose to study in private HEIs. Currently, students studying on a state scholarship and exempt from tuition constitute one-third of the student population (36%), and only 1.24% of these students study in private HEIs (State Student Admission Committee 2014).

HIGHER EDUCATION AND RESEARCH

The First Education Law (2003) declared the unification of research and teaching within higher education. There was a slow increase in HEI research activity, with still a strong role for the Azerbaijan National Academy of Sciences (ANAS) in overseeing research work. The MoE and the ANAS are the main bodies responsible for Doctoral programmes. In 2013, 106 institutions were carrying out research activities, of which 73 were scientific institutions and 33 HEIs. The cabinet, the MoE and the ANAS decide on the plan for Doctoral candidate admission and issue permits for establishing new Doctoral programmes. Only the six aforementioned autonomous universities are free to decide on their Doctoral programmes. The academic Doctorate is the only type of Doctoral programme that still reflects the practices of the Soviet period. The Doctorate degree is divided into two levels: (1) a PhD degree *(fəlsəfə doktoru)* that takes three to four years depending on the mode of study; and (2) a Doctor of Science degree *(elmlər doktoru)* that can be continued after the PhD degree with four to five years of study.

HIGHER EDUCATION LANDSCAPE IN AZERBAIJAN

Changes in the higher education system in Azerbaijan since its independence have developed and occurred at varying paces. Accelerated institutional differentiation in the early years after independence yielded good quality in private HEIs, as well as low calibre institutions that contributed to the aggravated corruption in the education system. Most in the latter category were phased out. On the one hand, the state still maintains strong control over the higher education market, and on the other it introduces incentives for HEIs to trigger competition.

During the academic year 2013–14, about 151,000 students studied in 53 HEIs (see Fig. 4.4). For that academic year, 40,884 students were admitted to universities, a majority of 87% at the Bachelor level with only 14% in private universities. The number of students paying tuition fees has

Fig. 4.4 Student body characteristics for 2014/2015 (Source: State Statistical Committee 2014)

been increasing every academic year; in 2000 only 45% of students were expected to pay for higher education, but this number grew to more than 60% by 2013. In addition to being able to study for free, students who score highest on admission exams are also awarded with a presidential scholarship. In 2013, 102 top scoring applicants received the scholarship (State Student Admission Committee 2014). Also in 2013, 96,720 students participated in admission exams, and about 35% were successful. About 60% of the applicants were high school graduates in the same year, and 70% of these high school graduates failed to score the minimum admission points required (150 out of 700) and therefore did not gain access to the higher education system.

Educational programmes in HEIs are offered in three languages: the official language, Azerbaijani, as well as Russian and English, although there are no programmes taught completely in English. Admission to HEIs, however, is carried out in Azerbaijani and Russian. In 2013, the majority of students (89%) were admitted to Azerbaijani language programmes, with 11% opting for Russian language programmes. The majority of public universities (32) and a few private universities (4) provide programmes in the Russian language (SSAC 2014).

The number of programmes at HEIs and their diversity has been increasing, with universities establishing new programmes that do not require much investment in infrastructure such as information technology, business administration and financial management. Often such courses are offered by most HEIs, which leads to duplication and overlap. HEIs offer educational programmes in eight areas that were defined by the Cabinet of Ministers in 2009: education; humanitarian and social sciences; arts and culture; economics and management; natural sciences; technical and technological sciences; agriculture; healthcare, well-being and service. The majority of students enrol in education, technical sciences and economics (70% for both Bachelor and Master degrees). HEIs try to expand their programmes in these qualification groups to attract more students.

Current Institutional Typology

Currently, HEIs in Azerbaijan can only be compared by using the state's institutional ranking. This ranking system incorporates only one dimension, student choice after the admission exam, and fails to reflect other major institutional functions. The current ranking does not provide any information on research quality, international orientation or institutional interaction with industry. The ranking also neglects the diversity of fields and educational programmes offered by the institutions. Although about 70% of HEIs in Azerbaijan can be defined as rather specialised institutions based on their title and educational study focus, each educational programme is offered by at least 10% of HEIs. Hence, the ranking does not sufficiently describe why students choose this or that specific university. The following dimensions were used within the research to classify HEIs in Azerbaijan (Table 4.4).

Table 4.4 State defined typology of HEIs

Type	Description	Number
Academy (*Akademiya*)	Implements higher and in-service training programmes, and conducts fundamental and applied scientific research	Public 11, Private 1
University (*Universitet*)	Leading multi-profile higher educational institution, which carries out a broad range of specialist training at all levels of higher education, in-service training programmes, and conducts fundamental and applied scientific research	Public 21, Private 14
Institute (*Institut, ali məktəb*)	Independent HEIs, independent research focused establishment, or a structural unit of a university, which carries out the training of specialists on specific specialties, as well as provides in-service training programmes	Public 1, Private 0
Conservatory (*Konservatoriya*)	Provides training for highly specialised experts in the field of music	Public 1, Private 0

Source: Education Law (2009)

In addition, HEI reputation and prestige levels are often mentioned in state documentation and policy papers, and were also incorporated into the typology (Table 4.5). University websites were also analysed to gauge HEIs' missions. Five public HEIs that require a special aptitude test as part of the admission process, which are affiliated with various defence and military ministries and state bodies, were excluded from this study. No data were accessible on research and education dimensions, and no international students were admitted to these institutions.

Flagship University. Baku State University (BSU) is the oldest university in Azerbaijan and is popular with prominent alumni and acclaimed professorial staff who are also active participants in the political and social life of the country. The current and former President of the country, as well as presidents and national leaders of various countries are honorary Doctors of the university. BSU is home to the highest number of students with the highest average scores and is considered "a leader of HEIs" and a "scientific and educational centre" of the higher education system. It is also one of the six completely autonomous HEIs in the country that attract the highest number of international students.

Leading public specialised HEIs. This group is comprised of eight HEIs popular among high scoring students with high cut-off scores and includes both recently established and older universities. These HEIs offer specialised studies in diverse fields such as diplomacy, executive education, languages, economics and oil engineering. This group is also diverse when the four dimensions are taken into account. Two of the institutions were established in the last 5 years: the Azerbaijan Diplomatic Academy, established in 2006, and Baku Higher Oil School, established in 2011. These are comparatively new HEIs and are popular among high scorers on the admission test. Both HEIs are selective and competitive, with the highest points required for admission and highest average points scored among admitted students (590 for ADA and 660 for BHOS).

Public specialised HEIs. This group makes up 70% of all public HEIs and enrols one-third of the total student body. Unlike the previous group, this cluster requires comparatively lower cut-off scores and enrols students with lower average scores. The group includes HEIs with a narrow focus that require a special aptitude test, for example the Painting Academy, Conservatory, and University of Art and Architecture. HEIs within the group have a relatively weak international focus and conduct mostly applied research. Although this group recently started providing PhD studies, there is still a limited research focus.

Table 4.5 Classification of HEIs in Azerbaijan

Title/number	Institutional characteristics	Example	Students
Flagship University (1)	Comprehensive, research focused institution which provides multi-profile educational programmes. Major provider of doctoral study programmes	Baku State University	16,988
Leading public specialised HEIs (8)	HEIs with high average admission scores and include research focused and teaching-focused institutions. Provider of specialised educational programmes for different areas of industry and social life	Diplomatic Academy, Medical University, Azerbaijan State University of Oil and Industry, etc.	37,143
Public specialised (12)	Provides specialised training on narrow fields, such as music, art, painting, languages, etc. Some of these HEIs have special aptitude test. Low focus on internationalisation, doctoral studies and research	Painting Academy, Music Academy, Slavic University, etc.	39, 137
Regional comprehensive (5)	Universities established on the basis of upgraded institutes. Carries a goal of serving a higher education centre for big region of the country and provide with training in various areas. Low focus on internationalisation, doctoral studies and research	Ganja State, Mingechevir State, Lankaran State, Nakhchivan State, Sumgayit State	18, 663
Regional specialised (3)	This group also includes 7 branches of Azerbaijan Pedagogical University. Teaching, Agriculture and technology focused institutions with low focus on internationalisation	Agrarian University, Technological University, Nakchivan Teachers' Institute	9473
Private leading comprehensive (4)	4 private comprehensive universities with higher average scored points compared to other private HEIs. High cut-off score. Choice of presidential scholarship holders. Holds at least 5 out of 8 educational programmes	Khazar U, Odlar Yurdu U, Qafqaz U, Western U.	17,987

(continued)

Table 4.5 (continued)

Title/number	Institutional characteristics	Example	Students
Private specialised and comprehensive (10)	Includes specialised and comprehensive private HEIs, with low international and research focus, lowest average admission scores. Also includes the HEI with the smallest student body—Baku Asia University, 200 students	Cooperation U, Azerbaijan U, Baku Islamic U, etc.	10,078
Regional comprehensive private (1)	The only private university in the region that provides educational programme in various areas. No focus on internationalisation and research	Nakhchivan University	972

The *regional comprehensive* group encompasses five comprehensive state universities operating in big cities such as Ganja, Sumgayit, Nakhchivan, Lankaran and Mingechevir. They were developed and upgraded from regional technicums into universities to serve as major comprehensive education providers in various regions. This group also includes two autonomous HEIs: Nakhchivan State University and Azerbaijan Agrarian University. This group has a low international and research focus, enrols students mostly from neighbouring regions and provides comprehensive educational programmes. This group requires lower admission scores and has a less intensive international and research focus.

The *regional specialised* group is comprised of HEI branches: three that provide specialised training in technology, agriculture and teaching and seven branches of teaching schools. However, the main campus and steering body of these branches, Azerbaijan Pedagogical University, is located in Baku. This group supports very few international students (seven students on average) and limited Doctoral studies (65 students on average). The major function of this group is meeting regional needs for a specialised work force.

Private leading comprehensive. Despite unequal competition conditions for private universities, some private HEIs perform with a strong portfolio and attract high-quality applicants each year. This group consists of four private universities in the capital city of Baku with higher average scored points compared to other private HEIs. These are also the first established private institutions, which function mostly on the basis of income from tuition fees. Being deprived of any kind of state funding, these HEIs can compete with other public HEIs. Qafqaz University, for example, was established by a Turkish foundation and has the biggest local and international student body with the highest number of research institutes and industry partnerships among private HEIs.

Private comprehensive and specialised. The remaining private comprehensive (six) and specialised (four) institutions require the lowest admission scores. This group is represented by the biggest (3900) and the smallest (200) student bodies amongst private institutions. HEIs within this group are teaching focused with very limited international activity. Although there are some research projects being conducted, none of these universities offer Doctoral degrees.

The *regional comprehensive private* group consists of only one private HEI, Nakhchivan University. It is located in the Nakhchivan Autonomous Republic with a student body of about 1000. This university provides no Doctoral study programme and enrols no international students. The role of the university is to provide alternative public education educational opportunities, mainly for local residents of Nakhchivan.

Conclusion

The higher education system in Azerbaijan was characterised by three primary types of institutions during the Soviet period and has now transformed into a more diverse system with seven types of HEIs. The number of HEIs has tripled and student enrolment has increased 68% in comparison with the highest enrolment rates in the 1980s. A major increase was also observed in the number of comprehensive universities as a result of the government's regional development policy. While during Soviet times there was only one comprehensive university (Azerbaijan State University), there are now 5 state and 11 private comprehensive universities.

Similar to the Soviet period, regional HEIs currently provide training in various areas to meet regional needs. When types of HEIs are compared, there is an apparent difference in relation to research and internationalisation policies between regional and capital institutions. Capital public and some private HEIs focus more on research and attract international students, while regional HEIs perform lower in these two dimensions.

The higher education system has changed and developed through internal (demographic, political, social and economic) and external factors (international relations, involvement of international development organisations). These factors have led to accelerated growth in the number of higher education institutions, educational programmes and opportunities. They include population increase, a large proportion of youth in society and an increased interest in higher education qualifications and the changed nature of the economy. This interest was also met by international organisations that contributed to the internationalisation and financing of higher education. Major drivers of change in the system were increased attention to privatisation and private institutions, emerging demand for skilled labour in the new open market, a recognised need for an education system upgrade based on international standards and a desire to participate more in student mobility. Similar to the Soviet period, changes in the economy and market dynamics are still driving major changes in the higher education system and shaping its diversity today.

Notes

1. In Nagorno Karabakh.
2. Technical vocational educational institution.
3. This institution was called Baku State University between 1919 and 1920. In 1991, the name was reintroduced.
4. This institution was called the Azerbaijan State Oil Academy between 1991 and 2015.
5. College—an educational institution that provides educational services based on secondary professional and vocational programmes and has the right to confer sub-bachelor vocational and professional degrees (Education Law 2009).
6. AZN- Azerbaijani New Manat (1400–1700 USD in 2015).

References

Ahmadov, N. 2014. *Azerbayjan Respublikasinin ali mekteblerinin reytingi. [Rating of Higher Education Institutions of the Azerbaijan Republic]*. Baku: Ministry of Education of the Azerbaijan Republic.

Aliyev, R. 2011. Azerbaijan: How Equitable is Access to Higher Education? *Khazar Journal of Humanities and Social Sciences* 14 (1): 20–37.

Ali Təhsil Pilləsinin Dövlət Standartı Və Proqramı [State Standarts in Higher Education]. http://edu.gov.az/az/page/299/1722. Accessed 23 May 2016.

Asian Development Bank (ADB). 2004. *Education Reforms in Countries in Transition: Policies and Processes. Six Country Case Studies Commissioned by the Asian Development Bank in Azerbaijan, Kazakhstan, Kyrgyz Republic, Mongolia, Tajikistan, and Uzbekistan*. Manila: Asian Development Bank.

Allahveranov, A., and E. Huseynov. 2013. *Costs and Benefits of Labour Mobility Between the EU and the Eastern Partnership Partner Countries. Country Report: Azerbaijan*. Baku: European Commission. http://www.iza.org/files/ENPIazerbaijan.pdf

Avakov, R., and A. Atakishiev. 1984. *Public Education in Soviet Azerbaijan: Appraisal of an Achievement*. Moscow-Unesco: Progress Publishers.

Azerbaijan Economists' Union and UNICEF. 2008. *Budget Investments in Health and Education of Azerbaijani Children*. Baku: Azerbaijan Economists' Union and UNICEF. http://www.unicef.org/azerbaijan/Budget_investments_in_health_and_education_of_Azerbaijani_children_ENG.pdf

Bayramov, F., N. Ibrahimova, and I. Babazadeh. 2014. *Azerbaijan's Accession to the WTO: Assessing the Macroeconomic Consequences for the Economy of Azerbaijan. The Center for Economic and Social Development (CESD)*. Baku: Konrad-Adenauer-Stiftung (KAS). http://www.kas.de/wf/doc/kas_39436-544-1-30.pdf?141107093345

Catterall, J., and J. McGhee. 1996. The Emergence of Private Postsecondary Education in the Former Soviet Republic of Azerbaijan. *International Higher Education* 5: 3–5.

Drummond, T.W., and S. Gabrscek. 2012. Understanding Higher Education Admissions Reforms in the Eurasian Context. *European Education* 44 (1): 7–26. doi:10.2753/eue1056-4934440101.

Education Law of the Republic of Azerbaijan. 2009. Retrieved 1 August 2014. http://www.edu.gov.az/view.php?lang=en&menu=72&id=5244

———. 1992. Retrieved 1 August 2014. http://e-qanun.az/files/framework/data/7/f_7956.htm

Isakhanli, H. 2014. Diversification of Post-Secondary Education in Azerbaijan. In *The Diversification of Post-Secondary Education*, ed. N.V. Varghese, 45–59. Paris: IIEP's Printshop.

Isaxanlı, H. 2006a. *In Search of Khazar*. Baku: Khazar University Press.

———. 2006b. *On Education System in Transition Economy: A View from Azerbaijan*. Baku: Khazar University Press.

Mehdi, M. 1980. *Azərbaycan Xalq Maarifinin Sürətli İnkişafı [Fast Development of Azerbaijani National Education]*. Baku: Maarif.

Salakov, M. 1990. *Vishee Obrazovanie V Azerbaydjane: Istoriya, Problemi, Perspektivi [Higher Education in Azerbaijan: History, Problems, Perspectives]*. Baku: Azerneshr.

Silova, I., and E. Kazimzade. 2006. Azerbaijan. In *Education in a Hidden Marketplace Monitoring of Private Tutoring*, ed. I. Silova, V. Būdiene, and M. Bray, 113–143. New York: Open Society Institute.

State Students Admission Commission (SSAC). 2014. *Highlights and Statistical Analysis of Examination Data for the Academic Year of 2013/2014*. Baku.

State Statistical Committee of the Republic of Azerbaijan. (SSC). 2014. *Statistical Yearbook 2014 "The State Statistical Committee of the Republic of Azerbaijan"*, January 2016. http://www.stat.gov.az/source/demoqraphy/ap/indexen.php. Accessed 1 Sept 2016.

Statistik Melumat [Statistical Information]. Baku: Study Abroad Program, 2015. http://xaricdetehsil.edu.gov.az/uploads/Statistika4.pdf

The World Bank Group. 2016. *Gross Enrolment Ratio, Tertiary, Both Sexes (%)*. http://data.worldbank.org/indicator/SE.TER.ENRR?locations=AZ&view=chart. Accessed 1 Sept 2016.

United Nations Economic Commission for Europe. 2010. *Country Profiles on the Housing Sector: Azerbaijan*. Geneva: United Nations Economic Commission for Europe. http://www.unece.org/fileadmin/DAM/hlm/documents/Publications/cp.azerbaijan.e.pdf

World Bank. 1997. *Azerbaijan Poverty Assessment Report*. Washington, DC: The World Bank.

World Education News & Reviews (WENR). 2015. *Bologna-Inspired Education Reform in Central Asia*. http://wenr.wes.org/2015/05/bologna-inspired-education-reform-central-asia/

Hamlet Isakhanli is a mathematician, poet, higher education researcher and founder of the first private university in Azerbaijan, Khazar University. Dr Isakhanli is Chairman of the Board of Directors and Trustees at Khazar University, founder of integrated primary, secondary and high schools and founder of a publishing house in Baku, Azerbaijan.

Aytaj Pashayeva is a researcher at the Institute of Education of the Republic of Azerbaijan. Ms. Pashayeva's current research foci include institutional research and institutional development of universities, quality assurance, research and innovation management in higher education institutions, and higher education participation in Azerbaijan.

Open Access This chapter is distributed under the terms of the Creative Commons Attribution 4.0 International License (http://creativecommons.org/licenses/by/4.0/), which permits use, duplication, adaptation, distribution and reproduction in any medium or format, as long as you give appropriate credit to the original author(s) and the source, provide a link to the Creative Commons license and indicate if changes were made.

The images or other third party material in this chapter are included in the chapter's Creative Commons license, unless indicated otherwise in a credit line to the material. If material is not included in the chapter's Creative Commons license and your intended use is not permitted by statutory regulation or exceeds the permitted use, you will need to obtain permission directly from the copyright holder.

CHAPTER 5

Belarus: Higher Education Dynamics and Institutional Landscape

Olga Gille-Belova and Larissa Titarenko

The HE system in Belarus has undergone important changes since the beginning of the 1990s under the pressure of various internal and external factors (including demographic, political, socio-economic changes and international cooperation). A study of changes in the HE system in the Republic of Belarus during the post-Soviet period can be made by using an analytical framework based on the conceptual distinction between three types of higher education system characteristics: horizontal diversification, vertical differentiation and organisational interrelationship (Teichler 1988). We will focus on these three dimensions in our analysis of main changes in the institutional landscape of Belarusian HE and discuss the issue of its diversity "as being about both similarities and differences" (Huisman et al. 2007, 565).

O. Gille-Belova
Department of Slavic Studies, University Bordeaux Montaigne, Bordeaux, France

L. Titarenko (✉)
Department of Sociology, Belarusian State University, Minsk, Republic of Belarus

Horizontal system diversification increased with the creation of new private and public HEIs, and changes in the functioning of the former Soviet HEIs. The vertical system differentiation inherited from the Soviet period was slightly changed by the end of the 1990s/beginning of the 2000s. It was strengthened, especially at the beginning of 2010, as a result of government policies (Educational Code 2011) and the introduction of national, regional and international rankings that made the existing vertical diversity more visible. The organisational interrelationship between HEIs has also changed from the logic of complementarity under the Soviet system to the logic of competition for students and resources.

This chapter will first analyse the HE system inherited from the Soviet period, because Soviet legacies still play an extremely important role in the Belarusian case. Then it will explore the main factors influencing the transformations in the HE landscape over more than 20 years. Finally, it will present the typology of existing Belarusian HEIs. The conclusion will draw some inferences about the further evolution of the national higher education system.

THE HE SYSTEM WITHIN THE SOVIET CONTEXT

If some Soviet republics inherited universities from the pre-Soviet period founded according to the German "Humboldt model" (Universities of Moscow, St. Petersburg, Kiev), it was not the case in Belarus. Under Russian Empire rule, only few secondary level establishments existed in this region (gymnasiums, vocational and parish schools), and three teachers' institutes were founded in Vitebsk in 1910, in Mogilev in 1913 and in Minsk in 1914. The HE system in Belarus was built from scratch during the Soviet period after the establishment of the Byelorussian[1] Soviet Socialist Republic (BSSR) in January 1919. This system was designed as a part of a larger Soviet "master plan".[2] From the beginning, it was intended as a vocational institutional structure with the main mission to train professionals for the needs of the Soviet command economy in the Byelorussian Republic. The main functions of the HE system included: (1) professional training for the needs of the national economy (according to the branches of the national economy in the BSSR); (2) reproduction of the Soviet managerial elite at all levels for the republic; and (3) Soviet ideological education for the younger generation.

The first university in Belarus was opened in the newly established republic in 1921. This university (Byelorussian State University, or BSU) was designed as the only one for the whole republic and it was a multidisciplinary comprehensive establishment with the main mission to train staff[3] for future BSSR HEIs and research institutes, as well as managers for the republic administration. Other HEIs were actively founded in the 1920–1930s, mainly as specialised institutes (*instituty*) to prepare cadres for particular sectors such as social infrastructure and economic development for the republic (teachers, doctors, economists, engineers). By 1940–1941, the BSSR had 25 HEIs with 21,500 students and 927 staff at different levels (Krasovskiï 1972). Some of these institutes were transformed from the former BSU faculties: the Medical Institute (BSMI)[4] in 1930, Minsk State Pedagogical Institute (MSPI)[5] in 1931 and the Byelorussian Institute of National Economy (BINE)[6] in 1933. The other institutes were built by upgrading secondary level vocational establishments (for example, Byelorussian Polytechnic Institute, BPI,[7] was transformed in 1920 from Minsk Polytechnic College) or regional pedagogical institutes transformed from former pedagogical colleges. Vertical differentiation selected five major establishments (BSU, BPI, MSPI, Medical Institute and BINE) as the core of the Byelorussian HE system; they performed the leading methodological functions for others and covered the training needs for main branches of republic professionals.

In the post-World War II period, expansion in the horizontal differentiation of the HE system continued: in 1958–1959 there were 56,700 students with more than 3,000 professorial teaching staff in 25 HEIs (Yearbook 1959). In order to develop the HE system in the regional (*oblast*) centres and introduce more balance, two new universities were opened, one in Gomel in 1969 and another in Grodno in 1972, on the foundations of existing pedagogical institutes. The separation of some faculties at Minsk State Pedagogical Institute gave birth to the Minsk State Pedagogical Institute of Foreign Languages[8] in 1948 and the Institute of Culture[9] in 1975. Some new stand-alone specialised industrial HE institutes were also founded. These included Minsk Radio Technical Institute (RTI)[10] in 1964, the Institute of Mechanization and Electrification of Agriculture[11] in 1954 and Belarusian Technological Institute,[12] which was reorganised from the Forest Technical Institute in 1961. Growth in the HE system mainly met new economic needs and was connected with labour market demands for new plants and factories; it also supported the development of agriculture, chemical and electronic industries and mechanical constructions.

Several institutes were opened in the regional centres: Mogilev Machine Building Institute[13] (1961) trained cadres for the Mogilev elevators plant (one of the biggest in Eastern Europe), and the Belarusian Institute of Railway Engineers[14] (1953) in Gomel prepared specialists for the transport sector. Other specialised regional institutes included Vitebsk Technological Institute of Light Industry[15] (1965) and Grodno State Medical Institute[16] (1958). Preparation of managerial personnel and professional ideological training were conducted by Minsk Higher Communist Party School in 1958. As everywhere in the USSR, it performed the important functions of reproducing the political elite and handling the regular ideological training of Soviet personnel with various educational backgrounds.

By the end of the Soviet period, the BSSR had 33 HEIs with 188,600 students and 15,400 staff including professors. BSU dominated the system as the oldest republican comprehensive university, followed by the main specialised republican institutes situated in Minsk. Outside Minsk, all administrative regional centres had either their own university (Grodno, Gomel) or pedagogical institute (Vitebsk, Brest, Mogilev); in some cases, this meant specialised institutes to train employees for a particular factory or meet other regional needs for society and the national economy (see Table 5.1). Like the universities, major specialised institutes and pedagogical institutes generally depended on the Ministry of Education of BSSR, while narrowly specialised institutes were under the control of the corresponding BSSR ministries. This vertical differentiation included general supervision by Soviet Union ministries in the relevant field from Moscow.

The increasing number of HEIs and staff during the Soviet period reflected the fast growth of young Soviet Byelorussians graduating from secondary schools with educational expectations that met the increasing needs of the national economy for professionals and well-trained personnel in the BSSR. In the last two to three Soviet decades, the BSSR was recognised as a manufacturing and industrial centre of the Soviet Union; therefore, all professionals for the factories and plants situated in the BSSR were trained mainly in the republic. As the republic was highly industrialised, most of its HEIs were oriented toward industry or other practical needs of the national economy including training for doctors, teachers, economists, and agronomists. Only the universities provided a limited space for education that was not directly connected with local needs (in philosophy, psychology, and sociology); therefore, young people had to move to other cities for education in fields not represented in Belarus.

Table 5.1 Main types of HEIs in the Byelorussian Republic, 1990/1991 academic year

Type of HEIs (number)	Examples	Location	Affiliation[a]	Main training function	Research activities	Number of students
Republic's Flagship University (1)	BSU	Minsk	ME	Staff for other HEIs and research, top management for republic administration	Some research institutes and centres	15,015
Leading regional HEIs (5)	2 regional universities and 3 pedagogical institutes	Grodno, Gomel, Vitebsk, Brest, Mogilev	ME	Teachers and management for regional administration	–	28,985
Specialised HEIs (14)	BPI, MSPI, Belarusian State Medical University (BSMI), BINE MRTI, etc.	Minsk	ME or corresponding BSSR Ministry (MH, MA, MC, etc.)	Specialists for particular sector of national economy (engineers, economists, doctors, teachers)	Few HEIs research centres	99,650
Narrowly specialised regional HEIs (13)	Regional Medical, Technological, Food, Pedagogical Institutes	Mogilev, Vitebsk, Gomel, Grodno, Brest, Mozyr, Polotsk	ME or corresponding BSSR Ministries (MH, MA, etc.)	Specialists for particular regional medical, teaching, technical needs	–	44,950
Total (33 HEIs)						188,600

Data from: *Narodnoe hozjajstvo* 1993: 123–124

[a]Affiliation: Ministry of Education (ME), Ministry of Health (MH), Ministry of Culture (MC), Ministry of Agriculture (MA)

Few Byelorussian HEIs had their own research centres and the level of financial support provided for research activities was rather low.

As for internationalisation, in 1988–1989 there were officially 6,800 (3.8 %) foreign students in the BSSR (including military students) (Vetokhin 2001, 91). They arrived mainly from African and Asian countries that formally followed the Marxist ideology and were therefore supported by the USSR authorities. Such exchange was part of the internationalisation activities conceived on the all-Union level in order to reinforce the ties between the USSR and its closest allies. Most foreign students studied for free and paid only for their living expenses.

In conclusion, Byelorussian HE existed in 1991 as a "Soviet legacy" based mainly on complementary interrelationships between HEIs, each designed to respond to the particular economic or social needs of the republic or the region. However, this system was designed for the out-of-date challenges of the Soviet political and industrial economic model, which led to requests for important reforms at the beginning of 1990.

Changes in the Higher Education System in Post-Soviet Belarus: Slow Evolution Under State Control

The end of the USSR and the formation of the new independent state, the Republic of Belarus, in 1991 marked the beginning of a long period of political, economic and social transformations in the country, which had an important impact on the HE system. In Belarus, like everywhere in post-Socialist states, ideas such as "democratisation" "decentralisation" "liberalisation" "pluralism" and "humanisation of learning" became very popular at the beginning of 1990 in regard to transformations in the field of education (Silova 2009, 296) and construction of the nation-state; some new liberal ideas coexisted with attempts by the ministerial authorities to preserve the "best practices" of the former Soviet system (Vetokhin 2001). It was particularly the new Law on Education (adopted by parliament on 29 October 1991) that played an important role in the transformation of the system inherited from the Soviet period.[17] It authorised the creation of private HEIs and the introduction of fees in state-owned public HEIs, granted more freedom in choosing programmes and disciplines offered by each HEI and replaced the nomination of university rectors with elections. Additionally, new specialties needed for the nation-state were introduced in new faculties at existing HEIs, such as "diplomacy" at the BSU Faculty of International Relations, and customs service at BSU and Belarusian National Technical University (BNTU). Despite these important changes in the legislative framework, Belarusian authorities had no clear ambition to create a radically new HE model; instead, they tried to adapt the former Soviet model to a new political, economic, social and international reality (Gille-Belova 2014).

This new legislative framework had an important impact on the HE system in breaking the state monopoly on education and stimulating system diversification. During the 1990s, many academic actors created new private HEIs or transformed existing public HEIs by creating new faculties and introducing new programmes. Ministry of Education officials did not have any particular "master plan" to guide the institutional changes, but they followed this spontaneous process. Their role was limited to the general supervision of the diversification process, mainly financed by Belarusian students and their families: in fact, students at not only private HEIs paid fees, but almost two-thirds of the students in public HEIs also paid[18] (NSCRB 2013, 147). Only one-third of students enjoyed public financial support provided by the Belarusian Ministry of Education in public HEIs (the limited number of state financed student places, mainly in "old traditional" fields of study, was fixed). In contrast, very few diplomas in the new fields (humanities, social sciences, management) were financed from the public budget, and therefore most students in these fields paid for their education. Within 20 years, the Belarusian state thus reduced its HE expenditure from 1 % to 0.7 % of GDP (IBK 2013, 20–22), despite the growing number of HEIs and students.

Horizontal diversification of HE during the 1990s–2000s was largely facilitated by demographic factors and corresponded to the massification of HE, which happened between the mid-1990s and the beginning of the 2010s. New HEIs were founded and new faculties opened in existing HEIs with a huge range of new programmes due to the growing number of students. In the academic year 1989–1990, the number of students was almost 190,000. It had increased to 250,000 by the end of the 1990s and almost doubled during the 2000s, reaching its peak at 445,000 in 2011–2012 (see Fig. 5.1).

New private HEIs started to appear from 1994 and the number of HEIs almost doubled in a few years, increasing from 33 in 1990–1991 to 59 in 1995–1996. This was largely because of private sector growth; there were 20 private HEIs by 1996/97 (see Fig. 5.2). Leading members of the teaching staff at main public HEIs were generally the founders of new

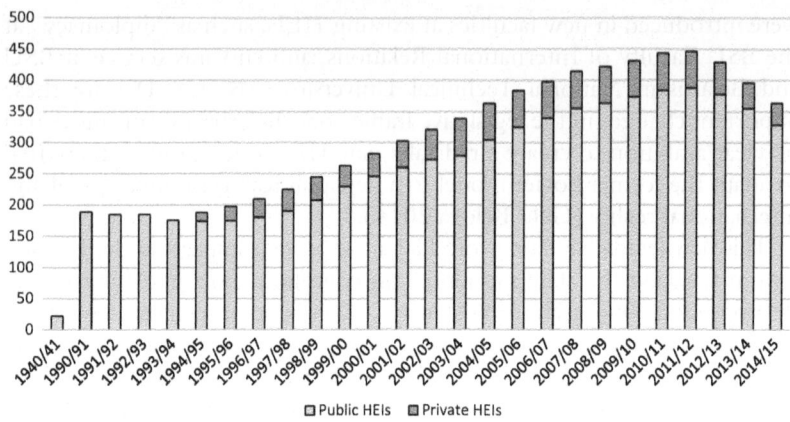

Fig. 5.1 Change in the number of HEI students in Belarus (thousands), 1940–2015 (Source: MORB 2001, 2013b; NSCRB 2013, 2014, 2015)

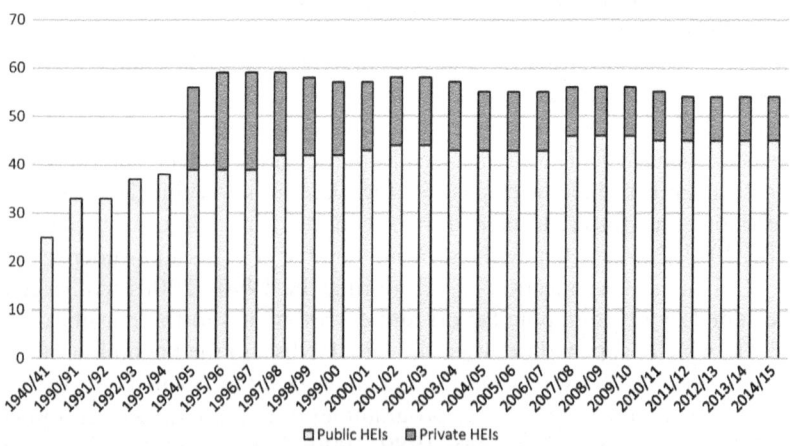

Fig. 5.2 Change in the number of HEIs in Belarus, 1940–2015 (Source: MORB 2001, 2013a; NSCRB 2013, 2014, 2015)

private HEIs, the staff of which was composed of part-time employees with full positions in nearby public HEIs. The number of students enrolled in private HEIs remained rather small and equal to about one-tenth of total student numbers (see Fig. 5.1). Private HEIs had a high proportion of part-time students (80 %) that was much higher than in public HEIs (under 50 %) by the end of the 2000s.[19] Most private HEIs were oriented toward training students in newly popular fields of study that represented a flux in education demands (management, economy, law and humanities). The disciplinary diversity in private HEIs was much more limited than in public HEIs, and competition between university enrolees was much lower than in public HEIs; tuition fees were generally lower as well.

The number of public HEIs did not increase until the end of 1990; most underwent significant changes by proposing new specialties and opening new faculties. Many public HEIs (in particular, the narrowly specialised ones) created so-called "non-profile" faculties of management and economics or humanities during the Soviet period. Their motivation was mainly financial, as all students of these new faculties paid relatively high fees while the demand for the traditional "profile" fields of study (engineers, agronomists, teachers) was less important and financed mainly by the state.[20] As state finances decreased during the economic crisis at the beginning of the 1990s, student fees became an important source of complementary revenue for public HEIs. At the same time, most of the former public HEIs called "institutes" were transformed into universities or academies. This ministry policy of "relabelling" responded to HEIs' leadership desire for higher symbolic recognition and prestige. These changes contributed to vertical and new horizontal differentiation.

Government policies started to change during the 2000s; as a result, the attitudes of Ministry of Education officials reoriented from supervision of a largely spontaneous HE system diversification to tighter control. The main reason for these changes was political, and related to the logic of consolidation by the authoritarian political regime searching to strengthen its ideological control over HE and prevent any student involvement in political initiatives (Gille-Belova 2015). As the Ministry actively used its right to control and check HEI performance, it became more difficult to obtain or renew accreditations as well as to secure compulsory official approval for programmes and specialisations. The election of rectors was replaced by Ministry of Education or presidential appointment, so that by the end of the 2000s the Belarusian HE system experienced a significant lack of academic freedom and university autonomy (IBK 2013, 2014).

During the 2000s, the number of private HEIs declined, some because they failed to renew their accreditation with the Ministry of Education.[21] The number of public HEIs, in contrast, increased to 46. New public

HEIs were opened by the state following two distinct trends. The first trend aimed to create public specialised non-university HEIs subordinated to various ministries and state agencies by changing the names of some colleges. Such "relabelling" was necessary for the government to raise the status of the colleges, because there has been almost no demand for special secondary education diplomas since the 1990s. These institutions were directly oriented to the preparation of cadres for a particular public administration sector (army, police, frontier guards) or economic branch (aviation, transportation). The second trend reflected the logic of encouraging regional development by creating small state universities in new places, as was the case with Baranovitchskiï university in 2004 and Polesskiï university in 2006, universities founded in the small cities of Baranovitchi and Pinsk. In both cases, the creation of new establishments responded mainly to demands from a particular ministry or regional authority and increased horizontal differentiation.

There were no foreign HEI campuses in Belarus, except two Russian HEI branches founded as official cooperation projects between the two countries within the framework of the Union of Belarus and Russia. Unlike the Baltic states, where the dominant language of instruction is Russian in all HEIs, there is no student differentiation by language (Belarusian is used primarily in faculties of Belarusian philology). The number of local branches of Belarusian national HEIs remained quite small in comparison with other post-Soviet countries. Only five branches of four public HEIs from Minsk were established: two in provincial cities, and three in the regional centres. However, like in Russia (Kuzminov et al. 2013, 33), these branches are specialised in economics, management and humanities, offering their educational services to students paying tuition fees. On the one hand, this adaptive strategy helped HEIs adjust to the conditions of restrictive state finances; on the other, the same strategy made higher education available for those living in small towns without time and money to spend on regular studies in regional centres or in the capital. Overall, branches became a new dimension of vertical differentiation.

Another important factor for HE diversification was strong social demand for higher education diplomas and high social expectations for the emergence of new occupations due to the transition to the market economy. The main rationale behind this social demand was the public opinion that a higher education diploma is necessary for career and life success. Most Belarusians were influenced by expectations of economic change and believed that the state-owned Belarusian economy might be progressively transformed following the pattern of Western post-industrial countries. This phenomenon explains why the most demanded professions since the 1990s have been lawyers, economists and managers. Official national statistics show that more than 40 % of students study economics, law and management (see Fig. 5.3); while in public HEIs this proportion is about 30 %, in private HEIs it is about 80 %. Engineering studies ("sciences" and "technology") offered by public HEIs attract only 20 % of students. Compared to the end of the Soviet period, the proportion of students in various fields of study has changed dramatically: in the 1990/1991 academic year, students in "industry" represented almost 50 % and in "economics" only 13 %.

However, these social expectations based on anticipated future changes in the structure of the economy did not match the reality. Belarusian authorities did not put in place any liberal economic reforms recommended by international financial organisations, in particular the IMF. The number of employees in the private sector grew in Belarus from 10 % in 1994 to almost 50 % in 2010, but the share of the private sector in GDP reached only 30 % in 2010, which was at least two times lower than in other post-Soviet states (OECD 2011, 34). Almost 80 % of the industrial and agriculture sectors remained public, dominated by state collective farms. The situation differs mainly in the service sector, which contains a large proportion of private enterprises. By the end of the 2000s, Belarusian authorities were forced to publicly recognise the problems connected with the fast growth of the HE system and admit the distortion between HE system output and the real needs of the Belarusian economy, which was unable to absorb such a high number of HE graduates; this was especially true in economics, law and management fields. At the same time, the growing number of persons with HE diplomas, which reached 467 per 10,000 at its highest level in 2011, was officially interpreted as an important indicator of strong socio-economic development, placing Belarus as a most developed country (MORB 2013a). However, this situation also raises the question of higher education quality, as many employers complain about the low level of graduate competencies and qualifications (Titarenko 2014).

The Belarusian state continues to play a main role in the structuring and functioning of the labour market, which implies maintaining a high level of employment and a low level of salary differentiation (Morgunova 2010, 100). A survey conducted by the Belarusian Institute for Strategic Studies in 2013 confirmed that a higher level of education does not

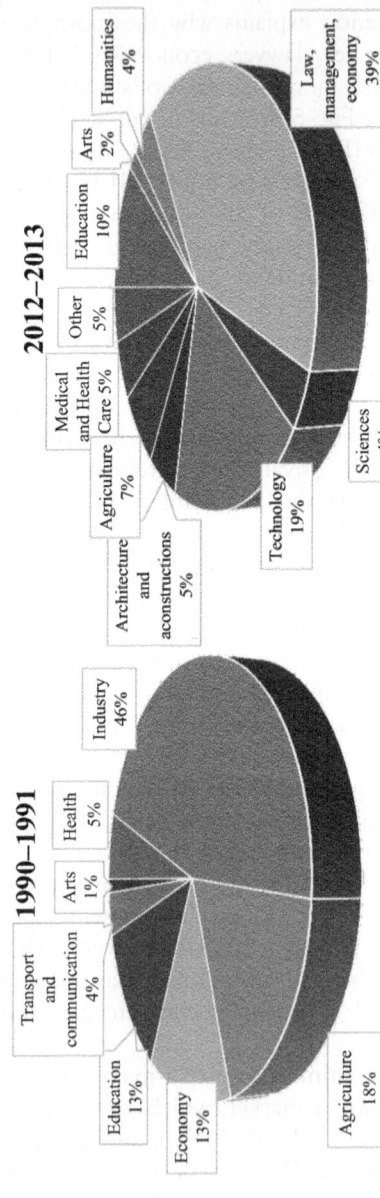

Fig. 5.3 Change in the number of students by study profile between 1990–1991 and 2012–2013 (Source: MORB 2001, 2013a)

produce a higher salary level for HEI graduates (Chubrik and Shimanovitch 2013). Under these conditions, HE diplomas cannot be converted into material values: persons with high school certificates could theoretically obtain almost the same salary while occupying low-qualified positions in the market, and there is no rational economic motivation to pursue HE diplomas (Sysoev 2010). Thus, the demand for HE could still be explained by social prestige, already important in the Soviet period, that seems to have become almost a social norm in contemporary Belarus.

While the social demand for HE still remains high in Belarus, the demographic situation has dramatically changed: from 2011 to 2012, the number of secondary school graduates decreased due to a low birth rate in the 1990s. The official government strategy for attracting foreign students could hardly compensate for the inevitable reduction in fees following the decrease in the number of potential students. These demographic and financial problems could have an important impact on the Belarusian HE system by increasing the competition between HEIs for students and financial resources. Some HEIs have better chances in this competition as they have better positions in terms of Belarusian HE vertical differentiation. This factor will be examined in the following.

THE HE INSTITUTIONAL LANDSCAPE IN CONTEMPORARY BELARUS

The typology proposed below defines six types of HEIs (see Table 5.2) and takes into account a variety of criteria regarding HEI educational, research and international activities (some of the criteria are presented in Table 5.3). The empirical data were gathered from official statistics on affiliation and number of HEIs, as well as size including number of faculties, number and characteristics of students (by study profile, level, CT admission score) and teaching staff (by age and scientific degree). As it is difficult to evaluate research activities (for the reasons mentioned above), we took into account the number of PhD students (*aspiranty* and *doctoranty*), the number of PhD Commissions,[22] the number of publications (if available) and the number of research centres and research projects (if available[23]). As for the level of internationalisation, we used official data on the number of foreign students and number of international cooperation agreements. We also took into account different official labels such as "leading" HEI status,[24] as well as the results of national official ratings

Table 5.2 Typology of Belarusian HEIs at the beginning of the 2010s[a]

Type	Number/location/particular official status	Type in 1990–1991 (Table 5.1)	Educational profile	Research activity	International activity
Flagship University (BSU)	1/ Minsk "Leading national HEI" status	Republic's Flagship University	Multidisciplinary biggest university with III levels[b] of study and highly qualified[c] teaching staff	High	High
National leading universities (BNTU, BSEU, BSUIR - high research and international; BelSTU, BSPU, BAA - low research and international)	6/Minsk "Leading field HEI" status	Specialised HEIs	Multidisciplinary big university with III levels of study and highly qualified teaching staff	Medium, above average for HEIs Lower	High Low
Regional comprehensive universities (GSU, GRSU, VSU, BRSU, MSU, PSU)	6/regional centres	Leading regional HEIs	Multidisciplinary medium-size university with II levels of study and qualified teaching staff	Medium	Low

(*continued*)

Table 5.2 (continued)

Type	Number/location/particular official status	Type in 1990–1991 (Table 5.1)	Educational profile	Research activity	International activity
National specialised HEIs (PAC, BSMU, MSLU, BSATU, BSAM, BSUCA, BSUT, BSUFK)	9/Minsk	Specialised HEIs	Medium-size HEI with few disciplines, II levels of study and qualified teaching staff	Low	Low
Regional specialised HEIs (BRU, BSTU, GSMU, GSTU, GRSMU, GGAU, MGUP, VSMU, VSAVM, VSTU)	10/regional centres	Narrowly specialised regional HEIs	Small-size HEI with few disciplines, II levels and qualified teaching staff	No	Very low
Private HEIs and local public HEIs (PolesSU, BarSU, MIU, MozyrPI, BIP-IP, BTEU, MITSO, IPP, IPD, ISZ, IMB, MGEI)	12/small cities or Minsk (in case of private HEIs)	–	Small-size HEI with few disciplines, II levels of study and commuting teaching staff	No	No (or very low)

[a]This typology does not take into account very small and narrowly specialised HEIs that prepare for one particular type of career in public administration (air force, police, frontier guards)

[b]By III levels of studies we mean the equivalent of undergraduate (*specialist*), graduate (*magistr*) and PhD studies (*aspirantura*, *doctorantura*). Officially, there are II levels, and PhD studies are not considered level III, keeping their specifics inherited from the Soviet period with the two scientific degrees *Kandidat Nauk* and *Doktor Nauk*

[c]Level of qualification means a particular proportion (>40 %) of teaching staff with the scientific degrees *Doktor Nauk* and *Kandidat Nauk*

Table 5.3 Characteristics of various HEI types (based on data for 2012–2013)

Type	No of full-time students	Average No of teaching staff	No of faculties/ specialisations	No of PhD commissions/ N of PhD students	No of research grants	No of foreign students/ international agreements
Flagship university	25,000	2400	16/260	22/800	336	2.324/376
National comprehensive universities	12–32,000	600–1700	9–17/20–120	5–16/150–300	120–300	40–1000/40–120
Regional comprehensive universities	9–17,000	500–600	10–12/35–50	0–4/20–60	70–80	30–600/20–130
National specialised HEIs	5–9000	200–500	4–9/5–40	0–3/0–100	0–50	0–100/7–60
Regional specialised HEIs	4–8000	300–500	6–8/5–30	0–2/0–30	0–30	0–200/0–50
Private HEIs and public local HEIs	2–9000	~200	3–5/10–20	0/–	0–8	0–150/0–35

introduced by the Ministry of Education in Belarus in 2013 as well as various international ratings, even if very few Belarusian HEIs figure into them (mainly BSU, BNTU, BSUIR).

BSU maintains its status as the leading national university in Belarus and the only one that can be qualified as a "research university". It has a significant size with 25 thousand students enrolled in more than 260 various programmes (*spetsializatsii*) offered by 16 faculties and 4 institutes. The staff has a very high level of qualification, more than 50 % with PhD degrees. The enrolment process is competitive, and BSU graduates can usually obtain employment with relative ease. BSU trains cadres for teaching and research in the sciences and humanities as well as for Belarusian public administration and the private sector. There are several research institutions belonging to BSU where students can gain research experience in parallel to their regular studies. BSU counts the largest number of PhD students (almost 800) and PhD Commissions (22), and confirms its leading position in the national system through both SCOPUS publication ranking and a high number of research grants. Several research institutions that belong to BSU have the highest national rankings in publications as well.[25] BSU has the highest number of international cooperation agreements and a significant proportion of foreign students (10 %). In comparison to other Belarusian HEIs, BSU occupies the best positions in various international rankings.[26]

A second group of "national comprehensive universities" is composed of six HEIs belonging to the "national specialised HEIs" group. These have managed their internal diversification and generally have a significant size: the smallest is Belarusian State Technological University (BelSTU) with 12,000 students and more than 600 teaching staff, and the biggest is BNTU with more than 32,000 students and more than 1,700 teaching staff (more than 40 % with scientific degrees). They have many faculties (from 9 to 17) with a high number of specialties varying from 20 at BAA to 121 at BNTU, and all of them host 150–300 PhD students and at least 5 PhD Committees. There are two sub-groups inside this category of "national universities": HEIs from the first sub-group (BNTU, BSEU, BSUIR) differ within the group by higher research levels and international activity; they attract students with high CT scores in their fields and have high positions in ministry ranks, sometimes even in regional and international rankings. These HEIs have "leading field" status and create programmes and manuals for corresponding disciplines.

The third group of "regional comprehensive universities" includes the six HEIs (former "leading regional HEIs") situated in regional centres. Two were transformed into universities in the 1970s (in Gomel and Grodno) and currently demonstrate a higher level of performance than the three (Vitebsk, Brest, Mogilev) that were relabelled as universities from pedagogical institutes in the 1990s. Only one, Polotsk State University (PSU), was founded in 1968 to serve the urgent needs of the country (USSR) in terms of new cadres of engineers for the chemical industry in the city of Novo-Polotsk; it was transformed into a university in 1993. They differ in size depending on the size of the region in which they operate and usually have 9–12,000 students enrolled in 10–12 faculties offering 35–50 specialties with 500–600 teaching staff (up to 40 % with scientific degrees).[27] They are almost totally oriented to the preparation of new teachers for all branches of education (pre-school, primary and middle school, high school). As they are no longer called "pedagogical", they established new programmes to attract talented ambitious students from their regions with new specialisations. However, overall enrolment is still a challenge as young people are free to decide whether they want to study in regional universities, in the capital, or abroad. Their research activity is generally low with some PhD students in a few fields; only Grodno and Gomel SU have their own PhD Commissions. Some host a low number of foreign students and conduct some international cooperation projects.

The next group of "national specialised HEIs" includes nine HEIs situated in the capital city of Minsk with variable size from ~1000 students at the smallest, the University of Arts and Culture (BSUCA) and the Academy of Music (BSAM), to ~11,000 at the technical-agrarian university Belarusian State Agrarian Technical University (BSATU); overall enrolment generally varies between 5000 and 9000 students. The number of teaching staff varies from 200 to 500 with the exception of MSLU university of foreign languages (~800) and medical BSMU (~1,100). The proportion of staff with scientific degrees is around 30–40 % with some exceptions. The number of faculties varies from four to nine and reflects the disciplinary specialisation of these HEIs. Despite the diversification of their programmes (from 5 to 40 specialisations), the majority of students are enrolled in major specialised profiles (medicine, foreign languages, art and culture, agriculture) and their main mission is to prepare specialists for the national labour market. Most do not host PhD students and only a few foreign students (with the exception of MSLU and Belarusian State Medical University (BSMU)).

The group of "regional specialised HEIs" is quite similar to the previous group but includes HEIs situated outside the capital, mainly in regional centres which already have regional universities. These HEIs are smaller in size with 4,000–8,000 students (except Brest technological Belarusian State Agrarian Technical University (BSTU) with 11,000 students), 300–500 teaching staff, 6–8 faculties and up to 30 specialisations.

If they are specialised in the same field as their "mother" national specialised HEIs, they are much less competitive and serve mostly regional needs (industries or particular plants/factories).

The last group is heterogeneous and includes nine private HEIs, two newly established public local universities and one pedagogical institute. They are generally small-sized with 2,000 to 9,000 students and 50–300 teaching staff, 30–40 % with scientific degrees. Private HEIs generally have 3–5 faculties with 10–20 specialties offering popular courses in management, economics and law, and provide educational service for almost anyone who can pay the tuition fee. Most do not have foreign students with few, if any, international cooperation agreements. Their major role is to provide diplomas and socialisation for the students, but their graduates generally have difficulty finding proper employment. This means that they are oriented only to receiving the diploma "paper" (*korotchki*) rather than acquiring professional knowledge and competences. As for the three public local HEIs, they are situated in relatively small cities and were opened in the 2000s to meet the demand of local authorities as well as to keep the provincial youth "in place" and to forestal that they move to regional centres or the capital to study. This always results in inter-regional youth migration with low chances of return after graduating. The "new local universities" do not have enough resources to attract qualified staff, but have good enrolment. The staff often commutes between these universities and the nearest regional universities, where most qualified staff are also employed.

The increasing number of HEIs and offered specialisations led to a higher horizontal diversification of the Belarusian HE system during the 1990s and early 2000s, but it kept the main patterns of differentiation inherited from the Soviet period. The leading state HEIs reinforced their positions at the beginning of the 1990s, while the private or recently created states HEIs have played a marginal role in the national HE system. Vertical differentiation increased: a few leading HEIs have the highest passing scores in the country, and the rest accept almost all enrolees (Dopnabor 2016).

Conclusion

If HE diversification in Western Europe was a failed attempt to deflect students from the elite university sector into the non-university sector during massification (Neave 2000, 12), the issue of diversification was much different in Belarus. The nature of the massification process was also different: it was not "the product of state intervention" following economic demand for a more qualified workforce like in Western countries, but rather a more spontaneous process in which the state abandoned "its monopoly on demand in higher education" and could not "fully control the supply side" (Froumin et al. 2014, 209). During the massification of Belarusian HE, new HEIs were opened and the existing ones tried to diversify their curricula, principally in response to social demand based on expectations of labour market changes as an outcome of economic reforms. Many HEIs used this situation as a chance to step away from the narrow specialisation imposed during the Soviet period.

The Belarusian authorities did not have a blueprint or particular design for the new HE system; they followed a process of spontaneous diversification during the 1990s, contributing more actively during the 2000s with the creation of new public HEIs in response to ministerial or regional authority demands. The expansion of the Belarusian HE system and its horizontal diversification were largely financed by students and their families. However, they became neither new stakeholders nor employers and had almost no influence on the main issues related to education. The Belarusian government remained the key stakeholder, reinforcing its control over the HE system since the 2000s, mainly for political reasons, and despite its incapacity to efficiently connect the HE system to labour market needs.

Regarding prospects for the development of the Belarusian HE system, it had already reached the limits of its expansion by the end of the 2000s, and it is likely that reductions will be reinforced in the near future. The decreasing number of national students and limited strategy results for exporting Belarusian HE services abroad will inevitably influence the number of HEIs. The Ministry of Education has already announced a new aim to cut the number of HEIs by 2020–2022, officially motivated by a desire to align with international standards (BELTA 2015). It is thus logical to expect the absorption of smaller state HEIs by the bigger regional or national institutions as well as the disappearance of some private HEIs. The number of study profiles at HEIs is likely to shrink, while their specialisations are likely to increase. As a result, the Belarusian state will strengthen its role as the main actor in remodelling the HE system; it will likely try to assign a particular role to every HEI and increase differentiation, so that few institutions will be able to compete on the international or even the regional level, while other institutions will respond to specific national and regional needs.

Notes

1. For the Soviet period we use "Byelorussian" and for the post-Soviet period "Belarusian" in accordance with the official name change: from the Byelorussian SSR to the Republic of Belarus in 1991.
2. For a detailed description of the general design of the Soviet "master plan" and its application in the Russian context, see Kuzminov et al. 2013, 14–26; Froumin et al. 2014.
3. Its own academic staff came mainly from Moscow, Kiev and Kazan Universities.
4. Belarusian State Medical University (BSMU). Most HEIs changed names in 1990 and their new (formal English) names used later in the text will be mentioned in the footnotes in the first part of this chapter.
5. Belarusian State Pedagogical University (BSPU).
6. Belarusian State Economic University (BSEU).
7. Belarusian National Technical University (BNTU).
8. Minsk State Linguistic University (MSLU).
9. Belarusian State University of Culture and Arts (BSUCA).
10. Belarusian State University of Informatics and Radioelectronics (BSUIR).
11. Belarusian State Agrarian Technical University (BSATU).
12. Belarusian State Technological University (BSTU).
13. Belarusian-Russian University (BRU).
14. Belarusian State University of Transports (BelSUT).
15. Vitebsk State Technological University (VSTU).
16. Grodno State Medical University (GSMU).
17. It was not replaced until 2007 by the new Law on Higher Education, which in turn was replaced in 2011 by the new Code on Education.
18. At the beginning of 2010, the fees varied from 600 to 1200€ per year depending on the HEI and the type of studies.
19. In mid-1990 this proportion was about 35 % in both private and public sectors.
20. In the latter case, students do not pay for their studies but should work for two years in a state-appointed workplace upon graduation. This practice, called *raspredelenie*, is inherited from the Soviet period.
21. The most famous example was European Humanities University (EHU), one of the rare private universities created in 1994 and financed mainly by international organisations, foreign governments and foundations. It was forced to close in Belarus in 2002 and moved to neighbouring Lithuania where it continued to teach Belarusian students via distance-learning programmes before reorienting its strategy in recent years, during which EHU has started to attract Russian-speaking students from the Baltic countries.

22. The PhD Commission (*dissertatsionnyï komitet*) is the official body in charge of granting the PhD degree in a particular discipline.
23. We assume that the number of projects shows that some HEIs are more active in the search for projects than others, even if this number does not directly reflect the scientific potential of the HEI.
24. The Code on Education (art. 209) introduced official differentiation inside the HE system through the creation of "leading" (*vedushtshii*) status "in the HE system", or "in a particular field of HE", accorded to two and six HEIs, respectively.
25. One such research institution, the Institute of Physics-Chemistry Problems, has the highest rating on the H-index in Belarus.
26. According to QS World University Rankings, BSU is placed between 491 and 500; according to EECA 2014/2015, BSU is in the top 50 for the region with the 38th position; according to the Russian ranking EXPERT RA, BSU belongs to class B (as do most of the best HEIs from other CIS countries). According to Webometrics Ranking of World Universities in 2014, BSU took position 612 and was in place 1461 according to Scimago Institutions Rankings (data source: SCOPUS publication numbers).
27. The exception is Grodno SU with more than 17,000 students and almost 1000 teaching staff as well as 13 faculties with 90 specialisations, 600 foreign students,131 international cooperation agreements, almost 130 research projects and 180 PhD students. Polotsk SU is also slightly bigger (~15,000 students) than other regional universities.

References

BELTA (Belarusian Telegraph Agency). 2015. *Tchislo Belorusskih vuzov sokratitsja s 54 do 20 [Number of Belarusian Institutions of Higher Education will be reduced from 54 to 20]*, February 26. Accessed 5 Oct 2015. https://news.mail.ru/inworld/belarus/society/21204616/?frommail=1

Chubrik, A. and G. Shimanovitch. 2013. *Otdacha na obrazovanie i otsenka chelovecheskogo kapitala v Belarusi [Return from Education and Evaluation of Human Capital in Belarus]*. Report SA#03/2013. http://www.belinstitute.eu/sites/biss.../BISS_SA03_2013ru_2.pdf

Dopnabor ne pomog: v belorusskih vuzah ostalis svobodnie mesta. 2016. *[Additional Set did not help: There are Vacant Places in Belarusian Universities]*. August, 10. Accessed 11 Aug 2016. https://news.mail.ru/society/26725125/?frommail=1

Education Code of Republic of Belarus. 2011. [*Kodeks Respubliki Belarus' ob obrazovanii*] № 243-3, Retrieved April 20, 2012. http://www.pravo.by/main.aspx?guid=3871&p0= Hk1100243&p2={NRPA}

Froumin I., Y. Kouzminov, and D. Semyonov. 2014. Institutional Diversity in Russian Higher Education: Revolutions and Evolution. *European Journal of Higher Education*. Published Online 09 June 2014, 209–234. http://dx.doi.org/10.1080/21568235.2014.916532

Gille-Belova, O. 2014. "Les réformes de l'enseignement supérieur en Biélorussie: entre poids de l'héritage soviétique et influence internationale diffuse" [The Reforms of Higher Education in Belarus: Between the Weight of Soviet Heritage and Diffuse International Influence]. *Revue d'études comparatives Est-Ouest* 45 (1): 55–90.

———. 2015. Beyond the Limits of the European Higher Education Area: The Case of Belarus. *European Journal of Higher Education* 5 (1): 83–95. http://dx.doi.org/ 10.1080/21568235.2014.979848.

Huisman, J., V.L. Meek, and F.Q. Wood. 2007. Institutional Diversity in Higher Education: A Cross-National and Longitudinal Analysis. *Higher Education Quarterly* 61 (4): 563–577.

IBK [Independent Bologna Committee]. 2013. *White Book. Reforming of the Belarusian Higher School in Accordance with the Aims, Values and Main Directions of the European Higher Education Area policy*. Minsk: IBK. Accessed 16 July 2013. http://bolognaby.org/?p=878&lang=en

———. 2014. *Alternative Report. Belarussian Higher Education: Readiness to EHEA Admission*. Minsk: IBK. Accessed 12 Dec 2014. http://bolognaby.org/?p=1872&lang=en

Krasovskiï, N.I. 1972. *Vysshaja shkola sovetskoï Belorussii [The Higher Education in the Soviet Bielorussia]*. Minsk: Vysheïshaja Shkola.

Kuzminov, Y., D. Semyonov, and I. Froumin. 2013. "Struktura vuzovskoï seti: ot sovetskogo k rossiïskomu masterplanu" [HEIs Network Structure: From Soviet to Russian Masterplan]. *Voprosy obrazovania* 4: 8–63.

MORB [Ministry of Education of the Republic of Belarus]. 2001. *Ustanovy vysheïshaï adukatsii Respubliki Belarus' na pachatak 2001/2002 navuchal'naga goda. Statystychny davednik [The HEIs of the Republic Belarus at the Beginning of the 2001/2002 Year. Statistics]*. Minsk: Galouny infarmatsiïna-analitychny tsentr Ministerstva adukatsii Respubliki Belarus'.

———. 2013a. *Belorusskoe obrazovanie v kontekste mezdunarodnyh pokazateleï [Belarussian Education in the Context of International Indicators]*. Minsk: Ministerstvo obrazovanija.

———. 2013b. *Ustanovy vysheïshaï adukatsii Respubliki Belarus' na pachatak 2013/2014 navuchal'naga goda. Statystychny davednik [The HEIs of the Republic Belarus at the Beginning of the 2013/2014 Year. Statistics]*. Minsk: Galouny infarmatsiïna-analitychny tsentr Ministerstva adukatsii Respubliki Belarus'.

Morgunova, A. 2010. "Zanjatost' v Belarusi: politika i povsednevnost'" [The Employment in Belarus: Policies and Realities]. *Vestnik obchtshestvennogomnenija* 4 (106): 98–115.

Narodnoe hozjaystvo Respubliki Belarus v 1991 godu [The National Economy of the Republic Belarus in 1991], ed. L. Sasnouski, D. Vasilenka. 1993. Minsk: "Belarus" publishing house.

NSCRB [National Statistical Committee of the Republic Belarus]. 2013, 2014, 2015. *Obrazovanie v Respublike Belarus. Statisticheskiï sbornik [The Education in the Republic Belarus. Statistics]*. Minsk: NSCRB.

OECD. 2011. *Competitiveness and Private Sector Development. Eastern Europe and Southern Caucasus 2011. Competitiveness Outlook*. OECD Publishing. http://dx.doi.org/10.1787/9789264112322-en.

Silova, I. 2009. Varieties of Educational Transformation: The Post-Socialist States of Central/South Eastern Europe and the Former Soviet Union. In *International Handbook of Comparative Education*, ed. R. Cowen and A.M. Kazamias, 295–320. Dordrecht: Springer.

Sysoev, S.A. 2010. "Institutsional'nye osobennosti investitsiï v chelovecheskiï kapital v Respublike Belarus'" [The Institutional Particularities of the Human Capital's Investements in the Republic of Belarus]. *Zhurnal institutsional'nyh issledovaniï* 2 (2): 109–117.

Teichler, U. 1988. *Changing Patterns of the Higher Education System*. London: Jessica Kingsley.

Titarenko, L. 2014. "Novye i starye problemy kachestva obrazovania v Belarusi" [New and Old Problems of Education Quality in Belarus]. *Sociologia* 2: 104–112.

Vetokhin, S. 2001. *Reformirovanie vysshego obrazovanija v Respublike Belarus' [The Reforms of the Higher Education in the Republic of Belarus]*. Minsk: RIVSh/BGU.

Yearbook of Big Soviet Encyclopedia, ed. L. Shaumjan. 1959. Moscow: Big Soviet Encyclopedia.

Olga Gille-Belova, PhD in Political Science, Professor in Russian Studies at University Bordeaux Montaigne (France) and researcher at the Center for Studies of Modern and Contemporary History (CEMMC). She is the author of publications on the politics and foreign relations in post-Soviet countries, and recently on emigration and higher education policies.

Larissa Titarenko, Dr. Hab in Sociology, Professor at the Department of Sociology at Belarusian State University (Minsk, Belarus). She is the author of numerous publications on history of social thought, education, youth and gender studies, urban sociology and political sociology.

Open Access This chapter is distributed under the terms of the Creative Commons Attribution 4.0 International License (http://creativecommons.org/licenses/by/4.0/), which permits use, duplication, adaptation, distribution and reproduction in any medium or format, as long as you give appropriate credit to the original author(s) and the source, provide a link to the Creative Commons license and indicate if changes were made.

The images or other third party material in this chapter are included in the chapter's Creative Commons license, unless indicated otherwise in a credit line to the material. If material is not included in the chapter's Creative Commons license and your intended use is not permitted by statutory regulation or exceeds the permitted use, you will need to obtain permission directly from the copyright holder.

CHAPTER 6

Inverted U-shape of Estonian Higher Education: Post-Socialist Liberalism and Postpostsocialist Consolidation

Ellu Saar and Triin Roosalu

INTRODUCTION

The Estonian Republic considers itself the continuation of the first Republic of Estonia, which was in place between 1918 and 1940. In the 50 years between 1940 and 1991, Estonia was part of the Soviet Union. Through the so-called 'Singing Revolution', independence was regained in August 1991. In 2004, Estonia became a NATO member state and a member of the European Union.

In almost 50 years of Soviet occupation, Estonia was subjected to the full force of Soviet ideological, political and economic policies as were other republics within the Soviet Union. While Estonia was afforded limited flexibility to adopt unique education policies reflecting language and culture, in all other respects it was fully integrated into the Soviet Union. The inevitable need to accommodate the heritage of the socialist regime when developing new institutions characterises all postsocialist countries in

---

E. Saar (✉) • T. Roosalu
Institute of International Social Studies/Tallinn University, Tallinn, Estonia

Europe (Bunce 1999). In addition to this, the previous Soviet republics also have to reconcile the experience of belonging to the Soviet Union, which in most cases, and especially in the Baltic republics, was not fully legitimised in society. For countries such as Estonia, this meant that not only was there a need for new ways to continue as a society and construct institutions fit for the new regime, but also that any traces of the old system were likely to be denied and destroyed as part of the colonial Soviet state and the previous regime itself. The major difference stemming from this in relation to the development of the education system lies in the fact that in Estonia, the previously well-established institutionalised systems were discontinued (see Saar et al. 2013a). The Estonian case is special in terms of the radical character of market reform, which has been deep, profound and swift in nature. However, given the fact that institutional solutions have often been 'imported', it would be very important to study what impact these have had on the higher education system. It is clear that the demand-led marketisation of higher education was taken up very quickly, illustrated by the fact that in 2002 there were 49 higher education establishments in Estonia, the majority of which later merged or closed down, but inevitably brought about system diversification on a different scale.

Therefore, not only what happened during the Soviet period but also what happened immediately after societal restructuring has had an impact on how higher education functions. The question remaining is if and when the latter period of 25 years has already become more important in understanding the current higher education era than the socialist period of 50 years; if so, it would become reasonable to replace the term 'postsocialism' with that of 'post-postsocialism' (see Ost 2009). Clearly, the roots of Estonian higher education existed long before the Soviet legacy.

Estonian Higher Education Before the Soviet Period

The development of education in Estonia has been influenced by many different countries which have ruled over its territory (Vaht et al. 2010). The conquest of Estonian territory by German, Swedish and Danish feudal lords in the thirteenth century may be regarded as the starting point of school education in Estonia. The first schools were then established in larger towns, so the development of the Estonian national school was due to the decline of feudalism.

In 1617 during the Swedish-Polish war, the territory of Estonia was incorporated into Sweden and Estonia remained under the rule of Swedish King Gustav Adolf II. This era was favourable for the development of education. In 1632, the Tartu Grammar School was reorganised and given the name Academia Gustaviana, which is now regarded as the establishment of the first university in Estonia: the University of Tartu. In the seventeenth century there were only students of Swedish and Finnish origin at this institution, and no Estonians. Academia Gustaviana operated until 1656 when the area was occupied by Russian troops.

An important event for the development of education in Estonia was the re-opening of the University of Tartu in 1802. Many outstanding scholars received their education there, among them the first native Estonians. Under the independent Estonian republic in 1919, instruction in the Estonian language was introduced and has remained the language of instruction since then. Between 1919 and 1939, 5,751 students graduated from the University of Tartu, a quarter of whom were women. In addition to providing Estonia with lawyers, doctors, clergymen and agronomists, the university also developed its own staff of lecturers and scientists. There were also a number of other higher education institutions (HEIs) that taught specialists. In the course of the brief existence of the independent republic, Estonia was thus able to produce a Western-style though nationally minded Estonian-language high intelligentsia that met the needs of the country at the time.

Using the classifications created by Dobbins (2011) it can be suggested that Estonian HEIs during the pre-Soviet period were between the Humboldtian and Statist tradition: there was freedom of study and teaching, because universities were governed by academic bodies, but also according to state budget decisions. Especially in the 1930s, state control seems to have intensified, with the Ministry of Education dictating student places, study fees, wages and salaries in the universities.

Soviet Period

After the occupation of Estonia by the Soviet Union in 1940, the introduction of the Soviet education system began and possibilities for developing independent education policy were very limited. Education in Estonia was part of the Soviet educational system, which was constructed as an integral part of the party-state institutional structure and organised on the basis of three main principles (see also Titma and Saar 1995; Saar 1997): centralisation, standardisation, utilitarian and egalitarian goals. A strong functional approach prevailed in education. However, the officially declared goal of education reforms provided more opportunities for previously disadvantaged groups.

The higher education system in Estonia was significantly redesigned in the Soviet period. Courses in dialectical and historical materialism and the history of the Communist Party were incorporated into study programmes, as was the Russian language. Military training also occupied a large share of higher education curricula (Tomusk and Tomusk 1993). Central authorities allocated disproportionally large quotas to engineering and science specialities (Terama et al. 2014). For example from 1975 to 1978, about 70 per cent of all higher education graduates in Estonia were educated in these specialisations (Titma et al. 1982, 45). This proportion stemmed not from the actual labour market dynamics but rather from the idea of industrialisation primarily for military purposes (Gerber and Schaefer 2004). Despite pressure to adopt the Soviet educational structure and curricula, the Estonian educational system nevertheless maintained Estonian as the language of instruction. While functioning within the ideology and constraints of the Soviet education system, Estonia was permitted to gradually develop more independent education policies, especially in the 1970s and 1980s.

By 1988, the higher education system in Estonia included six HEIs: one university, four special institutes (pedagogical, technical, agricultural institutes, institute for art) and one conservatory (see Table 6.1). While only one institution was officially called a university, their legal status was equal.

Reforms and Changes from the End of the 1980s

Upward Curve: Chaotic Liberalisation

Following independence from the Soviet Union, Estonian higher education underwent rapid changes from the late 1980s. These changes, which took place against the background of a general shift from a socialist planned economy to a market-based economy, were characterised by an increasing number of HEIs and developments in areas including funding, quality assurance, equity and links to the job market. The changes continued into the following decade, but by then many aspects of the changes were different. The neoliberal doctrine, which stressed the need to diminish the role of the state in public life, had a great impact by stimulating an explosion of private educational institutions and the development of insti-

Table 6.1 Main types of HEIs in Estonia in 1990/1991 and 1993/1994 academic year

Type of HEI	1990/1991	1993/1994	Students 1993/1994	Location	Affiliation	Main training function	Research activities
Public universities	1 state university[a]	6	7,624	Tartu	Ministry of education	Staff for other HEI and research, top management positions for administration	Research institutes and centres
	5 specialised institutes[b]		13,764	4 in Tallinn, 1 in Tartu		Staff in particular focus areas as well as teachers and management for administration	Fewer research centres
State professional HEIs	–	7[c]	1,824	3 in Tallinn, others regional: Tartu, Viljandi, Narva, Rakvere	Different ministries	Specialists for particular sector of national economy or society (e.g., teachers, engineers)	No significant academic research activity
Private professional HEIs	2[d]	7[e]	1,852	All in Tallinn	Privately owned	Specialists for businesses and managers; fields previously underdeveloped (theology, social sciences, humanities)	No significant academic research activity
Total	8	20	25,064				

Source: Statistics Estonia; Estonian education information system

[a]Tartu University

[b]Pedagogical University, Technical University, Agricultural University, Academy of Music and Theatre, Academy of Arts

[c]Maritime Academy, Academy of Security Sciences, College of Engineering, Teacher Education College, and two regional colleges, most reorganised from previously vocational institutions, except Estonian Academy of Security Sciences founded in 1992

[d]The Institute of Humanities and the Estonian Business School were newly established before 1990 as private HEIs that became private universities later in the 1990s

[e]Institute of Humanities, School of Social Sciences, three business schools and two theological institutes

tutional autonomy. The collapse of the communist regime in Estonia was reflected in a strong liberal discourse on education curricula, with explicit neoliberalism in attempts to introduce the notions of decentralisation, deregulation, market rules and values, the rhetoric of choice and an ideology of service provision (Aava 2009). The most significant development in Estonian higher education, however, was the emergence of new actors.

Tomusk (2004) identifies three periods in late and postsocialist reforms of Estonian higher education. He characterises *the first period* (1988–1992) as "a period of chaotic, individually and institutionally driven changes" (Tomusk 2004, 36). As the forces for greater freedom and, evidentially, independence began to build at the end of the 1980s, Estonia developed a strong, indigenous, grassroots movement for education renewal, even while still formally within the framework of the Soviet Union. Gorbachev's administration legalised cooperative enterprises in 1986. In this form, the first private HEI in Estonia was established, the Estonian Institute of Humanities. At the beginning of the 1990s this institute was very popular among young people. In 1989, a second private HEI emerged, the Estonian Business School (EBS). The EBS was clearly directed to the emerging class of newly rich and their children.

In 1989, the Council of Tartu State University deleted the word 'state' from the institution title and declared the university to be academically autonomous. Other public HEIs also changed their titles and became universities. In 1990, there were three types of HEIs: one university; five specialised institutes; and two private professional HEIs. By 1993 new types had emerged and there were now six universities; seven state-owned professional HEIs; and seven private professional HEIs (see Table 6.1). That indicates how rapidly the number of private HEIs increased, while also demonstrating that during this period, several formerly specialised secondary schools started to form a new sector in Estonian higher education, both as a result of pressure from economic and political insecurity and to boost their status: professional higher education (*rakenduskõrgkoolid*, ISCED 5b). The German higher education (*Fachhochschulen*) structure was taken as an example (Tomusk 2004).

This is an indication that institutions drifted towards higher status in an attempt to increase funding by opening higher education level tracks. There was confusion, because the government declared concern about this development and uncertainty regarding the structure of the higher education sector, but at the same time authorised these programmes (Tomusk 2004). As a result, the quality of teaching deteriorated because state-owned vocational schools did not have the capacity to provide higher education. It created a binary divide in Estonian higher education.

Reaching the Turning Point: Expand, Then Regulate

The second period (1993–1998) saw the expansion of the higher education system in combination with the development of legal frameworks and quality assurance mechanisms for the various sectors. Already by the academic year 1993/1994, the HEI landscape had changed considerably: from the previous six public HEIs (consisting of the state university, four specialised institutes and one conservatory in 1988), it had grown into 20 HEIs, with 2 private HEIs established at university level. The Law on Education was adopted in March 1992. Within the new higher education legislation, each institutional type was given its own law, but the University of Tartu was able to persuade the Ministry of Education to draft a law to protect its privileged and special status. According to Tomusk (2004), this indicates the level of political influence a single university can exert in a small country with regard to the national legislative process.

Regarding the management of the higher education system, there was a move from Soviet overly centralised education to extensive decentralisation. Universities became more autonomous from the government, with academic senates playing an increasing role in administration, while professional HEIs were under more direct financial control of the ministry than the universities (OECD 2001).

At the same time, a dramatic decrease in public funding not only made universities dependent on private sources of financing, including tuition fees, but also raised serious concerns about equity of access to higher education. The government introduced a formula funding mechanism: funds were distributed to universities according to student places, weighted by fields of study and level. However, the various weights of the funding formula reflected the power positions of particular universities more than any objective criteria (Tomusk 1995). Experts from the OECD (2007) point out two key issues in their review of the funding mechanism. The first is a misunderstanding of the modern 'knowledge' economy in Estonian policy-making in general, and the second is a public funding focus on the allocation of state-commissioned study places to the 'hard' disciplines (sciences and engineering) with inadequate funding for the service sector programmes (particularly financial and business services).

Due to the liberal HE policy, the number of HEIs grew very quickly to 49 institutions in 2002 (see Fig. 6.1). By 2001, 13 vocational schools offered HE programmes (now this number is much lower, only 2). For a population of just 1.3 million, Estonia probably had the highest ratio of HEIs per inhabitant in Europe at the time.

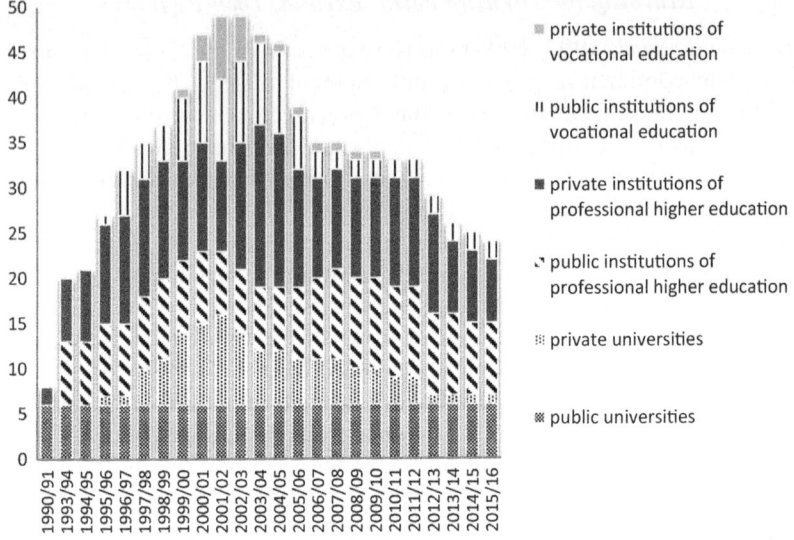

Fig. 6.1 Number of HEIs in Estonia 1990–2015 (Source: Statistics Estonia; Estonian ministry of education)

Expansion of higher education occurred through: (1) the establishment of new private universities and professional higher education schools; (2) the reorganisation of specialised secondary schools as public professional higher education schools; and (3) new legislation allowing foreign universities to establish branches in Estonia (Saar and Unt 2011). With the aim of maximising revenue and keeping costs low, private HEIs tend to concentrate on programmes in more lucrative professions such as law, business management and psychology, which do not require an expensive infrastructure. Parallel to the establishment of new, intellectually and socially exclusive HEIs, institutions emerged that have been referred to as diploma mills. These institutions attracted young people unable to find a place in public universities or meet the high fee requirements at elite private institutions. The Ministry of Education declined to issue an operating licence to some of them. By early 1996, eight private HEIs had been licenced. Most private HEIs were small: the number of students rarely exceeded 1,000. They often relied on part-time teaching staff coming from public universities. Many private HEIs were caught in a vicious cycle of limited funding, problems with recognition and low-quality students.

However, some private institutions were doing important work in offering alternative courses and serving non-traditional students who would otherwise have no access to higher education (see Saar et al. 2013c).

This rapid expansion of the higher education sector created a need for the establishment of a national higher education quality assurance system. Since 1996, the *Standard of Higher Education* has regulated the establishment of HEIs and determined the requirements that they and their programmes must meet in order to obtain an appropriate education licence. Quality assurance is a strange mixture of the new quality movement in European higher education and Soviet bureaucratic practices (Tomusk 2004). The accreditation process is run by the Higher Education Evaluation Council (HEEC, a unit under the auspices of the Ministry of Education). A negative decision by the Council means the closure of the programme or institution. However, several authors (Tomusk 1997; OECD 2007; Kroos 2010) have indicated that the HEEC seems to represent the quality perceptions of traditional universities and may be biased against private institutions.

While Estonian higher education policy seems to be part of the more general neoliberal agenda, there is a complexity in the approach used to steer Estonian higher education. "Far from being totally decentralised, its governance partially resembles the sovereign, rationality-bounded steering model. More specifically, in terms of political leadership and public (including EU) funds, the Estonian government, together with its Estonian Higher Education Quality Agency and various commissions, has an increasing will to intervene, as well as the power to do so" (Kroos 2013, 48).

From the mid-1990s in connection with the accreditation of HEIs and the introduction of state/national exams in upper secondary schools (in 1997), there has been evidence of some shift toward centralisation (see Loogma 1999). Since this time, a certificate of state examinations has been one of two general requirements for admission to higher education (another is a secondary school leaving certificate).

The number of students enrolled in higher education increased 2.7 times between the academic years 1994/1995 and 2008/2009, growing from 25,000 to 68,000 (Tõnisson 2011). Over the past decade, the number of higher education graduates has doubled as well. This expansion was accompanied by differentiation of the higher education system. The proportion of students enrolling in professional higher education increased until 2001, then started to slightly decrease (see Fig. 6.2). Since the

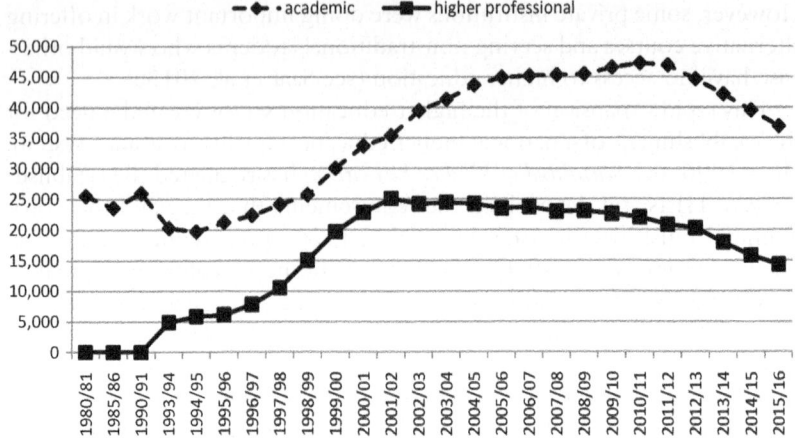

Fig. 6.2 Number of students in Estonian HEIs, 1980–2015 (Source: Statistics Estonia)

academic year 2005/2006, the proportions of students in academic and professional higher education (66 per cent and 34 per cent, respectively) have remained the same (Tõnisson 2011). Despite the large number of private HEIs in Estonia, less than one-quarter of students have studied in them.

From the 1990s, Estonia has experienced a substantial decrease in enrolment in engineering, manufacturing and construction; the proportion of students in these areas fell from 23 per cent in 1994 to 13 per cent in 2000. The agricultural fields also declined in popularity from 6 to 2 per cent in the same period. Enrolment also declined, but less significantly, in education. The number of students studying business increased dramatically between 1994 and 1999 and then levelled out at about 23 per cent (Saar and Lindemann 2008; Tõnisson 2011). Enrolment in social sciences and media can be seen as U-shaped, with higher proportions of students enrolling during the mid-1990s and mid-2000s. An inverted U-shape is evident for law specialities, with almost 10 per cent of all students choosing this subject area in 1999.

Characteristic for this phase was rapid growth in the numbers of tuition-paying students, both in terms of absolute numbers and as a proportion of all students. To obtain additional funding in the mid-1990s, universities began to admit fee-paying students. The Ministry of Education tried to

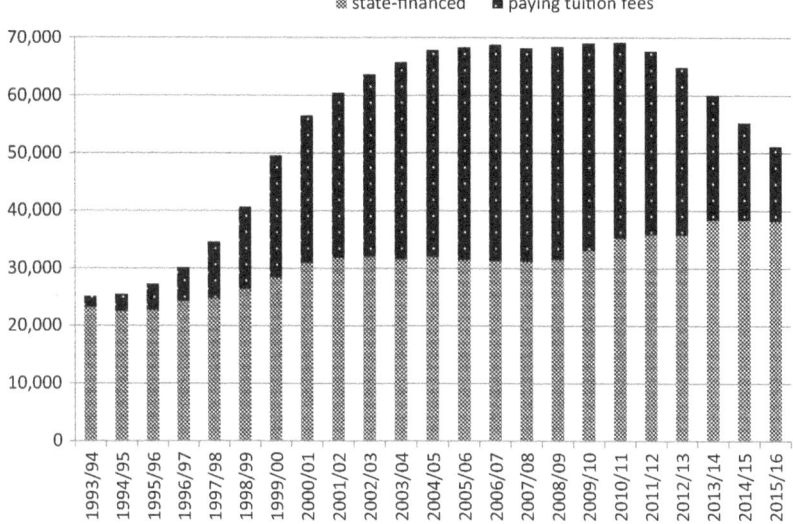

Fig. 6.3 Number of state-financed and fee-paying students in Estonian HEIs, 1993–2015 (Source: Ministry of education and research)

find a legal compromise that would allow universities to charge fees for some groups but at the same time maintain the official free-of-charge higher education policy (Tomusk 2004). As a result, the student admission quota was restructured, allowing universities to admit additional students (up to 20 per cent) on a fee-paying basis. The actual number of fee-paying students, however, exceeds this percentage. In the early 1990s, the majority of students were publicly funded, but by the end of the 1990s half of all students were fee paying. The proportion of students paying tuition fees increased from 7 per cent in 1993 to 54 per cent in 2004 (see Fig. 6.3).

Rapid Decline: Reform, Then Consolidate

The third period (1999–2005) indicated the next wave of reforms, hallmarked by a higher education reform plan in 2002. The growth of the system was considered too fast, and competition within the system was deemed fierce. In addition, the system was not fully geared towards the expectations established in the Bologna Declaration. Since 2000, changes in the higher education area have followed the principles of the Bologna

Process and have been primarily directed towards the new qualification structure and supporting mobility. The higher education reform was adopted by the Government of the Republic in the summer of 2001. Transition to new study programmes in Estonian HEIs took place in the academic year 2002/2003. The new system of higher education has two main cycles, following the bachelor/master model of the European Higher Education Area. The study programmes in some fields have been integrated into a single long cycle. Universities provide professional higher education, bachelor, master and doctoral programmes. Professional HEIs and some vocational education institutions provide professional higher education. A professional HEI may also provide master programmes. In terms of ownership, institutions are divided into state, public and private institutions. In 2004, a Diploma Supplement was introduced, as was a system of recognising how qualifications awarded under different qualification systems correspond to current degrees. The Bologna Process has, however, entailed changing the previous educational credential systems. Such a change has inevitable effects in undermining the value of bachelor-level higher education on the one hand, and not recognising the value of master-level education on the other hand. Compared to previous generations with more years spent in higher education, this is certainly unfair, even if the five-year higher education degrees are now considered comparable to master-level degrees.

Shrinking but Stable: Compete, Then Sustain, Then Excel?

The fourth period (2006-present) indicates new measures for strengthening the competitiveness and sustainability of the shrinking higher education sector. An overview of the changes in student numbers by study field is presented in Table 6.2.

It can be noted that the largest change occurred in the fields of social sciences, business and law, mostly due to the closure or merger of a number of private HEIs.

The Estonian Higher Education Strategy 2006–2015 was approved by the government in 2006. This strategy addressed four main challenges for the sector. First, the number of students entering higher education was expected to diminish by about 60 per cent by 2016. Second, the strategy indicated a clear need to strengthen the international dimension of HEIs. Third, additional funding for both infrastructure and human resources was mentioned as vitally important for the sustainability of the system.

Table 6.2 Number and share of students in Estonian HEIs by study field

Field of study	Number of students			Proportion of students, %		
	1993/1994	2005/2006	2013/2014	1993/1994	2005/2006	2013/2014
Educational sciences	671	1,457	1,013	11	7	7
Humanities and arts	724	2,401	1,888	12	12	13
Social sciences, business and law	1,954	7,180	4,081	32	37	28
Natural and exact sciences	499	2,251	2,316	8	12	16
Technical sciences, production, construction	1,498	2,586	2,295	24	13	16
Agriculture	198	480	328	3	2	2
Health and well-being	283	1,588	1,425	5	8	10
Services	328	1,677	1,260	5	9	9
Total	**6,155**	**19,620**	**14,606**	**100**	**100**	**100**

Source: Statistics Estonia 2014; Estonian education information system

Fourth, the strategy emphasised the needs of the Estonian economy and society. The following specific measures were planned: clarification of HEI profiles; a focus on quality issues; changing the recognition of diplomas (independent of accreditation results); advancing the Bologna Process; a new scheme for steering higher education by means of three-year contracts with individual HEIs; and more attention to career services and guidance to better inform young people about professional prospects. An overview of the institutional changes is presented in Annex 1.

As a result of these measures and general developments in society and the economy, and as an effect of the global economic crises of 2008, the current HEI landscape in Estonia can be described as presented in the following table (Table 6.3). In general, in the Estonian binary HE system the main differentiation is still between academic universities (*ülikool*) and professional HEIs (*rakenduskõrgkool*). This is similar to the situation in 2003, but also quite like the situation in 1993, when professional HEIs were not considered part of HE system, but six HEIs could be divided

Table 6.3 Main types of HEIs in Estonia in the 2013/2014 academic year

Type of HEI	2013/2014	Number of students	Examples	Location	Educational profile	Research activity	International activity
Public universities	1 national university (*with own Act*)	15,785	University of Tartu	Tartu, with regional colleges[a]	Multidisciplinary, full university, largest (Tartu)	High-level academic research activity	High
	1 university (*with own Act*)	12,903	Tallinn university of Technology	Tallinn, with regional colleges	Multidisciplinary big university		High
	4 other universities	16,077	Tallinn University, Academy of music and theatre, Academy of arts, university of life sciences	3 in Tallinn (1 with regional colleges), 1 in Tartu	Medium-size universities		High/medium
Private universities	1	1,508	Estonian business school	Tallinn	Small university, one field of study	Low	High (in teaching)/low (in research)

(*continued*)

Table 6.3 (continued)

Type of HEI	2013/2014	Number of students	Examples	Location	Educational profile	Research activity	International activity
State-owned professional HEI	9	8,520	Maritime Academy, aviation Academy, Academy of security sciences, College of Engineering, health care colleges, regional colleges	2 in Tallinn, others regional	Specialists for particular sector of national economy	Low	Low
Private professional HEIs	8	4,024	Business schools; theological institutes; ICT/computer science College	All in Tallinn, but some with regional branches	Specialists in narrow fields	Low	Low
State vocational education institutions	2	1,181	Tallinn School of Economics, Võru County vocational training Centre	Across country	Specialists in narrow fields	Low	Low
Total	26	58,817					

Source: Statistics Estonia; Estonian education information system

^aRegional colleges were previously independent state institutions of professional higher education (and sometimes vocational schools during the Soviet period), but by now have been merged with universities

between the general (state) university and five more specialised institutes. Formally, there is no differentiation within the group of public universities; they all provide education at all academic levels (bachelor, master and PhD) and are engaged in high-level, internationally visible research activities. However, as the universities differ by size and fields of (main) specialisation, their research profiles also differ.

In terms of further differentiating between public universities, it should be noted that funding varies greatly, including research grant-based funding (see Annex 2). In terms of both research as well as learning output, the University of Tartu as the state university appears the most productive, while different accounts place it as more or less comparable to Tallinn University of Technology. Other universities are smaller and have a much lower share of public funding. Therefore, it would be reasonable to distinguish between three types of universities: "flagship university"; two big universities (Tallinn University and Tallinn University of Technology); and four specialised universities, including the private university.

The Story of the Inverted U: Expansion and Vertical Differentiation of Estonian Higher Education

The expansion of higher education in Estonia was clearly demand-driven rather than designed by the system. Tomusk (2004) differentiates three types of demand. First, there is demand for alternative liberal education. Second, there is demand for studies in fields that state universities did not offer, for example business administration. Third, there is demand for exclusive elitist environments. There was also a fourth, hidden demand for diplomas of any kind requiring minimal effort. With the expansion of higher education, the need for a diploma becomes a symbolic threshold to be considered for certain jobs. On the other hand, the implications for higher education in light of the Bologna Process, by changing the system into three-year bachelor studies and two-year master studies, may make MA degrees more desirable in the labour market.

Rapid higher education expansion has led to vertical differentiation and inequalities. On the one hand, expansion opened up more places in HEIs, and these should have increased the opportunities for under-represented students to attend. On the other hand given the pattern of expansion, socially disadvantaged or otherwise less prepared students might have gained access to lower-status institutions, including those in smaller towns, and to fee-paying places either in the public or the private sector (see also Saar and Mõttus 2013). The OECD Review of Tertiary Education in Estonia (2007:63) indicates: "as is the case in many other countries, vocationally-oriented tertiary studies still suffer from a lack of parity of esteem relative to university studies". The best secondary education graduates, mostly with higher social origin and affluent urban families, were competing for a limited number of state-subsidied student places in public universities, while less affluent and less prepared students occupied fee-paying places, including those in private universities (Tomusk 2004).

According to the criteria offered by Arum et al. (2007) in their typology, Estonia has a diversified higher education system. While the primary tier is comprised of public university courses, the secondary tier is comprised of both professional higher education programmes as well as most academic programmes in private universities. First-tier institutions are typically rather selective in terms of academic staff and students ('status seekers') and enjoy higher prestige, thus contributing to vertical differentiation between universities. The less-selective, less-prestigious second tier consists of many private institutions, which rely on tuition fees for revenue ('client seekers'). Several authors have described Estonian higher education policy as oligopolistic (Tomusk 2003; OECD 2007; Masso and Ukrainski 2009). This means that even among the same type of HEI, some are more equal than others, for example with their own laws and ability to protect their special status. The leaders of these institutions have an important impact on higher education and research policy, from agenda setting to political leadership in reform implementation. Due to oligopolistic higher education policy, the University of Tartu has a special position in Estonian higher education.

Research indicates that employers also referred to the two-tier system of Estonian higher education (see Saar et al. 2013b). As there is an increasing range of higher education credentials available, employers seem to rely more on institutional status due to uncertainty about the value of various credentials. This indicates the importance of vertical differentiation in higher education. It is noteworthy that employers preferring graduates from the more prestigious, competitive public universities do not connect the preferred degree with better skills, but rather with the sorting power of the staff in these HEIs (Unt et al. 2013).

Conclusion: Post-Postsocialism Arrived

Higher education has gone through four major phases during the postsocialist period:

1. The first period, 1988–1992, can be considered a period of chaotic, individually and institutionally driven changes.
2. The second period, 1993–1998, saw a major expansion of the higher education system in combination with the development of legal frameworks and quality assurance mechanisms.
3. The third period, 1999–2005, indicated a wave of reforms, including following the principles of the Bologna Process.
4. In the fourth period, from 2006 onwards, new measures are being put in place to strengthen the (international) competitiveness and sustainability of the shrinking higher education sector.

We are inclined to say that the processes of the immediate postsocialist period may have had more impact on the current situation in Estonian HE system than the socialist period.

In the 1990s, the sector was growing rather chaotically in many directions, bringing about some vertical and horizontal differentiation between study programmes and institutions over time. In general, the Estonian binary higher education system differentiates only between academic track (universities) and professional track. While the size of the HE sector has changed over the past 25 years, the current number of HEIs is again comparable to that of 1993. On the other hand, it is worthwhile to distinguish between the (formally) similarly positioned universities: there is one so-called flagship university, and then there are others that can be classified differently depending on the dimensions chosen for comparison.

Expansion has thus led to a number of challenges which demand a priority shift from growth to quality improvement and equality. With respect to higher education access in Estonia, policy has emphasised an overall expansion in enrolment rather than equity of access, which relates more to differences in participation rates among groups of students (OECD 2007). The Estonian Higher Education Strategy 2006–2015 does not put enough emphasis on the equity dimension. Previous studies indicate that the impact of social origin on access to higher education has increased since the 1990s (Saar 2010; Saar and Unt 2011). Enrolment in higher education by students from poor backgrounds is particularly low (OECD 2012).

A review by the OECD (2007) also indicated that Estonian higher education was inequitable in its overall admissions policy and access to state-commissioned places (especially in the best institutions), which were disproportionately granted to students from families with well-educated parents. In Estonia, the main under-represented demographic group in higher education is the Russian-speaking population, which comprises about a quarter of the population. Increased variety in the supply of HE learning opportunities, in the form of both private institutions as well as more vocationally oriented professional learning facilities, has indeed provided those somewhat overlooked by the traditionally state-led educational system with better chances to acquire HE (Saar et al. 2012; Saar et al. 2014).

Among the main driving forces behind the developments in the Estonian higher education system are: the European political agenda, both in terms of a generally neoliberal European social agenda and reliance on foreign expertise in designing policies; the Estonian political agenda, with its neoliberalism and fragmentation but also subsequently re-established intervention patterns; demographic processes and shrinking population; changes in the system of higher education funding as well as in the qualification system and in labour market structure; missing feedback loops between education and the labour market; and internationalisation of both education and labour markets, as well as brain drain, together with the continuously high social value of higher education and the perceived inequality of access to it, which has also resulted in pressure on the system from lower levels of education.

While the main axis of differentiation for Estonian HEIs is between academic universities and professional HEIs, public HEIs are clearly privileged in terms of access to research funds as well as competition for students. Still, the time has inevitably arrived for supply-driven rather than demand-driven reorganisation of the HE system in Estonia, as evidenced by system-level restructuring decisions in all major HEIs suggested by state actors and the Ministry of Education. A report (Okk 2015) commissioned by the government and compiled by a CEO in private banking suggests further consolidation of HEIs as well as other major structural changes in the name of *efficiency* and *excellence* and has been met with rather mixed feelings in academia, as well as more critical analysis of neoliberal trends in academia (e.g. Aidnik 2014, 2015; Aavik and Marling forthcoming). Perhaps this, finally, indicates the arrival of the post-postsocialist period in Estonian HE. To what extent the underlying processes of further neoliberalisation will take hold in the postsocialist context in Estonia remains an open question, especially as the state is still a major player in defining and redefining the goals and structure of HE provision.

Acknowledgements Ellu Saar acknowledges the support of Estonian Research Council project IUT31-10 *Cumulative processes in the interplay of educational path and work career: explaining inequalities in the context of neoliberalization* and from European Commission Horizon2020 project EXCEPT: *Social Exclusion of Youth in Europe: Cumulative Disadvantage, Coping Strategies, Effective Policies and Transfer*. Triin Roosalu acknowledges the support received from Estonian Research Council personal research grant PUT106 *Alternatives at work and work organisation: flexible postsocialist societies* and project *Supporting the career track of female researchers in the academia* funded by the Estonian Ministry of Social Affairs through the small grants scheme *Mainstreaming Gender Equality and Promoting Work-Life Balance*, in the framework of Norway Grants 2009–2014.

ANNEX 1

Timeline of institutional changes in Estonian HE 1988–2015

First period—chaotic, individually and institutionally driven changes	1988	First private university, Estonian Institute of Humanities, established as a cooperative
	1989	June – ESSR CoEd discussed bill setting out new by-lays for Tartu (state) uni
		Second private university, Estonian business school, established
	1990	(during the period, other public HEIs became Unis, and specialised secondary schools—professional higher education)
	1991	Credit-based system reform (from academic year system) (bottom up)
		Introduction of MA study programmes
	1992	Education act passed in parliament
Second period—expansion of HE system, development of legal frameworks and quality assurance mechanisms = decentralisation	1993	
	1994	
	1995	Universities Act; **Tartu University Act**
		4+2 curriculum reform, start of 4-year BA programmes (not 5 year HE)
		HE Quality Assessment Council
	1996	
	1997	HE Accreditation Centre, launch of accreditation of curricula. Also, launch of nationally standardised state exams for high school graduates, later to be used as entrance exams in HE
	1998	Institution of Professional Higher Education Act

Third period—new wave of reforms, including initiating Bologna reforms	1999	4+2 MA degree in TUT equal to European PhD Rapid growth in student numbers, after "Universities Act" and "Professional HE Act" enabled demanding reimbursement by public entities. By 2002, 42 HEIs—up from 6 in 1988
	2000	Building of quality assessment systems at HEIs started
	2001	3+2 curricula reform concluded, legal acts amended, incl standard of HE
	2002	3+2(+4) reform introduced to universities—Bologna Estonian e-university programme launched
	2003	Uni "Quality Agreement Concerning Curricula, Acad. Professions and Academic Degrees" 2003–2010
	2004	Share of fee-paying students more than half, most in public Unis
	2005	Doctoral programmes reformed in all universities Launch of common electronic admissions platform (2014–15/22 HEI use it) Prof HEI declaration "Development of Professional HE system Quality Assurance"
Fourth period—strengthening competitiveness and sustainability of shrinking HE sector. Increasing inequality of access	2006	Strategy of HE 2006–2015/launch of curricula in English, promote student mobility, labour market demands set as objective
	2007	Agreement on good practice in internationalisation
	2008	Most numerous young cohorts enter HE, 82 % graduates in social sciences pay tuition
	2009	Inadequate HE financing—only 1.3 % of GDP—and downtrend HE Quality Agency formed. Bologna related outcome-based learning/ECTS reform deadline postponed from 2006 to 2009
	2010	Most Bologna goals declared achieved…
	2011	
	2012	Full-time, Estonian language HE programmes free of charge
	2013	Introduction of needs-based income support for students
	2014	**Tallinn University of Technology** Act + relaunch of entrance exams in HE

Annex 2

Typology of Estonian public universities, 2010s

		Public universities[a]						
		TU	TUT	TLU	EMÜ	EKA	EMTA	year
Size	N of study programmes opened	60	51	56	18	17	10	2014
	N of students	17,200	13,926	10,330	4,514	1,177	736	2012
	Students, compared to TUT	124%	100%	74%	32%	8%	5%	2012
	% of PhD graduates	60%	24%	8%	6%	0%	1%	2011
	Students/academic staff ratio	11	15	22	12	17	6	2012
Faculty	Total academic personnel	1,513	930	470	370	69	124	2012
	Academic personnel, compared to TUT	163%	100%	51%	40%	7%	13%	2012
	Share of professors + research professors	12%	16%	12%	10%	36%	23%	2012
	Share of foreigners among faculty	8%	8%	9%	4%	1%	3%	2012
	Relative pay of female faculty across academic positions	101%	86%	91%	90%	102%	103%	2012
Research intensity	% of public institutional support	55%	25%	9%	10%	0%	0%	2012
	% of project-based national funding of academic research	55%	26%	6%	8%	3%	3%	2012
	% of other R&D contracts	41%	40%	4%	14%	1%	0%	2011
	High-level peer-reviewed, internationally published academic publications per academic employee per year	1.2	1.16	1.26	0.8	n/a	n/a	2014

[a] *TU* University of Tartu, *TUT* Tallinn University of Technology, *TLU* Tallinn University, *EMU* Estonian University of Life Sciences, *EKA* Estonian Academy of Arts, *EMTA* Estonian Academy of Music and Theatre

REFERENCES

Aava, K. 2009. Haridusalaste tekstide võrdlev diskursusanalüüs [Comparative Discourse Analysis of Educational Texts; (in Estonian)]. *Eesti Rakenduslingvistika Ühingu Aastaraamat [Estonian Papers in Applied Linguistics]* 5: 7–17.
Aavik, K., and R. Marling. forthcoming/2017. Gender Studies at the Time of Neoliberal Transformation in the Estonian Academia. In *Gender Studies and Gender Research in the Times of the New Governance of Science*, ed. H. Kahlert. Springer VS.
Aidnik, M. 2014. Kas kõrgharidus on üksnes majanduse teener? [Is Higher Education Only a Servant for the Economy? (in Estonian)] *Eest Päevaleht [Estonian Daily]*, 25.11: 10.
———. 2015. Ülikoole koloniseerib manager'ide kultuur [Universities are Colonised by the Managerial Culture. (in Estonian)]. *Sirp [Estonian Weekly]*, 4.12.
Arum, R., A. Gamoran, and Y. Shavit. 2007. More Inclusion Than Diversion: Expansion, Differentiation, and Market Structure in Higher Education. In *Stratification in Higher Education*, ed. Y. Shavit, R. Arum and A. Gamoran, 1–35. Stanford: Stanford University Press.
Bunce, V. 1999. *Subversive Institutions: The Design and the Destruction of Socialism and the State*. Cambridge: Cambridge University Press.
Dobbins, M. 2011. *Higher Education Policies in Central and Eastern Europe – Convergence Towards a Common Model?* Basingtone: Palgrave Macmillan.
Gerber, T.P., and D.R. Schaefer. 2004. Horizontal Stratification in Higher Education in Russia: Rends, Gender Differences, and Labour Market Outcomes. *Sociology of Education* 77 (1): 32–59.
Kroos, K. 2010. *Kõrghariduse kvaliteet kehtivates riiklikes strateegia dokumentides [Higher Education Quality in the Existing National Strategy Documents*. (in Estonian)]. Unpublished Report.
———. 2013. Estonian Higher Education and Research Strategy: A Systematic Review and Policy Discussion. In *Higher Education in the Crossroad: The Case of Estonia*, ed. E. Saar and R. Mõttus, 27–70. Frankfurt: Peter Lang.
Masso, J., and K. Ukrainski. 2009. Competition for Public Project Funding in a Small Research System: The Case of Estonia. *Science and Public Policy* 36: 683–695.
OECD. 2001. *Reviews of National Policies of Education. Estonia*. Paris: OECD.
———. 2007. *Review of Tertiary Education in Estonia*. Paris: OECD.
———. 2012. *OECD Economic Surveys: Estonia*. Paris: OECD.
Okk, G. 2015. *Eesti ülikoolide, teadusasutuste ja rakenduskõrgkoolide võrgu ja tegevussuundade raport. [Report on the Landscape and Future Directions of Estonian Universities, Academic Institutions and Applied Higher Education Institutions*. (In Estonian)]. Tallinn: Teadus- ja Arendusnõukogu. https://riigikantselei.ee/sites/default/files/riigikantselei/strateegiaburoo/eutarkvt_loppraport.pdf

Ost, D. 2009. The Consequences of Postcommunism: Trade Unions in Eastern Europe's Future. *East European Politics and Societies* 23: 13–33.

Saar, E. 1997. Transitions to Tertiary Education in Belarus and the Baltic Countries. *European Sociological Review* 13: 139–158.

———. 2010. Changes in Intergenerational Mobility and Educational Inequality in Estonia: Comparative Analysis of Cohorts Born Between 1930 and 1974. *European Sociological Review* 26: 367–383.

Saar, E., and K. Lindemann. 2008. Estonia. In *Europe Enlarged: A Handbook of Education, Labour and Welfare Regimes in Central and Eastern Europe*, ed. I. Kogan, M. Gebel, and C. Noelke, 151–181. Bristol: Policy Press.

Saar, E., and R. Mõttus, eds. 2013. *Higher Education in the Crossroad: The Case of Estonia*. Frankfurt: Peter Lang.

Saar, E., and M. Unt. 2011. Education and Labour Market Entry in Estonia: Closing Doors for Those Without Tertiary Education. In *Making the Transition: Education and Labour Market Entry in Central and Eastern Europe*, ed. I. Kogan, C. Noelke, and M. Gebel, 240–268. Stanford: Stanford University Press.

Saar, E., A. Tamm, T. Roosalu, and E.-L. Roosmaa. 2012. *Mittetraditsiooniline tudeng kõrgkoolis [Nontraditional Student in Higher Education (in Estonian)]*. Tartu: Archimedes Foundation.

Saar, E., T. Roosalu, E.-L. Roosmaa, A. Tamm, and R. Vöörmann. 2013a. Developing Human Capital in Post-Socialist Capitalism: Estonian Experience. In *Lifelong Learning in Europe: National Patterns and Challenges*, ed. E. Saar, O.B. Ure, and J. Holford, 372–396. Cheltenham: Edward Elgar Publishing.

Saar, E., M. Unt, J. Helemäe, K. Oras, and K. Täht. 2013b. What is the Role of Education in the Recruitment Process? Employers' Practices and Experiences of Graduates from Tertiary Educational Institutions in Estonia. *Journal of Education and Work* 27 (5): 475–495.

Saar, E., K. Täht, T. Roosalu, and A. Tamm. 2013c. Wishing Welcome to the Nontraditional Student: How Institutions Create Barriers for Returning to Higher Education. In *Higher Education at a Crossroad: The Case of Estonia*, ed. E. Saar and R. Mõttus, 415–439. New York: Peter Lang Publishers House.

Statistics Estonia. 2014. *Statistical Database*. Available online: www.stat.ee

Terama, E., A. Kõu, and K.C. Samir. 2014. Early Transition Trends and Differences of Higher Education Attainment in the Former Soviet Union, Central and Eastern European Countries. *Finnish Yearbook of Population Research* XLIX: 105–122.

Titma, M., and E. Saar. 1995. Regional Differences in Soviet Secondary Education. *European Sociological Review* 11 (1): 37–58.

Titma, M., P. Kenkmann, A. Matulionis, and M. Taljunaite, eds. 1982. *Sozialnije peremeštšenija v studentšestvo Social [Mobility Into Higher Education (in Russian)]*. Vilnius: Mintis.

Tomusk, V. 1995. Nobody Can Better Destroy Your Higher Education Than Yourself: Critical Remarks About Quality Assessment and Funding in Estonian Higher Education. *Assessment and Evaluation in Higher Education* 20 (1): 115–124.

———. 1997. External Quality Assurance in Estonian Higher Education: Its Glory, Take-Off and Crash. *Quality in Higher Education* 3: 173–181.

———. 2003. Aristoscientists, Academic Proletariat and Reassembling the Mega-Machine: 21st Century Survival Strategies of the Estonian Academia. *International Studies in Sociology of Education* 13: 77–99.

———. 2004. *The Open World and Closed Societies. Essays on Higher Education Policies "in Transition"*. Houndsmills, Basingstoke, Hampshire: Palgrave.

Tomusk, V., and A. Tomusk. 1993. Teaching Psychology, Estonia: USSR Revisited. *Teaching of Psychology* 20 (3): 175–177.

Tõnisson, E. 2011. Kõrghariduse valdkonna statistiline ülevaade 2011 [Statistical Overview of Higher Education 2011 (in Estonian)]. Tartu: Estonian Ministry of Education and Research. Available Online: http://www.hm.ee/index.php?048183

Unt, M., K. Täht, E. Saar, and J. Helemäe. 2013. Educational Expansion: Devaluation or Differentiation of Higher Education? The Estonian Country Case. In *Higher Education in the Crossroad: The Case of Estonia*, ed. E. Saar and R. Mõttus, 367–390. Frankfurt: Peter Lang.

Vaht, G., L. Tüür, and Ü. Kulasalu. 2010. *Higher Education in Estonia*. 4th edn. Tallinn: Foundation Archimedes, Estonian Academic Recognition Information Centre.

Ellu Saar PhD, is Professor of Sociology at Tallinn University (Estonia). Her research focuses on life courses, social stratification and mobility, educational transitions, lifelong learning and ethnic inequalities. She has been involved in various international comparative projects, among these coordinating European Commission 6th Framework Project "Towards lifelong learning societies in Europe: the role of formal education", and has published several books and articles on these topics. Her edited books include *Higher Education in the Crossroad: the Case of Estonia* (2013, Peter Lang, with Rene Mõttus), *Lifelong Learning in Europe: National Patterns and Challenges* (2013. Edward Elgar, with Odd Bjorn Ure and John Holford) and *Towards a normal stratification order? Actual and Perceived Social Stratification in Post-Socialist Estonia* (2011, Peter Lang).

Triin Roosalu PhD, is Associate Professor and Researcher at Tallinn University (Estonia). Her research interests involve comparative social research on actual and perceived inequalities in the domains of work, education and lifelong learning systems; employment and care patterns; gender regimes; and studies of postsocialist welfare states. Her publications include *Rethinking Gender, Work and Care in a New Europe: Theorising Markets and Societies in the Post-Postsocialist Era* (2015, Palgrave, edited with Dirk Hofäcker) and *Learning in Transition: Policies and Practices of Lifelong Learning in Post-Socialist Countries* (2010, Nauka, edited with Vladimir Kozlovskiy and Rein Vöörmann).

Open Access This chapter is distributed under the terms of the Creative Commons Attribution 4.0 International License (http://creativecommons.org/licenses/by/4.0/), which permits use, duplication, adaptation, distribution and reproduction in any medium or format, as long as you give appropriate credit to the original author(s) and the source, provide a link to the Creative Commons license and indicate if changes were made.

The images or other third party material in this chapter are included in the chapter's Creative Commons license, unless indicated otherwise in a credit line to the material. If material is not included in the chapter's Creative Commons license and your intended use is not permitted by statutory regulation or exceeds the permitted use, you will need to obtain permission directly from the copyright holder.

CHAPTER 7

Georgia: Higher Education System Dynamics and Institutional Diversity

Lela Chakhaia and Tamar Bregvadze

Higher Education in Georgia at the Time of Independence

As one of the three South Caucasian post-Soviet republics, Georgia is located on the eastern coast of the Black Sea. Over 80 per cent of its 3.7 million inhabitants are ethnic Georgians. Other large ethnic and language groups residing in the country include Armenians, Russians, Azeris, Abkhazs and Ossetians. Even though the country has made significant strides towards improving the economic and social conditions of its citizens during the last decade, a large proportion of the population is still under the poverty threshold and economic inequality is substantial. With the officially declared state goal of joining the European Union and NATO, the Georgian government and the people of Georgia see themselves as an indispensable part of the Western world.

L. Chakhaia (✉)
European University Institute, Florence, Italy

T. Bregvadze
Ilia State University, Tbilisi, Georgia

Just before Georgia gained independence, higher education was part of the Soviet system and was accordingly standardised in terms of both form and substance. The higher education institutional landscape was very similar to those in the other Soviet republics (Sharvashidze 2005). All higher education institutions (HEIs) were exclusively owned by the state and the full course of studies was subsidised by the state; this was to achieve the ideal of total equality for all. In terms of disciplinary diversity, HEIs were often highly specialised and roughly divided into the following categories: comprehensive universities preparing professionals for a wide range of disciplines; specialised HEIs, which were institutes preparing professionals for specific professions (in most cases technical, medical and agricultural); pedagogical institutes established in regional centres with the dual purpose of preparing teachers and providing access at regional level; and institutes of art and culture. The number of HEIs in the country remained more or less constant throughout the entire history of the Soviet Union. Until the beginning of the 1990s there was only one HEI which bore the title of university and provided comprehensive education. This was the oldest and most well-known institution in the country, Tbilisi State University.

However, the number of students grew both nominally and as a share of the respective age group. In line with the Soviet trend of higher education massification that started at the end of the 1960s (Matthews 1972), this development was reflected in Georgia as well. As seen from Fig. 7.1, absolute enrolments as well as enrolments per 10,000 people doubled

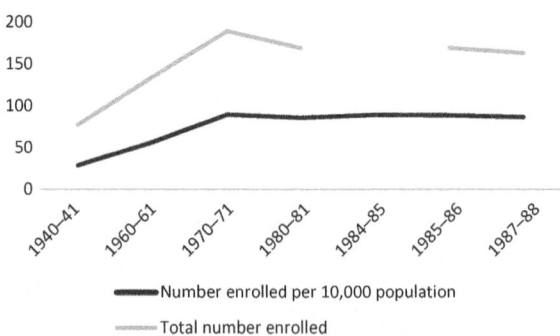

Fig. 7.1 Number of HEIs and enrolments in Soviet Georgia (Source: Savelyev et al. 1990)

from the beginning of the 1940s to the beginning of the 1960s, although the number of institutions remained stable.

Since the start of the 1970s, the number of enrolled students remained flat and by 1988 there were 19 higher education institutions (HEIs) enrolling some 86,400 students with more than 100 specialisations and 4 to 16 faculties at each university. With a gross tertiary enrolment ratio of 30 per cent, Georgia had one of the highest participation rates in the Soviet countries by the time it gained independence.

As mentioned above, the main distinction between HEIs during the Soviet period was in terms of fields of study, with some offering a comprehensive range of programmes (universities) and some confined to educating professionals for specific fields (institutes). Another important classification factor was the location of universities: to expand access to higher education geographically, the Soviet government encouraged the opening of institutes in various regions. In terms of study structure, all HEIs offered single-cycle programmes, which typically lasted for five years, and issued 'specialist' diplomas upon graduation. An exception to this rule were medical institutes, which provided longer courses of study although the degree conferred was the same. There was therefore no distinction between HEIs regarding the level of qualifications awarded. Another point of distinction was the possibility to receive a graduate research degree. It was possible to pursue graduate degrees at universities and at some institutes as well. There was no formal way of distinguishing quality differences between HEIs in Soviet Georgia, since there were no formal rankings in place. However, there was an informal understanding of which HEIs were 'prestigious' and because HEIs were in most cases highly specialised, the prestige of a particular HEI or programme was often equated with the prestige of the discipline.

To sum up, the higher education institutional landscape in Georgia in the final years of the Soviet Union just before independence can be described as follows (Table 7.1).

FRAMEWORK FOR CLASSIFICATION OF HIGHER EDUCATION INSTITUTIONAL LANDSCAPE IN GEORGIA

The transformation of Georgian higher education started immediately after the country gained independence. The changes that took place throughout the subsequent 25 years varied in scope, structure, agency and impact. There are several major dimensions along which the system developed and

Table 7.1 Classification of Georgian HEIs by the end of the 1980s

Type of HEI	Description	HEIs
University	HEI offering extensive range of disciplines; under the supervision of the Ministry of Education; opportunity for postgraduate study and research; varying prestige depending on the field of study	Tbilisi State University (the only university in Soviet Georgia)
Specialised professional institutes	HEI offering programmes in specific fields of study and preparing professionals to work in certain areas; under the supervision of various ministries; opportunity for postgraduate study and research; varying prestige depending on the institute and the field of study; located in Tbilisi	Technical Institute of Georgia Medical Institute of Georgia Agrarian Institute of Georgia Foreign Languages Institute of Georgia
Culture and arts institutes	HEI offering programmes and preparing professionals in various domains of arts and culture; under the supervision of various ministries; usually highly prestigious; located in Tbilisi	State Academy of Arts Tbilisi State Conservatory State Institute of Theatre and Film
Pedagogical institutes	HEI preparing school teachers in various subject disciplines; varying prestige depending on the institute and the field of study but usually less prestigious compared to most other HEIs; located in regions, one in Tbilisi	Tbilisi Pushkin Pedagogical Institute Kutaisi Pedagogical Institute Batumi Pedagogical Institute Sokhumi Pedagogical Institute Tskhinvali Pedagogical Institute Gori Pedagogical Institute

which are still shaping its current institutional landscape. In fact, these developments are reflected very accurately in the institutional setup of higher education.

Firstly, a distinction should be made between HEIs by *form of ownership*, meaning whether they are publicly or privately owned. Privatisation of higher education was perhaps the first major significant transformation of the system, resulting directly from the rapid transition from a centralised state-run economy to a market economy. The next distinction is *horizontal substantial differentiation* distinguishing between HEIs based on the variety of study fields offered. This dimension was influenced by the marketisation of the economy as well as by the changing demands of the labour market. The major trend in this regard has been diversification and broadening of narrow fields of specialisation. Further, there is *horizontal structural differentiation* between HEIs by degree of education offered and level of research and education integration. This is a more recent development that is closely tied with joining the Bologna Process and the related changes in the system. It is also important to highlight **vertical differentiation by quality**. This is more complicated in terms of suitable measurements, but we propose certain proxies.

Further distinctions can be made between HEIs by *location*: the capital city of Tbilisi is not only the biggest city in the country by more than eight times the population of the next biggest city (Kutaisi), but its economy is also far ahead of any other city or region. Therefore, it is perhaps no surprise that most of the HEIs in the country, 75 per cent, are located in Tbilisi. Next, there are important distinctions between HEIs based on *size*, ranging from a few hundred to several thousand students.

Overview of Socioeconomic and Political Developments

The development of higher education in post-Soviet Georgia mirrors the country's political and socioeconomic landscape and closely follows the timeline of major transformations. In Georgia, the economic and political hardships common to all post-Soviet countries were accompanied by a severe civil war in 1991–1992 and two violent ethnic conflicts in the autonomous regions of Abkhazia and South Ossetia. Nationalistic sentiments were on the rise and the country was in a state of chaos after the first democratically elected post-independence government was ousted by a military coup.

Together with Moldova, the Georgian economy suffered most with an average annual economic decline of 24 per cent between 1990 and 1994; the GDP in 1994 constituted only 28 per cent of its 1989 level (Mitra and Selowsky 2002). Total GDP composition, which in 1990 was roughly equally distributed between industry, agriculture and service sectors, was also radically asymmetric in 1994 with agriculture accounting for 65 per cent and industry a mere 10 per cent (World Bank 2009). These changes had crucial implications for labour market demands, and as a further consequence, for demands on formal education.

Unemployment rates increased in parallel with the economic decline. In addition, the economic decline did not affect all groups evenly. As a result, income inequality as measured by the Gini coefficient increased dramatically, soaring from 26 in 1990 to 43 in 1993 (Mitra and Selowsky 2002).

The political crisis resulting from the overthrow of the first elected president continued for almost three years, but the situation began to change in 1994 when a new government was installed. Central and local government institutions and agencies were slowly being restored and started functioning again, even if not efficiently. The economy grew rapidly as national assets were privatised, and the political situation was relatively stable except for the aforementioned cases of Abkhazia and South Ossetia. Conflict in these areas was at a standstill, but tensions arose from time to time. Meanwhile, income inequality continued to grow. Political discourse was largely dominated by the need to maintain stability after years of conflict, upheaval and disorder. Perhaps the most prominent feature of the public sector during this period was inefficiency and rampant corruption at every level (Transparency International 2002).

Starting in 2004 after the so-called Rose Revolution, the Georgian government undertook a set of sweeping countrywide reforms aimed at combatting corruption and increasing the efficiency of public services. A team of liberally minded young economic reformers set out to radically transform the country and make it a post-Soviet success story. The economy grew steadily with the exception of 2008–2009, when growth was hindered by both the global financial crisis as well as war with Russia.

The economic policies of the new government, especially during the first years, were based on the principles of deregulation and liberalisation. After privatising national assets, the privatisation of public services ensued. These reforms, which were commended by international organisations (World Bank 2009; OECD 2011), indeed succeeded in eradicating corruption at lower levels by limiting bureaucracy and improving efficiency in all public sectors.

The educational system, higher education in particular, was not only part of the extensive reform package that the new government implemented after the Rose Revolution; it was also one of the most prominent and highly debated. It is therefore deemed appropriate to divide the review of the Georgian higher education system development into two parts: before and after the Rose Revolution.

Higher Education System Development: An Overview Before 2005

As explained earlier in this chapter, developments in the higher education system have closely reflected the political and socioeconomic changes in the country since independence in 1991. All the features characteristic of the public governance system in the independent republic of Georgia during its first years of existence, as outlined above, were also relevant for its higher education system. The system functioned largely through inertia, and hence a number of defining features from the Soviet education system were retained. However, lack of experience in the planning and management of education systems resulted in somewhat haphazard developments.

From the outset, economic hardships in the country were reflected in the funding of the education system. Together with the dramatic economic decline described above, the share of educational funding as a percentage of GDP also shrank from about 7 per cent in 1991 to a mere 1 per cent in 1994 (Perkins 1998; Sharvashidze 2002).

In terms of institutional development and structural arrangement, the higher education system maintained many of the basic features of the Soviet period; changes, if there were any, were slow. There was no top-down effort to reform the system and no effort on the part of HEIs themselves to initiate substantive changes. As in other public sectors, the system was occupied with adjusting to new realities rather than substantially reforming. Rapid privatisation of the sector and disciplinary diversification of previously narrowly specialised HEIs were clear signs: these were unregulated and unplanned transformations to respond to the demands of the market economy and the labour market.

Privatisation and Ownership of HEIs

Privatisation of higher education was one of the most significant developments in the Georgian higher education system in the 1990s. Private educational institutions were opened alongside state institutions on the basis of the Decree of the Supreme Council of the Republic of Georgia, which was issued in June 1991. Privatisation also occurred through the introduction of tuition fees[1] at existing public HEIs, a change authorised by the government in 1993.

Growth and expansion of private higher education institutions in Georgia was spectacular; some 200 licenses for private HEIs were issued by the Ministry of Education and Science in 1991–1992. However, many of these were very short-lived and closed down within a year or two as shown in Fig. 7.2 below. The number decreased to 93 by 1993, but in the following years many more private HEIs were established for a total of 172 by 2004–2005. As Georgia had no history of managing a private higher education sector, there was no regulatory procedure in place for authorisation or accreditation of these newly established HEIs.

The structure, profile and status of the new HEIs were very diverse. Most of them were established as for-profit organisations by entrepreneurs who saw an opportunity to gain profit under the liberalised market system. There was a large segment of not-for-profit institutions as well, such as theological academies established by the Patriarchate of Georgia in various regions. Private HEIs received funding from tuition fees as well as endowments or other funds received from private sources such as gifts or donations, and funds received through agreements with the state and other legal entities. Tuition fees, however, constituted the largest part of their budgets (Sharvashidze 2005). No public institutional funding was available until major changes in the system in 2005.

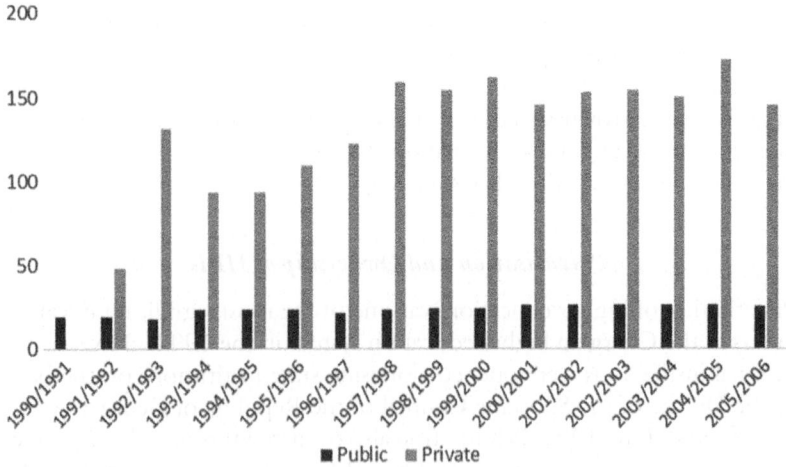

Fig. 7.2 Number of HEIs

The regional distribution of newly emerging private HEIs was another important issue. By the time of independence, almost all HEIs except for pedagogical institutes were located in Tbilisi. In the 1990s, even though the majority of new private HEIs were still located in Tbilisi, about one-third were in the regions. Figure 7.2 illustrates that while the number of private HEIs increased remarkably throughout the 1990s (with a small drop in 1995), the number of public HEIs remained stable.

On the other hand, the number of students enrolled in private universities, presented in Fig. 7.3, was much lower compared to public universities. To be more precise, at an earlier stage students at private HEIs constituted almost one-third of the entire student body. However, student numbers later dropped at private institutions and grew at public HEIs. It should be noted that the numbers presented in Figs. 7.2 and 7.3 regarding private HEIs and student numbers are only indications and should be considered with reservation. There are discrepancies in the numbers provided by the National Department of Statistics and the Ministry of Education and Science, which could result in possible inaccuracies.

The reasons for such dynamics are complex. Firstly, most of the newly established private HEIs had limited capacities due to lack of appropriate human and material resources. Facilities were in dire shape and inappropriate

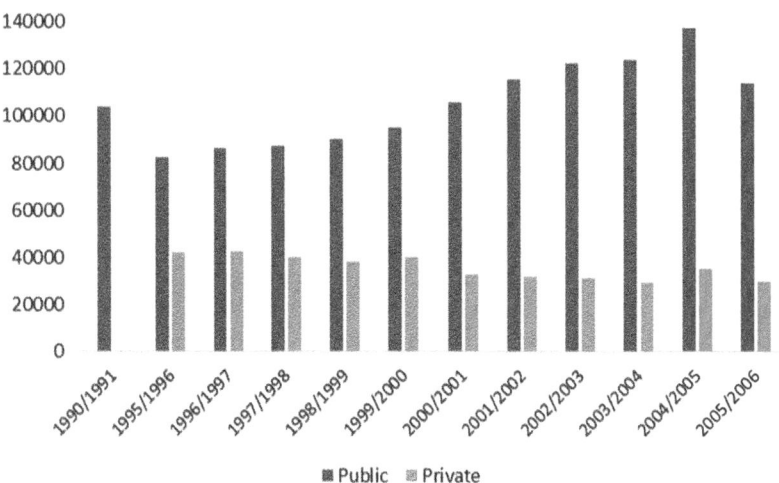

Fig. 7.3 Absolute student enrolments

for full operation. According to some accounts, about 30 per cent of all private HEIs shared premises with secondary schools or other organisations (Sharvashidze 2005).

Expansion in enrolment rates at public universities came largely at the expense of students themselves in the form of tuition fees. While in 1994–1995 fee-paying students constituted only 10.7 per cent of total enrolment, in 1997–1998 this number went up to 48 per cent and was stable till 2005. The number of students in tuition-free tracks, on the other hand, remained more or less constant.

It is important to point out that tuition fees constituted a substantial portion of income for public HEIs. In some cases, revenues received from tuition fees were more than double in volume compared to the funding provided by the state (Gvishiani and Chapman 2002).

Governance of Higher Education

As it was no longer under Soviet control, the education system was regulated by the laws of independent Georgia and supervised by the Ministry of Education. Universities enjoyed relative freedom in terms of designing teaching programmes and curricula, and in establishing tuition fees. However, the number of students admitted was still negotiated with the government. Centralised control of public HEIs was absent or weak, but this was not so much an expression of institutional autonomy as it was a result of poor governing capacity at the central administrative level. In fact, lack of unified vision and coherent national policy was a defining feature of Georgian higher education development during the first transition phase, until 2003. Most changes were restricted to the institutional level without substantively reforming the system.

One of the most prominent features of the Georgian higher education system during the 1990s and early 2000s was rampant corruption. Higher education was no exception to the common trend, as it was a deeply rooted practice in each public sector and inhibited many attempts at progress and efficiency. As testified by a series of reports and academic research (Orkodashvili 2009; Lorentzen 2000), corruption practices were present in admission procedures as well as during the academic process through different channels, most notably in the form of bribery and nepotism. The admissions exams administered by each university were a source of substantial income for those involved in the admissions process, as people were willing to pay large amounts in bribes; up to 20,000 USD in some cases, depending on the prestige of the university and the field of study. Corruption during admissions was largely limited to the tuition-free tracks in public universities. Only a very small number of top performing applicants were able to access prestigious universities or fields without paying bribes (Lorentzen 2000).

In general, the admissions system remained the same as it was during the Soviet period. Applicants were required to pass university-level, subject-specific competitive examinations. Until 2000 there was no possibility to register for examinations at different universities, thus limiting applicant chances to enrol in higher education. Once enrolled, students also had very limited opportunities to transfer to a different HEI or even to a different field of study.

The study structure remained unchanged until the late 1990s. This meant that the course of study in all universities and all departments consisted of five years, after which a graduate received a specialist diploma in the particular field. Those who wanted to work towards an academic degree stayed in the university or moved to a research institution.

As early as 1996, universities began shifting towards an Anglo-Saxon education model with a two-tier system comprised of a four-year bachelor cycle and a two-year master cycle. This was an attempt to bring the system closer to the standards of the Bologna Process. However, for a very long time this formal change did not translate into a fundamental reorientation of the system. In the initial stages of system transformation, the previous single-track five-year study programme was simply split without adapting the contents (Lorentzen 2000). This did not change until almost ten years later when the country formally joined the Bologna Process.

Rank and Prestige of Georgian HEIs

The issue of increasing access to higher education is tied to the question of returns to education. As attainment rates grow, returns might remain the same, they might shrink, or they might be affected differently based on the type and prestige of the degree. The ranking of universities according to quality is a helpful tool for both applicants and their parents wishing to distinguish themselves, as well as for employees wishing to recruit candidates with the best skills. But, it is difficult to assess whether higher-ranking universities actually help students develop better skills, or whether they receive 'better' applications in the first place because they are highly selective. In this respect, the argument resembles the distinction between 'human capital' and 'signalling' approaches to analysing returns to higher education.

In Soviet Georgia, as well as in the 1990s, there was an informal distinction between HEIs based on quality and prestige. It is hard to evaluate what exactly constituted the main reasons for HEI prestige during the Soviet period. However, since all HEIs except TSU were highly specialised, institutional prestige was strongly linked to the prestige of the discipline. For example, the Medical Institute was very prestigious as doctors enjoyed a high social status. The Institute of Foreign Languages was another popular HEI, albeit mostly for females. The Agrarian Institute and to a lesser extent the Polytechnic Institute, on the other hand, were considered less popular. Also within Tbilisi State University (TSU), certain disciplines were much more prestigious than others.

In the 1990s when all HEIs whether public or private introduced considerable disciplinary diversity, the situation changed and disciplinary competition was transformed into institutional competition. There were huge differences between the newly emerging private universities. As Pachuashvili (2009) describes, most small private HEIs served to simply absorb the demand for 'more education'. At the same time, by the end of the 1990s, a small group of more prestigious private HEIs had emerged. The success and prestige of these selected few private institutions was perhaps determined by the availability of extensive financial resources, and hence the possibility to attract better teaching staff for higher pay as well as offering better-equipped facilities. In many cases these prestigious private HEIs were co-funded by international foundations, donor organisations and large private companies. These HEIs were highly selective and completion rates were quite low due to demanding requirements. Employer appreciation of diplomas from this small set of private universities was therefore very high. This, in turn, cyclically contributed to the growth of their prestige. However, even these prestigious private HEIs were more focused on skills training and less on academic and research output (Gvishiani and Chapman 2002; Pachuashvili 2009). Table 7.2 shows completion rates as well as job placement rates for graduates from these prestigious private HEIs (at that time Georgian Institute of Public Affairs, GIPA, had a very high completion rate because it initially offered only MA level courses).

Tuition-free tracks in certain disciplines at some public HEIs enjoyed the same high social ranking as the prestigious private universities listed above. These public HEIs were also popular during the Soviet period.

Table 7.2 Performances of private HEIs

HEIs	Graduation rate (%)	Job placement (%)
Georgian Institute of Public Affairs (GIPA)	97	91
European School of Business (ESM)[a]	62	87
Caucasus School of Business (CSB)[b]	89	77
International Black See University (IBSU)	87	92
Alma Mater University[c]	90	86

[a]ESM later merged with the Free University of Georgia
[b]Currently a Caucasus University School
[c]Now Grigol Robakidze University
Source: Sharvashidze (2005)

First-tier
- Prestigious private HEIs (e.g. GIPA, ESM)
- Tuition-free tracks at some departments at prestugous universities (e.g. tuition-free track, Law department at TSU)

Second-tier
- Tuition-charging tracks of prestigious departments at 'good' public HEIs
- All tuition-free departments at 'good' universities

Third-tier
- Tuition-charging departments at 'good' public HEIs
- Other public HEIs

Fourth-tier
- 'Demand-absorbing' private HEIs

Fig. 7.4 Classification of Georgian HEIs in the 1990s by prestige and rank

At public universities, prestige and rank were defined by two factors: field of study and tuition fee status. The latter was important because students were admitted to 'free' tracks solely on merit. Merit was measured by admissions examinations, which were administered by HEIs themselves and highly corrupt. Overall, selectivity at admission was arguably the most important factor defining university prestige. In terms of prestige, HEIs and programmes were roughly ranked as presented in Fig. 7.4.

Disciplinary Diversification of Georgian HE

As described above in the section on higher education in Soviet Georgia, HEIs were classified by field of study and were usually narrowly specialised. There was only one HEI with formal 'university' status, Tbilisi State University, which offered programmes in diverse disciplines ranging from humanities to hard sciences. All other HEIs were specialised in a narrow set of disciplines. The basic classification of these HEIs was into technical institutes, medical institutes, agrarian institutes, teacher training institutes and art institutes.

However, immediately after the break-up of the Soviet Union, the education system became independent from central control and this situation changed. In fact, lax regulations and the virtual absence of an appropriate legal framework gave public HEIs the freedom to transform courses of study, structure and even status. Most began to adjust the contents of their educational programmes to meet the emerging demands of young people. Already in the 1990s, law and business studies proved to be the most popular fields (Lorentzen 2000). As funding from the public budget was reduced, public HEIs offered a growing number of places in these disciplines as fee-paying tracks.

As all HEIs except TSU were previously institutes with narrow specialisations, most changed their status from institute to university in order to offer new trendy disciplines. For example, the Polytechnic Institute became the Technical University of Georgia and Tbilisi Medical Institute became Tbilisi Medical University. This was in principle merely a name change, especially since no formalised definition was in place (Sharvashidze 2005; Pachuashvili 2009).

Similarly, pedagogical institutes were transformed into universities and started to offer undergraduate and graduate programmes in a wider range of disciplines. Since most of these pedagogical institutes were located outside the capital city of Tbilisi, they effectively became regional universities. The expansion of higher education into the regions was further enhanced by the establishment of eight TSU branches in various cities throughout the country. As previously pointed out, HE sector development was not strategised or planned in detail at the national level. Institutional-level changes were initiated by HEIs themselves and negotiated with the government, often through personal connections and power networks.

Developments After 2005

From 2004, the new government of Georgia that came into power after the Rose Revolution embarked on a comprehensive reform programme. As described earlier, reforms in public governance were aimed at fighting corruption, inefficiency and inflexibility. Underlying many of these reforms were the principles of the market economy and New Public Management. Guided by the drive toward marketisation and competitiveness and encouraged by an extremely positive response from the World Bank, the International Monetary Fund and other international agencies, many public institutions were fundamentally transformed in a seemingly very short period of time.

The changes that occurred in the higher education system in Georgia at the same time were no less dramatic. The system was entirely revamped by interwoven sets of reforms. Most notable were changes in higher education funding, admission mechanisms and quality control. All the changes were closely connected and took place simultaneously. Effective as the changes were in improving efficiency and eliminating corruption, they were truly top-down reforms; they were therefore part of larger reform efforts not driven by the HEI community.

Table 7.3 presents the typology of present-day HEIs in Georgia. The following sections will describe the processes that have shaped it during the last decade.

Accreditation and Quality Assurance

The development of external and internal higher education quality assurance systems started after the adoption of a new Law of Georgia on Higher Education in 2004 and coincided with joining the Bologna Process in 2005. In addition to making the three-tier HE system compatible with international systems, the enactment of the Bologna Process ensured that HE and scientific research would be brought closer together (Bakradze 2013).

The process of institutional accreditation was initiated in 2004 by the semi-autonomous National Accreditation Centre (later the National Quality Enhancement Agency) under the Ministry of Education and Science. The institutional accreditation procedure involved HEI compliance with certain requirements concerning their institutional capacity and physical facilities. As a result, the number of HEIs was dramatically

Table 7.3 Current typology of Georgian HEIs

Type of HEI	Research	Prestige	Disciplinary diversity	HEIs in this category
Leading public comprehensive universities	Integrated	High	Wide	TSU, Ilia State University
Leading private comprehensive universities	Integrated	High	Medium to wide	Free University, Black Sea International University, Caucasian University, GIPA, Georgian-American University
Specialised universities	Integrated	Medium to high	Narrow to medium	Tbilisi State Medical University, Agrarian University, Tvildiani Medical University, Academy of Arts, Theatre and Film University, Conservatory, Georgian Aviation University
Comprehensive universities	Integrated	Medium	Medium to wide	Georgian Technical University, University of Georgia, Robakidze University, Davit Aghmashenebeli University of Georgia, Saint Andria University
Highly specialised public teaching universities	Partly integrated	Medium	Narrow	Ministry of Internal Affairs Academy, Defence Academy
Regional comprehensive universities	Integrated	Medium	Medium to wide	Batumi State University, Gogebashvili University, Samtskhe-Javakheti University, Kutaisi State University, Sokhumi State University
Teaching universities	Partly integrated	Low	Medium to wide	All other teaching universities
Colleges	Not integrated	Low	Medium	All colleges

reduced. As shown in Fig. 7.5, so was the number of newly enrolled students, as the state imposed a cap on public university admission; this cap was among the accreditation requirements.

In 2010, the system was modified and since then universities have been required to obtain mandatory authorisation to operate as institutions. In addition, they can apply for the accreditation of individual programmes in order to be eligible for public funding to support students enrolled in those programmes. Although programme accreditation is not compulsory, HEIs are interested in this option because programmes with public funding are expected to attract more students.

Figure 7.5 also shows that the number of universities and enrolments has bounced back somewhat. This is because when the accreditation procedures were initially introduced in 2005, many HEIs were not ready to meet the new requirements; they have since adjusted their practices over time. Additionally, it can be argued that authorisation procedures are milder than those for institutional accreditation (Darchia 2013).

As described above, joining the Bologna Process in 2005 was a step towards transforming the higher education system into a three-cycle structure that would be easily recognised and comparable at the international level. By introducing research projects into the first and second cycles of higher education as well as introducing doctoral education, the Law of

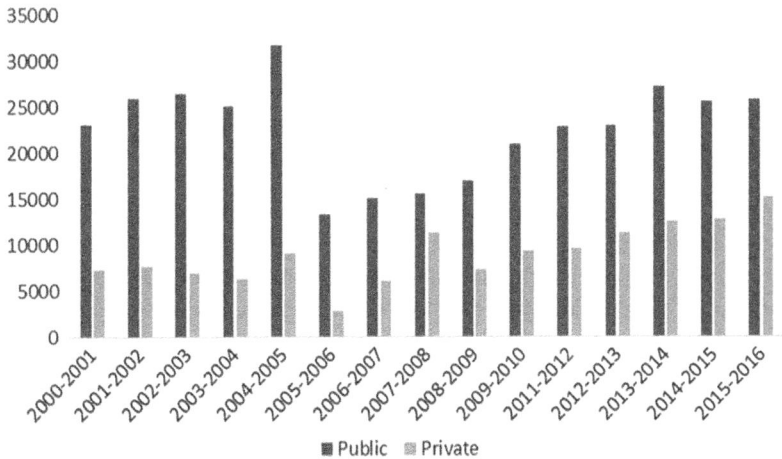

Fig. 7.5 Number of admitted students in HEIs

Georgia on Higher Education created a legal basis for integration of the higher education and science systems. PhD studies became an important element by integrating higher education and research.

As a result, all HEIs in Georgia are currently divided into groups by level of education and the degree of research and teaching integration. Universities offer bachelor, master and doctoral programmes; teaching universities offer master and bachelor programmes; and colleges offer only bachelor-level programmes. Accordingly, universities combine research and teaching, while teaching universities and colleges are solely focused on teaching. Such classification presents a remarkable break from the Soviet tradition, which considered HEIs primarily as places for teaching while most research was conducted at the Academy of Sciences.

Admissions Exams

Introducing centralised standardised examinations—Unified National Examinations (UNEs)—in 2005 was the single most important measure implemented by the government to fight corruption during the admissions process. Another major goal of introducing UNEs was to improve access for disadvantaged but talented students, as admission would be meritocratic. It was believed that the previous system disproportionately favoured those coming from families with ample financial resources and social capital. UNEs replaced exams previously administered by individual universities and became the sole admissions criterion (with minor exceptions, discussed below). The exams are administered in Georgian or English and focus on the relevant subject discipline (based on the study area selected by the applicant) and general aptitudes (verbal and mathematic). Seats are allocated based on the results. Another novelty of UNEs is that applicants became free to apply to several universities and various departments at the same time, unlike the previous system under which they had only one choice.

Since the introduction of UNEs, the number of admitted students as a percentage of the total number of school-leavers has been growing. The number of students applying to universities has increased as well: currently about 60 per cent of students from the relevant age-cohort register for UNEs and over 45 per cent are admitted.

UNEs continue to be one of the most well-received reform measures, widely supported by the public as well as representatives from the full political spectrum. A number of reports and research projects show that UNEs have effectively addressed the issue of corruption (Karosanidze and

Christensen 2005; Orkodashvili 2009). It is more difficult to assess whether or not the second goal of promoting equal chances for access has been achieved. This is due to lack of data on the social background of admitted students as well as lack of pre-UNE data. However, there are indications that the system still favours those from advantaged backgrounds, especially where funding is concerned, as elaborated in the subsequent sections.

There are legitimate concerns that the examination system results in 'teaching to the test' in the final years of secondary school. The International Institute for Education Policy, Planning and Management carried out a study which reports that the large majority of students attend private tutoring classes in their final secondary school years to better prepare for the test (Machabeli et al. 2011).

Furthermore, lack of HEI involvement in the admissions process is a serious issue. UNEs currently provide a necessary and sufficient channel to enrol in any HEI. Therefore, HEIs themselves have no authority to select students based on their own criteria and preferences. Interestingly, however, there was no opposition from HEIs against such a drastic imposition on their agency. This could have been the result of a heavy-handed approach adopted by the government in 2005 to fight corruption. However, a decade later, the time seems ripe to reconsider the admissions policies and give universities the right to decide which students they want to admit.

One side effect of the UNE is that it allowed for the division of universities by selection standards to be more standardised throughout the country. It is now possible to rank HEIs by level of selectivity with average UNE scores received for enrolled students. In her study on the effect of rural residence on university admissions, Chankseliani (2013) divides all HEIs into five categories based on mean student scores on three compulsory examinations. Such informal ranking of HEIs by average UNE scores has become popular. As the Examination Centre annually announces the highest scoring students and the HEIs in which they are enrolled, this evaluation of HEI rank and prestige is self-reinforcing.

Funding

Public expenditure on education as a share of GDP and as a share of total government spending remains among the lowest in the region. Despite the fact that overall public expenditure increased from 2004 onwards, the relative share of education has hardly changed. The share of education spending has varied between 2 and 3 per cent of GDP since 2000, and more recently the share of public spending on higher education has been estimated at around 1.2 per cent (Salmi and Andguladze 2012).

The introduction of standardised examinations coincided with a fundamental change in the higher education funding system. This change, in line with the government's liberal economic ideology, was carried out in two major ways. Firstly, the funding mode changed to exclusively per capita; secondly, the overall share of private (household) costs in funding higher education increased (Chakhaia 2013).

The government of Georgia has substantively changed its funding mechanisms to increase transparency and efficiency in allocating public resources. Previously, funds were allocated to HEIs based on several factors including number of students and staff, specific needs including capital repair, and negotiations and connections. This system was gradually replaced by one under which funds are allocated only to students who qualify for public funding as a result of UNE scores. The state established a ceiling for tuition fees at national universities and admitted students were awarded study grants based on UNE scores in the amount of 100 per cent, 70 per cent, 50 per cent, 30 per cent or 0 per cent of the maximum public university tuition. Those not able to secure 100 per cent funding have to cover the remaining costs themselves. Only about 30 per cent of all admitted students are currently receiving grants, and only about 5 per cent receive grants for 100 per cent. This effectively means that the overwhelming share of HE funding costs are generally borne by students and their families (Chakhaia 2013).

A major innovation and a step towards the economic liberalisation of the system was to include private universities in this scheme. Students who enrol in private universities are also entitled to state grants, conditional to their performance on the national exams. This way, private universities also receive state funding. Alongside improving transparency and efficiency, the system was designed to increase competitiveness among universities (both public and private), as attracting more students means receiving more funding.

A similar approach was used for funding research: direct allocations for research institutions were slowly replaced by competitive research grants based on quality criteria administered by a semi-independent agency under the Ministry of Education and Science of Georgia (MoES). Previously, research institutes (within the Academy of Science) received lump-sum funding. Such modification of the funding process for research activities additionally strengthens the research component at HEIs and supports the integration of research and instruction.

Conclusions

The development of the Georgian higher education system during the last 25 years has closely followed changes in the political and socioeconomic life of the country. Throughout the chapter, we have emphasised the usefulness of dividing this development trajectory into two periods: from 1991 to 2004, and from 2004 to the present.

The first period was characterised by somewhat haphazard and chaotic system development, as well as relative HEI freedom and lack of concerted reform effort. Governance of higher education, in fact, reflected the general pattern of public governance in the country: rampant corruption, lax regulations and lack of vision for development. It can be argued that during the period, particularly during the first years of independence, higher education developed in a legal and regulatory void.

The changes observed in higher education before 2004 were therefore largely determined by economic factors (i.e. transition to the market economy) and related changes in labour demand. The spectacular growth of private HEIs resulted from unrestricted supply without governmental regulations as a response to the growing demand for university education. Public HEIs were perhaps a little late in recognising the market potential of admitting fee-paying students. Both public and private HEIs had the freedom to adjust their programmes in accordance with market demands. Weak or absent quality assurance mechanisms were conducive to such developments.

Radical changes to this lax approach took place with the arrival of a new government in November 2003. With overwhelming support from the electorate and a vow to increase transparency and efficiency, sweeping reforms based on market principles were introduced in all public sectors. Higher education was a flagship of this crusade against corruption and inefficiency. Quality assurance mechanisms were introduced, corruption was eradicated and competition was encouraged. However, HEIs themselves have remained passive receivers of change throughout the process, as the changes were centrally planned and implemented.

Note

1. As opposed to the previously existing system under which all student studies were subsidised from the public budget.

References

Bakradze, L. 2013. *Strategic Development of Higher Education and Science – Integration of Teaching and Research*. Tbilisi: EPPM.
Chakhaia, L. 2013. *Funding and Financial Management of Educational Research*. Tbilisi: Education Policy, Planning and Management.
Chankseliani, M. 2013. Rural Disadvantage in Georgian Higher Education Admissions: A Mixed-Methods Study. *Comparative Education Review* 57: 424–456.
Darchia, I. 2013. *Strategic Development of Higher Education and Science in Georgia – Quality Assurance*. Tbilisi: EPPM.
Gvishiani, N., and D. Chapman. 2002. *Republic of Georgia: Higher Education Sector Study*. Washington, DC: The World Bank.
Karosanidze, T., and C. Christensen. 2005. A New Beginning for Georgia's University Admissions. In *Stealing the future. Corruption in the classroom. Ten real life experiences*. Georgia: Transparency International.
Lorentzen, J. 2000. *Georgian Education Sector Study – The Higher Education System*. Background paper. Washington, DC.: World Bank.
Machabeli, G., T. Bregvadze, and R. Apkhazava. 2011. *Examining Private Tutoring Phenomenon in Georgia*. Tbilisi: The International Institute for Education Policy, Planning and Management.
Mitra, P., and M. Selowsky. 2002. *Transition, the First Ten Years: Analysis and Lessons for Eastern Europe and the Former Soviet Union*. Washington, DC: World Bank.
OECD. 2011. *Development in Eastern Europe and the South Caucasus: Armenia, Azerbaijan, Georgia, Republic of Moldova and Ukraine*. OECD. Available from http://public.eblib.com/choice/publicfullrecord.aspx?p=746588
Orkodashvili, M. 2009. Corruption in Higher Education: Causes, Consequences, Reforms. *Online Submission*.
Pachuashvili, M. 2009. *The Politics of Higher Education: Governmental Policy Choices and Private Higher Education in Post-Communist Countries*. Budapest: Department of Political Science, Central European University.
Perkins, G. 1998. The Georgian Education System: Issues for Reform Management. In *Background Paper for the 1998 Georgia Education Sector Strategy Note*. Washington, DC: Europe and Central Asia Region, Human Development Unit, World Bank.
Salmi, J., and N. Andguladze. 2012. *Tertiary Education Governance and Financing in Georgia*. Unpublished.
Savelyev, A.Y., V.M. Zuyev, and A.I. Galagan. 1990. *Higher Education in the USSR*. Bucharest: CEPES.
Sharvashidze, G. 2002. Private Higher Education in Georgia: Main Tendencies. *Case Study Carried Out Under the IIEP Research Project on Structural Reforms in Higher Education: Private Higher Education*.

Sharvashidze, G. 2005. *Private Higher Education in Georgia: Main Tendencies*. Paris: UNESCO.

Transparency International. 2002. *Transparency International Corruption Perception Index Report*. Berlin: Transparency International.

World Bank. 2009. *Georgia Poverty Assessment*. Washington, DC: World Bank.

Lela Chakhaia is a doctoral researcher at European University Institute in Florence, Italy. She has extensive professional experience working for the Ministry of Education and Science of Georgia, UNICEF, Ilia State University, and so on. Her research interests include social stratification in post-soviet countries, inequalities in educational attainment and expansion of higher education.

Tamar Bregvadze is an Associate Professor at Ilia State University. At the same time, she is the member of the research team at Georgian National Examination Center coordinating a number of international and national educational assessments.

Open Access This chapter is distributed under the terms of the Creative Commons Attribution 4.0 International License (http://creativecommons.org/licenses/by/4.0/), which permits use, duplication, adaptation, distribution and reproduction in any medium or format, as long as you give appropriate credit to the original author(s) and the source, provide a link to the Creative Commons license and indicate if changes were made.

The images or other third party material in this chapter are included in the chapter's Creative Commons license, unless indicated otherwise in a credit line to the material. If material is not included in the chapter's Creative Commons license and your intended use is not permitted by statutory regulation or exceeds the permitted use, you will need to obtain permission directly from the copyright holder.

CHAPTER 8

Looking at Kazakhstan's Higher Education Landscape: From Transition to Transformation Between 1920 and 2015

Elise S. Ahn, John Dixon, and Larissa Chekmareva

In the past 25 years, Kazakhstan has undergone a period of rapid education reform. As it began transitioning from a Soviet Republic to an independent nation-state, President Nursultan Nazarbayev and the Kazakhstani government made it clear that the lynchpin to becoming a globally competitive market economy was education (Aitzhanova et al. 2014). Ideologically, this focus signified a watershed moment, as the philosophical underpinnings of Soviet higher education (HE) were uprooted, with the transition toward a market economy. However, this process of reforming Kazakhstan's HE system is situated amidst significant demographic, sociocultural and political shifts which have taken place in the last two decades.

E. S. Ahn (✉)
University of Wisconsin-Madison International Division, Madison, WI, USA

J. Dixon
Department of Political Science and Public Administration, Middle East Technical University, Ankara, Turkey

L. Chekmareva
University of Massachusetts, Amherst, MA, USA

Subsequently, while the path to education reform shares similarities to that of other states of the former Soviet Union (FSU), there are idiosyncrasies particular to the Kazakhstani context.

Starting with the establishment of its first HE institutions (HEI), this chapter provides a brief historical overview of HE in Kazakhstan starting from the Soviet period. The next section examines the education reforms that have been implemented since 1991 by examining three aspects of system transformation that the contributions in this edited volume are focusing on—horizontal diversification, vertical differentiation and inter-organisational relationships (Teichler 1988). Drawing from various sources, such as archival Soviet documents, Kazakhstani MoES reports and policy papers, along with interviews with different Kazakhstani administrators and faculty members, we found that at the macro-level there have, in fact, been departures from the Soviet HE apparatus vis-à-vis regulatory reform. However, despite this, much change remains to be implemented in terms of institutional, pedagogical and research practices in order to fulfil the teaching, learning and research mission of HE. The chapter concludes with a discussion on ongoing and emerging challenges facing the Kazakhstani HE system, as well examining its Soviet HE legacy.

THE FOUNDATIONS: KAZAKHSTAN'S SOVIET HIGHER EDUCATION LEGACY

The Soviet education apparatus began developing HE in the Kazakh SSR as part of its overall massification of education project in the 1920s and the emphasis on preparing local specialists during the *korenizatsia* period. Prior to this time, no HEIs existed in the territory of present-day Kazakhstan (Froumin et al. 2014; Kyzykeyeva and Oskolkova 2011). During the first phase of HE development starting in the 1920s, five institutions were established—Bukeev, Semipalatinsk, Kazakh, Orenberg Institutes of Public Education and the Kazakh Institute of Education in Alma-Ata (Dzholdasbekov and Kuznetsov 1975). Between 1927 and 1932, 15 more HEIs were established, expanding the focus to include medicine, agriculture and livestock, such as the Veterinary-Zoo Technical Institute (1928), Kazakh State Agricultural Institute (1930) and the Kazakh Medical Institute (1931).

The following 5-year period (1933–37) saw an expansion of pedagogical institutes throughout the Kazakh SSR, including the establishment of

Kirov Kazakh State University (1934), as well as the inclusion of postgraduate (*aspirantura*) studies in different institutes (Dzholdasbekov and Kuznetsov 1975). Following World War II (1946–63), 16 more institutes were established in the Kazakh SSR, along with the Kazakh Academy of Sciences.[1] In 1959, a state-level committee was formed to centralise the HE management within the Kazakh SSR, which would then eventually become the Kazakhstani MoES (Kyzykeyeva and Oskolkova 2011). By 1975, there were 47 HEIs, which offered programmes in 175 different areas for 200,000 students (Dzholdasbekov and Kuznetsov 1975).[2]

However, not only was the HE system undergoing transition during that time, but that was situated in the broader context of education reform. One of the early challenges facing HE was a bottleneck effect; because of limited access to quality primary and secondary education, access to HE was consequently limited. Moreover, as Kyzykeyeva and Oskolkova (2011) note, students' education trajectories were also affected by the rupturing of communities in the 1930s as a result of Stalin's social engineering strategy. Additionally, because HEIs expanded so rapidly between 1928 and 1975, they faced a number of pragmatic challenges including: classroom and student housing shortages, a lack of textbooks and various teaching materials and a shortage of qualified teaching faculty (Heynemann et al. 2007; Rumyantseva 2005; Silova 2011).

Like in the other SSRs, HE in the Kazakh SSR had several aims. The first was to produce specialists who could help sustain the Soviet Union's objectives, including education goals like universal literacy and sociopolitical ones like a commitment to the party ideology. Relatedly, the second aim was to reproduce specialists who would be able to work in industries that were being developed in various territories. For example, in the Kazakh SSR, this included the oil and gas sector (Froumin et al. 2014). In this way, the horizontal landscape of HEIs was an instantiation of these two pillars—ideological and industrial—and they were centrally determined in a command economy.

However, the high degree of specialisation also consequently resulted in resource inefficiency and knowledge compartmentalisation. This knowledge compartmentalisation was seen in the allocation of institutional functions—institutes focused on teaching or conducting applied research, and academies conducted more "pure" scientific research.[3]

By the end of the Soviet period, the Kazakh SSR had 55 HEIs that enrolled 287,400 students (NIIVO 1992). Table 8.1 provides an overview

Table 8.1 Kazakhstani HEIs (AY1988–89)

HEIs by academic focus	Quantity	Enrolled students
Engineering	12	80,989
Transport	2	7,153
Agriculture	7	40,455
Economy/law	3	18,452
Education	23	104,516
Health, medicine, sport	6	23,477
Arts	2	1,836
Total	55	276,878

Source: Narodnoe Obrazovanie i Kultura v USSR (1989, p. 142, 202)

of the institutional specialisations that were inherited by the nascent Kazakhstani government.

While no official taxonomy is available regarding the types of institutions and the corresponding quantity, Table 8.2 provides a general taxonomy of the types of HEIs that the Kazakhstani MoES inherited.

Al Farabi Kazakh National University (originally Kirov Kazakh State University) is the oldest university in the country and was the only HEI that could be considered a "classical" university with its multiple Faculties and Departments and an enrolment of 12,909 students (1988) (Moskva-Finansy i Statistika Razdel 1989). Most of the other HEIs could be categorised as either regional institutes or specialised institutes that were subject to shared oversight by the MoES and another Ministry (e.g., the Ministry of Transport, Internal Affairs or Defense). Regional institutes were primarily defined by geographical distribution, for example, pedagogical institutes were established throughout the country. This is in contrast to specialised institutes which, as mentioned earlier, were sector-specific—oil and gas, engineering and so on.

In sum, the Soviet HE legacy in the Kazakh SSR included: a system which was fundamentally undergirded by political ideology; isolation from international trends and practices, because of its ideological underpinnings; poor financing, which led to slow innovation; and systemically, the emphasis on specialisations, which were linked to the Soviet's raw economy (Rudista 2004). However, this legacy also included the network of 55 HEIs, of which the majority were engineering and pedagogy institutes, which provided the nascent Kazakhstani government a point of departure in 1991.

Table 8.2 Types of Kazakhstani HEIs in AY1990–91

HEI type (quantity)	Example	Location	Affiliation	Research activity
National university (2)	Al Farabi Kazakh National University[a]	Almaty	MoES	Pure
Regional institutes (24)	Kostanay Pedagogical Institute	Kostanay	MoES	Applied research/teaching only
Specialised institutes (29)	Kokshetau Technical Institute of the MoES Kazakhstan[b]	Kokshetau	Ministry of Internal Affairs; MoES	Applied research/teaching only

Note:
[a]The other university in the Kazakh SSR was Karaganda State University as noted earlier. It should be noted that while Karaganda State University did have the status of university, it was smaller in terms of number of faculties and student enrolment in comparison to Al Farabi Kazakh National University.

[b]See http://www.kti-tjm.kz/nash_instityt.html

THE EARLY YEARS: HIGHER EDUCATION REFORM IN THE 1990S

The dissolution of the Soviet Union brought about significant social, political and economic changes in Kazakhstan. Economically, from 1991 to 1996 the country's Gross Domestic Product dropped 39%, resulting in an overall collapse of the country's economy (World Bank 2005). But despite seemingly grim prospects, the economy eventually began recovering around 1999 and by 2007, achieved an annual growth rate of 10% and higher (Pomfret 2014). However, in spite of steady growth, Kazakhstan has not been exempt from the global economic downturn in the 2000s. Unsustainable levels of currency exchange rate control by the Kazakhstani Central Bank, combined with plummeting oil prices and economic sanctions on the Russian Federation starting in 2014, led to the de-dollarisation of Kazakhstan's currency, the tenge, and floated the exchange rate. This resulted in three significant rounds of currency devaluation (2009, 2014 and 2015). Consequently, the inflation forecast for 2016 is now 7.9% with a predicted GDP growth of 3.3% (Asian Development Bank n.d.).

Demographically, as the economy struggled, birth rates declined in the 1990s. This declining birth rate was reversed in the early 2000s, a shift which corresponds to the country's economic recovery and a period of relative sociopolitical stability as seen in Fig. 8.1.

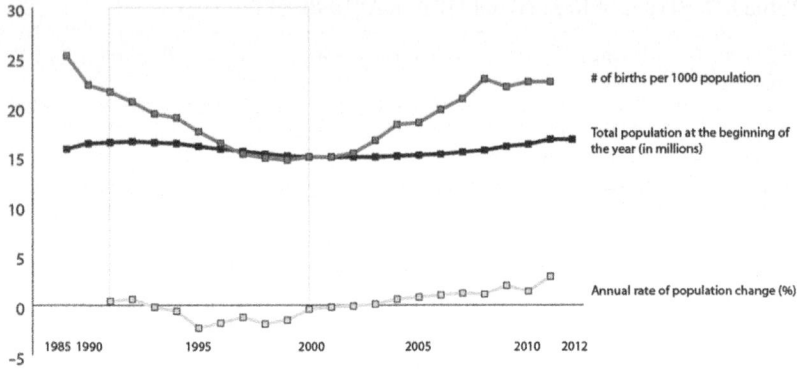

Fig. 8.1 Demographic trends (1985–2012) (Source: Adopted from the Agency of Statistics of the Republic of Kazakhstan (2013))

Socioculturally, with the establishment of its new Constitution in 1995, the Kazakhstani government began constructing a new civic identity.[4] This began by privileging the titular Kazakh language as the official state language, moving toward the conflation of an ethnic Kazakh and Kazakhstani civic identity.[5] This has resulted in changes in the language of instruction (LOI) in all schools—there was a shift in the LOI at the primary, secondary and tertiary level from Russian toward Kazakh (and more recently, the additional inclusion of English as the LOI).

In the 1990s, the Kazakhstani government began implementing a system-wide education reform amidst wide-scale sociopolitical-cultural reforms. The government's focus at the time was primarily on creating a regulatory structure that could create the conditions under which education reform could take place. The Constitution (1995) established the right to compulsory education for all Kazakhstani citizens, the Law on Education (1992) and the Law on Higher Education (1993),[6] along with other regulations and standards (Yakavets 2014). What did not change immediately was who "owned" education—HE remained a state-owned enterprise. Consequently, this meant that the government maintained the all-encompassing centralised control that had existed under the Soviet regime (Sarinzhipov 2013).

Figure 8.2 provides an overview of the main foci of the regulations initiated between 1991 and 2015.

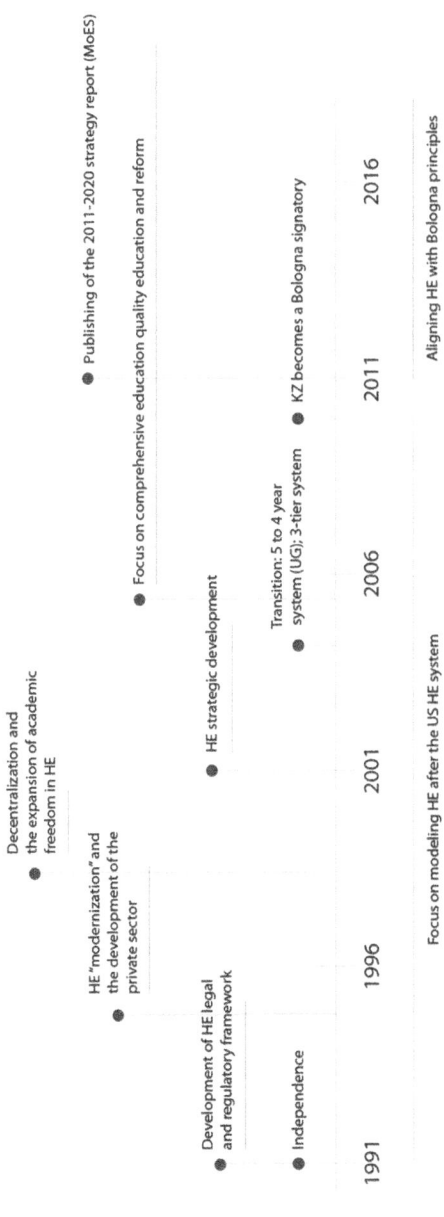

Fig. 8.2 Education reform timeline (1991–2020) (Source: Adopted from OECD (2007, 112))

Although there were a number of departures from the Soviet HE system and orientation in the new legislation and regulations, the most significant was the opening of private HEIs. The 1993 legislation "On Higher Education" permitted private universities to operate in Kazakhstan (albeit under the auspices of all MoES regulations).[7] During AY1990–91, there were 55 public HEIs. After the 1993 law was passed, 32 more HEIs opened, the majority of which were private (Sulima 2008). By AY1996–97, 43.2% of the HEIs were public and 56.8% were private (OECD 2007)—this distribution stayed similar through AY2013–14 (MoES 2014). The distribution of students enrolled in public and private HEIs was also similar (although there was some fluctuation). For example, in AY2012–13, 49.1% of students were enrolled in public HEIs. By AY2014–15, this percentage shifted, with 48.3% of students enrolled in public HEIs and 50.3% enrolled in private HEIs (MoES 2015). So while the proliferation of private HEIs was initially permitted through the enabling of regulatory reform, as seen in the enrolment distribution, there was a corresponding demand by Kazakhstanis who felt that acquiring a HE degree was essential to being employed in the new economic world order as demonstrated in Fig. 8.3.

Figure 8.3 reveals that the patterns of growth in student enrolment and the number of HEIs are similar. There are upward trends in both graphs with a particular peak in between AY2004–07. However, since then, there has been a decline in both the number of HEIs and enrolment due to increased accountability from the MoES (HEI decline) and demographic decrease (student enrolment). But despite these social and institutional shifts, the opening of HE to the private sector helped absorb the demand for HE particularly in the first 15 years of the Republic.

With an increased HE demand and the establishment of 114 HEIs in the 1990s, it is plausible to expect that geographical access to HE would have increased. This, however, did not happen. During the Soviet period, HEIs were primarily located in major urban areas (e.g., Almaty, previously Alma-Ata) or in oblasts with particular raw material factories (e.g., East Kazakhstan). However, when looking at the distribution of HEIs in the 1990s, the majority were established in Almaty city because it was previously the capital of the Kazakh SSR and for the first few years of independent Kazakhstan. Figure 8.4 shows that although Almaty is no longer the capital, it still has the highest proportion of HEIs in the country.

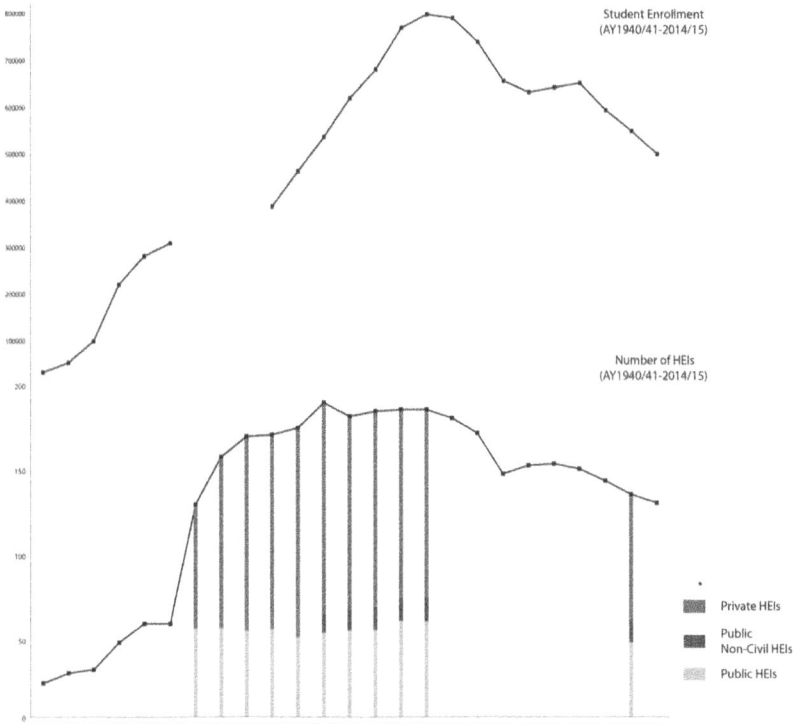

Fig. 8.3 HEI trends over time by institutions 1940–2014 (Sources: Adopted from Brunner and Tillett (n.d.); MoES (2014, 2015); Ministry of Economics (2015); Moskva-Finansy i Statistika [Moscow Finance and Statistics] (1989, 202); OECD (2007, 40); Zhakenov (n.d.))

Thus, in terms of the horizontal institutional diversification of HE after independence, although it remained completely under the auspices of the government through the MoES under the Law "On Education" (1993, 1997), the 1993 law did initially facilitate the establishment of private universities. This helped introduce financial diversity into the previously solely, state-funded sector. In turn, the proliferation of new private HEIs, along with the creation of new universities as a result of merging different institutes, helped to absorb the mass demand for HE.

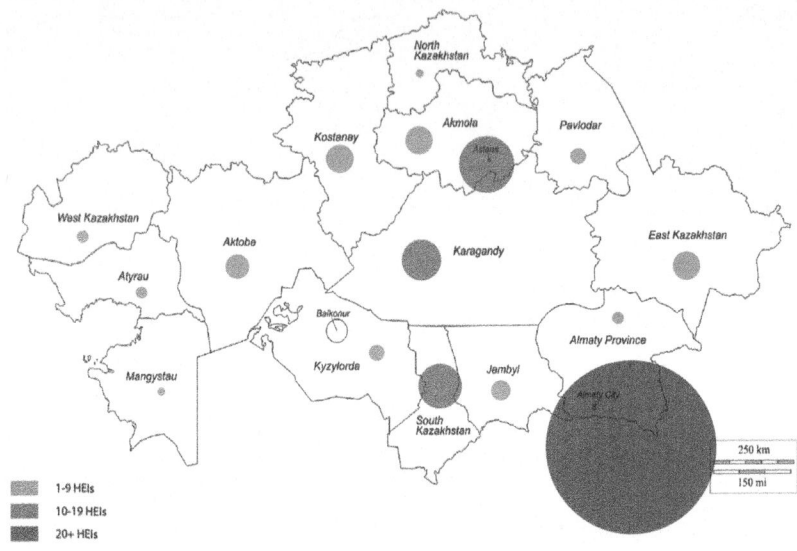

Fig. 8.4 Distribution of universities in Kazakhstan in AY2014–15 (Source: MoES (2015))

THE PRIVATISATION OF HE AND THE MODERNISATION OF HE: THE 2000S

While the 1990s introduced private HEIs into the system, the year 2000 began the process of privatising public HEIs. The general privatisation process of state-owned enterprises initiated in the 1990s was then extended to select HEIs with the passing of the law "On the List of the Republican State Enterprises and Institutions to be Privatised in 2000–01". The result was that 12 public HEIs became joint-stock companies (JSCs)[8]—a scheme where the Kazakhstani government shares ownership with other shareholders, which could be a private individual(s) or corporation. The privatisation of HEIs was (and continues to be) an attempt to diversification of the funding of higher education by introducing new revenue streams (including student tuition fees). Consequently, the privatisation of HEIs continued the process of horizontal HE diversification.

At that time, eight universities were given the status of "National University"—Al-Farabi Kazakh National University, Gumilyov Eurasian

National University, Kazakh National Agrarian University, K.I. Satpayev Kazakh National Technical University, S.D. Asfendiyarov Kazakh National Medical University, T.K. Zhurgenov Kazakh National Academy of Arts, Kurmangazy Kazakh National Conservatory and the Kazakh National University of Arts.

Thus, after diversifying the Kazakhstani HE horizontal institutional landscape with the inclusion of the private sector, the MoES then moved toward creating greater vertical differentiation. Generally, the type of HEI is determined by the institution's licencing, which is based mainly on the number of faculties that institution has—HEIs with three or more faculties can apply to become a university, while those with less than three are designated as an institute. An academy was a HEI that usually had one specialisation (e.g., the Academy of Civil Aviation). However, there are further distinctions which can be made via special Presidential Orders as seen above since the aforementioned Order granted eight universities the status of "National University". National universities are public HEIs that teach a wide gamut of programmes that have made a contribution to HE in the country.

Subsequently, 18 HEIs were established as regional centres of teaching learning (Zhankenov n.d.). These were also categorised as "state universities". Many of these regional or state universities were institutes that were merged in the 1990s in order to provide a diversity of taught program offerings and ultimately to attract more students. Table 8.3 is an overarching taxonomy of HEI types based on institutional mandate and scope and does not include all the different ways Kazakhstani HEIs are classified.

As the MoES continues with institutional privatisation and by extension, with the move toward a free market HE environment, it requires all HEIs to collect a percentage of the student fees which varies by institution in order to prepare them for eventual financial independence. Other policies and practices have been introduced to create an even "playing field" and to increase inter-institutional competition.

A significant part of increasing competition in the HE sector was the need to create a more transparent student admissions process (for both students and HEIs). In the 1990s, Kazakhstani HEIs were initially allowed to admit students based on their academic background and performance and how that fits with an institution's specialisation. In 2001, a new quality assurance system was implemented by the MoES, resulting in the establishment of the Committee for Supervision and Attestation; the National

Table 8.3 HEIs by type based on the law "On Education" (2007)

Type	Description	Example
	Universities	
National research university	A HEI which has a special status and programme of development for 5 years approved by the government, independently developed educational training programmes of higher education in three and more groups of specialties, using the outcome of pure and applied studies for generating, and in the transfer of, new knowledge	Al Farabi Kazakh National University (Almaty)
Research university	A HEI which implements programmes of development for 5 years, approved by the government and educational training programmes of higher education, in three and more groups of specialties. It uses the outcome of pure and applied studies for generating, and in the transfer of, new knowledge	Not defined
University	A HEI that implements educational programmes of higher education, master and doctoral programmes in three and more groups of specialties, carries out pure and applied research and is a scientific and methodological centre	Suleyman Demirel University (Kaskalen)
	Academy	
Academy	An educational institution that implements educational programmes of HE in one or two groups of specialties	Academy of Civil Aviation (Almaty)
	Institutes	
National higher education institute	A HEI which is a leading scientific and methodological centre in the country with a special status	Not defined
Institute	An institution that implements professional educational programmes of HE	Atyrau Institute of Oil and Gas (Atyrau)

Source: Law "On Education" (2007); National Tempus Office (2012)

Centre for Educational Quality Assessment; the National Accreditation Centre; the Centre for Certification, Quality Management and Consulting; and the National Centre of State Standards for Education and Tests (OECD 2007). To combat public perceptions regarding corruption linked to university admission, the Unified National Test (UNT) (*Edinoe*

Nacional'noe Testirovanie)—a 3-hour university entrance test and also an upper secondary school completion assessment—was developed for AY2003–04.[9] High scorers on the UNT would be guaranteed admittance to a public university and could receive a full scholarship via state grants. An alternative test—the Comprehensive Test (CT)—was later developed for students who attended: a non-Kazakh/non-Russian language of instruction secondary school, a school abroad but wanted to attend a Kazakhstani university or a vocational/technical secondary school but decided to enter university.

However, while the establishment of these tests addressed issues regarding the perceived corruption connected to university entrance by providing a more standardised measure of academic ability, there remain some unresolved issues. Neither test was or is calibrated to international university entrance standards. Consequently, students who take the UNT or the CT cannot use the scores earned toward admission into universities outside of Kazakhstan. From an assessment standpoint, they have been criticised because of their lack of subject matter depth due to the limits of the current format—30 multiple choice questions per section in 5 subject areas with an emphasis on language.[10]

A student's performance on the UNT not only has implications for their HE admission but also to whether students qualify for a government scholarship. These scholarships are "portable", which means that grant recipients have some choice(s) regarding which HEI they wanted to attend (EC 2010). But the government's priority areas for education and economic development, nationality and language of education determine grant availability. The other factor that is taken into consideration is membership of population categories that are under-represented in the HE student population, which include orphans, students from single-parent homes or from rural communities and young people with disabilities (EC 2010). The MoES also awards other types of scholarships for exceptionally high-achieving students (e.g., Presidential Scholarships). The MoES (2010) also established the "State Education Savings System", whereby parents can save money for their children's HE costs by providing a premium return on their savings. Note, however, HEIs can also provide different funding support to better attract students including institution-specific financial aid and loans, scholarships for high-achieving students and tuition and fee waivers or discounts.

Systemically, in AY2004–05, the Kazakhstani HE system changed from the 5-year Soviet-era bachelor degree to a 4-year degree. This was intended to facilitate increased student and faculty mobility in and out of Kazakhstan, as well as greater degree of recognition in alignment with international institutional structures (Piven and Pak 2006). This paved the way for discussions regarding the possibility of Kazakhstan joining the European Higher Education Area (EHEA). On 12 March 2010, Kazakhstan then became the first Central Asia Republic to sign the Lisbon Convention of the Bologna Process (BP) becoming its 47th signatory (Kazinform 2010).

Joining the BP has had the most comprehensive impact on the Kazakhstani HE system. Soon after joining the BP, the "State Programme of Education Development in the RoK for 2011–2020" was passed (MoES 2010). This outlined the government's plan to align all three tiers of education to international standards by the year 2020 in order to achieve its stated goal of "increasing [the] competitiveness of education and [the] development of human capital through ensuring access to quality education for sustainable economic growth" (MoES 2010, 1). The plan was comprehensive, covering everything from financing to the professional development of teacher faculty, along with intended structural and programme changes. The HE focus of this report was on re-aligning its structural, university governance and autonomy reforms to conform to BP priorities. In addition to legislation that was passed in the 1990s, the Law "On Education" (2007) and the Law "On Science" (2011) provided the legal framework that has been guiding HE reform.

In addition to system reform, one of the goals outlined in the MoES plan (2010) was the need to increase institutional and research output to meet international standards. In order to fund and support research, a number of laws have been passed, including the Law "On Science" (2001), Law "On Innovative Activities" (2003), Patent Law (2003) and the Law "On Support of Innovative Activities" (2006). In 2003, less than 100 articles were published per 10,000 researchers (Thomson n.d.; OECD 2007). The MoES (2010) stated that the goal was to have 2% of faculty members publish in international, peer-reviewed journals by 2015 and 5% by 2020. But according to MoES (2014), out of 41,636 faculty members, 541 (1.3%) have publications in international (peer-reviewed) journals. In terms of gender parity, there is an almost equal representation of genders among researchers, with the majority of researchers are in the STEM fields—Science, Technology, Engineering and Mathematics (UIS n.d.). However, in terms of researchers by sector, the HE and non-profit sectors have seen a gradual increase between 2005 and 2011 with a decrease in number of researchers in the governmental agencies (UIS n.d.).

The government remains the largest funder of research and development; it is responsible for between 25% (2011) and 61.5% (2003) of all related expenditures (UIS n.d.), which has limited the growth of research and development in HE. After independence, similar to the other post-Soviet countries, the Kazakhstani HE system faced a physically crumbling research infrastructure, in terms of laboratory space, equipment, resource centres and libraries, further constraining the ability of researchers to conduct research (MoES 2010). This is not surprising, given the reduction in the expenditure on research and development since 2003 (UIS n.d.). Relatedly, another systemic constraint on research output is the MoES's constrained funding priorities and by extension research outputs (OECD 2007). However, partnerships between international organisations like the British Council and individual universities (e.g., Al Farabi Kazakhstan National University), are moves to diversify research funding and have contributed to building deeper research capacity of Kazakhstani academics.

Another impetus for Kazakhstan joining the EHEA and committing to the implementation of BP was the internationalisation of HE through faculty and student mobility through programmes like ERASMUS MUNDUS. Systemically, this meant that HEIs would need to adopt the European Credit Transfer and Accumulation System (ECTS) and provide Diploma Supplements in order to facilitate mobility.[11] Moreover, in 1998, Kazakhstan signed an agreement between Belarus, Kyrgyzstan and Russia allowing for degree equivalence recognition, thereby increasing opportunities for student and graduate mobility between the four countries (Poletaev and Rakisheva 2011). Additionally, according to MoES (2010), as of 2010, over 20,000 Kazakhstani students had studied abroad, of whom 3000 were Bolashak scholarship holders.[12] In terms of in-bound student mobility, Kazakhstan is the second most popular destination to study in Central Asia (behind Russia) (Brunner and Tillet n.d.).

In terms of creating a more transparent system, MoES (2010) articulated a set of relevant HE policy aspirations—to establish a board of trustees at different HEIs to help provide stakeholder-informed governance, to continue the professionalisation of academic administrators (through various training programmes) and to institute a transparent rector-appointment system.[13] To support academic administrators, the MoES stated its intention of creating a comprehensive and easily accessible database of educational statistics, which would be made available to all universities to facilitate data-informed management decisions. While a database is not yet available, the MoES has been making yearly reports of aggregated HE data available on its website.[14] Also integral to the process of transforming HE provision is the development and implementation of lifelong learning through professional development opportunities for university administrators and leaders. Such training opportunities are being conducted through institutions like Nazarbayev University and KIMEP University.

Along the same vein of transparency, the proliferation of HEIs in the 1990s and 2000s is now being curbed by the emphasis on institutional quality assurance. At its peak, there were 182 HEIs in the system (2001) but by AY2015–16, there were 126 (MoES 2015). In 2011, the Independent Agency for Accreditation Rating (IAAR) was established as an independent national agency with a remit that includes the ranking of HEIs, the improving of their competitiveness, and their institutional and specialised accreditation. The Independent Quality Assurance Agency of Kazakhstan (IQAA) was established in 2012, also an independent national agency but with a remit to provide both institutional and programme accreditation for Kazakhstani HEIs. Out of the 131 universities in AY2014–15, only 3 universities (2%) had received institutional accreditation from the IAAR (www.iaar.kz), 4 (3%) from IQAA (www.iqaa.kz) and only 1 had all of its degree programmes accredited by an agency listed on the European Quality Assurance Register.[15]

While joining the BP has increased discussions regarding what constitutes "quality education", it has also foregrounded a number of policy tensions which were created in the first 20 years of education reform. One example of this is the tension between the MoES' centralised control over a significant portion of institutional operations and discourses on decentralisation and privatisation. Because one of the pillars of the BP is institutional autonomy, HEIs need to be given more procedural and substantive autonomy. "Procedural autonomy" refers to the ability for universities to make decisions related to higher-level administrative processes. "Substantive autonomy" refers to the ability to make decisions related to academic affairs. The later would include what degree programmes universities wanted to offer students and, subsequently, the curricular requirements (Soltys 2014). According to MoES (2010), it was intended that HEIs would be granted autonomy gradually—national research universities in 2015, national HEIs in 2016 and the rest by 2018. To date, this has not been the case; the exception is Nazarbayev University, which was established from its inception as an autonomous HEI by Presidential Order.[16]

Currently, the reach of the MoES still includes the types of degree programmes HEIs can offer through the list of state classifiers—HEIs cannot innovate degrees or programme titles which are not listed in the list of 342 state classifiers (OECD 2007; Sulima 2008), the standardisation of programme courses and core course curriculum through the State Compulsory Education Standards, the standardisation of faculty promotion and, for public HEIs, the constraints on tuition rates for fee-paying students. According to Sarinzhipov (2013), regardless of whether a HEI is public or private, they all need to comply with the MoES requirements regarding these aforementioned areas in order to maintain their institutional licences.

The centralised control of the MoES also affects research output. While academics need to conduct research and publish in order to receive promotion (according to the same criteria used pre-1991), there remain serious constraints on their time because of heavy teaching expectations, so faculty research output remains relatively low. Such constraints include 800–900 contact hours with students per academic year, mandatory office hours, thesis supervision, student consultations as well as being available for a variety of different activities related to university service, which are prescribed in various education laws. This, combined with low academic salaries and institutional corruption, has resulted in the phenomenon of faculty teaching at multiple universities—further limiting their time and their personal capacity to conduct original, independent research (Silova and Steiner-Khamsi 2008).

However, if the MoES does begin granting both substantive and procedural autonomy to HEIs, this would significantly change the dynamics between HEIs. Students would more freely be able to choose between meaningfully different programmes of study, educational experiences and curricula, and HEIs would have the ability to potentially innovate and engage directly with industry to produce graduates who would be able to aptly participate in the labour market.

Table 8.4 attempts to provide a comprehensive overview of the different categories that were created by the MoES to delineate and differentiate (horizontally and vertically) the emerging HE landscape between 1993 and 2010.

For potential students, such categories are important because they determine whether their choice of HE is an eligible host for a government scholarship, as well as the quality of education they might receive. But for university rectors and administrators, the categories presented in Tables 8.3 and 8.4 are marginally flexible. Private HEIs can move from being institutes to universities, but by virtue of being private, they currently cannot become national institutions. Because public HEIs are under the auspices of the MoES, there is little major institutional/structural changes which can be initiated by the institutions themselves. The table corresponding to this chapter in the Appendices provides an overview of the total number of HEIs that fit into the categories outlined in Table 8.4 as of AY2014–15.

In addition to the vertical and horizontal institutional distinctions that the MoES has made, it has also created another institutional taxonomy which highlights the university's expected research output based on the official institutional licence it has been granted. This research distinction was based on the Law "On Education" (2007). Logistically, public HEIs can be given the special status of "National University" or "National Higher Education Institute" by means of a Presidential Order. "Research University" is a title which is ostensibly open for both public and private HEIs under the auspices of the Law "On Education" (2007). However, it is noteworthy that to date, no HEI has been officially granted this status.

Table 8.4 The Kazakhstani HE landscape between 1993 and 2010

Type	Vertical	Licensing	Research	Example	Location
International	International	University		Yasawi International Kazakh-Turkish University[a]	Turkestan
Public	Autonomous National	University	x	Nazarbayev University Al Farabi Kazakh National University	Astana Almaty
		Institute			
		Academy		Academy of Public Administration under the President of the Republic of Kazakhstan	Astana
	State	University			
		Institute		Atyrau Institute of Oil and Gas	Atyrau
		Academy			
Private: JSC		University		KIMEP University	Almaty
		Institute			
		Academy		Academy of Civil Aviation	Almaty
Private		University		Almaty Management University	Almaty
		Institute		Eurasian Humanitarian Institute	Astana
		Academy		Kazakh Academy of Labor and Social Relations	Almaty

[a]Yasawi International Kazakh-Turkish University is unique because it is a joint education endeavour by the Kazakhstani and Turkish governments.

By default, then, all other HEIs fall under the conventional categories of "university", "academy" or "institute" with no official distinguishing descriptor. Table 8.5 provides an overview of the types of HEIs, profiles of exemplars and what they define as demonstrations of research in their institutional contexts.

Table 8.5 Characteristics of HEIs

Type (2015)	Type (1991)	Example	Institutional details		Education profile[*]	Research activity	International engagement
National research university	University	Al Farabi Kazakh National University Est. 1934[a]	Location Status # of students # of faculty	Almaty Public 18,000 2,000	14 faculties, 98 departments, 77 undergraduate, 80 master, 61 doctoral programmes	5 institutes, 1 science and technology park, 20 research centres	418 university partners, different university association international
Research university	Institute	Ablai Khan Kazakh University of International Relations and World Languages[**] Est. 1941[b]	Location Status # of students # of faculty	Almaty Private: JSC 4,750 135+	6 faculties, 15 undergraduate, 10 master, 3 doctoral programmes		14 different international organisations, student teaching/exchange 14 different universities
University	University	Sh. Ualikhanov Kokshetau State University Est. 1962[c]	Location Status # of students # of faculty	Kokshetau Public 5,000 345	5 faculties, 47 undergraduate, 28 master, 3 doctoral programmes	Lab, academic journal	Partnerships with universities in Germany, the USA, the UK, Malaysia, Russia
Academy	Academy	T. K. Zhurgenov Kazakh National Academy of Arts Est. 1955[d]	Location Status # of students # of faculty	Almaty Public N/A 400	6 faculties, 14 undergraduate, 13 master, 7 doctoral programmes	Creative production—performances, film production, etc.	63 universities in South Korea, Japan, China, EU, CIS, ME

(continued)

Table 8.5 (continued)

Type (2015)	Type (1991)	Example	Institutional details		Education profile[*]	Research activity	International engagement
National HEI	Institute	I. Altinsarin Arkalyk State Pedagogical Institute[**][c]	Location Status # of students # of faculty	Arkalyk Public – –	4 faculties, 19 undergraduate programmes		
Institute	Specialised institute	K. Satpaev Ekibastuz Engineering-Technical Institute (est. 1994)[f]	Location Status # of students # of faculty	Ekibastis Private 1,145 85	7 department, 14 undergraduate programmes	1 applied research and teaching lab	

NB: *A "faculty" [fakultet] is a group of "departments" [kafedra]; **indicates potential exemplars (not determined in an official regulation or Order)

[a] See www.kaznu.kz
[b] See www.ablaikhan.kz
[c] See http://kgu.kz/main/en/universitet
[d] See http://www.kaznai.kz/
[e] See http://www.api.kz/
[f] See http://citiekb.kz/index.php?option=com_content&view=category&layout=blog&id=11&Itemid=125

Conclusion

While joining the BP should lead to greater convergence across the EHEA, Kazakhstani HE has been embedded in a dynamic sociopolitical cultural context. For example, because the birth rate had declined in the 1990s (Fig. 8.1), HE enrolment is expected to decline from 2011 until around 2025. According to OECD (2007), the number of university-aged young people is expected to fall from 180,000 (2010) to below 120,000 (2025)—a 33% decline over 15 years. Even with the MoES's efforts to close for-profit diploma mill universities between 2001 and 2015, Kazakhstan's demographic drop-off has had serious implications for faculty and staffing at the remaining 126 HEIs, since the majority of Kazakhstani HEIs are private and since all institutions are expected to be financially autonomous by 2020.

From a systemic perspective, the Kazakhstani government has begun implementing many of the Bologna action points since joining the EHEA in 2010. Most notably, it has done the following: developed a necessary legal infrastructure; mapping out governmental and national-level organisational charts; and an array of procedural and substantive university autonomy and reform policies. But despite the plethora of HE reforms proposals and initiatives, there are a number of broad ranging challenges that the MoES continues to face, as Kazakhstan continues to navigate its way through its radical HE reform agenda (Heynemann 2010). For example, the "proliferation of actions, the plethora of agencies and committees and the frequent changes in the related regulations and processes are confusing and overburdening HE stakeholders" (OECD 2007, 117–118). This "proliferation of actions" and constant change are evident even in the way the MoES has been articulating its vision for an HE institutional infrastructure as seen in the MoES different organisational taxonomies presented in Tables 8.4 and 8.5.

Shifts in Kazakhstan's language policies also continue to change the linguistic context in which education is taking place. In AY1990–91, there was a greater percentage of students studying in Russian as compared to Kazakh. According to MoES (2014, 2015), there continues to be a shift in student enrolment from Russian to Kazakh-medium HEIs with a small, but growing number of enrollees in English-medium HEIs (2.6%) in AY2014–15 (MoES 2015).

What remains the most idiosyncratic element of Kazakhstani HE is the role of the government in making decisions regarding HE with little or no transparency. Despite the existence of education governance in the form of the MoES, moves toward greater transparency and (imminent) institutional autonomy, in actuality, Presidential Orders have been used to establish HEIs—L.I. Gumilyov Eurasian National University, KIMEP University and Nazarbayev University[17]—and have led to institutional mergers, Atyrau Institute of Oil and Gas and, most recently, the merger of K.I. Satpaev National Technical University with Kazakh-British Technical University (a JSC university).[18] The primacy of the government to make decisions in and across different sectors points to the reality that in many post-Soviet countries, despite the development of systems and infrastructure, it retains enough power to be able to establish (or dissolve) institutions, initiatives and policies with little or no stakeholder involvement or public debate.

In its first 15 years, the Kazakhstani government focused on establishing the framework for a new HE system—one that would be able to meet the needs of an emerging market economy, thereby pivoting away from the Soviet-style HE infrastructure which it inherited. It has laid the building blocks for its development through the creation of its education-related regulatory structure (1990s) and embracing the BP agenda (2000s). Moreover, it has made strides toward creating a more competitive HE landscape by allowing the establishment of private HEIs, the privatisation of existing public HEIs, and creating a more vertically differentiated structure which ostensibly acts to delineate between "elite" and "mass" HE (Trow 1970). However, areas that will lead toward long-lasting systemic and social change (e.g., curriculum content, programme structures and reporting and audit processes) still require significant amounts of reflection and change, with pre-independence HE organisational and institutional practices remaining entrenched. Moreover, because there has long been a lack of substantive stakeholder involvement in the HE reform process, there has been a lack of incentive to supporting reform implementation processes meaningfully, as evidenced by the disengagement from the reform process of both external stakeholders (business and civil society organisations) and internal stakeholders (faculty, lower- to mid-level administrators and students).

All this has been further problematised by the global economic crisis since 2009, particularly because of the recent downward trend in prices of oil and other natural resources, and the continued devaluation of the Kazakhstani tenge, following the footsteps of the Russian ruble. This has, inevitably, shifted government into austerity mode—cutting public funding for what it deems to be non-essential and non-time sensitive educational reforms, notably, the delay of implementing twelfth grade education on a larger scale, which has long-run implications for HE reform.

While signing up for the Bologna Process has somewhat clarified the HE vision, its implementation will test the resolve of government to persevere with the post-Soviet reform package. In this sense, Kazakhstan is, itself, a twenty-first century experiment in education reform (Kucera 2014), a process that is taking place in the context of both the geopolitical uncertainties and vulnerabilities in the Central Asia region and the transitional nature of the Kazakhstani economic, social and political environments.

In sum, the legacy of the Soviet Union in Kazakhstan is ambiguous. While there have been departures in terms of institutional types and education financing, its pedagogical legacy (approaches to teaching, learning and programme content) and administrative legacy (approaches to institutional reporting and accountability) remain. Continued change requires the MoES to continue its current trajectory of trying to aligning its HE agenda with the BP in order to continue innovating and preparing young people for work in the twenty-first century.

This chapter focused on the horizontal diversification, vertical differentiation and inter-organisational relationships among Kazakhstani HEIs. It is clear that, systemically, there have been significant departures from the Soviet-era institutions. But meeting future challenges cannot be done by one arm of the government in isolation; rather, it requires collaboration from all levels of governance and from the broad spectrum of HE stakeholders. It is in this area that we argue the lasting imprint of the Soviet legacy is more clearly evident, for example, the intra-institutional operational policies (e.g., student admissions) and the day-to-day practices within different HEIs. Thus, future research on intra-institutional reform could elucidate how transformation is experienced, interpreted and implemented at the local level and would provide a clearer picture regarding sustainable, meaningful and long-lasting transformation.

Notes

1. A number of schools and faculties were evacuated to the Kazakh SSR after World War II, along with many highly qualified faculty members due to political reasons.
2. Karaganda Pedagogical Institute became the second university in the Kazakh SSR, Karaganda State University in 1972 (http://www.euni.de/

tools/jobpopup.php?lang=en&option=showJobs&jobid=16693&jobtyp=7&university=Buketov+Karaganda+State+University&country=KZ&sid=61473).
3. It should be noted that many institutes conducted applied research for specific industries, for example, the Mining Institute (*Institut Gordnogo Dela*), under the auspices of the Academy of Sciences.
4. See http://www.constitution.kz
5. The move toward privileging the Kazakh language started before 1991—the Soviet 1989 Law "On Language" established Kazakh as the state language of the Kazakh SSR. This law was passed when 62% of Kazakhstan's ethnic Kazakh population indicated they fluently spoke Russian (Smagulova 2008).
6. See http://online.zakon.kz/Document/?doc_id=1001895
7. The exceptions were private institutes that were established by Presidential Order (1991), like the Kazakhstan Institute of Management, Economics and Research (KIMEP University since 2011) in Almaty.
8. See http://online.zakon.kz/Document/?doc_id=1018504
9. In the Kazakhstani education system, upper secondary includes grades 10 and 11.
10. There has been on-going discussion about cancelling both exams and replacing them with a more comprehensive and rigorous university entrance exam. In 2013, the MoES announced that the UNT would be cancelled by 2015 (Lee 2013). However, at the time this chapter was written, the MoES had yet to provide an alternative university entrance exam and so, the UNT and CT tests were still being administered.
11. A number of Kazakhstani universities have begun implementing the MoES guidelines on ECTS. However, at the degree level, the MoES is struggling to harmonise the ECTS learning-hour with its own teaching-hour credit system without diminishing its student workload requirements for graduation (Dixon and Soltys 2013).
12. The Bolashak scholarship programme was a governmental programme that was instituted in 1994 and selects high-achieving Kazakhstani students to study abroad at top universities on the condition that they would come back and work in-country for a minimum of 5 years to offset brain drain.
13. Currently, all public HEI rectors continue to be political appointees.
14. See http://www.edu.gov.kz/ru/analytics
15. Additionally, all HEIs are still currently subject to regular licensing and attestation inspections, which are under the MoES's purview.
16. See http://online.zakon.kz/Document/?doc_id=30914968
17. See http://online.zakon.kz/Document/?doc_id=30914968
18. See https://www.interfax.kz/index.php?lang=eng&int_id=10&news_id=8961

References

Agency of Statistics of the Republic of Kazakhstan. 2013. *Kazakhstan in Figures.* http://www.eng.stat.kz

Aitzhanova, A., S. Katsu, J.F. Linn, and V. Yezhov, eds. 2014. *Kazakhstan 2050. Toward a Modern Society for All.* Oxford: Oxford University Press.

Asian Development Bank. n.d. Kazakhstan: Economy. http://www.adb.org/countries/kazakhstan/economy

Brunner, J.J., and A. Tillett. n.d. *Higher Education in Central Asia. The Challenges of Modernization.* Washington, DC: World Bank.

Dixon, J., and D. Soltys, eds. 2013. *A Handbook to Understanding the Bologna Process for Kazakhstani Higher Education Administrators.* Almaty: Akadem Press.

Dzholdasbekov, U., and E. Kuznetsov. 1975. *Kazakh State University and Higher Education in the Kazakh SSR.* Alma-Ata: Kirov Kazakh National University.

European Commission [EC]. 2010. *Higher Education in Kazakhstan.* http://eacea.ec.europa.eu/tempus/participating_countries/reviews/kazakhstan_review_of_higher_education.pdf

Froumin, I., Y. Kouzminov, and D. Semyonov. 2014. Institutional Diversity in Russian Higher Education: Revolutions and Evolution. *European Journal of Higher Education* 2014: 1–26. doi:10.1080/21568235.2014.91653.

Heynemann, S.P. 2010. A Comment on the Changes in Higher Education in the Post-Soviet Union. *European Education* 42 (1): 76–87. doi:10.4934/EUE1056-4934420104.

Heynemann, S.P., K.H. Anderson, and N. Nuraliyeva. 2007. The Cost of Corruption in Higher Education. *Comparative Education Review* 52 (1): 1–25. http://www.jstor.org/stable/10.1086/524367

Kazakhstani Ministry of Economics. 2015. Statistics of the Kazakhstani Ministry of Economics. http://stat.gov.kz/faces/wcnav_externalId/homeNumbersEducation?_afrLoop=19040397582307102#%40%3F_afrLoop%3D19040397582307102%26_adf.ctrl-state%3D3v2o6ed7c_58

Kazakhstani Ministry of Education and Science [MoES]. 2010. *The State Program of Education Development in the Republic of Kazakhstan for 2011–2020.* Astana: MoES.

———. 2014. *Statistics of the Kazakhstani Education System.* 2014. Astana: MoES. http://www.edu.gov.kz

———. 2015. *Statistics of the Kazakhstani Education System.* 2015. Astana: MoES. http://www.edu.gov.kz

Kazinform. 2010. Kazakhstan Joined the Bologna Process at Sitting of Bologna Ministerial Forum. *Kazinform*, March 12. http://www.inform.kz/eng/article/2247114

Kucera, J. 2014. Can a Homegrown University in Authoritarian Kazakhstan Incubate Reform? *Al Jazeera*, June 20. http://america.aljazeera.com/articles/2014/6/20/kazakhstan-s-audaciousnazarbayevuniversity.html

Kyzykeyeva, A., and A. Oskolkova. 2011. Historical Aspects of Higher Education in the Republic of Kazakhstan. *The Kazakh-American Free University Academic Journal* 3(2011). http://www.kafu-academic-journal.info/journal/3/51/

Lee, D. 2013. Unified National Testing to be Replaced by Two Different Tests by 2015. *Astana Times*, September 23. http://www.astanatimes.com/2013/09/unified-national-testing-to-be-replaced-by-two-different-tests-by-2015/

Moskva-Finansy i Statistika Razdel [Moscow Finance and Statistics Unit]. 1989. *Narodniy Obrazovaniy i Kultura v USSR [Education and Culture in the USSR]*, 202. Moscow: Moscow Finance and Statistics Union.

National Tempus Office. 2012. *Higher Education in Kazakhstan*. Brussels: European Union.

Nauchno Isledovatelskii Institut Vishego Obrazavaniya [NIIVO][Scientific Institute of Higher Education Research]. 1992. *Universitet Rossii [Russia's Universities]*. Spravochnik. Moscow: Nauchno Isledovatelskii Institut Vishego Obrazavaniya.

Organisation of Economic Co-operation and Development (OECD). 2007. *Higher Education in Kazakhstan*. Paris: OECD Publishing.

Piven, G., and I. Pak. 2006. Higher Education in Kazakhstan and the Bologna Process. *Russian Education and Society* 2006: 82–91. http://www.international.ac.uk/resources/14325144ut378r7g.pdf

Poletaev, D., and B. Rakisheva. 2011. Educational Migration from Kazakhstan to Russia as an Aspect of Strategic Cooperation Within the Customs Union. *In Eurasian Integration—Historical and Social Aspects*, 198–219. Moscow: Eurasian Development Bank.

Pomfret, R. 2014. Kazakhstan's Progress Since Independence. *In Kazakhstan 2050. Toward a Modern Society for All*, ed. A. Aitzhanova, S. Katsu, J.F. Linn, and V. Yezhov, 15–35. Oxford: Oxford University Press.

Rudista, N. 2004. *Innovative Transformations of Higher Education in Far and Close Abroad Countries*. Tyumen.

Rumyantseva, N.L. 2005. Taxonomy of Corruption in Higher Education. *Peabody Journal of Education* 80(1): 81–92. http://www.jstor.org/stable/1493336

Sarinzhipov, A. 2013. *Opportunities for Faculty to Influence Academic Matters at Kazakh National University and Eurasian National University*. Unpublished Doctoral Dissertation, University of Pennsylvania, Philadelphia.

Silova, I. 2011. Higher Education Reforms and Global Geopolitics: Shifting Cores and Peripheries in Russia, the Baltics, and Central Asia. *Russian Analytical Digest*, 97 (May 30, 2011). http://www.css.ethz.ch/publications/pdfs/RAD-97.pdf

Silova, I., and G. Steiner-Khamsi, eds. 2008. *How NGOS React. Globalization and Education Reform in the Caucasus, Central Asia, and Mongolia*. Bloomfield: Kumarian Press.

Smagulova, J. 2008. Language Policies of Kazakhization and Their Influence on Language Attitudes and Use. *International Journal of Bilingual Education and Bilingualism* 11 (3–4): 440–475.

Soltys, D. 2014. Similarities, Divergence, and Incapacity in the Bologna Process Reform Implementation by the Former-Socialist Countries: The Self-Defeat of State Regulations. *Comparative Education* 51 (2): 179–195. doi:10.1080/03 050068.2014.957908.

Sulima, S. 2008. Quality and Effectiveness of the Higher Education System in Kazakhstan During the 'Pre-reform Period.' *Vestnik KASU* 4. http://www.vestnik-kafu.info/journal/16/604/

Teichler, U. 1988. *Changing Patterns of Higher Education Systems*. London: Jessica Kingsley.

Thomson. n.d. Web of Science Home Page. www.isiwebofknowledge.com

Trow, M. 1970. Reflections on the Transition from Mass to Universal Higher Education. *Daedalus* 90 (1): 1–42.

UNESCO Institute of Statistics (UIS). n.d. Country Profiles. Kazakhstan. http://www.uis.unesco.org/DataCentre/Pages/country-profile.aspx?code=KAZ&regioncode=40505

Yakavets, N. 2014. Educational reform in Kazakhstan: The First Decade of Independence. In *Educational Reform and Internationalisation. The Case of School Reform in Kazakhstan*, ed. D. Bridges, 1–27. Cambridge: Cambridge University Press.

Zhakenov, G. n.d. *Kazakhstan National Report on Higher Education System Development*. www.unesco.kz/education/he/kazakh/kazakh_eng.htm

Elise S. Ahn was an Assistant Professor at KIMEP University, Almaty, Kazakhstan, where she also worked as the Graduate Program Administrator in KIMEP's Language Center. Currently, she is the director of the Office of the International Projects at the University of Wisconsin-Madison (USA) and also an adjunct lecturer at Edgewood College's Doctorate of Education programme (Madison, WI). She has a PhD in Educational Policy Studies from the Education Policy and Organization Leadership Department at the University of Illinois at Urbana-Champaign (USA) with a concentration in Comparative and International Education and a specialisation in Programme Evaluation. She has been awarded a number of awards, including a Fulbright-Schuman award to the European Union (2006–07). She co-edited a recently published book, *Language Change in Central Asia* (2016, Mouton de Gruyter), and has a number of forthcoming articles on issues related to emergent education stratification in post-Soviet Kazakhstan.

John Dixon B Econ, M Econ, PhD, FAcSS, is a Professor of Public Policy and Public Administration at the Middle East Technical University in Ankara, Turkey. From 2009 to 2014, he was the Distinguished Professor of Public Policy and Administration at KIMEP University, where he was Dean of the College of Social Sciences (2009–12) and of the Bang College of Business (2013–14). He has held senior academic appointments in the UK (1997–2008), Hong Kong (1993–97) and Australia (1981–92). He is a fellow of the British Academy of the Social Sciences, and an honorary life member of the American Phi Beta Delta Honor Society for International Scholars.

Larissa Chekmareva is a PhD student in international education (University of Massachusetts, USA). She has served in the positions of the Deputy to the President, Dean for Enrollment Management and Registrar at KIMEP University (2000–14, Almaty, Kazakhstan). Her education consulting experience with UNESCO, UNICEF, World Bank, National Ministries of Education in Central Asia and so on include projects related to the quality of education, student assessment, international accreditation, academic credit system, Bologna Process, enrolment management and student information systems.

Open Access This chapter is distributed under the terms of the Creative Commons Attribution 4.0 International License (http://creativecommons.org/licenses/by/4.0/), which permits use, duplication, adaptation, distribution and reproduction in any medium or format, as long as you give appropriate credit to the original author(s) and the source, provide a link to the Creative Commons license and indicate if changes were made.

The images or other third party material in this chapter are included in the chapter's Creative Commons license, unless indicated otherwise in a credit line to the material. If material is not included in the chapter's Creative Commons license and your intended use is not permitted by statutory regulation or exceeds the permitted use, you will need to obtain permission directly from the copyright holder.

CHAPTER 9

Institutional Strategies of Higher Education Reform in Post-Soviet Kyrgyzstan: Differentiating to Survive Between State and Market

Jarkyn Shadymanova and Sarah Amsler

INTRODUCTION

Kyrgyzstan is a small, mountainous, landlocked, and relatively poor country in Central Asia. It is bordered by China to the east, Kazakhstan to the north, Uzbekistan to the west, and Tajikistan to the south and has a young, growing, and ethnically diverse population comprised of Kyrgyz, Uzbek, Russian, and German, Kazakh, Korean, Tajik, Tatar, Ukrainian, and other ethnic groups.[1] Following its independence from the Soviet Union in 1991, Kyrgyzstan experienced processes of change across all areas of social, political, and economic life. Higher education reform has been central to this agenda, and between 1991 and today, the Soviet-era system of state-funded and Communist Party-controlled higher education

J. Shadymanova (✉)
Department of Sociology, Bishkek Humanities University, Bishkek, Kyrgyzstan

S. Amsler
Faculty of Social Sciences, University of Nottingham, Nottingham, UK

© The Author(s) 2018
J. Huisman et al. (eds.), *25 Years of Transformations of Higher Education Systems in Post-Soviet Countries*, Palgrave Studies in Global Higher Education, https://doi.org/10.1007/978-3-319-52980-6_9

institutions (HEIs) in Kyrgyzstan has been transformed into an expansive, diverse, unequal, semiprivatized and marketized higher education (HE) landscape (Amsler 2011; Brunner and Tillett 2007; Mertaugh 2004; Narkoziev and Yanzen 2013). How should we make sense of these changes within the framework of institutional diversification?

Mindful of Fumasoli and Huisman's (2013) arguments that the marketization of higher education does not necessarily generate institutional diversification, that government regulation does not necessarily lead to homogenization among institutions, and that universities' own institutional strategies and responses to environmental changes shape processes of structural reform in complex ways, this chapter assesses the specific character of these changes to the landscape in post-Soviet Kyrgyzstan. After briefly describing the structure and financing of higher education in the Kirgiz Soviet Socialist Republic (KSSR) from 1917 to 1991, we consider some key factors which have shaped patterns of the differentiation and diversification of HE in the post-Soviet period. These include the historical legacies of Soviet HE infrastructures, new legal and political frameworks for HE governance and finance, changes to regulations for the licensing of institutions and academic credentials, the introduction of new multinational policy agendas for higher education in the Central Asian region, changes in the relationship between higher education and labor, the introduction of a national university admissions examination, and the adoption of certain principles of the European Bologna Process. The picture of HE reform that emerges from this analysis is one in which concurrent processes of diversification and homogenization are not driven wholly by either state regulation or forces of market competition, but mediated by universities' strategic negotiations of these forces in the context of historical institutional formations in Kyrgyzstan.

The analysis presented in this chapter focuses on trends, since 1991, in both 'external diversification' within the HE system (in which differences emerge between institutions) and 'systemic' and 'programmatic' differentiation, with particular attention to the relationship between this process and the dismantling, reinforcement, or emergence of hierarchy and stratification within the HE system. 'Systemic differentiation' refers to "differences in institutional type, size, and control found within a higher education system", and 'programmatic differentiation' refers to the "degree level, degree area, comprehensiveness, mission and emphasis of programs and services provided by the institutions" (Huisman 1995, 13). The chapter draws on national and international statistical indicators of higher education and educational reform in Kyrgyzstan, and qualitative data about the history and substance of these changes drawn from legislation, regulations, and policy statements concerning this period of reform. Statistical information about each university's structure, organization, and curricula during the post-Soviet period was obtained from the National Statistical Committee (NSC) of the Kyrgyz Republic; government educational databases from the Ministry of Education and Science (MoES), which is the main agency responsible for the quality of education and management of the education system in Kyrgyzstan; Accounting Chambers; the National Academy and National Testing Centre (for information about student enrollments) and institutional websites and annual reports.

THE DEVELOPMENT OF HIGHER EDUCATION IN THE KIRGIZ SOVIET SOCIALIST REPUBLIC

In the 1920s and 1930s, the new Soviet state implemented a violent process of forced settlement and collectivization in the KSSR and early Bolshevik programs for 'civilizing' the Central Asian steppe and incorporating its diverse tribal communities into a new empire included the creation of new universities and research centers in the region (Amsler 2007; Buyanin 2001); these existed side by side with traditional educational institutions such as the *maktab* and *madrassa* until the 1930s (Khalid 1999). Institutions of higher learning such as universities and filials of the Russian Academy of Science, which began to appear in Kirgizia in the 1930s following the establishment of the Central Asian University in Tashkent, Uzbekistan in 1920, were oriented primarily toward political and technical education rather than teaching or academic research and used as experimental sites for promoting literacy and disseminating pedagogies on science, politics and morality, or as 'bases' for Russian ethnographic and geographical research (Amsler 2007).

During the mid-Soviet period, due to large-scale campaigns for basic education which accompanied a process of rapid industrialization across the country, the literacy rate in the society jumped from 16.5% (1926) to 99.8% (1979) (Ibraimov 2001) and full systems of primary, secondary, professional, and higher education were created (Holmes et al. 1995; Shamatov 2015). By 1991, the country had 12 institutions of higher education, each of which served a different function within the educational system (Fig 9.1).

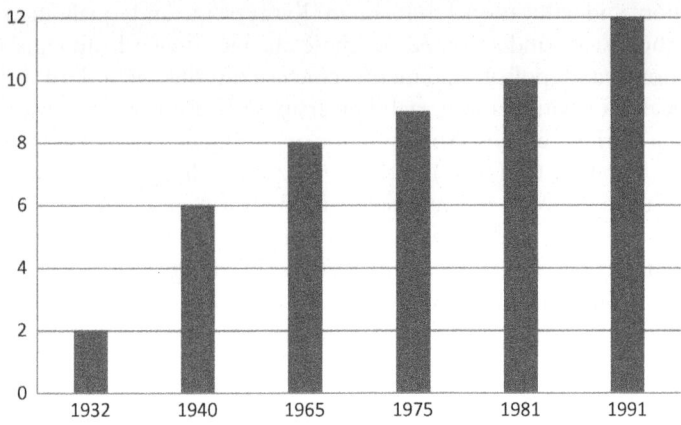

Fig. 9.1 Number of HEIs in the Kirgiz Soviet Socialist Republic, 1932–1991 (Source: Authors using data from Orusbaeva 1982 and NSC 2008)

The structural framework for Kyrgyzstan's educational system, like that in all Soviet republics, was shaped by centralized state policies in accordance with the country's economic needs and principles believed to define a general socialist education, including the eradication of illiteracy, the provision of vocational instruction in secondary school, the massification of educational opportunities, and the incorporation of state ideology and moral education into the curriculum and training processes (Clark 2005). Decisions about governance, curriculum content and organization, student admissions, and so on were made by the Ministry of Education in Moscow and, until the late 1980s, were similar across the 15 Soviet republics (Amsler 2007; DeYoung 2011; Heyneman 2010).

Each higher education institution had its own 'profile' or portfolio of specialized functions and purposes within the system (Table 9.1; Fig. 9.2). Contrary to current definitions of institutional positioning in which 'higher education institutions locate themselves in specific niches within the higher educational system' (Fumasoli and Huisman 2013, 160), this profiling was the responsibility of the Soviet state. There was no duplication of programs offered by each institution, although teachers with similar specializations were distributed throughout all regions. The state built HEI each with a specialized, profile-appropriate campus; for example, the Medical Institute had a study campus and anatomy building, the Polytechnic Institute had state-of-the-art technical labs, and so on. However, financial

Table 9.1 Higher education institutions in the Kirgiz Soviet Socialist Republic, 1980

	Higher education institution	Established	Location	Student numbers	Profile
1	Kyrgyz Veterinary Institute (later the Agricultural Institute named after Skryabin)	1933	Frunze	5,637	Agrarian
2	Kyrgyz State Medical Institute	1939	Frunze	4,488	Medical
3	Kyrgyz State University	1951	Frunze	12,869	Main state university with multidisciplinary profile
4	Osh Pedagogical Institute	1951	Osh	6,166	Teaching/pedagogy
5	Kyrgyz Women's Pedagogical Institute	1952	Frunze	4,771	Teaching/pedagogy
6	Prejevalsk Pedagogical Institute	1953	Prejevalsk	3,384	Teaching/pedagogy
7	Frunze Polytechnic Institute	1954	Frunze	14,324	Technical/construction/geology
8	Institute of Physical Culture and Sport	1955	Frunze	1,401	Sport
9	Kyrgyz State Institute of the Arts	1967	Frunze	1,117	Art and culture

(*continued*)

Table 9.1 (continued)

	Higher education institution	Established	Location	Student numbers	Profile
10	Frunze special secondary school, *militsiya* (police)	1969	Frunze	–	Protection of citizens and law
11	Frunze Pedagogical Institute of Russian Language and Literature	1979	Frunze	1,249	Preparation Russian language teachers/pedagogy
12	Osh Technical University	1990	Osh	–	Technical/construction/geology for southern regions

Source: Authors using data from Orusbaeva (1982)[2]

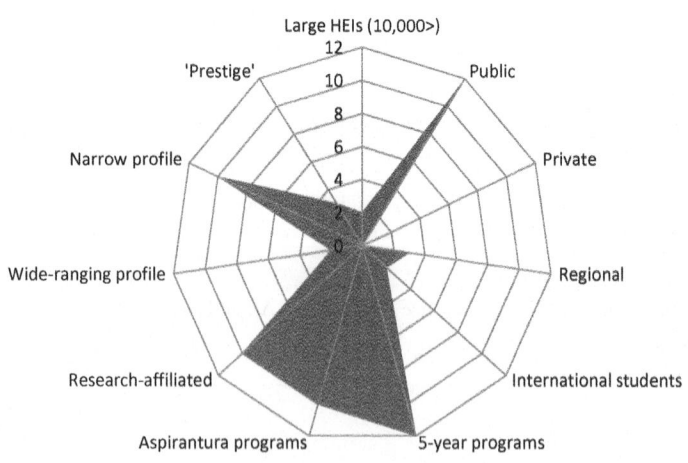

Fig. 9.2 The HEI landscape in Kyrgyzstan (Source: Authors using data from Orusbaeva 1982)

resources were not distributed evenly across the sector, and HEIs were geographically stratified such that central institutions located in Frunze (now the capital city of Bishkek) were more likely to obtain funding from the Central Committee of the Communist Party than regional institutions with small student populations and lower-priority profiles.

Student numbers were set by the State Planning Committee (*Gosplan*), which determined the demand for particular specializations in the national economy. All levels of education were state-funded, public and free of charge, and while enrollment was competitive it increased rapidly between 1965 and 1975 and then steadily until 1991 (Orusbaeva 1982; NSC 2012b; see Fig. 9.3). By the early 1990s, 58,023 students were studying across all HEIs in Kyrgyzstan—152 students per 10,000 citizens. As most of the institutions were located in Frunze, this urban center became the primary destination for higher education provision and many young people moved to the capital from rural locations across the country to obtain their qualifications.

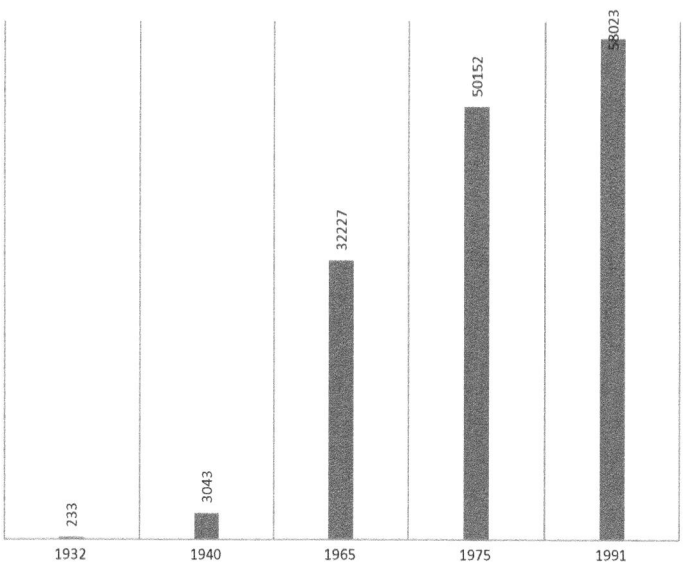

Fig. 9.3 Number of HE students in the Kirgiz Soviet Socialist Republic, 1932–1991 (Source: Authors using data from Orusbaeva 1982 and NSC 2008)

By 1990, the formal higher education system in the Kirgiz Soviet Socialist Republic was thus both differentiated and externally diversified (as different types of institutions, courses environments, and educational programs had been created in response to state-defined political and economic needs) and homogenous (as this process was directed through state planning and regulation, and all HEIs were state institutions).

Independence and New Patterns of Differentiation and Diversification in Higher Education

In December 1992, a year after Kyrgyzstan gained independence from the Soviet Union, the government adopted a Law 'On Education' to reorient educational reform in the new political-economic context; in particular, "changing to diversified educational programmes, seeking new learning forms and technologies, arranging multi-channel funding, involving various partners in providing educational services and developing non-governmental education" (MoESYP 2006; Tiuliundieva 2008, 78). This was followed by a series of new laws and strategies aimed at structurally transforming the system along these lines.[3] HEIs thus became partially autonomous and able to implement independent policies in areas such as human resources, student performance evaluation, educational methodology and technology, the identification of scientific research areas, and the management of organizational, financial, and other issues in accordance with their statutes, memoranda, legal, and other regulatory acts. Within these parameters, however, the state remained responsible for many core activities including providing basic funding for higher education according to individual's abilities and propensities (as determined by testing), setting standards for each level of formal education, approving priorities in curriculum development, training teachers, accrediting higher education institutions, collecting statistics on education, liaising with the National Academy of Sciences to set research priorities, and managing official international cooperation. Since independence, HEIs in Kyrgyzstan have remained accountable to the state for 'quality assurance' and must, at least formally, comply with its regulations in order to operate.

The new legal, financial and ideological frameworks for HE policy created conditions for a rapid diversification and expansion of the system, which grew from 12 HEIs in 1991 to 52 in 2015 (although this number can fluctuate from year to year as new institutions are opened and closed).

Table 9.2 Dynamics of institutional growth in Kyrgyz higher education, 1991–2016

	1991	1995	2002	2005	2015
Public HEIs	12	22	32	33	34
Private HEIs	–	10	16	18	18
Total HEIs	12	32	48	51	52

Source: Authors using data from NSC (2008, 2012a, 2016)

This was accomplished in a variety of ways, including the establishment of new institutions in all regions of the republic; the creation of new branches, departments, and educational centers with legal status in existing institutions; and the reorganization of vocational institutions (*technikums*) into higher education institutions that had a broader remit to offer market-oriented programs. For example, in the 1990s, the accounting vocational institute (*Frunzenskyi tecknicum sovetskoy torgovly*) changed its status to become the Bishkek High Commerce College (1997), then the Institute of Bishkek State University of Economics and Business (1999), the Bishkek State Institute of Economics and Commerce (2003), and the Kyrgyz Economic University (2007) (see Table 9.2).

Today, the Kyrgyz state classifies its 52 higher education institutions into four categories based on their teaching and research profiles. *Academies* are educational institutions that offer training programs and conduct fundamental and applied scientific research (public, 6; private, 5). *Universities* are multi-profile institutions which provide a wide range of specialist training at all levels of higher education including academic and in-service training and which conduct fundamental and applied scientific research (public, 19; private, 7). *Institutes* may be either independent or units in universities carrying out higher education training for specialists and in-service training programs at all levels (public, 4; private, 6). Finally, '*profiled HEIs*' offer more narrowly defined education and training programs in specific areas, such as the training of highly specialized experts in music or the military (conservatory, art and musical HEIs, 3; Military Institute of the Armed Forces and Interior HEI, 2). In this chapter, we offer a slightly more nuanced typology, focusing on processes of differentiation and diversification, which makes visible the impact of the emergence of new private and international HEIs (see Table 9.3).

Table 9.3 Dynamics of student population, public and private HEIs, 1991–2013

	1991	1995	2002	2005	2013
Public university students	58,023 (100%)	57,211 (88.5%)	184,879 (93%)	213,619 (92.5%)	196,232 (88%)
Private university students	–	7,430 (11.5%)	14,245 (7%)	17,476 (7.5%)	27,009 (12%)
Total university students	58,023	64,641	199,124	231,095	223,241

Source: Authors using data from NSC (2008, 2013a)

On one hand, this systemic differentiation and external diversification of the institutional landscape has broadened the range of HEIs in Kyrgyzstan. On the other hand, however, the setting of national curriculum standards by the MoES and the state regulations for institutional licensing means that there are still parameters for the differentiation or diversification of HE as all programs, regardless of whether they are located in public or private institutions, must demonstrate compliance with these state standards. This limits the scope for HEIs to develop genuinely independent profiles, which in turn limits the degree of diversity within the system (Fumasoli and Huisman 2013; Huisman 1995; Van Vught 2008; Teichler 1988). Nevertheless, institutional expansion has been coupled with an increase in the overall number of students enrolling in higher education. Despite economic hardship in post-Soviet Kyrgyzstan, public demand for higher education grew during the 1990s and has continued to do so to the present day, with nearly 40% of the current age cohort enrolling in higher education of some kind (NSC 2014b; Table 9.3).

According to official data (NSC 2008), student enrollment in HE reached its highest point in 2005 due to the growth in the number of HEIs in the country and the low cost of tuition fees (the average tuition fee being 8,000 Kyrgyz soms or USD $200 at the time). In 2008, however, more students began dropping out from universities due to the cost of tuition, and enrollments in vocational institutions—which charge lower fees, are more directly linked to employment, and offer shorter training periods—significantly increased (Fig. 9.4).

In 2008, the enrollment of secondary school graduate students to HEIs decreased because the tuition fees increased to a minimum cost of 17,000 Kyrgyz soms ($360), and it became mandatory for students to submit their

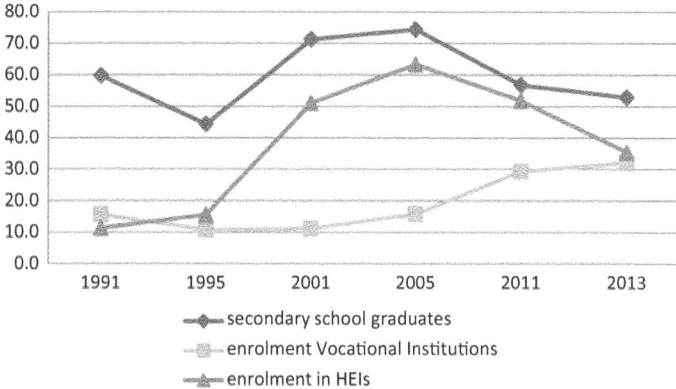

Fig. 9.4 Secondary school graduates and student enrollment in vocational and higher education institutions, 1991–2013 (Source: Authors using data NSC 2014c)

results from a new national admissions test to enroll in any university. Many graduates who did not pass the test found alternative pathways into higher education, such as enrolling in specialized colleges on the basis of their ninth-grade marks (see also DeYoung 2011, 44). Such colleges operate as parts of particular HEIs which do not require admission test scores because students take a special study program of study for credit and, upon completing it, continue two further years of study at the same HEI. Finally, secondary school graduates and their parents still often consider the 2-year Bachelor's degree, a post-independence credential which was introduced as part of Kyrgyzstan's efforts to join the Bologna Process, to be an incomplete higher education as compared with the Soviet 5-year specialized degree. This strategy for access has generated new relationships between vocational institutions and other types of HEI, and some institutions such as the Kyrgyz State University, Kyrgyz Technical University, International University of Kyrgyzstan, Slavonic University, and Bishkek Humanities University have internally diversified into multi-level complexes offering initial, secondary, and higher levels of vocational education.

Higher education in Kyrgyzstan also became more linguistically diverse after independence. With different logics of higher education reform operating in the country, from nation-building to regionalization and internationalization (Silova 2011), improving the quality of education in both a new national language (Kyrgyz) and English as well as Russian became a focus of educational policy. While post-independence language laws initially stipulated the development of national language literacy at all levels of education, with then-President Akayev signing a state language law in 2000, an acute lack of adequate textbooks, dictionaries, and teaching materials in Kyrgyz hindered the implementation of this policy (even the training manuals for the law were published in Russian). In 2013, although the legal status of state and official languages was altered again so that all official documents were to be prepared only in Kyrgyz, Russian remained the main language for most of the country's higher education programs. Therefore, while the Kyrgyz language was used in primary and secondary schools in the 1990s, it was not used at the university level except in linguistic specialisms.

While some universities have dedicated programs in English (such as degrees in Medicine or Information Technology for international students), there remains a shortage of both teaching materials and instructors who can teach diverse subjects in foreign languages in universities across the sector. Some institutions do now offer dual-language courses in other strategic languages. International HEIs such as the American University of Central Asia, the Kyrgyz–Turkish Manas University, and the Ata Turk Ala-Too University offer programs in English or Turkish and have degrees recognized jointly by both governments (the KRSU and KTU Manas universities work more generally in a new institutional form of intergovernmental agreement, which gives them more money for facilities and demands comparatively looser government oversight).

The Bologna Process: An External Driver of Diversification in Kyrgyz Higher Education

The Bologna Process project of 'harmonizing' and standardizing university awards across Europe and affiliated world regions has, in Kyrgyzstan, led to a certain type of diversification of education programs and the development of new types of relationship for training, financing, and partnerships in the provision of education services with European HEIs. In 2004, the Kyrgyz government, through a Working Group of the President of the Kyrgyz Republic on the Integration of HEIs of Kyrgyzstan into the Bologna Process and the National Office of the EU Tempus–Tacis program, signed a Memorandum of Agreement to integrate its HEIs into the Bologna Process (National Tempus Office Kyrgyzstan 2016). A number of universities (the International University of Kyrgyzstan, Bishkek Academy of Finance and Economics, Kyrgyz Economic University, and Kyrgyz National University) subsequently adopted projects to implement the requirements of the Bologna Process. Despite being denied membership to the Bologna Process in 2007, owing to the fact that Kyrgyzstan was not party to the European Cultural Convention of the Council of Europe, Kyrgyzstan still aspires to join and the state continues to create reform policies which are informed by the principles of the Bologna Process in order to increase opportunities for joint projects and international mobility among students and academic staff.

For example, the Bologna agenda had a significant impact on the structure of academic degree courses within the Kyrgyz higher education system, and on the status of existing and newer degree holders. Today, the Soviet-era two-cycle system, which consists of a specialist diploma degree and an advanced *aspirantura*, co-exists with the Bologna three-cycle system, which prepares students at Bachelor's, Master's, and PhD levels. While recognized PhD enrollment in Kyrgyzstan began only in 2013 in a small number of HEIs (e.g., the Kyrgyz–Turk Manas University, Kyrgyz National Agrarian University, and International University of Kyrgyzstan), by 2012 the MoES required all higher education institutions to offer Bachelor's and Master's degrees in order to enable future compliance with the Bologna Process. Seven HEIs are now licensed by the MoES to offer all three tiers of educational programs and seven to offer MAs, and while all universities offer BA programs, only 'profiled' HEIs can offer MA and PhD programs. The status of the PhD degree itself remains ambiguous in the country and at present only a few universities offer it, while the *aspirantura* award is still widely available. Such programs are thus offered alongside traditional 5-year specialized degrees in many parts of the country, although with more universities reducing these programs as required by government decree (Government of the Kyrgyz Republic 2011).

These courses are not, however, distributed evenly throughout the system and their availability varies across disciplines: Bachelor's and Master's degrees are in greater demand in economic and humanitarian fields, whereas within industry and agriculture, priority is still often given to specialists with what is considered 'full' (i.e., 5-year) higher education. Such degrees will thus remain part of the system for the foreseeable future and will not be shut down entirely, as according to a recent government resolution on education, by 2020 the proportion of students within the country's universities should be 70% BA, 20% MA, and 10% specialist (Government of the

Kyrgyz Republic 2012). Yet the differential value between these Bologna-compliant credentials and the previous two-tier cycle of awards, combined with the emergence of competition for students in public and private institutions alike, has become influential as a criterion for making hierarchical distinctions between the country's higher educational institutions. These different levels of license thus contribute to both diversification and vertical differentiation within the system, which in turn influences future developments in the academic profile, infrastructure, and focus of teaching and research within each institution.

Forces and Factors of Vertical Differentiation

The National Scholarship Test for University Admission

The higher education landscape in Kyrgyzstan has also been reshaped by the introduction of a National Scholarship Test, which is administered by a national testing center that is independent from both the MoES and individual HEIs. Kyrgyzstan was the first state in Central Asia to introduce a merit-based national university admission exam (following, in the wider CIS region, Azerbaijan in 1992 and Russia in 2001; see Drummond and Gabrscek 2012). It was introduced in 2002 in order to create a more transparent system for distributing state scholarships (National Tempus Office Kyrgyzstan 2016) and to replace institutional-based admission practices that had become regarded as problematic in the post-Soviet period because allowing universities to fill government-allocated student quotas and distribute government scholarships enabled some to be discriminatory, corrupt, and ineffective (Blau 2004; Heyneman et al. 2008; Mertaugh 2004; Osipian 2007; Shamatov 2012). From 2004, a new Center for Educational Assessment and Teaching Methods (CEATM), funded by the United States Agency for International Development, assumed responsibility for administering this exam. In 2012, the MoES made it mandatory for all students to have a national test certificate in order to enroll on any program, and the 50 applicants with the highest test scores from across the country receive a certificate enabling them to enroll in the discipline and university of their choice without further examination (National Tempus Office Kyrgyzstan 2016).

The National Scholarship Test (NST) has had dual implications for the structure of the higher education system in Kyrgyzstan. On the one hand, it is regarded as having the potential to reduce practices of corruption in university admissions processes and increase the participation of students from historically underrepresented social groups and geographical (particularly rural and mountainous) regions through the operation of a complex quota system (Shamatov 2012). On the other hand, it reinforces and produces vertical differentiation and inequalities within the system as students' academic performance is influenced by existing inequalities in language instruction, educational resources, type of school (public or private), and geographical opportunities (Tiuliundieva 2008). Elite students still have a better chance of winning a state scholarship for the program and university of their choice. This introduces a new form of hierarchy into the HE system as 'top choice' universities recruit more students with better scores and which, as they increase their prestige and 'value', are able to charge higher tuition fees for fee-paying students as well (DeYoung 2011, 13). Universities are therefore situated within a competitive market in which all strive to recruit state-funded students with high admission test scores, as the more students they recruit the more resources they will accumulate for improving facilities, hiring strong academics, and investing in research. Yet as state tuition grants are minimal and often do not cover the full costs of students' education, even state scholarships introduce an element of competition between institutions which all angle for economic survival amidst a "radical transformation of the whole market for higher education with the introduction of so-called *kontraktnyie*, or fee paying places" (Reeves 2005, 15). The introduction and reorientation of higher education financing toward private tuition fees is thus a major driver of both diversification and standardization in Kyrgyzstan today.

Commodification and Marketization: The Influence of Competition on Student Enrollments

Although 86% of students in Kyrgyzstan attend public HEIs, the majority still pay tuition fees as the government provides scholarships for only 21% of full-time students (NSC 2014a) in particular disciplines. As the demand for student-financed education has steadily increased, HEIs have sought new 'revenue streams' to attract fee-paying students with concerns that the emphasis on increasing fee-based revenues sometimes supersedes attention to the academic quality of the courses being taught. Various study formats—full-time, part-time, and evening classes—attract different types of students (Fig. 9.5) and international students who often pay more

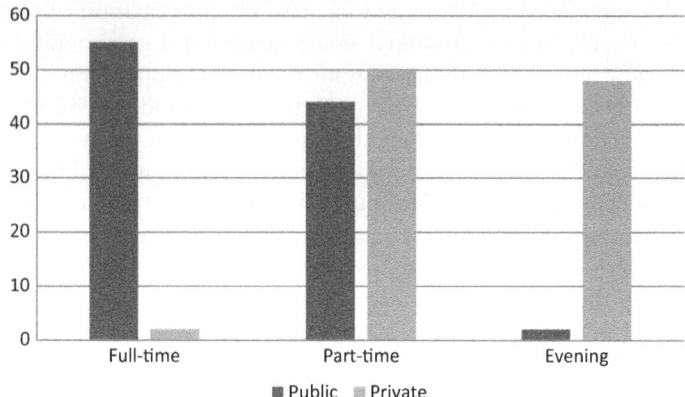

Fig. 9.5 Part-time and full-time, day, and evening-class students (Source: Authors using data from NSC 2014a)

unless they benefit from a bilateral agreement between countries co-sponsoring a university.

This form of educational commodification has been intensified as universities seek new means of financial survival in the absence of adequate state funding (Morgan et al. 2004). In contrast to the internally differentiated Soviet system of universities in which each institution served a particular function in relation to the others, many HEIs now thus offer a range of similar programs with minor modifications. For example, new disciplines which are associated with (or presumed to be associated with) market economics quickly gained prestige after independence, with economics, management, law, international relations, psychology, and foreign languages becoming oversubscribed as students and their families believed these professional qualifications would be lucrative; at the same time, HEIs have struggled to recruit and retain students for technical or teaching courses despite the allocation of state scholarships in such fields (Fig. 9.6).

This has created a problem of saturation in particular fields of study, in which universities educate more specialists than can be employed in a field and lead students to select courses of study instrumentally. By 2015, the state had already closed 23 university branches because they were deemed to be systemic 'duplications' (Bengard 2015). While the expansion of educational programs after independence was initially a process of diversification,

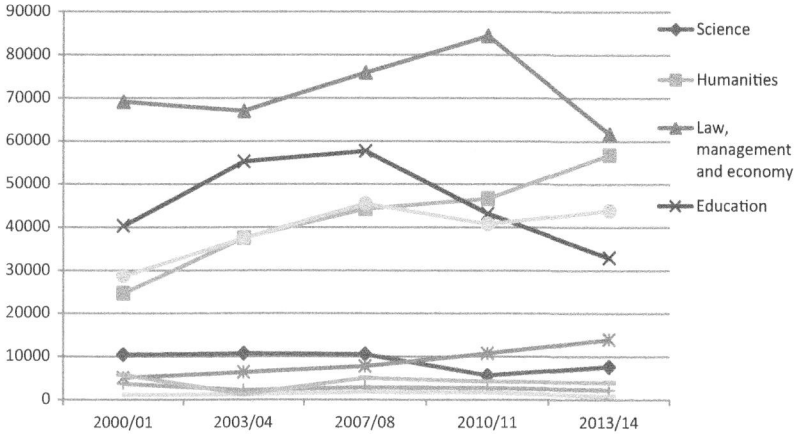

Fig. 9.6 Dynamics of higher education enrollment by fields of study, 2000–2014 (Source: Source: Authors using data from NSC 2008, 2015)

in other words, the unfolding of this process within a commercialized and marketized environment created a high degree of homogeneity across the system.

The Higher Education Landscape in Contemporary Kyrgyzstan

After independence, new legal and policy frameworks for university governance, financing, staffing, and educational programming created conditions for complicated new patterns of differentiation, diversification, and homogenization among higher education institutions in Kyrgyzstan.

The system of higher education now consists of 52 public and private HEIs under the MoES: 3 technical and technological ('specialized', or 'profiled') universities under the MoES; 1 medical university and 4 medical and healthcare institutes as branches of 2 public and 2 private HEIs, under the Ministry of Health; 1 agrarian institution, under the Ministry of Agriculture; 3 institutions in Arts and Culture, under the Ministry of Culture; 2 institutions in 'state security', under the Ministry of Defence and Ministry of the Interior Affairs, and the Ministry of Emergency Situations; 1 university in Sports and Tourism, under the State Agency for Youth, Physical Culture and Sports of the Kyrgyz Republic; 1 diplomatic academy and international relationship academy, under the Ministries of the Interior and Foreign Affairs; 1 Academy of Management, with the President's Administration; and 1 institute for social work and development, under the Ministry of Labour, Migration and Youth (Table 9.4, Fig. 9.7).

Figure 9.7 represents the current landscape of HEIs in Kyrgyzstan, illustrating each element of external and internal change which has been discussed previously in this chapter. This new landscape includes both historical and newly established public and private universities as well as HEIs which have been created by transforming technical institutes into universities. It also includes a number of institutions with new 'joint' forms of governance, such as those which are regulated by both the Kyrgyz Ministry of Education and Science and other government ministries, and joint-national universities such as the Kyrgyz–Russian (Slavic) and Kyrgyz–Turkish Manas universities. The two oldest universities in Kyrgyzstan are the largest, having had many years to build their material and academic infrastructure. Leading specialized public HEIs that have been working since the Soviet period have also had more opportunities and resources (such as space, staff, and students) and some of them

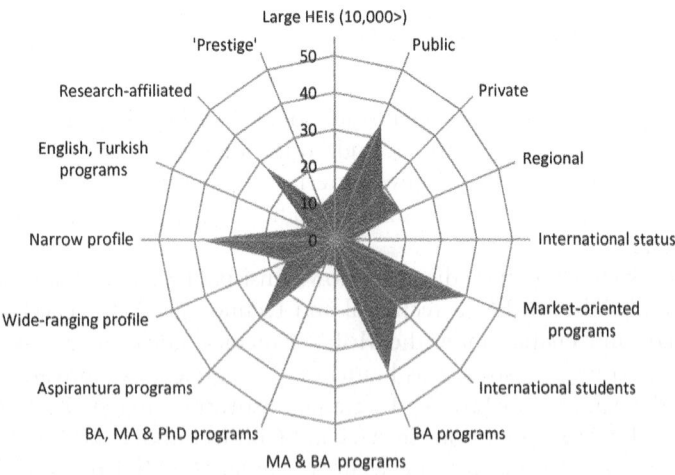

Fig. 9.7 The HEI landscape in Kyrgyzstan, 2015 (Source: Authors using data from NSC 2008, 2015)

Table 9.4 Classification of higher education institutions in Kyrgyzstan, 2015

Institution type (number)	Historical status	Description of institution type	Selected examples
Leading state comprehensive HEIs (2)	Soviet-era HEI type	The oldest universities in Kyrgyzstan, these have strong bases in both applied and fundamental research. They offer a diverse spectrum of undergraduate, graduate, doctoral, and specialized degree programs and are affiliated with other research and educational institutions, colleges, and regional branches. They are the major providers of candidate (PhD) and doctoral (DSc) degrees. These universities also have the largest student bodies	Kyrgyz National University named after J. Balasagyn (30,000 students) Osh State University (29,000 students) former Osh Pedagogical State Institute
Leading, specialized public HEIs (6)	Soviet-era HEI type	These 'profiled' HEIs carry out a broad range of specialist training at all levels of higher education (BA, MA, PhD, DSc) and in-service training, and conduct fundamental and applied scientific research in specific areas. They include research and educational institutions, research centers and colleges. Student bodies range from 10,000 to 20,000	Kyrgyz Technical University (19,000 students) Kyrgyz State University n.a. I. Arabaeva (17,000 students) Kyrgyz State University of Construction, Transport and Architecture (12,000 students) Bishkek Humanities University (10,000 students)

(*continued*)

Table 9.4 (continued)

Institution type (number)	Historical status	Description of institution type	Selected examples
Narrowly profiled state HEIs (10)	Soviet-era HEI type and post-Soviet-era HEI type	These leading 'profiled' HEIs carry out narrow specialist training at all levels of higher education and conduct fundamental and (primarily) applied scientific research in specific fields. They offer BA, MA, and PhD level programs, including aspirantura and doctorantura degrees. Some HEIs such as Kyrgyz State Juridical Academy and Kyrgyz Economic University changed their status by reorganizing HEIs of Soviet period	Kyrgyz State Juridical Academy (8,000 students) Kyrgyz state Agrarian University (7,000 students) Kyrgyz Medical Academy (4,000 students) Kyrgyz Economic University (4,600 students) The Kyrgyz State Academy of Physical Education and Sport (1,700 students)
	Soviet-era HEI type	Two military HEIs have a specific public function and offer training programs focused on military services. They require students to pass a special aptitude test as part of their admission process and are affiliated with military ministries and state bodies	Academy of the Ministry of Interior of the Kyrgyz Republic n.a. E. Aliev The Military Institute of the Armed Forces of the Kyrgyz Republic n.a. K. Usenbekova
	Soviet-era HEI type	Three arts-focused HEIs offer programs in the arts, music, painting, sculpture, acting, and other related specialties. They offer undergraduate, graduate, and postgraduate programs in these areas	Kyrgyz National Conservatory n.a. K. Moldobosanov (200 students) National Academy of Arts of the Kyrgyz Republic n.a. the Academic T. Sadykov Kyrgyz State University of Arts n.a. B. Beishenalieva

(*continued*)

Table 9.4 (continued)

Institution type (number)	Historical status	Description of institution type	Selected examples
Regional leading public universities (5)	Soviet-era HEI type	These universities are leading regional HEIs offering a wide range of programs at all levels, with the PhD being the highest award possible. They have a regional rather than international focus and conduct primarily applied research	Osh Technical Universities (11,000 students) Jalal-Abad State University (16,000 students)
Regional specialized small HEIs (9)	Post-Soviet HEI type	In this category of teaching-focused institutions are *technikums* or HEI branches established during the Soviet period, comprehensive state universities and specialized institutions, and 2 autonomous HEIs	Talas State University (3,000 students) Naryn State University (3,600 students)
Private comprehensive universities (18), including private international HEIs (7)	Post-Soviet HEI type	Private leading universities offer a wide range of programs focused on market demands for education, primarily in the areas of economics, management, law, and social science. This type includes international institutions such as the American University of Central Asia (AUCA) and the University of Ala-Too Ata Turk, which are regarded as prestigious despite charging high educational fees (e.g., $7000/year at AUCA)	International Academy of Management, Law, Finance and Business (3,000 students) Bishkek Academy of Finance and Economics (1,500 students) International University for Innovation Technologies (3,800 students)

(*continued*)

Table 9.4 (continued)

Institution type (number)	Historical status	Description of institution type	Selected examples
Leading comprehensive international universities (2)	Post-Soviet-era HEI type	These institutions, which work under agreement with two national governments, are highly prestigious and have strong educational infrastructures. They are funded by the Kyrgyz government with considerable funding from a foreign government. Both universities offer a wide range of programs at BA, MA, and PhD levels. They are top choices for students with the best National Test scores. KTU 'Manas' offers only scholarship study programs, while KRSU offers a small number of scholarships with a larger number of study programs being tuition fee based	Kyrgyz-Russian Slavonic University (11,000 students) KTU "Manas" (4,800 students)

Source: Authors

changed their statuses to develop in comparison with newly emerged private institutions, and after the collapse of the Soviet Union, these institutions used their advantages to become leading HEIs in their areas of specialization. Private HEIs are comparatively small and still need buildings and finance to operate. Regional HEIs, with the exception of the state universities (e.g., in Issyk Kul and Djalal-Abad), have developed from what were vocational institutions in regional branches of state HEIs and asserted their independence when education was redefined as a profit-making service in order to recruit local students. Leading comprehensive international universities work under bilateral agreements and are mainly funded by foreign countries. These universities build the landscape of HEIs in Kyrgyzstan.

Conclusion

For 25 years, higher education institutions in independent, post-Soviet Kyrgyzstan have undergone rapid, complex changes which are shaped by wider national and global projects to overhaul the social functions, financing, organizational structure, and intellectual content of higher education itself. The 1992 law 'On Education' was particularly influential in that it encouraged the creation or annexation of new public and private institutions, including 'international' or joint-governmental universities, which are neither dedicated to specific political and economic functions as in the Soviet system nor reliant on state funding for their survival. Yet the expansion of the system from 12 to 52 HEIs (at the time of writing) has not implied an immediate or totalizing diversification of institutional forms. For example, many of the country's original universities and institutes are still operating today (even if in altered form and under different names), and both Soviet and Bologna degree structures remain in operation across the sector. The development of higher education in post-Soviet Kyrgyzstan, while a process of expansion and diversification, remains located within historical and emergent hierarchies which separate older from newer, central from regional, public from private, generalized from specialized, larger from smaller, richer from poorer, and (increasingly) internationally connected from regionally oriented institutions.

These processes have been driven by economic, political and cultural reform agendas which seek to shift from state to private funding for higher education; to create economic and political mechanisms of competition for students, resources, and prestige; and to transform higher education from a public system into a field of autonomous entities which compete for revenue and prestige through the sale of commodified teaching and research products, goods, or services (Amsler 2008, 2013). Within this framework, the Kyrgyz Ministry of Education and Science officially regulates the functions of individual HEIs through its licensing and accreditation mechanisms (although deregulation of 'attestation' has been proposed; see Merrill 2016) and maintains control over some processes of institutional diversification such as the functional and hierarchical distinction between elite (PhD-awarding, state-scholarship recruiting) and non-elite (BA-awarding, 'contract'-focused) institutions.

At the same time, externally inspired reforms such as the US-led institutionalization of the National Scholarship Test and the government's ambition to participate in the European Bologna Process framework have introduced new forces of systemic homogeneity and convergence, largely by introducing and harmonizing mechanisms for 'quality control' in HEIs and through this also producing new distinctions (e.g., between HEIs which are more or less compliant, connected to European projects, etc.). As elsewhere in the world, HEIs in Kyrgyzstan are poised between "differentiation and compliance" in the "search for legitimacy" that will "make themselves different to elude competition" (Fumasoli and Huisman 2013, 160).

Yet for individual institutions, within this general context, differentiation, diversification, and market-led specialization are primarily a strategy for survival. As the public budget for higher education has been reduced and HEIs are forced to recruit greater numbers of fee-paying students in order to survive and thrive, they are under pressure to diversify and commodify the form and substance of their activities often regardless of whether such quantitative expansion enhances or damages the quality of educational activities and relationships. In this sense, they follow a familiar cross-national pattern in which universities are "compelled...to start positioning themselves, by constructing portfolios through setting priorities and a more explicit focus on specific competencies" (Fumasoli and Huisman 2013, 157, ADB 2004). However, as illustrated by the ballooning of student applications for and programs dedicated to 'market-oriented disciplines' promising (often elusive) individual return and the simultaneous difficulty of recruiting and retaining students to government scholarship-funded programs in core fields such as teacher training, this process in Kyrgyzstan may be more akin to "traditional positioning in for-profit sectors" (ibid., 160; Amsler 2011). In a competitive context where the most marketable niche to occupy is the capacity to occupy a range of marketable niches, the institutions with the greatest resources to do so—accumulated historically, by association with governmental and international power, or through reputation and prestige—have the most capacity for differentiating themselves strategically. This, in addition to the traditional forces of state and market, may have a significant impact on the further development of Kyrgyzstan's higher education landscape for the foreseeable future.

Notes

1. In 1991, the population was 4,422,000; in 2001, 4,968,119; in 2011, 5,551,888; and in 2015, 5,960,000. The ethnic composition of the population in 2013 was 72% Kyrgyz, 14.4% Uzbek, 6.5% Russian, and 7.1% others (Tajik, Kazakh, Ukrainian, Tatar, Korean, and German) (NSC 2013a, 2014a). Kyrgyzstan is, by World Bank classification, a 'lower-middle-income' country with 3.5% annual growth in 2015 (NSC 2015; World Bank 2016). The country's GDP is heavily dependent on agriculture; mineral resources such as gold, mercury, uranium, and electricity export; and migrants' remittances working in Russia, Kazakhstan, and other CIS countries. With a Gross Domestic Product of $6.57bn, Kyrgyzstan relies on official development aid, revenues from exporting mineral resources, and migrant labourers' remittances from work in Russia and other CIS countries.
2. Data for the Frunze special secondary school and Osh Technical University was not available.
3. Key legislation and policy include the Law On Education (1992) and its amendments in 1997, 2003, 2008, etc.; the creation of the 'Bilim' National Education Program (1996); the introduction of State Educational Professional Standards in Education (2000); the adoption of the 'Education for All' goals of the Dakar Agreement (2001); constitutional revisions (2003); the Development Strategy for Higher and Professional Education of the Kyrgyz Republic (2003); and National Education Strategies, 2007–2010 (2006) and 2012–20 (2012).

References

Amsler, S. 2007. *The Politics of Knowledge in Central Asia: Science Between Marx and the Market*. London: Routledge.

———. 2008. Higher Education Reform in Post-Soviet Kyrgyzstan: The Politics of Neoliberal Agendas in Theory and Practice. In *Structure and Agency in the Neoliberal University*, ed. J. Canaan and W. Shumar. London: Routledge.

———. 2013. The Politics of Privatisation: Insights from the Central Asian University. In *Educators, Professionalism and Politics: Global Transitions, National Spaces and Professional Projects*, Routledge World Yearbook 2013, ed. T. Seddon and J. Levin. London: Routledge.

Asian Development Bank. 2004. Education Reforms in Countries in Transition: Policies and Processes. Six Country Case Studies Commissioned by the Asian Development Bank in Azerbaijan, Kazakhstan, Kyrgyz Republic, Mongolia, Tajikistan, and Uzbekistan. http://www.pitt.edu/~weidman/2004-educ-reforms-countries.pdf. Accessed 16 Aug 2016.

Bengard, A. 2015. Kyrgyzstan pri VUZax zakryli 23 instituta [Universities in Kyrgyzstan Close 23 Institutes], 31 July 2015. http://24.kg/obschestvo/17092_v_kyirgyizstane_pri_vuzah_zakryili_23_instituta/. Accessed 21 Aug 2016.

Brunner, J.J., and A. Tillett. 2007. Higher Education in Central Asia: The Challenges of Modernization. In *Case Studies from Kazakhstan, Tajikistan, the Kyrgyz Republic, and Uzbekistan*. Washington, DC: World Bank and International Bank for Reconstruction and Development.

Buyanin, Y. 2001. The Kyrgyz of Naryn in the Early Soviet period: A Study Examining Settlement, Collectivisation and *dekulakisation* on the Basis of Oral History Evidence. *Inner Asia* 13 (2): 279–296.

Clark, N. 2005. Education Reform in the Former Soviet Union. *World Education News and Reviews*. http://www.wes.org/eWENR/PF/05dec/pffeature.html. Accessed 29 Aug 2016.

DeYoung, A. 2011. *Lost in Transition: Redefining Students and Universities in the Contemporary Kyrgyz Republic*. Charlotte NC: Information Age Publishing.

Drummond, T., and S. Gabrscek. 2012. Understanding the Higher Education Admissions Reforms in the Eurasian Context. *European Education* 44 (1): 7–26.

Fumasoli, T., and J. Huisman. 2013. Strategic Agency and System Diversity: Conceptualizing Institutional Positioning in Higher Education. *Minerva* 51 (2): 155–169.

———. 2011. Decree No. 496 of August 23, 2011 № 496. *On the Establishment of a Two-tier Structure of Higher Professional Education in the Kyrgyz Republic*, Bishkek.

———. 2012. Resolution No. 201 of March 23, 2012 on the Strategic Directions for the Development of the Education System in the Kyrgyz Republic. http://cbd.minjust.gov.kg/act/view/ru-ru/92984. Accessed 21 Aug 2016.

Heyneman, S.P. 2010. A Comment on the Changes in Higher Education in the Post-Soviet Union. *European Education* 42 (1): 76–87.

Holmes, B., G.H. Read, and N. Voskresenskaya. 1995. *Russian Education: Tradition and Transition*. New York: Garland Publishing.

Huisman, J. 1995. *Differentiation, Diversity and Dependency in Higher Education: A Theoretical and Empirical Analysis*. Utrecht: Lemma.

Ibraimov, O. 2001. *Kyrgyzstan: Encyclopedia. Bishkek: Center of National Language and Encyclopedia Publication*.

Khalid, A. 1999. *The Politics of Muslim Cultural Reform: Jadidism in Central Asia*. Berkeley: University of California Press.

Merrill, M.C. 2016. Kyrgyzstan: Quality Assurance – Do State Standards Matter? *International Higher Education* 85: 27–28.

Mertaugh, M. 2004. Education in Central Asia, with Particular Reference to the Kyrgyz Republic. In *The Challenge of Education in Central Asia*, ed. S. Heynemann and A.J. DeYoung. Greenwich: Information Age Publishing.

Ministry of Education, Science and Youth Policy of the Kyrgyz Republic. 2006. Education Development Strategy of the Kyrgyz Republic, Bishkek. Approved by the MoE on 19 October 2006 (order #658/1).

Morgan, A.W., E. Kniazev, and N. Kulikova. 2004. Organizational Adaptation to Resource Decline in Russian Universities. *Higher Education Policy* 17: 241–256.

Narkoziev, A., and V. Yanzen. 2013. '*Opyt i perspectivy reformirovania systemy obrazovania v Kyrgyzstane*' *[Experiences and Perspectives of the Education System in Kyrgyzstan]*. Bishkek: Kyrgyz Russian Slavonic University.

National Statistical Committee. 2008. *Education and Science in the Kyrgyz Republic, 2002–2006*. Bishkek: National Statistical Committee.

National Statistical Committee (NSC). 2012a. *Education and Science in the Kyrgyz Republic: 2007–2011*. Bishkek: National Statistical Committee.

———. 2012b. *Education and Science in the Kyrgyz Republic: 1991–2011*. Bishkek: National Statistical Committee.

———. 2013a. *Education and Science in the Kyrgyz Republic*. Bishkek: National Statistical Committee.

———. 2014a. *Education and Science in the Kyrgyz Republic, 2009–2013*. Bishkek: National Statistical Committee.

———. 2014b. *Socio-economic Position of Kyrgyz Republic*. Bishkek: National Statistical Committee.

———. 2014c. *Dynamic Statistics of Students in Educational Institutions*. Bishkek: National Statistical Committee.

———. 2015. *Kyrgyz Republic Financial Sector Stability Report*. Bishkek: National Statistical Committee.

———. 2016. *Socio-Economic Position of Kyrgyz Republic*. Bishkek: National Statistical Committee.

National Tempus Office, Kyrgyzstan. 2016. Higher Education in Kyrgyzstan. Last modified August, 18, 2016. http://eacea.ec.europa.eu/tempus/participating_countries/overview/Kyrgyzstan.pdf. Accessed 28 Aug 2016.

Orusbaeva, B. et al. 1982. *Encyclopedia of Kirgiz Soviet Socialist Republic*. Frunze: Glavnaya Redakzia Kirgizskoy Sovetskoy Enziclopedii.

Reeves, M. 2005. Of Credits, *kontrakty* and Critical Thinking: Encountering "Market Reforms" in Kyrgyzsatni Higher Education. *European Education Research Journal* 4 (1): 5–21.

Shamatov, D. 2012. Impact of Standardized Tests on University Entrance Issues in Kyrgyzstan. *Europe Education* 44 (#1): 71–92. (Special volume guest edited by T.W. Drummond and A.J. DeYoung: New Educational Assessment Regimes in Euroasia: Impacts, Issues, and Implications).

———. 2015. Teachers' Pedagogical Approaches in Kyrgyzstan: Changes and Challenges. In *Transforming Teaching and Learning in Asia and the Pacific: Case Studies from Seven Countries*, ed. E. Hau-Fai Law and U. Muira, 90–123. Paris: UNESCO.

———. 2011. Education and Postsocialist Transformation in Central Asia – Exploring Margins and Marginalities. In *Globalization on the Margins: Education and Postsocialist Transformations in Central Asia*, ed. I. Silova. Charlotte: Information Age Publishing.

Teichler, U. 1988. *Changing Patterns of the Higher Education System*. London: Jessica Kingsley.

Tiuliundieva, N. 2008. The Financing of Higher Education in Kyrgyzstan. *Russian Education & Society* 50 (1): 75–88.

Van Vught, F. 2008. Mission Diversity and Reputation in Higher Education. *Higher Education Policy* 21 (2): 151–174.

World Bank. 2016. Kyrgyz Republic. http://data.worldbank.org/country/kyrgyz-republic. Accessed 25 Aug 2016.

Jarkyn Shadymanova Jarkyn Shadymanova is an associate professor at the Department of sociology, Bishkek Humanities University. She has a doctoral degree in Sociology and has been a postdoctoral fellow at the Sociology of Consumption and Households Group, Wageningen University (2012, 2014) and Department of anthropology, University of Amsterdam (2017). She is author of the monograph The role of Mass Media in Social Change in Kyrgyzstan (2008). Her Research focuses higher education reform in Kyrgyzstan, ICT and sustainable consumption.

Sarah Amsler is a reader in Education at the University of Lincoln. She is author of *The Politics of Knowledge in Central Asia: Science from Marx to the Market* (2007), 'The politics of privatization: insights from the Central Asian university' (2013), and *The Education of Radical Democracy* (2015). Her research focuses on the politics of knowledge and higher education, neoliberal education reforms, critical and radical pedagogies, and the democratization of education.

Open Access This chapter is distributed under the terms of the Creative Commons Attribution 4.0 International License (http://creativecommons.org/licenses/by/4.0/), which permits use, duplication, adaptation, distribution and reproduction in any medium or format, as long as you give appropriate credit to the original author(s) and the source, provide a link to the Creative Commons license and indicate if changes were made.

The images or other third party material in this chapter are included in the chapter's Creative Commons license, unless indicated otherwise in a credit line to the material. If material is not included in the chapter's Creative Commons license and your intended use is not permitted by statutory regulation or exceeds the permitted use, you will need to obtain permission directly from the copyright holder.

CHAPTER 10

Latvia: A Historical Analysis of Transformation and Diversification of the Higher Education System

Ali Ait Si Mhamed, Zane Vārpiņa, Indra Dedze, and Rita Kaša

THE SOVIET HIGHER EDUCATION LANDSCAPE IN LATVIA

Several of the contemporary higher education institutions (HEIs) in Latvia emerged at the start of the twentieth century and even before. Higher education in Latvia, one of the Baltic States with a population of approximately two million, is more than 150 years old and has developed through several transformations in different political and socioeconomic contexts.

The first HEI in Latvia was Riga Polytechnicum, later renamed Riga Polytechnic Institute, which was established in 1862 under the Russian

---

A. A. S. Mhamed (✉) • R. Kaša
Nazarbayev University, Astana, Kazakhstan

Z. Vārpiņa
Stockholm School of Economics in Riga, Riga, Latvia

I. Dedze
Ventspils University College, Ventspils, Latvia

© The Author(s) 2018
J. Huisman et al. (eds.), *25 Years of Transformations of Higher Education Systems in Post-Soviet Countries*, Palgrave Studies in Global Higher Education, https://doi.org/10.1007/978-3-319-52980-6_10

Empire, first with German and then Russian as the language of instruction (RTU 2002, 2013). With the proclamation of the independent Republic of Latvia in 1918, the transformation of the higher education (HE) sector in Latvia continued. The first national HEI with Latvian as the language of instruction was established in 1919 on the foundations of Riga Polytechnic Institute (RTU 2013; LU 1999, 35). In 1923, this HEI was given the title University of Latvia. The development of the University of Latvia was a national priority, to which the government allocated 15% of the total national budget (LU 1999) between 1919 and 1940.

Several other HEIs were established during the first independence period. The Conservatoire of Latvia opened in 1919 and the Academy of Arts was established in 1921. These two institutions, like the University of Latvia, were located in the capital city of Riga. In 1939, the Department of Agriculture and Forestry separated from the University of Latvia (LU 2014) and became the Academy of Agriculture in Jelgava. The start of higher education in sports and teacher education in Latvia also dates back to the 1920s, when the government established the Latvian Institute of Physical Education and state teacher training institutes were opened in Daugavpils and Rezekne (LPE1 1981).

Political, social and economic shifts associated with the establishment of Soviet rule in Latvia prior to and after World War II shaped transformations in the higher education sector as well. In 1940, directly after the Soviet occupation, the University of Latvia was changed in name and structure: it became the State University of Latvia. Those occupying management and governance positions were replaced. The schools of theology were closed, other schools were renamed and departments were established for Marxism-Leninism and other political and military disciplines (LU 2009). The two-stream language model of instruction in Latvian and Russian was also introduced (LU 1999). In the Stalinist era of the Soviet period, higher education was characterised by ideological purges and the repression of faculty and students. It also marked the movement to separate science from higher education according to the Soviet model (LU 2009).

Ensuing transformations of the higher education sector involved continuing the diversification of the institutional landscape. It included relocating several HEIs from the supervision of the Ministry of Education to the supervision of the ministries of various sectors. Several new HEIs were established, some on the foundations of the existing structures established prior to 1940. Among those formed based on existing organisational structures were Rezekne State Pedagogical Institute established in 1941, the State Institute of Physical Culture established in 1946, Daugavpils Pedagogical Institute in 1952 and Liepaja Pedagogical Institute established in 1954. These HEIs were placed under the oversight of the Ministry of Education. In 1950, Riga Medical Institute was separated from the State University of Latvia and established as an independent HEI under the supervision of the Ministry of Healthcare (LPE1 1981, 485–487). Riga Polytechnic Institute, which initially formed the basis for the University of Latvia, was re-established as an independent HEI in 1958 (RTU 2002). A new institution was established in 1960, the Institute of Civil Aviation Engineering, the purpose of which was to prepare civil aviation professionals for the entire Soviet Union (LPE5 1984, 581). When Latvia proclaimed its independence from the USSR in 1990, the higher education system consisted of ten state HEIs; five HEIs were placed under the Ministry of Education and others were operating under the auspices of the ministries of healthcare, culture and agriculture (Table 10.1).

Higher education in Soviet Latvia was under full state control, organised to serve the needs of the centrally planned economy and the official Marxist-Leninist ideology. Institutional collaboration was limited to the HEIs of the Soviet bloc countries. The main focus of the higher education system was on the natural sciences and Soviet ideology, while social sciences and languages, except for Russian, were marginalised (Eglīte 2009; Heyneman 2000). Higher education in Latvia was expected to add to the building of the Soviet state, reshaping the social structure along socioeconomic and ethnic lines (Karklins 1984; Walder 1990).

The number of study places to be filled per HEI and study programme was determined by the state. Students could apply to either a Russian or Latvian language variant of a study programme (LU 1999). The most popular study programmes at HEIs did not have difficulties selecting the best applicants, but there were different approaches to filling vacant study slots in the least popular study programmes. During Soviet times, the State University of Latvia offered admission to the least popular study programmes to students who failed to enter their preferred study programme. It also organised additional admissions to unpopular programmes for applicants who had failed to enter other HEIs (LU 1999, 231–234). There was some student mobility taking place across the Soviet Republics; every year there were students from other parts of the USSR admitted to HEIs in Latvia, while a few students from Latvia were also admitted to other Soviet Republics with little to no HE entry competition (LPE5 1984, 581).

Table 10.1 Types of HEIs in Latvia by 1989 characteristics

Type of HEI	Number of HEIs	Ministerial oversight	Type of HEI
Flagship Public, located in Riga, multidisciplinary, undergraduate through advanced graduate study programmes	1 HEI State University of Latvia	Ministry of Higher and Specialized Secondary Education (MHSSE)	Multidisciplinary university
Public specialised HEIs Public, specialised or narrow specialisation, teaching, undergraduate, graduate and in some cases advanced graduate study programmes	9 HEIs Liepaja State Institute of Pedagogy	MHSSE	Specialised in teacher training
	Daugavpils Pedagogical Institute	MHSSE	Specialised in teacher training
	Riga Polytechnic Institute	MHSSE	Specialised in technical education
	Latvia Academy of Agriculture	Ministry of Agriculture	Specialised in agriculture
	Riga Medical Institute	Ministry of Healthcare	Specialised in medical education
	Conservatoire of Latvia	Ministry of Culture	Specialised in arts
	Art Academy of Latvia	Ministry of Culture	Specialised in arts
	State Institute of Physical Culture	MHSSE	Specialised in sports education
	Institute of Civil Aviation Engineering	Ministry of Civil Aviation	Specialised in aviation and transport

Source: Authors based on MoES data, bylaws and HEI websites

Although officially higher education in the USSR was free as it was entirely funded by the government, research documents the application of tuition fees and limited student financial assistance for various periods of time (DeWitt 1955; Dobson 1977). Tuition fees at the State University of Latvia were waived in 1957 and stipends were introduced (LU 1999, 259–260). Outstanding students had higher monthly stipends than average students (LVU 1982, 6). In 1989, tuition fees were reintroduced due to the admission of more students successfully passing the entrance examination than planned (LU 1999, 261).

Transformation of the Higher Education Sector Since 1990

The transition period from the centrally planned Soviet system to a democratic liberal market economy in Latvia involved challenging economic and social burdens. There was a dramatic collapse of production and real income, accompanied by a surge in poverty and social inequality. The restructuring of the economy involved massive declines in agriculture and industry, resulting in unemployment and a decline in individual well-being. The transition pushed 22% of the population in Latvia under the poverty line. The recession did not level off until 1994, while poverty and inequality remained a persistent attribute of the new system (Norgaard et al. 1999). These challenging socioeconomic conditions formed the context for the transformations of the higher education sector in Latvia after 1990. At the same time, the national political priority of integration into European structures, which eventually led to Latvia becoming a full member of the European Union (EU) in 2004, provided the direction for higher education reforms. Accession to the EU and acquired global openness strengthened the Europeanisation and internationalisation of higher education in Latvia (Kaša and Ait Si Mhamed 2013, 34).

Private Higher Education Institutions

The most important accomplishments of the higher education reform during the transition period from the centrally controlled Soviet system to a democratically governed system were the expansion of the HE sector in terms of the number of institutions and students, the creation of private HEIs, the introduction of HE quality assessment, the development of new study programmes and the modernisation of existing study programmes, and the intensification of international cooperation between HEIs in Latvia and abroad (Rivža 2004, 71–72).

After independence, higher education reforms in Latvia were in line with the Bologna process that started in 1999 and aimed at creating a European Higher Education Area (EHEA) with enhanced academic mobility (Štefenhagena 2012). As part of this process, Estonia, Latvia and Lithuania created a common higher education area in 2000 by agreeing to recognise the higher education qualifications of the others. In the following years, the integration of Latvia's higher education system into the EHEA progressed. In 2007, the European Credit Transfer System (ECTS) was introduced, which allows for higher education comparison and recognition across the EU. Since 2012, Latvia has been a full-fledged member of the EHEA. Figure 10.1 presents the milestones of the post-independence period.

In addition to European orientation, a liberal market has dominated the underlying steering philosophy of the post-independence higher education reforms in Latvia. This has allowed for the emergence of one of the largest private HE sectors in the region (Pachuashvili 2009). It also provided public HEIs in Latvia with rather high levels of institutional autonomy as compared to other countries in Europe (EUA 2012). As a result, in 2014 there were 60 HEIs in Latvia enrolling 184,132 students (MoES 2015). While private colleges were newly created, most public colleges were established on the foundations of vocational schools that existed prior to 1990. In 2004, these vocational schools were essentially renamed and reorganised into public colleges providing short-cycle higher education in order to achieve integration with the EHEA. Figure 10.2 indicates developments in the number of HEIs in the country.

Student Enrolment

Since 1991, all HEIs in Latvia have autonomously decided the total number of students admitted annually. Immediately after independence, total

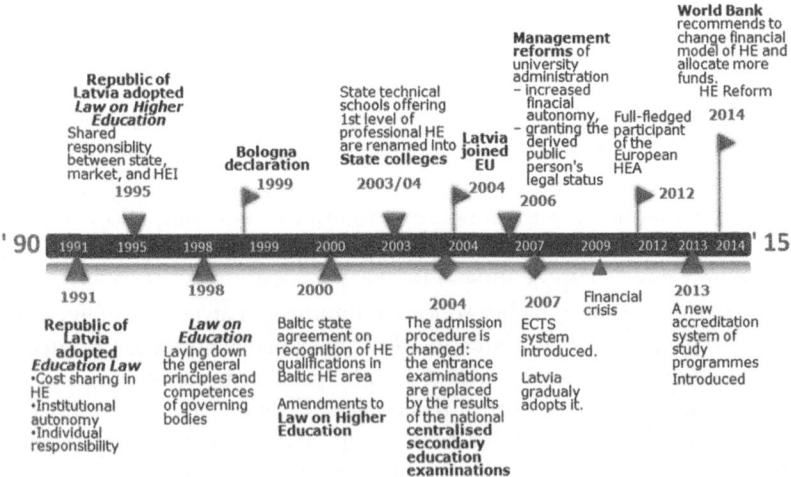

Fig. 10.1 Milestones in the development of the higher education system in Latvia, 1990–2014 (Source: Authors)

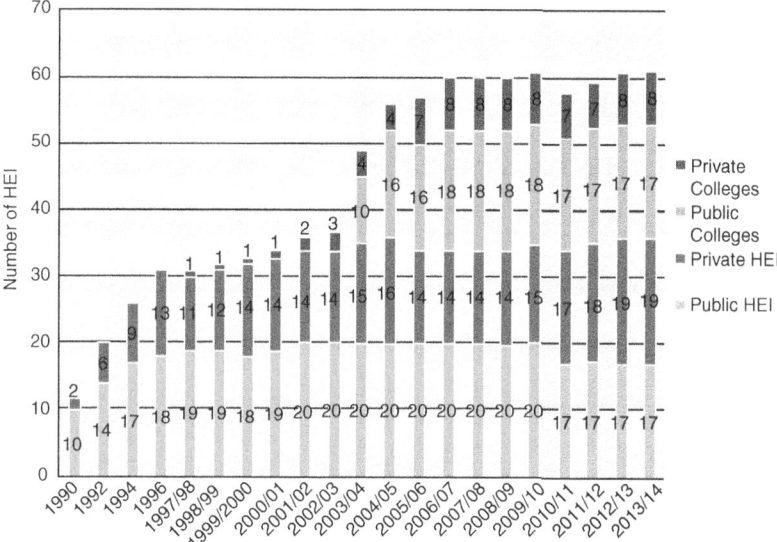

Fig. 10.2 The dynamics of HEIs in Latvia, 1990–2014 (Source: Authors based on data from MoES, 1991 to 2014)

student enrolment decreased from 42,000 in 1992 to 38,986 in 1993 because there were no more students coming in from the other former Soviet Republics (Latvijas Enciklopēdija 2002). However, in the mid-1990s, the increase in the number of students resumed to reach 46,680 in 1994. Between 2005 and 2014, the total number of students in Latvia declined by 34% (MoES 2015) (see also Fig. 10.3).

Participation in higher education increased due to tuition-paying students. All students at private HEIs, with negligible exceptions, paid tuition. Public HEIs reminiscent of the Soviet era applied a dual-track tuition approach based on the idea of public procurement in higher education (Kaša and Loža 2001). That is, the government continued to provide funding to educate a certain number of students free of charge who studied alongside students paying tuition. Admission to these publicly funded study slots remained merit-based, taking into account only the applicant's grades (Kaša 2007). In 2004, admission to HEI undergraduate studies changed from independently organised entrance examinations to the standardised national secondary school leaving exams (Cabinet Regulations 846 2006; Saeima 1995a). In 2005, the number of fee-paying students as

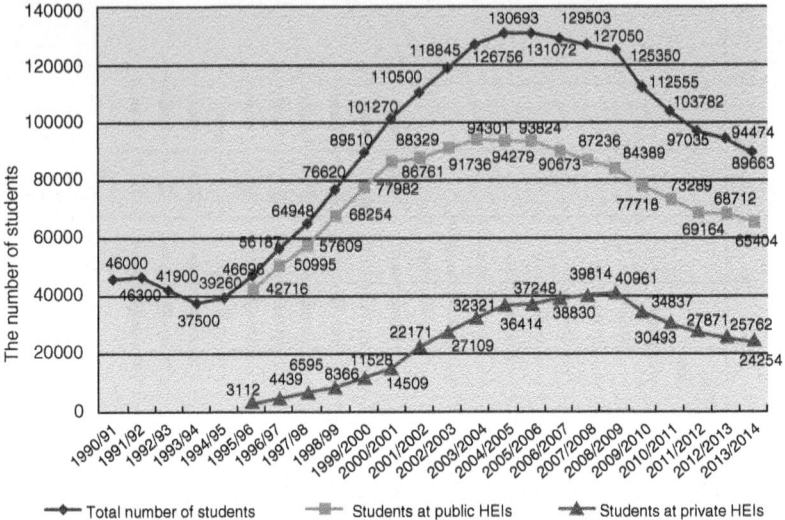

Fig. 10.3 The dynamics of HE student enrolment in Latvia, 1990–2014 (Source: Authors based on data from MoES, 1991 to 2014)

a proportion of the total number of students in the country reached 70%, but this share started to decrease later, reflecting a demographic decline in traditional-age cohort students. In 2014, the proportion of tuition-paying students was 40% of all students in Latvia (MoES 2015).

Legislation Regarding the Higher Education System

According to the Law on Higher Education Establishments (Saeima, 1995a), Latvia has a binary higher education system, which pertains mostly to the level of study programmes and is not strictly institutionalised. This means that both university and non-university institutions in Latvia can run academic and professional study programmes, and most HEIs choose to do so. The only exceptions to this rule are colleges (first-level professional higher education institutions) which offer short-cycle tertiary education (ISCED 5) in the form of professional study programmes only (Eurydice 2014). Legislation in Latvia supports the mobility of higher education graduates from professional to academic higher education programmes and vice versa.

The law of higher education institutions established the division of university and non-university institutions in 1995, prescribing conditions for the use of specific terms in HEI titles. The types of HEIs according to the law in Latvia are universities, academies, institutions of higher education and colleges (Saeima 1995a). The legislation allows for institutions to change their status and evolve over time from one type of institution to another. The process of a non-university institution becoming a university institution is illustrated by the example of Liepaja University, which was initially a narrowly specialised HEI that eventually transformed into a university (see Text Box 10.1).

> **Text Box 10.1. The Case of Liepaja University**
> Liepaja University is the youngest university in Latvia. It was established in 1954 as Liepaja Institute of Pedagogy and has since changed its name seven times, eventually acquiring university status in 2008 (Saeima 2008):
>
> 1. Liepaja Institute of Pedagogy (01.08.1954–19.06.1961)
> 2. Liepaja State Institute of Pedagogy (20.06.1961–27.04.1966)
> 3. V.Lāča Liepaja State Institute of Pedagogy (28.04.1966–January, 1990)
> 4. Liepaja Institute of Pedagogy (February,1990–10.02.1993)
> 5. Liepaja Higher School of Pedagogy (11.02.1993–08.06.1998)
> 6. Liepaja Academy of Pedagogy (09.06.1998–15.07.2008)
> 7. Liepaja University (since 16.07.2008)
>
> In 2014, Liepaja University was accredited as a state higher education institution offering study programmes on all three levels: Bachelor, Master, and Doctoral. It was the only university located in the Western part of Latvia, in the Kurzeme region, and can be considered a small, regional higher education institution.
> Initially, this HEI offered teacher training for preschools, primary schools and teachers specialising in mathematics and Latvian language and literature. Since 1990 it has also added non-pedagogical study programmes, with the aim of shifting from a single-profile HEI to a multi-profile institution offering a broad spectrum of study programmes. Eventually in 2008, it became Liepaja University and

> by 2014 had four faculties and offered 34 study programmes in social sciences, business, humanities and arts, natural sciences, mathematics, IT, pedagogic and educational sciences, and social welfare. The university employed 101 academic staff, of which 53 had a PhD degree.
>
> Source: Developed by authors based on Saeima 2008.

The state steers the differentiation of the higher education system through accreditation and licencing. Licensed study paths encompass various study programmes offered by HEIs (Saeima 1995a). The primary purpose of this process is higher education quality assurance, confirming that HEIs have sufficient resources to carry out their intended study programmes rather than enforcing a specific profile (Cabinet Regulations 407 2015; Cabinet Regulations 408 2015). The higher education quality assurance system, which is primarily based on accrediting study paths rather than study programmes, was introduced in Latvia in 2011 in the context of reforms related to the Bologna Process (Saeima 1995a).

The HEI quality assurance reform was a result of ongoing effort to achieve better performance. Substantial institutional autonomy was regarded as another way to improve the quality of higher education, allowing institutions more flexibility in their institutional development decisions. From the start in 1995, there was an emphasis on HEI institutional autonomy, but substantial transformation only took place in 2006 when HEI law (Saeima 1995a) was amended to increase the autonomy of public HEIs.

Despite substantial financial autonomy, public HEIs in Latvia found themselves in very challenging circumstances between 2009 and 2014, because overcoming the economic crisis of 2009 required significant cuts in the public budget (Aslund and Dombrovskis 2011). The World Bank found the Latvian HEI funding system to be contingent on basic funding only, and thus it does not follow the European trend. Based on the recommendations of the World Bank, the government of Latvia initiated a reform of the national higher education funding model to eventually introduce a three pillar financing model (World Bank 2014b). The introduction of the new funding model was gradual and started in 2015. Public funding to HEIs became available on the basis of the first and the second pillar, that is, basic funding and ex post performance funding (Cabinet

Regulations 994 2006). The third pillar is organised around innovation-oriented funding.

While public HEIs in Latvia enjoy a high degree of financial autonomy in comparison with their European counterparts, public HEIs remain more regulated by the state than private HEIs. As recipients of public funding, public HEIs are, for instance, required to observe more restrictive rules on the language of instruction than private HEIs.

Language of Instruction and Internationalisation

In 1998, the Parliament of Latvia passed the Law on Education (Saeima 1998), which in combination with the Official Language Law (Saeima 1999) and the Law on Higher Education Establishments (Saeima 1995a) stipulated Latvian as the language of instruction in public HEIs. One of the key reasons for such a national language policy in public higher education was to ensure that Latvian as the official state language is used and developed in national higher education (Klava et al. 2010, 14). It was also argued that the aim of such a language policy is to avoid English becoming the single language used in higher education and research in the country, given its international dominance. A further but related aim is to maintain and develop terminology in the national language to be used in research in order to ensure the quality of higher education studies. Also, there was acknowledgement of the fact that the level of English language among academic staff and students might not be sufficient for effective use (Davidsen-Nielsen 2010; Druviete 1998). By 2014, several amendments to the law enabled public HEIs in Latvia to carry out study programmes in the official EU languages, including English, if certain preconditions are met.

Private HEIs on the other hand were more advantaged regarding the use of a foreign language of instruction in Latvia. They were able to offer HE study programmes not only in English but also in Russian, which is not an official EU language. Although there was a portion of international students at private HEIs in Latvia studying in Russian, evidence shows that these programmes mainly catered to the local Russian-speaking student population (Kaša and Ait Si Mhamed 2013). Restrictions on the use of foreign languages in higher education instruction for public HEIs have contributed to the diversification between public and private HEIs in Latvia; each caters to different pools of the student population. However, it should be mentioned that there are exceptions with English-taught public higher education in social sciences, law and business. These academic entities were established in the 1990s with special governmental support in order to modernise instruction in the aforementioned fields (Dovladbekova et al. 2006; Riga Business School 2015; RGSL 2014; Saeima 1995b). All of these cases involved collaboration with Western HEIs and presented another trajectory in post-Soviet higher education system diversification.

With the exception of the Stockholm School of Economics in Riga (SSE Riga), which from the very start was established to educate students from all three Baltic countries (Saeima 1995b), all other public institutions offering study programmes in a foreign language of instruction have evolved to enrol an increasing number of international students. In 1995, there were 648 international degree-seeking students studying at public and private HEIs in Latvia, compared to 5293 in 2014 (MoES 2014). Internationally mobile students in Latvia originated from a vast number of countries in the East and West (Kaša and Ait Si Mhamed 2013). By the end of the first decade of the new millennium, international students from former Soviet Union countries acquiring higher education in the Russian language mainly enrolled in the private HE sector (Priednieks and Kukliča 2012). The majority of degree-seeking international students studying in English mainly come from other EU countries and choose the HE public sector. The most popular study programmes in the English language among internationally mobile students were programmes in business, medical sciences and social sciences. The most popular programmes in Russian among international students included information technologies, logistics and business (Kaša and Ait Si Mhamed 2013).

Nearly all international students as well as the largest share of local students study at HEIs located in the capital of Riga (MoES 2014). Riga is home to the largest public and private HEIs in the country. However, the availability of higher education in other regions during the post-Soviet period increased with the opening of new public HEIs in the Western and Northern parts of the country. Some HEIs outside the capital that were narrowly specialised in Soviet times have also evolved into universities. In addition, many private and public HEIs have branches operating in major regional towns. From the perspective of institutional diversity, the regionalisation of higher education in post-Soviet Latvia has contributed to more choices for higher education seekers. However, Riga is still the central destination for students and its attractiveness contributes to migration from the regions.

Factors of Diversification

Since national independence in 1990, there has been a steep increase in the demand for modern higher education training in the social sciences, which was not available during the Soviet era driven by Marxist-Leninist ideology. This contributed to the expansion of higher education in the social sciences (see Fig. 10.4). Another factor driving student demand in the social sciences was the secondary education reform in the early 1990s, which gave high school students the choice of focusing on the social sciences and humanities or mathematics and natural sciences. As the government did not incentivise private HEIs to develop study programmes in the hard sciences, this HE sector is limited to study programmes in social sciences, commerce and information technology. Study programmes in natural sciences and engineering are clustered in the public HE sector only.

Another aspect of higher education diversification by student characteristics is age. As explained earlier, higher education participation in post-Soviet Latvia doubled and tripled at its peak in 2005 as compared to 1990 (Fig. 10.3). In the 2000s, the prevalence of traditional students aged 17–23 started diminishing and the proportion of non-traditional or mature-age students increased. This shift in the demographic composition of higher education students was driven by demographic changes in terms of smaller youth cohorts, as well as the necessity of engaging in life-long

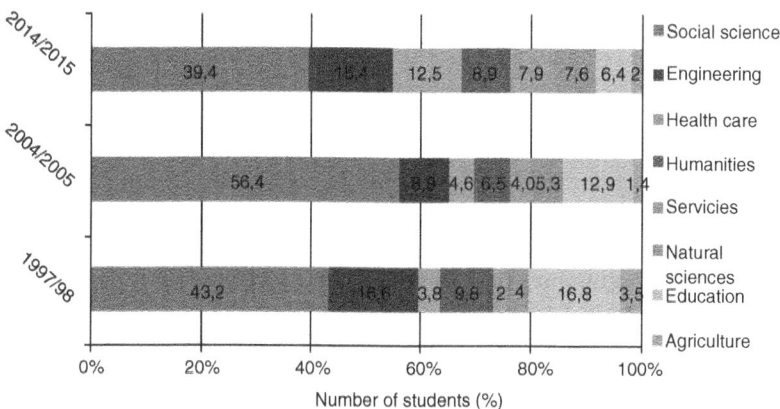

Fig. 10.4 Proportion of the number of students in different fields of study (Source: Authors based on data from MoES 1998 to 2014)

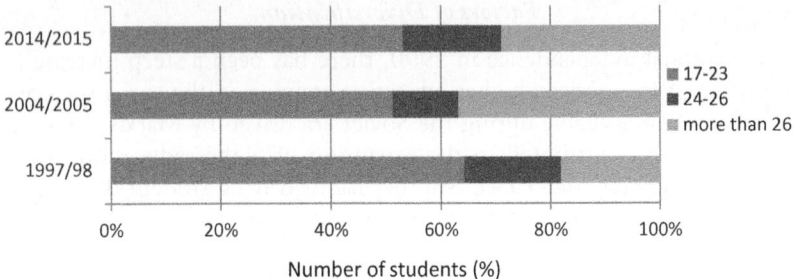

Fig. 10.5 Proportion of students by age group (Source: Authors based on data from MoES 1998 to 2014)

learning to upgrade education obtained during Soviet times. In 2014, nearly 30% of all students in Latvia were older than 26 (Fig. 10.5).

At the HEI level, however, there have not been significant differences in student clustering by age. In 2014, all HEIs showed a relatively similar distribution of students by age (MoES 2015). Thus, while there was a system-level trend towards a more diverse age composition of HE students, there was no significant diversification by this factor among HEIs in Latvia.

The overall observation about HE system diversification from 1990 to 2014, with a focus on programme provision and student characteristics, suggests that institutional autonomy has enabled most HEIs in the country to engage with demands and expectations in rather similar ways. An exception here is language policy in higher education, which has limited public HEIs in delivering study programmes in non-official EU languages such as Russian. This has instead been an area of activity for private HEIs in Latvia. On the other hand, private HEIs did not have the capacity to offer study programmes in natural sciences, as such institutional development was not incentivised by the government. Although there were formal governmental regulations allowing private HEIs to request public funding for programmes that are unique and competitive in the national HE market (World Bank 2014a), the government continued to provide direct funding to public HEIs only. Cases in which private HEIs receive public funding to implement study programmes are therefore the exception rather than the rule. Because public funding was also limited in the public HEI sector, all HEIs were sensitive to the market demand for higher education.

Typology of Higher Education Institutions in Latvia

By 2014, several types of HEIs in Latvia had emerged in terms of the range of study programmes offered. One type includes specialised HEIs offering study programmes in only one area, like the National Defence Academy or the College of Medicine. The second type of HEI offers study programmes in two to four areas, and the third type is multidisciplinary, offering study programmes in five or more areas. Changes in study programmes offered in various areas by HEIs reflect institutional ability to develop new study programmes in new areas in an attempt to develop competitiveness in higher education markets.

The type of specialisation, however, was not the only characteristic which distinguished different types of institutions, especially since they reacted to market pressures in similar ways. There were additional characteristics such as primary function: teaching or research, location, ownership, size, levels of study. When taking into account this set of characteristics, HEIs in Latvia can be placed into seven groups consisting of flagships, regional HEIs, public specialised HEIs, internationally developed specialised HEIs with English as the language of instruction, private HEIs, both public and private colleges, and branches of foreign HEIs (see also Table 10.2).

In 2014, the University of Latvia and the Riga Technical University qualified as flagships of the HE system. They enrolled one-third of all students in Latvia (MoES 2015). Both of these HEIs have a history that precedes the Soviet era. In the years after independence since 1990, the University of Latvia has developed into the most comprehensive HEI in the country. While the focus of the Riga Technical University (RTU) has remained largely on technical sciences, it has also expanded since 1990 by developing study programmes in social sciences and business. Both the University of Latvia and RTU are multidisciplinary HEIs which offer undergraduate, graduate and advanced graduate/PhD study programmes. They are important research centres of national and international orientation.

The second type of HEI, regional HEIs, encompasses public institutions established both prior to and after the independence of Latvia in 1990. These HEIs are located outside the capital of Riga in the regional centres of the country. The University of Applied Sciences and Ventspils University College are both newly established regional HEIs with the primary objective of developing regionally accessible higher education. The remaining

Table 10.2 Types of HEI in Latvia by 2015 characteristics and ministerial affiliation

Type of HEI	Number of HEIs	Ministerial oversight
Flagships Public, located in Riga, multidisciplinary, important research centres, undergraduate through advanced graduate study programmes, national and international orientation	2 HEIs University of Latvia Riga Technical University	 The Ministry of Education and Science (MoES) MoES
Regional HEIs Public, located in regional centres, multidisciplinary, teaching and research, undergraduate and advanced graduate study programmes, significant regional orientation	5 HEIs Vidzeme University of Applied Sciences Ventspils University College University of Liepaja, Daugavpils University, Rezekne Higher Education Institution	 MoES MoES MoES
Public specialised HEIs Public, specialised or narrow specialisation, teaching, research, undergraduate, graduate, and in some cases advanced graduate study programmes, national and international orientation	10 HEIs Latvia University of Agriculture Riga Stradins University Jāzeps Vītols Latvian Academy of Music, Art Academy of Latvia Latvian Academy of Culture Latvian Maritime Academy Latvian Academy of Sports Education Riga Teacher Training and Educational Management Academy (RPIVA) BA School of Business and Finance National Defence Academy	 The Ministry of Agriculture The Ministry of Health The Ministry of Culture The Ministry of Culture MoES MoES MoES MoES The Ministry of Defence

(*continued*)

Table 10.2 (continued)

Type of HEI	Number of HEIs	Ministerial oversight
Specialised HEIs with English as language of instruction Public or private, specialised, teaching, research, undergraduate and graduate study programmes, national and international orientation, international and national founders, English as language of instruction	3 HEIs	
	Stockholm School of Economics in Riga	MoES
	Riga Graduate School of Law	MoES
	Riga International School of Economics and Business Administration (RISEBA)	MoES
Private HEIs Private, specialised and narrow specialisation, teaching, research, undergraduate, graduate, advanced graduate study programmes, national and international orientation, study programmes in official EU languages and in Russian	13 HEIs	
	Transport and Telecommunication Institute (established on the bases of former Institute of Civil Aviation Engineering)	MoES
	Riga Aeronautical Institute (established on the basis of former Institute of Civil Aviation Engineering)	MoES
	ISMA University of Applied Sciences (established on the basis of former Institute of Civil Aviation Engineering	MoES
	Ten other private HEIs with specialisation in social sciences, humanities, commerce, and services	MoES
Colleges Public and private, specialised and narrow specialisation, teaching, professional study programmes only, national and international orientation	25	
	17 public colleges	MoES for the majority, one for the Ministry of Health, one for the Ministry of Culture, three for the Ministry of Interior, one for Ministry of Welfare
	Eight private colleges	MoES

(*continued*)

Table 10.2 (continued)

Type of HEI	Number of HEIs	Ministerial oversight
Branches of foreign HEIs	3 HEIs Riga Higher Institute of Religious Sciences affiliated to the Pontifical Lateran University (RARZI) Lateran Pontifical University Branch—Riga Institute of Theology Moscow State University of Economics, Statistics and Informatics (MESI) Riga branch	MoES

Source: Authors based on MoES data 2015, bylaws and HEI websites

three HEIs have evolved from an initially specialised focus on teacher education during Soviet times into multidisciplinary institutions. In 2014, all five HEIs were multidisciplinary in orientation and delivered undergraduate, graduate and PhD study programmes. While these HEIs are engaged in international projects and have a national orientation, they also have a strong regional focus in terms of responding to regional policies and human capital and cultural needs. The mission of these institutions includes both teaching and research.

The group of public specialised HEIs is comprised of ten institutions, six of which share past Soviet experiences and four of which were established after 1990. The newly established specialised HEIs each serve a specific purpose: national security, the development of the financial sector, the modernisation of pedagogical and management education, and the development of international intercultural relations. Among the other six HEIs, the most significant transformation took place with Riga Stradins University (RSU), known as the Riga Medical Institute during Soviet times. While this HEI has continued to provide education and research in medicine, it has also developed study programmes in social sciences. Other HEIs in this group have also somewhat diversified their offer of study programmes, but within their primary subject areas. All of these HEIs are focused on teaching, with various degrees of international and research engagement.

Specialised HEIs with English as the language of instruction form a group of three institutions which were established as the result of major international collaboration. The Stockholm School of Economics in Riga was established in 1994, endorsed by the Latvian and Swedish governments with the purpose of providing state-of-the-art education in business and economics for the Baltic region (SSE Riga 2015). Providing state-of-the-art education in law and related social science fields, the Riga Graduate School of Law was established 1998 and is also supported by the governments of Latvia and Sweden (RGSL 2014). All of these HEIs teach exclusively in the English language, providing undergraduate and graduate education to students from Latvia and abroad. They have a strong international orientation and are also engaged in research.

The set of private HEIs in Latvia represents a diverse group of specialised and narrow specialisation institutions. This group is diverse in terms of historical heritage and contemporary focus. Three HEIs in this group have emerged from the former Soviet Institute of Civil Aviation Engineering. These HEIs maintain a focus on aviation and transportation systems. Other private HEIs have emerged in response to the post-1990 demand for higher education in social sciences, services, commerce and humanities. Most private HEIs in Latvia offer undergraduate and graduate study programmes, while others also offer PhD study programmes. Some are predominantly teaching oriented, although many are engaged in research activities with a national and international scope. An orientation to attract both national and international students is another characteristic of private HEIs in Latvia, which offer study programmes in English and Russian.

Colleges represent the sixth type of HEI. Both private and public colleges are the result of post-1990 legislative amendments in Latvia. While most public colleges share a Soviet past as vocational educational institutions, private colleges are the outcome of attempts to satisfy market demand in higher education after Latvian independence. All the colleges offer specialised first-level professional higher education. Although colleges predominantly enrol local students, some have a strong international orientation and all are engaged in international collaboration networks.

The last type of HEI, branches of foreign HEIs, is quite distinguished. In 2014, there were three such HEIs in Latvia. Of these, two were theological HEIs and one was a branch of the Moscow State University of Economics, Statistics and Informatics. The presence of such an HEI form did not exist in Soviet Latvia. Ministries overseeing HEIs remain the same as during Soviet times, creating unequal conditions for public HEIs depending on the wealth of each sector (World Bank 2014a). However, all HEIs in Latvia face similar higher education market conditions in terms of attracting tuition-paying students to their institutions.

Conclusion

Institutional history and the ability to respond to higher education market conditions have influenced how various HEIs have developed in Latvia. Compared to the Soviet period, the HE landscape has diversified. The Soviet HEI model with exclusively public and predominantly specialised HEIs has been replaced by a model of public and private specialised and multidisciplinary HEIs. The main drivers for this development were the liberalisation of the higher education sector and intensified demand for higher education among both traditional and non-traditional student age cohorts, especially in the social sciences (Kaša et al. 2016).

By 2014, the higher education landscape in Latvia consisted of 35 university and non-university HEIs offering both academic and professional study programmes, as well as 25 colleges offering short-cycle or professional first-degree higher education programmes. Furthermore, after 1990 HEIs in Latvia were longer operating in a secluded higher education space. On the contrary, integration into the EHEA and the internationalisation of higher education became an important national goal in the scope of higher education reform. EU membership provided conditions for the free movement of persons in Europe and supported student ability to travel abroad. Hence, Latvian HEIs no longer compete only on the national level (Cunska 2012). They face global competition for both local and international students, a condition unknown prior to 1990.

Given the context of a demographically shrinking student age cohort as well as national engagement with European higher education policy initiatives, migration and fluctuating economic conditions, it is likely that transformations of the institutional landscape in Latvia have only just begun.

References

Aslund, A., and V. Dombrovskis. 2011. *How Latvia Came Though the Financial Crisis*. Washington, DC: Peterson Institute for International Economics.
Cabinet Regulations 407. 2015. Augstskolu, koledžu un studiju virzienu akreditācijas noteikumi [Regulations on the Accreditation of Higher Educational

Institutions, Colleges, and Study Directions]. *Latvijas Vēstnesis* 146(5464). http://likumi.lv/ta/id/275560-augstskolu-koledzu-un-studiju-virzienu-akreditacijas-noteikumi. Accessed 1 Oct 2015.

Cabinet Regulations 408. 2015. Studiju programmu licencēšanas noteikumi [Regulations on the Licensing of the Study Programmes]. *Latvijas Vēstnesis* 146(5464). http://likumi.lv/ta/id/275563-studiju-programmu-licencesanas-noteikumi. Accessed 1 Oct 2015.

Cabinet Regulations 846. 2006. Noteikumi par prasībām, kritērijiem un kārtību uzņemšanai studiju programmās [Regulations on the Requirements, Criteria and Procedure for Admission to Study Programmes]. *Latvijas Vēstnesis* 172(3540). http://likumi.lv/ta/id/275563-studiju-programmu-licencesa-nas-noteikumi. Accessed 1 Oct 2015.

Cabinet Regulations 994. 2006. Kārtība, kādā augstskolas un koledžas tiek finansētas no valsts budžeta līdzekļiem [Regulations on the Procedure of State Budget Financing to Institutions of Higher Education and Colleges]. *Latvijas Vēstnesis* 200(3568). http://likumi.lv/doc.php?id=149900. Accessed 27 Sept 2015.

Cunska, Z. 2012. Iedzīvotāju izglītības līmenis Latvijā. [Level of Education of Inhabitants of Latvia]. In *Universitāšu ieguldījums Latvijas tautsaimniecībā [The Contribution of Universities to the Economy of Latvia]*, 17–29. Rīga: Latvijas Universitāšu asociācija.

Davidsen-Nielsen, N. 2010. Language in Higher Education: A Danish View. In *National Languages in Higher Education*, ed. M. Humar and M.Ž. Karer, 87–90. Ljubljana: ZRC Publishing.

DeWitt, N. 1955. *Soviet Professional Manpower: Its Education, Training and Supply*. Washington, DC: National Science Foundation.

Dobson, R. 1977. Social Status and Inequality of Access to Higher Education. In *Power and Ideology in Education*, ed. J. Karabel and A.H. Halsey, 245–274. New York: Oxford University Press.

Dovladbekova, I., T. Muravska, and T. Paas. 2006. Transformation of Higher Education as the Precondition for Competitive Development in Estonia and Latvia. *European Legacy* 11 (2): 171–184. doi:10.1080/10848770600587953.

Druviete, I. 1998. *Latvijas valodas politika Eiropas Savienības kontekstā*. Rīga: Latvijas Zinātņu Akadēmijas Ekonomikas insitutūts.

Eglīte, P. 2009. Padomju okupācijas demogrāfiskās, sociālās un morālās sekas Latvijā. *Latvijas Zinātņu Akadēmijas Vēstis* 63(1/2): 86–106. http://www.lza.lv/LZA_VestisA/65_3-4/6_Eglite_Padomju okupac.pdf. Accessed 1 Oct 2015.

EUA. 2012. *EUA's Public Funding Observatory*. Brussels: European University Association.

Eurydice. 2014. *The Structure of the European Higher Education Systems 2014/15: Schematic Diagrams.* http://eacea.ec.europa.eu/education/eurydice/facts_and_figures_en.php#diagrams. Accessed 1 Oct 2015.
Heyneman, S.P. 2000. Educational Evaluation and Policy Analysis. *Educational Evaluation and Policy Analysis* 22(2): 173-191. http://www.jstor.org/stable/1164394. Accessed 4 Dec 2015.
Karklins, R. 1984. Ethnic Politics and Access to Higher Education: The Soviet Case. *Comparative Politics* 16 (3): 277-294.
Kaša, R. 2007. Devolution of Student Financial Assistance in Latvia. Unpublished PhD dissertation, SUNY Buffalo, Buffalo.
Kaša, R., and A. Ait Si Mhamed. 2013. Language Policy and Internationalization of Higher Education in the Baltic Countries. *European Education* 45 (2): 28-50.
Kaša, R., and Z. Loža. 2001. The State Financing for Higher Education: Financial Flow Mechanisms. In *A Passport to Social Cohesion and Economic Prosperity: Report on Education in Latvia 2000*, ed. G. Catlaks, I. Dedze, S. Heyneman, and K. Krēsliņš, 14-26. Riga: Soros Foundation – Latvia.
Kaša, R., A. Ait Si Mhamed, I. Dedze, and Z. Cunska. 2016. Trajectories of Higher Education Massification in Latvia. *HERB* 2 (8): 27-28.
Klava, G., K. Klave, and K. Motivāne. 2010. *Latviešu valodas prasme un lietojums augstākās izglītības iestādēs: mazākumtautību izglītības satura reformas rezultāti [Knowledge and Use of Latvian Language at the Institutions of Higher Education: The Results of the Curriculum Reform at Ethnic Minority Schools].* Rīga: Latviešu valodas agentūra.
LE. 2002. Latvijas Enciklopēdija [*Encyclopaedia of Latvia*], Volume 1, Entry "Augstākā izglītība" pp: 378-379. SIA "Valērija Belokoņa izdevniecība", Rīga.
LPE1. 1981. In *Latvijas padomju enciklopēdija. 1. Sējums [Encyclopaedia of Soviet Latvia. Volume 1]*, ed. P. Jērāns and S. Ziemelis. Rīga: Galvenā enciklopēdiju redakcija.
LPE5. 1984. In *Latvijas padomju enciklopēdija. 5. Sējums [Encyclopaedia of Soviet Latvia. Volume 5]*, ed. P. Jērāns and S. Ziemelis. Rīga: Galvenā enciklopēdiju redakcija.
LU. 1999. In *Latvijas Valsts universitātes vēsture, 1940-1990 [History of the State University of Latvia, 1940-1990]*, ed. H. Strods. Rīga: Latvijas Universitāte.
———. 2014. Latvijas Universitāte. Vēsture. [History of the University of Latvia]. http://www.lu.lv/par/vts/vesture/. Accessed 12 Jan 2014.
LVU. 1982. *P. Stučkas Latvijas Valsts Universitāte. [Latvia State University of P. Stučka].* Riga: Avots.

MoES. 1998. *Pārskats par Latvijas augstskolu darbību 1998. gadā. [Annual Report on Latvia's Higher Education in 1998]*. Riga: The Ministry of Education and Science.

———. 2014. *Pārskats par Latvijas augstāko izglītību 2013. gadā (galvenie statistikas dati) [Review on Higher Education in Latvia in 2013: Main Statistical Indicatotrs]*. Riga: Ministry of Education and Science.

———. 2015. *Pārskats par Latvijas augstāko izglītību 2014. gadā [A Review on Higher Education in Latvia in 2014]*. Rīga: Izglītības un zinātnes ministrija.

Norgaard, O., L. Johannsen, M. Skak, and R.H. Sorensen. 1999. *The Baltic States After Independance*. 2nd ed. Northampton: Edward Elgar Publishing.

Pachuashvili, M. 2009. The Politics of Higher Education: Governmental Policy Choices and Private Higher Education in Post-Communist Countries. http://web.ceu.hu/polsci/dissertations/Marie_Pachuashvili.pdf. Accessed 25 Oct 2011.

Priednieks, A., and I. Kukliča. 2012. Augstākās izglītības eksports. [Export of Higher Education]. In *Universitāšu ieguldījums Latvijas tautsaimniecībā [The Contribution of Universities to the Economy of Latvia]*, 56–65. Rīga: Latvijas Universitāšu asociācija.

RGSL. 2014. Riga Graduate School of Law (RGSL) History. http://www.rgsl.edu.lv/en/inside-rgsl/about/history/. Accessed 5 Dec 2015.

Riga Business School. 2015. RTU Riga Business School. http://www.rbs.lv/about-rbs/about-rbs. Accessed 5 Dec 2015.

Rivža, B. 2004. The Structure of the Higher Education System and the Role of Research. In *UNESCO Forum Occasional Paper Series Paper No. 6. Diversification of Higher Education and the Changing Role of Knowledge and Research* (ED-2006/W ed.), 70–82. Paris: UNESCO.

RTU. 2002. *Augstākās tehniskās izglītības vēsture Latvijā, 1. daļa [The History of Technical Higher Education in Latvia: Part One]*. Rīga: Rīgas Tehniskā universitāte.

———. 2013. Rīgas Tehniskā Universitāte. Vēsture [History of Riga Technical University]. http://www.rtu.lv/content/view/19/924/lang,lv/. Accessed 3 Dec 2015.

Saeima. 1995a. Augstskolu likums [The Law on Higher Education Establishments]. *Latvijas Vēstnesis* 179(462). http://likumi.lv/doc.php?id=37967. Accessed 27 Sept 2015.

———. 1995b. Par Rīgas Ekonomikas augstskolu [About Stockholm School of Economics in Riga]. *Latvijas Vēstnesis* 164/165. http://likumi.lv/doc.php?id=37448. Accessed 5 Dec 2015.

———. 1998. Izglītības likums [The Law on Education]. *Latvijas Vēstnesis* 343/344. http://likumi.lv/doc.php?id=50759. Accessed 1 Oct 2015.

———. 1999. *Valsts valodas likums* [Official Language Law]. *Latvijas Vēstnesis* 428/433. http://likumi.lv/doc.php?id=14740. Accessed 1 Jan 2015.
———. 2008. Likums "Par Liepājas Universitātes Satversmi" [Law 'On the Constitution of Liepaja University']. *Latvijas Vēstnesis* 100(3884). http://likumi.lv/doc.php?id=177519. Accessed 10 Oct 2015.
SSE Riga. 2015. SSE Riga Mission and History. http://www.sseriga.edu/en/about/overview/mission-and-history/. Accessed 5 Dec 2015.
Štefenhagena, D. 2012. Universitātes regulējošais tiesiskais ietvars [The Legal Regulatory Framework of Universities]. In *Universitāšu ieguldījums Latvijas tautsaimniecībā [The Contribution of Universities to the Economy of Latvia]*, 39–49. Rīga: Latvijas Universitāšu Asociācija.
Walder, A. 1990. The Political Dimension of Social Mobility in Communist States: Reflections on the Soviet Union and China. In *The Political Sociology of the State: Essays on the Origins, Structure, and Impact of the Modern State*, ed. R. Braungart and M. Braungart, 49–66. London: JAI Press Inc.
World Bank. 2014a. *Higher Education Financing in Latvia: Analysis of Strengths and Weaknesses*. World Bank Reimbursable Advisory Service on Higher Education Financing in Latvia. http://www.izm.gov.lv/images/izglitiba_augst/03.pdf. Accessed 22 Aug 2015.
———. 2014b. *Higher Education Financing in Latvia: Final Report*. World Bank Reimbursable Advisory Service on Higher Education Financing in Latvia. http://www.izm.gov.lv/images/izglitiba_augst/06.pdf. Accessed 22 Aug 2015.

Ali Ait Si Mhamed is currently an Associate Professor at Nazarbayev University Graduate School of Education, Astana, Kazakhstan, where he also serves as a member of the Policy Research Project "Development of Strategic Directions for Education Reforms in Kazakhstan", 2015–2020. He has a PhD in Comparative Education from the State University of New York in Buffalo, USA, and extensive teaching experience internationally (USA, Morocco, Latvia and Kazakhstan). Moreover, he was a World Bank Consultant on issues of finance of higher education. He has examined financial aid systems in Moroccan and Latvian higher education. Dr. Ali Ait Si Mhamed was a Fulbright Scholar from the USA to Latvia in 2011–2012.

Zane Vārpiņa obtained a PhD in Demography with specialisation in socioeconomic demography (Dr.demogr.) from the University of Latvia and has an MA of Science in Mathematical Economics from the same university. She also has an Inter-university Diploma in EU Studies, Université Nancy II, Aix-en-Provence Institute of Political Science. Zane Vārpiņa is Assistant professor at Stockholm School of Economics, Riga, since 2013. Zane Vārpiņa has research experience in the Baltic International Centre for Economic Policy Studies (BICEPS). Her main research interests include higher education and demography.

Indra Dedze holds a PhD degree in International Comparative Education from Stockholm University. Currently she is working at the University of Latvia. From 2009 to 2013, she was national research coordinator for Latvia for the EUROSTUDENT IV project. For several years she worked at NGOs: the Soros Foundation—Latvia, Centre for Public Policy PROVIDUS in Latvia and the Open Society Institute in Budapest. In all these organisations, Dedze was responsible for research projects in the field of Education Policy including cooperation with the NGO networks in Central Asia and Eastern Europe and international organisations. As a Fulbright fellow, Dedze carried out research on the evaluation of higher education management at Vanderbilt University, USA (2004–05).

Rita Kaša holds a PhD in Comparative Education from the State University of New York in Buffalo (SUNY Buffalo), USA, and MA and BA in Political Science from the University of Latvia. Her research interests concern educational policy, finance and governance. She especially focuses on student financial assistance policies, equity and equality in educational access in the context of intensifying transnationalism and migration. Prior to her current position as an Assistant Professor at Nazarbayev University Graduate School of Education in Kazakhstan, Rita held academic and administrative positions at the Stockholm School of Economics in Riga, Latvia.

Open Access This chapter is distributed under the terms of the Creative Commons Attribution 4.0 International License (http://creativecommons.org/licenses/by/4.0/), which permits use, duplication, adaptation, distribution and reproduction in any medium or format, as long as you give appropriate credit to the original author(s) and the source, provide a link to the Creative Commons license and indicate if changes were made.

The images or other third party material in this chapter are included in the chapter's Creative Commons license, unless indicated otherwise in a credit line to the material. If material is not included in the chapter's Creative Commons license and your intended use is not permitted by statutory regulation or exceeds the permitted use, you will need to obtain permission directly from the copyright holder.

CHAPTER 11

Lithuanian Higher Education: Between Path Dependence and Change

Liudvika Leišytė, Anna-Lena Rose, and Elena Schimmelpfennig

INTRODUCTION

This chapter provides an overview of transformation of the higher education landscape in post-Soviet Lithuania. Our special focus is on the vertical and horizontal system differentiation in an attempt to explain the main forces leading to such system dynamics. Lithuanian higher education has changed from an elite system with one flagship university towards a mass system with various institutions—both of university and non-university type. Vertical differentiation exists in terms of private higher education providers, regional providers as well as alliances between universities both on a national and international scale. Much of this differentiation was brought by political, economic and social changes, including the Soviet occupation of the country, the re-establishment of Lithuanian independence, the signing of the Bologna Declaration and the accession

L. Leišytė (✉) • A.-L. Rose
TU Dortmund, Center for Higher Education (zhb), Dortmund, Germany

E. Schimmelpfennig
Oskar Kämmer school, Hildesheim, Germany

© The Author(s) 2018
J. Huisman et al. (eds.), *25 Years of Transformations of Higher Education Systems in Post-Soviet Countries*, Palgrave Studies in Global Higher Education, https://doi.org/10.1007/978-3-319-52980-6_11

to the EU. Besides, a set of higher education reforms revealed the state's ambition to boost higher education quality and to ensure access to higher education to various segments of population.

EMERGENCE OF THE HIGHER EDUCATION SYSTEM IN LITHUANIA

Lithuanian Higher Education Before 1940

Lithuania has had a long-lived tradition of elite higher education. One of the oldest universities in Europe, Vilnius University, was established in the country's capital in 1579. Yet, Lithuania's turbulent history and political developments, on the one hand, and the nature of the industrialization and the dominance of agricultural sector in the country, on the other hand, had a significant impact on the development of the higher education system. Under the rule of the Russian Tsar, Vilnius University was shut down for almost a century from 1831 until 1919 and the Lithuanian language was banned. Lithuania regained independence in 1918, which led to the most important period for establishment and development of general, vocational and higher education in the country. New specialized professional training institutions, both regional and national, were central to the development of the Lithuanian nation state and were fostering Lithuanian culture, language and economy. After the end of World War I in 1918, Vilnius and the region surrounding it were annexed by Poland, but Vilnius University continued to function on Polish territory as Stefan Batory University until 1939. Therefore, a new 'University of Lithuania' (later named Vytautas Magnus University, VMU) was established in Lithuania's interim capital, Kaunas (Bumblauskas et al. 2004; Mašiotas 1923).

By 1940, the time of the Soviet annexation, Lithuania had the following institutions of higher education: Vilnius University (VU, which became Lithuanian after the territory of Vilnius was returned to Lithuania in 1939), the Vilnius Art School (established in 1940 on the basis of an VU department), the Vytautas Magnus University (established as the University of Lithuania in 1922 in Kaunas), the Agricultural Academy (1924, Dotnuva), the Conservatoire of Kaunas (1933), the Institute of Commerce (1934, Klaipėda, 1939–1944 in Šiauliai), the National Pedagogical Institute (1935, Klaipėda), the Veterinary Academy (1936, Kaunas) and the Kaunas Art School (1922, renamed the Kaunas School of Applied Arts in 1940) (OECD 2002; Leišytė 2002).

Lithuanian Higher Education During the Soviet Period (1940–1941 and 1944–1990)

Based on a political agreement between the Soviet and German governments, the Baltic States became part of the Soviet Union in June 1940. Although the first period of Soviet control over Lithuania lasted only 1 year (1940–1941), it was the time when a formal restructuring of the Lithuanian higher education system based on the Soviet standards commenced (Procuta 1967; Šakalys 1985). Vytautas Magnus University lost its Faculties of Theology and Philosophy. Many academics were relieved from their duties, and those engaged in intellectual resistance were arrested and sent to Siberian Gulags (OECD 2002; Zulumskytė 2014, 118; Leišytė 2002; KTU 2016b; VMU 2016). Teaching and research activities were separated into different institutional settings with the establishment of the Lithuanian Academy of Sciences. After the end of WWII, the higher education sector was redesigned according to the Soviet model and became subject to Moscow's centralized control (Leišytė 2002). Vytautas Magnus University was closed in 1950, and its medical and technological faculties were re-established as independent institutes. However, many other higher education institutions that had existed before the war were re-opened and new faculties covering the Soviet agricultural and industrial needs were founded. A restructured Lithuanian higher education, which followed the Soviet model of higher education, was achieved by the mid-1950s and specialized institutions in the main cities and their subsidiaries in the regions performed the major task of preparing teachers, engineers and doctors for the Soviet-industrialized economy (Šakalys 1985). Universities, which traditionally acted as centres of teaching and research according to a Humboldtian model, were thus redefined as centres for professional training, and academic freedom and autonomy were eliminated, while the curriculum was controlled by the state (Suchodolski 1971; Želvys 2004). The goal of higher education was mainly focused on polytechnic education and training the 'socialist man', and the traditions of Lithuanian higher education aimed at educating Lithuanian citizens according to Christian values were eradicated (Leišytė 2002). Despite this, Lithuanian remained the main language of instruction (ibid.) (Fig. 11.1).

In Lithuania, industrialization was not as rapid and heavy compared to Estonia and Latvia (Willerton 1992). In the 1960s, however, industrialization in Lithuania started to pick up in the regions, which triggered the geographical spread of some of the higher education institutions. For example,

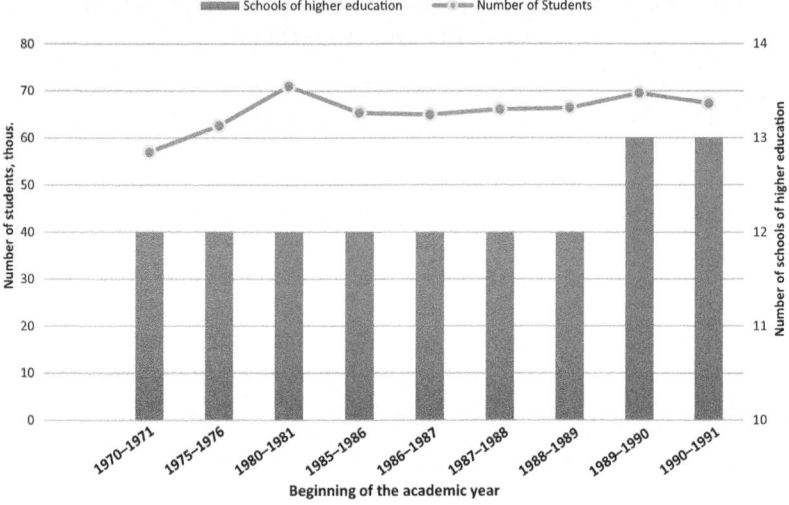

Fig. 11.1 Number of schools of higher education and number of students in Lithuanian SSR (1970–1990) (Source: Statistics Lithuania: Official Statistics Portal)

to cater for the needs of electrical and mechanical engineering in the north of the country, which hosted a Soviet military airport, key factories producing electronics, as well as bicycles and naval engineering in the west of the country, Kaunas Technology Institute faculties or extramural programmes were established in the cities of Panevėžys, Šiauliai and Klaipėda. Thus, we can observe some horizontal differentiation in this period.

By the end of the Soviet era in 1989, the Lithuanian higher education system consisted of one university (Vilnius University, centrally funded from Moscow to prepare the academic and party elites), one music conservatory, five institutes, four academies and one Higher Party School. VMU, which was a symbol of independent Lithuania and its intellectual elite, was destroyed. The role of the state was severely interventional. All processes, including core academic activities, were controlled by the Ministries of Education either in Vilnius or in Moscow. Higher education in the Soviet period was free, while access to higher education was based on merits for the Communist party, affiliation to it being an important requirement. By 1990, the gross enrolment ratio in higher education was

33.25%, which is slightly higher than in the other Baltic states at that time: to compare, Estonia (24.75%) and Latvia (24.87%).

Lithuanian Higher Education in 1990

The Lithuanian higher education landscape in 1990 inherited the legacy of a diversified system from the Soviet period and pre-WWII Lithuania. In contrast to many other Soviet republics, Lithuania had already begun to act independently from the Soviet Union prior to its official dissolution in 1990. In the 1980s under the policy of *glasnost*, Lithuanian democracy movements started to weaken the Soviet institutional base of government establishments. It served as a foundation for and laying the basis for the new higher education system (OECD 2002). The first step towards transformation of the Soviet model of higher education in Lithuania took place in 1989–1990, when Vytautas Magnus University (VMU) in Kaunas was re-established. It was supported by Lithuanian expats who returned to their fatherland at that time, predominately from the USA and Canada. The institution was designed as a liberal arts university, adopted the US-American academic degree system with bachelor's and master's degrees and offered programmes in English. As such, the re-establishment of VMU was a symbol for both the imminent breakdown of the Soviet Union and the profound changes that would occur within the Lithuanian higher education system in the years to come. At that time, in 1989, many higher education establishments already prepared the new statutes (OECD 2002).

The first and most significant political step towards the restructuring of the Lithuanian higher education sector was to reform the higher education legal basis. The Constitution of Lithuania ensured the autonomy of universities and free higher education for qualified students. The first enacted laws were the Law of the Republic of Lithuania concerning the Approval of the Status of Vilnius University (1990), the Framework Law on Education and the Law on Higher Education and Science (LHE) (1991). The most important aspect for higher education institutions in Lithuania was to clear themselves from Soviet ideology and become autonomous from the state. The 1991 LHE defined the governance, autonomy and financing of higher education institutions in broad terms and showed confidence regarding quality and academic freedom of academics in Lithuania (OECD 2002). It allowed specialized institutes, which were preparing students for certain professions (such as medicine or engineering) to be renamed into universities or academies. In this way, the Academy of Music and Vilnius Art Academy were born. This trend of seeking prestige and rebranding into universities or academies was also noted as 'universification' (Želvys 2004), as it was rather obvious that the trend of relabelling the institutions could enhance their prestige. It also allowed some institutions to be 'upgraded' into universities, such as the former police professional school, which was reorganized into a university in Vilnius (Mykolas Romeris University at present). Regional institutes and technical colleges ('technicums') also took the chance to upgrade themselves. That is how two regional universities were created: Šiauliai University (based on former Pedagogical Institute and pre-war Commerce School moved from Klaipėda) and Klaipeda University (which had three faculties: Humanities and Education, Marine Technology, Social and Health Sciences). Further horizontal differentiation was allowed as the first private institutions appeared, although they were not officially recognized as part of the higher education sector until 2000. Another important development in 1990 in terms of horizontal differentiation was the establishment of religious higher education institutions, as well as Lithuanian Military Academy. These were institutions that embodied the economic, political and academic freedoms Lithuania regained: for instance, the military training was no longer taking place in Russia or Ukraine, at the bases for the Soviet Army, but in Lithuania for the Lithuanian Army. Lithuania, being a predominantly Catholic country, also got an opportunity to profess its religion, which meant that apart from the Catholic Seminary in Kaunas, Telšiai and Vilnius Seminaries were opened.

Thus, the preconditions for promoting the geographical spread of higher education institutions and horizontal differentiation were created in 1991 with the enactment of the first regulatory frameworks. At the same time, the system experienced chronic underfunding, low wages, high inflation and decreasing quality, although still having the features of elite higher education (with only 50,000 students in the system of 3.7 million population of Lithuania in 1990). The task of governing higher education institutions was given to a newly created Department for Science and Higher Education of the Republic of Lithuania and the government of Lithuania. The following table presents a typology of institutions in 1990 (Table 11.1).

Table 11.1 Typology of higher education institutions in Lithuania in 1990

Traditional flagship university	Vilnius	**VU:** comprehensive, high prestige, traditional, strong links with Soviet academic elites, had national university status during Soviet times, many professors got their doctorates abroad (mainly in Russia)
Re-established liberal arts comprehensive university	Kaunas	**VMU:** re-established in 1989 following the liberal arts model of the US higher education, high percentage of foreign educated academic staff, very international and dynamic
Specialized technological universities	Vilnius Kaunas Šiauliai Panevėžys Klaipėda	**VGTU and KTU:** focus on technology and engineering, architecture with faculties and departments in many other cities, strong traditional links with Soviet industry and research institutes, well established and prestigious, traditional
Specialized other universities	Vilnius Kaunas Šiauliai Klaipėda	**KMA, VDA, LMA, VPU, LŽUA:** focus on pedagogy, sports, arts, agriculture, medicine, veterinary science, music, religion. Well established, nationally known, traditional

POLICY DEVELOPMENTS AND OTHER FACTORS INFLUENCING STRUCTURAL CHANGE IN LITHUANIAN HIGHER EDUCATION AFTER 1990

Since 1990, significant changes have taken place within the Lithuanian higher education system in terms of horizontal and vertical differentiation as well as inter-organizational collaborations (Leišytė and Kiznienė 2006; Leišytė et al. 2015; Želvys 2004). The main advances of higher education transformation included system expansion in terms of the amount and types of higher education institutions, as well as the number of students, the creation of binary higher education system, the agglomeration of research institutes into universities and the mergers of faculties and institutions. These developments were partly caused by increasing competition between institutions, changes in funding models of higher education, demographic downturn and immigration partly facilitated by access to Western European higher education markets and academic mobility due to EU membership. Changes were brought about by incremental legislative changes (Laws on Science and Higher Education, 1991, 2000 and 2009), numerous bylaws, as well as constant policy developments related to the Europeanization of the system (Bologna Process, EU accession, EU

Structural Funds availability), international donor influences (the World Bank, Nordic Council of Ministers, Soros Foundation in Lithuania), transformation of the academic system after the collapse of the Soviet Union (dismantling the Lithuanian Academy of Sciences research institutes), and the collapse of certain industries and a consequent lack of demand for certain graduates and certain types of research. In the following sections, we provide a policy development account during the main three periods of structural change of the system: 1990–2000, 2001–2009, 2010 to present.

Years 1990–2000: Regained Autonomy and Sporadic Expansion

The main changes in the Lithuanian higher education sector in the early 1990s were rather sporadic and focused on renaming and 're-establishment' of universities and academies. The foundation of two regional universities followed the logic of regional revival, because due to the economic downturn, regional authorities were pressing for 'having university in their city'. At the same time, the former technical institutes in Kaunas and Vilnius, which were training engineers and architects for the Soviet economy, were rebranded into Technology universities (in this way Kaunas University of Technology and Vilnius Gediminas Technical University were created). While in 1989, the majority of students in Central and Eastern European countries studied natural sciences and engineering, the 1990s saw a decrease in these fields and an increasing demand for programmes in the humanities and the social sciences (Scott 2015). As a consequence, some universities in Lithuania, such as Kaunas University of Technology, expanded their profiles by adding the social sciences and the humanities in order to absorb large numbers of fee-paying students, especially in management and business, as well as humanities.

In 1991, universities in Lithuania were granted a high degree of autonomy to relinquish the Soviet political grip on higher education. The Law on Science and Higher Education (1991) defined the boundaries of state regulation (Leišytė 2002). The two instruments which remained at the state's disposal were the funding of higher education as well as the demand for certain type and number of graduates. The governmental bodies controlling universities were dispersed, which allowed a sporadic expansion of the system and led to chronic underfunding. This was soon compensated by the introduction of tuition fees (a merit-based system was established, where a certain number of study places at the entrance to higher education were state funded, while others could enter the university, but had to pay). From the mid-1990s onwards, student numbers started to increase substantially, as did the share of fee-paying students, which changed from 3.5% in 1995–1996 to 33.1% in 2000–2001. Universities started to compete for students, as they were bringing in extra cash. Due to sporadic expansion, the quality of higher education was deteriorating. As international support from the PHARE programme, the Council of Europe and foreign donors started coming in, the Centre for Quality Assessment in Higher Education was established in 1995 to ensure the quality as well as to accredit the study programmes (ibid.). The Centre also took over the role of recognizing foreign degrees, as this became a necessity due to increasing outgoing mobility of students. This development indirectly showed that the state was coming back into the game of supervising higher education sector and monitoring via intermediary agency.

The funding of foreign donors was highly important for the process of re-establishment and change not only in terms of global structural landscape but also for introducing institutional changes. Based on the US system, bachelor (4 years) and master's (2 years) system was foreseen in study programmes of universities since 1991. In contrast to Soviet times, universities were expected to carry out research and grant doctoral degrees again, which increased their power vis-à-vis other higher education institutions and called for the implementation of a stronger teaching-research nexus than before. The governance of higher education in the 1990s was carried out between university rectors and the Department for Science and Higher Education (which was later incorporated into the Ministry of Education and Science of Lithuania) (ibid.). The Lithuanian Science Council acted as an advisory body, while the Parliament and its education committee were approving the budget. These were the actors with which university leaders had to constantly engage in discussions about the future of the system. The Academy of Sciences was restructured: it lost its research institutes and remained as a 'club' of elite professors. Nevertheless—although it did not possess its main instruments anymore, namely, research governance and funding—it continued to exert some of its power in the policy networks.

The University Rectors' Conference has been a very central and powerful actor in higher education policy decision-making in Lithuania since 1990, lobbying the government and parliament committees to ensure that their interests were met (ibid.). It was strongly opposing the creation of a private sector in higher education and was initially successful. As shown by

Leišytė (2002), attempts to introduce reforms in management and governance structures, funding and teaching methods in higher education remained rather unsuccessful. Universities also opposed the establishment of colleges to minimize competition. Consequently, in contrast to the other Baltic states (Estonia and Latvia), where the private sector had emerged at early stages of independence, the Lithuanian higher education sector initially saw a slow growth in private universities.

In 1999 and 2000, however, after many years of resistance by other actors, the first private universities gained official state recognition. Moreover—partly driven by the significant expansion of the number of students, which was caused both due to higher number of high school graduates and the entrance of older students, who needed new types of diplomas in order to requalify themselves for the new market—the LHE passed in 2000 fostered the expansion of the system by creating the non-university higher education sector. First plans to establish a non-university higher education sector and to reorganize technicums (technologically oriented professional schools established during Soviet times) and professional colleges, which were counted as post-secondary vocational education institutes back in the 1990s, into colleges were made. After long debates between the Rectors' Conference, the Higher Education Department and the leaders of former technicums, the big structural change—the creation of a binary system of higher education—took place in 2000. The Law foresaw university (doctorate granting) and non-university (colleges or universities of applied sciences, providing undergraduate degrees) institutions of higher education. The non-university colleges were allowed to offer undergraduate level degrees. A high demand for new degree programmes, especially in the field of management and law studies, was filled in by private colleges, which started to mushroom after 2000.We can say that this Law set the conditions for deregulation and increased autonomy of higher education institutions towards the corporate state model to use Gornitzka and Maassen's typology (2000). It also provided a framework for student fees within the auspices of the contract between the Ministry of Education and Science (MoES) and the higher education institutions according to different disciplines that covered the full costs of studies (Mockienė 2004). On October 1, 2000, there were **92,800** students in public higher education institutions of which **28,600** were self-financed (DeSHE 2001; Leišytė 2002).

Hence, we can observe that after regaining independence in 1990, Lithuanian higher education shifted between academic elite coordination and sporadic state interference. Student numbers were decreasing until 1995–1996 from 67,000 in 1990 to 54,000 in 1995 as many high school graduates preferred to go to the 'new market' and earn money as the prestige of higher education was dwindling. However, after the first worst transition period, the numbers of students rose sharply from 59,000 in 1996–1997 to 96,000 in 2000–2001 (Leišytė 2002). Though the OECD (2002) notes that the acceleration has not been as drastic as in other countries in the region, the demand for higher education has risen and even enhanced with the expansion and diversification of the system (OECD 2002). Due to the increase in the number of students and high demand for retraining, extramural courses flourished, which was a good source of funding for institutions, very often to the detriment of programme quality (Dobbins and Leišytė 2014).

Years 2001–2009: The Main System Expansion and EU Accession

Since the adoption of the LHE in 2000, no explicit strategic goals or priorities for higher education policy were formulated. At the same time, in 2001 the demand for higher education was rising: the gross enrolment ratio in the tertiary education in Lithuania was about 70% (UNESCO 2002/2003). This phenomenon was accompanied by concerns about the quality of higher education, the mismatch between market/society needs and university outputs (Leišytė and Kiznienė 2006). Various proposals how to address higher education's problems were made by the Science Council of Lithuania, the Rectors' Conference and the Ministry of Education. Policy rhetoric called for the more efficient use of scarce funding, for more accountability and better management (ibid.). According to Žalys (2004), the government programme of 2001–2004 envisaged a higher education development plan, outlining the state's aims and objectives. However, the government did not approve the development plan drawn up by the Department of Higher Education and Science—allegedly due to a lack of political determination on the one hand and an inability to reach consensus among the main interest groups on the other. Thus, for five years higher education developed without clearly stated aims and without a clear government higher education policy except for the tacit aim of expansion.

An important development in the period of 2001–2009 included the expansion of the number of institutions as a number of private universities and colleges were created. The first private institution to be officially recognized as a university in 1999 was Vilnius St. Joseph Seminary, followed by the Lithuanian Christian College and ISM University of Management and Economics (1999), Vilnius University International Business School (2000) and Telšiai Bishop Vincentas Borisevičius Priest Seminary (2001). The real expansion of private sector did, however, take place in 2002, when the college sector saw the boom of private colleges. Traditionally, private colleges were rather small in size and narrowly oriented. They used to specialize in social sciences, management and economics offering law and business bachelor's degrees or professional education, such as nursing. Recently, the focus of the colleges has however somewhat broadened. The private college sector served 20% of the Lithuanian college student body and was quite an important alternative in Lithuanian higher education. In the university sector, however, public universities had the majority of students, as only around 4,000 students were enrolled in private universities in 2005 (Leišytė and Kiznienė 2006).

Not only private colleges, but the whole college sector saw a boom in the early 2000s. The seven first public and private colleges were established in 2000. They offered 41 study programmes to about 3,500 students. By 2002, there were 16 public and private colleges which offered 242 study programmes to 26,000 students. A year later, the total number of colleges had grown to 27. A decrease in this number can be witnessed only after 2008/2009, when several colleges merged (Official Statistics Portal 2015).

After the first wave of significant system expansion and differentiation in early 2000, some new institutions also became part of the system. Despite the debates against private universities, one more specialized institution was created (Vilnius Academy of Business Law in 2003; renamed as Kazimieras Simonavičius University in 2012). Furthermore, two international universities became part of Lithuanian higher education system in this period. The European Humanities University (EHU) was initially founded in Minsk in 1994 in Belarus and—after having been shut down by the national authorities in 2004—was re-established in exile in Vilnius in 2005 with support from the European Union funds. The university has a strong sense of Belarusian identity and—while also admitting international academic staff and students—primarily serves as a 'haven of academic freedom' for Belarusian students and staff. Another example of international presence in Lithuanian higher education was the opening of a branch of the Polish University of Bialystok in Vilnius 'Faculty of Economics-Informatics' in 2007. It was opened following an initiative to increase the level of higher education among the Polish minority in Lithuania.

As Lithuania joined the EU in 2004, EU Structural Funds became available to the country's higher education via the Ministry of Education and Science. As a result, a number of initiatives with implications for system differentiation and inter-organizational dynamics took place from 2006. First of all, to use the EU Structural Funds the Ministry established the Research and Higher Education Monitoring and Analysis Centre (MOSTA), which monitors the system dynamics and collects data on higher education trends in Lithuania. It has carried out various monitoring studies of higher education institutions and has provided information to the Ministry of Education and Science on demand. The most recent research evaluation of all fields in Lithuania using the methodology developed by consultants from Technopolis and carried out by MOSTA in 2014–2015 shows that the state uses this centre as a monitoring instrument which may contribute towards vertical stratification in the long run. Further, a crucial development based on the availability of the EU Structural Funds that had implications on vertical differentiation was the strengthening of the Lithuanian Research Council. Its budget was more than doubled and it has become the main provider of competitive basic research grants for academics and research groups at Lithuanian research institutions.

After 2009: Increasing Competition, Demographic Decline and Internationalization

The most recent reforms in the Lithuanian higher education were brought along by the 2009 Law on Higher Education and Research (2009). It extended the autonomy of universities even further and significantly increased competition for research funding and students due to a funding mechanism based on strong performance, as well as changed student financing system (Researchers' Report, 2014). University status was changed into a not-for-profit institution, which entailed the need to approve new statutes of universities and to appoint rectors according to the new procedure. Besides, universities started to own their assets and became responsible for their maintenance. However, with regard to matters related to the curriculum and student admissions, academics and university management retained a strong say. Thus, academic elites still have considerable influence on the power balance of higher education governance in Lithuania, despite the indicated shifts towards the market-based paradigm. With European Union funding schemes as well as increased tuition fees, the institutions have diversified their funding base and do not depend as much on state budget allocations as they did in 2000. Given the above factors, competition in the system has significantly increased, and although we can still see the presence of the state in steering, there has also been a 'discharging' of state responsibility to the university management and stakeholders (Dobbins and Leišytė 2014).

In terms of institutional landscape, proposals for mergers became even more present on the policy agenda. In 2005–2006, policy rhetoric and some initiatives for an agglomeration of faculties as well as integration of research institutes into universities were observed (Žalys 2006). Imperatives of mergers of colleges and universities have been around also in 2008 (Valinčius 2008; Viliūnas 2009). After 2009, the MoES put forward financial incentives for universities from EU Structural Funds to facilitate mergers. A governmental committee was created to prepare scenarios for mergers of universities with two conflicting goals: to rescue the weak institutions which will massively loose students and, at the same time, to improve the quality of higher education. The proposal developed by the commission with the participation of the ministry basically implied a scenario of having one or two big institutions in each big city: Vilnius and Kaunas. Strong lobbies from certain university rectors were observed. However, this remained only a committee proposal, as the Minister was highly criticized for the overall reform process and did not pursue further implementation of this proposal. Especially the destiny of regional and small, specialized universities was questioned. Overall, the attempt to facilitate mergers of universities did not work as only two institutions stepped forward. In 2010, Kaunas University of Medicine and the Lithuanian Veterinary Academy merged to form the Lithuanian University of Health Sciences. This happened both under pressure and with the financial assistance from the Lithuanian government (Švaikauskienė and Mikulskienė 2016).

However, mergers took place at a larger scale among research institutes, which also affected the university landscape. Mergers of research institutes into universities followed the carrot of the EU Structural Funds (e.g. the

Vilnius University merger with the Biotechnology Institute). Clustering of science institutions as well as university faculties in 'Valleys' took place due to infrastructural financing from the EU Structural Funds in Vilnius, Kaunas and Klaipėda. After these mergers, the binary higher education system consists of 22 universities (14 public and 8 private) and 24 colleges (13 public and 11 private). Altogether, the higher education sector educated 148,389 students and employed 13,532 researchers in 2014 (Eurostat 2017a, 2017b).

In addition to these reforms, significant changes have taken place in the context of higher education institutions, including dynamics of student demand, internationalization and increasing competition for resources fuelled by demographic downturn as well as global rankings and prestige imperatives.

The student numbers in Lithuania peaked in 2008 with the prospects of a 40% demographic decline in the coming years. Partly due to this fact, internationalization has been influencing the policy agenda since the accession to the EU and the availability of the Structural Funds from 2006 onwards. A number of development plans at the MoES as well as policy discourses have focused on increasing internationalization. The acceptance of double-degree programmes, promotion of English language programmes as well as agreements between Lithuanian higher education institutions and the institutions abroad are the examples of these developments. Historically, among the private higher education institutions we have seen a strong influence of foreign institutions and funders, as well as the strong influence of Lithuanian diaspora in reviving the Vytautas Magnus University in Kaunas. In terms of structures of higher education institutions, Mykolas Romeris University stands out as in the past couple of years it has strongly geared towards creation of double-degree programmes with foreign universities in France, Ukraine, Portugal, Austria, Finland, Latvia and Estonia.

THE HIGHER EDUCATION LANDSCAPE IN CONTEMPORARY LITHUANIA

The current Lithuanian higher education system follows to a large extent a 'state supervision model' (Leišytė 2002) where we have observed a policy shift in the state's role from 'sovereign state' to a 'corporate state'. Higher education institutions enjoy a high degree of organizational autonomy while facing lower levels of political and especially financial autonomy (Ritzen 2013). The European University Association (2012) has rated the Lithuanian higher education system as 'medium low' in financial and academic autonomy, 'medium high' in organizational autonomy and 'high' in staffing autonomy. The autonomy of universities is strongly influenced by the bureaucratic financial reporting rules as well as quality assurance arrangements, which have shifted from input- to output-based funding and from a priori to ex-post quality evaluation over the years (see Dobbins and Leišytė 2014). In terms of Gornitzka and Maassen's (2000) typology, the state in the past decade has played a corporate role with some supermarket state features. Market-driven orientation and increased competition for resources and students were key features of the past decade (Leišytė and Kiznienė 2006; Dobbins and Leišytė 2014). In order to counteract quality deterioration, low institutional accountability during the phase of expansion and privatization in 1990s and 2000, the state "re-emerged as a monitor of quality, while at the same time trying to relinquish previous legacy of bureaucratic and procedural control" (Dobbins and Leišytė 2014).

Demographic change, fuelled by high levels of emigration, lead to increasing competition for students among a large number of higher education institutions in Lithuania (Rose and Leišytė 2017). Taking this into consideration, efforts to restructure the universities' landscape are currently made by individual higher education institutions as well as politicians. Again, it is planned to propose higher education institutional mergers concentrating them in Vilnius and Kaunas. In 2016 Kaunas University of Technology decided to acquire shares of the private ISM University of Management and Economics. Furthermore, Kaunas University of Technology and the Lithuanian University of Health Sciences put forward the intentions to merge by 2020 with the declared goal of belonging to the top-250 universities worldwide in 2025 (KTU 2016b). Moreover, the International Business School, a private entity established by Vilnius University (IBS) became an integral part of Vilnius University in 2016. This shows that institutions are aware that competition is increasing and that institutional profiling and inter-organizational links are ever more important. While some institutions gain visibility and rankings by publications and research projects (VU is the leader here), the other ones, with no strong hard science base to compete, attempt to internationalize and find international alliances in order to strengthen their market position (e.g. Mykolas Romeris University).

Thus, today we observe the following higher education institutional types in Lithuania (see Table 11.2).

Table 11.2 Typology of higher education institutions in Lithuania in 2016

Type	Number/location	Type in 1990–1991 (see Table 11.1)	Profile	Research activity	International activity
Flagship comprehensive public research university Vilnius University	1 Vilnius	Traditional flagship comprehensive university	Large, comprehensive, high prestige institutions; III degree levels, attracting students on national scale	High	High
Comprehensive public research university Vytautas Magnus University	1 Kaunas	Re-established liberal arts comprehensive university	Medium size, comprehensive, high prestige institution; III degree levels, attracting students on national scale	High	High
Comprehensive public university Mykolas Romeris University	1 Vilnius	Specialized professional school	Large, offers a range of social sciences, business and law, security studies, moderate prestige, III degree levels, attracting students on national scale	Moderate	High
Technical public universities 1. Vilnius Gediminas Technical University	2 Vilnius	Specialized technological universities	Large institutions, moderate (VGTU) to high (KTU) prestige, III degree levels, main focus on technology, but broadened their focus in the past decade	1. Moderately high	1. Moderate
2. Kaunas University of Technology)	Kaunas			2. High	2. Moderately high

(*continued*)

Table 11.2 (continued)

Type	Number/location	Type in 1990–1991 (see Table 11.1)	Profile	Research activity	International activity
Specialized public universities 1. Vilnius Academy of Arts, Lithuanian Academy of Music and Theatre, Lithuanian University of Health Sciences	7 Vilnius Kaunas	Specialized other universities	Small to medium size, offer a range of specialized study programmes, moderate to high prestige, III degree levels, attracting students on a national scale	1. Moderately high	1. Moderately high
2. The General Žemaitis Military Academy of Lithuania, Lithuanian University of Educational Sciences, Lithuanian Sports University, Aleksandras Stulginskis University				2. Slightly moderate	2. Slightly moderate
Regional public universities Klaipėda University, Šiauliai University	2 Klaipėda Šiauliai	Specialized other higher education institutions	Medium-sized, offer a reduced range of study programmes, moderate prestige, III degree levels, regional focus in teaching and research	Slightly moderate	Low
Foreign (private) universities 1. European Humanities University 2. Branch of the University of Białystok	2 Vilnius	n/a	Belarusian University in exile (III degree levels)/Branch of Polish university (II degree levels), high prestige, catering for specific groups of students and staff (Belarusians/Polish Lithuanian minority)	1. Moderate 2. Low	Low

(continued)

Table 11.2 (continued)

Type	Number/location	Type in 1990–1991 (see Table 11.1)	Profile	Research activity	International activity
Private specialized universities 1. ISM University of Management and Economics 2. LCC International University 3. Kazimieras Simonavičius University, Vilnius St. Joseph Seminary, Telšiai Bishop Vincentas Borisevičius Priest Seminary	6 Vilnius Kaunas Klaipėda Telšiai	n/a	Small institutions with few disciplines, strong focus on teaching, ISM has III degree levels, others II degree levels Attract students on a national (ISM) and international (LCC) or regional (especially theological seminaries) scales	1. High 2. Low 3. Low	1. Moderate 2. High 3. Low
Public colleges	13 All regions	Technicums (professional, non-higher education)	Medium size, usually include programmes in technology and/or social sciences, I degree level, strong focus on teaching	Low	Moderate
Private colleges	11 Vilnius Kaunas Klaipėda Šiauliai	n/a	Small in size, narrow, specialized focus in business administration, I degree level, strong focus on teaching, strong regional focus	Low	Slightly moderate

Conclusion

Over the past century, Lithuanian higher education has experienced a steady horizontal differentiation. It started with a moderate differentiation in the Soviet times and intensified after 1990 when two regional universities and new specialized universities were created, many universities opened new programmes, and Vytautas Magnus University was re-established. Horizontal differentiation was especially fostered by the Law on Higher Education and Science in 2000, as it created a binary higher education system and allowed the establishment of private universities and institutions of a non-university type. This development opened the door to a number of small private and public colleges which strongly focused on management, business and law—the subjects which were in high demand at that time. These subjects were also taught at different universities, with new management and social sciences programmes being introduced at all universities, even though they could be, for instance, specialized in sports or agriculture. This blossoming of programmes and rapid system expansion catered for the ever increasing number of students, when up to 70% of high school graduate cohorts were going to obtain higher education. Issues of quality as well as funding through tuition fees were often the topic of policy debates. The state used quality assurance instruments of programme accreditation as well as institutional evaluations to 'tame' the expansion of programmes and to ensure minimum quality. As the demographic reality started to change and student numbers started to drop (with the prognosis of 40% drop until 2020) the vertical differentiation started to increase even further. Some institutions in Lithuania have changed their names quite a few times, sometimes to ensure that the same rector will be in office for a longer period of time than usual (e.g. Lithuanian University of Educational Sciences, Mykolas Romeris University). At the same time, renaming institutions has served the symbolic purpose of 'relabelling' into a new profile, which may reflect institutions' intentions to 'abandon' earlier legacies and specializations (in the case of Mykolas Romeris—former police school, and then law and social sciences orientation) and to signal that the profile of the institution has become broader.

The Lithuanian higher education system was vertically differentiated from the outset—with one main classical comprehensive university catering for the needs of the nation. This trend has been maintained after

1990. However, the stratification of the institutions has increased due to the creation of the binary system, as well as the appearance of private higher education institutions. The prestige of public traditional universities and technological universities has remained the same, with Vilnius University still being the top university in terms of research output and student numbers. The specialized public institutions are stratified into two main categories. The well-established and prestigious specialized Arts and Music Academies and the Lithuanian University of Health Sciences recruit students on a national basis and have good reputation both nationally and internationally. At the same time, regional universities as well as some private higher education institutions and public colleges serve regional needs. They enjoy moderate prestige and have certain research strengths, but their main focus is on teaching and contribution to regional economy and knowledge transfer. Recent national rankings, a variety of international rankings of study programmes and the attempt of the Ministry of Education and Science to evaluate research quality at Lithuanian universities in 2014–2015 show that the government is keen to identify 'winners and losers' in the system. Further, the Centre for Quality Assessment in Higher Education with its programme and institutional accreditations has indirectly sustained the system's vertical differentiation. However, it is not that easy to establish a thoroughly stratified system in Lithuania as there are many lobby forces and a strong tradition of higher education funding on historical basis, which is not easy to uproot (Leišytė 2002). The main developments towards performance-based funding and especially the availability of science funding via Lithuanian Research Council for basic research using EU Structural Funds seem to be one of the main instruments to boost the prestige of researchers and research groups from Lithuanian universities. Teaching and research at universities have been 'reconnected' in stronger ways due to external research funding. In this respect, the role of the Lithuanian Research Council as well as EU funding in the stratification of the system should not be neglected.

A great number of policy actors played a crucial role in the dynamics of system expansion and contributed to horizontal differentiation. University rectors and college directors were extremely influential in lobbying the necessary amendments and opposing policy changes in order to not allow private universities to get established in Lithuanian higher education. Moreover, the binary system creation and the fact that colleges can offer only professional bachelor's degree today demonstrate that the traditional university status is maintained. Over the years, the Ministry of Education and Science did not have much power over the higher education institutions due to the broad autonomy granted back in 1990. However, the laisser-faire period of 1990s showed that certain instruments of state steering, like the power of the purse and quality assurance, are important to try to 'reign' some of the system dynamics which went somewhat 'out of hand' in the period of 2001–2009.

The 2009 Law on Higher Education and Research was extremely important in terms of giving even more flexibility to universities in owning their assets, charging tuition fees and having the ability to act strategically and profile themselves. At the same time, it was buttressed with the power of the purse that has had an effect in terms of clustering scientific and educational base in big cities in Lithuania. Here we observe the role of the state shifting towards a corporate state as the power is given to students, their parents as well as other actors, such as the Lithuanian Research Council and university management.

However, brain drain to Western European universities as well as the demographic decline of young people in the Lithuanian higher education system call for significant policy initiatives as well as institutional actions. Students, their parents and employers are having their say in shaping the system of higher education in Lithuania. Students voting with their feet opting for certain universities or going abroad determine the destiny of quite a few higher education institutions which are at the bottom of the pecking order pyramid. Further, rankings and league tables of study programmes and universities appear to be increasingly significant for policymakers as well as institutional leaders. This is another impetus for competitive behaviour and strategic gaming for the institutions. We can see that in the past years, some rectors have been active in promoting mergers and alliances, thus contributing to vertical differentiation. In the years to come, it seems that the trend of agglomeration of faculties, programmes and further alliance building between institutions is inevitable, which will lead to even further vertical differentiation and agglomeration in the Lithuanian higher education system.

As shown in our earlier studies (Leišytė 2002; Dobbins and Leišytė 2014), many developments in higher education in the 1990s and early 2000 were strongly path dependent. Taking initiatives and introducing competitive funding were the notions that took time to be accepted in the higher education policy and practice. State steering approaches and governance arrangements took a lot of time to change. A lack of trust in governmental authorities and institutional resistance to change persisted. Initiatives to monitor the higher education system have always been perceived as a form of control by higher education institutions. At the same time, the notion of academic freedom and professional autonomy among Lithuanian academia has become stronger than ever, in this way placing the Soviet past aside.

REFERENCES

Bumblauskas, A., B. Butkevičienė, S. Jegelevičius, P. Manusadžianas, V. Pšibilskis, E. Raila, and D. Vitkauskaitė. 2004. *Universitetas Vilnensis 1579–2004 – Vilnius University 1579–2004.* Vilnius: Vilnius University. http://www.vu.lt/site_files/InfS/Leidiniai/Vilnius_University_1579_2004.pdf. Accessed 12 Dec 2014.

DeSHE. 2001. Lietuvos aukstojo mokslo sistemos 2001–2005 metu pletros plano projektas [The Draft Development Plan of Lithuanian Higher Education System in the Period from 2001–2005].

Dobbins, M., and L. Leišytė. 2014. Analysing the Transformation of Higher Education Governance in Bulgaria and Lithuania. *Public Management Review* 16 (7): 987–1010.

Gornitzka, Å., and P. Maassen. 2000. Hybrid Steering Approaches with Respect to European Higher Education. *Higher Education Policy* 13 (3): 267–268.

KTU. 2016a. Kaunas University of Technology Virtual Museum. http://muziejus.ktu.lt/. Accessed 1 Sept 2016.

———. 2016b. *Project of the Merger Between KTU and LSMU Was Introduced at the Ministry of Education and Science.* January 22. http://ktu.edu/en/newitem/project-merger-between-ktu-and-lsmu-was-introduced-ministry-education-and-science

Leišytė, L. 2002. *Higher Education Governance in Post-Soviet Lithuania,* Studies in Comparative and International Education. Vol. 10. Oslo: Institute for Educational Research, University of Oslo.

Leišytė, L., and D. Kiznienė. 2006. New Public Management in Lithuania's Higher Education. *Higher Education Policy* 19 (3): 377–396.

Leišytė, L., R. Želvys, and L. Zenkienė. 2015. Re-contextualization of the Bologna Process in Lithuania. *European Journal of Higher Education* 5 (1): 49–67.

Mašiotas, P. 1923. Švietimo reikalai Lietuvoje [Public Instruction in Lithuania]. In *Visa Lietuva: Informacinė knyga 1923 metams* [Lithuania: Information Book for 1923], ed. K. Pruida, 237–243. Kaunas: Centralinis Statistikos Biuras prie Finansų, Prekybos ir Pramonės Ministerijos.

Mockienė, B.V. 2004. Multipurpose Accreditation in Lithuania: Facilitating Quality Improvement, and Heading Towards a Binary System of Higher Education. In *Accreditation and Evaluation in the European Higher Education Area*, eds. S. Schwarz and D.F. Westerheijden, 299–322. Dordrecht: Springer.

OECD. 2002. *Review of National Policies for Education: Lithuania 2002.* Paris: OECD.

Official Statistics Portal. 2015. Database of Indicators: Number of Colleges. Last Modified May 15, 2015. http://osp.stat.gov.lt/en/statistiniu-rodikliu-analize1?epoch=ML

Procuta, G. 1967. The Transformation of Higher Education in Lithuania During the First Decade of Soviet Rule. *Lituanus* 13 (1): 71–92.

Ritzen, J. 2013. *Challenges for University Policy in Lithuania.* Presentation at the EIB Round Table on the Future of Higher Education, Vilnius, October 22.

Rose, A.-L., and L. Leišytė. 2017. Integrating International Academic Staff into the Local Academic Context in Lithuania and Estonia. In *International Faculty in Higher Education: Comparative Perspectives on Recruitment, Integration, and Impact*, eds. L. Rumbley, M. Yudkevich and P.G. Altbach. New York: Routledge.

Šakalys, J. 1985. Higher Education in Lithuania: An Historical Analysis. *Lituanus: Lithuanian Quarterly Journal of Arts and Sciences* 31 (4): 5–22.

Suchodolski, B. 1971. The East European University. In *World Yearbook of Education 1971/2: Higher Education in a Changing World*, eds. B. Holmes, D.G. Scanlon and W. R. Niblett, 120–134. Milton Park, Abingdon, Oxon: Routledge.

Švaikauskienė, S., and B. Mikulskienė. 2016. Autonomy Produces Unintended Consequences: Funding Higher Education Through Vouchers in Lithuania. In *(Re)Discovering University Autonomy: The Global Market Paradox of Stakeholder and Educational Values in Higher Education*, eds. R.V. Turcan, J.E. Reilly, and L. Bugaian, 137–147. New York: Palgrave Macmillan.

UNESCO, Institute of Statistics. 2002/2003. Education: Gross Enrolment Ratio by Level of Education. http://stats.uis.unesco.org. Accessed 1 Sept 2016.

Valinčius, G. 2008. *Mokslo ir studijų institucijų įrangos, žmogiškųjų išteklių koncentracijos teritorijų analizė* [The Analysis of Infrastructure and Human Resources Concentration in Science and Higher Education]. Vilnius: Nacionalinės plėtros institutas.

Viliūnas, G. 2009. Kaip pertvarkyti Lietuvos universitetus [How to Reform Lithuanian Universities]. Section: Sankirtos. Bernardinai.lt. August 11. http://www.bernardinai.lt/straipsnis/-/2989

VMU. 2016. Vytautas Magnus University Now and Before. http://www.vdu.lt/en/about-vmu/vmu-now-and-before/. Accessed 1 Sept 2016.

Willerton, J.P. 1992. *Patronage and Politics in the USSR*. Vol. 82. Cambridge: Cambridge University Press.

Žalys, A. 2004. Lietuvos mokslo ir studijų perspektyvos po gegužės 1-osios [Perspectives of Lithuanian Science and Higher Education After May 1]. Presentation at the DAAD Club Lietuvos mokslo ir mokymo politika, Lietuvai tampant Europos Sąjungos nare, April 17.

———. 2006. Kodėl vis dar naujai vertiname dešimties metų senumo vertinimo rezultatus? [Why Are We Evaluating the Ten Year Old Evaluation Results in a New Way?] Presentation at the Round Table Discussion "Ką pasiekėme ir ko siekiame?" [What Have We Achieved and What Are We Striving For?] at the Lithuanian Presidency, May 10.

Želvys, R. 2004. Development of Education Policy in Lithuania During the Years of Transformation. *International Journal of Educational Development* 24: 559–571.

Zulumskytė, A. 2014. Aukštųjų mokyklų sistema Lietuvoje 1940–1990 metais: raidos bruožai [The System of Higher Education Institutions in Lithuania in 1940–1990: Features of Development]. *Tiltai* 66 (1): 105–120.

Liudvika Leišytė is Professor of Higher Education at the Center for Higher Education (zhb) at TU Dortmund University, Germany. Previously she worked at Vilnius University, Oslo University and Center for Higher Education Policy Studies (CHEPS), University of Twente. She did her postdoctoral research at the Minda de Gunzburg Center for European Studies at Harvard University in 2008/2009. Her research focuses on academic work and organizational transformation in the context of changing institutional environments in various countries. Prof. Leišytė is a member of editorial boards of higher education journals and board member of various non-profit organizations (e.g. Futura Scientia, German Higher Education Research Association, Hungarian Accreditation Committee). She is co-convener of Network 22 (Research in Higher Education) at the European Conference on Educational Research of the European Educational Research Association (EERA/ECER). Her publications include four books, numerous articles in higher education and public administration journals as well as chapters in volumes such as the *Handbook of Higher Education Theory and Research*.

Anna-Lena Rose is a research assistant and PhD student at the Professorship of Higher Education at the Center for Higher Education (zhb) at TU Dortmund University, Germany. Her PhD research focuses on the development of interdisciplinary structures in academic project settings in German higher education. Furthermore, she is interested in the internationalization of higher education and issues of brain drain/brain gain in Central and Eastern European countries and is involved in the Lithuanian country study for the APIKS (Academic Profession in the Knowledge Society) project.

Elena Schimmelpfennig works in the adult education sector and supervises a teaching programme in the Oskar Kaemmer Schule in Hildesheim, Germany. Previously she was a lecturer at European Humanities University and was involved in the Network for the Development of Higher Education Management Systems (DEHEMS).

Open Access This chapter is distributed under the terms of the Creative Commons Attribution 4.0 International License (http://creativecommons.org/licenses/by/4.0/), which permits use, duplication, adaptation, distribution and reproduction in any medium or format, as long as you give appropriate credit to the original author(s) and the source, provide a link to the Creative Commons license and indicate if changes were made.

The images or other third party material in this chapter are included in the chapter's Creative Commons license, unless indicated otherwise in a credit line to the material. If material is not included in the chapter's Creative Commons license and your intended use is not permitted by statutory regulation or exceeds the permitted use, you will need to obtain permission directly from the copyright holder.

CHAPTER 12

Moldova: Institutions Under Stress—The Past, the Present and the Future of Moldova's Higher Education System

Lukas Bischof and Alina Tofan

INTRODUCTION

This chapter introduces the higher education system (HES) in the Republic of Moldova and discusses the changes it underwent between 1991 and 2015. The case of Moldova is characterised by competing forces such as the oscillating political priorities of often-changing governments, labour market changes, emigration and demographic decline. Political blockades and interdependences in such a small country have only allowed hesitant consolidation of the higher education system.

L. Bischof (✉)
Institute of Education, Higher School of Economics, Moscow, Russia
Graduate School of Global Studies, University of Leipzig, Leipzig, Germany

A. Tofan
University Leipzig, Leipzig, Saxony, Germany

The Republic of Moldova

The Republic of Moldova is a post-Soviet state, situated between Romania and Ukraine, with a long and controversial history of shifting borders and a short history as an independent state. Regarding higher education, the quasi-permanent peripheral status the region had for centuries was not favourable to the establishment of centres of higher learning before the mid-twentieth century.

The territory of modern-day Moldova between the area's two main rivers, the Dniester and the Prut, was part of a Romanian principality (Principality of Moldova) from 1359 until 1538, when it became a vassal state of the Ottoman Empire. In 1812, the Russian Empire annexed the eastern part of medieval Moldova from the Ottoman Empire and renamed the annexed region "Bessarabia". After World War I, the area became part of the Romanian State until the German-Russian non-aggression pact allowed the Soviet Union to re-annex Bessarabia in June 1940. In August 1940, the Soviet authorities created the Moldovan Soviet Socialist Republic (MSSR), encompassing mostly the interwar Bessarabia annexed territory as well as a strip of land on the eastern bank of the Dniester from an earlier-established "Moldavian SSAR". Simultaneously, the southern and northern areas of Bessarabia and almost 60% of the MSSR territory were incorporated into Ukraine. In addition to reconfiguring the ethnic and linguistic landscape of the MSSR in this way, the Soviet government sought to reshape the identity of the republic's remaining population through the creation of a distinct national Moldovan identity. On the one hand, this presupposed a distinctive "Moldovan" language with Cyrillic letters, distinct and separate from the Romanian language. On the other, Russian was imposed as the predominant language at all levels of social organisation. This process was not specific to the Republic of Moldova, but part of the much larger Sovietisation taking place across the Soviet Union (Worden 2014, 49).

The Republic of Moldova became independent from the Soviet Union in 1991, retaining its Soviet-defined borders. During the dissolution of the USSR, the region on the eastern bank of the Dniester with its predominantly Russian-speaking population self-proclaimed an independent "Pridnestrovian Moldavian Soviet Socialist Republic" (Transnistria) in 1990; its capital was located in Tiraspol. In 1992, the political tension degenerated into a military engagement and evolved into a frozen conflict. As of 2015, the Moldovan government still has no control over the territory and higher education in Transnistria will not be addressed in this chapter. The total population of Moldova within its internationally recognised borders was 3,940,000 in 2014 (National Bureau of Statistics of the Republic of Moldova 2014) with 78% Moldovan/Romanian, followed by Ukrainian (8%), Russian (4%), Gagauz (4%) and Bulgarian (2%).

Higher Education in the MSSR

The history of higher education in the modern Republic of Moldova is relatively young, the bulk of its development occurring during the Soviet period with support from professors from Leningrad, Odessa, Kiev and Moscow (Tiron et al. 2003, 23). As in other Soviet republics, not only were the HES organisational structure and governance arrangements of the USSR replicated in Moldova but also the contents of the courses, study programmes, teaching methods and recruitment policies. The lack of academic traditions prior to the Soviet period and the import of established Soviet institutional types (as well as staff) into Moldova accentuated the typical characteristics of the Soviet educational system in the Moldovan case. The immigration of professors and scientists from other Soviet republics, especially Russia and Ukraine, raised the educational levels of the population but also promoted the use of the Russian language, which became the predominant language of education.[1] By 1988 the HES of the MSSR included nine state HEIs (Yagodin 1990, 76): one university, seven specialised institutes (three pedagogical institutes, one medical institute, one technical institute, one agricultural institute and one art institute) as well as one conservatory (Table 12.1).

On the one hand, ample state funding to HEIs created unprecedented growth and "a 'golden' period in the development of Moldavian cultural life" (Padure 2009, 234), a well-developed technical and material base (Stati 2002) and internationally comparable educational standards (Cojocaru 1995, 74). On the other hand, the high centralisation of the Soviet educational system made it static and unable to adequately respond to the changing needs of the dynamic labour market (Smolentseva 2012, 16–17). The strict centralisation of education led to the bureaucratisation of management, authoritarianism, excessive uniformity, a lack of understanding of local conditions, a stifling of "bottom up" initiatives (Cojocaru 1995, 74), and a lack of academic mobility (Galben and Cogan 2003; Padure 2009). Participation in HE was still the third lowest of all Soviet republics (Yagodin 1990).

Table 12.1 HEIs in Moldova during the Soviet period

Year	Name	Location	Profile	Number of students ('91/'92)
1926	Moldavian Institute of Public Education in Tiraspol	Tiraspol	Teacher training	2,720
1940	Agricultural Institute in Chisinau, based on pre-existing Agronomy Department at the University of Iasi[a]	Chisinau	Agricultural education	4,220
1940	Pedagogical State Institute "Ion Creangă" Chisinau	Chisinau	Teacher training	4,335
1940	State Conservatory in Chisinau, based on pre-existing Chisinau "Unirea" Conservatory	Chisinau	Musical education	2,017
1945	The State Medical Institute as a successor of Medical Institute No.1 in St. Petersburg	Chisinau	Medicine and pharmacy	5,113
1945	The Pedagogical Institute of Balti, based on the Primary School Teachers Institute in Balti (1945) and renamed in 1959 to "Alecu Russo Balti State Pedagogical Institute"	Balti	Teacher training	4,030
1946	The Chisinau State University, integrating the Chisinau-based Departments of the Moscow Economics Institute and the Moscow Institute for Legal Studies in 1953 and 1959	Chisinau	Classical comprehensive university	6,015
1946	Moldovan Affiliate for Scientific Research of the Academy of Sciences of the USSR (1949 converted into Moldovan Branch of the Academy of Sciences of the USSR, and in 1961 reorganised as the Academy of Sciences of MSSR)	Chisinau	Research institute	n/a
1963	Moldavian State Institute of Arts	Chisinau	Belle arte education	2,158
1964	The Polytechnic Institute in Chisinau, which emerged from the Faculties of Engineering and Economics at Chisinau State University	Chisinau	Technical education	9,765

[a]The Agrarian University became the only institution with "all-Union significance" (Vsesoyuznogo znacheniya) in the MSSR. The other HEIs educated specialists primarily for the local labour market.

Transformation of the Higher Education System in the Republic of Moldova

The Republic of Moldova declared its independence on 27 August 1991. This marked the beginning of radical political, economic and social changes aiming at developing a market economy based on private and public property, entrepreneurship and competition. As a consequence, the political, economic and social changes also created the necessity to align the social and educational institutions the young country had inherited from the Soviet Union.

As did other countries, Moldova faced the multiple challenges of maintaining and building a self-sufficient HE system in a small country under the conditions of a rapidly deteriorating planned economy. Challenges also included adapting the higher education system to support nation and state building as well as harmonising the education system with European and international practices. These sometimes competing objectives all shaped the transition process, which did not turn out to be a smooth one.

Indeed, compared to the neighbouring post-Socialist states in terms of HE expansion and diversification, curricula de-ideologisation, governance democratisation and European integration in the Republic of Moldova, the transition from the Soviet system to a distinct national HES occurred in several abrupt and often contradictory steps, with policy shaped by often-changing governments and education ministers. Educational policy was thus often subject to contradictory oscillations between the divergent political vectors in language politics (pro-Romanian vs. pro-Russian) and ideological orientation (pro-Communist and pro-Western) (Padure 2009, 335–37) (Fig. 12.1).

The following timeline gives an overview of important steps in the development of the HES in the Republic of Moldova.

The development and institutional diversification of the HE system in Moldova are characterised by the direct involvement of the main political forces; the parliament of the Republic of Moldova was a strong driving force shaping the higher education system. The many changes of parties in power were thus reflected in different policy initiatives promoted by parliament, which reflected the different political factions in power during each phase.

The first post-Soviet years (1989–1994) were characterised by conceptualisation, experimentation and the emergence of private HE in a young independent republic. Until 1989, all HEIs in the MSSR were state institutions exclusively funded by the state. In 1989, the first groups of students

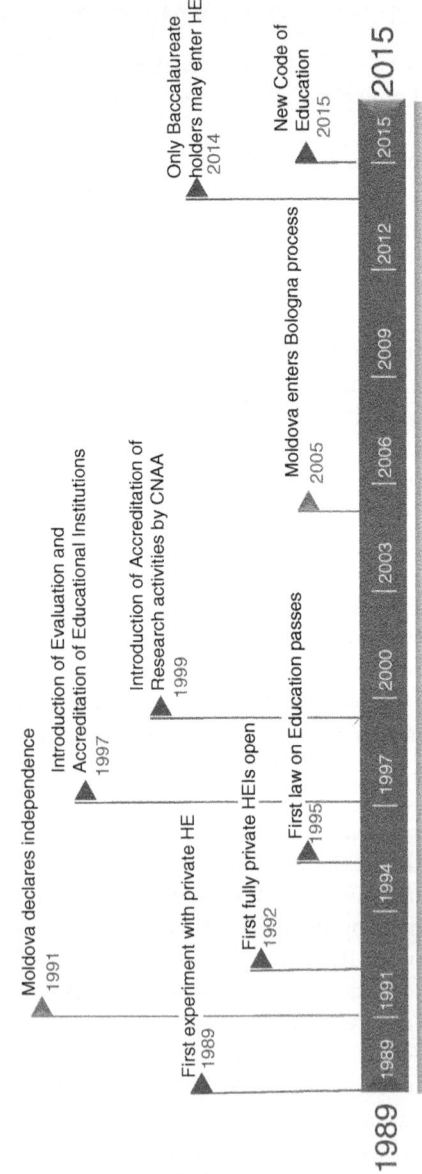

Fig. 12.1 Timeline of important developments in higher education policy in the Republic of Moldova

were enrolled on a tuition basis in a special English-language engineering and technical programme designed as a private entity within existing state institutions at the Polytechnic Institute in Chisinau.[2] In September 1992, the first two private educational institutions opened their doors in Chisinau almost simultaneously: the University of Humanities and the Free International University of Moldova (Galben and Cogan 2003, 28–30). This marked the actual start of an institutional diversification process of the national higher education system. Prior to the 1995 Law on Education, private HEIs operated based on the Soviet Law of Education (1972, repealed in 1992) along with government decisions.

The development of a new conceptual and legal framework for the national HE system began with the Concept on the Development of Education in the Republic of Moldova (1994) and the Law on Education (The Parliament of the Republic of Moldova 1995) which established post-Soviet educational policy and regulated the organisation and functions of national education. Especially during the 1990s, higher education reforms were often modelled on Romanian examples.[3] Moldova's ascension to the Bologna Process and the European Higher Education Area (EHEA) in 2005 marked the beginning of the gradual integration of the Moldovan HES into the European area. As summarised by Ciurea, Berbeca, Lipcean and Gurin (2012), reforms aimed at three priority areas: (1) changing the structure of the university system, organising higher education in three cycles, introducing the diploma supplement and the European Credit Transfer and Accumulation System; (2) organising an internal and external quality evaluation and monitoring system by creating a quality assurance agency independent of the government, and quality management centres at each university; and (3) connecting the university curricula to the market by tracing graduate employment, creating links with employers and professionalising education. While most actors welcomed the accession to the European Higher Education Area, the related action programme proved to be a serious challenge. This was the implementation of broad structural reforms in financing, quality assurance, stricter regulation of access to HE, greater institutional autonomy, the development of a national qualification framework and the elaboration and adoption of a new legal framework for higher education (Code of Education).

In summary, the Republic of Moldova is a country which essentially did not have an HES prior to its establishment by the Soviet Union and inherited its institutional architecture. For almost two decades, the country perpetuated many Soviet HES institutional arrangements, first of all centralised governance (Toderaș 2012). The following sections describe the key structural changes in the Moldovan higher education system between 1989 and 2015.

STRUCTURE, CHANGE AND CONTINUITY OF THE HIGHER EDUCATION SYSTEM IN MOLDOVA

Degree Structure

After joining the Bologna Process in 2005, Moldova reorganised its former Soviet-style degree structure into a two-cycle degree system (Turcan et al. 2015, 19), consisting of Bachelor (3–4 years) and Master's degrees (1–2 years). This was accomplished by 2011. Only medical, pharmaceutical and architectural education retain their one-tier structure. Study programmes can be organised as day, evening or extramural. The new Code of Education (2014) extends the tertiary education cycles and introduces cycle III: Higher Education PhD. Within cycle III, the Soviet "*kandidat*" and "*doktor nauk*" degrees are still in place as "*Doctor*" and "*Doctor Habilitate*".

Classification of HEIs

By law, Moldovan HEIs are classified by ownership as either public or private and, as unchanged since the Soviet era, by the scope of their disciplinary offers as universities, academies or institutes. However, between 1990 and 1999 as an attempt to restructure and optimise the HE landscape in accordance with new social and economic needs, almost all public specialised HEIs (institutes) were converted into "classical universities" with the possibility to offer study programmes outside their previous area of specialisation.[4] Newly founded regional public universities (in Comrat, Taraclia, Cahul) were designed as classic universities from the beginning. The only exceptions were the new public specialised HEIs, which were founded to serve the needs of state building, especially for international relations, police and armed forces.

With the exception of the University of the Academy of Science, the different types of HEIs are considered equal in terms of academic organisation, governance and state standards and requirements. All HEIs are coordinated by the Ministry of Education. Since Soviet times, each HEI has been affiliated to and supervised by a particular ministry. For the vast majority of HEIs, this is the Ministry of Education. Specialised universities and academies are affiliated to other ministries (e.g., the State University of Medicine and Pharmacy reports to the Ministry of Health, the State Agrarian University to the Ministry of Agriculture and Food Industry, and the Academy of Public Administration to the President of the Republic of Moldova). However, the Ministry of Education still remains their institutional supervisor for education and research activities. As with the official classification, the ministry affiliation in itself does not have an effect on status or reputation.

Admission to Higher Education

For each state university and for all study cycles, the government sets admission quotas for state-funded (budgets) and tuition-based study places. Competition for admission is based on grades achieved during and at the end of secondary education (Baccalaureate exams). Depending on the number of study places determined by the state and the score obtained on school leaving certificates, applicants can either enrol in state-funded or tuition-based places. The share of state-funded places is considerably smaller; about one-third of students are financed by the state, whereas the rest pay tuition fees (self-financed) (Ruffio et al. 2012). The entrance regulations are the same for private and public HEIs.

Until 2014, admission to higher education was possible for graduates from different secondary education schools including lyceums, general schools and vocational schools and colleges. Since 2014, however, the exclusive entry requirement is the Baccalaureate Diploma issued by lyceums.[5] This restricts the number of eligible potential students for HEIs and has had an effect on admission numbers (Fig. 12.3).

The Development of the Public and Private HE Sector

As of 2015/2016, there are 30 HEIs in operation in Moldova, 19 of them state institutions and 11 private institutions. The development of private higher education as an alternative to state education started in 1992 with the inauguration of two classic (humanistic) universities. In 2000, the number of private HEIs had risen to 32 compared to only 15 public institutions. The lack of a stringent quality assurance system allowed universities to multiply (especially private HEIs) and significantly internally expand (especially state HEIs). Expansion was greatest for HEIs benefitting from preferential allocations or on the basis of political affinity (as in the case of ASEM or Institute of International Relations of Moldova (IRIM)) or political

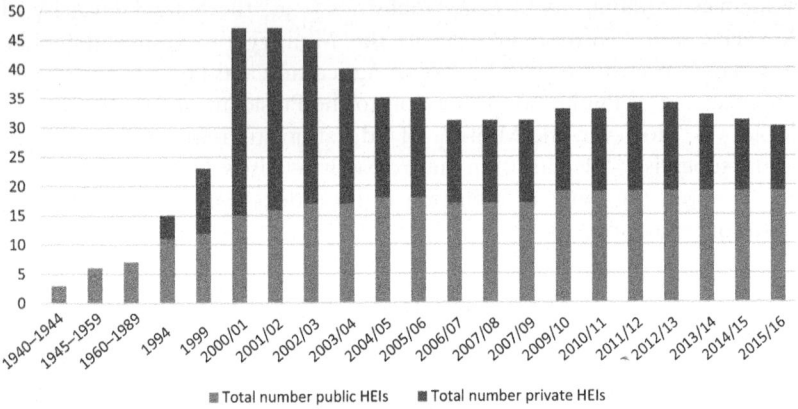

Fig. 12.2 Number of public and private HEIs in the Republic of Moldova

centrality (as with the University of the Academy of Science). During the 2000s this number was substantially reduced again when many private HEIs failed to survive the intermittent economic crisis and the competition with the public education sector, in which they were at a disadvantage.

The emergence in the 1990s of private HE as an alternative to public HE was a response to the pressures of socioeconomic and political demand and new opportunities at a time of rapid economic and social change. The institutional mission of the first private HEIs was to train specialists for the market-oriented economy and under (new) conditions of the market-oriented economy. Over the years, the environment which generated HES transformations has changed, as has the strategic focus of many private HEIs. Only one private HEI (The Free International University of Moldova) corresponds to the profile of a "classical" comprehensive university. The rest of the private sector seems to be guided primarily by economic considerations, which seem to be the decisive factor in establishing new graduate degree programmes.

"Public" HEIs, however, also changed their behaviour in similar ways to the non-public HEIs. The Law on Education (1995) stipulated that state education is generally tuition-free ("free of charge"), but insufficient state funding has in fact forced HEIs to find new income sources to fill this gap (Secrieru 2007, 12–14). State HEIs have accomplished this since

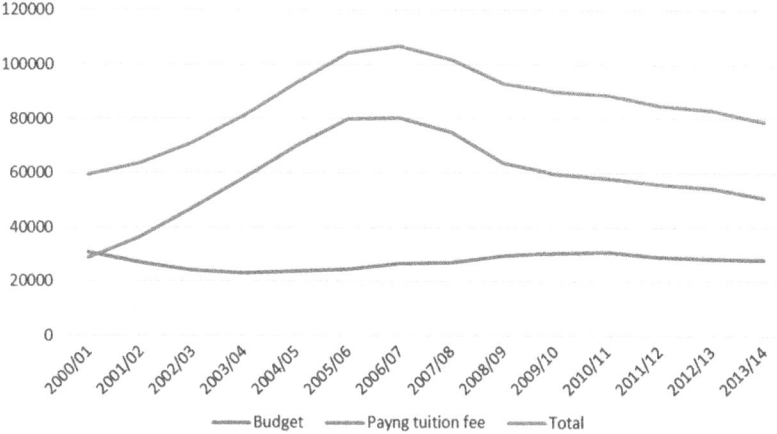

Fig. 12.3 Development of the total number of students enrolled on a budget and tuition-fee basis (in both private and public HEIs)

1993–1994 by enrolling students on a "contract basis", which requires those students to pay tuition fees. The following graph illustrates these developments (Fig. 12.3):

While the law distinguishes HEIs by ownership status, higher education policy requires private HEIs to fulfil the same criteria as public HEIs. Private HEIs are subject to the same accreditation requirements as public institutions and have to conform to the same admission regulations. In the 2013–2014 academic year, private HEIs in Moldova made up 39% of the total number of HEIs while only enrolling around 20% of all students. Their role is thus relatively modest. Their emergence, however, represents an important increase in the institutional differentiation of the Moldovan HES.

Differentiation of HEIs Based on Research Activity

Another "historical" legacy of the Soviet Union is the perception of universities as primarily teaching institutions, leaving research to the Academy of Science. The one exception to this rule is the University of the Academy of Science itself, which was founded with the express objective of conducting both teaching and research. This, however, does not mean that its reputation within the HE system is better than that of other HEIs. Until 2014, doctoral studies at other universities always depended on the Academy of Science for examination and oversight and were tolerated rather than welcomed at universities. To what degree the new Law on Education of 2014 will change this remains to be seen.

Moldovan HEIs report a relatively large volume of annual scientific production to the Ministry of Education. Most of this data, however, is published in local journals and collections; to the authors' knowledge, there is no database for a reliable comparative analysis of research productivity or funding. The non-inclusion of most local publications in international databases (ISI-Thomson and Scopus) means they are mostly invisible to the international scientific community (Cuciureanu 2014, 63). As a consequence, Moldovan HEIs are currently not represented in the internationally recognised rankings by Academic Ranking of World Universities (ARWU), THE, Quacquarelli Symonds World University Rankings (QS), University Ranking by Academic Performance (URAP) and CWTS Leiden. An indication for research performance is accreditation by the *National Council of Attestation and Accreditation* (CNAA), which conducts an assessment of HEI research activity and acts as a precondition to receiving public funding for research.[6] Of 30 HEIs in the Republic of Moldova, currently only 14 public universities and 4 private universities have been accredited by the CNAA and may thus receive public funding for research. Since the new Code of Education (2014), PhD programmes need to be conducted in doctoral schools, which need to be accredited. As of November 2015, 43 doctoral schools had received temporary authorisation. Of all 30 Moldovan HEIs, only the 18 with CNAA accreditation were permitted to establish doctoral schools. All but two of these are located in Chisinau.[7]

International Cooperation

There is an ongoing process of differentiation between Moldovan HEIs in terms of international activities. While some HEIs (especially USM, UTM, USMF, ULIM, UPS and the Agrarian University) are actively developing internationalisation activities, the HES overall is still very weakly internationalised (Cuciureanu 2014, 63). While the number of foreign students reached a low point in 2008/2009 and has since been increasing again, the overall share of foreign students remains around 2% and the number of teachers from abroad remains insignificant.

Typology of HEIs in the Republic of Moldova in 2015

Although all HEIs operate under the same legal framework, their status, quality and performance vary. This variation exists in regard to accreditation status, size (in terms of number of students and staff), the degree of research activities, the level of international activities and, as a result of these factors, financial situation. Based on size (in terms of student number), scope (in terms of study programmes), research activity, prestige and internationalisation as discussed above, a number of distinct types of Moldovan HEIs can be distinguished (Table 12.2)[8].

The large high-prestige comprehensive universities (type I) have developed a good reputation in teaching and partially in research. They also have developed infrastructure and a collective of teachers. Except for two (The Free International University of Moldova and the Academy of Economic Studies of Moldova), all of them already existed before 1991. This historical heritage combined with their mostly public status and government education policies favoured their development during the post-Soviet period. All of them have active doctoral schools, are accredited by CNAA in different research areas and are partners in various regional or international academic cooperation projects. Over two-thirds of all students are enrolled at these universities. Except for one (Balti), all are located in the capital city of Chisinau.

Specialised middle- to high-prestige universities (type II) offer high-quality study programmes in a small range of subjects such as medicine, economics or the arts. These universities have managed to develop a good reputation in their respective fields. All of them have active doctoral schools, are accredited by CNAA in specific research areas and are partners in various regional or international academic cooperation projects. All of them are located in the capital city of Chisinau.

Between 1991 and 2004, three regional public universities were founded in small cities in the south (type III). Only about 3% of all Moldovan students study at the newly established regional universities in Cahul (1.6%), Comrat (1.8%) and Taraclia (0.28%). These type III HEIs are characterised by a small number of students (between 300 and 700 in total), a reduced range of studies and relatively little research; their long-term survival has been put into question (Turcan and Bugaian 2015).

Table 12.2 Types of HEIs in 2015

Type/label	#	HEIs in this category	Description
I. Large high-prestige comprehensive universities	8	Moldova State University, Technical University of Moldova, Free International University of Moldova, Academy of Economic Studies of Moldova, State Agrarian University of Moldova, Chisinau Pedagogical State University "Ion Creanga", Tiraspol State University, Balti "Alecu Russo" State University	5k+ students, large number of study programmes, developed infrastructure, good international contacts and partnerships, public or private, doctoral programmes
II. Specialised middle- to high-prestige universities	6	European University of Moldova, "Constantin Stere" University of European Political and Economic Studies, Trade Co-operative University of Moldova, State University of Medicine and Pharmacy "N.Testemiteanu", Academy of Music, Theatre and Fine Arts, State University of Physical Training and Sports	Large number of specialised study programmes, developed infrastructure, good international contacts and partnerships, public or private, doctoral programmes
III. Regional public universities founded after independence (in Comrat, Cahul, Taraclia)	3	Cahul State University "Bogdan Petriceicu Hasdeu", Comrat State University, Taraclia "Grigore Țamblac" State University	Small number of students, reduced range of study programmes and a predominantly regionally oriented teaching activity
IV. Highly specialised state HEIs	5	Academy of Transports, Computer Sciences and Communications, Military Academy of the Armed Forces "Alexandru cel Bun", Academy of Public Administration; The Academy "Stefan cel Mare" of Minister of Internal Affairs, Institute of International Relations of Moldova	Specific affiliation to a particular ministry, highly specialised study programmes to meet demand of state services
V. Small private HEIs	4	University "Perspectiva—INT", Institute of Applied Criminology and Criminal Sciences of Moldova, Dniestr University of Economics and Law, University "Higher Anthropological School"	Small number of students, reduced range of cost-effective study programmes

(continued)

Table 12.2 (continued)

Type/label	#	HEIs in this category	Description
VI. Special HEIs	4	IMI-Nova International Management Institute, Slavonic University, Institute of Education Sciences, University of the Academy of Science	Very specific profile, unique HEIs

Type III institutions were established to serve regional labour market needs and linguistic particularities (in the case of Taraclia).

There are five highly specialised state HEIs (type IV). These were founded with the objective of educating future staff for government-related institutions such as the Ministry of Internal Affairs (Academy of the Ministry of Internal Affairs), Ministry of Foreign Affairs (Institute of International Relations of Moldova), the armed forces (Military Academy of the Armed Forces "Alexandru cel Bun") and the Academy of Science (University of the Academy of Science).

Of the 32 private HEIs that existed in 2000, only 11 survived. The remaining small private HEIs (type V) play only a marginal role. They often struggle with lack of infrastructure (they often have to rent premises), a small number of students and the absence of research activity.

In addition to these HEIs, there are four with a unique profile which do not fit into any type. These special HEIs include two highly specialised institutions offering postgraduate education (the Academy of Public Administration (APA) trains civil servants and the Institute of Education Sciences conducts graduate research and training in education), as well as the University of the Academy of Science and the Slavonic University that offer study programmes in the Russian language.

FORCES AFFECTING THE DEVELOPMENT OF THE HES IN MOLDOVA

A number of forces have affected the development of the HES in the Republic of Moldova, which will be explored in this section.

Political Will to Break with the Soviet Past and Orientation Towards Romanian and European Models

During the short history of the Republic of Moldova, political priorities have been oscillating between a strong orientation towards Romanian and Western models and more conservative tendencies in favour of preserving the model of higher education inherited from the Soviet Union. During the 1990s, higher education reforms were often modelled on Romanian examples. The tendency may have been promoted further by the substantial number of Moldovan students who have studied at Romanian universities since the 1990s. During the 2000s, the "European model of higher education" promoted by the Bologna Process became the most important point of reference for the public discourse on higher education reform, and European Union funded projects helped to introduce new curricula and management structures at many HEIs.

Demands for New Skills (e.g. in Business, Economics, Political Science) and Shifting Employment Prospects

An important factor driving the differentiation of curricula offered by Moldovan HEIs is market demand for new skills. This became particularly evident during the large wave of newly founded HEIs after 1992 (see Annex 6.1). Private HE pioneered the import of Western curricula while new public HEIs were primarily established to train public servants for the young state. Of the ten HEIs founded between 1990 and 1995, seven were focused on economics, business administration, law or political science. These new skills were in high demand and soon most HEIs adapted to market demand by offering their own study programmes in these sought-after disciplines.

On the other hand, the economic collapse of substantial parts of the industrial and agricultural base of the country led to a decline in student interest in studying exact sciences, agriculture, medicine and engineering. This was sometimes to the ruin of the involved faculties which further suffered from brain drain due to emigration of highly qualified specialists.

Maintained Public Funding for Education

As in other CIS countries, the break-up of the economy in the early 1990s decreased government revenues and in consequence the public

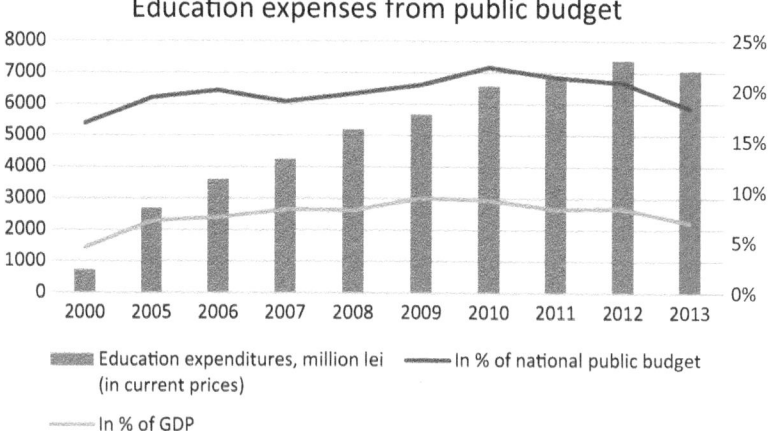

Fig. 12.4 Government expenditure on education 2000/2005–2013

funds available to HEIs (The World Bank 1997). On the other hand, public spending on education (as % of GDP) is higher than in other post-Socialist states, in fact, almost double the average of peer countries. Not only did Moldova establish and fund very small regional universities in cities such as Taraclia or Cahul; since 2000, Moldova has also increased spending on education each year, even in the face of a decreasing number of students. Without this continued public funding, several public HEIs may have disappeared, as did several private ones. While the survival of all public HEIs was assured, government funding was almost entirely subsistence-oriented and was used to pay for salaries and maintain existing infrastructure rather than investing in infrastructure quality and teaching staff. The following figure shows education funding in absolute and relative terms (Fig. 12.4).

Demography, Stricter Admission Requirements and Attractive Alternatives Lead to Declining Student Numbers

As described above, a demographic decline is reducing the number of potential students. In addition, reforms in secondary education have also had effects on the HES. The Code of Education (2014) enforced the Baccalaureate exam as a compulsory admission requirement, which has considerably reduced the number of potential students. In addition, an

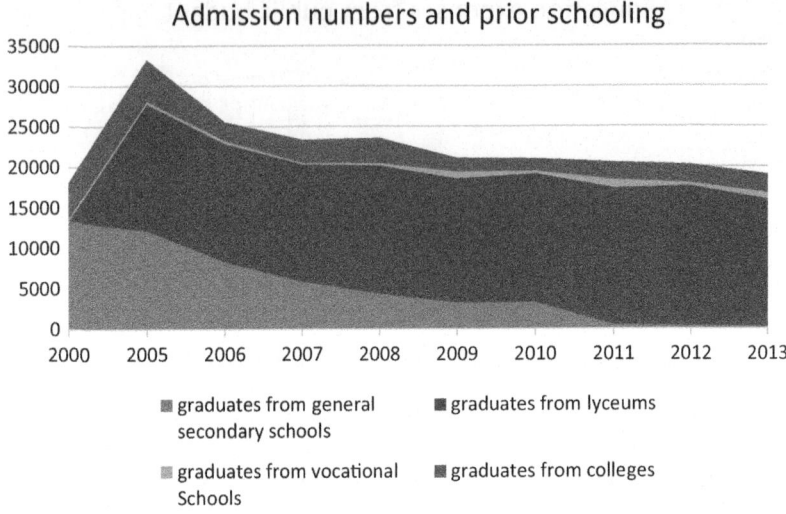

Fig. 12.5 Admission numbers by type of prior schooling (2000/2005–2013)

anti-fraud campaign conducted during the Baccalaureate exams in 2014 caused a sudden drop in the number of high school graduates who succeeded, resulting in a 2014 Baccalaureate pass rate of 56% compared to 96% in 2010.[9] The following figure shows the decline in admission numbers by type of school leaving certificate (Fig. 12.5).

The HEI "crisis" due to lack of potential students is exacerbated by attractive alternatives to studying at home. Bilateral agreements and scholarship programmes with Romania, Russia, Ukraine, Bulgaria and Turkey are options for Moldavan students, mostly in specific ethnic groups. As of 2014, over 4000 fully funded study places were open in Romania, 574 in Russia, 128 in Bulgaria and 100 in Ukraine. Scholarships for high school graduates are also provided by Turkey, Greece, China, Hungary, the Czech Republic, Slovakia and Lithuania. Moldovan graduates can continue their studies at universities in any country in the world, with the most preferred countries being Germany, Italy, France, the UK and the USA. According to mass media statistics,[10] every year approximately 6000 young Moldovans are choosing to study abroad, although no official numbers seem to exist to confirm this. The demographic downshift has already led to the closing of two HEIs and is threatening many others.

Internationalisation and Reform Driven and Supported by International Funding

Foreign funding has undoubtedly had an effect on the development of the higher education system in Moldova. Actors such as the Soros Foundation, the World Bank, the European Union, the Chinese government, the Council of Europe and others have provided *funding for exchange programmes, scientific publications and conferences, as well as curricula modernisation and governance reform.* While it is difficult to quantify the impact of these projects, their number, often-stated strategic purposes[11] and feedback from personal communication make it reasonable to assume that they do indeed shape higher education policy.

The most visible impact of international funding has been the establishment of the *International Management Institute "IMI-NOVA"* in 1995 by USM, ASEM, ASM, Pierre Mendes University (Grenoble, France) and two large local Moldovan enterprises. The institute specialises in social sciences (law, international relations). It is active in various international partnerships, especially with the francophone world, and has introduced a double-degree programme which allows students to obtain a French as well as a Moldovan degree.

CONCLUSIONS

In summary, the development of the HES from its Soviet past can be described as a process of expansion and (still ongoing) consolidation. The 1990s were a time during which tremendous economic change (mostly decline) coincided with the sudden disappearance of governance structures (and indeed of government itself) that regulated and assured the quality of the higher education system. HEIs were faced with strong demand for new types of knowledge, while at the same time their ideological and economic foundations were in a state of rapid deterioration. Education entrepreneurs and (a little later) public HEIs took advantage of this situation by setting up new programmes and establishing new HEIs, which led to a tripling in the number of HEIs between 1989 and 1999. Not only newly founded HEIs but also established ones set up "trend" faculties teaching law, business administration, economics or international relations. Because of the speed of this expansion and the resulting scarcity of qualified teaching staff, HEIs often had to make do with less than qualified personnel. Student numbers soared, in part driven by a market need for the qualifications HEIs had to offer, in part for the prestige HE conferred on graduates and in part because the bleak economic situation offered few alternatives to young people. The lack of adequate state funding for HEIs created an incentive to attract and retain any fee-paying students while the lack of (rigorous) regulation made HE easy to enter, including for those who lacked the appropriate qualifications. As a consequence, the quality and, in turn, the reputation of HE began to suffer, in particular that of young HEIs in the provinces or non-publicly owned. Emigration of qualified teaching staff and the practice of teaching at more than one HEI for more income further contributed to this decline in quality.

The expansion phase reached a turning point around 2005. Several factors contributed to this, the most powerful of which is demography. The HES had expanded to such a degree that the available number of HEI study places had become saturated and even exceeded demand. On the other end of the supply-demand equation, high incidences of emigration and low birth rate led to a decline in the number of potential students. The state as a regulation agency had further consolidated structures and was implementing stricter forms of quality assurance; these were restricting the ability of sub-par HEIs, but also clamping down on corrupt practices in school-leaving and university entrance examinations, which were reducing the number of potential students. The poor reputation of some HEIs made them less attractive to students eligible for HE with increasing opportunity to choose between affordable options, not only in Moldova but also abroad. The consequences of declining student numbers have long been visible in the declining number of private HEIs, while public HEIs have so far been kept alive by maintained state funding.[12]

Comparing the situation in 1991 and 2015, one cannot help but note that the Soviet-era institutions still form the core of the HE system. Only two truly new HEIs have grown to resemble the "old" institutions in terms of size, scope and quality, while most newer HEIs are smaller and focus on serving the regions or very specific market niches and make up only a small part of the higher education system.

The demographic and economic situation makes it unlikely that all HEIs will continue to thrive or even survive in their present form. In some cases, they may disappear altogether. HEIs with the least fortunate geographical and demographic potential in the regions as well as those with the worst reputations will likely be hardest hit. More fortunate HEIs may be facing fiercer competition for the remaining students. This competition may be based on quality, or it may be based on the ease of attaining a qualification. Seen in the light of more challenging prerequisites for students to gain HE eligibility combined with the potentially devastating effects of a bad reputation, the first strategy seems more likely; however, it cannot be ruled out that some HEIs may try to pursue the second. Regional HEIs may not be able to maintain the full range of programmes and may be forced to cooperate in consortia lest they perish. Like with the number of HEIs, a number of "trend faculties" established during the boom of the 1990s will be forced to close, either as a consequence of stricter accreditation and quality assurance requirements or because they will not be able to attract enough students. To the degree that this consolidation decreases the practice of teaching at more than one HEI, such a development may even contribute to the quality of teaching elsewhere.

All of these internal trends point towards further consolidation and decreasing internal quantity and possibly diversity, albeit arguably gaining in quality. In the macrosystem, the process towards European integration through the Bologna Process, student and staff mobility and joint research activities will make further internationalisation probable, although likely still on a relatively low level.

Notes

1. For instance, according to King (2002, 99), the share of Russians in the MSSR increased from 7% in 1941 to 13% in 1989, and Russian became the native language of 4% of Romanians, 37% of Ukrainians, 7% of Gagauz, 18% of Bulgarians and 73% of Jews, and these numbers were higher among younger people (King 2002, 123).
2. The force behind this first initiative was professor Ion Groza, who in the past had benefited from a series of fellowships in the United States, France and the United Kingdom. On the basis of these first two student groups, the first private HE institutional structure was created by an official government decision within the auspices of a public institution. However, this private sub-division (named "private university") of a public university existed for only 3 years and had to suspend activity because of legal contradictions and personal opposition by university administration.
3. A noteworthy example of this knowledge transfer from Romania is the invitation of a Romanian professor to act as rector of the newly founded Academy of Economic Studies of Moldova.
4. Specifically, in 1990 the Pedagogical State Institute "Ion Creangă" became the Pedagogical State University "Ion Creanga"; in 1991 the Beltsy "Alecu

Russo" State Pedagogical Institute was reorganised into the Beltsy "Alecu Russo" State University, the State Institute of Medicine to the State University of Medicine "N.Testemiteanu" (since 1996 the State University of Medicine and Pharmacy "N.Testemiteanu"), and the State Agrarian Institute "M. Frunze" of Moldova was nationalised and became the State Agrarian University of Moldova. In May 1992, the Tiraspol State Pedagogical Institute "T. Sevcenko" was reorganised into the Tiraspol State University. In 1993, the Polytechnical Institute "S.Lazo" of Moldova became the Technical University of Moldova. The two specialised HEIs in the field of culture and arts have supported a triple reorganisation: in 1993 the "Gavriil Musicescu" Moldovan State Conservatory became the Academy of Music "Gavriil Musicescu", which in 1999 merged with the Moldavian State Institute of Arts to become the State University of Arts in Moldova; in 2002 this university was reorganised into the Academy of Music, Theatre and Fine Arts of Moldova.

5. The 2014 Education Code allows graduates of other types of secondary education to participate in an external examination for the Baccalaureate upon application.
6. Accreditation results in recognition of an HEI as a "*profile member*" of the Academy of Science, which grants them the right to conduct independent research in a specific area. Alternatively, HEIs may become "*affiliate members*" of the Academy of Science, which allows them to conduct research in cooperation with the Academy of Science.
7. The exceptions are the Universities of Balti and Cahul.
8. A list of Moldovan HEIs can be found in Annex 6.1.
9. http://bloguvern.md/2013/11/11/rezultatele-finale-ale-examenului-de-bac-2013/
10. http://www.zdg.md/editia-print/social/peste-sase-mii-de-burse-pentru-tinerii-din-r-moldova-care-doresc-sa-studieze-in-strainatate
11. The Ministry of Education lists all ongoing cooperation projects on its website: http://edu.md/ro/cooperare-internationala/
12. Some experts argue that in favour of long-term viability, quality and efficiency, the number of public HEIs should be reduced from the current 19 to only 7, with 3 in the regions and 4 in the capital of Chisinau (Turcan et al. 2015).

References

Ciurea, C., V. Berbeca, S. Lipcean, and M. Gurin. 2012. *Higher Education System in the Republic of Moldova in the Context of the Bologna Process: 2005–2011*. Chişinău: Soros Moldova-Foundation.

Cojocaru, V. Gh. 1995. *Reforma învăţămîntului: orientări, obiective, direcţii*. Chişinău: Ştiinţa.

Cuciureanu, G. 2014. *Country Reports 2013: Moldova//ERAWATCH Country Reports 2013: Moldova*, EUR, Scientific and Technical Research Series. Vol. 26763. Luxembourg: Publications Office.
Galben, A., and A. Cogan. 2003. *ULIM [Universitatea Libera Internationala din Moldova]: 1992–2002: pagini de istorie = ULIM: 1992–2002: stranicy istorii*. Chișinău: [s. n.].
King, C. 2002. *Moldovenii: România, Rusia și politica culturală*. Chișinău: ARC.
National Bureau of Statistics of the Republic of Moldova. 2014. Educational in the Republic of Moldova: Statistical Publication, 2013/2014. http://www.statistica.md/public/files/publicatii_electronice/Educatia/Educatia_RM_2014.pdf
Padure, L. 2009. *The Politics of Higher Education Reforms in Central and Eastern Europe. Development Challenges of the Republic of Moldova*. PhD Thesis. https://tspace.library.utoronto.ca/bitstream/1807/19157/6/Padure_Lucia_200911_PhD_thesis.pdf
Republica Moldova Parlamentul. 1995. Law of Education of the Republic of Moldova. http://www.see-educoop.net/education_in/pdf/law_on_education_mol-enl-t04.pdf. Accessed 5 June 2014.
Ruffio, P, A. Giorgio, J. Gierach, and A.S. Ballart. 2012. *Overview of the Higher Education Systems in the Tempus Partner Countries: Eastern Europe*, Tempus Studies. Vol. 11. Luxembourg: Publications Office.
Secrieru, D. 2007. *Integrarea sistemului educațional din Republica Moldova în spațiul european Studiu elaborat în cadrul Programului "Politici Educaționale"*. Chișinău: Institutul de Politici Publice.
Smolentseva, A. 2012. *Access to Higher Education in the Post-Soviet States: Between Soviet Legacy and Global Challenges*. Unpublished.
Stati, V. 2002. *Istoria Moldovei*, Biblioteca Pro Moldova. Chișinău: Vivar-Editor.
The Parliament of the Republic of Moldova. 1995. Law of Education of the Republic of Moldova, No. 547-XII of 21.07.1995. http://www.see-educoop.net/education_in/pdf/law_on_education_mol-enl-t04.pdf
———. 2014. Education Code of the Republic of Moldova, No. 152 of 17.07.2014. http://edu.gov.md/sites/default/files/education_code_final_version.pdf
The World Bank. 1997. Staff Appraisal Report: Republic of Moldova General Education Project. http://www-wds.worldbank.org/servlet/WDSContentServer/IW3P/IB/1997/03/21/000009265_3980420170717/Rendered/PDF/multi_page.pdf
Tiron, Ș., V. Arion, M. Paiu, V. Scalnîi, and V. Stan. 2003. *Higher Education in the Republic of Moldova*, Monographs on Higher Education/UNESCO CEPES. Bucharest: UNESCO CEPES.

Toderaş, N. 2012. The Governance of Higher Education System in Moldova: The Case of a Failed Institutional Change: Synopsis. http://www.doctorat.snspa.ro/sites/default/files/doctorat/nicolae%20toderas/Abstract%20%20Eng.pdf

Turcan, R., and L. Bugaian, eds. 2015. *Restructuring, Rationalizing and Modernizing Higher Education Sector in the Republic of Moldova*. Chisinau: Cuvântul ABC.

Turcan, R.V., L. Bugaian, A. Niculita, A. Cotelnic, D. Pojar, and P. Todos. 2015. Draft Legislative Proposals. In *Restructuring, Rationalizing and Modernizing Higher Education Sector in the Republic of Moldova*, ed. R. Turcan and L.Bugaian, 11–43. Chisinau: Cuvântul ABC. http://vbn.aau.dk/files/218934776/Restructuring_HE_in_Moldova.pdf.

Worden, E.A. 2014. Moldova: Challenges and Opportunities. In *Education in Eastern Europe and Eurasia*, Education Around the World, ed. N. Ivanenko, 47–64. London: Bloomsbury.

Yagodin, G.A., ed. 1990. *Higher Education in the USSR*. Bucharest: CEPES.

Lukas Bischof is a visiting research fellow and advisor at the Higher School of Economics (Moscow) and an associated consultant with CHE Consult (Berlin). Between 2011 and 2016 he worked as a consultant for universities, foundations, ministries of education and the European Commission. He has worked and published on the regulation and quality assurance of national and international higher education systems, institutional quality management and project management in higher education. As part of the Development of Quality Assurance in Higher Education in Moldova (QUAEM) project in Moldova, he supported universities and the government of the Republic of Moldova in the reform of the country's institutions of quality assurance.

Alina Tofan is a senior research fellow at the Moldova-Institut Leipzig at the University of Leipzig, Germany. Previously she was an associate professor at Moldova State University. She received a PhD in Philology from the Academy of Sciences of Moldova and a PhD in Philosophy from the University of Leipzig, Germany. She is author of numerous publications on literary and cultural history, sociolinguistics, migration and education.

Open Access This chapter is distributed under the terms of the Creative Commons Attribution 4.0 International License (http://creativecommons.org/licenses/by/4.0/), which permits use, duplication, adaptation, distribution and reproduction in any medium or format, as long as you give appropriate credit to the original author(s) and the source, provide a link to the Creative Commons license and indicate if changes were made.

The images or other third party material in this chapter are included in the chapter's Creative Commons license, unless indicated otherwise in a credit line to the material. If material is not included in the chapter's Creative Commons license and your intended use is not permitted by statutory regulation or exceeds the permitted use, you will need to obtain permission directly from the copyright holder.

CHAPTER 13

Russia: The Institutional Landscape of Russian Higher Education

Daria Platonova and Dmitry Semyonov

INTRODUCTION

In this chapter we explore changes in the higher education institutional landscape, analysing the case of the largest post-Soviet higher education system. In the post-Soviet period, Russian higher education (HE) has expanded tremendously. Dramatic growth in the number of students and institutions has been facilitated by the introduction of additional tuition-paying tracks in the public as well as the new private higher education sector. Shifts in social and economic demand for professional fields have affected the disciplinary and organisational structure of higher educational institutions (HEIs).

External forces (economic, political and social conditions) and higher education policy have been changing during the last decades. In the first part of the transitional period, the state provided limited regulation for the higher education system, but in the 2000s it has regained its role as the main agent of change in the design of the higher education system. The variety of institutional types that have evolved in Russian higher education

D. Platonova (✉) • D. Semyonov
Institute of Education, National Research University Higher School of Economics, Moscow, Russia

© The Author(s) 2018
J. Huisman et al. (eds.), *25 Years of Transformations of Higher Education Systems in Post-Soviet Countries*, Palgrave Studies in Global Higher Education, https://doi.org/10.1007/978-3-319-52980-6_13

illustrates the consequences of massification and marketisation, such as a new "demand-absorbing" segment of the higher education system and institutional programme drift. Also, the governmental role in shaping the landscape has been reflected in attempts to increase vertical diversity (e.g. the excellence initiative) on the one hand, and to restrain it by closing down lower-tier institutions on the other.

The first part of the chapter presents a brief description of the HE landscape by the time of independence as the starting point of post-Soviet transformations. In the second part, we will discuss the key socioeconomic changes and major trends in higher education including massification, privatisation of costs and changes in the subject mix at HEIs. The key HE policy changes that affected the institutional landscape since independence are discussed in the next part. In the final part we present the results of an analysis of the recent HE landscape.

THE HIGHER EDUCATION LANDSCAPE IN SOVIET RUSSIA

In the last decades of the USSR, Russian higher education played a major role in the whole Soviet "machinery". The Russian Soviet Federative Socialist Republic (RSFSR) was a part of the Soviet Union (USSR), and the Union spent about 39% of expenditure on higher education in its largest republic. This higher education expenditure represented 17% of all education expenditure in Soviet Russia (compared to 10% for the Soviet Union, Table 13.1).

Table 13.1 Expenditure on education (total and higher education) in the USSR and Russian SFSR in 1981 and 1987 (in billion rubles and %)

Year		1981/1982	1987/1988
USSR	Expenditure on education (total), billion rubles	31.9	42.5
	Expenditure on higher education, billion rubles	3.86	4.17
	Percentage of expenditure on higher education in all expenditure on education	12%	10%
Russian SFSR	Expenditure on education (total), billion rubles	7.2	9.9
	Expenditure on higher education, billion rubles	1.54	1.64
	% of expenditure on higher education in all expenditure on education	21%	17%

Source: *Statistical Book on Higher Education* (1992, 100)

In contrast to higher education trends in Western Europe and North America, during the last decade of Soviet Russia enrolment decreased (by about 6% in 1980–1990). The number of students per 10,000 inhabitants also dropped by 13.2% (*Statistical Book on Higher Education* 1992, 166).

The federal design was a distinctive feature of the RSFSR from other Soviet republics. It consisted of several dozen regions, which affected the deliberate dispersion of HEIs within the Russian "subjects of federation" (hereafter referred to as regions). Moscow and Saint Petersburg were the two largest regions (they were in fact cities with the status of regions) and accumulated more than 28% of students (528.7 and 272.9 thousand students, respectively) in 82 HEIs in Moscow and 41 in Saint Petersburg.

Each region had at least one HEI, but often more. The regular set consisted of a comprehensive university, a polytechnic institution, a pedagogical institution and a specialised HEI (described below). This "package" varied according to the size of the population and the distribution of industries across the regions. By 1990 there was a group of regions with 10–18 HEIs and a large number of regions with 3–4 HEIs (*Statistical Year Book* 1992, 278–280).

By the end of the Soviet era, 2,825 million students studied in 514 HEIs within Russia. About 58% of the student population were full-time, about 10% took evening courses and about 32% studied in correspondence courses[1] (Statistical Book on Russian Federation 1993, 276). There were 42 comprehensive universities with 328.1 thousand students. Yet, the majority of HEIs were highly specialised and affiliated to a relevant industrial ministry or department.

Thirty-seven per cent of all students studied in 135 specialised industrial HEIs (the largest group of HEIs), with 26% in 94 pedagogical HEIs (the second specialised); most of the other HEIs were small institutes (see Table 13.2).

The number of HEIs specialised in economics and law was limited. Moreover, these institutions mostly provided part-time education. About 70% of students took evening and correspondence courses in such institutions, while in all other types of HEIs the percentages ranged from 30% to 50%. The exception were medical institutions where the share of full-time students was about 92%.

In general, the Soviet Russian higher education system, as in the rest of the Soviet system, reproduced the German-style industrial education model (strict segmentation of vocational and higher education) and the Humboldtian academic tradition (although with a Soviet slant). The

Table 13.2 Number of HEIs by type, number of students by form of learning and their shares, 1990

Sector	Number of HEIs	Total number of students	Students in evening and correspondence courses	
		Number of students, thousand	Number of students, thousand	Percentage of total student numbers
Industry	135	1,026	406	40
Construction	21	104	49	47
Transport	23	143	76	53
Communication	5	31	16	52
Agriculture	60	261	119	46
Economics	31	170	119	70
Law	4	27	21	78
Healthcare	46	186	14	8
Physical training and sport	9	28	13	46
Education	14	52	32	62
Pedagogical HEIs	94	446	179	40
Art and cinema	30	21	7	33
Universities	42	328	125	38

Source: *Statistical Book on Higher Education* (1992)

model reflected "a merger between the need for speedy mass education with the reality of few university centers in the country" (Kuraev 2016, 182). These centres of knowledge were established by the most prestigious universities, such as the Lomonosov Moscow State University. With regard to the typology of Soviet HEIs (Froumin et al. 2014), we can distinguish six types of HEIs in Soviet Russia (Table 13.3).

Major Changes in Higher Education Under New Conditions

The 25 years of Russian HE can be divided into three periods with different key policy intentions. The major HE reforms are shown in Fig. 13.1.

The first post-Soviet decade can be characterised as "laissez-faire". After the adoption of the main federal laws on education in the early 1990s that set the framework for HEI activities, the government did not intervene in the higher education system until the early 2000s.

Table 13.3 Types of HEIs in Soviet Russia

	Leading	General
Comprehensive universities	Old prestigious universities, research centres, located in capital/regional centres, subordinated by MoE ~5–10 universities ~80–120 thousand students For example, Lomonosov Moscow State University	Established for regional socioeconomic development; some were opened on the basis of pedagogical HEIs, graduates, faculty for other HEIs, and staff for research institutes, widespread within regions, subordinated by MoE ~32–37 universities ~180–240 thousand students For example, Tyumen State University
National industrial HEIs	Specialised HEIs related to the Soviet industrial clusters, performed the role of curriculum development centres, subordinated by the particular ministries, located in Moscow, Leningrad or other large industrial cities ~ 20–30 HEIs ~ 200–250 thousand students For example, Moscow Aviation Institute	Specialised HEIs related to the Soviet industrial clusters and particular factories, subordinated by the particular ministries, located in large industrial cities, widespread within regions ~100–110 HEIs ~750–800 thousand students For example, Kazan Aviation Institute
Regional HEIs: Agricultural, pedagogical, medical, economic, polytechnics, arts and theatre	Established for socioeconomic development of the region; the role of methodological centres, Specialised HEIs, subordinated by the particular ministries, located in Moscow, Leningrad or other large industrial cities ~10–20 HEIs ~100–150 thousand students For example, Moscow Timiryazev Agricultural Academy	Established for socioeconomic development of the region; Specialised HEIs, subordinated by the particular ministries, spread within all regions ~280–300 HEIs ~1,150–1,300 thousand students For example, Chelyabinsk State Pedagogical Institute

Source: Developed by the authors based on Froumin et al. (2014)

The period of reforms in the 2000s started with the introduction of a unified national exam. In this period, the government also stimulated institutional reforms, such as meeting the expectations of the Bologna Process and the integration of education and research. Moreover, the state

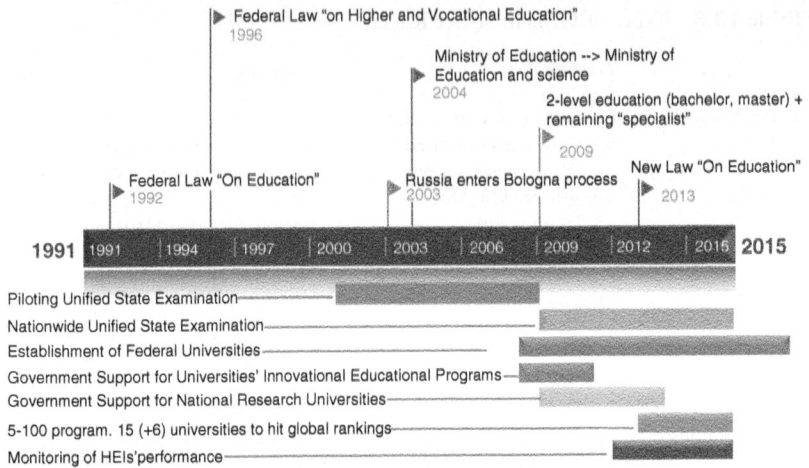

Fig. 13.1 Timeline of key higher education reforms in Russia, 1991–2015 (Source: Developed by the authors)

launched its first support programmes for federal universities and national research universities.

Since 2012, the government has taken the reins even more explicitly regarding the reform of the Russian HE system and its institutional landscape. It started with the performance-based monitoring of HEIs, which led to mergers and reorganisation. Excellence programmes urged more internationally oriented research activity in selected universities. The ideas of new public management including performance evaluation, transparency of data and managerialism were key drivers for change in this period.

Higher education transformations have been closely related to the political and socioeconomic changes in Russia since the USSR dissolution. Liberalisation and the establishment of a new market economy inevitably affected the education system (Balzer 1994). Within the framework of wider socioeconomic changes, we emphasise three main trends in HE development in Russia that significantly influenced the landscape: massification, privatisation of costs (cost-sharing) and changes in the subject mix.

Shift in Demand for Educational Fields

The Russian economy has experienced explicit structural transformations, with a major expansion of the tertiary sector (services) (see Table 13.4). From

1990 to 2002, the cumulative loss in the number of employees in the industry sector was extremely dramatic, amounting to about 36%. There were comparable changes in other production sectors such as agriculture (−20%), construction (−23%) and transport and communication (−16%) (Gimpelson et al. 2010, 4). These changes in the labour market generated a perception of low demand for "hard sciences" and led to a decline in the popularity of engineering HEIs. The services and healthcare sector grew significantly. Employment in the trade sector increased by 85%, in the financial sector by 103% and in public management by 85% (Gimpelson et al. 2010, 4).

Such changes in the economy and the labour market also affected student choices. Figure 13.2 shows the dramatic increase in social science graduates.

Table 13.4 Structural transformations of the Russian economy 1991–2014

	1991	1995	2000	2005	2010	2014
Agriculture, value added (% of GDP)	14.3	7.2	6.4	5.0	3.9	4.2
Industry, value added (% of GDP)	47.6	37.0	37.9	38.1	34.7	35.8
Services, value added (% of GDP)	38.1	55.9	55.6	57.0	61.4	60.0

Source: World Bank: World Development Indicators

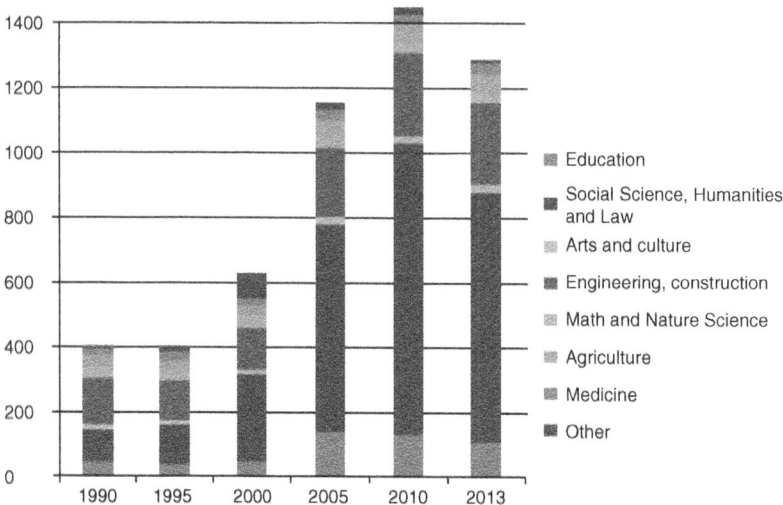

Fig. 13.2 Number of graduates by study field (Source: Aggregative groups calculated by authors based on data from the Federal State Statistics Service (2015))

Massification

New economic conditions and changes in social attitudes underlie the rapid massification of higher education in independent Russia. Contrary to the previous period (1990–1995) when student enrolments were declining, from the mid-1990s new social values led youth to invest in long-term targets, such as continuing their education. This phenomenon, which can be explained by the quick rise of the wage premium after central control on salaries was abolished (Kapeliushnikov 2006; Gimpelson et al. 2007), is defined as *"proobrazovatel'nyi sdvig"* (the shift towards education in the life strategies of young people) (Magun and Engovatov 2004).

Figure 13.3 shows the pace of massification in absolute numbers and the gross enrolment rate according to national statistics. All indicators have been growing since 1994, and it was only after 2008 that the trend turned downward. Today, the age cohort participation among 17- to 25-year-olds in higher education is about 32%. OECD data show the same upward trend. The tertiary[2] enrolment rate among 20- to 24-year-olds increased from 28.8% to 30.3% between 2005 and 2014 (OECD 2016). Russian higher education has thus become "universal" in the last decade according to Trow's terminology (Trow 1973).

As a response to the massive demand, the number of HEIs doubled from 1991 to 2011. Moreover, the establishment of HEI branches (satellite HEIs[3]) provided wider access to higher education in the regions. The

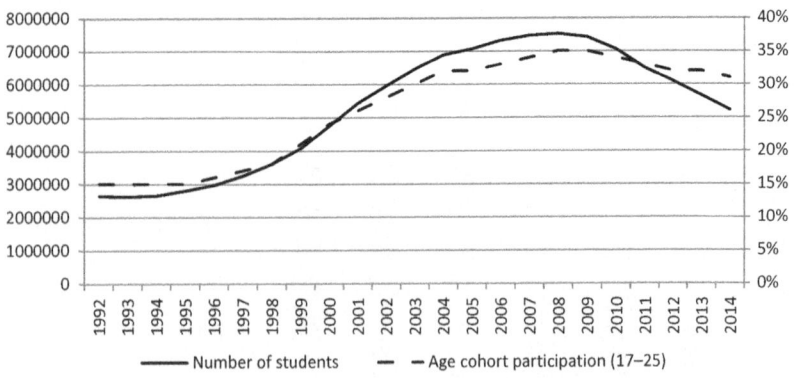

Fig. 13.3 Number of students in HEIs and age cohort participation (17–25), 1991–2014, Russia (Source: Calculated by the authors. Data from Federal State Statistics Service (2015))

majority of satellite HEIs has shaped a demand-absorbing segment along with small private HEIs. In 1993 there were only about 200 public satellite HEIs (National Centre for Public Accreditation n.d.), but in 10 years the number increased more than six times; taking into account private establishments as well increases the number to eight times. The growth originated from local initiatives for new HEIs as well as a liberal governmental attitude towards newcomers on the higher education market. Moreover, the demographic situation and the financial abilities of some households to enrol in higher education also contributed to the expanding supply.

The government had concerns about the quality of education provided by satellite HEIs and there was a general perception that the number of satellites increased too fast. Hence, the government limited the growth of these entities in 2006 by revoking the licence of several dozen satellites. In 2005 there were about 2200 satellite HEIs (1823 public and 378 private), while in 2007 there were only 1646 (1114 public and 532 private). The same concerns in the period between 2012 and 2015 led the Ministry of Education and Science (MoES) to once again reduce the number of satellites, this time on the basis of performance evaluation.

Massification is also associated with the influential trend of expansion in part-time HE. The number of part-time students increased three times over the 25-year period. In 1991, the share of students learning in evening and correspondence courses was 39%, and by 2014 it had risen to 53%. The majority of part-time programmes are not supported by state funding.

Private Sector and Cost-Sharing

The new legislation adopted in 1992 allowed the establishment of private HEIs (the Federal Law "On Education"). The expansion of the HE system was therefore partially due to the growth of the private higher education sector. The number of private HEIs grew to 358, although only 7% of students were enrolled in the private sector.

After 2000, the private sector formed a substantive part of the higher education system, not only in terms of the number of HEIs (there were more than 400 private HEIs) but also in terms of student body. About 14% of students were in private HEIs in 2014. Moreover, private education expanded through the privatisation of public HEIs. New legislation adopted in 1992 allowed public HEIs to attract so-called non-budgetary funding. In line with that regulation, HEIs started to introduce a *dual tuition track system* (Johnstone 2004). This means that in public HEIs the state provides tuition-free student places and that HEIs can add private tuition tracks. A student can apply for either state funding (more competitive) or pursue a self-paid place in public or private HEIs (less competitive). The competition for state-funded places is based on merit. In general, students with the highest entry exam scores enrol in public HEIs for state-funded places, and students with the lowest exam scores enrol in third-rate private HEIs. The latter are less competitive HEIs that accept the majority of low performers.

As Fig. 13.4 depicts, the balance between the numbers of state-funded students and students paying tuition is inverted when the 1990s are compared with the 2000s. In 1995 only 13.7% students enrolled in public HEIs without state support, but since 2000 more than 40% of students enrolled in public HEIs are paying fees. If private HEI enrolment is included, more than 60% of students in Russia are paying for their education by themselves (since 2002).

Most of the higher education private sector is oriented towards providing popular programmes (e.g. economics, law and management). The government made several attempts to restrain the growing supply, including quotas for privately funded places in public HEIs in 1996, but the quota was abolished (Klyachko et al. 2002, 17).

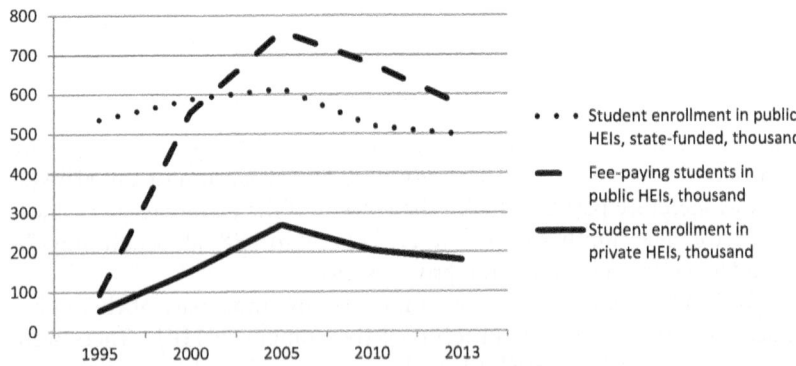

Fig. 13.4 Enrolment by source of financing and type of HEIs, 1995–2013, Russia (Source: Calculated by authors. Data from: before 2000, Education in the Russian Federation (2006); for 2000–2010, Education in the Russian Federation (2012); after 2010, Federal State Statistics Service (2015))

The explicit higher education financial policy was thus cost-sharing that took the form of a double tuition fee track system. Students with high exam scores almost automatically get free access to a public HEI, whereas students with lower grades can register for a tuition fee track. The support for regularly admitted students at public HEIs has not changed since Soviet times and is implemented through the dispersion of state-funded slots to HEIs. In the mid-2000s, there was an attempt to introduce a student grant system; however, it faced opposition from academics and society in general (Zaretskaya and Kapranova 2003).

The lingering economic crisis partially determined the financial policy directions during the first decade of independence. By 1998, the funding allocated per student decreased by 70% compared with the end of the 1980s (Klyachko and Rojdestvenskaya 1999, 4). Figure 13.5 shows the gap in HE funding during the late 1990s. Compared with Soviet Russia, the importance of HE in public expenditure on education dropped from 17% in 1987 to less than 10% in 1995–1999.

Public resources, or lack thereof, affected the operation of HEIs. Most HEIs accumulated bad debts due to inability to pay for utilities. Financial

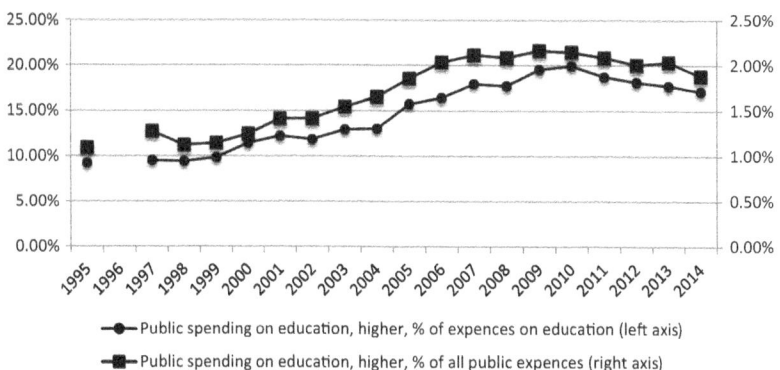

Fig. 13.5 Public spending on higher education as a share of total public expenditure on education and public spending on education as a share of total public expenditure (*per cent*) (Source: Calculated by authors. Data for expenditure from: before 2003, Education in the Russian Federation (2006); after 2003, Roskozna (2015) and FSSS (2015))

Note: Due to the reform of the financial system in 2003, the data before and after 2003 cannot be directly compared.

distress and new legal abilities provided a catalyst for active fundraising through the creation of fee-paying slots and the leasing of facilities (Klyachko and Rojdestvenskaya 1999).

From the beginning of 2000, government policy was focussed on education as a priority (Johnson 2008). The new legal basis for the development of HE (e.g. National Doctrine for Education, 2000; the Concept of Modernisation for Russian Education, 2001; and the Federal Strategic Programme for the Development of Education, 2005) along with rapid economic growth enabled large-scale changes in the design of the HE system (Abankina and Abankina 2013). Firstly, these circumstances conditioned substantial growth of public expenditure on HE from 2000 to 2010 (see Fig. 13.5), although this share dropped between 2009 and 2014.

The described developments affected the horizontal differentiation of Russian higher education. Before 2010, the main changes took place in the field of HEI education activities (mix of subjects, as addressed earlier). Economy and labour market transformations, along with lack of public financing and state deregulation, urged HEIs to find new sources and broaden their supply. Liberalisation and decentralisation supported "natural" differentiation by legitimising the emergence of a private sector, a dual tuition track system and relatively unrestricted internal programme diversification.

HIGHER EDUCATION GOVERNANCE AND REFORMS

Governance Structure

Despite the fact that Russia is a federal country, the decentralisation of state authority over higher education did not go far. In the 1990s some regions established their own HEIs, but very few HEIs were actually under regional control. Since the early 2000s, greater centralisation has affected the HE system. There are few HEIs subordinated by regional authorities (70 HEIs, including satellite HEIs with only 2.5% of students, see Table 13.5) and more than 95% of budgetary funding is federal (Froumin and Leshukov forthcoming).

HEIs report directly to the various bodies of executive power. By the end of Soviet times, there were 28 different ministries supervising HE. In modern Russia there are still 21 different bodies, including the MoES. In general, the MoES provides a broad framework for HE system operation through its right to grant licences, accredit institutions, assign admission quotas and implement federal programmes for HE development.

Table 13.5 Distribution of HEIs by ministry and other agencies, Russia, 2014

	Number of HEIs (satellites and parent)	Number of parent HEIs	Share of students (head count) in total number of students
Ministry of Education and Science	825	274	58.49%
Private HEIs	816	368	14.89%
The Russian Government	88	7	4.30%
Ministry of Agriculture	76	55	7.47%
Regional authorities	70	53	2.54%
Ministry of Culture	55	45	1.32%
Federal Agency for Railway Transport	51	9	2.64%
Ministry of Health and Social Development	48	46	4.13%
Ministry of Sport	22	14	0.78%
Federal Agency for Marine and River Transport	20	6	0.76%
Ministry of Justice	13	1	0.33%
Supreme Court	11	1	0.29%
Federal Communications Agency	11	4	0.53%
Federal Fishery Agency	8	6	0.77%
Federal Air Transport Agency	5	3	0.32%
Federal Customs Service	4	1	0.17%
Russian Academy of Arts	3	2	0.05%
The Ministry of Foreign Affairs	2	2	0.16%
Ministry of Economic Development	2	1	0.06%
Russian Science Academy	1	1	0.00%
The Federal Service for Intellectual Property, Patents and Trademarks	1	1	0.01%

Source: Calculated by the authors. Data from Monitoring (2015)

Most HEIs (catering for 60% of all students) report directly to the MoES. The two other major ministries are the Ministry of Agriculture and the Ministry of Health and Social Development (medical HEIs).

Higher Education and Science

After two reforms of the ministerial body that oversees higher education (1991–1995, the State Committee of Higher Education; 1996–2004, the Ministry of Education), the governance structure changed profoundly in

2004. The new Ministry of Education and Science united two former separate spheres, which are higher education and science. However, the Academy of Science was not abolished. In 2013 the government launched an academy reform, which faced considerable resistance and has not brought crucial changes yet.

In general, in contrast to Soviet HE, research activity in universities is receiving ample support in modern Russia. For example, the federal programme "Integration of Science and Higher Education" (2002–2006) supported the involvement of graduate and postgraduate students in large research projects and leading research centres. The development of HEI research activities and the research university as a model for leading HEIs is legitimated by direct support for research projects from several state foundations, special federal programmes and requirements for academic performance. With the introduction of a new federal law (2012), the qualification framework supports a three-cycle education system.

Although there are no PhD programmes in Russia, the government moved *aspirantura* (corresponding level to PhD) from the postgraduate to the higher education level. Before the reform, *aspirantura* was a specific learning track more focussed on self-directed learning in preparation for a dissertation. Now, as a part of higher education, *aspirantura* programmes are more oriented toward training research skills.

Bologna Process

The Bologna Process is considered one of the major institutional reforms with a direct internationalisation aim and involvement in the global higher education system. Although the government's intention to join the Bologna Process was much debated and faced strong opposition among university leaders and faculty as well as students and parents, Russia signed the Bologna Declaration in 2003 (Telegina and Schwengel 2012).

Since that time, the European Credit Transfer and Accumulation System (ECTS) along with a three-cycle degree system and quality assurance systems have been gradually introduced. The bachelor/master degree structure was optional for HEIs parallel to the 5-year specialist degree (gradually introduced since 1989, in 1992 proposed as the national multilevel degree structure) (Luchinskaya and Ovchynnikova 2011). From 2009, all educational programmes were expected to transform into two-cycle degree programmes (with some exceptions). Half of all master students are enrolled in 65 HEIs, suggesting a high level of master student concentration in a relatively small set of HEIs. In 2015, 12% of all bachelor graduates transferred to master programmes. The government has emphasised the importance of master programmes by allocating about 40% of all publicly funded places to master degree programmes in 2016.

Admission: National State Examination

The admission reform started in 2001 and was implemented nationwide in 2009. It included the abolishment of university-specific exams and the introduction of the state entry exam (Unified State Examination, USE). The reform aimed at increasing accessibility, equality and transparency of higher education (Bolotov 2004).

The exam is called "unified" as schools and HEIs use the same exam. The USE is designed for the assessment of all results for secondary education graduates and for the enrolment of prospective HE students. The USE is administered in test form and school graduates must choose several subjects to enter an HEI (two are obligatory, mathematics and the Russian language). Due to the double track tuition system with publicly and privately funded slots, students with lower grades can choose to study on a payment basis, yet "passing" scores vary between HEIs.

The USE project is considered one of the most influential institutional reforms in Russian higher education. A high score on the exam has become the aim of most school leavers. Selectivity became a measurable indicator of perceived educational success at HEIs. The higher the average entry exam score of the HEI, the more successful it is in attracting talented students and (presumably) the higher the quality of teaching; this is the guiding logic of the MoES. Selectivity has always been in place, during Soviet times as well, but transparency brought a clear framework for HEI hierarchy based on prestige and demand.

The distribution of HEIs by average exam scores is far from normal:

- Only a few HEIs accept students with very high exam scores (most of these HEIs are medical);
- Only 10% of HEIs have an average entrance score of more than 67.5 (out of 100);
- And 40% of HEIs have very low average exam scores (under 55), with a dominance of private HEIs.

Normative Types of HEIs in Russia

The Federal Law (1996) defined the structure of the higher education system, considering the types of HEIs: universities, academies and institutes (see Fig. 13.6). According to this law, the distinguishing characteristics of these formal types were:

- University—wide range of education fields
- Academy—focussed on graduate education in one or more fields (often medical HEIs)
- Institute—HEIs mostly with a particular specialisation (inherited from Soviet times)

Due to the loss of federal funding in the 1990s, many institutes upgraded themselves to university status, expect those with more stable public financing and attractiveness for tuition-paying students (Bain 2003). As the upgrades had to be permitted by the state, the acquisition of university status was associated with diversification of fields.

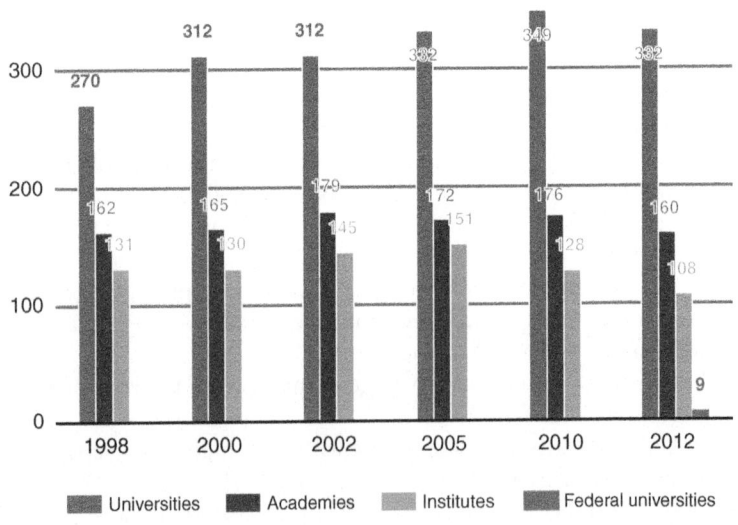

Fig. 13.6 Russian HEIs by nominal types, 1998–2012 (Source: Education in the Russian Federation 2006; Federal State Statistics Service, 2015)

Soviet diversity with reference to specialisation is also rooted in the description of the HE landscape in post-Soviet Russia. Until 2004 the Federal Statistical Agency collected data on the number of students within such groups as engineering HEIs, agricultural HEIs, transport HEIs, pedagogical HEIs, arts HEIs and medical HEIs. The classification reflects merely path dependence, but does not reflect the actual subject mix.

As mentioned, the new Federal Law was adopted in 2012. It suspended the three HEI categories. In addition to proposing a general HEI category ("organisation of higher education"), the law labels Moscow State University and Saint Petersburg State University as leading classic universities with special status. Other categories included federal universities and national research universities (Federal Law 2012).

Leading University Programmes

From the mid-2000s, the government made efforts to select a group of leading universities. In 2004, two universities (Moscow State University and Saint Petersburg State University) were assigned a special status, which implied a particular model of autonomy and funding. From 2006, the government has frequently launched special programmes to shape an elite higher education segment.

In 2006 the government started establishing "federal universities" by merging several regional institutions (e.g. comprehensive, teacher training and arts HEIs). The model implied a special focus on the regional economic context and special funding. Currently, there are ten federal HEIs.

In 2006–2007, 57 institutions received special funding for the implementation of "innovative education programmes". This was the first example of targeted funding for selected universities.

In 2008–2009, 29 HEIs obtained national research university status with special government funding for research, internationalisation and curriculum development. The programme set incentives for research intensiveness and was intended to stimulate the strategic development of university R&D missions through annual performance evaluations.

Furthermore, in 2013, Russia launched its Excellence Initiative ("5–100"). The Russian government, with the help of the International Council, selected 15 Russian universities to receive special funding in efforts to place these universities among the top 100 universities (in major global rankings) by 2020. In 2015, the programme was extended by adding six more universities.

Although the number of institutions decreases from one project to another, in general the policy trend is to establish a benchmark for leading institutions, modelled on the idea of the research university.

Universities with special status differ considerably from all other HEIs in terms of size, funding, research activity and enrolments. Federal universities are the largest in the higher education system in terms of student numbers and federal funding. Research universities in the 5–100 programme rely mainly on federal funding. Moreover, the excellence programme spurs the internationalisation of education activity and research. The number of publications indexed in Scopus and the Web of Science is several times higher than in other universities. Vertical diversification, initiated by the structural reforms, has increased. The most talented students choose these universities. Almost 50% of school Olympiad winners enrol in 5–100 and national research universities.

Post-massification: Quality and Performance

The topic of insufficient quality and quality assurance is a recurrent theme on the agenda in public and policy debates, fed by nostalgia with reference to the Soviet past. The government has made an attempt to reshape the accreditation system. The authorities decided to establish a special department inside the federal ministry which now exists as the Federal Service of Inspection and Control in Education and Science.

In 2012, the MoES launched HEI Performance Monitoring, an annual institutional assessment of HEIs. The MoES collects and publishes about 150 indicators for each HEI, and six to eight indicators that vary through the years are also selected as performance indicators. They describe all fields of activity such as education (average entry exam score), research (share of R&D revenues), international activity (share of international students), financial stability (revenues per faculty) and faculty salaries (ratio between average faculty salary and average salary in the region). High results on at least four indicators are considered critical for efficient HEIs.

A radical policy was implemented when the first results of the Monitoring Project were published. In 2012–2013, 52 HEIs and 373 satellite HEIs were either reorganised through mergers, or the Federal Service of Inspection and Control in Education and Science revoked their licences. In subsequent years, more than 200 HEI satellites were reorganised and even private HEIs could not avoid reforms.

Current Higher Education System Landscape in Russia

As the Russian higher education system is large, we employ a quantitative analysis to identify the types of HEIs by implementing a cluster technique to categorise the classification of HEIs. In previous sections we described the major changes that influenced the HE landscape in post-Soviet Russia, and on this basis we suggest key indicators for the quantitative analysis in the table below (Table 13.6).

Approach, Sample and Data

The general sample consists of 1,653 parent and satellite HEIs. For the quantitative analysis, we take only 772 parent HEIs, excluding the satellite HEIs as a relatively homogeneous group. We exclude some organisations that are in the process of reorganisation, as well as HEIs with unreliable data (according to the Monitoring Project), arts and military schools (due to the specificity of their activities) and significant outliers.

We use Ward's agglomerative hierarchical clustering technique. Euclidean distance is chosen as a metric, and all variables are standardised into Z-scores. Several parameters have high (and significant) levels of correlation.

All data are retrieved from HEI Performance Monitoring 2015 (Monitoring 2015). Considering the programme diversification index and

Table 13.6 Indicators and measurement

Indicator	Measurement
Size of student body	Number of students, headcount
Part-time education	Share of full-time students in all students, %
Privatisation of costs	*Non-state revenues* from education activities as a share of overall revenues from education activity
Subject mix	Herfindahl-Hirschman index
Research	R&D revenues per faculty
	Number of publications in Scopus per 100 faculty
Balance between bachelor/ specialist and master programmes	Share of master students in all students, %
Unified state exam	Average exam scores
Selectivity	The number of students, admitted by the school Olympiad
State support	The share of federal funding in all revenues

following previous studies on programme diversification in universities (e.g. Rossi 2009), we use the Herfindahl-Hirschman index.

Empirical Results

The hierarchical clustering technique is flexible in terms of arriving at the number of clusters. A step-by-step analysis of relevance for each division revealed five clusters. Hence, Table 13.7 shows the contemporary classification of HEIs in Russia.

Table 13.7 Classification of HEIs in Russia, 2015

Type		Features	1—# of HEIs 2—% of HEIs 3—% of students[a]
1	Research universities	Diversified subject mix, research-productive, selective, attract talented students, MA students, attract fee-paying students, location—particularly in Moscow and Saint Petersburg	1–22 2–3% 3–4%
2	Public regional universities	Very large, diversified subject mix, selective, large part-time, large state support, some R&D	1–84 2–11% 3–32%
3	Specialised HEIs	Small, highly selective, highly specialised, full-time, mostly medical	1–88 2–11% 3–8%
4	Public mass universities	Diversified subject mix, selective, large part-time, large state support, do not attract fee-paying students	1–248 2–32% 3–36%
5	Private HEIs	Small, only fee-paying students, large part-time, very low selectivity	
5a	Specialised	Specialisation in popular programmes	1–167 2–22% 3–5%
5b	Diversified	Diversified subject mix	1–95 2–12% 3–5%
6	Part-time HEIs	Only part-time fee-paying students, very small, specialisation in popular programmes	1–68 2–9% 3–10%

[a]Share in the sample
Source: Calculated by the authors

Government policies resulted in the segregation of a group of research-intensive universities. *Research universities* (cluster 1) pursue high selectivity, are oriented towards the provision of master programmes and cater mostly for full-time enrolment. Despite the long history of division between research institutes and universities during Soviet times, the global movement towards world class is reflected in the Russian higher education landscape. However, very few of these universities have achieved global recognition yet.

Post-Soviet expansion also provided an opportunity for some universities to grow into large institutions alongside an internal diversification and growth of part-time enrolment. These large *regional public universities* (cluster 2) are often situated in provincial centres and are usually significantly supported by the state. Examples of such giants can be found worldwide, but mostly in big federal countries. In Russia, these HEIs attract talented students and focus on their teaching mission but still engage in some research.

The Soviet legacy of specialised training in particular fields remained vital for another group of institutions. The peculiarity of *specialised HEIs* (cluster 3) is their limited internal diversity, relatively small size and high selectivity. These are mostly medical institutions accompanied by Soviet-type industrial universities that managed to sustain their narrow orientation in the reconfigured economy.

The next groups represent the consequence of higher education expansion that can be identified in all high-participation systems worldwide as a reaction to the growth of demand. In order to achieve economic sustainability, the higher education system grew through internal diversification in Soviet institutions, as well as through the emergence of new institutions, an increase in part-time education and privately funded places (both in traditionally public HEIs and others). *The demand-absorption HEIs* constitute a large share of the higher education system.

The group of *mass public universities* (cluster 4) is close to the group of regional giants (cluster 2), but they are smaller, less selective and more dependent on public funding. With regard to their funding model, we can assume they represent the state's function of providing widened access to higher education.

Three groups of privately funded institutions (clusters 5 and 6) represent different aspects of popular demand. The small specialised HEIs (5a) provide education in particular low-cost popular fields (usually economics, management and social sciences). The diversified HEIs (5b) also have a low level of selectivity and a low share of full-timers, but a broader range of fields. The group of "open" HEIs (cluster 6) focusses entirely on part-time distance education and provides credentials in popular fields.

Conclusion

The post-Soviet social and economic higher education environment along with massification, new regulations and targeted government activities have shaped the institutional landscape in Russia in the past decades. Decreased funding pushed existing HEIs to seek new sources in order to survive. Old and newly established institutions, both public and private, entered a new competition that went along with regulatory liberalisation. The expansion was moreover fed by popular demand in reaction to the new social and economic conditions. Yet, many HEIs continued playing the "higher learning tradition" card by addressing their legacy, mostly Soviet, in order to legitimate their existence in current times. Many internally diversified HEIs even kept their old names in order to demonstrate their commitment to parent industries. This conservatism combined with general organisational adaptability has sustained path dependency.

From the 2000s, the comeback of the state as financially stronger and more managerial brought several policies that introduced new rules of the game: the Unified National Examination, and two-level (later three-level) degrees.

The initiatives that aimed at system segmentation (from 2006 on) shaped the Russian institutional landscape even more, in both the vertical and horizontal dimension. The creation of federal universities and assignment of national research universities resulted in the coercive adoption of new functions: regional labour market supply, research efficiency, and international recognition.

Public claims for education quality and the governmental intention to spend resources efficiently drove the system to the "optimisation" period (from 2012 on). Along with licence withdrawals, the state widely used mergers to correct the system to a manageable size and assumed higher levels of efficiency. The government is continuing with system segmentation to build an institutional hierarchy.

The aspiration of a clearly arranged structure for the higher education system is not new. The Soviet design also outlined clearly defined functions. However, the size of the system and the emergence of popular demand as defining factors closed the door on a renaissance of the Soviet masterplan, but also on a wholesale introduction of Western concepts and structures. For the state and society, it is still a work in progress to find balance in the institutional landscape with regard to regional differentiation, the country's global ambitions, its path dependency from historical developments and the relevance of higher learning in the contemporary and future socioeconomic environment.

Notes

1. There are two forms of part-time education in Soviet and post-Soviet countries. Here we use correspondence courses to indicate the form of education in which students visit HEIs twice per year. Part-time education was also called "on-site education" (study without leaving the workplace).
2. The tertiary system includes both the higher education and secondary vocational education systems in Russia.
3. It should be noted that in Russia a satellite HEI operates as a representative of the parent HEI, but it is a separate (independent) legal entity. The ties and relationships with parent HEIs can vary from direct "supervision" to absolute independence.

References

Abankina, I., and T. Abankina. 2013. Mesto vuzov v novoy ekonomike: strategii i ugrozy [Place of Universities in the New Economy: Strategies and Threats]. *Otechestvennyye zapiski* 4 (55): 171–181.

Bain, O.B. 2003. *University Autonomy in the Russian Federation Since Perestroika*, Studies in Higher Education, Dissertation Series. New York: RoutledgeFalmer.

Balzer, H.D. 1994. Plans to Reform Russian Higher Education. In *Education and Society in the New Russia*, eds. A. Jones. Armonk, NY: M.E. Sharpe, 27–46.

Bolotov, V. 2004. EGE: promejutochnye itogi [The USE: Interim Results]. *Voprosy obrazovaniya* 2: 155–167.

Education in the Russian Federation. 2006. *Obrazovanie v Rossijskoj Federacii: 2006. Statisticheskij ezhegodnik* [Education in the Russian Federation: 2006. Statistical Yearbook]. Moscow: SU-HSE, 528. isbn 5-7218-0885-3.

———. 2012. *Obrazovanie v Rossijskoj Federacii: 2012. Statisticheskij ezhegodnik* [Education in the Russian Federation: 2012. Statistical Yearbook]. Moscow: National Research University "Higher School of Economics", 444. isbn 978-5-7218-1275-0.

Federal Law. 1996. Federalnyi zakon ot 22 avgusta 1996 g. N 125-FZ g. Moskva "O vysshem i poslevuzovskom professionalnom obrazovanii" [Federal Law on August 22, 1996 N125 FZ Moscow "About Higher and Postgraduate Professional Education"].

———. 2012. Federalnyi zakon ot 29 dekabria 2012 g. № 273-FZ "Ob obrazovanii v Rossiiskoi Federatcii" [Federal Law on December, 29 2012 N273-FZ "About Education in Russian Federation"].

Federal State Statistics Service. 2015. *Federalnaya sluzhba gosudarstvennoy statistiki. Ofitsialnaya statistika. Naselenie. Obrazovanie* [Federal State Statistics Service. Official Statistics. Population. Education]. http://www.gks.ru/

Froumin, I., Y. Kouzminov, and D. Semyonov. 2014. Institutional Diversity in Russian Higher Education: Revolutions and Evolution. *European Journal of Higher Education* 4 (3): 209–234.

Froumin, I., and O. Leshukov. forthcoming. Federal – Regional Relationships in Higher Education in the Russian Federation. In *Federalism and Higher Education: A Comparative Study*, eds. M. Carnoy, I. Froumin, S. Marginson, and O. Leshukov. Palgrave Macmillan UK.

Gimpelson, V., R. Kapelyushnikov, and A. Luk'yanova. 2007. Spros na trud I kvalifikatsiyu v promyshlennosti: mejdu defitsitom i izbytkom [Demand for Labor and Skills in the Industry: Between Deficit and Surplus]. *Ekonomicheskii jurnal Vysshei Shkoly Economiki* 11 (2): 163–199.

———. 2010. Uroven' obrazovanija rossijskih rabotnikov: optimal'nyj, izbytochnyj, nedostatochnyj? [The Level of Education of Russian Workers: Optimal, Excessive, Inadequate?] *Working Paper WP3/2010/09.* Moscow: Publishing House of the Higher School of Economics, 64.

Johnson, M.S. 2008. Historical Legacies of Soviet Higher Education and the Transformation of Higher Education Systems in Post-Soviet Russia and Eurasia. In *The Worldwide Transformation of Higher Education*, eds. D.P. Baker, A.W. Wiseman. Emerald Group Publishing Limited UK, 159–176.

Klyachko, T., and I. Rojdestvenskaya. 1999. *Obrazovanie* [Education]. Moscow: Institut ekonomiki perehodnogo perioda.

Klyachko, T., N. Titova, A. Kryshtanovsky, M. Mikhailyuk, M. Drugov, D. Vasiliev, L. Kapranova, A. Zaborovskaya, and S. Zaretskaya. 2002. *Strategii adaptatsii vysshikh uchebnykh zavedeniy: ekonomicheskiy i sotsiologicheskiy aspekty* [Adaptation Strategies of the Higher Education Institutions: An Economic and a Sociological Aspects]. Moscow: HSE.

Kuraev, A. 2016. Soviet Higher Education: An Alternative Construct to the Western University Paradigm. *Higher Education* 71 (2): 181–193. doi:10.1007/s10734-015-9895-5.

Luchinskaya, D., and O. Ovchynnikova. 2011. The Bologna Process Policy Implementation in Russia and Ukraine: Similarities and Differences. *European Educational Research Journal* 10 (1): 21–33.

Magun, V., and M. Engovatov. 2004. Mezhpokolennaia dinamika zhiznennykh pritiazanii molodezhi i strategii ikh resursnogo obespecheniia: 1985–2001 [Intergenerational Change in Life Aspirations and in Strategies of Their Realization in the Young]. In *Otsy i deti. Pokolencheskii analiz sovremennoi Rossii* [Fathers and Children: Cross-Generational Analysis of Contemporary Russia], ed. T. Shanin and I. Levada, 180–234. Moscow: NLO.
Monitoring. 2015. Monitoring effektivnosti dejatel'nosti obrazovatel'nyh organizacij vysshego obrazovanija [The Monitoring of HEIs' performance 2015]. http://indicators.miccedu.ru/monitoring/
National Centre for Public Accreditation. n.d. Systema vysshego obrazovaniya v RF [Higher education system in Russian Federation]. http://ncpa.ru/index.php?option=com_content&view=article&id=251&Itemid=375&lang=ru
OECD. 2016. *Education at a Glance 2016*. Education at a Glance. OECD Publishing. http://www.oecd-ilibrary.org/education/education-at-a-glance-2016_eag-2016-en
Roskozna. 2015. *Konsolidirovannyj bjudzhet Rossijskoj Federacii i bjudzhetov gosudarstvennyh vnebjudzhetnyh fondov* [The Consolidated Budget of the Russian Federation and Budgets of the State Off-Budget Funds]. http://www.roskazna.ru/ispolnenie-byudzhetov/konsolidirovannyj-byudzhet/
Rossi, F. 2009. Increased Competition and Diversity in Higher Education: An Empirical Analysis of the Italian University System. *Higher Education Policy* 22 (4): 389–413.
Statistical Book on Higher Education. 1992. *Vysshaya shkola v 1991: Ezhegodnyj doklad o razvitii vysshego i srednego special'nogo obrazovanija*. [Higher School in 1991: Annual Report on Higher and Secondary Specialized Education]. NIIVO Moscow.
Statistical Book on Russian Federation. 1993. *Rossiiskaya Federatsiya v 1992. Statisticheskii eshegodnik* [Russian Federation in 1992. Statistical Yearbook]. Rosstat Moscow.
Statistical Year Book. 1992. *Statisticheskiy ezhegodnik* [Statistical Year Book]. Rosstat Moscow.
Telegina, G., and H. Schwengel. 2012. The Bologna Process: Perspectives and Implications for the Russian University. *European Journal of Education* 47 (1): 37–49.
Trow, M.A. 1973. *Problems in the Transition from Elite to Mass Higher Education*. University of California, Institute of International Studies US.
Zaretskaya, S., and L. Kapranova. 2003. Vysshaya Shkola i Reforma Obrazovaniya: Vzglyady Rukovoditelei Vuzov Rossii [Higher School and Education Reform: HEIs' Management View]. Retrieved. http://ecsocman.hse.ru/text/18240963/

Daria Platonova is a research fellow and Head of the Laboratory for Universities Developmentat the Institute of Education, National Research University Higher School of Economics, Moscow, Russia.

Dmitry Semyonov was Head of the Laboratory for Universities Development at the Institute of Education and an Advisor to Rector at National Research University Higher School of Economics, Moscow, Russia.

Open Access This chapter is distributed under the terms of the Creative Commons Attribution 4.0 International License (http://creativecommons.org/licenses/by/4.0/), which permits use, duplication, adaptation, distribution and reproduction in any medium or format, as long as you give appropriate credit to the original author(s) and the source, provide a link to the Creative Commons license and indicate if changes were made.

The images or other third party material in this chapter are included in the chapter's Creative Commons license, unless indicated otherwise in a credit line to the material. If material is not included in the chapter's Creative Commons license and your intended use is not permitted by statutory regulation or exceeds the permitted use, you will need to obtain permission directly from the copyright holder.

CHAPTER 14

Higher Education in Tajikistan: Institutional Landscape and Key Policy Developments

Alan J. DeYoung, Zumrad Kataeva, and Dilrabo Jonbekova

Higher education in Tajikistan has undergone substantial changes over the past 25 years. After an educational degradation in the early 1990s, a long period of educational reforms began aiming at dismantling the Soviet model and creating a new system of education based on national values, traditions and culture—while simultaneously responding to the challenges of globalization and transitioning toward world education space. The process of internationalization, however, was slower in Tajikistan compared to most of the Newly Independent States (NIS).

In this chapter, we examine progression of the Tajik system of higher education from the Soviet time throughout independence (1991–2015)

A. J. DeYoung
Educational Policy Studies and Evaluation, University of Kentucky, Lexington, KY, USA

Z. Kataeva (✉)
Institute of Education, Higher School of Economics, Moscow, Russia

D. Jonbekova
Graduate School of Education, Nazarbaev University, Astana, Akmola, Kazakhstan

in terms of its growth, the emerging institutional landscape and diversification, and key policy developments and issues. We analyze the impact of changes in the relevant economic, social and political spheres which is particularly important in the case of Tajikistan. The system of higher education is highly centralized, yet greatly affected by a complex mixture of cultural, religious, demographic and regional factors. Political decisions made under certain political circumstances influence it significantly. The landscape of higher education in Tajikistan has commonalities but also differences with others among the NIS. This writing is based on a variety of sources—statistics, educational laws, institutional documents, reports published by international organizations; English-language press accounts; and ethnographic interviews conducted by the authors in Tajikistan between 2011 and 2014.

THE SOVIET LEGACY AND A SYSTEM OF HIGHER EDUCATION AT THE TIME OF INDEPENDENCE

Soviet education, with all its shortcomings, has been widely praised as a success in the USSR, including Tajikistan. Although lagging behind in most major educational outcomes compared with other Soviet republics, by the time of its independence in 1991, Tajikistan was a country with almost 100% literacy and 10 years of compulsory secondary education. An especially important (early) Soviet education legacy was bringing girls to school, under the auspices of a wider movement known as "The liberation of a woman of the East." Before 1917, there were no formal higher education institutions in Tajikistan. Schooling took place in religious schools (*madrasas*), where students learned the Quran and other religious books and read masterworks written in Persian and Arabic. Students were also able to learn geography, geometry, algebra and other sciences. Graduates of these religious schools such as Avicenna made significant contributions to modern science. After the socialist revolution, the Soviet government closed all *madrasas* due to their religious connections and created a system of new public and postsecondary schools. Over the decades, various sorts of post-secondary education opportunities were also created for high-achieving secondary school graduates to become skilled workers and professionals.

The first higher education institutions in Tajikistan were these pedagogical institutes. The first established were in Dushanbe (then Stalinabad), the republican capital (1931) and Khujand (1932), a more than 2000-year-old cultural center of the country, renamed Leninabad during the Soviet era. Also in the 1930s, an agrarian institute was separated from an institute in Tashkent (Uzbekistan) and placed in Khujand. Later (1939), a medical institute was founded in Dushanbe (Tajik State Medical University www.tajmedun.tj). Further developments were slowed due to World War II, but were resumed in the late 1940s and 1950s. Evacuated from the European part of the USSR during the war (1941–1945) and also exiled by the Stalin regime, many professors and academicians came to work in Tajik HEIs, helping to lay the foundation for a high-quality system of education.

The first and only university in Soviet Tajikistan—Tajik State University—was created in 1947 in Dushanbe (Tajik National University www.tnu.tj). The agrarian institute was relocated to the capital (1944) (Tajik Agrarian University www.tajagroun.tj), and a polytechnic institute was established there in 1956. In the 1960s and 1970s, two regional pedagogical institutes in Khatlon were founded—Kulob Pedagogical Institute (1962) and Dushanbe Branch of the Pedagogical Institute in Kurghon-Teppa (1978), bringing the total number of pedagogical institutes in the country to four. In Dushanbe, meanwhile, the Institute of Physical Culture (1971), the Institute of Arts (1973) and the Tajik Pedagogical Institute of Russian Language and Literature (1980) were added to the system.

The last wave of transformation happened during *perestroika* and immediately before independence. In 1987, the Institute of Russian Language and Literature was reorganized into the Tajik State Institute of Languages. Around the time of announcing independence, some institutional upgrades happened quickly. For example, the now prestigious Technological University of Tajikistan (TUT) traces its history back to 1990 when the Tajik High Technological College was founded, renamed later (1991) as Tajik Institute of Food and Light Industry and eventually as the Technological University of Tajikistan in 1993.

There were ten HEIs in Tajikistan by the end of the 1980s. Higher education was free, and students received stipends. As graduates, they were then assigned by the government to work for 2 or 3 years in schools and HEIs. There were also quotas which advantaged rural students who may not have had high-quality preparation in secondary schools to enter HEIs. Apart from teachers, engineers, doctors and agricultural specialists—requiring higher education diplomas—other specialists for the economy were prepared at lower educational levels—secondary specialized education (*technicums* and *uchilischa*) and vocational training schools (*uchilischa*).

Using Teichler's (1988) framework of horizontal and vertical system differentiation and organizational interrelationships, the most prominent bifurcation in Tajikistan was the "university" versus the "institute." However, the university was not exactly commensurate with those of the West, as it was more tightly controlled by the government and primarily focused upon teaching at the expense of independent research. Tajik State University, however, did have better funding and more freedom and enjoyed much greater prestige than did the institutes. The other primary axis of differentiation occurs at the level of region. Initially, the higher education system started as "dual-centered"—with HEIs operating in Dushanbe and Khujand; but the educational dominance of the capital eventually gained momentum. Meanwhile, the fact that a pedagogical institute in Khujand is one of the first Soviet era institutes greatly impacted the regional landscape. Throughout Soviet history and today, "in its scientific and pedagogical potential and the number of students, it is considered second only to the Tajik (National) University" (websites, KhSU).

Sectoral expansion of the system was specifically tied to the needs of the socialist economy. There was one institute per sector in agrarian, medical and polytechnic fields (except, as we have seen, for the last year before independence). The rest of the system was overwhelmingly pedagogical: Not only were there four pedagogical institutes and one branch of Dushanbe in Kurghon-Teppa, but the graduates of the Physical Culture Institute and (most) graduates of the State University were assigned to work as secondary school teachers. And as a Soviet state, no private HEIs were allowed. Table 14.1 represents the classification of HEIs by the time of independence (1989/1990).

In sum, the Tajikistan higher education system during Soviet period was maintained as a response to the direct need of the planned economy with well-developed technical, engineering, medical and pedagogical education. However, the high centralization of the Soviet educational system was not responsive to changes in the labor market. A number of other characteristics contributed to the weaknesses of higher education such as restrictions on faculties and student enrollments in fields like history, linguistics, genetics and sociology; poor management of financial and human resources; and narrow and rigid vocational and professional curricula (Johnson 2008; Anderson et al. 2004). This would all change with independence.

Table 14.1 Classification of HEIs as of 1989/1990

#	Name	Year	Location	Profile	# of students
1.	Tajik Agrarian Institute	1931 in Khujand/then moved to Dushanbe in 1944	Leninanabad (now Khujand) and then moved to Dushanbe	Agricultural education	5,916
2.	Tajik Medical Institute	1939	Dushanbe	Medicine	5,816
3.	Tajik State University named after V.I. Lenin	1947	Dushanbe	Comprehensive university	12,128
4.	Tajik Polytechnic Institute	1956	Dushanbe	Technical and engineering education	7,046
5.	Institute of Physical Culture	1971	Dushanbe	Physical/sport education	1,055
6.	Institute of Arts	1973	Dushanbe	Art and cinematography education	2,180
7.	Tajik State Pedagogical Institute named under T.G. Shevchenko	1931	Dushanbe	Pedagogical	31,445
8.	Leninabad State Pedagogical Institute named under S. Kirov	1932	Leninabad (now Khujand)	Pedagogical	
9.	Kulyab State Pedagogical Institute	1940	Kulyab	Pedagogical	
10.	Tajik State Pedagogical Institute of Languages	1980	Dushanbe	Pedagogical	

Changes in the Higher Education Landscape: Rise of the Universities

After the events of 1991, the higher education landscape significantly changed in Tajikistan. Its growth and diversification were challenging during the time of the Civil War (1992–1997), considered another major factor in the history of independent Tajikistan. During the war tens of thousands of people were killed, and hundreds of thousands more displaced. It also destroyed the economy and much of the educational infrastructure; and subsequently led hundreds of thousands of (mostly) men to out-migrate to Russia, where they have been seasonal and unskilled workers remitting wages home. These remittances continue to be substantial, comprising almost half (42%) of Tajikistan's GDP, and making the country vitally dependent on Russia (Eurasia Net 2014). The narcotics trade has also flourished (Olcott 2005). In terms of financial provisions, funding allocated for the educational sector in the state budget declined from 11.6% (1989) to 2.3% (2000) and rose again to 4.0% in 2014 (World Bank 2005, 2014). It is below the OECD average of 4.8%, but just about the average of countries with similar economic development status and demographic compositions of the former Soviet Union (Moldova, Kyrgyzstan, Georgia, Azerbaijan) (World Bank 2014). The government intends to increase educational spending up to 6% of GDP by 2015 and not less than 7% of GDP by 2020 (NSED). The higher education enrollment rate of 13% is lower than most Europe and Central Asian countries, but much higher than many countries at a similar level of economic development.

The transition from the planned to the market economy has led to a number of key policy decisions, which also has led in the Tajik case to a quadrupling of the number of higher education institutions since 1990. The graphs below illustrate this "massification" of higher education in Tajikistan since independence; however, it also shows that while the number of HEIs grew rapidly in the 1990s, enrollments did not—until more recently. By the academic year 2014/2015, there were 38 institutions enrolling 167,660 students, with 10,675 faculty members (Figs. 14.1 and 14.2). Of the 167,660 students, 69% were enrolled in full-time programs and 31% in part-time correspondence programs; 62% of 2013/2014 full-time graduates of HEIs received a specialist diploma (master's degree equivalent) and 38% a bachelor's degree.

The rapid emergence of universities (13 by the mid-1990s) significantly changed the Tajik higher education landscape. A list of the previous Soviet

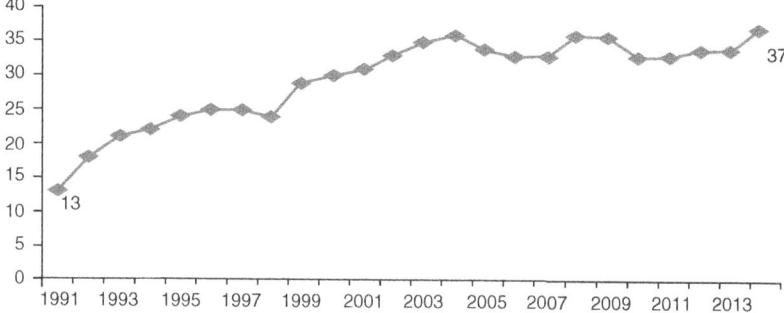

Fig. 14.1 HEIs in Tajikistan, 1991–2013

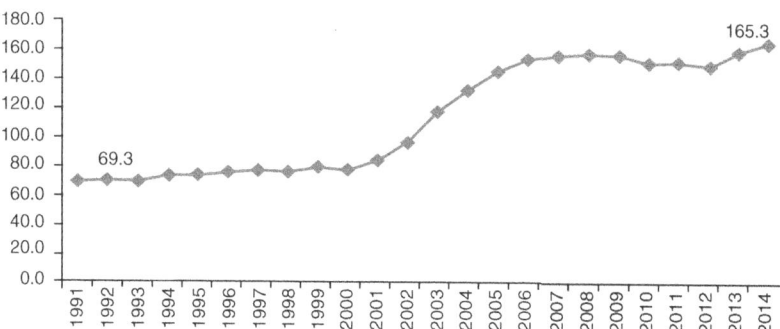

Fig. 14.2 Student enrolments in Tajikistan (in thousands): 1991–2013

institutes has quickly become a list of the universities, as all the institutes commonly known as *ped*, *med*, *politech* and *selkhoz* (originated in student slang from the beginning of institutes' types) have been transformed (see Table 14.2). Four pedagogical institutes have been reorganized into state universities (three regional and one "pedagogical" in Dushanbe) and have become the largest HEIs, enrolling currently from 8000 to 15,000 students—Khujand State University (Khujand State University www.hgu.tj), Tajik State Pedagogical University, Qurghonteppa State University and Kulob State University. The medical institute has become the Tajik State Medical University. The rest of the transformed—the Tajik Technical University, the Tajik Agrarian University, the Tajik State University of Commerce and the Technological University of Tajikistan—are also among the now largest universities, enrolling from 5,000 to 9,000 students.

Table 14.2 Typology of higher education institutions as of 2014/2015

Type	Number/location	Example/prestige	Educational profile
1. National flagship university	1/Dushanbe	TNU (programs in law and economics among the most prestigious)	The largest university (118 programs) with bachelor, specialist, master's degrees and candidate of science; PhD will start in 2015/2016
2. State specialized universities	8/Dushanbe (7) and Khujand (1)	TSPU, TAU, TTU, TSMU (prestigious), TUT (prestigious), TSUC, TSIBPL	Multidisciplinary large- and medium-size universities with bachelor, specialist and master's degrees and PhD will start in 2015/2016
3. Regional state universities	5/regional centers	KhSU, KSU, KTSU, Khorog SU, DSU	Multidisciplinary large- and medium-size universities; with bachelor, specialist and master's degrees; PhD will start in 2015/2016
4. International bilateral institutions	4/Dushanbe	RTSU; MSU; MISA, MIE—All highly prestigious	Multidisciplinary medium-size university with bachelor, specialist, master's degrees and candidate of science; and small recently established branches of prestigious Russian universities and institutes with bachelor's degree: PhD only in RTSU
5. Institutes in the capital	12/Dushanbe	TSIL,TSIA, TIAD, TIPC, TIEF, TIES, IPA (prestigious), MIMD, AMIA, HSBPNCS, HSNCS	Small- and medium-size HEI with specialist, bachelor and few master's degrees
6. Regional institutes	8/regional centers	EIKT, TMMI, PPI, PIR, KulobTUT, IsfaraTUT, IET, PITTU	Small-size HEI with few disciplines with bachelor, specialist and few master's degrees

Three new universities were born in the mid-1990s: the Russian-Tajik Slavonic University (RTSU), The Tajik State University of Law, Business and Politics (TSULBP) in Khujand and the Khorog State University. Established by a bilateral agreement between the two governments and now one of the most prestigious, RTSU offers instruction in Russian (arguably understood to be of better quality just because of that) and has technology better than most; and its degrees are recognized in both countries (Russian Tajik Slavonic University www.rtsu.tj). Its "founding" rector A. Sattarov, reported the history of its founding. While working for the Ministry of Education, parents often complained to him that Russian language groups in HEIs were being closed. So he came up with the idea of creating an HEI, where Russian was the only language of instruction. Then in 1992, the Russian minister of Foreign Affairs, A. Kozyrev, visited Tajikistan: and with his support and the support of the government of the RT, the RTSU was founded (Asia-Plus 2011). "Slavonic" has symbolized a trend—still less common in Tajikistan compared to the NIS and or its Central Asian neighbors—the establishment of international universities.

The creation of TSULBP was the result of a merger of the branches of the two higher education institutions in Khujand. It represents yet another trend—capitalizing on the popularity of law and business degrees that would attract "contract" or fee-paying students (in this case, in a regional setting). Continuing the institutional expansion into the regions, the establishment of Khorog State University (where Tajik is the language of instruction) has provided historic opportunity for Pamirian people in the Gorno-Badakhshan Autonomous Oblast (GBAO) to receive higher education for the first time without going to the capital.

The latest (2013) addition to the system—the Danghara State University (2,000 students)—started as a branch of the Agrarian University with 200 students in 2005. It represents a recent trend (seen also with institutes and branches) to go beyond the large regional centers (Kulob, Qurghonteppa and Khujand) to reach smaller towns. There are currently 14 universities—8 in Dushanbe and 6 in the regions. Ten of them existed as HEIs before the 1990s. All of them are "state" universities, meaning that they belong to the state system of education of Tajikistan. Some universities also have "state" in the title—reflecting a vertical hierarchy among them. Importantly, there will be one more university soon in Dushanbe. Tajik Islamic Institute (2000 students) is expected to be transformed into a university. It prepares specialists in Islamic studies: Quran study, History of Islam and Arabic language study.

Some of the newly born universities were small, with only several hundred students. They were modest attempts (sometimes private) to start from scratch that did not survive. One of the latest private universities (2003–2009) was originally known as the University of International Relations. It kept changing titles under the pressure of the Ministry of Education, but was widely known by an unofficial name—"American" University. It was founded by a Tajik-born US citizen and funded primarily from Western sources. It also was the home of several prominent opposition leaders who were on the faculty, proclaimed to be transparent in a national sea of corruption and provided higher quality and more affordable education than the others. Its founder, S. Akramov, insisted the reasons it was closed were all political, but he lost his court battle against the Ministry of Education (Najibullah 2009). In neighboring Kyrgyzstan, the Kyrgyz-American University had a different experience. Ironically—or not—the Moscow State University appeared on the Tajik map at approximately the same time as the "American" university was being closed.

"Branching-In," "Branching-Out" and the Growth of Institutes in a Changing Landscape

Established in 2009 under the initiative and by the Decree of the President Emomali Rahmon, who personally attended the opening ceremony, the Dushanbe Branch of the Moscow State University (now one of the most prestigious HEIs in Tajikistan) provides a "fundamental, classical university education," based on the latest Moscow educational standards. Highly qualified instructors are from Tajikistan (30%) and the Russian Federation (70%) who work in changing rotation. Students (600) have digital access to the Moscow State University (MSU) library and cutting-edge technology. And it seems that they have already acquired an elitist mindset: Those in International Relations, for example, see their future careers as working no less than for the UN, European Council, government and the largest analytical think tanks (websites, MSU, Gazeta 2014). Recently, the Dushanbe MSU has been given a new status—a "regional branch." (Branch of the Moscow State University in Dushanbe www.msu.tj) As the President Emomali Rahmon has envisioned, it has been developing into a regionally significant HEI for neighboring Asian countries. With this move, another attempt of creating an international HEI can be seen. Although there will soon (2018) be a functioning international university in Tajikistan, the University of Central Asia, this university is being subsidized by the Aga

Khan Foundation and will be in distant Khorog. International student enrollments (for 2014–2015) in Tajikistan remain small: Around 900 students—mostly from Afghanistan, Iran and India.

"Branching-in" and "branching-out" has been a prominent feature on the Tajik education landscape. "Branching-in" is the Moscow HEIs: In addition to the first comer (Dushanbe Moscow State University (MSU)), two more branches have settled in the Tajik capital—the Branch of the Moscow Institute of Steel and Alloy and the Branch of the Moscow Energy Institute. "Branching-out," on the other hand, is the Tajik universities—from Dushanbe into the regions. There are two branches of the Technological University—in Kulob and in Isfara (Sughd); The Tajik State University of Commerce and the Tajik Technical University have their branches in Khujand. With regard to student enrollment, Dushanbe universities expanded overwhelmingly into Khujand. Notably, as well, moving to the regions were the branches of other than "pedagogical" institutions; and no branches crossed the mountains to reach GBAO.

Sixteen institutes operate in the country, including institutes remaining from the Soviet times. Established in the 2000s the Pedagogical institute in Rasht and the Penjikent Pedagogical Institute in Sughd demonstrate a trend of reaching to the smaller towns. They also symbolize a (modest) attempt "to revive" pedagogical education in the regions, that is, "to correct" at the regional level a largely unfavorable development in teacher training, when all the former regional pedagogical institutes have become universities. Yet "university" graduates in pedagogical specializations are often in no hurry to actually teach—given the economic situation. Teachers have little salary or prestige to work in the education sector. Teacher shortage, especially in rural places, has become a serious problem. The Penjikent Pedagogical Institute occupies a unique place in the higher education system of Tajikistan. It is a "non-state" institution. It does not proclaim it is "private" in its charter (*ustav*); but still, it is the only "non-state" institute out of 38 HEIs.

The Tax-Law Institute in Dushanbe, with more than 13,000 students in 2003–2004, was an exception among the institutes with regard to enrolment. "Tax" and "law" programs have become magic words in Tajikistan. Meanwhile, we heard during an interview with a respected and skeptical senior higher education administrator that even the MoE was having trouble obtaining exact numbers of students enrolled there. It was a puzzle to figure out how so many thousands of students could physically sit at the desks in the available building space (interview, Dushanbe 2011). Clearly an educational "bubble" previously, it was eventually reorganized into the Tajik Institute of Economy and Finance. We summarize the current higher education landscape in Table 14.2.

Looking at the regional distribution of HEIs, it must be noted that the expansion into the regions, although important, has not solved the historically established center-periphery gap in Tajikistan, as almost 60% of students enrolled in higher education institutions located in the capital of Dushanbe.

Moreover, instructors with advanced degrees and best qualifications are clustered in the six largest universities in Dushanbe. In 2014–2015, 10,675 faculty members were employed in HEIs. Only 25% of them hold candidate of science or doctor of science degrees; and most of those with degrees are approaching retirement age (Mirzoev 2014; Kataeva 2014). The ministerial affiliations affirm the increased horizontal differentiation of the HEIs. It can be seen, in particular, by the fact that the number of the institutions under the auspice of the Ministry of Industry and New Technologies has increased; and that RTSU and Russian branches brought with them an oversight of the Russian Minister of Education (MoE)—in addition to the MoE of RT. The number of the programs offered by universities and institutes has also increased. The most significant enrolment growth (by almost 30%) has occurred in "economics and law" programmes: from 1% in these specializations in 1991 to 29% in 2011 (see Fig. 14.3).

However, the existing market cannot absorb graduates from these programmes. "Who needs so many lawyers and economists?" has been a rhetorical question among educators for two decades now. Furthermore, a disconnect between the production of graduates by specialty and the actual job market has brought about new discussions centering not only

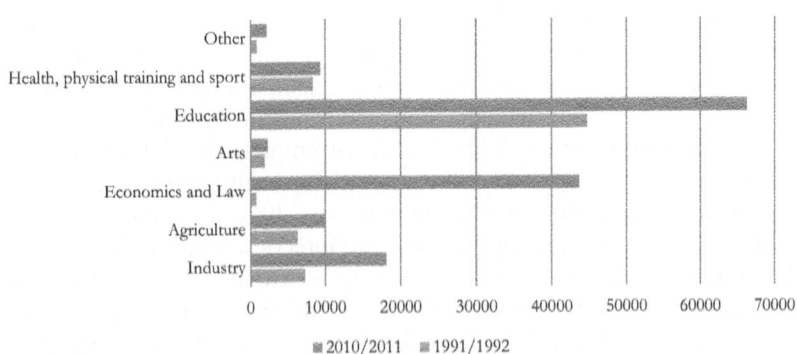

Fig. 14.3 Number of enrolled students by specialization, 1991 and 2010 (Source: The Ministry of Education and Science)

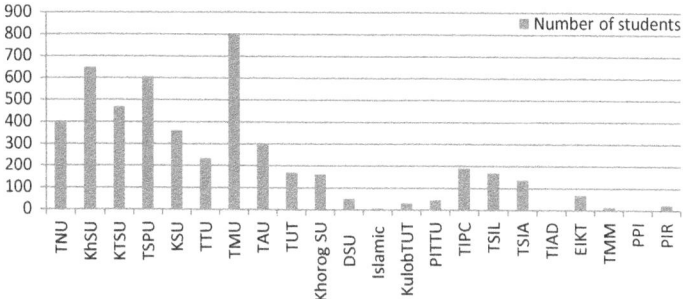

Fig. 14.4 Higher education institutions by presidential quota, 2014/2015

on the lawyers and economists, but upon higher education specialists in general. The current discourse about interrelationships between higher education and market now finds many asking the question, "who needs so many higher education graduates at all?" There are also quality concerns. Employers are often dissatisfied with the skills of new graduates, especially in terms of subject areas (see Jonbekova 2015).

Among the social and cultural factors affecting higher education has been the role of women in society. Since independence, a more traditional definition of the role of women in Muslim society has been reintroduced as a part of national identity building (Johnson 2004; Whitsel 2009; DeYoung 2012). These include strong cultural traditions and values where extended multi-generation and patriarchal families are the norm, and expectations and opportunities for young women outside the household limit their involvement in secondary and higher education. Arranged marriages are typical, and young women are now marrying at younger and younger ages, affecting women's enrolment in the HEIs. Therefore, in 2006 the Presidential Quota was introduced into the higher education system to provide free places for girls and boys from disadvantaged families and those residing in remote mountain areas to provide them with the opportunity to obtain higher education. Though it is still very small, the number of Presidential quotas since 2008/2009 has been increasing and in 2014/2015, 3.4% of students in HEIs of Tajikistan were awarded scholarships under this quota. The chart below (Fig. 14.4) shows that 21 HEIs out of 38 receive places funded from the state budget for quotas. Most of quota seats are distributed among medical, pedagogical and two regional universities (KhSU and KTSU); a bit lower number for national and technical universities to cover the labor market needs with physicians, teachers and engineers.

University Status and University Autonomy: The Case of Tajik National University

The rise of the universities has brought an end to a higher educational landscape overwhelmingly populated with institutes. The vertical "university"-"institute" differentiation has become more profound and nuanced—regionally, as well as nationally. Importantly, all the universities have come into existence by the decree of the Tajik government. Back in Soviet times, HEIs were founded and regulated by the government, and this *modus vivendi* continues now. State university relationships, although under international pressures to introduce serious changes, are still managed and operated as they were during Soviet times.

Meanwhile, higher education system expansion has not changed the leading position of the university that used to be the only university in the country—Tajik State University. Currently enrolling over 21,000 students, it offers the largest number (188) of programmes (22 bachelor's, 68 specialist and 28 master's) and continues to be the republican HEI flagship. To distinguish this (only) pre-independence university in Tajikistan from all those which appeared later—and to re-enforce its higher status—the Tajik State University was first renamed (in 1997) "Tajik State National University" (TSNU); and then, in 2008, "Tajik National University" (TNU). Both decisions were made by a Decree of the President of Tajikistan; and the university's charter, or *Ustav* (2008), was approved by the government (Ustav TNU, 2008).

TNU was the first and for some time the only university that was given university autonomy. The 1997 Decree of the President of RT "On the Status of the Tajik State University" has declared TNU as an "autonomous, self-governing higher education institution." A new status has brought more funding and—importantly—*directly* from the republican budget. Notably, the Decree came at a time when the national system of higher education was operating on the legal base of the "Law on Education," adopted in 1993 (Tajikistan, 1993). University autonomy was not specified there, but was included later into the Law on Higher and Professional Education (Tajikistan, 2003).

The definition of university autonomy in the Law on Higher Education differs profoundly from what is generally understood in Western higher education (DeYoung and Valyayeva 2013). In Tajikistan, "university autonomy is the highest form of the learning process and academic activities, determining the state responsibility of the institutions of higher professional education before their founder" (Law on Higher Education, definitions; we used the amended 2009 version). Unless a HEI is private—which does not apply in Tajikistan—"the founder" is always "the government." As part of university autonomy, students and instructors are given "academic freedoms" defined in Tajikistan as "freedom of delivering the content of learning in one's own way – within the learning programmes" and "a freedom of those who study [students] to acquire knowledge in accordance with their own inclinations – within the learning programmes" (Law on Higher Education: Definitions; Article 5).

There is very minimal academic freedom or university autonomy in Tajikistan. If we apply the European University Association (EUA 2009) university autonomy framework—which employs indicators of financial, staffing, organizational and academic autonomy—most observations in the Tajik case would yield scores of "none" to "low." In reality, it is only rectors who now have some autonomy. Universities are governed by rectors' orders; and in most of the interviews with faculty and administrators, it became clear that few members of the academic community in the country can speak or comprehend the language of university autonomy. Yet, the concepts of university autonomy and academic freedom are now in the Tajik Law on Higher education and in the TNU *Ustav*.

Being the most powerful within the university governance structures, rectors at the same time are vulnerable to political changes. They are appointed to and dismissed from their positions by the government (President) of the country. The events of 2012 provide an illustration of the extent the higher education system has been politicized, and the vertical power hierarchy within universities. In January, A. Rahmonov was "relieved from his position" as a Minister of Education—and later appointed to be the rector of the Tajik State Pedagogical University. Following this, TNU rector N. Saidov was elevated to become the education minister. At that time he had been TNU rector for approximately 3 years and, prior to that, the Tajik State Pedagogical University rector for less than a year. In August, H. Odinaev, who was then the TNU rector was "relieved from his position" to "be transferred to another job." The vacant chair of the rector of the main HEI was given to M. Imomov, former rector of Slavonic University. The rector of the Tajik State Kulob University, in turn, became the rector of Slavonic (Asia-Plus 2012). During these domino effect changes, all rector appointments, as required by the law, were made by decrees signed by the President.

Key Education Policy Issues and Challenges

Being the poorest among the NIS, Tajikistan is a country with relatively young and fast growing population. Approximately 44% of its eight million people are under the age of 18. The estimated 2.2 million labor force is divided mostly between agriculture and services, with only about 11% in industry. Industry is dominated by a small number of state-owned enterprises, and consists basically of an aluminum plant (one of the ten largest aluminum smelters in the world), several large hydropower plants and small factories in food processing and light industry. Tajikistan's exports are primarily cotton and aluminum.

Although the Civil War delayed the beginning of the reforms and transition to market economy, even during the war, a *Law on Education* (1993) was adopted. The adoption of the new Law was a part of the series of legislation reforms in Tajikistan, which were initiated by the parliament. Just 1 year before the adoption of this Law, the presidential system of governance was abolished. Then President Nabiev had resigned, and parliamentary power was established and lasted until the first after-war presidential elections in 1996. The turning point in educational policy decision-making was the process of signing the Peace Agreement with the United Tajik Opposition in 1997, which officially ended the Civil War, and the development of new educational policies then commenced.

The Law on Education of 1993 allowed a number of changes in education (Tajikistan, 1993; ERSU, 2006). Private education institutions were legally allowed and some were established; but those in higher education eventually closed in 2000s. As throughout the NIS, "contract places" for students who paid tuition has become a key higher education development (DeYoung 2011). By the 2000s, the formation of the new government was completed, and the Ministry of Education started adopting several policy documents, under the influence of key supra-national agencies such as the World Bank, UNICEF and OSI. The Ministry's efforts were driven by the rhetoric of including Tajikistan's education system into the "world educational space." Although the reasons for these policy decisions were made in an effort to democratize the system, equalize and diversify access to quality education, the educational system still remains under the tight control of the government. For instance, decentralization of the system of education and its management is widely perceived as incomplete. *The National Strategy for Educational Development of Tajikistan* (Ministry of Education, 2005, 2012) acknowledges that "today the system of public management of education is a legacy of a highly centralized and planned system of the former Soviet Union and to a considerable extent remains unreformed. ... The dominant position in education belongs to the Government and participation of non – governmental and private sector is minimal" (p. 11). International agencies are also concerned that the country has "a centralized" and "non- participatory governance structure" which is "one of the main obstacles to effective educational change" that "policy key stakeholders, including NGOs, teachers, parents and students are rarely involved, and they have only very limited influence on key decisions at the national level" (OSI 2002).

Language of instruction issues were and remain contentious. Adopted during Gorbachev's *perestroika*, the *Law on Languages* (1989) declared Tajik the "state" language and Russian a "language of international communication." The current ethnic breakdown of Tajikistan is 84.3% Tajiks and 13.8% Uzbeks. The rest include Russians, Kyrgyz, Tatars and others. It also includes Pamiris, a small ethnic group primarily living in GBAO. Dozens of local language dialects are spoken there—Shugni being the most popular (see Niyosov 2002).

Over a quarter of century into independence, working knowledge of Russian among the Tajiks has almost been eliminated. While many from an older generation still speak Russian fluently (especially in Dushanbe), and while Russian is still used in business and government transactions, the younger generation as a group—especially in rural places—has limited Russian language skills. This process was also facilitated by a mass exodus of Russians during the Civil War. Following the process of a national identity building and cultural de-*russification*, secondary schools with Tajik as the language of instruction effectively replaced Russian language schools, and Tajik eventually also became predominant in HEIs. In 2014/15, approximately 82% of the students studied in Tajik and 17% in Russian. Meanwhile, replacing Russian as the language of instruction with Tajik has become an important challenge, especially for Medical and Technical Universities(ERSU, 2006). Now some subjects are being taught in Russian, although "officially" Tajik is required.

Today, an instructional language policy has re-emerged as a divisive political issue throughout all education levels. In Dushanbe, many ethnic Tajik parents now pay bribes to enroll their kids into Russian language schools, resisting the Ministry of Education's "suggestions" that only ethnically Russian are eligible. This parents' movement is driven by a quest for education quality and concerns about *Tajification* of the country (Parshin 2014). Elites and the upper classes in the country often still believe that Russian fluency is a prerequisite to upward social mobility.

Russian fluency is also essential now at the other end of the scale. Annually, almost a million Tajiks (mostly men) go to Russia as seasonal workers; about half of the labor age males. The Russian Federation has adopted a new law (in 2015) requiring a Russian government Certificate of Knowledge of Russian for those who apply for a working visa. This makes Russian fluency important even for those not going to HEIs. Seizing upon the opportunity, the Dushanbe Branch of Moscow State University has already opened a testing center, issuing such a certificate and offering Russian language classes (websites; MSU branch).

Along with the *National Strategy for Education Development of the Republic of Tajikistan* (2006–2015) and the *National Strategy for Education Development of the Republic of Tajikistan until 2020*, there is also the *National Concept of Up-bringing of the Republic of Tajikistan*, adopted in 2006. Accordingly, HEIs constitute stage four in the process of the up-bringing of youth; the preceding stages accomplished by the family, pre-school and secondary education. Therefore, *vospitatelnaya rabota* (the system of up-bringing) is an essential responsibility of each university and institute; and they should organize activities to contribute to the moral, national, patriotic, ideological and physical upbringing of students. HEI websites in Tajikistan invariably contain a separate rubric—"*vospitatelnaya rabota.*" The MoE, in its turn, is responsible for continuously reviewing the programs "to strengthen" this component. Symptomatic of these developments is the imposition of a dress code for students, mandating conservative attire for both boys and girls, and a controversial decision prohibiting the hijab on campus.

The latest education policy initiative is the creation of the Unified Entrance Exam (UEE) for HEI admission. Developed by The National Testing Center founded in 2008 by the Tajik government and funded mostly by grants from the Russian Federation, World Bank and the Open Society Foundation, it was administered nationwide for the first time in 2014—replacing the previous Soviet practice. The rational for this center and UEE relates to the rampant corruption in higher education widely understood in the country (Transparency International 2013). Other considerations have been the improvement of quality and equity throughout the entire system of education. The National Testing Center is considered to be the first step in establishing national education assessments.

While other countries, like Russia (2003) and Kazakhstan (2010), have already joined the Bologna Process, Tajikistan is currently a "non-Bologna signatory." The Bologna Process is "being implemented by ad hoc groups under the supervision of the Ministry of Education." (TEMPUS 2012) The level of implementation of the Bologna cycle structure is judged "extensive but gradual," according to TEMPUS (2012). Introduced Bachelor's and Master's degrees widely coexist with the previous (Soviet) degrees of *Specialist*, Candidate of Science and Doctor of Science. Ironically, graduates with Western PhDs sometimes report difficulty in having these degrees formally recognized in Tajikistan. Credit hours (European System of Transferred Credits, ESTC) are also being gradually adopted. In an inherited Soviet system curriculum, however, not all the classes are created equal, and to recalculate hours from the exiting learning plans into the required credit hours without revamping the curriculum has been difficult. For that matter, researchers find the borrowing of higher education policies and strategies in Central Asia poorly understood and applied (Merrill 2011). Adapting Bologna structures, like many other changes, often conflicts with the existing educational cultures and internal administration. Tajikistan is building Bologna structures basically within the MoE, instead of creating independent monitoring and implementation agencies. The "2020 National Strategy" envisions Tajikistan joining Bologna after this strategy has been implemented—thus by 2020. In official speeches, joining Bologna is cast as achieving "world standards" in higher education. In reality though, no Tajik HEIs has made it to the "Emerging Europe and Central Asia" (EECA) 150 top universities in 2015 rankings (QS 2015).

CONCLUSION

Higher education in Tajikistan has undergone substantial changes over the past 25 years as a result of both its internal crises and those social and economic transition challenges seen throughout the NIS. Transforming major Soviet institutes into universities and establishing new ones has significantly changed the higher education landscape. Now universities—not institutes—dominate this landscape, enrolling most of the students. The only university from Soviet Tajikistan, TNU, retains its leading position. The number of HEIs and student enrollments have significantly increased. This has been fueled partly by the mass creation of new programmes that reflect the needs of an emerging knowledge-based economy but also the result of parental craving for higher education for their children—regardless of market demands. Specific features of the massification of higher education in Tajikistan are further explained by internationalization according to the Bologna Process and other globalization agendas, the establishment of international HEIs under bilateral government agreements (with Russia) and significantly increasing the number of HEI programs and enrollments in far-flung regions of the country—especially those programs related to industry and technology. A deeper look at the higher education landscape reveals, however, that the major changes have occurred mostly within the preexisting Soviet structures and frameworks. Relationships between the HEIs and the state have not changed much, although nominally university autonomy was given to them. The system remains highly centralized; and MoE governance generally follows the old Soviet pattern. Tajikistan does not have private HEIs; and most important landmarks of the current educational landscape are the former Soviet institutions.

References

Anderson, K.H., R. Pomfret, and N. Usseinova. 2004. Education in Central Asia During the Transition to a Market Economy. In *Challenge of Education in Central Asia*, ed. S. Heyneman and A. DeYoung, 131–153. Greenwich: Information Age Publishing.

Asia-Plus. 2011. Hokim, M. RTSU – 15 Years. Retrieved from: http://www.news.tj/ru/news/rtsu-15-let

———. 2012. Mannonov, A. *Rokirovka rektorov. Kto vozglavlyaet vuzy Tajikistana* [Rectors' "Musical Chair": Who Are the Heads of the HEIs in Tajikistan]. Retrieved from: http://news.tj/ru/news/rokirovka-rektorov-kto-vozglavlyaet-vuzy-tadzhikistana

DeYoung, A. 2011. *Lost in Transition: Redefining Students and Universities in the Contemporary Kyrgyz Republic*. Charlotte: Information Age.

———. 2012. Gender and the Pedagogical Mission in Higher Education in Tajikistan: From Leninabad Pedagogical Institute into Khujand State University. *European Education: Issues and Studies* 44 (2): 44–64.

DeYoung, A., and G. Valyayeva. 2013. University Autonomy and Academic Freedom: Are They Included in Transforming Universities in Tajikistan? *AUDEM: The International Journal of Higher Education and Democracy*. 4: 4–25.

Education Reform Support Unit (ERSU). 2006. *Baseline Study of Higher Education in Tajikistan*. Dushanbe: Irfon.

Eurasia Net. 2014. Tajikistan: Migrant Remittances Now Exceed Half of GDP (by D. Trilling). Retrieved from: http://www.eurasianet.org/node/68272

European University Association (EUA): *University Autonomy in Europe 1*. 2009. Exploratory Study by Estermann, T. and Nokkala, T. Retrieved from: http://www.rkrs.si/gradiva/dokumenti/EUA_Autonomy_Report_Final.pdf

Government of the Republic of Tajikistan. *The National Concept of Up-Brining.* 2006. Reprieved from: http://tajmedun.tj/

Johnson, M. 2004. The Legacy of Russian and Soviet Education and Shaping of Ethnic, Religious, and National Identities in Central Asia. In *Challenges for Education in Central Asia*, ed. S. Heyneman and A. DeYoung, 21–37. Greenwich: Information Age Publishing.

———. 2008. Historical Legacies of Soviet Higher Education and the Transformation of Higher Education Systems in Post-Soviet Russia and Eurasia. In *The Worldwide Transformation of Higher Education*, ed. D. Baker and A. Wiseman, vol. 9, 159–176. International Perspectives on Education and Society. Bingley: Emerald Group Publishing, Ltd.

Jonbekova, D. 2015. University Graduates' Skills Mismatches in Central Asia: Employers' Perspectives from Post-Soviet Tajikistan. *European Education* 47 (2): 169–184.

Kataeva, Z. 2014. PhD Dissertation. The Changed Status of the Academic Profession and Quality of Faculty Life in the Contemporary Republic of Tajikistan.

Merrill, M. 2011. Internationalizing Higher Education in Central Asia: Definitions, Rational, Scope and Choices. In *Globalization on the Margins: Education and Post-Socialist Transformations in Central Asia*, ed. I. Silova, 145–173. Charlotte: Information Age Publishing.

Ministry of Education of the RT. 2005. *National Strategy for Education Development of the Republic of Tajikistan* (2006–2015). Retrieved from: http://planipolis.iiep.unesco.org/upload/Tajikistan/Tajikistan%20 Education%20Plan%202006-2015.pdf

———. 2012. *National Strategy of Education Development of the Republic of Tajikistan till 2020*: Retrieved from: http://planipolis.iiep.unesco.org/upload/Tajikistan/Tajikistan_ED_Sector_Plan_2012-2020.pdf

Mirzoev, S. 2014. *The Joint Education Sector Review.* UNICEF and the Ministry of Education and Science. Dushanbe, Tajikistan.

Najibullah, F. 2009. Tajikistan's Lone Private University Defies Order, Opens For New School Year. Retrieved from RFE: http://www.rferl.org/content/Tajikistans_Lone_Private_University_Defies_Order/1812474.html

Niyozov, S. 2002. Understanding Teaching in Post-Soviet, Rural, Mountainous Tajikistan: Case Studies of Teachers' Life and Work (Doctoral Dissertation). Retrievedfrom:www.proquest/pqdtft/docview/304767630/E949EF668C17498EPQ/-

Olcott, M. 2005. *Central Asian's Second Chance.* Washington, DC: Carnegie Endowment for International Peace.

Open Society Institute (OSI). 2002. *Education Development in Kyrgyzstan, Tajikistan and Uzbekistan: Challenges and Ways Forward Prepared by Open Society Institute – Education Support Program* Retrieved from: https://www.opensocietyfoundations.org/sites/default/files/education_development.pdf

Parshin, K. 2014. Tired of Tajikistan's Deplorable Schools, Parents Want Russian. http://www.eurasianet.org/node/70211 (29 Sept 2014).

QS Top Universities. 2015. *QS University Rankings: EECA 2015*. Retrieved from: http://www.topuniversities.com/university-rankings/eeca-rankings/2015

Teichler, U. 1988. *Changing Patterns of the Higher Education System*. London: Jessica Kingsley.

Tempus. 2012. *State of Play of the Bologna Process in the Tempus Partner Countries*. Retrieved from: http://eacea.ec.europa.eu/tempus. DOI 10.2797/90379

Transparency International. 2013. *Overview of Corruption and Anti-corruption in Tajikistan*. Retrieved from: http://www.transparency.org/whatwedo/answer/overview_of_corruption_in_tajikistan

Ustav TNU. 2008. Retrieved from: http://www.tnu.tj/index.php/ru/2012-02-15-12-41-27?layout=edit&id=31

Whitsel, C.M. 2009. *Growing Inequality: Post-Soviet Transition and Educational Participation in Tajikistan* (Doctoral Dissertation). Retrieved from http://search.proquest.com.ezproxy.uky.edu/pqdtft/docview/304898863/85A526F

WEBSITES (2015) OF THE UNIVERSITIES

Branch of the Moscow State University, Dushanbe http://www.msu.tj/ru; http://msu.tj/sites/default/files/newspapers/gazeta_001.pdf; http://www.msu.tj/ru/msu/istoriya-sozdaniya-filiala-v-gorode-dushanbe

Khujand State University. http://www.hgu.tj/en.html

Russian-Tajik Slavonic University. http://www.rtsu.tj/

Tajik Agrarian University. http://www.tajagroun.tj/en/

Tajik National University. http://www.tnu.tj/index.php/ru/

Tajik State Medical University. http://tajmedun.tj/

Tajikistan 1993. Law on Education 1993. Dushanbe, Tajikistan.

Tajikistan 2003. Law on Higher and Professional Education. 2003. (amended in 2009). Dushanbe, Tajikistan.

Alan J. DeYoung is Professor Emeritus of Education Policy and Sociology at the University of Kentucky. His teaching and research interests are in education and higher education reform/change in Central Asia. He has authored or edited three books on these subjects, and his other publications appear in such journals as *Central Asian Survey*, *European Educational Research Journal* and *Communist and Post-Communist Studies*.

Zumrad Kataeva is a postdoctoral research fellow at the Institute of Education of the National Research University Higher School of Economics, Moscow, Russia. She obtained her *kandidat nauk* degree in Tajikistan, and her PhD at the University of Kentucky, USA. Dr. Kataeva is a recipient of the Doctoral Fellowship

Program of the Open Society Foundation. She has also served as a consultant for the World Bank, UNDP and UNICEF. Dr. Kataeva's research interests focus upon various aspects of higher education transformation in post-Soviet countries including academic profession and faculty life, gender and higher education, and effects of globalization on higher education.

Dilrabo Jonbekova is Assistant Professor at the Graduate School of Education at Nazarbayev University in Astana, Kazakhstan. She obtained her PhD in Education and an MPhil from the University of Cambridge and an MA in Management from the University of Leeds in England. Dr. Jonbekova's research interest is in the area of higher education, where her current projects focus upon the relationship between higher education and labor market outcomes.

Open Access This chapter is distributed under the terms of the Creative Commons Attribution 4.0 International License (http://creativecommons.org/licenses/by/4.0/), which permits use, duplication, adaptation, distribution and reproduction in any medium or format, as long as you give appropriate credit to the original author(s) and the source, provide a link to the Creative Commons license and indicate if changes were made.

The images or other third party material in this chapter are included in the chapter's Creative Commons license, unless indicated otherwise in a credit line to the material. If material is not included in the chapter's Creative Commons license and your intended use is not permitted by statutory regulation or exceeds the permitted use, you will need to obtain permission directly from the copyright holder.

CHAPTER 15

The Transformation of Higher Education in Turkmenistan: Continuity and Change

Victoria Clement and Zumrad Kataeva

INTRODUCTION

Turkmenistan is a Central Asian country that has experienced significant reforms in its higher education system since the end of the Soviet Union. Because Turkmenistan's state archives are not available to researchers, this chapter is based on limited available information such as statistical information of CIS countries, NGO reports, mass media reports and the reports of international agencies.

Turkmenistan is one of the largest holders and exporters of gas in the world. The country is comparable to the size of France in territory, but it is sparsely populated by approximately five million people. The country possesses the world's fourth largest reserves of natural gas. According to the World Bank (2014), Turkmenistan has become an upper middle-income economy driven by hydrocarbon exports: GDP per capita rose from 970 USD in 2002 to nearly 7,000 USD in 2013. Among Central Asian countries, Kazakhstan has a larger GDP per capita (10,508 USD),

V. Clement (✉)
Woodrow Wilson Center for International Scholars, Washington, DC, USA

Z. Kataeva
Institute of Education, Higher School of Economics, Moscow, Russia

with Kyrgyzstan and Tajikistan the lowest: 1,103 USD and 926 USD, respectively.[1] Living standards of the Turkmenistan population have improved over the past years, supplemented by massive investment in physical capital. Natural gas exports, which consist of 90 percent of overall export, have pushed national economic growth. The extractive sector accounts for nearly half of Turkmenistan's GDP.

Although the country has made a significant progress in macroeconomic indicators, the quality of Turkmenistan's human capital—its health and education systems—lags behind most other comparable nations, such as Azerbaijan or Ukraine. Moreover, "the Human Development Index (HDI), a composite statistic of life expectancy; education; and income, shows that despite the enormous increase in income per capita experienced in recent years, improvements of health and education outcomes are not remarkable." The people of Turkmenistan have lower life expectancy than most neighbors, let alone the populations of more developed resource-rich countries around the world. Current employment rates of 55 percent and a labor force participation rate of 61 percent for the 15–64-year-old population are low by international standards. According to the same study, with the working age population projected to increase by one-third in 2030, investment in human capital is insufficient to allow the next generation of Turkmen citizens to find jobs.

Despite this wealth, affluence has not trickled down enough to the general population. Rural areas remain notably poor and underdeveloped. The state budget provides funds to subsidize citizens' home heating, gasoline, electricity, water, flour and salt. However, people in rural areas do not have guaranteed access to clean drinking water and electricity outages are not unusual.

Although Turkmenistan does not participate in global assessments such as PISA or TIMSS, the quality of education and its alignment to the present and future needs of the economy are questionable. Education transformation under the first president of Turkmenistan led to decreasing educational provision on all levels. Relatively recently the Turkmen government has made an attempt to reverse this negative trend. The Turkmenistan President's Decree on the "Improvement of the Education System in Turkmenistan" (2013) and the "Concept of Transition to 12-year General Secondary Education in Turkmenistan" were adopted, which aim at radical reforms in the education sector. These reforms are reaching a great number of the population. They include costly projects, ranging from introduction of internet access to building new campuses for HEIs that are made possible by the government's access to energy wealth.

The challenge of modernization is significant, particularly in higher education. Turkmenistan's population is extremely young with 46 percent under age 24 and 20 percent between ages 15 and 24. This demographic situation has implications for all social systems, especially education. Taking in just over 7,000 first year students in the 2014/2015 academic year, HEIs are only able to accommodate around 7 percent of the 100,000 annual graduates. There are approximately 25,600 students currently enrolled in HEIs.

Turkmenistan as other post-Soviet republics attempted to build its education system according to national interests, which were identified by the government. According to the model developed by the first President of Turkmenistan, Niyazov, the country has had to emphasize transformation from the Soviet model to what he called a democratic model, which was declared in the first Constitution of independent Turkmenistan. However, according to this political model, the state should be the main driver and guarantor of this process (Horak 2005). Building the education system, which had to respond to the national interests identified by Niyazov, has driven many reforms in this country. In Turkmenistan, the state plays a major role in the transformation of the economic, social and political institutions including secondary and higher education systems.

The purpose of this chapter is to provide an analysis of the changes that took place in higher education and its institutional landscape in Turkmenistan from the late Soviet years to the present day. Most prominent in this examination will be the differences between Soviet and post-Soviet Turkmen higher education institutions (HEIs) as well as the salient characteristics of reform during the first presidency of Saparmurat Niyazow (1990–2006) and that of the second president, Gurbanguly Berdimuhamedow (2007–present).

This chapter starts with an overview of the Soviet era education and continues with the analysis of two periods of independence (1991–2007) and 2007 to the present day.

Soviet Era Education

Overall it was the Soviet state rather than any independent entities that modernized education in Turkmenistan (also known by its Russian name "Turkmenia"), which was established as part of the 1924 delimitation of Central Asia. Though reliant on Russian language, the Soviet higher education system was free, secular and available to all. In the final years of the Soviet Union, before Turkmenistan gained independence on 27 October

1991, adult literacy approached 99 percent and education was universal. When the Turkmen Soviet Socialist Republic did become independent Turkmenistan, the education system was "Soviet." Textbooks still featured works of the Bolshevik leader Lenin, and HEIs continued to rely on Russian language vocabulary for technical, scientific and medical terminology.

Prior to 1917, there were no universities in the region that became Turkmenistan. Turkmens went to Ufa, Bukhara, Istanbul and sometimes St. Petersburg for higher education. The Soviet administration developed the higher educational system in the Turkmen SSR as part of the Union-wide infrastructure designed for mass tertiary education.

By the end of the Soviet era, there were 9 higher education institutions (Table 15.1) and 41,800 students, with 8,000 of those at the Turkmen State University alone. Most of those institutions (8) were located in the capital, the city of Ashgabat, enrolling 31,000 students (1988). There was one regional pedagogical institution located in the city of Chärjew (currently Turkmenabat). Additionally, established in 1931, the Ashgabat Pedagogical Institute became known as the Turkmen State University named after the Russian writer Maxim Gorky in 1950.

It is important to note that number of students enrolled in higher education institutions in Turkmen SSR was the lowest: number of students per 10,000 equaled 112 in the republic versus 174 on average in the USSR, while the competition at entrance examinations was among the highest: 301 students per 100 places (the average in the USSR was 192). Apparently, the social aspirations of the population to get higher education were much higher than the opportunities created within the republic. It is worth noting that during the Soviet period, Turkmenistan achieved relatively high indicators in terms of gender parity: 44 percent of overall numbers of students were female as of 1988. Two tables below show the institutional landscape of higher education in Turkmenistan where the

Table. 15.1 Number of higher education institutions in Turkmenistan during 1940–1990

	1940	1950	1960	1970	1980	1985	1988	1990[a]
Number of HEIs	5	6	4	5	7	9	9	9
Number of students, thousands	3	6,6	13,1	29,1	35,8	38,8	40,2	41,8

[a]Narodnoe khozyaistvo SSSR v 1990 godu. Moscow: Finansy i statistika, 1991

Source: Narodnoe obrazovanie i kultura v SSSR 1989, Moscow: Financy i statistika)

Table 15.2 Distribution of higher education institutions by sector (1988)

HE by sector, 1988	Number of HEIs	Number of students, thousands
Industry and construction	1	6.0
Transportation and communication	0	0
Agriculture	1	5.8
Economics and law	1	3.5
Education	3	18.3
Incl. Pedagogical HEIs	(2)	(10.2)
Healthcare, physical education and sport	2	5.3
Art and cinema	1	6.6

Source: Narodnoe obrazovanie i kultura v SSSR 1989, Moscow: Financy i statistika

majority of HEIs were specialized institutions. At the same time their composition reflected the main manpower needs of the republic and needs of maintaining Turkmen language and culture (Table 15.2).

However, as in some other Soviet Union republics, the pedagogical institutions in Turkmenistan enrolled relatively large numbers of students: two (2) pedagogical higher education institutions enrolled 25 percent of the total number of students (Table 15.3).

First Years of Independence: Closing "Borders"

The first post-independence years were a period of new state building under the leadership of President Niyazow. According to Niyazow, a new democratic society could appear only through the state taking responsibilities for the well-being of the nation, which led to the total control of overall economic, social and political life of the country (Horak 2005). Post-independence reform of education was intimately tied to language and alphabet reform (Clement 2008). Encouraged by Gorbachev's reforms, the Turkmen SSR adopted the law "On Language" on 24 May 1990. Announcing, "Turkmen is the state language of Turkmenistan," this law made Turkmen the official language and removed Russian's official status.[2] From 1 September 1998 the main language of instruction throughout Turkmenistan became Turkmen. To underscore this, an exam in the Turkmen language—with both written and oral parts—became a mandatory part of the entrance exam for universities and institutes (Meredova 2013). In 1993, President Niyazov announced that Turkmenistan would, over a 3-year period, adopt the Latin-based "New Turkmen National Alphabet" in place of the Cyrillic-based one (Soyegow and Rejepow 1993).

Table 15.3 Classification of Soviet HEIs (1988)

#	Name	Year	Location	Profile	# of students
1.	Turkmen State University named after M. Gorky (now—TSU named after Magtumguly)	1931	Ashgabat	Comprehensive university	8100
2.	Turkmen State Medical Institute	1931	Ashgabat	Medicine	5300
3.	Turkmen Institute of Physical Culture	1981	Ashgabat	Physical/sport education	
4.	Turkmen Agricultural Institute	1930	Ashgabat	Agriculture	5800
5.	Turkmen Institute of National Economy	1980	Ashgabat	Economy fields	3500
6.	Turkmen Polytechnic Institute	1963	Ashgabat	Technical and Engineering	6000
7.	Turkmen State Pedagogical Institute	1950	Chardjew (current Turkmenabat)	Pedagogical	10,200
8.	Turkmen State Institute of Russian Language and Literature	1984	Ashgabat	Pedagogical	
9.	Turkmen state Institute of Culture	1972	Ashgabat	Culture/arts	6600

In the early 1990s, policy on education was laid out in Niyazow's 1993 program "*Bilim*" (Education) and corresponding law. This policy is unique for the beginning of twenty-first century. It manifested a radical reform that contradicted pedagogical norms. For example, the length of secondary education in Turkmenistan was reduced from 10 to 9 years.

Curriculum reform in all levels of education was also radical. From the first grade of school education to the last year of university education the core of the curriculum was President Niyazow's *Ruhnama*, a two-volume work combining history, philosophy and ideology. He wrote this text to instruct Turkmen in their moral, spiritual and political lives. The books contained President Niyazow's personal version of Turkmen folk history, spiritual guidance as well as his own autobiography. Courses on *Ruhnama* replaced fully or partially such courses as History, Social Studies, Philosophy and Geography. Students memorized passages from it, wrote essays on the history it recorded and lived their lives according to *Ruhnama's* moral guidelines. Learning became severely limited when study of *Ruhnama* was combined with the intense cult of personality surrounding Niyazow, which required students to participate in frequent public festivals, sing the praises of the president in their school work and take exams on his writings. Niyazow labeled this period the "Golden Era" and the students of the time the "Golden Generation." However, local teachers referred to their students as the "Lost Generation," witnessing the decline of education (Ahn and Jensen 2016; Clement 2004). Many teachers and university professors lost their jobs. Niyazow's language policies caused non-Turkmen specialists to leave the country. This was one way that Turkmenistan used education for nation-building.

The structure of the tertiary education sector was strongly affected by this policy. The length of study in vocational schools was also reduced from 3 years to 1 year; most vocational schools were reprogramed into 1-year agricultural schools, which provided only certificates after graduation. The study term in higher education was also reduced from 5 years to 2 years. In addition, in 1995 the evening and correspondence learning in higher education was totally dismissed. The Academy of Science and all research institutes under the Academy were also closed blocking any postgraduate studies such as *aspirantura*.

One could expect that such drastic reduction of the number of years to study might lead to greater access to higher education. It was not the case. The access to higher education has become very restrictive because the enrollment to higher education institutions required at least 2 years of practical experience before entering institutes and universities, let alone becoming very competitive. This system has also reproduced inequality in access to higher education because most poor families could not afford paying private tutors to prepare them for higher education as the quality of secondary higher education spiraled downward.

In 2003, the Cabinet of Ministers announced that in order to gain practical experience university students would be required to obtain 2-years' work experience in their selected area of study before they could graduate. Thus, students who wished to pursue higher education were expected to find an internship in a country where unemployment was estimated to be between 40 percent in urban areas and 60 percent in rural areas.[3] When the Ministry of Education announced this program, urban youth lined up at state administration offices while rural students sought work in areas connected to wheat or cotton in the hope of later entering the Agricultural University.[4] Students studying at the Medical Institute found themselves mopping floors in hospitals (Clement 2004). A fundamental problem with the program was that the state provided banks, hospitals, schools and businesses with little guidance as to how to mentor these young people. An example of this was the cohort assigned to the banks, which was supposed to be engaged in daily bank activities, learning managerial skills. However, many reported that they were assigned simple tasks such as filing or running errands (Clement 2004). The general conditions around the country hampered the feasibility of even marginal success when high unemployment was keeping qualified individuals from obtaining work. Locals labeled this the "two-plus-two program," referring to the fact that the 2 years of internship left students of 4-year programs with only 2 years of formal learning (there are some exceptions, such as Architecture, which are 5-year programs). The students received their stipends from the government, and criteria for the program were met on paper, but in reality it suffered from weakness in implementation.

However, under President Niyazow the number of HEIs increased from 9 to 16. The isolated country needed to ensure supply of trained graduates in the areas where Turkmenistan did not have higher education programs in the Soviet times. Some new universities and specialized institutes were opened including Turkmen State Institute of Transport and Communications, International Turkmen-Turkish University, Turkmen State Academy of Arts, the National Institute of Sport and Tourism of Turkmenistan, and the National State Institute of Manuscripts.

The governance of higher education in Turkmenistan is centralized; the higher education institutions are regulated and governed by the Cabinet of Ministers of Turkmenistan. The Cabinet has a wide array of responsibilities including developing and implementing state policy in the field of education. It also ensures that the system of education is in line with the constitution of Turkmenistan, the legal provisions governing education and international treaties. The Cabinet of Ministers also develops all strategies and state education standards; coordinates the activities of education institutions; participates in setting the budget for education; develops quality assurance models and sets requirements for admission to higher education institutions.

The implemented reforms have made a significant impact on the general indicators of higher education. Although the number of higher educa-

Table 15.4 Number of higher education institutions and number of students from 2000 to 2011

	2000	2007	2008	2009	2010	2011
Number of HEIs	16	17	18	19	21	23
Number of students, thousands	16.6	17	20.7	22.1	23.7	25.6

Source: Turkmenistan Statistical Yearbook 2012

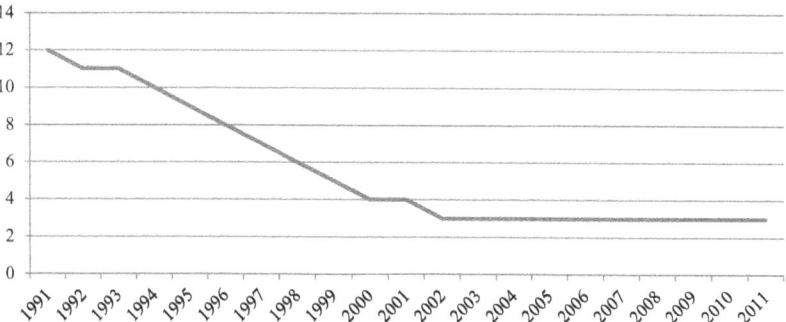

Fig. 15.1 Higher education participation rate 1991–2011, in % (age cohort 20–24) (Sources: http://www.cisstat.com)

tion institutions doubled from 1991 to 2000 the number of students has significantly declined. For instance, in 1990 the number of students was 41,800, but in 2000 the number of students declined to 17,000 (Table 15.4).

Consequently, the participation rate in higher education for youth aged from 20 to 24 years has declined by almost 75 percent (Fig. 15.1).

From 2007 to the Present: From Isolation to Participation?

The political and policy agenda in Turkmenistan has changed with the new (second) President, Gurbanguly Berdimuhamedow. Since then the education sector has been a focus for reorganization and development. The president has repeatedly declared education reform to be one of his top priorities. After his election to the presidency in February 2007, Berdimuhamedow launched a major reform of Turkmenistan's education system starting with his 15 February 2007 decree "On improvement of the education system in Turkmenistan." This decree manifested a departure from Niyazow's reforms. With that decree the school system was restructured from 9 to 10 years, higher educational institutions to 5 years, and medical and some art institutes to 6 years.[5] He also raised the salaries of those in the education sector while decreasing the number of hours worked, reducing class sizes and increasing access to computers. On 30 March 2007, he instructed that the salaries of Turkmenistan's teachers increase by 40 percent.[6] Starting 1 September 2007 a presidential decree reduced the annual work hours from 1250 to 850 for teachers, instructors and professors. Of that time, 490 hours are contact hours (14 hours per week), the rest is time for preparation.[7]

Perhaps President Berdimuhamedow's most important initiative in education was his 1 March 2013 extension of secondary schooling to 12 years.[8] This initiative has had ramifications for higher education as well since it has meant that there are a greater number of students graduating with the credentials that will allow them to pursue higher education both domestically and abroad.

Since 2008, President Berdimuhamedow has emphasized the role of higher education in providing "abundant inflow of highly qualified specialists in a few years."[9] The new Law on Education adopted in 2009, and modified in 2013, has made a significant change in higher education policies. It allowed the introduction of tuition fees in educational sector including higher education; it also regulated issues regarding quality assurance. The International University of Humanities and Development (IUHD), which was opened in 2014, has become a pilot university for introduction of tuition fees. The first university to charge tuition was the International Turkmen-Turkish University. Recently opened (2016), the University of Engineering Technologies of Turkmenistan, named after Oguz Khan, has been also introduced as a pilot university. There is no public information about the amount of tuition; however, according to some mass media resources it varies from $1,300 to $2,000 dollars per academic year. Legally public HEIs have the right to charge tuition fees in cases when (a) students whose education is not being funded from the state budget, (b) students admitted to part-time, evening or correspondence courses and (c) students admitted to the second cycle of higher education (TEMPUS 2012). The minimum annual tuition fee will amount to 3,700 *manats* ($1,300), average, 4,200 *manats* ($1,470) and maximum, 4,700 *manats* ($1,645). The amount of the fees will be determined by the higher educational establishment.[10]

The other significant peculiarity of the Turkmen education system is that although the Law on Education allows private educational organizations all higher education institutions are still the public ones.

Since 2007, Turkmenistan opened four new universities including the Institute of International Relations under the Ministry of Foreign Affairs of Turkmenistan (2008), the International University of Oil and Gas (2012), the International University of Humanities and Development (2014), and most recently the University of Engineering Technologies named after Oguz Khan (2016). In the meantime, the government closed the Branch of the Russian Oil and Gas University (2012) and International Turkmen–Turkish University (2016).

One of President Berdimuhamedow's earliest promises was to reduce the status of *Ruhnama*. Between 2008 and 2011, schools and universities phased out lessons based on *Ruhnama*. Entrance exams on based on *Ruhnama* were ended in August 2014 by declaration of the president. However, the new president's books have replaced the writings of President Niyazow, and Berdimuhamedow's ideological statements now fill the public sphere.[11]

In 2014, a new university opened that is somewhat experimental for Turkmenistan: the International University of Humanities and Development (IUHD). The experimental aspects are that it is organized according to the Bologna model and the language of instruction is English. Thus, the university has been hiring faculty who have obtained their degrees abroad as well as foreign faculty (in spring 2016 there were two foreign professors working there). Other HEIs do not hire foreign faculty, but some, such as the International Oil and Gas University and the Turkmen Institute of Economics and Public Administration, do invite guest lecturers from abroad, in alignment with the Erasmus Program.[12] The philosophy behind IUHD's founding was to create a Turkmen HEI that would meet international standards and compete with the internationally recognized Nazarbayev University in Kazakhstan. It is intended to become "a national brand for academic excellence."[13] With over 500 students, it is operating below its capacity for 2500, but plans to take in more students each year. IUHD will train specialists in 14 areas of study: philosophy, sociology, international public law, private law, international relations, journalism, international economy, management, finances, insurance, commerce and computer programming, information technology and communication technologies. This university's education is based on a 5-year program, with the first year devoted to language learning and practice. With the establishment of IUHD we see a new form of education in Turkmenistan. The new university represents institutional differentiation of a new sort: international criteria, use of ECTS (European Credit Transfer and Accumulation System) and the Bologna model. The 2013 Law on Education has also introduced a two-tier system such as Bachelor and Master degrees.

Turkmenistan is not a signatory to the Bologna Process. However, there are long-term plans to bring HEIs in line with the Bologna model. This is significant as officially neutral Turkmenistan does not often join coalitions or unions. It signals that the government is growing more comfortable with the importation of outside ideas. It is not clear how it will affect the higher education system and the institutional landscape in the country.

In 2014, the state began to recognize foreign diplomas earned after 1993, which in 2004 Niyazow had declared invalid in an effort to discourage students from studying abroad.[14] In 2012, Turkmenistan's Ministry of Education estimated that there were 42,000 citizens studying abroad in foreign universities.[15] There were 13,000 Turkmenistani students in Ukraine; 10,000 in Belarus; while Russia, Turkey and Malaysia also each were taking in a great many. The government of Turkmenistan paid tuition for only 2,000 of these individuals, the rest were privately funded.[16] In addition, there is some demand for Russian language education within Turkmenistan itself. To help satisfy this desire, Russia's Oil and Gas University opened a branch in Ashgabat in 2008 (closed later). Except for at this university, Russian is no longer a language of instruction at HEIs, it is taught only in Russian language classes as a foreign language.

In spring 2009, when there were 4,275 students entering their first year at Turkmenistan's HEIs and 2,700 leaving to study abroad, President Berdimuhamedow referenced the country's reliance on graduates from foreign universities and the knowledge they bring home, saying that Turkmenistan would continue the practice of sending students abroad "until the country gets fully staffed with specialists with high qualifications."[17] Citizens of Turkmenistan holding a foreign degree may have their diploma recognized with a certificate after successful completion of two exams: one in Social Studies and one in the applicant's field of specialization. These exams were offered in the Turkmen language.[18]

In terms of gender policies Turkmenistan's Constitution and laws declare equality between women and men and guarantee equal rights to education. However, the available statistics of 2008/2009 shows that the proportion of women in higher education is decreasing annually. For example, as of 2008/2009 academic year, only 35 percent of total students were female which is 2 percent lesser than in 2006/2007 academic year.

Current Institutional Landscape in Higher Education

Turkmenistan represents unequal regional distribution of higher education. All institutions, except three, are located in the capital of the country, Ashgabat. For instance, Turkmen National University named after Magumguly, Turkmen State Medical University, Turkmen Agricultural University, International University of Oil and Gas, the newest University of Engineering Technologies of Turkmenistan, the International University of Humanities and Development, the Turkmen State Institute of Culture, the Turkmen State Institute of Transport and Communication, the National Institute of Sport and Tourism of Turkmenistan, the Turkmen National Institute of World Languages, the Institute of International Relations under the Ministry of Foreign Affairs, Turkmen State Institute of Finance, Turkmen State Institute of Architecture and Construction as well as Turkmen National Conservatory and Turkmen Academy of Arts. The three regional higher education institutions include Turkmen State Pedagogical Institute in Turkmenabad, Turkmen State Institute of Energy in Mary city and Turkmen Agricultural Institute in Daşoguz.

The typology, which is proposed below, represents four types of HEIs (see Table 15.5) and takes into account criteria with regard to educational activities and majors and specialties they include. The data were gathered from available internet information on number of HEIs, their size and major and specializations they represent. It is difficult to gather information on number of students, research activities and involvement in international projects of these HEIs. The Turkmen State University named after Magumguly (former Maksim Gorky) still holds the status of leading university and remains the flagship in Turkmenistan. The second type includes large state specialized universities such as Agricultural and Medical, which were specialized institutes during Soviet times, as well as the new University of Engineering Technologies named after Oguz Khan. The third category represents two international universities, International University of Humanities and Development and International University of Oil and Gas. While we were working on this chapter one international university (Turkish–Turkmen University) was

Table 15.5 Current classification of higher education institutions (2016)

Type	Number/location	Example	Educational profile
1. National flagship university	1/Ashgabat	Turkmen State University	The largest university
2. State large specialized universities	3/Ashgabat	Agricultural and medical Universities; University of Engineering Technologies named after Oguz Khan	Multidisciplinary large- and medium-size universities
3. International universities	2/Ashgabat	International University of Oil and Gas; International University of Humanities and Development	International university
4. Small and specialized institutes in the capital	15/Ashgabat	Turkmen Institute of Economics and Management; Institute of World Languages; Institute Architecture and Construction	Small- and medium-size HEI
5. Regional specialized institutes	3/regional centers	Seyitnazar Seydi Turkmen State Pedagogical Institute(Turkmenabat city) Turkmen State Power Engineering Institute (Mary city) Turkmen State Agricultural Institute (Daşoguz city)	Small- and medium-size HEI

closed by the decree of President Berdimuhamedow, while the proclaimed International University of Humanities and Development was launched under the guise it would play a lead role in preparing highly qualified graduates according to international standards, using English as the instructional language. It is composed of six faculties and 13 departments and has programs in philosophy, sociology, international relations, journalism, economic, finances and computer science. The IUHD is also the first university preparing students according to the two-tier education system with Bachelor and Master degrees, theoretically aligned with requirements of the Bologna Process.[19] The International University of Oil and Gas was opened due to Turkmenistan's specific need for specialists in the oil and gas industries.

The fourth type of HEIs represents small and specialized institutes, which prepare students in narrow areas for specific jobs. Some of them include institutes from the Soviet period, which were renamed such as the National Institute of Sport and Tourism of Turkmenistan (former Institute of Physical Culture) and Turkmen National Institute of World Languages (former Institute of Russian Language and Literature). Other institutes include new ones such as Turkmen State Institute of Transport and Communication, Turkmen State Institute of Finance, Turkmen State Institute of Architecture and Construction, Turkmen National Conservatory, Turkmen Academy of Arts and the Institute of International Relations under the MFA. This institutional type also includes five military institutes located in the capital city of Ashgabat. Finally the last category includes regional institutions. One of these institutes inherited from the Soviet time is the pedagogical institute named after Seyitnazar Seydi and two other new institutions, Pedagogical Institutions in Mary and Daşoguz city.

The research and development in Turkmenistan has been revived and coordinated by both higher education institutions and the Academy of Science, where the Academy of Science still carries the large part of the research and is still responsible for training of doctoral students. At the same time, although the university programs were extended in accordance with international standards, it became clear that the dismissal of former researchers and/or teachers from the universities in the past decade has created a gap in qualified staff from which the country has not been able to recover.

Conclusion

Turkmenistan's higher education has undergone significant changes since the Soviet era. These changes were driven mainly by state policies under total centralization of the system. The political leaders were main drivers of the transformations. Two periods of presidency in Turkmenistan have also played a major role in its current institutional landscape. Turkmenistan had only 9 higher education institutions by the end of the Soviet times and now the country has 24 higher education institutions to have a full spectrum of higher education programs in the country through the specialized universities. For the main sector of the economy—oil and gas—Turkmenistan's government even allowed the establishment of an international university. The challenge of the territorial development also forced the government to establish two new regional universities.

The demand of higher education is very high—five applicants for one place in 2014. At the same time the wealth of the country and total control allow the government to ignore this growing demand and to prohibit the private higher education sector to grow.

For almost three decades of independence Turkmenistan's higher education has undergone reforms and transformations, and the dynamics of those changes were not smooth. Compared to other post-Soviet countries where the number of higher education institutions and number of students have raised significantly, Turkmenistan did not have such rapid growth. During the first years of independence, the number of students decreased considerably. However, after the second phase and arrival of President Berdimuhamedow, the education system started to see some growth in terms of student enrollments, opening new universities and emphasis on internationalization. Turkmenistan was able to open more specialized institutes and relatively expand its regional higher education. However, Turkmenistan higher education does not have any private higher education institutions and the system remains under the tight control of the government.

Notes

1. World Bank (2015). GDP data per country
2. *Turkmenistan's Constitution*, 1992, Section I, Article 13
3. "2004 Country Report on Human Rights Practices in Turkmenistan," Bureau of Democracy, Human Rights, and Labor, U.S. Department of State, 28 February 2005. More recent estimates remain high, and the BBC reports 50% of urbanites unemployed with rural areas suffering even higher rates; see *BBC Monitoring Central Asia*. 26 February 2012.
4. Until 2005 it was typical for school children to work in the cotton fields each fall. But after the 1 February 2005 adoption of the law "On guarantees of the rights of youth to work" only rural areas still saw children working in the fields. See *Neitral'nyi Turkmenistan*, No. 28, 2 February 2005.
5. http://www.turkmenistan.ru/en/node/7038
6. http://www.turkmenistan.ru/en/node/6072
7. The typical academic year is 34 weeks long, although HEIs with international status, such as International Turkmen-Turkish University, work on a 35-week academic calendar. Recently there has been discussion at some

universities of reducing the number of contact hours to 12–13 per week, but that has yet to be agreed upon.
8. http://www.turkmenistan.ru/en/articles/17173.html
9. http://www.turkmenistan.ru/en/print/node/7467
10. http://chono-tm.org/en/2014/05/tuition-fees-to-be-introduced-in-turkmen-universities/
11. http://rferl.org/articleprintview/25237344.html
12. http://Turkmenistan.gov.tm/_eng?id=4031
13. IUHD brochure
14. According to Presidential Decree 13430, issued 9 January 2014, only diplomas earned through full-time study will be acknowledged in educational establishments. Degrees earned through part-time study, at HEIs or secondary vocational educational establishments, will not be recognized. This is problematic for thousands of students studying abroad as well as via correspondence.
15. http://chrono-tm.org/en/2015/02/turkmenistan-resumes-validation-of-foreign-diplomas/
16. www.thediplomat.com/2015/07/in-turkmenistan-border-woes-trump-education/
17. http://www.turkmenistan.ru/en/node/8188
18. http://www.chrono-tm.org/en/2014/03/turkmenistan-to-impose-severe-restrictions-on-foreign-diplomas/
19. http://www.infoabad.com/obrazovanie-nauka-i-tehnika/v-ashhabade-otkrylsja-mezhdunarodnyi-universitet-gumanitarnyh-nauk-i-razvitija.html

References

Ahn, E.S., and A. Jensen. 2016. Language Teaching in Turkmenistan: An Autoethnographic Journey. In *Language Change in Central Asia*, ed. E.S. Ahn and J. Smagulova, 59–99. Boston/Berlin: Mouton de Gruyter.

BBC Monitoring Central Asia. 2012. Has Turkmenistan Changed at All? Retrieved from http://www.bbc.com/news/world-asia-16958817

Clement, V. 2004. Secular and Religious Trends in Turkmen Education. Unpublished Policy Paper for Eurasia Policy Studies Program at the National Bureau of Asian Research (NBR).

Clement, V. 2008. Emblems of independence: script choice in post-Soviet Turkmenistan. *International Journal of the Sociology of Language* 192, 171–185.

Horak, S. 2005. The Ideology of the Turkmenbashy Regime. *Perspectives on European Politics and Society* 6 (2): 305–319.

Horak, S. 2013. Educational Reforms in Turkmenistan: Good Framework, Bad Content? Central Asia Policy Brief, September 2013, No. 11.

Law on Guarantees of the Rights of Youth to Work. 2005. *Neitral'nyi Turkmenistan*, Number 28, 2 February.
Meredova, M. 2013. Turkmenistan: Reforming the Education System. In *Education in West Central Asia*, ed. M. Ahmed, 273–287. London: Bloomsbury.
Narodnoe obrazovanie i kultura v SSSR. 1989. Moscow: Financy i statistika.
Narodnoe khozyaistvo SSSR v 1990 godu. 1991. Moscow: Finansy i statistika.
Söýegow, M., and N. Rejepow. 1993. *Täze Türkmen elibiýi*. Aşgabat: Ruh.
TEMPUS. 2012. Higher Education in Turkmenistan. Retrieved from http://eacea.ec.europa.eu/tempus/participating_countries/overview/Turkmenistan.pdf
Turkmenistan. 2014. Presidential Decree 13430 "About Foreign Diplomas", Issued 9 January 2014.
US Department of State. 2005. Country Report on Human Rights Practices in Turkmenistan.
World Bank (2014). Turkmenistan – Diversifying the Turkmen Economy. Retrieved from http://documents.worldbank.org/curated/en/887311468111849090/Turkmenistan-Diversifying-the-Turkmen-economy

ELECTRONIC SOURCES

http://www.chrono-tm.org/en/2015/02/the-results-of-census-in-turkmenistan
http://www.indexmundi.com/turkmenistan/demographics_profile.htm
http://www.mfa.gov.tm/en/tukrmenistan/education
http://www.stanradar.com/news/full/21712-sistema-obrazovanija-v-turkmenistane.html

Victoria Clement is a research scholar at the Woodrow Wilson International Center for Scholars in Washington, DC. Her work explores the intersection of political and social power in modern Central Asia. Her book on the history of modern language and education reform, entitled *Learning to Become Turkmen: Literacy, Language, and Power*, 1914–2014, will be published by the University of Pittsburgh Press. Dr. Clement's research has been published in the *International Journal of the Sociology of Language*, the edited volumes *Daily Life in Central Asia* (2007) and *Muslim World in Transition* (2007) as well as several encyclopedias and two Central Asian publications: *Türkmen Dili* (2003) and *Owadan* (1997). She has lived in Turkmenistan, Russia and Turkey and works with primary sources in Turkmen, Turkish and Russian languages.

Zumrad Kataeva is a postdoctoral research fellow at the Institute of Education of the National Research University Higher School of Economics, Moscow, Russia. She obtained her *kandidat nauk* degree in Tajikistan and her PhD at the

University of Kentucky, USA. Dr. Kataeva is a recipient of the Doctoral Fellowship Program of the Open Society Foundation. She has also served as a consultant for the World Bank, UNDP and UNICEF. Dr. Kataeva's research interests focus upon various aspects of higher education transformation in post-Soviet countries including academic profession and faculty life, gender and globalization and higher education.

Open Access This chapter is distributed under the terms of the Creative Commons Attribution 4.0 International License (http://creativecommons.org/licenses/by/4.0/), which permits use, duplication, adaptation, distribution and reproduction in any medium or format, as long as you give appropriate credit to the original author(s) and the source, provide a link to the Creative Commons license and indicate if changes were made.

The images or other third party material in this chapter are included in the chapter's Creative Commons license, unless indicated otherwise in a credit line to the material. If material is not included in the chapter's Creative Commons license and your intended use is not permitted by statutory regulation or exceeds the permitted use, you will need to obtain permission directly from the copyright holder.

CHAPTER 16

Ukraine: Higher Education Reforms and Dynamics of the Institutional Landscape

Nataliya L. Rumyantseva and Olena I. Logvynenko

INTRODUCTION

The developmental trajectory of the HE system in Ukraine has mirrored the large-scale transformations that have been taking place in the country since the collapse of the Soviet Union. Rapid change in the socioeconomic and political environments and dramatic demographic changes as well as vicissitudes in foreign relations have all formed the wider context in which the HE system has been evolving.

This chapter views the changes in the HE landscape through the lens of horizontal and vertical diversification and organisational interrelationships (Teichler 1988). Ukraine's HE followed a trajectory that is both similar and different to developments in other post-Soviet states (Huisman et al. 2007, 565), facing a shared communist past, bringing back to life pre-Soviet institutions and achievements and looking for the ways forward.

N. L. Rumyantseva (✉)
Business School University of Greenwich, London, UK

O. I. Logvynenko
National University of Life and Environmental Sciences, Kyiv, Ukraine

© The Author(s) 2018
J. Huisman et al. (eds.), *25 Years of Transformations of Higher Education Systems in Post-Soviet Countries*, Palgrave Studies in Global Higher Education, https://doi.org/10.1007/978-3-319-52980-6_16

We will review how horizontal institutional differentiation has been jumpstarted with the introduction of private universities and other structural changes in the system. We will also discuss changes in the vertical differentiation amongst institutions of HE based on their status and ranking system. The interrelationships amongst old and new universities have inevitably shifted towards being more competitive, which presents not only a new practice for the system but also an additional challenge in the face of negative demographic trends.

Brief Historical Overview of the Pre-Soviet HE System in Ukraine[1]

The first HEIs in Ukraine appeared in the West of the country and, in Kyiv, the capital of Kyivan Rus. Towards the end of the sixteenth century, Western Ukraine was experiencing religious and national identity struggles whilst seeking to position itself between the influence of Orthodox Christian Russia and Roman Catholic Poland and Austria. The Ostrozska Academy, established in 1576, was the first HEI established in the territory that is now Ukraine. The Academy was closed in 1636. In 1632 Petro Mohyla, Metropolitan of Kyiv, founded a later well-known Kyiv-Mohyla Academy whose main purpose at the time was to 'benefit the Orthodox Rus' religious and ethnic communities' (Yershova and Gordiichuk 2013, 474). The Academy became an influential centre of innovation and research and served as a model for universities in Eastern territories established in the nineteenth century (Bunina 2013). In 1817, however, the Academy closed down soon after Russian Empress Catherine II withdrew her financial support.

In the mediaeval city of Lviv, the Roman Catholic Jesuits order actively pursued the approval of the Polish King John II Casimir who eventually granted permission to establish the University of Lviv in 1661. The University facilitated the development of this region (Bunina 2013) and produced several graduates of national impact. Over a 100 years later, another university in the western part of the country was opened in 1875 in the city of Chernivtsi. Although the University teaching was originally delivered in German, it gradually became a multicultural and multilingual institution.

In the modern Eastern Ukrainian territories, the first HEIs appeared at the beginning of the nineteenth century. These HEIs were established in territories that at that time were under the jurisdiction of the Russian Empire. Hence, they reflected different principles and traditions. Osipian (2008) describes the Russian tradition in HE as one of 'weak university self-governance', compensated by 'strong state control'. The first university in these territories was opened in the city of Kharkiv in 1805. Other national universities were open in Kyiv (1834) and Odessa (1865).

Institutions established under Western European influence differed in many ways from their Eastern counterparts in the underlying autonomy models that underpinned institutional relationships with the corresponding governments. In the West, the impact of religion on HEIs was given considerable importance by the state (whether Polish or Austrian) and often resulted in clashes with the religious beliefs of the Ukrainian population. In the East, issues concerning institutional autonomy were the key source of tension in university-government relations.

A parallel trend of systematic development of teacher training institutions started in the 1860–1870s. This development introduced the first elements of differentiation into the HE system as these institutions combined elements of vocational training with advanced studies and attracted a specific student population interested in the teaching career. Initially, not all of them were HEIs. The first teacher training HEI opened in Gluhiv in 1874 (Bunina 2013) putting a start to what is now a robust net of pedagogical universities.

By the beginning of the twentieth century, student numbers in higher education had doubled by comparison to the late 1800s, although access for poorer working class and peasant youth was still severely restricted (Bunina 2013). Immediately prior to 1917, the Ukrainian HE system amounted to 27 institutions that educated more than 35,000 students (Kurbatov 2014). During the brief period of Ukraine's independence and the Civil War of 1917–1920, additional HEIs were opened in the capital, including the Academy of Pedagogy, as well as in Kamyanets-Podilsky in the West and an early form of Tavrida University in the Crimea. By the time most of the current Ukraine's territory became part of the USSR in 1939, Ukraine had 129 HEIs. In 1941, Ukraine had 162 HEIs and around 130,000 students. Table 16.1 presents a simple typology of the HEIs by extent and type of specialisation. At this point, Ukraine had six comprehensive universities. Technical and industrial institutions were leading the way along with their pedagogical counterparts, reflective of the needs of the economy and the high emphasis placed on access to secondary education.

Table 16.1 Typology of HEIs by specialisation in 1941

Type of HEI	Number of HEIs
Comprehensive universities	6
Industrial/technical institutes	40
Agricultural institutes	19
Economics institutes	6
Pedagogical institutes	69
Medical institutes	15
Art, music and theatrical institutes	7
Total	162

Source: Buhalo (1945)

UKRAINIAN HIGHER EDUCATION SYSTEM BETWEEN 1940 AND 1990

Not unlike other post-Soviet states, the Soviet Ukrainian HE system was designed and developed to supply the manpower needs of the economy. In a highly centralised social system, HE was controlled and coordinated in relation to the industry and economic needs of the USSR. The military needs during the war and then the post-war arms race mirrored themselves in the growing numbers of engineering and other technical specialisations. Centralised control and manpower planning enabled institutional inter-relationships that were primarily based on the principles of complementarity rather than competition. Ukrainian HEIs during the Soviet period were producing graduates for the needs of other Soviet republics as well as Ukraine itself. Two institutions, in particular, were noteworthy for their all-USSR student body: the Ivano-Frankivsk National Technical University of Oil and Gas and the Mykolayiv Shipbuilding Institute.

Disciplinary orientation and geographical location in part determined HEIs' role in the overall system and national economy. In addition, student mobility was not very high but policy measures were implemented over time to boost the HE participation rate for low-income applicants, especially from the countryside. Higher education was free of charge and all students were admitted on a competitive basis. Students also received a modest stipend to cover living expenses. This gradually boosted student mobility.

After World War II and Stalin's death in 1953, Khrushchev's government undertook a reform of the HE system. In the 1950s–1960s, the HE system was slightly downsized, with some institutions closed or merged, leaving 135 HEIs instead of 160. The student numbers, however, doubled in comparison with the pre-war period. Diversity in the form of delivery grew, including the delivery by correspondence (*zaochyi fakultet*), further opening opportunities for older individuals already in the labour force.

Vertical institutional differentiation had become particularly clear by this time. Comprehensive universities enjoyed higher status, a wider range of disciplines and more privileges, including opportunities to engage in research, whilst specialised institutes focused primarily on teaching within their chosen fields. Polytechnics, however, received additional support and funding from the government at this time, fuelled by the need to rebuild the country (USSR) after the war, whilst maintaining its technologically competitive status in the international political arena. Many of these polytechnics grew into well-recognised and prestigious institutions of the time. Table 16.2 presents the state of the system in 1988, shortly before the collapse of the Soviet Union. Horizontal diversity is evident in the different types of specialisation within universities. Technical HEIs attracted the largest number of students at the time, followed by pedagogical HEIs, suggesting a possible element of vertical differentiation based on their importance in the overall social system.

Table 16.2 Typology of HEIs by type of specialisation in 1988

Type HEI	Number of HEIs	Number of students
Comprehensive universities	10	98,734
Pedagogy and education	42	257,014
Technical (industry and construction)	40	318,181
Transport and communication	10	56,284
Agriculture	17	90,372
Economics and law	10	68,964
Medicine and sport	18	56,591
Art and cinema	9	6,572
Total	156	952,712

Source: Goskomstat (1989)

Changes in the HE System Since Ukraine's Independence: Policy, Practice and Agency

With the onset of independence, Ukraine's HE system had 156 HEIs at the beginning of the 1991/1992 academic year. The system was then about to enter a long and turbulent period of reforms with varying levels of success in implementation.

Initially, the only active agency in the reform process belonged almost exclusively to the President, the Parliament and the Cabinet of Ministers. Fimyar (2010), in her analysis of policy rationales in HE, argues that the primary policy documents reveal that the sources of all policy documents were Presidential Decrees, whilst Educational Laws, directives of the Cabinet of Ministers and Ministry of Education laws and directives were derivatives of the latter. It is in part understandable why the president of a highly centralised country so inexperienced in self-governance would be reluctant to delegate important decisions, but such high levels of centralisation in policy sources excluded important stakeholders from having a voice for at least two decades, having an inevitable impact both on the institutional diversity, institutional interrelationships and the quality and relevance of higher education to the country's economy and social development. The reform processes have been underpinned by three key rationales: *nation and state building, comparison and critique, and finally catch-up Europeanisation* (Fimyar 2010). The following three sub-sections explain the nature of each rationale in more detail.

Nation and State Building

The *nation and state building* rationale is grounded in the concerns of separation from the Soviet past, establishing a differentiated system, reviving pre-Soviet traditions and history as well as pursuing active ukrainianisation of the educational process to ensure that the historically vulnerable Ukrainian language (Janmaat 2008) continues to develop and shape the national identity of the Ukrainian people. The proportion of university students instructed in Ukrainian in the 1995/1996 academic year was 51%. In 2002/2003 this figure grew to 78%, with Western (99%) and Central Ukraine (approximately 96%) taking the lead. Even in the traditionally Russian-speaking East and South, these figures grew from 23% to 58.9% and from 26.9% to 55.5%, respectively (Ministry of Statistics 2003). The use of language presents a more complex picture, however, if we consider formal and informal use, the use of *Surzhyk* (a mixture of Russian and Ukrainian) and the ideological dimensions of linguistic diversity (Bilaniuk and Melnyk 2008). The government's language policies sparked much controversy and, some believe, ate up valuable time and resources, leaving other goals disadvantaged (Byron 2001). Others argue that ethno-linguistic self-identification is crucial for second wave Wilsonian states, which derive their legitimacy for independence primarily through ethnic and linguistic markers (Janmaat 2008). Regardless of how one evaluates these changes, they undoubtedly became a source of horizontal institutional differentiation, with Western and Central Ukrainian HEIs being more ukrainianised than their Eastern and Southern counterparts. In addition to language as a marker of ethnic identity, shared Ukrainian history was revived via symbolic (but also very practical) rebirth out of mediaeval ruins of two HEIs: the Kyiv-Mohyla Academy in 1991 and the Ostrozska Academy in 1994. Several new HEIs were opened to supply qualified staff for the newly created state organs of the independent Ukraine: the University of Customs and Finance (1996), the National Academy of Internal Security of Ukraine (1992) and the University of the State Fiscal Service (1999).

In addition to the revival of language and history, the Law of Ukraine on Education (1991) and the Law on Higher Education (2002) made the statement that Ukraine's HE system was to be structured differently and to some extent mirror the growing liberalisation of the economy and of property rights. The most radical change at this stage was the introduction of the private or non-state HEIs. This set the precedent for an alternative private HE system. By 2013, the proportion of private HEIs mounted to 21% of all the HEIs in the system. According to UkrStat, Ukraine had 162 private institutions in the 2015/2016 academic year, comprising around 130,000 students (State Office of Statistics of Ukraine 2016). New institutions have only loosely been regulated and were largely left to their own devices to find their way in the market. The impact of private HE providers on the quality of education in the system remains unclear. They appear to be a lot less competitive than traditional public institutions but tap into the same intellectual potential of the academic staff thus, according to some reports in the Ukrainian press, diluting the system. A more systematic approach, however, is needed to assess how this form of institutional differentiation is influencing the quality and relevance of HE in the country. From the students' perspective, the division between private and public higher education becomes less clear as more and more students across all institutional types pay the cost of their studies out of their own pocket. On the whole, 52.3% of all students, across all types of institutions, were paying tuition fees in the 2014/2015 academic year, whilst 46.1% were funded from the state budget, with a small minority being funded from city budgets (0.9%) and from the budgets of private companies (0.7%) (State Office of Statistics of Ukraine 2015).

The second prominent feature of systemic changes in the onset of independence has been the merging of parts of the vocational education system with higher education. Secondary specialised educational institutions (*uchilischa* and *technikumy*) were reclassified as HEIs of I and II levels of accreditation, and more established HEIs as level III and level IV. By changing the status of these institutions, the Law on Higher Education (2002) increased the institutional diversity of the HE system. HEIs at different levels served different functions and attracted different types of students (horizontal differentiation) but also enjoyed different levels of prestige and status (vertical differentiation) both with the government and students. This becomes particularly obvious when we consider that the number of HEIs of levels I and II exceeded that of the III and IV levels throughout the period of independence (Fig. 16.1), though the latter were leading in student numbers by 1995 (Fig. 16.2).

In addition to increased institutional differentiations and choice, the new structure incorporated a more diverse set of degrees, starting with junior specialist granted in HEIs of levels I and II and the new-for-the-system Bachelor's degrees, which left graduates qualified to enter Master's programmes, alongside specialist degrees inherited from the Soviet system which in principle enabled graduates to enter doctoral-level studies. Doctoral-level degrees were left unchanged from the Candidate of Science and Doctor of Science until later reforms (specifically the Law on Higher Education passed in 2014). At this stage, the new structure thus combined elements of Western degrees with the Soviet heritage. The second Law on Higher Education (2014) has left the status of level I and II institutions undefined, although the practice of students' direct entry from college into the second year of university continues, which implies that level I and II institutions remain a part of the HE system. The Soviet doctoral-level degrees were replaced at this stage with the more familiar to the Western reader Doctor of Philosophy (PhD). The licence to grant this higher-level degree serves as an additional source of institutional differentiation, with the academies and the universities having the exclusive right to bestow it.

UKRAINE: HIGHER EDUCATION REFORMS AND DYNAMICS... 415

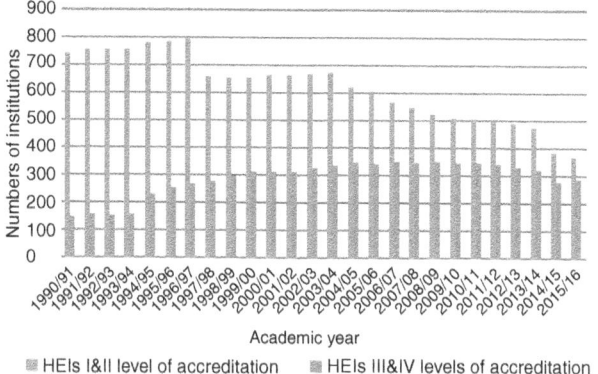

Fig. 16.1 Numbers of HEIs by levels of accreditation, 1990–2015 (The data for 2014–2015 and 2015–2016 are not fully comparable to data from previous years as they do not take into account institutions that remained in the occupied territories and the zone of military conflict in Donetsk, Lugansk and Crimea. Source: State Office of Statistics of Ukraine (2016))

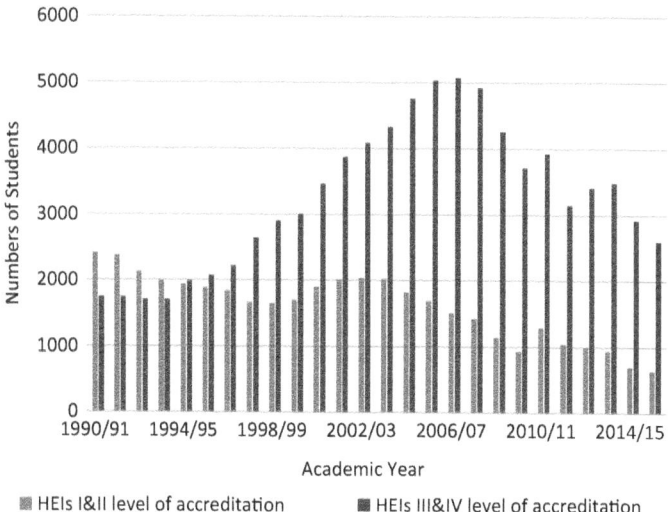

Fig. 16.2 Numbers of students in HEIs by levels of accreditation, 1990–2015 (The data for 2014–2015 and 2015–2016 are not fully comparable to data from previous years as they do not take into account institutions that remained in the occupied territories and the zone of military conflict in Donetsk, Lugansk and Crimea. Source: State Office of Statistics of Ukraine (2016))

Whilst the number of HEIs continued to grow along with the student numbers, the demographic situation in Ukraine took on a negative turn from the early 1990s onwards. Whilst 1990 saw 657,000 children born, in 2001 when the birth rate hit its lowest, there were only 376,000 births. This trend has been accompanied by high emigration and brain drain rates. The first decline in student numbers can be seen in 2008 for level III–IV institutions, which corresponds to the 1991 born cohort. At the same time, the number of HEIs of III–IV accreditation levels increased from 156 in 1991/1992 to 351 in 2006/2007, a 125% increase.

Although the negative demographic trend has been partly offset by growing participation rates and increasing popularity of second HE degrees amongst already employed university graduates, on the whole, these trends taken together represented a time bomb for the HE system. Unfortunately, very few Ukrainian policy makers and university managers chose to acknowledge them with any strategically developed response. Hence, the inevitable oversupply of HEIs posed a serious problem and the question of mergers has arisen for the recent and the current Ministers of Education, Serhiy Kvit and Liliya Grynevych.

Comparison and Critique

The second policy rationale—*comparison and critique*, or more precisely *self-critique*—has generated discourse around the desired states of decentralisation, quality control, modernisation, democratisation, internationalisation and equal access, often noticed by Western observers as positive developments (Johnston and Bain 2002; Silova 2009). Such aspirational goals on the one hand and acute awareness on the other of the real state of affairs—which is seen as lacking in all these qualities by the Ukrainians themselves—are what generates most of the self-critique and the notion of a persistent educational crisis. Specific facets of the crisis are described in Presidential (1995) and Parliamentary Decrees (2002) and admit to the low status of the academic profession, unacceptably low salaries, the low and decreasing level of prestige of higher education, limited diversity in the forms of ownership and declining interdisciplinary links (Fimyar 2008). This policy discourse identifies the reasons for the crisis highlighted in the Law on Education of 1991 (Fimyar 2008) as significant reduction in educational spending, lack of implementation of policies on social protection of teachers, the legacy of the Soviet system of education (specifically politicisation and bureaucratisation) and, at the same time, nostalgic whining about the weakness of the modern state's control over quality of education. A large step from a highly centralised system to a more democratic and self-governing one is perhaps not possible without some ambivalence and hesitation, which comes across in the early educational discourse. What is troublesome, however, is that an 'impersonal' critique is fostered, 'limited to critical evaluation of the processes but not the actors behind these processes; the identification of which is crucial for understanding and overcoming the crisis' (Fimyar 2010, 80).

Interestingly, similar types of issues pertaining to the notion of crisis in HE were raised by academic staff and administrators in the case study by Shaw et al. (2013), conducted a decade after these weaknesses were originally noted in official documents. The study additionally documented the complaints of university administrators on low levels of autonomy in terms of financial self-management and of academic staff in terms of the structure and content of degree programmes. Levels of autonomy are not identical across the system, however, serving as a source of vertical institutional differentiation. Currently, three state HEIs have the status of autonomous/self-managed universities with greater powers over their budgets, academic curriculum and capacity to forge external links (Table 16.3). There is also a plethora of private institutions that enjoy relatively high levels of autonomy from the government in terms of their own income generation and spending, and to a certain extent over curriculum planning and implementation.

Respondents in the case study conducted by Shaw et al. (2013) were drawn from a HEI that is less autonomous by formal criteria. Unsurprisingly, the accuracy of understanding of the status quo evident in the interviews was accompanied by an acute awareness of the informers' own helplessness with regard to reality, with only occasional sparks of optimism and sense of agency from selected top-level administration or very experienced academic staff.

The Law on Higher Education (2014) has made some notable steps in the direction of creating an explicit sense of agency in the system by introducing actors apart from the government and charging them with specific responsibilities. Specifically, in creating provisions for a Quality Assurance Agency, which is expected to function as an arms-length body, similarly to its UK namesake, the Law makes an effort to delegate important monitoring functions away from the Ministry. The Agency has not started functioning at the time of this writing, however, which makes it impossible to comment on the actual realities of its work and division of responsibilities.

Table 16.3 Typology of higher education institutions in Ukraine in 2016

Type	Examples of HEIs	Quantity	City or region	Educational profile	Research activity	International activity	Form of governance/form of ownership/source of budget	Ministerial jurisdiction[a]
				Nationwide HEIs				
				Comprehensive				
Flagship universities	Kyiv National University of Taras Shevchenko; Kharkiv National University of Vasyl Karazin; National University 'Ostrog Academy'	3	Kyiv, Kharkiv, Ostrog	Multidisciplinary	High	High	Autonomous/self-managed/state and own budget	Ministry of Education and Science
National comprehensive universities	Ivan Franko National University of Lviv; National University of Kyiv-Mohyla Academy; Donetsk National University[b]; Taras Shevchenko National University of Luhansk; Lesya Ukrainka East European National University; Khmelnytskyi National University	19	Lviv, Kyiv, Odessa, Chernivtsi, Dnipro, Zakarpattia, Vinnytsia, Luhansk, Khmelnytskyi, Poltava, Zaporizhia, Volyn, Mykolaiv, Cherkasy, Ivano-Frankivsk	Multidisciplinary	Medium but above average for HEIs	High	State	Ministry of Education and Science

(continued)

Table 16.3 (continued)

Type	Examples of HEIs	Quantity	City or region	Educational profile	Research activity	International activity	Form of governance/form of ownership/source of budget	Ministerial jurisdiction[a]
				Specialised				
Academies/state	Bogdan Khmelnytskyi's National Academy of State Border Service; Academy of Internal Troops of Ukraine; Ukrainian Academy of Internal Affairs; National Metallurgical Academy of Ukraine	10	Khmelnytskyi, Kharkiv, Kyiv, Dnipro	Sectoral speciality	High to medium	High	State	Ministry of Education and Science
Academies/non-state	National Academy of Management	1	Kyiv	Sectoral speciality	Medium	Medium	Private	Ministry of Education and Science
				Nationwide specialised				
Technical HEIs/state	Kharkiv Petro Vasylenko's National Technical University of Agriculture; Lviv National Polytechnic; Kharkiv National Polytechnic; Kyiv National Polytechnic; Donetsk National Polytechnic; Central Ukrainian National Polytechnic; Ivano-Frankivsk National Technical University of Oil and Gas; Donbas State Technical University	15	Kharkiv, Lviv, Kyiv, Donetsk, Kirovohrad, Kherson, Volyn, Poltava, Zaporizhia, Ternopil, Vinnytsia	Technical	Medium but above average for HEIs	High	State	Ministry of Education and Science

(continued)

Table 16.3 (continued)

Type	Examples of HEIs	Quantity	City or region	Educational profile	Research activity	International activity	Form of governance/form of ownership/source of budget	Ministerial jurisdiction[a]
Sectoral HEIs/state	National University of Pharmacy; Odessa National Economics University; Sumy National Agrarian University; Tugan-Baranovsky's Donetsk National University of Economics and Trade'; National University "Yaroslav the Wise Law Academy of Ukraine"; National Aviation University; National Pedagogical Dragomanov University; Ukrainian National Forestry University; South Ukrainian National Pedagogical University; Admiral Makarov National University of Shipbuilding; Tchaikovsky National Music Academy of Ukraine; Banking University; Ukrainian Academy of Banking of the National Bank of Ukraine[c]	65	Kharkiv, Kyiv, Mykolayiv, Donetsk, Lviv, Vinnytsia, Zhytomyr, Dnipro, Ternopil, Ivano-Frankivsk, Volyn, Sumy	Sectoral speciality	Medium	High to medium	State	Ministry of Education as well as a corresponding Sectoral Ministry (e.g. Ministry of Healthcare for Medical HEIs)
Total nationwide and flagship HEIs		113						

(continued)

Table 16.3 (continued)

Type	Examples of HEIs	Quantity	City or region	Educational profile	Research activity	International activity	Form of governance/form of ownership/source of budget	Ministerial jurisdiction[a]
				Regional HEIs				
				Comprehensive				
Regional comprehensive universities	Sumy State University; Kherson State University; Zhytomyr State University; Nizhyn Gogol State University; Mariupil State University; Mukachevo State University	6	Sumy, Kherson, Zhytomyr, Chernihiv, Mariupil, Zakarpattya	Multidisciplinary	Medium to low	Medium	State	Ministry of Education
Regional comprehensive universities/ non-state	Ukrainian Catholic University; Alfred Nobel University; European University; Lutsk University Institute of Human Development "Ukraine"; Classic Private University; International Solomon University; Bukovyna University	11	Dnipro, Lviv, Kyiv, Volyn, Zaporizhia, Odessa, Chernivtsi	Multidisciplinary	Medium to low	Medium	Non-state	Ministry of Education
				Specialised				
Academies/ state	Dnipropetrivsk State Medical Academy; Donbas State Machine-Building Academy; Academy of Municipal Management; Ukrainian Engineering Pedagogics Academy; Odessa State Academy of Civil Engineering and Architecture; Prydniprovska State Academy of Civil Engineering and Architecture; Military Academy; Kirovograd Flight Academy	29	Dnipropetrivsk, Donetsk, Kyiv, Kharkiv, Odesa, Poltava, Zaporizhia, Lviv, Kherson, Kirovograd, Poltava, Dnipro	Sectoral speciality	Medium	Medium	State	Ministry of Education as well as a corresponding Sectoral Ministry (e.g. Ministry of Healthcare for Medical Academies)

(continued)

Table 16.3 (continued)

Type	Examples of HEIs	Quantity	City or region	Educational profile	Research activity	International activity	Form of governance/form of ownership/source of budget	Ministerial jurisdiction[a]
Academies/ non-state	Lawyer Academy of Ukraine; Interregional Academy of Personnel Management; Academy of Work; Social Relations and Tourism	3	Kyiv	Sectoral speciality	Medium to low	Medium	Non-state	Ministry of Education as well as a corresponding Sectoral Ministry (e.g. Ministry of Healthcare for Medical Academies)
Regional HEIs Specialised								
Academies/ municipal	Kremenets Regional Humanitarian Pedagogical Academy; Vinnytsia Academy of Continuous Education; Kharkiv Humanitarian Pedagogical Academy of Regional Council	3	Kharkiv, Ternopil, Vinnytsia	Sectoral speciality	Low	Low	Municipal	Ministry of Education
Technical HEIs/state	Podilsky Technical University of Agrarian Science; Mykolaiv Polytechnic; Pryazovskyi State Technical University; Dneprodzerzhinsk State Technical University; Zhytomyr State Technological University	5	Mariupil, Khmelnytskyi, Donetsk, Mykolaiv, Zhytomyr	Technical	Medium to low	Medium	State	Ministry of Education
Technical HEIs/ non-state	International Science Technical University of Yuri Bugay; Mykolaiv Polytechnic Institute	2	Kyiv, Mykolaiv					

(continued)

Table 16.3 (continued)

Type	Examples of HEIs	Quantity	City or region	Educational profile	Research activity	International activity	Form of governance/form of ownership/ source of budget	Ministerial jurisdiction[a]
Sectoral HEIs/state	Bukowinian State Medical University; State University of Telecommunications; Ternopil State Medical University; Zaporizhia State Medical University; Podilsky Technical University of Agrarian Science; Izmail State University of Humanities; Tavria State Agrotechnological University; Kosiv Institute of Applied and Decorative Art	87	Chernivtsi, Kyiv, Ternopil, Zaporizhia, Dnipro, Ivano-Frankivsk, Khmelnytskyi, Kherson, Odessa, Kharkiv, Poltava, Dnipro, Lviv, Chernihiv, Luhansk, Zaporizhia, Zhytomyr, Kropyvnytskyi, Donetsk	Sectoral speciality	Medium to low	Medium		Ministry of Education
				Regional specialised				
Sectoral HEIs/ non-state	Kyiv Medical University of Ukrainian Academy of Untraditional Medicine; International University of Business and Law; International University of Finance; Kyiv University of Law; KROK University; Hungarian Institute of Ferenc Rákóczi II; Kyiv School of Economics; Tourism Institute of Federation of Trade Unions of Ukraine[d]	40[c]	Kyiv, Kherson, Ternopil, Khmelnytskyi, Zakarpattia, Rivne, Odessa, Kropyvnytskyi, Lviv, Volyn, Kharkiv, Dnipro	Sectoral speciality	Low	Medium	Private/ cooperative/joint ownership	Ministry of Education

(continued)

Table 16.3 (continued)

Type	Examples of HEIs	Quantity	City or region	Educational profile	Research activity	International activity	Form of governance/form of ownership/source of budget	Ministerial jurisdiction[a]
Sectoral HEIs/ municipal	Zhytomyr Institute of Nursing; Institute of business "Strategy"; Kyiv Cooperative Institute of Business and Law	3	Zhytomyr, Dnipro, Kyiv	Sectoral speciality	Low	Low	Municipal	Ministry of Education
Total regional		189						
Other types of IHE (branches of overseas or joint HEIs)	Wisconsin International University in Ukraine; Central European University (Ukrainian-Polish)	2	Kyiv	Specialised (economics and business)	Low	High	Private	Ministry of Education
Total HEIs		304						

[a]According to Order No. 1191-p of the Cabinet of Ministers of Ukraine (2011), all HEIs in Ukraine will be transferred over time to the jurisdiction of the MoE which licences their operations. However, in practice, sectoral HEIs have to coordinate and agree their curriculum with sectoral Ministries before seeking approval from the MoE.

[b]These and several other institutions from the Donetsk and Luhansk Regions have been evacuated from the region of military operations to other areas of Ukraine. In some cases, parallel versions of these institutions continue to operate in their original locations but their formal identification with Ukraine (through licencing) is not recognised by the Ukrainian side.

[c]These HEIs come under the jurisdiction of the National Bank of Ukraine.

[d]This institution is also under the jurisdiction of the Federation of Trade Unions of Ukraine.

[e]The total number of non-state institutions in this typology amounts to 59, which is considerably fewer than the 169 reported to exist in Ukraine by the State Office of Statistics of Ukraine (2016).

Another thought-provoking phenomenon apparent in the most recent legislative changes is a tendency for policy makers to blame academic staff for poor implementation of the changes and a corresponding resentment of academic staff towards the government for not creating sufficient legal and system-wide provisions to enable the implementation processes. For instance, although universities are allowed in principle to hold their own bank accounts, the legal and procedural details of this change have not yet been implemented, making it impossible for universities to take advantage of this opportunity. These conversations appear to be happening at cross purposes and much gets lost in translation (e.g. Fedorchenko 2016; National Aviation University 2015). On the positive side, there is evidence of dialogue between the power and the people, which had previously been suppressed.

In addition to the most obvious stakeholders in HE, government, academic staff and university administrators who find themselves in strenuous and difficult relationships with one another, the discourse of comparison and critique also pervades the minds of students, many of whom prefer to study abroad and often fail to return to Ukraine after completion of their studies. This creates a problem known as 'brain drain' or 'brain waste' (Semiv and Hvozdovych 2012). At the time of writing, this exit appears to be the primary if not the only mechanism accessible to students to communicate their views on the state of the national HE system.

Employers are equally dissatisfied. According to the World Economic Forum Global Competitiveness Report (2011), despite relatively comprehensive higher education coverage (8th place out of 142 countries), Ukraine takes the 51st place in terms of perceived quality. According to the survey, employers complain about the lack of important employability skills, including critical analysis, emotional, technical and even basic mathematical skills. Despite this documented dissatisfaction, the Federation of Employers in Ukraine's involvement in higher education reforms remains minimal. In stark opposition are the views of rectors on the quality and state of higher education in the country. According to a survey conducted by the Ukrainian Democratic Initiatives Foundation, most rectors report high quality of education in their institutions and raise concerns around poor funding and disinterested students (Democratic Initiatives Foundation 2015). One may conclude that the views and opinions of various stakeholders on the state of quality of the HE system in Ukraine are akin to those of the fabled blind men touching an elephant, though most agree on the notion of crisis. Responsibility for the crisis, however, is pushed around like a football on a playing field. On the whole, the *comparison and critique* discourse lacks a clear sense of agency and, as a result, has not had any significant impact on the structure or extent of differentiation of the HE system. The Soviet legacy remains largely untouched.

Catch-Up Europeanisation

If the HE system is seen as being in crisis, Europeanisation or rather *catch-up Europeanisation*, the third policy rationale identified by Fimyar (2010), is seen as the strategy by which to emerge from crisis. Based on extensive study of policy documents pertinent to higher education reform, Fimyar (2020, 81) concludes that this narrative is widespread and all-pervading, seeking to reach 'every subject, organisation, as well as the system of education as a whole, to align existing Ukrainian norms, capacities, and ethos with those in 'Europe' and the "world"'. The most obvious manner in which this narrative is manifested in practice is Ukraine's joining the Bologna Process in 2005. Experiments with Bachelors' degrees inspired by the Bologna Process started as early as the year 2000. More widely, this policy rationale pervades all strategies of moving from the 'old' system to the 'new', bridging the gap between the 'ideal' and the 'real', as well as all the tools and changes aimed at resolving the educational crisis described above. The practical implementations, however, are riddled with difficulties and often encounter insurmountable resistance from various actors in the system. In fact, resistance appears to be the most common way for various stakeholders to respond to changes implemented from above. A case study by Shaw et al. (2013) presents multiple examples of academics trapped by competing external pressures as well as the internal need for meaning derived from their work. These tensions lead to selective adaptation of the Bologna requirements. Clearly, the role of lower-level stakeholders should not be underestimated in the process of changes. Although the approach to the reforms has gradually become more democratic (as part of the catch-up Europeanisation narrative) as more and more information is shared with lower-level stakeholders and some consultations are taking place (e.g. with the Council of Rectors), the relationship between the government, institutions and academic staff within them appears to be pervaded with low levels of trust. This, in turn, causes difficulties in communication and panic amongst the lower levels as a response to changes, and possibly a hesitation to communicate more openly on the part of such strategic actors as the Ministry. Such tensions may be indicative of more deeply seated problems described by Kovryga and Nickel (2006) as a cycle of false necessities in the reform processes in Ukraine, for which they partly blame excessive pressures for reform from the West and the very high speed of change.

Admittedly, Europeanisation has impacted different parts of the system to different degrees. Larger, national-level HEIs have had better access to student mobility programmes, staff professional development opportunities which often bring Western notions into the Ukrainian realities (e.g. empowerment) and joint degrees with overseas institutions. HEIs located in Kiev also tend to have an advantage due to their relatively better accessibility for foreign visitors. Smaller institutions located in smaller towns tend to have less contact with their EU counterparts, less funding to finance international conferences or institutional visits and, as a result, develop fewer international links. International links and academic staff with overseas backgrounds form an attractive and prestigious feature for students. Hence, to a certain extent, Europeanisation policies have contributed to the vertical diversification of the institutional landscape.

The Law on Higher Education (2014) and the Most Recent Changes in the Institutional Landscape

The recently adopted Law on Higher Education (2014) has a special significance in the process of HE reform in Ukraine and comes at a significant time in Ukrainian history, following the Revolution of Dignity and the assertive stance Ukraine adopted on national self-governance. As insufficient time has yet to pass from its adoption it would be unreasonable to expect fully fledged implementation at the time of writing. It is, however, important to note several aspects which weave in the above-mentioned changes, leading to already noticeable alterations in the institutional landscape.

First of all, there is an explicit effort to engage all the most immediate stakeholders of HE with the quality assurance process. The newly created Quality Assurance Agency is expected to draw on representatives of academic staff (excluding senior managers), employers and students. Secondly, rectors will once again be elected, with students' voices having a greater impact (15% in proportional representation) on the outcome than before, which democratises the system. The Ministry of Education will be obliged to appoint rectors who have been elected in this fashion, regardless of the Ministry's own views. This is a clear step towards supporting institutional autonomy and self-governance. The Law abolishes the concept of levels of accreditation, which simplifies the typology of HEI and leaves four types of institutions: comprehensive universities, specialised institutes, academies and colleges. This change has not yet been fully implemented. Moreover, the Ministry of Education is planning to discontinue the direct financing of colleges, leaving them attached to the municipal budgets. Expert observers predict that this will cause colleges to merge with higher status HEIs, thus reducing their overall number. Given the extremely high number of level I and II colleges at the time of writing (over 1500) and the high likelihood of forthcoming comprehensive changes in this part of the system, the authors have chosen to present only level III and IV institutions in the most up to date typology of Ukrainian HEIs. Although this part of the overall system appears to be more stable than institutions with lower levels of accreditation, it is not completely shielded from changes. The recent Minister of Education Serhiy Kvit had tackled the rather high numbers of HEIs of III and IV levels of accreditation with plans and some actions to reduce their numbers via closures and mergers. For example, the Lugansk State Institute of Housing and Utilities and Building was closed in 2015 (Cabinet of Ministers 2015). Moreover, the Accreditation Commission that functions under the jurisdiction of the Ministry of Education announced a list of 60 HEIs in 2015 that may be closed following quality control revisions of their curriculum and study programmes. The process is on-going and the full impact on the institutional landscape remains to be seen.

At the time of writing, the Ukrainian HE system amounted to around 300 HEIs of levels III and IV of accreditation with clear elements of vertical and horizontal differentiation. Flagship institutions present the most successful ones, both in terms of the status granted by the government (highly autonomous with their own budgets) as well as consolidated independent rankings (a market element of the system) (Osvita.ua 2016). These institutions, however, occupy very low positions in the Times Higher Education Rankings of HEIs worldwide (Times Higher Education Rankings 2016). The overall picture suggests that the number of technical HEIs has been considerably reduced in comparison with 1988 (Table 16.2), with only 22 institutions remaining, 20 of which are state owned. The total number of comprehensive universities amounts to 28 state (22 national and 6 regional) and 11 non-state establishments, whereas specialised institutions are much more numerous, with 181 state-owned, 44 non-state-owned and 6 supported by municipal budgets.

Conclusions

Ukrainian HE developments inevitably testify to the path dependency and reliance on the post-Soviet legacy as the point of departure—either by seeking to overcome it or to incorporate it into the new realities. Similarly, the fascination with EU developments and the zeal to modernise the system represent an equally strong driver that impels Ukraine to implement changes, assimilate Bologna alterations and seek developmental inspiration from the West. The black box in the middle between these two drivers represents authentic and unique Ukrainian concerns, aspirations and visions of how and why the HE system has to function for the distinctive needs of Ukrainian economy and society. Like most other post-Soviet but also European nations, Ukraine is seeking to reshape its system of Higher Education to fit into the globalised world, whilst ensuring the country's interests are sufficiently protected.

The chaotic 1990s released a great amount of creative resources, which up until then had been securely hidden under Soviet regulatory pressure. This, in turn, unleashed the process of growth and institutional diversification along with the increased participation rates, resulting in a somewhat hectic and overgrown higher education system. The diversity of institutional types and horizontal differentiation in the system has also increased with the proliferation of non-state and municipal universities, academies and institutes. The number of technical institutions has decreased in comparison with the late Soviet period, whereas institutions specialising in the social sciences have outperformed the needs of the economy to a certain extent. On the other hand, many HEIs have achieved a fairly respected status, thus driving vertical differentiation, both as recognised by the government and in the market driven rating systems, and they continue to perform critical functions in supplying the nation with qualified graduates.

Multiple political, demographic, economic and social currents underpin the dynamics of the HE system in the country. Although the most visible agency of change remains in the hands of the government, the role of the academic staff, students and employers is becoming more and more noticeable and impactful, which is being gradually recognised via official mechanisms (the Quality Assurance Agency). Still, many of the factors influencing change are not fully incorporated into conscious decision-making processes or influential debates, which perpetuates the bottleneck in the communicating vessels metaphorically representing various stakeholders. Low levels of trust, divergent points of view on the suitability of quality and functions of higher education and lack of dialogue amongst stakeholders hold the developments back but may also be maintaining an illusory equilibrium which is needed for stability and continuity. Having outgrown the country's needs, the HE system is now viewed as being in need of closures and mergers of individual HEIs. This process is inevitably painful and fear-inducing at the institutional level as well as that of individual academics and university graduates. It may be a necessary undertaking but how it is managed will make a big difference for the future health and stability of the system. Top-down threats, even when justified, still echo painfully in the post-communist mindset and demand special care in the implementation process. Ironically, the government appears to lack precisely the understanding of the implementation processes and mechanisms required to ensure a smoother and less traumatic experience for stakeholders at the lower levels. Although the Western literature is full of such recommendations concerning implementation of reforms, it rarely takes into account the depth of pre-existing disturbances that proliferate in post-Soviet societies (e.g. Bittner 2014). Ukraine, like other post-Soviet states, needs to find its own path to continue modernising and organising the HE system more effectively, reflecting its specific geographical location, demographic trends, including the levels of mobility amongst young and intelligent students, history and future prospects, whilst maintaining a fragile equilibrium. The uniqueness of one's path, however, does not preclude collaboration or seeking support from outside actors, both Western and from fellow post-Soviet states. The devil as always hides in the details.

Note

1. This chapter refers to contemporary Ukraine's territory as recognised by the United Nations unless explicitly stated otherwise.

Bibliography

Bilaniuk, L., and S. Melnyk. 2008. A Tense and Shifting Balance: Bilingualism and Education in Ukraine. *International Journal of Bilingual Education and Bilingualism* 11 (3–4): 340–372.

Bittner, S. 2014. *Myth, Memory, Trauma – The Stalinist Past and the Post-Soviet Present*. Russian History Blog. Available at: http://russianhistoryblog.org/2014/05/myth-memory-trauma-the-stalinist-past-and-the-post-soviet-present/. Accessed 3 Oct 2016.

Buhalo, C.M. 1945. Sostoyanie i Ocherednye Zadachi Vyzov Ukrainy. *Vestnik Vyschey Schkoly.*
Bunina, L.M. 2013. Istoriya Vyshoi Osvity Ukrainy. *UDK* 378 (09): 477.
Byron. 2001. Conflicts Over Language Impede Ukraine's Higher-Education System. *Chronicle of Higher Education* 00095982, 47(21).
Cabinet of Ministers of Ukraine. 2011. *Deyaki Putannya Upravlinnya Vyschymy Navchalnumu Zakladamy.* 1191-p,Kiev, November 16.
———. 2015. *Pro Likvidaciyu Vyschogo navchalnogo Zakladu 'Luhanskyi Derzhavnyi Institut Zhytlovo-komunalnogo gospodarstva i budivnyctva'.* № 656-p, Kiev, June 26.
Democratic Initiatives Foundation. 2015. *Survey of Rectors Results.* Available at: www.dif.org.ua. Accessed 30 Sept 2016.
Fedorchenko, Y. 2016. *Reform of Higher Education.* Available at: http://osvita.ua/vnz/reform/50808/. Accessed 30 Sept 2016.
Fimyar, O. 2010. Policy Why(s): Policy Rationalities and the Changing Logic of Educational Reform in Post-communist Ukraine. Post-socialism Is Not Dead: (Re)Reading the Global in Comparative Education. *International Perspectives on Education and Society* 14: 61–91.
Huisman, J., V.L. Meek, and F.Q. Wood. 2007. Institutional Diversity in Higher Education: A Cross-National and Longitudinal Analysis. *Higher Education Quarterly* 61 (4): 563–577.
Janmaat, J.G. 2008. Nation Building, Democratization and Globalization as Competing Priorities in Ukraine's Education System. *Nationalities Papers* 36 (1): 1–23.
Johnston, D.B., and O. Bain. 2002. Universities in Transition: Privatisation, Decentralisation, and Institutional Autonomy as National Policy with Special Reference to the Russian Federation. In *Higher Education in the Developing World*, ed. D. Chapman and A. Austin, 45–68. Westport: Greenwood Press.
Kovryga, O., and P.M. Nickel. 2006. In a Cycle of False Necessity? escaping from Embedded Quasi-Institutions and Building a New System of Public Administration and Management in Ukraine. *International Journal of Public Administration* 29 (13): 1151–1166.
Kurbatov, S. 2014. Before Massification: Access to University Education in Ukraine in 1950s–1980s. *International Review of Social Research* 4 (2): 75–86.
Law on Education. 1991. Kyiv: Parliament of Ukraine.
Law on Higher Education. 2002. Kyiv: Parliament of Ukraine.
———. 2014. Kyiv: Parliament of Ukraine.
Ministry of Statistics. 2003. *Statystychnyi shchorichnyk Ukrainy za 2002 rik.* Kiev: Konsul'tant. (statistical yearbook of Ukraine for 2002).
Narodnoe Obrazovanie i Kultira v SSSR. 1989. *Statisticheskiy Sbornik.* Moscow: Finansy i Statistika.

National Aviation University. 2015. Sergiy Kiv is lying. *Reiderske Zahoplennya*. Available at: Reider-nau.com. Accessed 30 Sept 2016.

Osipian, A. 2008. Transforming University Governance in Ukraine: Collegiums, Bureaucracies, and Political Institutions. *Munich Personal RePEc Archive Paper*, No. 11058. Available at: http://mpra.ub.uni-muenchen.de/11058. Accessed 3 Oct 2015.

Osvita.ua. 2016. *Consolidated University Rankings*. Available at: http://osvita.ua/legislation/Vishya_osvita/25395/. Accessed 30 Sept 2016.

Parliamentary Decrees. 2002. *On the Results of the Parliamentary Hearings 'On the Implementation of the Education Laws'*. No. 210–215, October.

Presidential Decree. 1995. *On the Main Directions of Higher Education Reform in Ukraine*. No. 832/95, September.

Semiv, L., and Y. Hvozdovych. 2012. The Intellectual Migration of the Youth in Ukraine: The Backgrounds for 'Brain Circulation'. *Journal of International Studies* 5 (2): 72–81.

Shaw, M., D. Chapman, and N. Rumyantseva. 2013. Organizational Culture in the Adoption of the Bologna Process: A Study of Academic Staff at a Ukrainian University. *Studies in Higher Education* 38 (7): 989–1003.

Silova, I. 2009. Varieties of Educational Transformation: The Post-socialist States of Central/South Eastern Europe and the Former Soviet Union. In *International Handbook of Comparative Education*, ed. R. Cowen and A.M. Kazamias, 295–320. Dordrecht: Springer.

State Office of Statistics of Ukraine. 2015. *Publikacia Dokumentov Gosudarstvennoi Sluzhby Statistiki Ukrainy*. Available at: http://ukrstat.org. Accessed 30 Sept 2016.

———. 2016. *Publikacia Dokumentov Gosudarstvennoi Sluzhby Statistiki Ukrainy*. Available at: http://ukrstat.org. Accessed 30 Sept 2016.

Teichler, U. 1988. *Changing Patterns of the Higher Education System*. London: Jessica Kingsley.

Times Higher Education. 2015–2016. World University Rankings. Available at: https://www.timeshighereducation.com/world-university-rankings/2016/world-ranking. Accessed 30 Sept 2016.

World Economic Forum. 2011–2012. *World Economic Forum Global Competitiveness Report*. Geneva, Switzerland.

Yershova, O., and A. Gordiichuk. 2013. University Autonomy in Ukraine: International Experience and National Interests. *American Journal of Educational Research* 1 (11): 472–476. doi:10.12691/education-1-11-3.

Nataliya L. Rumyantseva is a senior lecturer at the University of Greenwich, London, United Kingdom. Her research interests include higher education management and policy, leadership development and ethics in education in the developing nations. Nataliya is very sympathetic to the struggles that Former Soviet Union nations are confronting in order to overcome the setbacks and develop their own sense of identity whilst at the time fitting in with the international and global developments. Her research aims to offer a compassionate and yet critical approach in order to enable growth and development beyond imagination. She is particularly interested in enhancing understanding of inner workings of the higher education systems through the lens of ethical issues, paradoxes and professional development of academic staff and management. She is currently involved in the Tempus Project (ELITE) on Higher Education Leadership Development with seven Ukrainian partner institutions.

Olena I. Logvynenko is a *dotsent* at the Department of Theory and History of State at the National University of Life and Environmental Sciences, Ukraine. A lawyer by training, Olena has served as a professor and a Head of Department in several Ukrainian institutions for over 5 years. A prolific researcher, Olena concentrates on the issues of women's rights, children's rights and broader ecological human rights from the contemporary and the historical perspectives. Olena is now extending her interests into the area of higher education studies applying the principles of ecological perspective.

Open Access This chapter is distributed under the terms of the Creative Commons Attribution 4.0 International License (http://creativecommons.org/licenses/by/4.0/), which permits use, duplication, adaptation, distribution and reproduction in any medium or format, as long as you give appropriate credit to the original author(s) and the source, provide a link to the Creative Commons license and indicate if changes were made.

The images or other third party material in this chapter are included in the chapter's Creative Commons license, unless indicated otherwise in a credit line to the material. If material is not included in the chapter's Creative Commons license and your intended use is not permitted by statutory regulation or exceeds the permitted use, you will need to obtain permission directly from the copyright holder.

CHAPTER 17

Uzbekistan: Higher Education Reforms and the Changing Landscape Since Independence

Kobil Ruziev and Umar Burkhanov

INTRODUCTION

Higher education (HE) played an important role in the pre-independence period under central planning, as it helped to provide the economy with specialist skills to support the country's industrialisation drive; it also served as a means through which the prevailing ideology was promoted. HE plays a no less important role in modern market-based economies. In well-functioning meritocratic economic systems, HE can serve as a catalyst for achieving social mobility and cohesion, matching individual aspirations and societal goals in the process.

Uzbekistan has a long tradition of HE, albeit in a narrower sense of the term. It inherited territory mostly comprising the three independent khanates (kingdoms ruled by *Khans*) centred in Bukhara, Khiva

---

K. Ruziev (✉)
Bristol Business School, University of the West of England, Bristol, UK

U. Burkhanov
Tashkent Institute of Finance, Tashkent, Uzbekistan

© The Author(s) 2018
J. Huisman et al. (Eds.), *25 Years of Transformations of Higher Education Systems in Post-Soviet Countries*, Palgrave Studies in Global Higher Education, https://doi.org/10.1007/978-3-319-52980-6_17

and Kokand, which ruled central Asia between the sixteenth and nineteenth centuries. The education system in pre-Soviet times in central Asia, also known as Turkistan at the time, included *maktabs* (schools) and *madrasas* (colleges), both funded by landed estates and charitable donations. *Maktabs* taught basic reading and writing skills, and more talented students went to study at *madrasas* by the age of 14, where they would spend another 10 years studying theology, literature, law, philosophy and other worldly wisdom (Allworth 1994; Majidov et al. 2010). One of the universities in modern Uzbekistan, Samarkand State University, claims to be a spiritual heir to Samarkand's well-known fifteenth century *Madrasai Oliya* (Higher Madrasa) established by Timurid king and astronomer Ulugbek, where advanced math and astronomy were also taught. The country's first modern and secular HE institution, Turkistan National University, was created in April 1918 in Tashkent under Soviet rule. The name of the university has changed several times since then: to Central Asian State University in 1923, Tashkent State University in 1960 and finally to the National University of Uzbekistan in 2000.

This chapter is the first study that carefully documents the evolution of higher education reforms in Uzbekistan since the demise of the Soviet Union (SU). It examines key HE reforms undertaken in Uzbekistan since independence and analyses the impact of these reforms on the changing landscape of the HE system in the country. The study highlights complex interactions between policy legislation and its implementation on the one hand, and the demands of the new market-based economic system and the requirements of building and strengthening state institutions on the other hand.

In the next section, we provide brief background information on Uzbekistan's unique approach to transition, as it closely resonates with the country's HE system reforms. The basic determinants of HE demand since independence are discussed in the section 'Determinants of HE Demand'. In the section 'Key HE Reforms Since Independence', we discuss the key characteristics of the HE system at the time of independence and examine fundamental and systematic HE reforms introduced since 1991. The impact of HE reforms in shaping the current HE landscape in the country is analysed in the section 'Reforms and the Current Landscape of HE'. Finally, discussions and concluding remarks are presented in the section 'Discussion and Concluding Remarks'.

Uzbekistan's General Approach to Economic Reforms

Unprecedented political and economic developments that swept across the former communist bloc countries in the late 1980s and the early 1990s did not leave Uzbekistan unaffected. Similar to other former Soviet republics, the country gained its independence in 1991 after the dissolution of the SU. The disintegration of the SU was seen by many as final proof of the triumph of a market-based economic system over one that is centrally planned. Following the prevailing euphoric expectations at the time about the advantages of a market-based economic system, Uzbekistan also joined other post-communist economies and committed itself to a transition towards a market economy.

Transition from a centrally planned economy to a market-based economy, as promoted by influential international financial institutions such as the International Monetary Fund and the World Bank, required fundamental and comprehensive reforms in both sociopolitical and economic spheres of life. In terms of the former, this entailed a move away from a single-party administrative bureaucratic system towards a multiparty civil society based on democratic institutions and a replacement of communist ideology with a national ideology that was consistent with free market principles. In terms of the latter, this involved the introduction and protection of private property rights, privatisation of state-owned enterprises and facilitation of private entrepreneurial initiatives. Further institutional reforms in the monetary, banking, fiscal and judiciary systems, as well as price liberalisation and the achievement of macroeconomic stabilisation, were needed to support the transformation process. Changing the structure and composition of disciplines taught at higher education institutions (HEIs) and reorienting the priorities of the HE system were equally important as the system prepared personnel for the new economic system and social order.

Although the Uzbek government agreed with the essence of this comprehensive reform package, its gradualist approach to transition was unique in terms of the pace, sequencing and prioritisation of reforms, resulting in the so-called Uzbek model of economic development (Pomfret 2000). The Uzbek model emphasised, among other things, the guiding role of the state during transition, the precedence of economics over politics and a gradualist approach to reform implementation (Karimov 1995, 1998). Hence, in principle, Uzbekistan adopted a 'developmental state' approach to transition: the authorities decided to maintain complete control over the 'commanding heights' of the economy, including the HE sector as well as the transport, communications and media industries and the financial, agricultural and extractive sectors.

The regulations allow the entry of small-scale private enterprises to certain sectors such as finance and agriculture, but large organisations with systemic importance remain state-owned and hence state-controlled. In other sectors, such as HE and extractive industries, no direct private sector participation is permitted. It is therefore not surprising that Uzbekistan's general approach to HE reforms has been described as top-down and strictly centralised, offering little or no autonomy to HEIs in matters concerning course design, student intake and management of own finances (Weidman and Yoder 2010).

Determinants of HE Demand

The supply of and demand for HE services play equally important roles in shaping the structure of a national HE sector. Public policy and regulation ultimately determine the quantity of HE supply and at what cost it will be provided. The key demand-side factors, on the other hand, include structural transformation of the economy, improvements in per capita income levels, demographic conditions, and the changing aspirations and preferences of the general public. Before embarking on a detailed analysis of HE policy and regulation, we will briefly discuss some of these demand-side phenomena.

With a population of over 20 million, Uzbekistan was the third largest former Soviet republic in 1990 after the Russian Federation and the Ukraine. It was, however, one of the poorest and least industrialised countries of the Soviet Union: its per capita income level in 1988 was only 62 % of the USSR average and the share of industrial production in GDP was 33 % in 1990 (Ruziev et al. 2007). The country's population increased from around 21 million in 1991 to around 31 million in 2014 (ADB 2015). Further, the share of 14- to 24-year-olds in the general population expanded by over 1 million between 1990 and 2015, which highlights a significant growth in demand for HE services during independence.

Figure 17.1 shows data on the changing structure of the economy during independence. In 1993, in terms of the national income, agriculture accounted for 36 %; manufacturing, mining, energy and construction jointly accounted for 35 %; public administration, trade and transport for

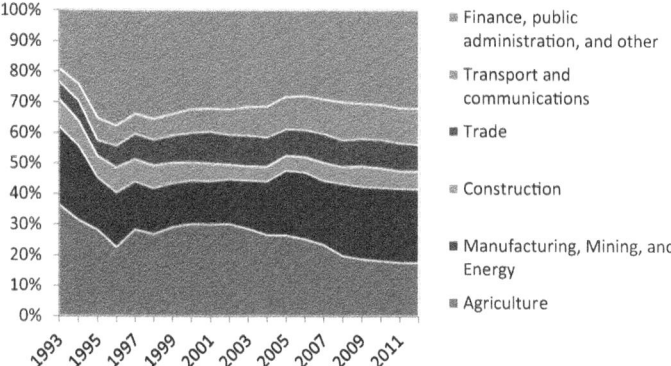

Fig. 17.1 Share of GDP by industrial origin in Uzbekistan, 1993–2012 (Source: ADB (2015))

around 10 %; and financial and other services for the remaining 19 %. As the economy slowly moved towards a free market system, some sectors shrunk and others expanded in relative size. The most notable changes can be observed in relation to agriculture, which fell by almost half, to 17 % of GDP by 2012, and services, which increased from around 30 % of GDP in 1993 to more than 50 % of GDP in 2012. Although the share of manufacturing, mining and energy in the national income remained relatively stable during this time, the composition changed. While some industries shrank in size or disappeared (agricultural machine building shrank, and airplane building industries disappeared), others emerged and expanded (a strong automotive industry emerged, and the mining and energy sectors expanded).

As the composition of the economy changed, so did the structure of the demand for labour. As can be seen in Fig. 17.2, in 1991 more than 40 % of the employed labour force worked in agriculture, 14 % in industry and the rest in other sectors. By 2012, only 27 % of the employed labour force worked in agriculture, 13 % in industry and the remaining 60 % in the services sector. The growing importance of services is a natural phenomenon, as the sector was underdeveloped in the centrally planned economy. Further, the demand for services is expected to increase even more with rising per capita income levels: it is estimated that four of every five new jobs created in the economy between 2010 and 2030 will be in the services sector (World Bank 2014, 28).

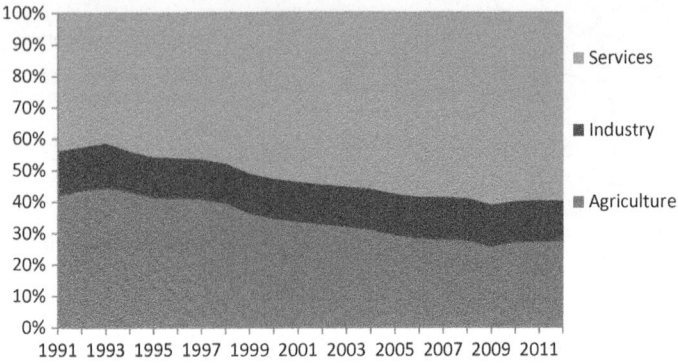

Fig. 17.2 Employment by economic sector in Uzbekistan, 1991–2012 (Source: ADB (2015))

In terms of economic performance, the size of the economy expanded and per capital income levels also rose notably during transition, after a slight dip in the early 1990s (Ruziev et al. 2007). The economy has experienced strong and sustained growth of around 8 % per year since the mid-2000s. The country's GDP, measured in current US dollars, grew from around $US13 billion in 1990 to more than $US63 billion in 2014. In PPP dollar terms, it grew from $US62 billion in 1990 to around $US165 billion in 2014 (World Bank 2015). Per capita income levels also rose during this period. GDP per capita rose from around $US650 in 1990 to more than $US2000 in 2014 in current US dollars, and from around $US3000 in 1990 to $US5300 in 2014 in PPP dollar terms. In terms of income distribution, limited available data indicate an inverted U-shaped behaviour for the period between 1988 and 2003: the Gini coefficient was 24 in 1988, 44 in 1998, 36 in 2000 and 35 in 2003 (World Bank 2015).

The demand for HE increased strongly during independence in response to changing economic conditions and demographic dynamics, necessitating a supply-side transformation in the HE sector. In line with a generally cautious and gradualist approach by the authorities to transition, however, HE sector reforms were introduced only slowly and gradually. Some important changes, although ad hoc in nature, were introduced in the first half of the 1990s. These included the enactment of the Law on Education in 1992 combined with growth of student intakes in accounting, banking, economics and other business related disciplines, which were deemed particularly important in the early years of transition. Truly fundamental and systematic reforms, however, were not introduced until the second half of the 1990s.

Key HE Reforms Since Independence

Upon independence in 1991, Uzbekistan inherited an education system that was organisationally and structurally similar to those found in other members of the Former Soviet Union (FSU). As can be seen in Table 17.1, in 1988–89 there were 43 HEIs in Uzbekistan, including 40 specialised institutes and 3 comprehensive universities. Around 310,000 students studied 5-year taught degree courses in these HEIs, of which around 45 % were enrolled in evening and correspondence courses (Brunner and Tillett 2007, 158). Almost half of the student population specialised in education, a quarter in industry and construction, around 10 % in agriculture, and the rest in other areas such as healthcare and sports, transport and communications, and economics and law (Goskomstat 1989). With approximately 15 % of the relevant age cohort studying at HEIs in 1991, access to higher education in the country was among the lowest in the former Soviet Union (UNDP 2008).

Of the 40 specialised institutes that concentrated on specific fields of knowledge such as agriculture and medicine, 14 were teacher-training institutes specialising in education, 10 in engineering and technical studies, 7 in medical-pharmaceutical studies, 3 in agricultural studies, 3 in arts and culture, 3 in national economy and cooperative services, and 1 in physical training and sports. The three comprehensive universities offered HE courses in a wide range of specialisations, except for medicine, and were also larger, collectively accounting for around 12 % of the overall student population. The universities were better funded in terms of physical infrastructure and human capital, more prestigious and located in major politically and economically important cities such as Tashkent (the capital city since 1930), Samarkand (Uzbekistan's first capital city until 1930 and the country's cultural centre) and Nukus (the capital of the Karakalpak Autonomous Republic).

Another peculiar feature of the pre-independence HE system in Uzbekistan was that almost half of all HEIs were located in Tashkent, where around 60 % of the student population studied (see the last two columns of Table 17.1). The concentration of HEIs in Tashkent was influenced by a combination of factors. First, most manufacturing industries in

Table 17.1 Horizontal diversity by HEI type in 1988–89

HE types	Number	Student population	Located in Tashkent	Student population in Tashkent
Comprehensive universities	3	36,964	1	19,300
Specialised institutes	40	271,908	18	162,900
Total	43	308,872	19	182,200

Source: Goskomstat (1989)

pre-independence Uzbekistan were concentrated in and around Tashkent, which made the city the most prosperous administrative region in the country; its per capita output exceeded the national average by more than two and a half times. Second, Tashkent was the largest regional city in central Asia with a population of around 2 million in 1990 and had been historically seen as a higher education hub for the country and the central Asian region. For example, the National University of Uzbekistan bore the name the Central Asian University until 1960, and the Tashkent Institute of Paediatric Medicine was called the Central Asian Institute of Paediatric Medicine until 1988. Both played regionally important roles in central Asia at certain points in their history. Third, as a rule, almost all regions had teacher-training institutes. Regionally important agricultural and medical institutes existed only in some regions such as Samarkand and Andijan. Other regions such as Bukhara and Qashqadarya, which had strong natural gas and associated processing industries, also hosted technical institutes.

Reforms were introduced to the general education system only gradually, particularly the HE sector. The Law on Education, which was enacted on 2 July 1992, provided the legal foundations and laid the underlying philosophical principles for carrying out further reforms in the education system. It emphasised, among other things, a secular and ideology-free nature for the new education system. The timeline of the key HE changes since independence is illustrated in Fig. 17.3 below.

Several new HEIs were created in quick succession in the early 1990s, taking the total number of HEIs in the country to 58 by 1995–96. Twelve of these new HEIs were institutes which specialised in business studies, law, engineering and medicine. Two were specialised universities which focussed on foreign languages and international relations, respectively, and only one was a comprehensive university established on the foundations

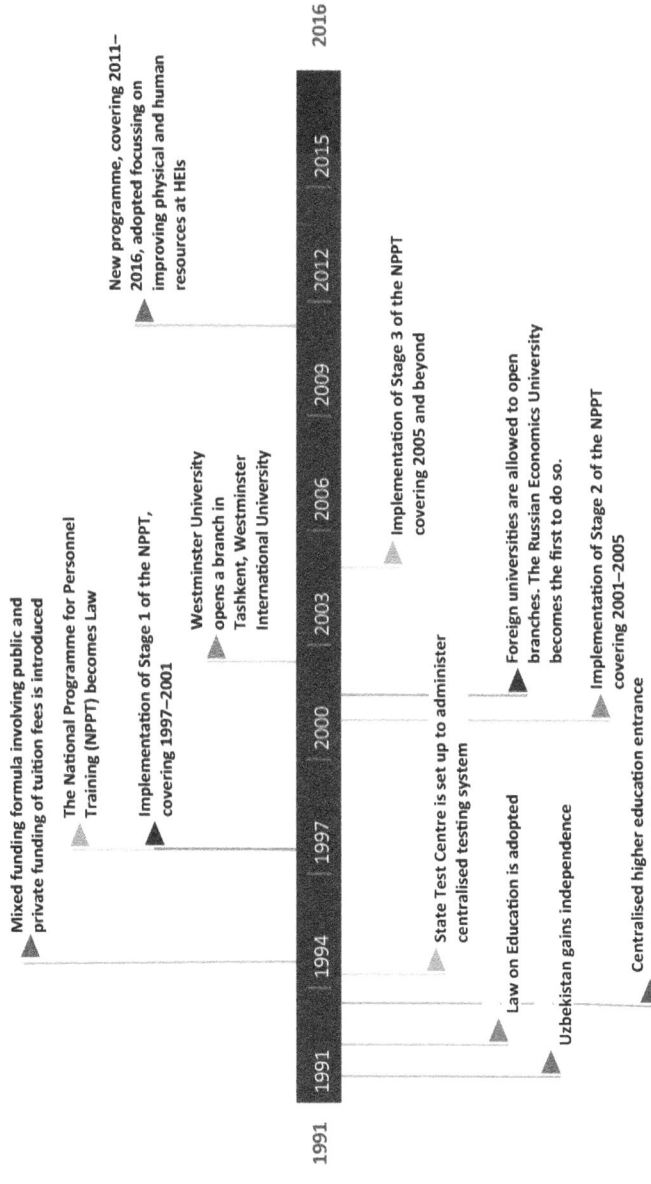

Fig. 17.3 Timeline of key changes in HE since independence

of a regional teacher-training institute. The rationale for setting up these new HEIs was dictated by the demands of the new economic system and new statehood, which necessitated strengthening and expanding state institutions. For example, transition to a market economy required a considerable expansion of the financial sector to ease the financing constraints of the emerging private sector. Further, the decentralisation of inter-enterprise relations, coupled with the exponential increase in the number of small and medium enterprises, necessitated the enlargement of the tax collection apparatus to fill the state coffers. In response, some new HEIs were established such as the Tashkent Institute of Finance and the Tax Academy, and new finance departments were created in comprehensive universities and other HEIs specialising in business studies. Likewise, independent statehood also required establishing new state ministries and agencies such as the Ministry of Foreign Affairs, the Ministry for Foreign Economic Relations and the State Customs Agency. It also required expanding others such as the Ministry of Internal Affairs, and the Ministry of Defence to maintain the law and patrol the national borders. In the short term, personnel shortages in these areas were filled by selecting and retraining teacher-training graduates who were in relatively abundant supply by default. The authorities set up new specialist HEIs, also expanding the profiles of existing ones, as a longer-term solution to prepare specialists for new and emerging sectors. The decision-making process was centralised at the top of the government structure and each decision was supported by an individual presidential decree. Most of the new HEIs were created by dividing existing HEIs and only a few were created as entirely new institutions.

For example, the Tashkent Institute of Finance and the Tashkent State University of Economics emerged from the foundations of the former Public Economy Institute. The World Economy and Diplomacy University, which focussed on preparing specialists for state institutions in the areas of international economic and political affairs, was freshly established in 1992 at a venue previously occupied by the former Communist Party School in Tashkent. The Samarkand State Institute of Foreign Languages was created in 1994 to prepare specialists for tourism industries. The Navoiy State Institute of Mining was set up in 1995 to prepare specialists for mining and other related industries in the region. The Andijan State Institute of Mechanical Engineering was created in 1995 to prepare specialists for the emerging automotive industry in the Andijan region, where the government had previously established an automobile production plant in 1992.

The Tashkent State Aviation Institute (TSAI) was created in 1995 on the basis of several institutions, including the Aviation Engineering Faculty of the Tashkent Polytechnic Institute, the Tashkent branch of the Kiev International Institute of Civil Aviation Engineering and the Tashkent Aviation College, to cater for the needs of the country's aviation industry. However, the aviation industry struggled to survive in the post-independence period and the country's only airplane construction plant went bankrupt in 2010. Anticipating this outcome, the authorities disbanded TSAI and merged it with the Tashkent State Polytechnic University in 2008.

Several private HEIs briefly emerged in the first few years of independence. Generally, these institutions had low entry requirements, and most were not adequately resourced in terms of personnel and physical infrastructure. Only one of these institutions, the Tashkent Institute for International Economic Relations and Entrepreneurship (TIIERE), was able to obtain an official licence. However, fearing sub-standardisation of HE degrees, the government soon decided not to allow any private sector involvement in HE, resulting in the demise of a newly emerging market segment. TIIERE's licence was also revoked just a few weeks after the start of the academic year in 1993. To this day, all HEIs in the country with the exception of foreign university branches remain publicly owned.

The reorganisation of HE entrance examination rules, which attempted to remove abusive discretion from the HE examination process, was arguably the most significant reform of the early 1990s. Admissions to HEIs before independence were based on oral and/or written entrance examinations, usually in three relevant subject areas, administered locally at each HEI. However, public concerns about the subjectivity of such exams and their susceptibility to corruption grew especially strong in the late 1980s and the early 1990s. In order to radically improve fairness of access to HE and to limit widespread corruption practices, a new centralised testing system based on multiple choice questions and an automated marking system was piloted in selected HEIs in 1993. The new system of testing HE candidates was formally adopted across all HEIs (except those specialising in performance-based disciplines such as arts and sports) in 1994. The State Test Centre (STC), accountable directly to the Cabinet of Ministers, was formally set up in May 1994 to administer the new HE entrance examination system. The new system is meritocratic, at least in principle, which contributes to the deepening of vertical differentiation amongst HEIs. As a rule, applicants need to score more than 85 % to study traditionally lucrative fields such as law, medicine and business in HEIs specialising in these fields, and the competition for places at Tashkent-based HEIs offering similar subjects is usually even fiercer.

As elsewhere in the FSU, HE was universally free in pre-independence Uzbekistan: there were no tuitions fees and students were paid stipends, scaled on academic performance, to cover living expenses. But the Uzbek authorities changed this tradition partially in 1994 by introducing a dual-track funding formula for HE tuition fees. Under the new funding scheme, only some HE places were publicly funded, the so-called grant places, and the remaining places were privately funded, the so-called contract places. The Cabinet of Ministers centrally determines the total number of grant and contract places. It takes into account HE demand as well as labour market conditions in its decision making (World Bank 2014). The allocation of fixed grant places, which are subject to an annual review, are merit-based depending on entrance examination results, with top performers being offered government grants. The distribution of grant places varies across disciplines depending on demand conditions and market rewards for graduates. For example, in 2015–16, the share of grant places in total student places was around 10 % for law and jurisprudence, 16 % for economics, 35 % for medicine, 50 % for mathematics and around 55 % for physics and chemistry. However, the process is not transparent, which makes it difficult to judge whether or not the authorities also take into account institutional selectivity in their decision making. Whether they are funded publicly or privately, students are still offered merit-based monthly stipends as in the past. Those with government funding are expected to work in government-owned enterprises once they graduate, usually for about 2 years. But in practice this is not monitored strictly, as neither government bodies nor HEIs can guarantee work placement opportunities to graduates.

Although the reforms of the early 1990s changed the nature of the HE system to a considerable extent, the institutional structure of the system remained relatively intact. Comprehensive reforms requiring a complete overhaul of the entire education system were initiated only in the second half of the 1990s. The government's vision for the education system was formulated in an official reform programme, 'The National Programme for Personnel Training' (NPPT), which became law in August 1997. The programme was born from government belief in the non-reversibility of the move towards a market-based economy and an appreciation of the fact that developing an education system consistent with market principles was vital in pursuit of economic prosperity (ADB 2004, 94). Nevertheless, the NPPT was still an embodiment of the government's strictly top-down approach to HE reforms, as it did not grant HEIs any autonomy in important matters such as designing new HE courses and managing own finances.

The NPPT aimed at creating an education system that reflected national values, met personal aspirations and produced highly qualified specialists that the new economic system demanded; it was also seen as an opportunity to formally and comprehensively de-ideologise the education curriculum, and to increase the range and structure of degree programmes offered at HEIs. The NPPT was a state-initiated and fully funded programme involving a strict top-down implementation plan coordinated by the Cabinet of Ministers and aided by other government institutions such as the Ministry of Higher and Secondary Specialised Education (MHSSE), and various other ministries linked to particular HEIs (e.g. the Ministry of Health is linked to medical HEIs).

The NPPT set out clear timescales to achieve its reform targets. Stage 1, which covered 1997–2001, involved the creation of an appropriate infrastructure necessary for the implementation of the programme, which included developing new curricula, teaching and learning resources, and exploring alternative HE funding sources. Stage 2, which covered 2001–2005, set out to promote a nationwide drive for the development of teaching content including textbooks as well as electronic and online learning materials. It also reorganised the existing 5-year academic degree courses, and research-based *aspirantura* and *doktorantura* programmes into Bologna Process Bachelor degrees (4 years), Master degrees (2 years) and PhD programmes. And Stage 3, which covered the period beyond 2005, was intended to fine-tune the programme after the first 5 years of implementation. In May 2011, the government adopted a new programme, covering 2011–2016, which focusses on improving physical and human resources at HEIs including upgrading information-technology facilities and raising the quality of HE degrees and courses. Despite its importance, the NPPT only set the general direction of reforms; establishing new HEIs and expanding existing ones were determined on the basis of individual presidential decrees and resolutions from the Cabinet of Ministers.

Reforms and the Current Landscape of HE

As a result of the reforms mostly associated with the NPPT, both HEI and full-time student numbers increased significantly in the post-independence period. The number of HEIs affiliated with the MHSSE increased from 43 in 1989 to 78 in 2015, and the number of full-time students increased from around 180,000 to around 250,000 during this time. However, HE courses offered in the evenings and by correspondence were gradually phased out by the late 1990s, thereby effectively making HE study a full-time preoccupation. The relatively poor quality of these programmes in terms of design, delivery and student engagement was the main rationale behind the government's decision. The reforms also affected the vertical and horizontal organisational structure of the HE system. Table 17.2 provides some information about the horizontal diversity of the HE sector in terms of types of HEIs. HEIs can be classified into six types under the new HE system, which are comprehensive universities, specialised universities, institutes, academies, regional branches of specialised HEIs and branches of foreign universities. Of the 78 HEIs in Uzbekistan in 2015, 11 were comprehensive universities, 9 were specialised universities, 36 were specialised institutes (including the Higher School of National Dance and Choreography and the Uzbek State Conservatoire), 2 were academies, 13 were regional branches of domestic HEIs and 7 were branches of international HEIs. All domestic HEIs in Uzbekistan are state-owned.

With the exception of the three universities that existed before independence, the new comprehensive universities were created on the foundations of the former regional teacher-training pedagogic institutes.

Table 17.2 Horizontal diversity by HEI type in 2015

HE types	Number	Average student population	Average number of subject specialisation
Comprehensive universities	11	6,242	35
Specialised universities	10	5,054	23
Institutes[a]	35	3,236	17
Regional branches of domestic HEIs	13	671	4
Academies	2	2,305	3
Branches of foreign universities	7	820	na

Note: [a]Includes the State Conservatoire and the Higher School of Dance and Choreography
Source: Author calculations from various official sources

Comprehensive universities, for example, the National University, the Samarkand State University and the Ferghana State University, are the largest of the HEIs in terms of both student numbers and the number of taught specialisations. As a rule, institutes considered relatively important in their area of specialisation with large student populations are given official 'university' status. These specialised universities, for example, the Tashkent State University of Economics, the University of the World Economy and Diplomacy and the Tashkent State Technical University, offer programmes in narrower areas of specialisation and are smaller in size compared to comprehensive universities.

In terms of regional branches of domestic HEIs, these belong to Tashkent-based HEIs and are established by government decrees in regional capitals to improve HE access in the regions. For example, the Tashkent Institute of Pediatric Medicine opened a branch in Nukus in 1991, and the Tashkent Academy of Medicine opened branches in Urgench in 1992 and Ferghana in 1998. The Tashkent University of Information Technologies opened branches in Samarkand, Ferghana, Qarshi, Nukus and Urgench in 2005. The Uzbek State Institute of Arts and Culture opened a branch in Nukus in 2008. The Tashkent Institute of Irrigation and Melioration opened a branch in Bukhara in 2010. And finally, the Tashkent State Dental Institute opened branches in Andijan and Bukhara in 2015.

Academies are leading scientific-methodological centres in specific fields, so their status is more superior compared to that of universities and institutes. They offer postgraduate degrees and continuous professional development (CPD) as well as executive retraining courses; some, for example, the Academy of Medicine, also offer undergraduate degrees. For example, the Banking and Finance Academy, considered to be the most prestigious HEI in the area of banking and finance, offers postgraduate studies and regularly runs CPD workshops and executive retraining courses for banking and finance specialists.

Foreign university branches (FUBs), which are set up as public-private partnerships (World Bank 2014), are a relatively new phenomenon in Uzbekistan's HE system and are the result of a government initiative. In the late 1990s, the government experimented with competitively selecting up to 800 HE students annually from Uzbek HEIs and funding their HE studies in advanced economies such as the USA, the UK, Germany and Japan. The government saw the establishment of FUBs as a cost-effective alternative to this scheme, as they offered internationally recognised HE courses at home, and hence ensured greater positive externalities and spill-over in terms of specialist preparation.

The Russian Economics University was the first FUB to establish a branch in Uzbekistan in 2001. London-based Westminster University established a branch in Tashkent in 2002. The next FUB was opened in 2006 by the Moscow State University. The Russian Oil and Gas University and the Management Development Institute of Singapore opened Tashkent branches in 2007. The Turin Polytechnic University, Italy, opened a branch in 2009, and Inha University, South Korea, opened a branch in 2014. FUBs administer their entrance tests independently and enjoy complete autonomy on curriculum design. However, mostly due to regulation, FUBs have not yet grown into serious players in the HE market: their combined student population was less than 6000 in 2015–16, which is less than 3 % of the country's HE student population.

Figure 17.4 illustrates a peculiar HE sector structure that emerged in the post-independence period. HEIs are subject to multiple layers of

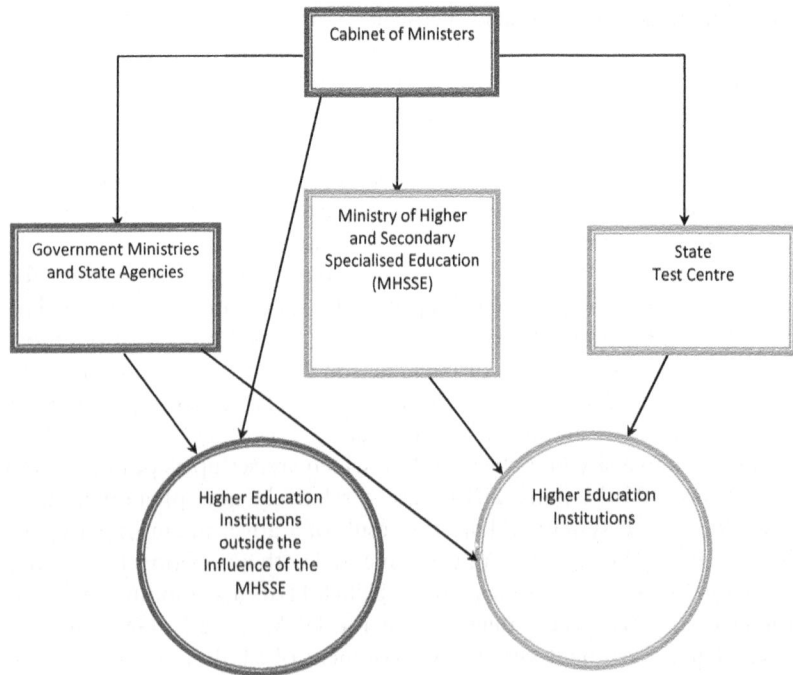

Fig. 17.4 Hierarchical structure of the higher education system in Uzbekistan

accountability, resulting in the duplication of administrative control, which limits the capacity of the MHSSE to strategically manage the HE system. It also limits the HE system's ability to flexibly adapt to changes (Weidman and Yoder 2010, 63). The Cabinet of Ministers, which sits at the top of the governance hierarchy, is in charge of all key decisions concerning the HE system. It sets the state educational standards and determines funding methods, number of study streams and student enrolment numbers including the proportion of enrolment places that are publicly funded. It also approves senior management appointments at HEIs and sets HEI strategies. The STC administers HE entrance examinations and carries out HEI accreditation and ranking. The role of the MHSSE in managing the HE sector is therefore mostly complementary and limited to HEI supervision, approval of secondary legislation, provision of methodological guidance and organisation of the academic year. The administrational influence of the MHSSE over HEIs is further weakened by the fact that of the 78 HEIs supervised by the MHSSE, 27 are also accountable to various ministries and state agencies to which they are formally attached. For example, the Academy of Medicine is attached to the Ministry of Health and the University of Agriculture is attached to the Ministry of Agriculture and Water Resources.

In addition to the 78 HEIs affiliated with the MHSSE, there are several other providers of specialist HE training which are outside the influence of the MHSSE, as depicted in the bottom left corner of Fig. 17.4. These institutions specialise in personnel preparation for various state departments and agencies. Some of the HEIs belonging to this category are directly linked with various government offices serving national security and upholding the rule of law, such as the National Security Service and the Ministry of Internal Affairs. Others have more civilian credentials, for example, the Academy for State and Social Construction under the Office of the President, the Graduate School of Business under the Cabinet of Ministers and the Banking and Finance Academy affiliated with the Bankers' Association. All of these HEIs are accountable directly to the Cabinet of Ministers and respective government ministries to which they are attached, and little information is publicly available on internal factors such as student enrolment figures and funding models.

Given Uzbekistan's peculiar context, it is difficult to differentiate HEI diversity in terms of status and prestige afforded by legislature. For example, all HEIs with the exception of regional HEI branches are allowed to offer undergraduate, postgraduate and PhD courses. In de facto terms, however, specialist institutions supporting state bodies are considered the most prestigious by both the general public and civil service institutions, as they play an important role in elite regeneration. As proxies for talent, HE certificates from these institutions are often used as the minimum requirement for appointment to relatively important bureaucratic positions. They are followed in order of importance by academies, comprehensive universities, specialist universities and institutes. Anecdotal evidence from HE insiders at the time of this study suggests that the most senior positions in academies and universities are appointed by the president, while those in institutes are decided by the Cabinet of Ministers.

Due to data limitations, we cannot construct any robust measures of quality ranking indicators across HEIs. However, the information presented in Table 17.3 can provide a rough guide on the diversity of quality across HEIs. The results are based on our judgement in terms of demand, selectivity and general public perception of prestige accorded to individual HEIs. As can be seen from Table 17.3, academies and branches of foreign universities are all highly regarded. Most of the comprehensive and specialised universities in the table are ranked 'medium' on the basis of 'average' quality perception across all fields with varying popularity. Institutes score the most variable ranking and this is mostly related to area of specialisation; those specialising in lucrative fields are in high demand, and hence are more selective and highly regarded by the general public.

Figure 17.5 illustrates the geographic distribution of HEIs and their student populations across the country in 2012–13, another measure of

Table 17.3 HE quality diversity based on demand, selectivity and public perception

	Tashkent			Regions			
	High	Medium	Low	High	Medium	Low	Total
Academies	2	0	0	0	0	0	2
Comprehensive universities	1	0	0	1	8	1	11
Specialised universities	3	5	1	0	0	0	9
Institutes	9	4	3	3	2	15	36
Branches of domestic HEIs	0	0	0	0	6	7	13
Foreign university branches	7	0	0	0	0	0	7
Total	22	9	4	4	16	23	78

Note: Based on author judgement

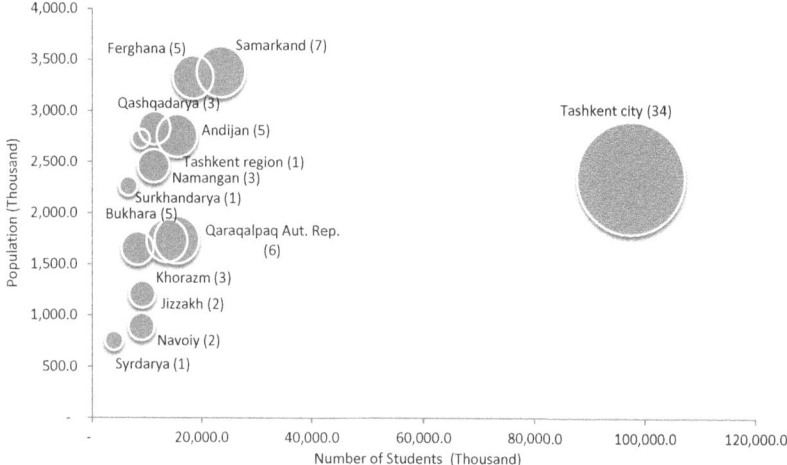

Fig. 17.5 Geographic distribution of HEIs and student population in 2012–13 (Source: MHSSE (2013))

horizontal diversity. The vertical axis measures the population and the horizontal axis measures the number of students studying in each of the 14 administrative regions in the country. The size of the bubbles measures the number of HEIs in each region. Almost half of all HEIs were based in Tashkent in the pre-independence period. Although a number of HEIs have been created across the regions since the early 1990s, a disproportionately high number of HEIs are still located in Tashkent city: 34 out of 78. Of the approximately 252,000 students enrolled in HEIs in 2012–13, around 40 % studied in Tashkent. The figure is a slight improvement from the pre-independence figure of 60 %, which is mainly due to the transformation of regional teacher-training institutes into comprehensive universities and size expansion as a result of the government's attempt to improve HE access in periphery regions.

The number of full-time students studying at HEIs increased noticeably during the post-independence period. However, more robust measures of HE access that take into account population demographics and HE demand dynamics depict a gloomy picture. The number of HE graduates per 10,000 people dropped from around 28 in 1993 to around 14 in 2001; similar, but less dramatic, trends can be observed regarding the gross enrolment rates (number of HE students divided by the number of

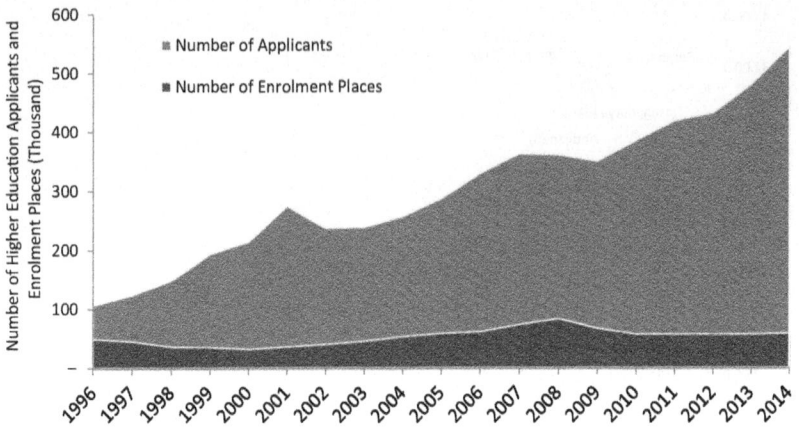

Fig. 17.6 Demand for and supply of higher education places, 1996–2014 (Source: MHSSE (2015))

19- to 24-year-olds), which fell from around 15 in 1991 to around 9 in 2012 (World Bank 2014, 23).

Additional data that sheds further light on this matter is presented in Fig. 17.6, which illustrates the growing mismatch between the demand for and the supply of HE places between 1996 and 2014. The number of HE applications, which measures the effective demand for HE, increased from 106,000 in 1996 to more than 540,000 in 2014; a more than fivefold increase in demand. Unfortunately, HE enrolment places as a measure of supply increased only modestly during this period, from around 49,000 in 1996 to 58,000 in 2014. As a result, the mismatch between HE demand and supply has widened significantly since 1996. Furthermore, the number of applicants per 100 HE places increased from 342 in 1989 (Balzer 1992, 178) to 938 in 2014; an almost threefold increase.

The observed mismatch between HE supply and demand can be explained partly by the changes observed in population demographics and improvements in per capita income levels since independence. However, the authorities' conscious choice to expand secondary specialised education (SSE) at the expense of HE also contributed to the increasing mismatch between HE demand and supply. The implicit argument behind the government's choice was that, given the relatively unsophisticated state of the national economy which relied largely on commodity production, services and small-scale manufacturing, the economy would be best served by the expansion and modernisation of the vocational education sector (Ruziev and Burkhanov 2016). The expansion of the SSE sector lowered the labour market return on middle education and encouraged a greater number of SSE graduates to seek entry into HE. This, coupled with the rigidity of HE supply and the fact that applicants are given only one single university choice each year, created a bottleneck effect as unsuccessful but ambitious applicants attempted HEI entry the following year. Therefore, it is no surprise that in 2014 the number of applicants for HE places exceeded the number of secondary and SSE graduates by about 8 %.

Furthermore, the data on HE student specialisations from 2007 to 2012 shows that the distribution of specialisations was driven mostly by the government's policy priorities rather than being in line with changing economic conditions (World Bank 2014). Despite the changing structure of the economy as described in Figs. 17.1 and 17.2, the distribution of the student population across most of the broad specialisation areas did not change notably during this period: around 5–7 % of students specialised in transport and communications, 7–10 % in economics and law, around 8 % in healthcare and around 1 % in other disciplines such as arts. Furthermore, although the share of agricultural production in the country's output nearly halved, the share of students specialising in agriculture fell only marginally from 9 % in 1989 to 7 % in 2012. The most dramatic changes, however, occurred in relation to education. The success of the government's decision to fundamentally reform and expand the SSE sector depended on the availability of subject-specialist teacher trainers for professional colleges. Subsequently, more than half of HE entrance places were allocated to education. Of the approximately 300,000 HE students studying in the peak period in 2009, around 170,000 specialised in education. Since then the number of students specialising in education has fallen by about 45,000, also driving the overall student population down to around 250,000 by 2012.

The analysis of supply and demand factors in HE indicates an urgent need for the expansion of HE supply. However, this has to be done without sacrificing quality standards. The existing human resource capacity of the HE system seems inadequate for this task; as can be seen in Table 17.4, which details the highest academic qualifications of full-time academic HEI staff in 2013, almost two-thirds had no scientific qualifications. In addition, Uzbekistan's HE system scores low in important human capital indicators such as the number of patent applications and journal publications. In 2009, the number of patent applications per million people was

Table 17.4 Academic qualification of full-time HEI staff in 2013

	Domestic HEIs		International HEIs	
	Number	% of total	Number	% of total
Doctor of philosophy/science	1,314	6.1	21	9.7
Candidate of science	7,491	34.5	56	25.9
No scientific qualification	12,893	59.4	139	64.4
Total	21,698	100.0	216	100.0

Source: MHSSE (2013)

only 19, and the number of technical and scientific journal publications per million was only 5 (World Bank 2014, 8). The relatively poor quality of human capital at HEIs hinders the HE sector's contribution to overall economic performance in terms of research and innovation; more importantly, it also significantly constrains the government's future attempts to expand access to HE.

Uzbekistan spends around 8–10 % of GDP on its education system, a relatively high figure given Uzbekistan's per capital income level (Weidman and Yoder 2010; World Bank 2014). However, only a small proportion of this budget is spent on HE; in fact, the share of HE spending on education declined from 10 % in 1990 to around 5 % in 2013 (World Bank 2014, 72). This is partly explained by the authorities' conscious attempt to fund an increasingly higher proportion of HE expenditure through private (personal) financing. With the introduction of private funding in the form of HE tuition fees, the share of government funding for HE enrolment places decreased from 100 % in 1990 to around 33 % in 2015 (MHSSE 2015). In 2013, the average tuition fee for domestic HEIs was around US$1400 and for international HEIs around US$4400 (World Bank 2014, 62). Another peculiarity of Uzbekistan's HE funding model is that up to 40 % of the HE system budget is spent on student stipends, of which only one-third comes from the state budget (World Bank 2014, 80).

Discussion and Concluding Remarks

Uzbekistan has undertaken important reforms in its HE sector since becoming independent in 1991, which significantly changed the country's HE landscape. Initially in the early 1990s, some important albeit ad hoc reforms were implemented. But this changed when the NPPT was formulated and made into a national law in 1997, transforming the structure and organisation of the HE system drastically. The most important changes since independence can be highlighted as follows: introduction of an automated entrance examination scheme overseen by the STC; adoption of a Bologna Process-style three-cycle HE system comprised of Bachelor, Master and Doctorate programmes; allowing the entry of foreign HEIs into the HE system; and moving away from a fully public HE funding model towards a system that increasingly relies on personal financing. The variety of HEIs and the number of students studying full time also changed during this period. HEI numbers increased from 43 in 1989 to 78 in 2015 and types of HEIs now include academies, comprehensive universities, specialised universities, institutes, regional branches and FUBs.

The demands of the new market-based economic system and the requirements of building and strengthening state institutions to support the transition process were the key drivers for HE reforms; these are factors inspired by global events beyond the control of the national authorities. Uzbekistan's general approach to transition has been about managing, rather than resisting, the prevailing 'winds of global change'. Therefore, although the creation of new HEIs, including expanding taught HE subject disciplines, was dictated by global trends, ultimately the state is still the main initiator and implementer of HE sector reforms. This strictly top-down approach to reforms, however, has not been successful in improving a number of key areas including management and organisation of HEIs, access to HE, and quality of human and physical capital at HEIs.

The current structure of HE management, with several levels of official control over HEI activity, is too rigid to adjust the provision of HE services to the changing needs of a dynamic market economy. To date, student enrolment numbers as well as the number of study streams and subject areas, and even curriculum content, are all presided by various government departments. Despite generating more than two-thirds of their funding from the private sector, HEIs are unable to use these funds freely, including in matters concerning staff remuneration. As a result, staff salaries are generally low and do not incentivise a sufficient number of talented individuals to commit themselves to, invest in, and remain in the long-term. Further, although HE enrolment numbers increased during the early years of independence, this did not take into account demographic factors and changing demand conditions. As a result, the mismatch between the demand for and supply of HE increased considerably in the post-independence period.

References

Asian Development Bank. 2004. Education Reforms in Countries in Transition: Policies and Processes Six Country Case Studies, Azerbaijan, Kazakhstan, Kyrgyz Republic, Mongolia, Tajikistan, and Uzbekistan. http://www.pitt.edu/~weidman/2004-educ-reforms-countries.pdf. Accessed 21 Sept 2015.

———. 2015. Key Economic Indicators for Asian and the Pacific. Country Tables: Uzbekistan. http://www.adb.org/publications/key-indicators-asia-and-pacific-2015. Accessed 21 Sept 2015.

Balzer, H. 1992. Educating Scientific-Technical Revolutionaries? Continuing Efforts to Restructure Soviet Higher Education. In *Soviet Education Under Perestroika. Papers from the 4th World Congress for Soviet and East European Studies*, ed. J. Dunstan, 165–195. Harrogate: Routledge.

Brunner, J.J., and A. Tillett. 2007. *Higher Education in Central Asia: The Challenges of Modernization: Case Studies from Kazakhstan, Tajikistan, the Kyrgyz Republic, and Uzbekistan*. Washington, DC: World Bank.

Goskomstat. 1989. *Narodnoe Obrazovanie i kultura v USSR* [Statistical Collection of the National Education and Culture in the USSR]. Moscow: Financi i Statistika.

Karimov, I. 1995. *Uzbekistan on the Way of Deepening Economic of Reforms*. Tashkent: Sharq.

———. 1998. *Uzbekistan on the Threshold of the Twenty First Century*. New York: Saint Martin.

Majidov, T., D. Ghosh, and K. Ruziev. 2010. Keeping Up with Revolutions: Evolution of Higher Education in Uzbekistan. *Economic Change and Restructuring* 43: 45–63.

Ministry of Higher and Secondary Specialized Education of the Republic of Uzbekistan. 2013. *Statistical Collection: Main Activities of the Higher Education Institutions 2012–13*. Tashkent: MHSSE.

Pomfret, R. 2000. The Uzbek Model of Economic Development, 1991–1999. *Economics of Transition* 8: 733–748.

Ruziev, K., and U. Burkhanov. 2016. Higher Education Reforms in Uzbekistan: Expanding Vocational Education at the Expense of Higher Education? *Higher Education in Russia and Beyond* 2: 14–15.

Ruziev, K., D. Ghosh, and S. Dow. 2007. The Uzbek Puzzle Revisited: An Analysis of Economic Performance in Uzbekistan Since 1991. *Central Asian Survey* 26: 7–30.

United Nations Development Programme. 2008. *Education in Uzbekistan: Matching Supply and Demand*. Tashkent: United Nations Development Programme.

Weidman, J., and B. Yoder. 2010. Policy and Practice in Education Reform in Mongolia and Uzbekistan During the First Two Decades of the Post-Soviet Era. *Excellence in Higher Education* 1: 57–68.

World Bank. 2014. *Uzbekistan: Modernizing Tertiary Education*. Washington, DC: World Bank.
———. 2015. World Development Indicators: Uzbekistan. http://data.worldbank.org/data-catalog/world-development-indicators. Accessed 25 Oct 2015.

Kobil Ruziev is Senior Lecturer in Economics at the University of the West of England, Bristol, England. He obtained his master's degree from Vanderbilt University, Nashville, USA, and PhD degree from Stirling University, String, Scotland. His main research interests include financial development and reform in emerging economies, institutional economics and economic transformation in the former Soviet Union.

Umar Burkhanov is a consultant at the Ministry of Higher and Secondary Specialized Education of Uzbekistan and Associate Professor of Finance at the Tashkent Institute of Finance, Uzbekistan. Dr Burkhanov also worked as the Chief Consultant on Education at the President's Office (2012–13) and Pro-rector of the Tashkent Institute of Finance (2014–15). He obtained his PhD from the Tashkent Banking and Finance Academy, Uzbekistan.

Open Access This chapter is distributed under the terms of the Creative Commons Attribution 4.0 International License (http://creativecommons.org/licenses/by/4.0/), which permits use, duplication, adaptation, distribution and reproduction in any medium or format, as long as you give appropriate credit to the original author(s) and the source, provide a link to the Creative Commons license and indicate if changes were made.

The images or other third party material in this chapter are included in the chapter's Creative Commons license, unless indicated otherwise in a credit line to the material. If material is not included in the chapter's Creative Commons license and your intended use is not permitted by statutory regulation or exceeds the permitted use, you will need to obtain permission directly from the copyright holder.

Appendix

Daria Platonova

Key Data on Pre-Soviet, Soviet and Post-Soviet Higher Education

This Appendix consists of the statistical data that is considered to be the most important for the study of Soviet and Post-Soviet higher education. Here we talk about general trends and aggregate numbers that provide a broad view on higher education changes. The Appendix contains three parts. The first part includes data on higher education in Russian empire (until 1917). Second part covers Soviet period (1917–1991): statistics on higher education institutions (HEIs), numbers of students by field of education, forms of studies and across the USSR Republics as well as age cohort participation in the Republics. The third part consists of post-Soviet changes of HEIs in state and non-state sector, student body, privatisation of costs (fee-paying students) and participation in higher education.

The Appendix includes not only tables but also brief comments on data sources, major points that should be considered for data analysis and descriptions of key facts.

D. Platonova
Institute of Education, National Research University Higher School of Economics, Moscow, Russia

Higher Education in the Russian Empire

Tables A.1, A.2 and A.3 describe the landscape of higher education just before the Russian Revolution. It should be noted that the data differs considerably between sources. Thus, we present two reliable sources. Tables A.1 and A.2 refer to the year 1913 and accumulate data from Ivanov (1991). Table A.3 consists of information on 1914/15 academic

Table A.1 State HEIs in Russia in 1913

Types of HEIs	Number of HEIs	Number of students
Comprehensive universities	10	35,695
Law	4	1036
Oriental studies	3	270
Medical	2	2592
Pedagogical	4	894
Military and naval	8	894
Theological	6	1185
Engineering	15	23,329
Agriculture	6	3307
Veterinary	4	1729
Art	1	260
Total	63	71,379

Russian empire included territories which were not a part of the USSR, such as territories of Poland, so the date includes respective HEIs, for example, Warsaw University and Warsaw polytechnic institute

Source: Russia 1913 year. *Statistical and document handbook* [Rossiya 1913 god Statistiko-dokumental'nyy spravochnik]. (1995). Russian Academy of Science Institute of Russian history [Rossiyskaya Akademiya Nauk Institut Rossiyskoy istorii]. Saint-Petersburg

Table A.2 Non-governmental HEIs in 1913

Types of non-state HEIs	Number of HEIs	Number of students
Higher female university courses	18	23,534
Higher female medical institutions	4	1254
Higher female and male universities	5	7659
Pedagogical	6	1237
Art	8	7189
Commercial	6	8364
Agricultural	4	2274
Industrial	2	624
Total	54	52,153

Source: Russia 1913 year. *Statistical and document handbook* [Rossiya 1913 god Statistiko-dokumental'nyy spravochnik]. (1995). Russian Academy of Science Institute of Russian history [Rossiyskaya Akademiya Nauk Institut Rossiyskoy istorii]. Saint-Petersburg

Table A.3 State and non-state HEIs, number of students and share of women by types of HEIs in the Russian Empire in 1914/15

	Number of HEIs	Number of students	Share of women
Universities and other 'comprehensive' HEIs	35	60,437	39.9%
Theological seminary	6	1264	0.0%
Medical	10	5534	58.1%
Pedagogical	10	2632	88.3%
Agricultural	9	4192	5.3%
Technical	14	21,216	0.9%
Art and music	7	4099	54.0%
Commercial	6	10,563	11.5%
Total	97	109,937	30.5%

Includes universities in St. Petersburg, Moscow, Kazan, Tomsk, Saratov (later in Soviet and modern Russia), Kharkov, Kiev, Odessa (later in Soviet and modern Ukraine), Tartu (later in Soviet and modern Estonia) and Warsaw (later in modern Poland)

Source: Narodnoe obrazovanie v SSSR po dannym tekushchikh obsledovaniy na 1 yanvarya 1922, 1923 i 1924 gg. i kratkiy svod statisticheskikh dannykh za pyatiletie 1921–1925 gg. [Education in the Soviet Union according to the current survey on January 1, 1922, 1923 and 1924 and a short set of statistics for the five-year period 1921–1925 gg.] (1926) Trudy Tsentral'nogo Statisticheskogo Upravleniya, № XXVIII, V. 1, Moskva. Available here: http://istmat.info/node/22102

year. Data comes from the Appendix of the statistical handbook on education, published in 1926. In this appendix there are data on different parts of the Russian Empire and Russian regions. In these statistical tables, the general data on the whole country in 1914/15 is marked as the USSR instead of the Russian Empire (Table A.3), so one might assume it pertains to the borders of later USSR.

Table A.1 presents data on state HEIs and Table A.3 includes communal and private higher education institutions (HEIs). In his book Ivanov points out that by 1917 there were more than 120 HEIs (65 state HEIs and 59 communal and private) (Ivanov 1991, 3). Data on non-state sectors from two sources (Tables A.2 and A.3) differs considerably.

In Table A.3 the share of women is calculated by the author on the basis of absolute numbers.

Soviet Higher Education

According to Narodnoye obrazovaniye... [Education...] (1926), in 1922–1925 the number of HEIs gradually decreased from 278 to 160 (Table A.4). Although the number of all HEIs declined, the number of

Table A.4 Number of HEIs and students by types of HEIs in the USSR in 1922 and 1925

	1922		1925	
	Number of HEIs	Number of students	Number of HEIs	Number of students
Total	278	224,229	160	165,440
Universities	22	84,467	21	54,368
Other 'comprehensive' HEIs	23	6497	9	2932
Pedagogical	80	24,816	38	17,975
Medical	24	19,888	22	19,492
Agricultural	27	15,333	23	17,935
Technical	44	46,383	23	37,624
Social science and economics	16	12,623	9	8535
Art and music	42	14,222	15	6578

Source: Narodnoe obrazovanie v SSSR po dannym tekushchikh obsledovaniy na 1 yanvarya 1922, 1923 i 1924 gg. i kratkiy svod statisticheskikh dannykh za pyatiletie 1921–1925 gg. [Education in the Soviet Union according to the current survey on January 1, 1922, 1923 and 1924 and a short set of statistics for the five-year period 1921–1925 gg.] (1926) Trudy Tsentral'nogo Statisticheskogo Upravleniya, № XXVIII, V. 1, Moskva. Available here: http://istmat.info/node/22102

students in medical and agricultural HEIs was stable and even increased. The most significant decrease was within universities, other comprehensive, and art and music HEIs.

In Tables A.1, A.2, A.3 and A.4 we use the term pedagogical HEIs as a direct translation from the statistical handbooks. Thereafter (from Table A.5) pedagogical HEIs are included into the group "Education".

Universities are also included in this group of education HEIs. Thus, if we compare 1925 and 1940 (Tables A.4 and A.5), we see that number of universities, pedagogical and other comprehensive HEIs increased from 68 to 407. The share of students in these HEIs had grown from 45 % to 60 % during the 15 years since 1925. After the next 15 years the share of students in HEIs dropped to 37 % (Table A.6). Table A.6 is calculated by the author on the basis of absolute numbers on enrolment.

Every issue of the statistical yearbook *Narodnoe khozyaystvo SSSR...* [National economy of the USSR...] is available for the years 1956–1990. In 1989 the statistical book *Narodnoye obrazovaniye i kultura...* [Education and culture...] (1989) was published. Most of the data overlaps, except statistics on engineers (Tables A.7 and A.8).

Tables A.9, A.10, A.11, A.12, A.13, A.14, A.15, A.16 and A.17 refer to the heterogeneity between Soviet republics with a special focus on pre-1991 years. The tables use Soviet republic names for the Soviet period. The number of universities in Table A.11 is calculated by the author. Calculations in Table A.13 were prepared by the author on the basis of absolute numbers.

Table A.5 Number of HEIs in the USSR in 1940–1988

	1940/41	1950/51	1960/61	1970/71	1980/81	1988/89
Total	817	880	739	805	883	898
Industry and construction	136	147	169	201	228	235
Transport and communications	28	35	37	37	46	45
Agriculture	91	94	96	98	103	106
Economics and law	47	47	51	50	57	57
Healthcare, physical culture and sport	78	89	98	99	104	106
Education	407	417	241	268	287	287
Art and cinema	30	51	47	52	58	62

Source: Narodnoye obrazovaniye i kultura v USSR: Statisticheskiy ezhegodnik [Education and Culture in the USSR: Statistic Yearbook] (1989). Moscow: Finansy i statistika.; Narodnoe khozyaystvo SSSR v 1960 godu Statisticheskiy sbornik [National economy of the USSR in 1960]. (1961). Gosstatizdat TsSU SSSR. Moskva

Table A.6 Share of enrolment by the types of HEIs, %

	1940	1955	1960	1970	1980	1988
Industry and construction	17	31	38	40	40	38
Transport and communications	3	6	6	5	5	5
Agriculture	5	11	11	9	10	10
Economics and law	5	6	7	8	8	6
Healthcare, physical culture and sport	9	7	6	7	7	7
Education	60	37	31	30	30	33
Art and cinema	1	1	1	1	1	1

Source: Narodnoye obrazovaniye i kultura v USSR: Statisticheskiy ezhegodnik [Education and Culture in the USSR: Statistic Yearbook] (1989). Moscow: Finansy i statistika.; Narodnoe khozyaystvo SSSR v 1960 godu Statisticheskiy sbornik [National economy of the USSR in 1960]. (1961). Gosstatizdat TsSU SSSR. Moskva

Table A.7 Engineers in the USSR, thousand students

	1960	1970	1980	1988
Total number of graduates	343,3	631	817	775
Number of engineers	120,4	257	359	315
Share of engineers, %	35	41	44	41

Source: Narodnoye obrazovaniye i kultura v USSR: Statisticheskiy ezhegodnik [Education and Culture in the USSR: Statistic Yearbook] (1989). Moscow: Finansy i statistika

Table A.8 Graduates by the forms of education, thousand students

	1940	1960	1980	1988
Total	126,1	343,3	817,3	775,2
Full time	97,8	228,7	518	447,1
Part time	4,4	15,4	85,3	77,7
Correspondence	23,9	99,2	214	250,4

Source: Narodnoye obrazovaniye i kultura v USSR: Statisticheskiy ezhegodnik [Education and Culture in the USSR: Statistic Yearbook] (1989). Moscow: Finansy i statistika.; Narodnoe khozyaystvo SSSR v 1960 godu Statisticheskiy sbornik [National economy of the USSR in 1960]. (1961). Moscow: Gosstatizdat TsSU SSSR

Table A.9 Number of HEIs in the Soviet Republics

	1940	1960	1970	1980	1990
USSR	817	739	805	883	911
Armenian SSR	9	10	12	13	14
Azerbaijan SSR	16	12	13	17	17
Belorussian SSR	25	24	28	32	33
Estonian SSR	5	6	6	6	6
Georgian SSR	21	18	18	19	19
Kazakh SSR	20	28	44	55	55
Kyrgyz SSR	6	8	9	10	9
Latvian SSR	7	10	10	10	10
Lithuanian SSR	7	12	12	12	11
Moldavian SSR	6	6	8	8	9
Russian SFSR	481	430	457	494	514
Tajik SSR	6	6	7	10	10
Turkmen SSR	5	4	5	7	9
Ukrainian SSR	173	135	138	147	149
Uzbek SSR	30	30	38	43	46

Source: Narodnoye hozyaistvo SSSR v 1985. [National economy in the USSR in 1985]. (1986). Moscow: Finansy i statistika; Narodnoye hozyaistvo SSSR v 1990. [National economy in the USSR in 1990]. (1991). Moscow: Finansy i statistika

Table A.10 Number of HEIs in 1988

	Total	Industry and construction	Transportation and communications	Agriculture	Economics and law	Education	Healthcare, physical culture and sport	Art and cinema
USSR	898	235	45	106	57	287	106	62
Armenian SSR	13	1	0	2	1	5	2	2
Azerbaijan SSR	16	4	0	1	1	6	2	2
Belorussian SSR	33	9	1	4	3	10	4	2
Estonian SSR	6	1	0	1	0	2	0	2
Georgian SSR	19	2	0	3	1	8	2	3
Kazakh SSR	55	12	2	7	3	23	6	2
Kyrgyz SSR	10	1	0	1	0	5	2	1
Latvian SSR	10	1	1	1	0	2	3	2
Lithuanian SSR	12	2	0	2	1	3	2	2
Moldavian SSR	9	1	0	1	0	1	4	2
Russian SFSR	507	154	28	60	33	148	55	29
Tajik SSR	10	1	0	1	0	5	2	1
Turkmen SSR	9	1	0	1	1	3	2	1
Ukrainian SSR	146	40	10	17	10	42	18	9
Uzbek SSR	43	5	3	4	3	20	6	2

Source: Narodnoye obrazovaniye i kultura v USSR: Statisticheskiy ezhegodnik [Education and Culture in the USSR: Statistic Yearbook] (1989). Moscow: Finansy i statistika

Table A.11 Number of universities and university students in 1988

	Number of universities
USSR	69 (with 593,716 students enrolled)
Armenian SSR	1
Azerbaijan SSR	1
Belorussian SSR	3
Estonian SSR	1
Georgian SSR	2
Kazakh SSR	2
Kyrgyz SSR	1
Latvian SSR	1
Lithuanian SSR	1
Moldavian SSR	1
Russian SFSR	40
Tajik SSR	1
Turkmen SSR	1
Ukrainian SSR	10
Uzbek SSR	3

Source: Narodnoye obrazovaniye i kultura v USSR: Statisticheskiy ezhegodnik [Education and Culture in the USSR: Statistic Yearbook] (1989). Moscow: Finansy i statistika

The estimations of age cohort participation in higher education (Table A.16) were also developed by the author. The indicator is calculated as the ratio of the number of students in the Republic and number of 20- to 24-year-olds in the Republic. The estimations are limited by the fact that the relevant cohort for higher education students is closer to 17- to 25-year-olds. The data for this cohort within republics is not available. Nevertheless, the estimations are considered useful for overall evaluation and comparison of participation in higher education within republics.

Regarding competition at entrance exams (Table A.17), we would like to include a comment from Narodnoye obrazovaniye i kultura ... [Education and Culture ...] (1989, 230) (Table A.18):

> In 1988 the lowest level of competition was in economic HEIs in Lithuanian SSR that was 106 people per 100 slots, in industrial HEIs in Estonian and Lithuanian SSR that was 116 and 120 people per 100 slots (correspondingly), and in agricultural HEIs in Lithuanian, Latvian and Belorussian SSR that was 121–123 people per 100 slots. The most popular were art and cinema HEIs in Russian SFSR, medical and education HEIs in Georgian SSR, and economic HEIs in Tajik SSR where competition was 519–652 people per 100 slots.

Table A.12 Number of students in 1988

	Total	Industry and construction	Transportation and communications	Agriculture	Economics and law	Education	Healthcare, physical culture and sport	Art and cinema
USSR	4,999,167	1,835,578	264,412	513,323	355,093	368,456	1,611,819	50,486
Armenian SSR	98,771	41,239	158	7561	4570	8612	33,989	2642
Azerbaijan SSR	57,927	22,205	0	5930	4715	4602	19,204	1271
Belorussian SSR	178,595	53,868	4872	21,482	18,252	13,894	64,775	1452
Estonian SSR	85,594	33,395	0	11,392	1921	6422	30,223	2241
Georgian SSR	24,275	8677	0	3642	0	0	10,912	1044
Kazakh SSR	276,878	80,989	7153	40,455	18,452	23,477	104,516	1836
Kyrgyz SSR	57,109	13,946	0	5434	0	6786	30,129	814
Latvian SSR	44,247	11,695	3782	6032	0	3558	17,889	1291
Lithuanian SSR	66,341	19,857	0	9651	430	4116	29,207	3080
Moldavian SSR	53,068	11,261	0	6886	0	5015	28,076	1830
Russian SFSR	2,795,336	1,136,326	171,578	263,890	213,636	196,092	791,818	21,996
Tajik SSR	58,553	6179	0	5069	326	6871	38,069	2039
Turkmen SSR	39,623	5991	0	5798	3512	5347	18,318	657
Ukrainian SSR	853,978	318,181	56,284	90,372	68,964	56,591	257,014	6572
Uzbek SSR	308,872	71,769	20,585	29,729	20,315	27,073	137,680	1721

Source: Narodnoye obrazovaniye i kultura v USSR. Statisticheskiy ezhegodnik [Education and Culture in the USSR: Statistic Yearbook] (1989). Moscow: Finansy i statistika

Table A.13 Number of students and share of full-time students in 1990

	# of students, total, thousand	% of students, full time
USSR	5161.6	59.2
Armenian SSR	68.4	70.6
Azerbaijan SSR	105	57.4
Belorussian SSR	188.6	61.5
Estonian SSR	25.9	66.4
Georgian SSR	103.9	62.5
Kazakh SSR	287.4	60.8
Kyrgyz SSR	58.8	69.4
Latvian SSR	45.9	63.4
Lithuanian SSR	65.6	64.6
Moldavian SSR	54.7	62.3
Russian SFSR	2824.5	58.3
Tajik SSR	68.8	68.5
Turkmen SSR	41.9	67.3
Ukrainian SSR	881.3	59.0
Uzbek SSR	340.9	53.8

Sources: Statisticheskiy ezhegodnik: Vyssheye obrazovaniye v 1990 [Statistic Yearbook: Higher education in 1990]. (1991) Moscow: NIIVO

Table A.14 Dynamics of student number in the Soviet Republics, thousand

	1960	1970	1980	1990
USSR	2396.1	4580.6	5235.2	5161.6
Armenian SSR	20.2	54.4	58.1	68.4
Azerbaijan SSR	36	100.1	107	105
Belorussian SSR	59.3	140	177	188.6
Estonian SST	13.5	22.1	25.5	25.9
Georgian SSR	56.3	89.3	85.8	103.9
Kazakh SSR	77.1	198.9	260	287.4
Kyrgyz SSR	17.4	48.4	55.4	58.8
Latvian SSR	21.6	40.8	47.2	45.9
Lithuanian SSR	26.7	75	71	65.6
Moldavian SSR	19.2	44.8	51.3	54.7
Russian SFSR	1496.7	2671.1	3045.8	2824.5
Tajik SSR	20	44.5	56.8	68.8
Turkmen SSR	13.1	29.1	35.8	41.9
Ukrainian SSR	417.7	806.6	880.4	881.3
Uzbek SSR	101.3	232.9	278.1	340.9

Source: Narodnoye hozyaistvo v SSSR v 1985. [National economy in the USSR in 1985]. 1986. Moscow: Finansy i statistika; Statisticheskiy ezhegodnik: Vyssheye obrazovaniye v 1990 [Statistic Yearbook: Higher education in 1990]. (1991) Moscow: NIIVO

Table A.15 Dynamics of student number per 10,000 population in the Soviet Republics

	1940	1960	1970	1980	1990
USSR	41	111	188	196	178
Armenian SSR	82	106	214	186	203
Azerbaijan SSR	44	91	191	173	147
Belorussian SSR	24	72	154	183	184
Estonian SSR	45	111	161	172	164
Georgian SSR	77	134	189	169	190
Kazakh SSR	16	75	151	173	171
Kyrgyz SSR	19	79	162	152	133
Latvian SSR	52	101	171	186	171
Lithuanian SSR	20	95	180	206	176
Moldavian SSR	10	63	124	128	125
Russian SFSR	43	124	204	219	190
Tajik SSR	15	94	149	142	128
Turkmen SSR	22	81	131	124	113
Ukrainian SSR	47	97	170	176	172
Uzbek SSR	28	116	192	172	165

Sources: Narodnoye hozyaistvo v SSSR v 1985. [National economy in the USSR in 1985]. 1986. Moscow: Finansy i statistika; Statisticheskiy ezhegodnik: Vyssheye obrazovaniye v 1990 [Statistic Yearbook: Higher education in 1990]. (1991) Moscow: NIIVO

Table A.16 Age cohort participation in higher education (20–24 age cohort) in Soviet Republics

	1960	1970	1980	1990
USSR	11%	26%	22%	26%
Armenian SSR	10%	32%	16%	24%
Azerbaijan SSR	9%	34%	16%	15%
Belorussian SSR	8%	23%	21%	27%
Estonian SSR	14%	21%	22%	24%
Georgian SSR	14%	29%	20%	26%
Kazakh SSR	7%	21%	18%	22%
Kyrgyz SSR	9%	27%	16%	16%
Latvian SSR	12%	24%	24%	25%
Lithuanian SSR	11%	35%	25%	24%
Moldavian SSR	7%	19%	14%	19%
Russian SFSR	12%	26%	23%	30%
Tajik SSR	10%	27%	16%	15%
Turkmen SSR	9%	21%	12%	12%
Ukrainian SSR	10%	25%	22%	26%
Uzbek SSR	12%	33%	18%	19%

Source: Narodnoye hozyaistvo v SSSR v 1985. [National economy in the USSR in 1985]. 1986. Moscow: Finansy i statistika; Statisticheskiy ezhegodnik: Vyssheye obrazovaniye v 1990 [Statistic Yearbook: Higher education in 1990]. (1991) Moscow: NIIVO; United Nations, Department of Economic and Social Affairs, Population Division (2015). World Population Prospects: The 2015 Revision, custom data acquired via website

Table A.17 Competition at entrance exams per 100 places in 1988

	Competition at entrance exams per 100 places
USSR	192
Armenian SSR	245
Azerbaijan SSR	307
Belorussian SSR	177
Estonian SSR	154
Georgian SSR	394
Kazakh SSR	226
Kyrgyz SSR	304
Latvian SSR	159
Lithuanian SSR	164
Moldavian SSR	195
Russian SFSR	169
Tajik SSR	328
Turkmen SSR	301
Ukrainian SSR	187
Uzbek SSR	291

Source: Narodnoye obrazovaniye i kultura v USSR: Statisticheskiy ezhegodnik [Education and Culture in the USSR: Statistic Yearbook] (1989). Moscow: Finansy i statistika

Table A.18 Share of women in student body in the Soviet Republics in 1988

	% of women
USSR	54
Armenian SSR	39
Azerbaijan SSR	33
Belorussian SSR	59
Estonian SSR	56
Georgian SSR	49
Kazakh SSR	48
Kyrgyz SSR	46
Latvian SSR	64
Lithuanian SSR	62
Moldavian SSR	59
Russian SFSR	53
Tajik SSR	43
Turkmen SSR	36
Ukrainian SSR	54
Uzbek SSR	44

Source: Narodnoye obrazovaniye i kultura v USSR: Statisticheskiy ezhegodnik [Education and Culture in the USSR: Statistic Yearbook] (1989). Moscow: Finansy i statistika

Post-Soviet Transformations: Higher Education Institutions

Table A.19 provides information on higher education institutions in post-Soviet states. Most countries conserved Soviet types of organizations that are included to higher education level. They are universities, academies, institutes and conservatoriums. Yet, there are exceptions. For Estonia as HEIs we include universities, professional higher schools and vocational education institutions. For Latvia and Lithuania as HEIs we include universities and colleges. Ukrainian HEIs are considered as HEIs of III and IV accreditation levels.

Tables A.20, A.21 and A.22 present countries with available statistics for the selected years. The statistics on private higher education institutions and tuition fee-paying students are very limited, thus most of the tables lack some countries and years. Here we use term 'non-state' higher

Table A.19 Number of higher education institutions

	1991	1995	2000	2005	2010	2011	2012	2013
Armenia	14	56	98	89	74	68	65	63
Azerbaijan	18	43	47	47	51	51	52	52
Belarus	33	59	57	55	55	55	54	54
Estonia	6[a]	26	46	39	33	33	29	26
Georgia	19	132	171	170	52	57	66	73
Kazakhstan	61	108	170	181	149	146	139	128
Kyrgyz Republic	12	35	45	51	56	53	54	55
Latvia	14	28	33	57	58	59	61	61
Lithuania	n.a.	15	26	49	45	47	47	47
Republic of Moldova	11	20	47	35	33	34	34	32
Russia	519	762	965	1068	1115	1080	1046	969
Tajikistan	13	24	30	36	33	33	34	34
Turkmenistan	9	15	16	16	21	23	n.a.	n.a.
Ukraine	156	255	315	345	349	345	334	325
Uzbekistan	52	58	61	62	62	n.a.	64	n.a.

[a]Year 1990

Source: CIS Statistics (http://www.cisstat.com/); for Estonia – Statistics Estonia; for Georgia since 2009 – National Statistics Office of Georgia (http://www.geostat.ge/); for Latvia – Central Statistical Bureau of Latvia (http://www.csb.gov.lv/); for Lithuania – Official Statistics Portal (http://osp.stat.gov.lt/); for Turkmenistan (2010–2011) – Statistical Yearbook of Turkmenistan 2012

Table A.20 Number and share of non-state HEIs

	1995		2001		2005		2010		2015	
	# of non-state HEIs	% of non-state HEIs	# of non-state HEIs	% of non-state HEIs	# of non-state HEIs	% of non-state HEIs	# of non-state HEIs	% of non-state HEIs	# of non-state HEIs	% of non-state HEIs
Armenia	41	46	71	70	68	76	n.a.	n.a.	37	62
Azerbaijan	20	43	18	45	15	32	15	29	13	24
Belarus	20	34	14	24	12	22	10	18	9	17
Estonia	11	34	20	41	18	46	15	45	8	33
Georgia	109	76	145	81	140	82	33[a]	58[b]	52	71
Kazakhstan	41	37	112	61	130	72	103[a]	71[a]	85	67
Kyrgyz	10	23	16	33	18	35	23	41	19[c]	36[c]
Latvia	n.a.	n.a.	19	53	36	63	34	59	34	59
Lithuania	n.a	n.a.	n.a.	n.a.	n.a.	n.a.	16[b]	37[b]	n.a.	n.a.
Moldova	7	29	32	68	17	49	14	42	12	39
Russia	193	24	358	36	409	38	452	41	366	41
Tajik	n.a.	n.a.	5	16	5	14	n.a.	n.a.	1	3
Ukraine	64	25	92	29	113	33	106	30	80	28

[a]Year 2011
[b]Year 2012
[c]Year 2014

education that is less deterministic than 'private'. So we distinguish between different HEIs (state and non-state) according to founding bodies.

In Table A.20 for Kazakhstan for the 1995–2005 data comes from CIS Statistics.[1] On the basis of the National Education Report for 2010 and 2015 we define non-state HEIs as all HEIs except National University and public HEIs according to the National Education Report 2012[2] and National Education Report 2015.[3] Latvian non-state HEIs are included.

Data on Lithuanian non-state HEIs is calculated on the basis of statistics on individual HEIs, which is collected within the European Tertiary Education Register (ETER) project (Tables A.20 and A.21).

APPENDIX   475

Table A.21 Number and share of enrolment in non-state HEIs

	1995		2001		2005		2010		2015	
	# of students in non-state HEIs	% of students in non-state HEIs	# of students in non-state HEIs	% of students in non-state HEIs	# of students in non-state HEIs	% of students in non-state HEIs	# of students in non-state HEIs	% of students in non-state HEIs	# of students in non-state HEIs	% of students in non-state HEIs
Armenia	n.a.	n.a.	18,200	28	n.a.	n.a.	n.a.	n.a.	9198	11
Azerbaijan	n.a.	n.a.	28,664	24	23,951	18	19,753	14	20,592	13
Belarus	23,200	12	41,800	14	58,200	15	60,100	14	28,100	8
Estonia	n.a.	n.a.	n.a.	n.a.	14,756[a]	21[a]	8974	13	4737	9
Georgia	n.a.	n.a.	31,887	22	30,078	21	24,188[b]	22[b]	42,492	32
Kazakhstan	n.a.	n.a.	n.a.	n.a.	n.a.	n.a.	311,817[b]	50[b]	236,700	52
Kyrgyz Republic	7430	11	15,513	7	17,476	8	27,848	12	25,616[c]	12[c]
Latvia	n.a.	n.a.	20,776	19	37,383	29	30,490	29	20,656	25
Lithuania							15,194[c]	10[c]		
Republic of Moldova	n.a.	n.a.	19,654	23	21,706	17	19,022	18	14,731	18
Russia	n.a.	n.a.	470,600	9	1,079,300[a]	15[b]	1,283,300	18	705,077	15
Tajikistan	n.a.	n.a.	n.a.	n.a.	n.a.	n.a.	n.a.	n.a.	2582	2
Ukraine	n.a.	n.a.	n.a.	n.a.	n.a.	n.a.	266,023	12	115,895	8

[a]Year 2006
[b]Year 2011
[c]Year 2012

Table A.22 Share of students paying tuition fees

	1995	2000	2005	2010	2015
Belarus	n.a.	n.a.	59%	66%	60%
Estonia	n.a.	n.a.	55%[b]	49%	25%
Kazakhstan	n.a.	71%	n.a.	79%[c]	73%
Kyrgyz Republic	n.a.	n.a.	n.a.	87%	85%[d]
Latvia	34%	66%	77%	66%	59%
Lithuania	n.a.	40%[a]	45%	53%	49%
Republic of Moldova	n.a.	61%	81%	71%	67%
Russia	13%	41%	56%	63%	60%
Tajikistan	n.a.	n.a.	n.a.	61%	59%[e]
Ukraine	n.a.	n.a.	n.a.	12%	8%

[a]2002
[b]2006
[c]2011
[d]2013
[e]2014

In Table A.22 tuition fee-paying students in Estonia are indicated as enrolments in the category 'NSC/compensation' (non-state-commissioned student place or the student required to compensate study costs). The estimations for the cases of Moldova and Russia are made by the author as a sum of state HEIs' enrolment paying tuition fees and non-state HEIs' enrolment.

STUDENTS AND PARTICIPATION IN HIGHER EDUCATION

Since 1991 the number of students in post-Soviet states increased up to 3.9 times, except Uzbekistan and Turkmenistan where the number of students decreased (Table A.23). We also calculated how the share of full-time students changed. Only in Armenia, Belarus, Kyrgyz Republic and Russia the share of full-time students decreased 10–14 percent points. The data comes from CIS statistics, except Estonia, Latvia, Lithuania and after-2008 Georgia.

According to national statistics, in Table A.24 for Estonia we use 'full-time students' as enrolment on daily courses before 2001 (after 2005 – full-time courses). For Lithuania full-time courses are daily courses in 2000–2008 and after 2009 – regular courses.

Table A.23 Number of students in 1991–2013

	1991	1995	2000	2005	2010	2011	2012	2013
Armenia	66,079	41,968	60,726	97,765	111,003	95,308	90,145	85,922
Azerbaijan	107,945	98,812	119,683	129,948	140,241	143,146	145,584	151,274
Belarus	184,565	197,381	281,742	383,045	442,890	445,576	428,448	395,268
Estonia	25,899[a]	27,126	56,036	68,286	69,113	67,607	64,806	59,998
Georgia	102,818	124,236	138,960	143,879	95,110	109,533	117,710	124,223
Kazakhstan	288,371	272,715	440,715	775,762	620,442	629,507	571,691	527,226
Kyrgyz Republic	58,023	64,641	188,820	231,095	230,379	239,208	231,562	223,241
Latvia	46,279	46,680	101,270	131,125	103,856	97,041	94,474	89,671
Lithuania	n.a.	n.a.	99,140	197,720	186,861	174,823	159,465	148,473
Republic of Moldova	52,191	54,765	79,082	126,132	107,813	103,956	102,458	97,285
Russian Federation	2,762,800	2,790,723	4,741,341	7,064,577	7,049,815	6,490,002	6,073,887	5,646,671
Tajikistan	69,345	73,987	77,701	132,405	151,680	152,222	150,156	159,415
Turkmenistan	41,738	32,138	16,597	16,100	23,700	25,600	n.a.	n.a.
Ukraine	876,228	922,838	1,402,904	2,203,830	2,129,835	1,954,789	1,824,906	1,723,685
Uzbekistan	337,433	192,070	183,576	278,700	274,500	253,000	258,300	n.a.

[a]Year 1990

Source: CIS Statistics (http://www.cisstat.com/); for Estonia – Statistics Estonia; for Georgia since 2009 – National Statistics Office of Georgia (http://www.geostat.ge/); for Latvia – Central Statistical Bureau of Latvia (http://www.csb.gov.lv/); for Lithuania – Official Statistics Portal (http://osp.stat.gov.lt/); for Turkmenistan (2010–2011) – Statistical Yearbook of Turkmenistan 2012

Table A.24 Share of full-time students, %

	1991	1995	2000	2005	2010	2011	2012	2013
Armenia	72%	94%	95%	85%	74%	66%	64%	62%
Azerbaijan	58%	70%	80%	75%	81%	81%	83%	85%
Belarus	63%	65%	61%	50%	50%	50%	49%	50%
Estonia	66%[a]	83%	76%	68%	87%	86%	85%	85%
Georgia	60%	70%	79%	87%	100%	100%	100%	100%
Kazakhstan	62%	64%	58%	49%	53%	57%	63%	69%
Kyrgyz Republic	70%	73%	54%	54%	56%	55%	54%	56%
Latvia	63%	724%	58%	59%	69%	71%	73%	73%
Lithuania	n.a.	n.a.	72%	57%	62%	67%	72%	74%
Republic of Moldova	65%	72%	69%	63%	72%	71%	69%	66%
Russia	60%	63%	55%	50%	44%	44%	45%	46%
Tajikistan	69%	72%	62%	64%	66%	69%	69%	70%
Turkmenistan	68%	88%	n.a.	n.a.	n.a.	n.a.	n.a.	n.a.
Ukraine	61%	67%	61%	56%	59%	59%	61%	62%
Uzbekistan	55%	61%	77%	n.a.	98%	100%	100%	n.a.

[a]Year 1990

Source: CIS Statistics (http://www.cisstat.com/); for Estonia – Statistics Estonia; for Georgia since 2009 – National Statistics Office of Georgia (http://www.geostat.ge/); for Latvia – Central Statistical Bureau of Latvia (http://www.csb.gov.lv/); for Lithuania – Official Statistics Portal (http://osp.stat.gov.lt/)

Table A.25 Age cohort participation in higher education (17–25 age cohort) in 1991–2013

	1991	1995	2000	2005	2010	2011	2012	2013
Armenia	15%	12%	15%	21%	24%	21%	20%	20%
Azerbaijan	10%	9%	11%	10%	10%	10%	10%	11%
Belarus	16%	17%	23%	30%	37%	39%	39%	38%
Estonia	15%[a]	17%	36%	41%	44%	45%	45%	45%
Georgia	16%	21%	25%	25%	17%	20%	22%	24%
Kazakhstan	13%	13%	21%	34%	26%	27%	25%	24%
Kyrgyz Republic	9%	10%	25%	27%	25%	26%	25%	25%
Latvia	16%	17%	38%	46%	38%	37%	38%	39%
Lithuania	n.a.	n.a.	25%	48%	45%	43%	40%	39%
Republic of Moldova	10%	10%	16%	23%	19%	19%	19%	19%
Russian Federation	17%	17%	26%	36%	40%	39%	39%	39%
Tajikistan	9%	9%	8%	12%	12%	12%	11%	12%
Turkmenistan	7%	5%	2%	2%	3%	3%	n.a.	n.a.
Ukraine	16%	16%	24%	37%	39%	38%	37%	37%
Uzbekistan	11%	6%	5%	6%	6%	5%	5%	n.a.

[a]Year 1990

Source: Developed by the author on the basis of following data sources: CIS Statistics (http://www.cisstat.com/); for Estonia – Statistics Estonia; for Georgia since 2009 – National Statistics Office of Georgia (http://www.geostat.ge/); for Latvia – Central Statistical Bureau of Latvia (http://www.csb.gov.lv/); for Lithuania – Official Statistics Portal (http://osp.stat.gov.lt/); for Turkmenistan (2010–2011) – Statistical Yearbook of Turkmenistan 2012; World Bank. Education Statistics – All Indicators

Table A.26 Gross enrolment ratio, tertiary, %

	1990	1995	2000	2005	2010	2011	2012	2013	2014
Armenia	23	19	35	38	51	51	44	43	44
Azerbaijan	23	18	n.a.	n.a.	19	20	20	21	23
Belarus	49	41	55	67	79	86	90	91	89
Estonia	25	25	55	68	68	70	72	73	n.a.
Georgia	n.a.	44	38	47	29	31	29	35	39
Kazakhstan	39	35	32	n.a.	46	48	51	50	48
Kyrgyz Republic	27	20	35	42	42	41	n.a.	47	46
Latvia	25	23	57	79	70	67	66	67	67
Lithuania	33	26	50	80	86	81	77	72	69
Republic of Moldova	35	30	33	36	38	39	40	41	n.a.
Russian Federation	55	43	56	73		76	76	78	79
Tajikistan	22	21	18	21	23	22	22	23	24
Turkmenistan	12	n.a.	n.a.	n.a.	n.a.	n.a.	n.a.	n.a.	8
Ukraine	49	42	49	71	82	83	82	80	82
Uzbekistan	17	n.a.	13	10	9	9	n.a.	n.a.	n.a.

Source: UNESCO Institute for Statistics (http://www.uis.unesco.org/)

Participation rates in higher education in post-Soviet states are presented by two Tables A.25 and A.26. Table A.25 shows calculation by the author similar to estimations for Soviet times but we take better estimations of relevant age cohort (17- to 25-year-olds). The limitations are the same. As age cohort is not very precise and does not take into account countries' differences, calculations are rough. UNESCO statistics on gross enrolment ratio have similar limitations (Clancy 2010, 73). As Clancy shows while analysing developed countries, dispersion of students by ages is very different across the countries. Thus, any measure of the participation rate within countries without comprehensive data on student ages seem to be quite arbitrary. Moreover, regarding Table A.26 with UNESCO statistics provides estimations for tertiary education. For most post-Soviet states it means both secondary professional (specialised) and higher education.

Data Source for Non-state Higher Education Sector (e-sources)

Armenia	Annual Statistical Report on Social Sphere – http://www.armstat.am/file/article/14.soc-6new.pdf; Slancheva and Levy (2006)
Azerbaijan	The State Statistical Committee of the Republic of Azerbaijan (http://www.azstat.org/)
Belarus	Statistical Annual Books. Education in Belarus 2013, Education in Belarus 2015/2016 (http://www.belstat.gov.by/ofitsialnaya-statistika/solialnaya-sfera/obrazovanie/publikatsii_8/)
Estonia	Statistics Estonia (http://www.stat.ee/en)
Georgia	National Statistics Office of Georgia (http://www.geostat.ge/)
Kazakhstan	National Education Report 2012 (http://edu.gov.kz/storage/1d/1d88ba85588878820bbe4f514fd9c097.pdf); National Education Report 2015 (http://edu.gov.kz/ru/page/deyatelnost/statistika_i_analitika/natsionalnii_doklad/natsionalnii_doklad__o_sostoyanii_i_razvitii_sistemi_obrazovaniya_respubliki_kazahstan_po_itogam_2015_goda); Statistics of education system in the Republic of Kazakhstan (http://edu.gov.kz/storage/31/3157bb93472cf16b5768b83dddcd3923.pdf)
Kyrgyz Republic	National Statistical Committee of the Kyrgyz Republic (http://www.stat.kg/ru/statistics/obrazovanie/); Education and Science in the Kyrgyz Republic, 2014 (http://www.stat.kg/media/publicationarchive/e92fa220-6092-4b80-ab66-9941553f73e3.pdf)
Latvia	Central Statistical Bureau of Latvia (http://www.csb.gov.lv/)
Lithuania	Official Statistics Portal (http://osp.stat.gov.lt/); The ETER project (https://www.eter-project.com)

Republic of Moldova	National Bureau of Statistics of the Republic of Moldova (http://www.statistica.md/category.php?l=ru&idc=116)
Russia	Federal Statistical Agency (http://www.gks.ru/)
Tajikistan	Education in the Republic of Tajikistan (http://stat.tj/ru/img/695c206e2b1ce86f333f33fdc268a469_1433502622.pdf)
Ukraine	1995–2010: key performance indicators of HEIs in Ukraine in 2010/11 (https://ukrstat.org/uk/druk/publicat/Arhiv_u/15/Arch_vnz_bl.htm); 2015: key performance indicators of HEIs in Ukraine in 2015/16 (https://ukrstat.org/uk/druk/publicat/Arhiv_u/15/Arch_vnz_bl.htm) CIS Statistics (http://www.cisstat.com/)

References

Clancy, P. 2010. Measuring Access and Equity from a Comparative Perspective. In *Access and Equity: Comparative Perspectives*, ed. H. Eggins. Rotterdam/Boston/Taipei: Sense Publishers.

Ivanov, A. 1991. *Vysshaya shkola Rossii v kontse XIX – nachale XX veka* [Russian Higher School at the End of XIX – Beginning of XX Century]. Moscow: Akademiya Nauk SSSR Institut istorii SSSR.

Narodnoe khozyaystvo SSSR v 1960 godu Statisticheskiy sbornik [National Economy of the USSR in 1960]. 1961. Moscow: Gosstatizdat TsSU SSSR.

Narodnoe obrazovanie v SSSR po dannym tekushchikh obsledovaniy na 1 yanvarya 1922, 1923 i 1924 gg. i kratkiy svod statisticheskikh dannykh za pyatiletie 1921–1925 gg. [Education in the Soviet Union According to the Current Survey on January 1, 1922, 1923 and 1924. and a Short Set of Statistics for the Five-Year Period 1921–1925 gg.]. 1926. Trudy Tsentral'nogo Statisticheskogo Upravleniya, № XXVIII, V. 1, Moskva. Available here: http://istmat.info/node/22102

Narodnoye hozyaistvo SSSR v 1985. [National Economy in the USSR in 1985]. 1986. Moscow: Finansy i statistika.

Narodnoye hozyaistvo SSSR v 1990. [National Economy in the USSR in 1990]. 1991. Moscow: Finansy i statistika.

Narodnoye obrazovaniye i kultura v USSR: Statisticheskiy ezhegodnik [Education and Culture in the USSR: Statistic Yearbook]. 1989. Moscow: Finansy i statistika.
Russia 1913 Year. Statistical and Document Handbook [Rossiya 1913 god Statistiko-dokumental'nyy spravochnik]. 1995. Saint-Petersburg: Rossiyskaya Akademiya Nauk Institut Rossiyskoy istorii.
Statisticheskiy ezhegodnik: Vyssheye obrazovaniye v 1990 [Statistic Yearbook: Higher Education in 1990]. 1991. Moscow: NIIVO.

Notes

1. http://www.cisstat.com/
2. http://edu.gov.kz/storage/1d/1d88ba85588878820bbe4f514fd9c097.pdf
3. http://edu.gov.kz/ru/page/deyatelnost/statistika_i_analitika/natsionalnii_doklad/natsionalnii_doklad__o_sostoyanii_i_razvitii_sistemi_obrazovaniya_respubliki_kazahstan_po_itogam_2015_goda

The manufacturer's authorised representative in the EU is Springer Nature Customer Service Centre GmbH, Europaplatz 3, 69115 Heidelberg, Germany. If you have any concerns regarding our products, please contact ProductSafety@springernature.com

Printed and bound by CPI Group (UK) Ltd, Croydon, CR0 4YY
23/03/2026
02076672-0015